Welsh–English
English–Welsh

Teach
Yourself®

Essential
Welsh
Dictionary

Welsh–English
English–Welsh

Edwyn C. Lewis

Essential Welsh Dictionary

Welsh–English
English–Welsh

Edwin C. Lewis

Consultant Editor: Cennard Davies

For UK order enquiries: please contact Bookpoint Ltd, 130 Milton Park, Abingdon, Oxon OX14 4SB. *Telephone:* +44 (0) 1235 827720. *Fax:* +44 (0) 1235 400454. Lines are open 09.00–17.00, Monday to Saturday, with a 24-hour message answering service. Details about our titles and how to order are available at www.teachyourself.com

For USA order enquiries: please contact McGraw-Hill Customer Services, PO Box 545, Blacklick, OH 43004-0545, USA. *Telephone:* 1-800-722-4726. *Fax:* 1-614-755-5645.

For Canada order enquiries: please contact McGraw-Hill Ryerson Ltd, 300 Water St, Whitby, Ontario L1N 9B6, Canada. *Telephone:* 905 430 5000. *Fax:* 905 430 5020.

Long renowned as the authoritative source for self-guided learning – with more than 50 million copies sold worldwide – the *Teach Yourself* series includes over 500 titles in the fields of languages, crafts, hobbies, business, computing and education.

British Library Cataloguing in Publication Data: a catalogue record for this title is available from the British Library.

Library of Congress Catalog Card Number: on file.

First published in UK 1992 as *Teach Yourself Welsh Dictionary* **by** Hodder Arnold, part of Hachette UK, 338 Euston Road, London NW1 3BH.

First published in US 1993 as *Teach Yourself Welsh Dictionary* **by** The McGraw-Hill Companies, Inc.

This edition published 2010.

The *Teach Yourself* name is a registered trade mark of Hodder Headline.

Typeset by Transet Ltd, Coventry, England.
Printed in Great Britain for Hodder Education, an Hachette UK Company, 338 Euston Road, London NW1 3BH, by CPI Cox & Wyman, Reading, Berkshire RG1 8EX.

The publisher has used its best endeavours to ensure that the URLs for external websites referred to in this book are correct and active at the time of going to press. However, the publisher and the author have no responsibility for the websites and can make no guarantee that a site will remain live or that the content will remain relevant, decent or appropriate.

Hachette UK's policy is to use papers that are natural, renewable and recyclable products and made from wood grown in sustainable forests. The logging and manufacturing processes are expected to conform to the environmental regulations of the country of origin.

Impression number 10 9 8 7 6 5 4 3 2 1
Year 2014 2013 2012 2011 2010

Contents

Credits

Foreword

The Essential Welsh Dictionary is a modern dictionary specifically designed for use by Welsh learners. The Welsh–English section is based on a basic vocabulary formulated to meet their particular needs. It differs significantly from the traditional type of dictionary, in as much as it also contains mutated forms of nouns, verbs, adjectives and prepositions integrated into the main alphabetical structure. Learners thereby are able to trace the standard form of a mutated word without difficulty. Irregularly formed plural nouns are systematically included, and each Welsh verb is complete with its first person singular form in the present tense. In addition, many of the prepositions governed by various verbs are included.

An attempt has been made to supply sufficient grammatical detail with each entry in the English–Welsh section to facilitate cross-reference and easy access to the fuller definition in the Welsh–English section.

Throughout, the dictionary is well illustrated with examples of language in action, with an emphasis on Welsh idiomatic usage.

The supplement contains a short introduction to some of the salient features of Welsh grammar including the conjugation of verbs and prepositions, the comparison of adjectives, forms of personal pronouns, and a summary of the main rules of consonantal mutation.

I am indebted to Mr Cennard Davies, M.A., for his sustained interest and encouragement during the preparation of the work, for reading the manuscript, and for his many valuable suggestions.

I gratefully acknowledge that a section of the dictionary was awarded First Prize at the 1989 Llanrwst National Eisteddfod. Its completion was commissioned by the Eisteddfod Council, and it is now published by kind permission of the National Eisteddfod Court.

Edwin C. Lewis
Rhydargaeau
Carmarthen

Meet the author

I was born next door to my maternal Grandfather, who hailed from Herefordshire, and who persistently refused to utter one word of Welsh. He loved my Welsh-speaking Grandmother and their four Welsh-speaking children. As a child, I grew up unaware that I was bilingual. Later, I entered Trinity College, Carmarthen, trained as a teacher, was claimed by the Army and taught for some two years with the Royal Army Education Corps as a Warrant Officer. I returned then to the schools of West Glamorgan and ever since I have been a teacher of languages: Welsh and English. The introduction to Latin gained at Pontardawe Grammar stood me in fine stead when I strove later to master New Testament Greek in order to translate 'The Gospel according to Mark' into a vernacular Welsh version for school use.

While teaching, I gained two university degrees through the medium of English, but with a Welsh flavour. I retired early from teaching and completed my research for a doctorate based on an overview of the provision and development of bilingual education in Wales. Of a dozen books that I have published since 1960, only one bears an English title, though half of it is in Welsh. Note its contents: A Pocketbook of Welsh House-Names. My children, Heledd and Ioan, are thoroughly Welsh-speaking. Both phone me regularly from the uttermost ends of the earth, in Welsh, of course!

This is a dictionary with a difference!
It has been compiled specifically with the Welsh learner in mind. Its word-base includes the nouns, adjectives, verbs, etc., needed by the reader in order to begin learning the Welsh language.

The pronunciation section has been given pride of place and should be well rehearsed. A page of abbreviations follows which is informative and important. Every Welsh noun listed usually has its gender and plural form, and should be read as a 'drill'. For example:

cot *e.b. ll.* - **iau** *coat*

The drill for this word is:

cot *enw benywaidd, lluosog* **cotiau** coat

Once the 'drill' is established each new noun will have three parts: **name**/gender/plural.

Consider this example: afal *e.g. 11.* -**au** apple

Expanded, it reads: **afal** *enw gwrywaidd* (noun masculine) *lluosog* (plural) **afalau** apple.

Adjectives are generally masculine; some also have a feminine form, and a few have a plural form.

The verb **bod** (to be), is one of the first that the learner will meet. Not only is it versatile in its own right, but it is normally used to construct a periphrastic combination of nearly every other verb.

In the Dictionary's Supplement there is a short introduction to grammar, together with a summary of the main rules of mutation. The Dictionary's Welsh text abounds with examples of mutated nouns, adjectives, verbs, prepositions.

A valuable companion volume is *Complete Welsh*.

The ten most important things for the learner to remember:

1   It was a former Prime Minister (Rt Hon Tony Blair MP) who declared, 'Education, Education, Education!' The learner must engage daily with pronunciation, pronunciation, pronunciation!

2   Repeat daily drills: phrases, opening gambits, polite
    questions, weather observations, simple introductions ...
3   Listen to *Radio Cymru* at home or in the car and become
    immersed in the Welsh ethos throughout the week. View
    the S4C television channel and especially its long-running
    soap opera, *Pobol y Cwm*.
4   Equipped with *Essential Welsh Dictionary* and *Complete
    Welsh*, join a Welsh Learners' group; contact your LEA for
    a local group, or find an online group.
5   Visit a variety of Welsh functions such as a *Noson Lawen*,
    the Royal Welsh Show, a *Cymanfa Ganu*. The annual
    week-long National Eisteddfod welcomes and caters
    especially for Welsh learners, and is an encouraging and
    exciting week (the first full week in August).
6   Visit the annual *Urdd* National Eisteddfod – the greatest
    youth festival in Europe – during the Spring Bank Holiday
    week for the thrill of your life; or perhaps call at the
    Llangollen International Musical Eisteddfod in July.
7   Be innovative, join a Welsh choir.
8   Listen to Dafydd Iwan, *Gwibdaith Hen Frân* or other
    Welsh pop groups, and learn the words of their songs.
9   Befriend a Welsh speaker. You will be surprised how much
    help a 'personal tutor' can provide.
10 Visit a Welsh chapel on a Sunday. Join the congregation
    there after you have explained that you are a Welsh learner.
    (This simple act of visiting on your part may seriously alter
    the rest of your life!)

Only got a minute?

Welsh is a revered and rich language; it is also a phonetic language. In the Welsh alphabet there are 29 letters, including several 'digraphs' (two letters which represent one sound, such as 'ch', as in Scots 'loch'). Nine of the letters of the Welsh alphabet are pronounced exactly as in English:

b, d, j, l, m, n, p, s, t.

Of the remaining 20 letters, only one has two sound values, namely the letter 'y'.

The seven vowels are:

a   as the **a** sound in **a**t
e   as the **e** sound in **e**bb
i   as the **ee** sound in gr**ee**t
o   as the **o** sound in **o**dd
u   as for the sound of **i** above
w   as the **w** sound in **w**ill
y   (i) as the sound of **i** above
    (ii) as the **e** sound in th**e**rmal

The following Welsh words using the vowels and the above consonants may now be pronounced with confidence:
a, am, at
ben, bu
da, dan, di, doli, dot, du, dyn (i), dy (ii)

jam, Jim
lan, lu
man, mi, map
na, neb, ni
pa, pan, pen
cas, mis, Sul, tost
ti, to, ton, top, Twmi

Thirteen remaining Welsh consonants require attention:

c	as in **c**andle
ch	as in lo**ch** (Scottish), Johann Sebastian Ba**ch** (German)
dd	as in brea**the**
f	as the **v** sound in **v**ery
ff	as the **f** sound in **f**oe
g	as in **g**ive
ng	as the **ng** sound in pi**ng**
h	as in **h**atch
ll	Place tongue as though to sound **l** emitting only breath – **ll**o, **ll**u
ph	as in **Ph**ilip
r	as in **r**ag
rh	with a greater expulsion of breath and rolled, as by Scots
th	as the **th** sound in hea**th**

The Anglesey village name should be kept for a later occasion:
Llanfairpwllgwyngyllgogerychwyrndrobwllllantysilio gogogoch!

5 Only got five minutes?

Equipped with this *Essential Welsh Dictionary* and with plenty of practice, the Welsh learner is able to converse daily with other Welsh speakers, and also have access to a noble literature that was established as early as the sixth century of the first millennium. Such early Welsh poets as Aneirin and Taliesin flourished in that period, and the tradition of learning and precedent has continued through successive centuries until the present day, yielding incomparable treasures of Welsh prose and poetry. (Contrast these early origins with the fact that the long Anglo-Saxon elegy *Beowulf*, one of the oldest poems in the English language, was not composed until the eighth century of that first millennium!)

Today's vibrant Welsh language is accessible in many different media formats. The Welsh-speaking television channel S4C (*Sianel 4 Cymru*) offers viewers a wide range of programmes, from the serious to the entertaining: news bulletins, political debates, nature and sports programmes, travelogues, magazine programmes, soap operas, chat shows, concerts, farming, children's programmes. Such a miscellany enrichens much of the day-to-day life of the Welsh speaking population. Added to this is the radio output of the BBC's Radio Cymru and Radio Wales, plus local radio stations such as Radio Ceredigion and Sain Abertawe (Swansea Sound).

There are many weekly or monthly publications for Welsh readers, such as the newspaper Y Cymro (weekly), Christian denominational weeklies (*Y Goleuad, Y Seren, Y Tyst*) and magazines such as Golwg, Barn, Cristion, Barddas, Llafar Gwlad. Welsh publishers also keep a steady supply of new books on the market to attract readers of all ages.

The word-processing software package Microsoft Word is now available in Welsh, and a telecoms company launched the first Welsh predictive text facility for mobile phones during the National Eisteddfod in Bala in 2009.

Eisteddfodau are an important element of Welsh culture. Every year the *Eisteddfod Genedlaethol* (National Eisteddfod) is hosted by a different town or city, alternating annually between North and South Wales. The youth festival *Eisteddfod yr Urdd* is the largest gathering of its kind in Europe, and also alternates between towns in North and South Wales. In addition to this, many smaller *eisteddfodau* are held annually in towns and villages. These have fostered the careers of many successful Welsh performers; the opera-singer Bryn Terfel always pays tribute to the opportunities that the Urdd Eisteddfod gave him to perform and compete when he was younger.

Regular Sunday worship at Welsh chapels and churches is still respected by many families. Affiliation to Welsh choirs, whether male, female or mixed voice, is witnessing a huge surge in popularity. This is reflected by the success of Welsh choirs in the BBC's 2008 programme *Last Choir Standing*, in which the winning choir (Only Men Aloud) and runners-up (Ysgol Glanaethwy) were from Wales.

The renowned Edward Llwyd Walkers' Society (*Cymdeithas Edward Llwyd*) publishes annually a programme of walks for North and South Walians. They also welcome Welsh learners to join them on their walks and organize continental walks regularly.

With the continued demand for more Welsh schools at both primary and secondary level, Parents' (and Friends) Associations have much lobbying to do, and welcome Welsh learners to their midst. The enthusiasm of Welsh language classes for Welsh learners is insatiable and rewarding, reflecting the current climate in which an ability to speak Welsh is preferable if not essential for many jobs in Wales.

10 Only got ten minutes?

The Welsh language along with Scottish Gaelic, Irish, Cornish, Manx and Breton make up the Celtic group of languages, and are related to Gaulish and other Western European Iron Age languages.

In Wales, parts of Ireland, Scotland and Brittany four of the above languages still exist. It is little short of miraculous that *Cymraeg* (the Welsh language) has survived to date, when the pressures that the language has borne over the centuries are fully considered: it was joined territorially to England, conquered by the English armies, governed with English laws by the English Crown, overrun with the conqueror's castles, and existed next-door to one of the greatest and most successful empires the world has known, the British Empire.

Henry VIII did his best to extirpate the Welsh language in Wales. In his 1536 'Act for Laws and Justice to be Ministered in Wales', he conferred on all persons born or to be born within 'the Principality, Country or Dominion of Wales' the opportunity to enjoy the same rights as English people, provided that they became Englishmen. It further stated that the people of Wales 'do daily use a speech nothing like nor consonant with the natural tongue used within this realm' and deliberately declared its intention 'utterly to extirpe all and singular the sinister usages and customs differing from the laws of this realm'. The Act went further, as Wales was to be merged with England and its people to become English-speaking. The Welsh language was robbed of its status and its prestige began to decline; Anglicization had now begun in earnest. The worst was to follow. If the Welshman and his children adopted the English language, they could become socially elevated and become equal to Englishmen. English was the key to every position and privilege.

However, despite the demoralizing effect of the legislation of Henry VIII, the Welsh language yet derived considerable impetus from action initiated during the reign of the last of the Tudors. G. M. Trevelyan wrote in 1946 that 'In Queen Elizabeth's reign, the Church, by translating the Bible and the *Book of Common Prayer* into Welsh, began unconsciously to counteract the Anglicising policy of the State'. The translation of the Bible in 1588 by William Morgan (1545–1604) was described by Glanmor Williams in 1941 as 'the true foundation of the literature (and Protestantism) of modern Wales', and was in a way the crowning achievement of Welsh Renaissance scholarship. David Williams (1963) has acknowledged, 'This was undoubtedly the most important event in the history of the Welsh nation, for the Bible has been the most powerful medium in keeping the language alive, and it is the language, above all else, which has preserved for Wales a consciousness of its distinct nationality ... and has preserved Welsh from the decay which befell the other Celtic languages.'

In this brief overview of 'the State versus the Welsh language' no précis could be complete without reference to another fantastic phenomenon that was particularly Welsh and which contributed considerably to the preservation of the language. It was the arrival of the Welsh Circulating Schools, founded and organised by Griffiths Jones (1683–1761), Llanddowror, Carmarthenshire. These were Welsh schools organised on a three-monthly basis at a place, mainly during the winter period, when least work needed to be done on the farms. Children were taught to read the Bible and the *Book of Common Prayer* in Welsh, and drilled in the Church Catechism using the Welsh language. Evening classes were held for those unable to attend during the day. The schools were very successful from the start. Numbers for the years 1737–61 show that 3,495 schools had been founded and that 158,237 pupils had attended them, in addition to the unrecorded numbers of adults who had come to evening classes.

Geraint H. Jenkins wrote in 1983 that 'by giving education through their mother tongue to people who had never before been given any form of education, Griffith Jones rescued the

Welsh language. His great achievement was in creating a body of Welsh readers at a time when more than 90% of the world's population was illiterate'.

Such was the fame of the schools that they were worthy of mention in the report of the Russian Commissioner authorized by Catherine the Great to investigate the state of English education in 1764.

Before the end of that century, yet another phenomenon closely related in many respects to the Circulating Schools came into being, namely the Sunday School Movement pioneered by Thomas Charles (1775–1814) of Bala. His aims for these new schools closely resembled those of his predecessor Griffith Jones. The schools were to teach children to read their native language correctly, and to instruct them in the principles of Christianity. This summed up the whole purpose of the education offered, and was akin to the English Sunday School Movement started by Robert Raikes (1735–1811), but the Welsh counterpart differed significantly. Children only were taught in the English Sunday Schools, whereas in the Sunday Schools of Wales children and adults were taught. This became a very successful movement in Wales, with the Sunday School Society in 1799 in London reporting that in the previous year in Wales 8,000 children had attended for instruction at the existing 140 Sunday Schools. The movement continued to grow and flourish throughout the nineteenth century. It was with much affection that many people referred to it as *Prifysgol y Werin*, the University of the People.

Massive industrialization, emigration and consequent rural depopulation occurred in the nineteenth century. Religious and social cohesion was rocked by the devastating wars of the twentieth century, as the disillusionment of the returning servicemen and women to civilian life combined with the steady growth of secularism to weaken the already decimated congregations of both church and chapel in Wales.

In the early 1940s, a small, bright light was kindled at Aberystwyth – the birth of the first Ysgol Gymraeg, the Welsh school sponsored and fostered by Urdd Gobaith Cymru (Welsh

League of Youth). It was an experiment that was to blossom into an experience – the birthright of every Welsh child. Far-sighted parents and others noted that the 1944 Education Act contained the following clause in Section 76:

> '... the Minister and local education authorities shall have regard to the general principle that, so far as is compatible with the provision of efficient instruction and training and the avoidance of unreasonable public expenditure, pupils are to be educated in accordance with the wishes of their parents.'

The resounding success of the 'private' *Ysgol Gymraeg* at *Aberystwyth*, plus the above Section 76 clause spurred on eager, well-intentioned parents to press local education authorities to implement the expressed wishes of parents: to have their children educated through the medium of the Welsh language. Some local authorities were slow to respond, although most authorities in North Wales acquiesced and took up the challenge gallantly. Local authorities in the south such as Swansea, Cardiff, Glamorgan and Gwent put obstacles and devised delaying tactics to daunt the Parents' Association representatives. Several authorities behaved in a cavalier manner towards these representatives, but after many years the parents have succeeded, and now all local authorities have to make provision for Welsh-medium education within their specified areas – some, grudgingly!

Today, the parental cry is for more provision, more places and for smaller class sizes. Since its inception at the turn of the new millennium, the Welsh Assembly has pursued a different educational model for schools in Wales, with the introduction of the pioneering Foundation phase (Cyfnod Sylfaenol) for Key Stage 1 pupils (from nursery to year two) where the emphasis is on 'learning through play'. Recent media reports have highlighted the pressures that the English academic system places on children; the Welsh model may lead the way.

The above represents much of our past and part of our present. The Welsh learner is welcomed with open arms into the midst of our society to read, mark, learn, engage and profit from some or all aspects of our esteemed Welsh culture. *Croeso!*

Pronunciation

As Welsh is a vibrant phonetic language, learners who master the basic sounds early find that they are able to pronounce Welsh words right from the start. Of the 29 letters in the Welsh alphabet, nine share the same sound value as their counterparts in English, these are: **b, d, j, l, m, n, p, s, t.**

Vowels

a   as the **a** sound in **a**pple
e   as the **e** sound in **e**lf
i   as the **ee** sound in de**e**p
o   as the **o** sound in n**o**t
u   as for the sound in **i** above
w   as the **w** sound in **w**ood
y   (i)   as for the sound in **i** above. It occurs in monosyllables as in bys, and in the final syllable of polysyllables, diferyn
    (ii) as the **e** sound in th**e**. It occurs in polysyllables (except for final syllables) such as dynion, and in such words as y, yng, ym.Consonants

Consonants

a   see **Vowels**
b   as in English
c   as in **c**ap, **c**o**c**onut
ch   as in German A**ch**tung!
d   as in English
dd   as the **th** sound in brea**the**
e   see **Vowels**
f   as in the **v** sound in **v**iola
ff   as in the **f** sound in **f**ury
g   as in the **g** sound in **g**ift
ng   as the **ng** sound in cli**ng**
h   as in the **h** sound in **h**elp
i   see **Vowels**
j   as in English
l   as in English
ll   Place tongue as though to sound l emitting only breath. Try these words: **ll**o, **ll**i, **ll**w, **Ll**ane**ll**i

m	as in English
n	as in English
o	see **Vowels**
p	as in English
ph	as the **ph** sound in trium<u>ph</u>
r	as in <u>r</u>ed
rh	with greater expulsion of breath and rolled, as by the Scots
s	as in English
t	as in English
th	as the **th** sound in dea<u>th</u>
u	see **Vowels**
w	see **Vowels**
y	see **Vowels**

Ideally, the learner should practise pronunciation regularly with a native Welsh speaker. Welsh communities in town and country districts abound with such possibilities. Weekly programmes for learners are broadcast by Radio Cymru (FM 92–95, 96–98MHz), Radio Wales (AM 882 kHz) and by local radio stations such as Radio Ceredigion (FM 96.9, 103.3MHz) and Swansea Sound (AM 1170 kHz). The Welsh television channel S4C adds daily to the Welsh environment. Groups of Welsh-speaking walkers invite learners to join them on their walks. Welsh language courses at all levels of ability are comprehensively organized throughout each local education authority. The University is interested and involved in every aspect of the work. Competitions are arranged, new course-books are published, **Twmpath** dancing is celebrated and **Cymanfaoedd Canu** are joyfully attended. Facilities at the annual National and Urdd **Eisteddfodau** attract learners worldwide. **Nosweithiau llawen, Dawnsio gwerin**, CDs, tapes, records, videos, the Web. . . The list is endless as is the energy and enthusiasm of specialist teachers who devise these enjoyable events in order that learners may experience at first hand the joy of speaking their new language in as natural an environment as possible. For our children, Welsh-medium education from nursery group to degree level is flourishing.

Croeso i'n plith!   (Welcome to our midst!)

Welsh–English
dictionary

Abbreviations

a.	ansoddair	*adjective*
a.b.	ansoddair benywaidd	*feminine adjective*
ad.	adferf	*adverb*
a.g.	ansoddair gwrywaidd	*masculine adjective*
ardd.	arddodiad	*preposition*
At.	Atodiad	*Supplement, Appendix*
b.	benywaidd	*feminine*
be.	berfenw	*verb-noun (followed in brackets by the first person present tense)*
bf.	berf	*verb*
c.	cysylltair	*conjunction*
D.C.	De Cymru	*South Wales (S.W.)*
e.b.	enw benywaidd	*feminine noun*
* *e.b.g.*	enw benywaidd/gwrywaidd	*feminine/masculine noun*
ebych	ebychiad	*interjection*
e.e.	er enghraifft	*for example*
e.g.	enw gwrywaidd	*masculine noun*
* *e.g.b.*	enw gwrywaidd/benywaidd	*masculine/feminine noun*
e.ll.	enw lluosog	*plural noun*
e.p.	enw priod	*proper noun*
e.torf.	enw torfol	*collective noun*
g.	gwrywaidd	*masculine*
G.C.	Gogledd Cymru	*North Wales (N.W.)*
geir.	geiryn	*particle*
geir. gof.	geiryn gofynnol	*interrogative particle*
geir. perth.	geiryn perthynol	*relative particle*
gw.	gweler	*see*
lit.	yn llythrennol	*literally*
ll.	lluosog	*plural*
N.W.	Gogledd Cymru	*North Wales (dialect)*
[pron.]	dywedir	*[pronounced]*
rhag.	rhagenw	*pronoun*
rhagdd.	rhagddodiad	*prefix*
rhag. gof.	rhagenw gofynnol	*interrogative pronoun*
rhag. perth.	rhagenw perthynol	*relative pronoun*
S.W.	De Cymru	*South Wales (dialect)*
S.W.W.	De Orllewin Cymru	*South West Wales (dialect)*
y fan.	y fannod	*definite article*
ymad. ad.	ymadrodd adferfol	*adverbial phrase*

*The gender of some nouns varies in different dialects, for example: munud (*minute*); llygad (*eye*).

1

a

A

a *geir. gof. o flaen berf (interrogative particle before a verb).* **A oes heddwch?** Is there peace?

a *rhag. perth. (followed by soft mutation)* who, whom, which (**a** *is often omitted in everyday speech, but the mutated form of the verb remains).* **Y ferch a welais** The girl whom I saw; **y llyfr a ddarllenais** the book which I read

a:ac [ac *pronounced* ag] *c.* (**a** *before a consonant,* **ac** *before a vowel;* **a** *followed by spirant mutation)* and. **du a gwyn** black and white; **pensil a phapur** pencil and paper; **afal ac oren** apple and orange

â *bf.* he/she/it goes. *gw.* **mynd**

â: ag 1 *ardd,* (**â** *before a consonant,* **ag** *before a vowel;* **â** *followed by spirant mutation)* with (*an instrument*), by means of. **torri cig â chyllell** cutting meat with a knife; **crynu ag ofn** shivering with fear. 2 *c.* (**â** *before a consonant,* **ag** *before a vowel;* **â** *followed by spirant mutation)* as. **cyn goched â thân** as red as fire; **mor ysgafn â phluen** as light as a feather; **mor wyn ag eira** as white as snow

aber *e.g.b. ll.* **-oedd** estuary, mouth of river; confluence; stream

Abertawe *e.b.* **(Dinas a Sir)** Swansea City and County

aberth *e.g.b. ll.* **-au** sacrifice

aberth *be.* **(aberthaf)** to sacrifice

absennol *a.* absent

ac *gw.* **a: ac**

acen *e.b. ll.* **-nau, -ion** accent; intonation

act *e.b. ll.* **-au** act; statute

actio *be.* **(actiaf)** to act

acw: cw *ad.* (**cw** *in everyday speech)* there, yonder

achlysur *e.g. ll.* **-on** occasion; cause, opportunity

achos 1 *e.g. ll.* **-ion** reason, cause; action; case, factor. 2 *ardd.* because, for

achosi *be.* **(achosaf)** to cause

achub *be.* **(achubaf)** to save. **achub bywyd** to save life; **achub cyfle** to seize an opportunity

adael *gw.* **gadael**

adain: aden *e.b. ll.* **adenydd** wing

adar *gw.* **aderyn**

adeg *e.b. ll.* **-au** opportunity; period of time. **adeg y Nadolig** Christmas time; **ar adegau** at (certain) times

adeilad *e.g. ll.* **-au** building

adeiladu *be.* **(adeiladaf)** to build, to construct

adeiladwr *e.g. ll.* **adeiladwyr** builder

adenydd *gw.* **aden**

aelwyd

aderyn *e.g.* *ll.* **adar** bird
adfer *be.* **(adferaf)** to return; to
revive; to restore *(to health,
former condition, etc.)*
adferf *e.b.* *ll.* **-au** adverb
adlais *e.g.* *ll.* **adleisiau** echo
adleisiau *gw.* **adlais**
adloniannau *gw.* **adloniant**
adloniant *e.g.* *ll.* **adloniannau**
entertainment; recreation
adnabod *be.* **(adnabyddaf)** to
recognise; to be familiar
with; to identify; to know
(person or place); to diagnose
adnod *e.b.* *ll.* **-au** verse *(in
Bible)*; clause; section
adran *e.b.* *ll.* **-nau** division,
section; department. **Adran
Addysg** Education
Department

byddwn yn mynd. I promised
him that I would go
addoldai *gw.* **addoldy**
addoldy *e.g.* *ll.* **addoldai**
place of worship
addoli *be.* **(addolaf)** to
worship
addoliad *e.g.* *ll.* **-au** worship;
religious service
addysg *e.b.* *ll.* **-au** learning,
knowledge; education,
instruction. **addysg grefyddol**
religious education;
addysg gynradd primary
education; **addysg uwchradd**
secondary education
aeaf *gw.* **gaeaf**
aeddfed *a.* ripe, mature

Insight

Pronunciation is our goal: let's start with **aer**; **air**; **aur**. They're
all pronounced as the **-air** sound in the girl's name Mair.
aelwyd *e.b.* (with **ae** pronounced as **ai**) a noun meaning
fireplace or hearth, and a cosy venue for a family gathering.
Often seen as a house-name and bearing an earlier meaning –
home or dwelling.

adref *ad.* homewards
adrodd *be.* **(adroddaf)** to
relate; to recite; to report
adroddiad *e.g.* *ll.* **-au** account,
report; recitation; narration
addas *a.* fitting, suitable,
proper
addewid *e.g.b.* *ll.* **-ion**
promise
addo (i), *be.* **(addawaf)** to
promise. **Addewais iddo y**

ael *e.b.* *ll.* **-iau** brow
aelod *e.g.* *ll.* **-au** limb;
member. **Aelod Seneddol**
Member of Parliament;
Aelod o'r Cynulliad
Assembly Member
aelodaeth *e.b.* membership
aelwyd *e.b.* *ll.* **-ydd** hearth;
home

aer

aer 1 *e.g.* air, atmosphere.
2 *e.g. ll.* **-(i)on** heir
aeres *e.b. ll.* **-au** heiress
aerion *gw.* **aer**
aeron *gw.* **aer, aeronen**
aeronen *e.b. ll.* **aeron** berry,
fruit. **aeron cochion** red
berries
aeth *gw.* **mynd**
afael *gw.* **gafael**
afaelgar *gw.* **gafaelgar**
afal *e.g. ll.* **-au** apple
afan(s)en *e.b. ll.* **afan(s)**
raspberry *(S.W.)*
afiach *a.* unhealthy, sick;
dirty, unwholesome
afiechyd *e.g. ll.* **-on** disease,
illness
afon *e.b. ll.* **-ydd** river; straits.
Afon Tawe River Tawe; **Afon
Menai** Menai Straits
afonydd *gw.* **afon**
afr *gw.* **gafr**
agor *be.* **(agoraf)** to open
agored *a.* open; unobstructed;
liable. **Y Brifysgol Agored**
The Open University
agoriad *e.g. ll.* **-au** key
(N.W.); opening, aperture.
agoriad llygad eye-opener
agos *a.* **(at** person, **i** place)
near. *gw.* **At. Ansoddeiriau**
agosach *gw.* **agos**
agosaf *gw.* **agos**
agosáu (at, i) *be.* **(agosâf)** to
draw near to, to approach.
agosáu at *(person);* **agosáu i**
(place)
agosed *gw.* **agos**
agwedd *e.g. ll.* **-au** attitude

angau *e.g. ll.* **angheuoedd**
death
angel *e.g. ll.* **angylion, engyl**
angel
angenrheidiau *gw.* **anghenraid**
angenrheidiol *a.* necessary
anghenraid *e.g. ll.*
angenrheidiau necessity
angheuoedd *gw.* **angau**
anghofio (am) *be.* **(anghofiaf)**
to forget
anghyfarwydd *a.* unfamiliar,
unaccustomed.
anghyfarwydd â unfamiliar
with, unaccustomed to
anghywir *a.* inaccurate,
wrong; false
angladd *e.g.b. ll.* **-au** funeral
angylion *gw.* **angel**
ai 1 *geir. gof. heb dreiglad ar
ei ôl, a geir o flaen enw,
rhagenw, berfenw ac
ansoddair (interrogative
particle not followed by
mutation, and used before a
noun, pronoun, verb-noun,
or adjective)* **(ai** *is often
omitted in spoken Welsh).* **Ai
te sy'n y cwpan?** Is it tea in
the cup? **Ai Twm sy yno?** Is
it Twm that's there? **2** *c.*
either . . . or; **naill ai Marc
neu Ioan** Either Marc or
Ioan
âi *bf.* he/she/it was
going/would go/used to go;
gw. **mynd**
ail *a. (followed by soft
mutation)* second; like,
similar. **yr ail fachgen** the

4

second boy; **yr ail dŷ** the
second house; **yr ail gadair**
the second chair; **heb (ei) ail**
unequalled; **bob (yn) ail**
alternate, alternately
ail *rhagdd.* re-, second;
secondary. **ail achos**
secondary cause; **ailadroddiad**
repetition; **ailfeddwl** second
thought, afterthought;
ailgyfrif a recount; **ail-law**
second-hand; **ailystyried** to
reconsider
ailgylchu *be.* **(ailgylchaf)** to
recycle
air *gw.* **gair**
alar *gw.* **galar**
alarch *e.g. ll.* **-od, elyrch** swan
alaru *gw.* **galaru**
alaw *e.b. ll.* **-on** music; air,
melody, tune; lily. **alaw werin**
folk tune
Alban, Yr *eb.* Scotland
Almaen, Yr *eb.* Germany
alw *gw.* **galw**
alwad *gw.* **galwad**
alwedigaeth *gw.* **galwedigaeth**
alwyn *gw.* **galwyn**
allan *ad.* out, outside
allanfa *e.b. ll.* **allanfeydd** exit
allanfeydd *gw.* **allanfa**
allanol *a.* external, outward,
exterior
allt *e.b. ll.* **elltydd** hill *(N.W.)*;
cliff *(N.W.)*; wood *(S.W.)*
alltud *e.g. ll.* **-ion** exile; alien
alltudion *gw.* **alltud**
allu *gw.* **gallu**
alluog *gw.* **galluog**
allwedd *e.b. ll.* **-au, -i** key
(S.W.); clef

allweddell *e.b. ll.* **-au**
keyboard
am 1 *ardd. (followed by soft
mutation) (personal forms:*
**amdana, amdanat,
amdano/amdani, amdanon,
amdanoch, amdanyn)** about,
at, around, for, on. **am ddeg
o'r gloch** at ten o'clock;
Galwodd am Emyr He called
for Emyr; **am y tro** for the
time being; *gw.* **At.
Arddodiaid.** 2 *c.* because, for,
since; provided that
amaethwr *e.g. ll.* **amaethwyr**
farmer; *gw.* **ffarmwr: ffermwr**
amaethyddiaeth *e.b.*
agriculture
amau 1 *be.* **(amheuaf)** to
doubt; to suspect; to dispute.
2 *e.g. ll.* **amheuon** doubt
ambell *a. (followed by soft
mutation)* occasional. **ambell
waith** occasionally,
sometimes; **ambell un** an
occasional one
ambiwlans *e.g. ll.* **-ys**
ambulance
amcan *e.g. ll.* **-ion** purpose,
notion, guess
amcanion *gw.* **amcan**
amddiffyn 1 *be.* **(amddiffynnaf)**
to defend; to protect. 2 *e.g.
ll.* **-ion** defence
Americanwr *e.g. ll.*
Americanwyr an American
amgaeëdig *a.* enclosed
amgáu *be.* **(amgaeaf)** to
enclose; to envelop

amgueddfa

amgueddfa *e.b. ll.*
amgueddfeydd museum;
Amgueddfa Genedlaethol
National Museum;
Amgueddfa Werin Folk
Museum
amgueddfeydd *gw.*
amgueddfa
amgylch *e.g. ll.* **-oedd** circuit,
environs; **o amgylch** round
about, about
amgylchedd *e.g. ll.* **-au, -ion**
environment
amharod *a.* unprepared,
unready, unwilling
amherffaith *a.* imperfect
amheuaeth *e.b. ll.* **-au** doubt,
suspicion
amheuon *gw.* **amau**
amhosibl *a.* impossible
aml *a. (followed by soft
mutation)* frequent,
abundant; **aml (i) gyfle**
frequent opportunity; **gan
amlaf** most often, mostly
amlen *e.b. ll.* **-ni** envelope
amlenni *gw.* **amlen**
amlosgfa *e.b. ll.* **amlosgfeydd**
crematorium
amlosgfeydd *gw.* **amlosfga**
amlosgi *be.* **(amlosgaf)** to
cremate
amlwg *a.* evident, clear, plain;
famous; prominent
amod *e.g.b. ll.* **-au** condition;
term; proviso
amrwd *a.* raw, crude
amryw *a. (followed by soft
mutation)* several; various.
amryw fath various kinds

amrywiaeth *e.g. ll.* **-au** variety;
variation
amrywiol *a.* miscellaneous
amser *e.g. ll.* **-au, -oedd** time,
period; season; tense;
rhythm, measure *(in music
and poetry)*
amserau *gw.* **amser**
amserlen *e.b. ll.* **-ni** timetable
amseroedd *gw.* **amser**
amynedd *e.g.* patience
amyneddgar *a.* patient
anabl *a.* disabled
anabledd *e.g.* disability
anadl *[pron.* **anal** *in S.W.]*
e.g.b. ll. **-au, -on** breath
anadlu *be.* **(anadlaf)** to breathe
anaddas *a.* unfit, unsuitable
anafu *be.* **(anafaf)** to receive
hurt or injury; to injure, to
wound, to mutilate
anaml *a.* infrequent; scarce,
rare
anarferol *a.* unusual
anawsterau *gw.* **anhawster**
aned *gw.* **ganed**
aneffeithiol *a.* ineffectual
aneglur *a.* obscure
anerchion *gw.* **annerch**
anferth *a.* huge, gigantic,
monstrous, prodigious
anfodlon *a.* unwilling,
discontented
anfoesgar *a.* rude, ill-
mannered
anfon *be.* **(i** *place,* **at** *person)*
(anfonaf) to send; to transmit
anffodus *a.* unfortunate
anhapus *a.* unhappy; unlucky
anhawster *e.g. ll.* **anawsterau**
difficulty

anhwyldeb *e.g. ll.* **-au** sickness
anhwylder *e.g. ll.* **-au** sickness
anhwylus *a.* unwell;
inconvenient
anialwch *e.g.* desert,
wilderness
anifail *e.g. ll.* **anifeiliaid**
animal, beast. **anifail anwes**
pet; **anifail dof** tame animal
anifeiliaid *gw.* **anifail**
anlwcus *a.* unlucky
annerch 1 *be.* **(anerchaf)** to
greet; to address. **2** *e.g. ll.*
anerchion greetings
anerchiadau addresses,
speeches
annhebyg *a.* unlike, dissimilar,
different
annheg *a.* unfair, unjust
annheilwng *a.* unworthy
anniben *a.* untidy
annibyniaeth *e.b.*
independence
Annibynnwr *e.g. ll.*
Annibynwyr Independent,
Congregationalist
annoeth *a.* unwise
annwyd *e.g. ll.* **-au, -on** cold,
chill. **Mae annwyd arno fe(fo)**
He has a cold
annwyl *a. (when the adjective
precedes the noun soft
mutation occurs)* dear,
beloved; precious. **Annwyl
Blant** Dear Children; **Annwyl
Gyfaill** Dear Friend *(used to
begin a speech or a letter).*
anwylyd darling
anochel *a.* unavoidable,
inevitable

anodd *a.* difficult, hard
anos *a.*more difficult, harder
anrheg *e.b. ll.* **-ion** gift,
present
anrhydedd *e.g. ll.* **-au** honour
ansicr *a.* uncertain, doubtful
ansicrwydd *e.g.* uncertainty,
doubt
ansoddair *e.g. ll.*
ansoddeiriau adjective
ansoddeiriau *gw.* **ansoddair**
antur *e.g.b. ll.* **-iau, -iaethau**
adventure; danger, risk
anturus *a.* adventurous
anweledig *a.* invisible, unseen
anwes *e.g. ll.* **-au** fondness,
pampering, fondling;
indulgence. **anifail anwes** pet
anwesu *be.* **(anwesaf)** to
fondle, to cherish
anwiredd *e.g. ll.* **-au** untruth,
iniquity
anwyd *gw.* **ganwyd**
anwylaf 1 *a.* dearest. **2** *e.g. b.*
beloved one
anwyliaid *e.ll.* beloved ones
ar *ardd. (followed by soft
mutation) (personal forms:*
**arna, arnat, arno/arni, arnon,
arnoch, arnyn)** on, upon; by,
in, at. **ar fynydd Epynt** on
Epynt mountain; **ar lawr y
gegin** on the kitchen floor; **ar
hap a damwain** by chance; **ar
ddi-hun** awake; **ar ôl** after;
gw. **At. Arddodiaid**
araf *a.* slow, leisurely. **yn araf
deg** slowly, gently; by degrees
arafu *be.* **(arafaf)** to slow, to
retard, to decelerate

araith

araith *e.b. ll.* **areithiau** speech, address

arall *a. ll.* **eraill** another, other, else. **bachgen arall** another boy; **bechgyn eraill** other boys

arbed *be.* **(arbedaf)** to spare, to save. **arbed amser** to save time

arbennig *a.* specialist, distinct

arch 1 *e.b. ll.* **eirchion** request, petition. 2 *e.b. ll.* **eirch** coffin, ark

arch- *rhagdd.* chief, principal, high, arch-; worst. **archesgob** archbishop; **archdderwydd** archdruid; **archoffeiriad** chief priest; **archelyn** worst enemy

archeb *e.b. ll.* **-ion** order *(especially for goods); gw.* **gorchymyn 2**

archebu *be.* **(archebaf)** to order. *ew.* **gorchymyn 1**

archfarchnad *e.b. ll.* **-oedd** hypermarket

ardal *e.b. ll.* **-oedd** region, district, area

ardd *gw.* **gardd**

arddangosfa *e.b. ll.* **arddangosfeydd** show, exhibition

ardderchog *a.* excellent, splendid

arddio *gw.* **garddio**

arddodiad *e.g. ll.* **arddodiaid** preposition

arddodiaid *gw.* **arddodiad**

arddwr *gw.* **garddwr**

arddwrn *e.g. ll.* **arddyrnau** wrist

areithiau *gw.* **araith**

arf *e.g.b. ll.* **-au** weapon; tool; **arfau** arms

arfer 1 *be.* **(arferaf)** to use; to practise; to accustom; to partake of. 2 *e.g.b. ll.* **-ion** usage, custom, practice; rule; habit

arferion *gw.* **arfer**

arferol *a.* usual, customary

arfog *a.* armed

arfordir *e.g. ll.* **-oedd** seacoast, maritime district

arglwydd *e.g. ll.* **-i** lord. **Tŷ'r Arglwyddi** House of Lords

arglwyddes *e.b. ll.* **-au** lady

arglwyddi *gw.* **arglwydd**

argraff *e.b. ll.* **-iadau, -au** impression, imprint

argraffiad *e.g. ll.* **-au** edition

argraffu *be.* **(argraffaf)** to print, to impress

argymell *be.* **(argymhellaf)** to urge

arholiad *e.g. ll.* **-au** examination. **arholiad llafar** oral examination; **arholiad ysgrifenedig** written examination; **sefyll arholiad** to take *(sit)* an examination

arian *e.g.* silver; money, coin, cash. **arian byw** quicksilver, mercury; **arian gleision** small change, **arian parod** cash; **arian pen** exact money; **arian poced** pocket money

arlleg *gw.* **garlleg**

arllwys *be.* **(arllwysaf)** to pour, to empty. **arllwys y glaw** to pour with rain *(S.W.)*

arogl *e.g. ll.* **-au** scent, perfume *(N.W.)*

arogli: aroglu *be.* **(aroglaf)** to scent, to smell *(N.W.)*.

aros (am) *be.* **(arhosaf)** to wait (for), to stay; to stop, to remain

arth *e.g. ll.* **eirth** bear

arw *gw.* **garw**

arwain *be.* **(arweiniaf)** to lead, to guide, to conduct

arweinydd *e.g. ll.* **-ion** leader, guide, conductor

arwydd *e.g. ll.* **-ion** sign

arwyddo *be.* **(arwyddaf)** to sign

asesu *be.* **(asesaf)** to assess

asgellwr *e.g. ll.* **asgellwyr** wing: **blaenasgellwr** flanker *(rugby)*

asgwrn *e.g. ll.* **esgyrn** bone

asiant *e.g. ll.* **-au** agent

asiantaeth *e.b. ll.* **-au** agency

asyn *e.g. ll.* **-nod** ass, donkey

asynnod *gw.* **asyn**

at *ardd. (followed by soft mutation) (personal forms:* **ata, atat, ato/ati, aton, atoch, atyn)** to, towards, for, at, by. *gw. At. Arddodiaid*

atal (rhag) *be.* **(ataliaf)** to stop; to prevent; to withhold. **atal dweud** to stammer

ateb 1 *be.* **(atebaf)** to answer, to reply. **2** *e.g. ll.* **-ion** answer, reply

atebion *gw.* **ateb**

atgoffa *be.* **(atgoffaf)** to recall, to remind

atodiad *e.g. ll.* **-au** appendix

atyniadol *a.* attractive

athrawes *e.b. ll.* **-au** female teacher

athrawon *gw.* **athro**

athro *e.g. ll.* **athrawon** teacher, professor: **yr Athro Thomas Parry** Professor Thomas Parry

aur *e.g.* gold

awdur *e.g. ll.* **-on** author

awduraeth *e.b. ll.* **-au** authorship

awdurdod *e.g.b. ll.* **-au** authority. **awdurdod iechyd** health authority

awduron *gw.* **awdur**

awel *e.b. ll.* **-on** breeze

awelon *gw.* **awel**

awgrymu *be.* **(awgrymaf)** to suggest

awn *bf.* we go. *gw.* **mynd**

awr *e.b. ll.* **oriau** hour; time

Awst *e.g.* August

awtomatig *a.* automatic

awyddus *a.* desirous, eager, zealous. **yn awyddus i fynd** eager to go

awyr *e.b.* air; sky. **awyr agored** open air; **awyr iach** fresh air

awyren *e.b. ll.* **-nau** aeroplane

B

ba *gw.* **pa**

bab *gw.* **pab**

baban *e.g. ll.* **-od** baby

babanaidd *a.* babyish, childish, puerile

babell *gw.* **pabell**

babi *e.g.* baby; *gw.* **pabi**

babydd

babydd *gw.* pabydd
bac *gw.* pac
baced *gw.* paced
bacio *be.* (baciaf) to back; to move backward; to bet (on). bacio car to reverse a car; bacio ceffyl to bet on success of a horse; *gw.* pacio
bach 1 *e.g. ll.* -au hook, hinge. 2 *a.* small, little; dear. araf bach slowly, very slowly; bore bach very early morning, crack of dawn
bachau *gw.* bach; bachyn
bachgen *e.g. ll.* bechgyn boy
bachgennaidd *a.* boyish, childish, puerile
bachu *be.* (bachaf) to hook, to grapple
bachyn *e.g. ll.* bachau hook
bad *e.g. ll.* -au boat. bad achub lifeboat
badell *gw.* padell
bader *gw.* pader
bae *e.g. ll.* -au bay. Bae Abertawe Swansea Bay
baent *gw.* paent
bafiliwn *gw.* pafiliwn
bafin *gw.* pafin
bag *e.g. ll.* -iau bag
bagan *gw.* pagan
bagiau *gw.* bag
bai *e.g. ll.* beiau fault, blame; defect
baich *e.g. ll.* beichiau load, burden
bais *gw.* pais
bâl *gw.* pâl
balas *gw.* palas
balch *a.* proud, fine, stately; glad. Roedd e'n falch ein

gweld ni he was glad to see us
balchder *e.g.* pride, glory
baled *e.b. ll.* -i ballad
baledwr *e.g. ll.* baledwyr composer of ballads, ballad-monger
balot *e.g. ll.* -au ballot
balu *gw.* palu
balŵn *e.b. ll.* balwnau balloon
ballu *gw.* pallu
bamffled *gw.* pamffled
ban *e.g.b. ll.* -nau peak, mountain, beacon, height; top, summit; corner, quarter; arm, branch; verse, section of line. Bannau Brycheiniog Brecon Beacons; o bedwar ban y byd from the four corners of the world
banana *e.g. ll.* -s, bananâu banana
banasen *gw.* panasen
banc 1 *e.g. ll.* -iau bank. gŵyl banc bank holiday. 2 *e.g. ll.* bencydd mound, bank, hillock
bancio *be.* (banciaf) to bank
band *e.g. ll.* -au, -iau band, binding. band pres brass band
banel *gw.* panel
baner *e.b. ll.* -i banner, flag
bannas *gw.* panasen
bannau *gw.* ban
bannod *e.b. ll.* banodau 1 line, clause, part. 2 definite article *gw.* y, yr, 'r
banodau *gw.* bannod

bant *gw.* pant

bapur *gw.* papur

bapuro *gw.* papuro

bar *e.g.* *ll.* -rau bar

bâr *gw.* pâr

bara *e.g.* bread. **bara brith** currant bread; **bara lawr** laver bread; **bara menyn** bread and butter. *gw.* **para**

baragraff *gw.* paragraff

baratoi *gw.* paratoi

barbeciw *e.g.* *ll.* **barbeciwiau** barbecue

barc *gw.* parc

barcut coch *e.g.* red kite

barch *gw.* parch

barchedig *gw.* parchedig

barchu *gw.* parchu

barchus *gw.* parchus

bardwn *gw.* pardwn

bardd *e.g.* *ll.* beirdd bard, poet

barddoniaeth *e.b.* poetry

barf *e.b.* *ll.* -au beard

barhad *gw.* parhad

barhau *gw.* parhau

barn *e.b.* *ll.* -au opinion, judgement. **Dydd y Farn** the Day of Judgement

barnwr *e.g.* *ll.* **barnwyr** judge

barod *gw.* parod

barrau *gw.* bar

barsel *gw.* parsel

barti *gw.* parti

bas 1 *e.g.* bass *(voice)*; base. 2 *a.* shallow

Basg, Gwlad y *e.b.* the Basque Country. *gw.* **Pasg**

basged *e.b.* *ll.* -i basket. **basgedaid** basketful

basiant *gw.* pasiant

basn *e.g.* *ll.* -au, -ys basin. **basn siwgr** sugar basin

basnau *gw.* basn

basnys *gw.* basn

baswn i. *bf.* I would (be). *gw.* **bod**

baswr *e.g.* *ll.* **baswyr** bass *(singer)*

bat *e.g.* *ll.* -iau bat

batrwm *gw.* patrwm

batrymau: batrynau *gw.* **patrwm**

bath 1 *e.g.* *ll.* -au kind; bath; such a. **Dim byd o'r fath** nothing of the kind; **Welais i erioed y fath le.** I never saw such a place. 2 *a.* minted

bathdai *gw.* bathdy

bathdy *e.g.* *ll.* **bathdai** mint

bathodyn *e.g.* *ll.* -nau badge

bathu *be.* (**bathaf**) to form, to shape, to coin, to mint. **bathu gair** to coin a word

baw *e.g.* dirt *(S.W.)*, dung, filth, mucus

bawb *gw.* pawb

bawd *e.g.* *ll.* **bodiau** thumb; big toe. **bys bawd** thumb, big toe

bawen *gw.* pawen

becso *be.* (**becsaf**) to worry, to vex *(S.W.)*

becyn *gw.* pecyn

bechadur *gw.* pechadur

bechan *a.b.* little, small. *gw.* **bychan**

bechgyn *gw.* bachgen

bechod *gw.* pechod

bechu *gw.* pechu

bedair

bedair *gw.* pedair
bedol *gw.* pedol
bedw *gw.* bedwen
bedwar *gw.* pedwar
bedwaredd *gw.* pedwaredd
bedwen *e.b. ll.* bedw birch.
  gwialen fedw birch-rod
bedwerydd *gw.* pedwerydd
bedyddio *be.* (bedyddiaf) to
  baptize
Bedyddiwr *e.g. ll.* Bedyddwyr
  Baptist. **Ioan Fedyddiwr** John
  the Baptist
bedd *e.g. ll.* -au grave, tomb
beg *gw.* peg
begwn *gw.* pegwn
beiau *gw.* bai
Beibl *e.g. ll.* -au Bible. **Y Beibl**
  Cymraeg Newydd The New
  Welsh Bible
beic *e.g. ll.* -iau bicycle
beicio *be.* (beiciaf) to cycle
beichiau *gw.* baich
beichiog *a.* pregnant;
  burdened
beidio *gw.* peidio (â)
beiddio *be.* (beiddiaf) to dare,
  to venture
beilot *gw.* peilot
beint *gw.* peint
beintio *gw.* peintio
beintiwr *gw.* peintiwr
beio *be.* (beiaf) to blame, to
  accuse, to censure
beirdd *gw.* bardd
beiriant *gw.* peiriant
beirniad *e.g. ll.* beirniaid
  adjudicator, critic
beirniadu *be.* (beirniadaf) to
  adjudicate, to criticize

beirniaid *gw.* beirniad
beisiau *gw.* pais
bêl *gw.* pêl
belydr *gw.* pelydr
bell *gw.* pell
bellach *ad.* now, at length,
  further. *gw.* pell
bellaf *gw.* pell
belled *gw.* pell
bellter *gw.* pellter
ben *gw.* pen
benaethiaid *gw.* pennaeth
benawdau *gw.* pennawd
ben-blwydd *gw.* pen-blwydd
bencadlys *gw.* pencadlys
bencampwr *gw.* pencampwr
bencydd *gw.* banc
bendant *gw.* pendant
benderfyniad *gw.*
  penderfyniad
benderfynol *gw.* penderfynol
benderfynu *gw.* penderfynu
bendigedig *a.* blessed,
  glorious, wonderful
bendith *e.b. ll.* -ion blessing
bendithio *be.* (bendithiaf) to
  bless
benelin *gw.* penelin
benfoel *gw.* penfoel
ben-glin *gw.* pen-glin
benigamp *gw.* penigamp
benillion *gw.* pennill
ben-lin *gw.* pen-glin
benlinio *gw.* penlinio
bennaeth *gw.* pennaeth
bennaf *gw.* pennaf
bennau *gw.* pen
bennawd *gw.* pennawd
bennill *gw.* pennill
bennod *gw.* pennod

benodau *gw.* pennod
benodi *gw.* penodi
benodiad *gw.* penodiad
benrhyn *gw.* penrhyn
bensaer *gw.* pensaer
bensil *gw.* pensil
bensiwn *gw.* pensiwn
bensiynau *gw.* pensiwn
bensiynwr *gw.* pensiynwr
benteulu *gw.* penteulu
bentref *gw.* pentref
bentwr *gw.* pentwr
bentyrrau *gw.* pentwr
benthyca *be.* **(benthycaf)** to
  borrow, to lend
benwythnos *gw.* penwythnos
benyw *e.b.* *ll.* **-od** woman,
  female
benywaidd *a.* female, feminine
ber *a.b.* short, brief. *gw.* **byr**
bêr *gw.* pêr
berchen: berchennog *gw.*
  perchen
beren *gw.* peren
bererin *gw.* pererin
berf *e.b.* *ll.* **-au** verb
berfa *e.b.* *ll.* **berfâu**
  wheelbarrow (*N.W.*); *gw.*
  whilber
berfedd *gw.* perfedd
berfenw *e.b.* *ll.* **-au** verb-noun
berffaith *gw.* perffaith
berffeithio *gw.* perffeithio
beri *gw.* peri
berl *gw.* perl
berlysiau *gw.* perlysiau
berllan *gw.* perllan
bersli *gw.* persli
berson *gw.* person
bersonol *gw.* personol

bersonoliaeth *gw.*
  personoliaeth
bert *gw.* pert
berth *gw.* perth
berthnasau *gw.* perthynas
berthnasol *gw.* perthnasol
berthyn *gw.* perthyn
berthynas *gw.* perthynas
berw 1 *e.g.* boiling, tumult,
  turmoil. 2 *a.* boiling,
  seething; **dŵr berw** boiling
  water. 3 *e.g.* cress: **berw'r**
  dŵr water cress
berwi *be.* **(berwaf)** to boil
bergyl *gw.* perygl
beryglus *gw.* peryglus
beswch *gw.* peswch
besychiad *gw.* pesychiad
betrol *gw.* petrol
beth *rhag.* what? **beth am**
  ginio? what about dinner?
  beth mae e'n wneud? what's
  he doing? **beth sydd yma?**
  what's here? **beth ydy ei**
  enw? what's his name? **beth**
  bynnag anyway. *gw.* **peth**
biano *gw.* piano
bianydd *gw.* pianydd
bib *gw.* pib
biben *gw.* piben
bicil: bicl *gw.* picil
bictiwr *gw.* pictiwr
bicwnen *gw.* picwnen
bigfain *gw.* pigfain
bigiad *gw.* pigiad
bigo *gw.* pigo
bigog *gw.* pigog
bil *e.g.* *ll.* **-iau** bill. *gw.* **pil**
biler *gw.* piler
bilio *gw.* pilio
bilion *gw.* pil

bili-pala

bili-pala *gw*. pili-pala
bilsen *gw*. pilsen
bilyn *gw*. pilyn
bin *e.g*. *ll*. -iau bin. *gw*. **pin**
bîn *gw*. pîn
bînafal *gw*. pînafal
binc *gw*. pinc
binnau *gw*. pin
binsio *gw*. pinsio
binwydden *gw*. pinwydden
bioden *gw*. pioden
bioleg *e.b*. biology
bisged *e.b*. *ll*. **bisgedi** biscuit
bisgïen *e.b*. *ll*. **bisgis** biscuit
bisyn *gw*. pisyn
biti *gw*. piti
bitw *a*. tiny. **bws bitw** minibus
blaen 1 *e.g*. *ll*. -au, -ion point,
  end, top, tip; front, van;
  edge; source, limit, lead. 2 *a*.
  foremost, front, first
blaendal *e.g*. *ll*. -iadau deposit
blaenor *e.g*. *ll*. -iaid leader;
  deacon; predecessor
blaenwr *e.g*. *ll*. **blaenwyr**
  forward (*rugby and soccer*);
  leader (*of orchestra*)
blaguro *be*. (**blaguraf**) to bud
blaguryn *e.g*. *ll*. **blagur** bud
blaid *gw*. plaid
blaidd *e.g*. *ll*. **bleiddiaid,**
  bleiddiau wolf
blan *gw*. plan
blanced *e.b*. *ll*. -i blanket.
  blanced wlân woollen
  blanket; **blanced drydan**
  electric blanket
blanhigyn *gw*. planhigyn
blannu *gw*. plannu
blant *gw*. plant

blas *e.g*. taste, flavour;
  fervour, zest. **colli blas ar** to
  lose one's taste for. *gw*. **plas**
blasty *gw*. plasty
blasu *be*. (**blasaf**) to taste, to
  relish
blasus *a*. tasty, delicious,
  savoury
blât *gw*. plât
blawd *e.g*. *ll*. **blodiau, blodion**
  flour, meal; **blawd codi** self-
  raising flour; **blawd llif**
  sawdust
ble *rhag*. where?
bleidiau *gw*. plaid
bleidlais *gw*. pleidlais
bleidleisio *gw*. pleidleisio
bleidleisiwr *gw*. pleidleisiwr
bleiddiaid: bleiddiau *gw*.
  blaidd
blentyn *gw*. plentyn
blentynnaidd *gw*.
  plentynnaidd
bleser *gw*. pleser
bleserus *gw*. pleserus
blesio *gw*. plesio
blew *gw*. blewyn
blewyn *e.g*. *ll*. **blew** hair (*on
  body, not on head*), fur;
  small fish bone. **hollti blew** to
  split hairs
blin *a*. tired, tiresome, cross;
  sorry
blinder *e.g*. *ll*. -au weariness,
  trouble, adversity
blinedig *a*. wearisome, tired
blino *be*. (**blinaf**) to tire, to
  vex, to weary. **Rydw i wedi
  blino** I am tired; **Mae e wedi
  blino** he is tired; **blino ar** to
  grow tired of
blisgyn *gw*. plisgyn

blisman: blismon *gw.* **plisman**
blith *gw.* **plith**
blodau *gw.* **blodyn**
blodeugerdd *e.b.* *ll.* **-i**
  anthology
blodfresychen *e.b.* *ll.*
  blodfresych cauliflower
blodiau: blodion *gw.* **blawd**
blodyn *e.g.* *ll.* **blodau** flower,
  blossom, bloom
bloedd *e.g.* *ll.* **-iau, -iadau**
  shout
bloeddio *be.* **(bloeddiaf)** to
  shout (*N.W.*)
blows *e.b.* *ll.* **-ys** blouse
blog *eg.* *ll.* **–iau** blog
blogio *be.* **(blogiaf)** to blog
blogiwr *e.g.* *ll.* **blogwyr** a
  blogger
blu *gw.* **pluen**
bluen *gw.* **pluen**
bluf *gw.* **plufyn**
blufyn *gw.* **plufyn**
blwc *gw.* **plwc**
blwch *e.g.* *ll.* **blychau** box,
  chest
blwg *gw.* **plwg**
blwm *gw.* **plwm**
blwydd 1 *e.b.* *ll.* **-i** year-old,
  year of age. **tair blwydd oed**
  three years of age. 2 *a.* year
  old. *gw. At. Treiglad-
  Trwynol*
blwyddyn *e.b.* *ll.*
  blynyddoedd year. **dwy
  flynedd** two years; **tair
  blynedd** three years; **pedair
  blynedd** four years; **pum
  mlynedd** five years. *gw. At.
  Treiglad Trwynol*
blwyf *gw.* **plwyf**

blychau *gw.* **blwch**
blygu *gw.* **plygu**
blynedd *gw.* **blwyddyn**
blynedd *e.b.* *ll.* years (*used
  usually after cardinal
  numbers*)
blynyddoedd *gw.* **blwyddyn**
bob *gw.* **pob. bob bore** every
  morning; **bob nos** every
  night; **bob dydd** every day
bobi *gw.* **pobi**
bobl *gw.* **pobl**
boblogaeth *gw.* **poblogaeth**
boblogaidd *gw.* **poblogaidd**
bobman *gw.* **pobman**
bobydd *gw.* **pobydd**
boced *gw.* **poced**
bocedi *gw.* **poced**
bocs *e.g.* *ll.* **-ys** box
boch *e.b.* *ll.* **-au** cheek
bod 1 *e.g.* *ll.* **-au** existence;
  being. **Y Bod Mawr** God.
  2 *be.* **(rydw i/rwy i /dw i)** to
  be; **rydw i**
  I am, **rwyt ti** you are, **mae e/o**
  he/it is, **mae hi** she/it is, *etc.*
  gw. At. Berfau
bodau *gw.* **bod**
bodiau *gw.* **bawd**
bodio *be.* **(bodiaf)** to thumb,
  to finger
bodlon: boddlon *a.* willing,
  pleased, content. **bodlon ar**
  satisfied with
bodloni *be.* **(bodlonaf)** to
  please, to satisfy, to be
  contented
bodd *e.g.* will, pleasure;
  consent. **rhyngu bodd** to
  please; **trwy fodd** with
  consent or permission; **wrth
  ei fodd** happy, contented

boddhad

boddhad *e.g.* satisfaction, pleasure

boddi *be.* **(boddaf)** to drown, to be drowned, to flood

boddlon *gw.* **bodlon**

boen *gw.* **poen**

boeni *gw.* **poeni**

boenus *gw.* **poenus**

boenydio *gw.* **poenydio**

boer: boeri *gw.* **poer, poeri**

boeth *gw.* **poeth**

boeth *gw.* **poethi**

bol *e.g.* *ll.* **-iau** belly, stomach, abdomen

bola *e.g.* *ll.* **bolâu, boliau** belly, stomach, abdomen

bolâu *gw.* **bola**

boliau *gw.* **bol, bola**

bolion *gw.* **polyn**

boliticaidd *gw.* **politicaidd**

bolyn *gw.* **polyn**

bollt *e.g.b.* *ll.* **-au, byllt** bolt, dart; thunderbolt

bolltau *gw.* **bollt**

bolltio *be.* **(bolltiaf)** to bolt

bom *e.g.* *ll.* **-iau** bomb

bôn *e.g.* *ll.* **bonau, bonion** base, trunk, stump, counterfoil. **yn y bôn** basically, in reality

boneddiges *e.b.* *ll.* **-au** lady

boneddigion *gw.* **bonheddwr**

bonheddig *a.* noble, gentle

bonheddwr *e.g.* *ll.* **bonheddwyr, boneddigion** gentleman, nobleman. **foneddigion a boneddigesau** ladies and gentlemen *(in addressing an audience)*

bonion *gw.* **bôn**

bont *gw.* **pont**

bontydd *gw.* **pont**

bopeth *gw.* **popeth**

bopty *gw.* **popty**

bord *e.b.* *ll.* **-ydd, -au** table *(S.W.)*, board *(S.W.)*

bordau: bordydd *gw.* **bord**

bore *e.g.* *ll.* **-au** morning. **yn fore** early; **bore trannoeth** next morning

borfa *gw.* **porfa**

borfeydd *gw.* **porfa**

borffor *gw.* **porffor**

bori *gw.* **pori**

bortread *gw.* **portread**

borth *gw.* **porth**

borthladd *gw.* **porthladd**

bos *e.g.* *ll.* **-ys** boss, chief. **Pwy ydy'r bos yma?** Who's the boss here?

bos *gw.* **pos**

bosibilrwydd *gw.* **posibilrwydd**

bosibl *gw.* **posibl**

bost *gw.* **post**

bostio *gw.* **postio**

bostman: bostmon *gw.* **postman**

bostmyn *gw.* **postman**

bostyn *gw.* **postyn**

bosys *gw.* **bos**

botel *gw.* **potel**

botwm *e.g.* *ll.* **botymau** button

botymu *be.* **(botymaf)** to button

bowdr: bowdwr *gw.* **powdr**

bowdrau *gw.* **powdr**

bowlen: powlen *e.b.* *ll.* **-ni, bowliau: powliau** bowl

bresenoldeb

braf *a.* fine, nice, pleasant.
bore braf a fine morning;
Mae hi'n braf (*no mutation*),
it is fine (*weather-wise*)

bragdy *e.g.* *ll.* **bragdai**
brewery

braich *e.b.g.* *ll.* **breichiau** arm

braidd *ad.* near, almost, just,
rather, scarcely. **o'r braidd**
hardly. *gw.* **praidd**

brain *gw.* **brân**

braint *e.b.* *ll.* **breintiau**,
breiniau privilege, right,
honour, status.

bram *gw.* **pram**

brân *e.b.* *ll.* **brain** crow

bras *a.* thick, fat; greasy;
coarse; rich; rough,
approximate

braslun *e.g.* *ll.* **-iau** outline,
sketch

braster *e.g.* *ll.* **-au** grossness,
fat

braw *e.g.* *ll.* **-iau** terror, fright

brawd *e.g.* *ll.* **brodyr** brother

brech *e.b.* *ll.* **-au** eruption,
vaccination, pox. **brech goch**
measles; **brech yr ieir**
chickenpox

brechdan *e.b.* *ll.* **-au** slice of
buttered bread, sandwich

brechiad *e.g.* *ll.* **-au**
inoculation, vaccination

bregeth *gw.* **pregeth**

bregethu *gw.* **pregethu**

bregethwr *gw.* **pregethwr**

breichiau *gw.* **braich**

breichled *e.b.* *ll.* **-au** bracelet,
bangle

breiddiau *gw.* **praidd**

breifat *gw.* **preifat**

breiniau: breintiau *gw.* **braint**

bren *gw.* **pren**

brenhines *e.b.* *ll.* **breninesau**
queen

brenhinoedd *gw.* **brenin**

brenhinol *a.* royal

brenin *e.g.* *ll.* **brenhinoedd**
king

brennau *gw.* **pren**

Insight
> brawd *e.g.* (pronounced as bra-wd) brother; friar. **Brawd Du**
> Black Friar or Dominican Friar; **Brawd Gwyn** White Friar or
> Carmelite Friar; **Brawd Llwyd** Grey Friar or Franciscan Friar.

brawddeg *e.b.* *ll.* **-au** sentence

brawf *gw.* **prawf**

brawiau *gw.* **braw**

brecwast *e.g.* *ll.* **-au**
breakfast. **wy i frecwast-**
egg for breakfast

brentis *gw.* **prentis**

brentisiaeth *gw.* **prentisiaeth**

bres *e.g.* *ll.* **-i,-ys** brace. *gw.*
pres

breseb *gw.* **preseb**

bresennol *gw.* **presennol**

bresenoldeb *gw.* **presenoldeb**

bresgripsiwn

bresgripsiwn *gw.*
 presgripsiwn
brest *e.b.* *ll.* **-iau** breast; chest
breswyl: breswylfod *gw.*
 preswyl
breswylfeydd *gw.* **preswyl**
bresychen *e.b.* *ll.* **bresych**
 cabbage
brethyn *e.g.* *ll.* **-nau** cloth.
 brethyn cartref home-spun
 cloth
breuddwyd *e.b.g.* *ll.* **-ion**
 dream
breuddwydio *be.*
 (breuddwydiaf) to dream
breuddwydion *gw.* **breuddwyd**
bridwerth *gw.* **pridwerth**
bridd *gw.* **pridd**
brif *gw.* **prif**
brifardd *gw.* **prifardd**
brifathrawes *gw.* **prifathrawes**
brifathro *gw.* **prifathro**
brifddinas *gw.* **prifddinas**
brifeirdd *gw.* **prifardd**
brifio *gw.* **prifio**
brifo *be.* **(brifaf)** to hurt, to
 wound; to crumble *(N.W.)*
brifysgol *gw.* **prifysgol**
briffordd *gw.* **priffordd**
briffyrdd *gw.* **priffordd**
brig *e.g.* *ll.* **-au** top, summit;
 outcrop; twig(s). **brig y don**
 crest of the wave; **brig y**
 goeden the tree top; **brig y**
 nos dusk; **brig y to** the roof-
 top; **o'r brig i'r bôn** from top
 to bottom; **glo brig** open-cast
 coal; **ar frig yr agenda** at the
 top of the agenda
brigau *gw.* **brig, brigyn**

brigyn *e.g.* *ll.* **brigau** twig
brin *gw.* **prin**
brinder *gw.* **prinder**
brintio *gw.* **printio**
briod *gw.* **priod**
briodas *gw.* **priodas**
briodi *gw.* **priodi**
briodol *gw.* **priodol**
bris *gw.* **pris**
britho: brithio *be.* **(brithaf:**
 brithiaf) to turn grey (of hair,
 beard)
briwsionyn *e.g.* *ll.* **briwsion**
 crumb, fragment
bro *e.b.* *ll.* **bröydd** region,
 country, vale, lowland. **bro a**
 bryn vale and hill; **Bro**
 Morgannwg Vale of
 Glamorgan
broblem *gw.* **problem**
brodor *e.g.* *ll.* **-ion** native
brodorol *a.* native
brodyr *gw.* **brawd**
brofi *gw.* **profi**
brofiad *gw.* **profiad**
brofiadol *gw.* **profiadol**
brofion *gw.* **profion**
broffid *gw.* **proffid**
broffidiol *gw.* **proffidiol**
broffwyd *gw.* **proffwyd**
broffwydo *gw.* **proffwydo**
broga *e.g.* *ll.* **-od** frog. *gw.*
 ffroga: llyffant *(S.W.)*
bron 1 *e.b.* *ll.* **-nau** breast.
 2 *e.b.* *ll.* **-nydd** breast of hill.
 3 *ad.* almost nearly, just
 about to
bronfraith *e.b.* *ll.* **bronfreithod**
 thrush
bronnau: bronnydd *gw.* **bron**

brotest *gw.* protest

Brotestant *gw.* Protestant

brown *a.* brown

bröydd *gw.* bro

brudd *gw.* prudd

brwdfrydig *a.* enthusiastic

brwnt *a.* dirty (*S.W.*), foul,
cruel (*N.W.*)

brws: brwsh *e.g. ll.* brwsys:
brwshys brush, broom

brwsio: brwshio *be.* (brwsiaf:
brwshiaf) to sweep, to brush

brwsys: brwshys *gw.* brws

brwydr *e.b. ll.* -au battle,
conflict

brwydrau *gw.* brwydr

bryd *e.g. ll.* -iau mind,
thought, intent. *gw.* pryd

Brydain *gw.* Prydain

brydau *gw.* pryd

Brydeinig *gw.* Prydeinig

bryder *gw.* pryder

bryderu *gw.* pryderu

bryderus *gw.* pryderus

brydferth *gw.* prydferth

brydferthwch *gw.*
prydferthwch

brydiau *gw.* bryd, pryd

brydlon *gw.* prydlon

bryf: bryfedyn: bryfyn *gw.*
pryf

bryfed *gw.* pryf

bryfocio *gw.* profocio

bryfyn *gw.* pryf

bryn *e.g. ll.* -iau hill

brynhawn *gw.* prynhawn

bryniau *gw.* bryn

brynu *gw.* prynu

brynwr *gw.* prynwr

brys *e.g.* haste, hurry. **ar frys**
in haste, hurriedly; **ar frys
gwyllt** in a mad rush

brysio *be.* (brysiaf) to hasten,
to hurry

brysurdeb *gw.* prysurdeb

brysuro *gw.* prysuro

brysur *gw.* prysur

buan *a.* swift, quick, fast;
soon. *gw. At. Ansoddeiriau*

buarth *e.g. ll.* -au farmyard,
yard

buchod *gw.* buwch

budr *a.* dirty (*N.W.*), nasty
(*N.W.*), foul (*N.W.*), vile
(*N.W.*). **bachgen budr** a bit
of a lad (*S.W.*)

budd-dâl *e.g. ll.* budd-daliadau
benefit *(payment)*

buddsoddi *be.* (buddsoddaf)
to invest

buddugol *a.* victorious,
winning

buddugoliaeth *e.b. ll.* -au
victory

bues i *bf.* I was, I have been.
gw. bod

bugail *e.g. ll.* bugeiliaid
shepherd; pastor

bugeiliaid *gw.* bugail

bugeilio *be.* (bugeiliaf) to
shepherd, to watch

bulpud *gw.* pulpud

bum: bump *gw.* pump

bûm: bues *bf.* I was, I have
been. *gw.* bod

b'un *gw.* p'un

bunnau: bunnoedd *gw.* punt

bunt *gw.* punt

bupur *gw.* pupur

bur

bur *gw.* pur
burfa *gw.* purfa
buro *gw.* puro

bwthyn *e.g. ll.* bythynnod
cottage, cabin
bwy *gw.* pwy

Insight
bwyd *e.g.* (a true diphthong: 'wy' with emphasis on w and pronounced as 'bŵeed') food, nourishment. bwyd y duwiau 'ambrosia'.

busnes *e.g.b. ll.* -ion, -au
business, affairs
buwch *e.b. ll.* buchod, da
(*S.W.*) cow
bwced *e.g.b. ll.* -i bucket
bwdin *gw.* pwdin
bwdr *gw.* pwdr
bwdryn *gw.* pwdryn
bwdu *gw.* pwdu
bwlch *e.g. ll.* bylchau gap,
pass
bŵer *gw.* pŵer
bwll *gw.* pwll
bwmp *gw.* pwmp
bwnc *gw.* pwnc
bwrdd *e.g. ll.* byrddau table
(*N.W.*); board, plank; deck.
bwrdd brecwast breakfast
table; bwrdd du blackboard
bwriad *e.g. ll.* -au purpose,
intention, resolution
bwriadu *be.* (bwriadaf) to
intend
bwrpas *gw.* pwrpas
bwrs *gw.* pwrs
bwrw *be.* (bwriaf) to cast; to
shed; to strike. bwrw glaw to
rain; bwrw cesair to hail;
bwrw eira to snow
bws *e.g. ll.* bysiau, bysys bus

bwyd *e.g. ll.* -ydd food
bwyda *gw.* bwydo
bwydlen *e.b. ll.* -ni menu
bwydo: bwyda *be.* (bwydaf) to
feed, to nourish. bwydo'r
adar to feed the birds
bwydydd *gw.* bwyd
bwyll *gw.* pwyll
bwyllgor *gw.* pwyllgor
bwyllo *gw.* pwyllo
bwynt *gw.* pwynt
bwys *gw.* pwys
bwysedd *gw.* pwysedd
bwysig *gw.* pwysig
bwysigrwydd *gw.*
pwysigrwydd
bwyslais *gw.* pwyslais
bwyso *gw.* pwyso
bwyta: byta (*S.W.*) *be.*
(bwytâf) to eat; to consume,
to ravage; to corrode (*S.W.*).
Bwytâf ginio bob dydd I eat
dinner every day. *gw. At.
Berfau*
bwyty *e.g. ll.* bwytai
restaurant
bwyth *gw.* pwyth
bychan *a.g.* little, small,
petty. *gw.* bechan

byd *e.g. ll.* **-oedd** world; life;
state. **byd caled** a hard
struggle; **byd da** good living,
a sumptuous life; **byd o
wahaniaeth** a world of
difference; **gwyn ei fyd!**
blessed is he, how fortunate!
beth yn y byd. . .? what in
the world. . .? what on
earth. . .?

bydoedd *gw.* **byd**

bydru *gw.* **pydru**

bydd (e/hi) *bf.* he/she/it will
be. **Bydd Mair yno** Mair will
be there; **bydd plant yno
hefyd** children will be there
also. *gw.* **bod**

byddar 1 *e.g. ll.* **-iaid** deaf
person
2 *a.* deaf

byddin *e.b. ll.* **-oedd** army,
host

byddinoedd *gw.* **byddin**

byg *e.g. ll.* **bygiau** bug

bylchai *gw.* **bwlch**

byllau *gw.* **pwll, pyllyn**

byllt *gw.* **bollt**

byllyn *gw.* **pyllyn**

bymtheg: bymtheng *gw.*
pymtheg

bymthegfed *gw.* **pymthegfed**

bynciau *gw.* **pwnc**

bynnag *rhag.* -ever, -soever.
beth bynnag whatsoever; **ble
bynnag** wherever; **pryd
bynnag** whenever; **pwy
bynnag** whoever

byped *gw.* **pyped**

byr *a.g. ll.* **-ion** short, brief.
dyn byr a short man; **stori fer**
a short story; **straeon byrion**
short stories. *gw.* **ber**

byrbryd *e.g. ll.* **-iau** snack

byrddaid *e.g. ll.* **byrddeidiau**
tableful

byrddau *gw.* **bwrdd**

byrfodd *e.g. ll.* **-au**
abbreviation

byrsau *gw.* **pwrs**

byrth *gw.* **porth**

bys *e.g. ll.* **-edd** finger. **bys
bawd** thumb, big toe; **bysedd
y blaidd** lupins; **bysedd y
cŵn** foxgloves. *gw.* **pysen**

bysedd *gw.* **bys**

bysen *gw.* **pysen**

bysgod *gw.* **pysgodyn**

bysgodyn *gw.* **pysgodyn**

bysgota *gw.* **pysgota**

bysgotwr *gw.* **pysgotwr**

bysiau *gw.* **bws**

byst *gw.* **post**, *gw.* **postyn**

bysys *gw.* **bws**

byta *(S.W.) gw.* **bwyta**

byth 1 *ad.* ever, still, always.
am byth for ever; **byth a
hefyd** continually. **2** (**byth** *is
frequently used in negative
sentences in the present,
future, imperfect and
conditional tense to convey
the meaning* never). **Ddaw e
byth** He will never come;
Doedd hi byth yn hwyr She
was never late. **3** *e.g. ll.*
-oedd eternity. **byth
bythoedd** for ever and ever,
world without end

bythefnos *gw.* **pythefnos**

bythynnod *gw.* **bwthyn**

byw

byw 1 *be.* **(bywiaf)** to live, to exist, to dwell, to inhabit; to animate, to revive, to restore to life. **byw a bod** to be habitually present; **Mae e'n byw yma** He lives here. 2 *a.* alive, living. **Ydy e'n fyw?** Is he alive? 3 *e.g.* life. **yn fy myw** for the life of me

bywiog *a.* lively, vivacious

bywyd *e.g. ll.* **-au** life, existence

bywydeg *e.b.* biology

C

caban *e.g. ll.* **-au** booth, cabin, hut

cacen *e.b. ll.* **-nau, -ni** cake *(N.W.)*

cacwn *gw.* **cacynen**

cacynen *e.b. ll.* **cacwn** wasp *(N.W.).* **yn gacwn gwyllt** furious

cadach *e.g. ll.* **-au** cloth, rag; handkerchief, bandage *(N.W.).* **cadach llawr** cloth for wiping floor; **cadach llestri** dish cloth

cadair *e.b. ll.* **cadeiriau** chair. **cadair esmwyth** easy chair; **cadair freichiau** arm chair

cadeirio *be.* **(cadeiriaf)** to chair

cadeiriol *a.* chaired. **eglwys gadeiriol** cathedral

cadeirydd *e.g. ll.* **-ion** chairman

cadno *e.g. ll.* **cadnoaid, cadnawon** fox. **cadnawes: cadnöes** vixen *(S.W.)*

cadw (rhag.) *be.* **(cadwaf)** to keep, to preserve (from). **cadw ar gof** to keep on record; **cadw draw** to stay away; **cadw sŵn** to make a noise, to complain; **cadw'n heini** to keep fit; **cadw ystafell** to reserve a room; **cadw-mi-gei** money box; **cyfrif cadw** deposit account

cadwrol *a.* conservative

cadwyn *e.b. ll.* **-au, -i** chain; series

cadwyno *be.* **(cadwynaf)** to chain, to enslave

cae *e.g. ll.* **-au** field

caeau *gw.* **cae**

cael *be.* **(caf)** to have, to find. **ar gael** in existence, available; **cael annwyd** to catch a cold; **cael blas ar** to enjoy; **cael a chael** a close call. *gw. At. Berfau*

Insight

caer *e.b.* ('ae' pronounced as 'ai') fort or castle as in **Caernarfon** or **Caerfyrddin**. The former *has* a castle, the latter *had* a fort a long, long time ago!

caer *e.b. ll.* **-au, ceyrydd** fort, castle

Caer *e.b.* Chester

Caerdydd *e.b.* **Prif Ddinas a Sir** Cardiff (Capital City and County)

Caeredin *e.b.* Edinburgh

Caerfyrddin *e.b.* (Tref a Sir) Carmarthen (Town and County)

Caergybi *e.b.* Holyhead

Caerloyw *e.b.* Gloucester

Caersalem: Jerwsalem *e.b.* Jerusalem

caets *e.g. ll.* **-ys** cage

caf *bf.* I have, I shall have. *gw.* **cael**

cafodd *bf.* he/she/it had. *gw.* **cael**

caffe *e.g. ll.* **-s** café

cangen *e.b. ll.* **canghennau** branch

canghennau *gw.* **cangen**

caiff *bf.* he/she/it will have. *gw.* **cael**

cais *e.g. ll.* **ceisiadau, ceisiau** attempt; try *(rugby)*; request; application. **gwneud cais** to make an application, to apply

calan *e.g. ll.* **-nau** first day *(of month or season)*. **Dydd Calan** New Year's Day; **Calan Gaeaf** All Saints' Day; **Calan Mai** May Day

caled *a.* hard, hardy, difficult. *gw. At. Ansoddeiriau*

caledi *e.g.* hardship, severity

caledu *be.* **(caledaf)** to harden; to dry. **caledu dillad** to air clothes; **caledu gwely** to air a bed

caledwch *e.g.* hardness; difficulty

calendr *e.g. ll.* **-au** calendar

calenigion *gw.* **calennig**

calennig *e.g. ll.* **calenigion** New Year's gift

caletach *gw.* **caled**

caletaf *gw.* **caled**

caleted *gw.* **caled**

calon *e.b. ll.* **-nau** heart. **diolch o galon** heartfelt thanks; **calon lân** pure heart; **calon y gwir** the absolute truth. **trawiad ar y galon** heart attack

call *a.* wise, sensible, **hanner call a chrac** foolish, stupid. *gw. At. Ansoddeiriau*

callach *gw.* **call**

callaf *gw.* **call**

called *gw.* **call**

cam 1 *e.g. ll.* **-au** stride, step; injury. **o gam i gam** step by step. 2 *a.* crooked, false. **coesgam** bandy-legged

camarwain *be.* **(camarweiniaf)** to mislead

camddeall *be.* **(camddeallaf)** to misunderstand

camera *e.g. ll.* **camerâu** camera

camp *e.b. ll.* **-au** feat, game; excellence. **campau** sports

campfa *e.b. ll.* **campfeydd** gymnasium

campfeydd *gw.* **campfa**

campus

campus *a.* excellent, splendid
campwaith *e.g. ll.*
  campweithiau masterpiece
campweithiau *gw.* **campwaith**
camsyniad *e.g. ll.* **-au**
  mistake *(S.W.)*
camu *be.* **(camaf)** to step, to
  stride; to bend, to stoop
cân *e.b. ll.* **caniadau,**
  caneuon song, poem. **cân**
  actol action song; **cân bop**
  pop song; **cân serch** love
  song; **cân werin** folksong;
  cân ysgafn ballad
can 1 *a.* white; hundred.
  canpunt a hundred pounds
  (sterling); **canmlwydd** a
  hundred years old; **canmil** a
  hundred thousand; **canrif** a
  century. *gw.* **cant.**
  2 *e.g.* white flour, flour;
  bara can white bread. **3** *e.g.*
  ll. **-iau** *(tin)* can
caneuon *gw.* **cân**
canfed *a.* hundredth
canhwyllau *gw.* **cannwyll**
canhwyllbren *e.g. ll.* **-nau, -ni**
  candlestick
caniad *e.g. ll.* **-au** song,
  singing; ring *(telephone).*
  Rhowch ganiad i fi
  Telephone me
caniadaeth *e.b.* music,
  singing. **Caniadaeth y Cysegr**
  Songs of Praise
caniadau *gw.* **cân, caniad**
caniatâd *e.g.* permission,
  consent
caniatáu *be.* **(caniatâf)** to
  allow

caniedydd *e.g. ll.* **-ion** song-
  book, hymn-book
canmlwydd *e.ll. & e.b. ll.* **-i** a
  hundred years old, hundred
  years; century
canmlwyddiannau *gw.*
  canmlwyddiant
canmlwyddiant *e.g. ll.*
  canmlwyddiannau centenary
canmol 1 *be.* **(canmolaf)** to
  praise. **2** *e.g.* praise
canmoliaeth *e.b. ll.* **-au** praise
cannoedd *gw.* **cant**
cannu *be.* to bleach, to
  whiten
cannwyll *e.b. ll.* **canhwyllau**
  candle. **cannwyll y llygad**
  pupil of the eye; apple of the
  eye
canol 1 *e.g. ll.* **-au** centre,
  middle. **canol dydd** midday;
  canol nos midnight. **2** *a.*
  middle. **canol y ffordd**
  middle of the road
canolbarth *e.g. ll.* **-au**
  midland; **Canolbarth Cymru**
  Mid Wales; **Canolbarth**
  Lloegr The Midlands;
  Canolbarth Ffrainc Central
  France
canolbwyntio (ar) *be.*
  (canolbwyntiaf) to
  concentrate, to focus (on)
canoldir *e.g. ll.* **-oedd** inland
  region. **Y Môr Canoldir**
  Mediterranean Sea
canolfan *e.b. ll.* **-nau** centre.
  canolfan ddinesig civic
  centre; **canolfan hamdden**
  leisure centre

canolog *a.* central

canolwr *e.g. ll.* **canolwyr** referee, umpire

canradd *a.* centigrade

canran *e.b. ll.* **canrannau** percentage

canrif *e.b. ll.* **canrifau, canrifoedd** century

canrifau: canrifoedd *gw.* **canrif**

cant: can *e.g. ll.* **cannoedd** hundred. **cant a mil** a hundred and one, a large number; **cant y cant** hundred per cent; **deg y cant** ten per cent; **can diolch** many thanks; **canwaith** a hundred times

cantor *e.g. ll.* **-ion** precentor. *gw.* **cantores; canwr**

cantores *e.b. ll.* **-au** female singer, female vocalist. *gw.* **cantor; canwr**

canu *be.* **(canaf)** to sing, to play. **canu cloch** to ring a bell; **canu'n iach** to bid goodbye; **canu'r piano** to play the piano; **wedi canu ar** too late, all up. *gw. At. Berfau*

canŵ *e.g. ll.* **-od** canoe

canŵio *be.* **(canŵiaf)** to canoe

canwr *e.g. ll.* **canwyr** male singer, vocalist. *gw.* **cantor; cantores**

canwriad *e.g. ll.* **canwriaid** centurion

cap *e.g. ll.* **-iau** cap

capel *e.g. ll.* **-i, -au** chapel

capteiniaid *gw.* **capten**

capten *e.g. ll.* **-iaid, capteiniaid** captain

capteniaid *gw.* **capten**

car *e.g. ll.* **ceir** car. **car heddlu** police car; **car rasio** racing car; **car llusg** sled

carafán *e.b. ll.* **-au** caravan

carafana *be.* **(carafanaf)** to go caravanning

carbon *e.g.* carbon

carco *be.* **(carcaf)** to take care of *(S.W.)*

carcus *a.* careful *(S.W.)*

carchar *e.g. ll.* **-au** prison

carcharor *e.g. ll.* **-ion** prisoner

carcharu *be.* **(carcharaf)** to imprison

cardiau *gw.* **cerdyn**

caredig *a.* kind

caredigrwydd *e.g.* kindness

cariad *e.g.b. ll.* **-on** love, lover. **Dere 'ma, cariad!** Come here, love!

cariadon *gw.* **cariad**

cariadus *a.* beloved; loving

cario *be.* **(cariaf)** to carry

carlamu *be.* **(carlamaf)** to gallop

carol *e.b. ll.* **-au** carol. **carol Nadolig** Christmas carol

carped *e.g. ll.* **-i** carpet

carreg *e.b. ll.* **cerrig** stone. **carreg aelwyd** hearthstone; **carreg fedd** tombstone; **carreg filltir** milestone; **carreg y drws** doorstep; **cerrig mân** pebbles, chippings

cartref

cartref *e.g. ll.* **-i** home. **gartref** at home; **adref** homewards

cartrefi *gw.* **cartref**

cartrefu *be.* **(cartrefaf)** to dwell

cartŵn *e.g. ll.* **cartwnau** cartoon

caru *be.* **(caraf)** to love, to like, to court

carwriaeth *e.b. ll.* **carwriaethau** affair, romance

cas *e.g.* enmity, hated person or thing; case. 2 *a.* nasty

casáu *be.* **(casâf)** to detest

casgen *e.b. ll.* **casgenni** barrel

casgenni *gw.* **casgen**

casgliad *e.g. ll.* **-au** collection; gathering; conclusion. **Fe ddaeth i'r casgliad** He came to the conclusion

casglu *be.* **(casglaf)** to collect, to infer. **casglu dros** to collect on behalf of

Cas-gwent *e.b.* Chepstow

Casllwchwr *e.b.* Loughor

Casnewydd *e.b.* Newport (*Mon.*)

castell *e.g. ll.* **cestyll** castle

Castell-nedd *e.b.* Neath

cath *e.b. ll.* **-od** cat. **cath fach** kitten; **cwrcath, cwrcyn** tomcat

cau 1 *be.* **(caeaf)** to close. 2 *a.* enclosed; hollow

cawl 1 *e.g.* soup, broth. **cawl cennin** leek broth; **cawl pys** pea soup. 2 *e.g.* mess. **Fe**

wnaeth e gawl o'r trefniadau He made a mess of the arrangements

cawod *e.b. ll.* **cawodydd** shower. **cawodydd Ebrill** April showers

cawr *e.g. ll.* **cewri** giant. **cawr o wleidydd** a great politician

caws *e.g.* cheese. **caws Caer** Cheshire cheese; **caws Caerffili** Caerffili cheese; **cael caws o fola ci** to get blood out of a stone; **caws llyffant** toadstool. *gw.* **cosyn**

cefn *e.g. ll.* **-au** back; ridge; support. **cefn gwlad** heart of the countryside. **Roedd e'n gefn i'r teulu** He was a great help to the family

cefnder *e.g. ll.* **-wyr, cefndyr** cousin (*male*); *gw.* **cyfnither**

cefnderwyr *gw.* **cefnder**

cefndir *e.g. ll.* **-oedd** background

cefndiroedd *gw.* **cefndir**

cefndyr *gw.* **cefnder**

cefnogi *be.* **(cefnogaf)** to support

cefnu (ar) *be.* **(cefnaf)** to turn one's back upon, to forsake

cefnwr *e.g. ll.* **cefnwyr** back, full-back

ceffyl *e.g. ll.* **-au** horse. **ceffyl blaen** leading horse, pushy person; **ceffyl brith** piebald horse; **ceffyl gwinau** bay (horse); **ceffyl siglo** rocking horse; **ar gefn ei geffyl** on his high horse, exultant

ceg *e.b. ll.* **-au** mouth. **(cael, rhoi) llond ceg** *(to receive, to give)* a telling off

cegin *e.b. ll.* **-au** kitchen **cegin fach** kitchenette; **cegin gefn** back kitchen

cei *e.g. ll.* **ceiau** quay. *gw.* **cael**

ceidwad *e.g. ll.* **ceidwaid** keeper.

ceiliog *e.g. ll.* **-od** cockerel. **ceiliog y gwynt** weathercock; **ceiliog y rhedyn** grasshopper

Ceinewydd *e.b.* Newquay

ceiniog *e.b. ll.* **-au** penny. **heb geiniog goch** without a brass farthing or penny

ceir *gw.* **car**

ceiriosen *e.b. ll.* **ceirios** cherry

ceisiadau: ceisiau *gw.* **cais**

ceisio *be.* **(ceisiaf)** to seek, to ask. **ceisio am** to try for, to apply for

celf *e.b. ll.* **-au** art, craft; **Adran Celf** Art Department

celfi *gw.* **celficyn**

celficyn *e.g. ll.* **celfi** a piece of furniture; a tool

Celt *e.g. ll.* **-iaid** male Celt

Celtaidd *a.* Celtic

Celteg *e.b.* language of the Celts

Celtes *e.b. ll.* **-au, -i** female Celt

celwydd *e.g. ll.* **-au** lie, untruth. **celwydd golau** white lie; **celwydd noeth** barefaced lie; **celwyddgi** a liar

celwyddog *a.* untruthful

celyn *gw.* **celynnen**

celynnen *e.b. ll.* **celyn** holly. **llwyn celyn** holly bush

cell *e.b. ll.* **-oedd, -au** cell **cellau: celloedd** *gw.* **cell**

cemeg *e.b.* chemistry

cenadaethau *gw.* **cenhadaeth**

cenedl *e.b. ll.* **cenhedloedd** nation; species, kind; gender *(grammar).* **Cenedl y Cymry** the Welsh nation; **Y Cenhedloedd** the Gentiles; **y Cenhedloedd Unedig** the United Nations; **cenedl enwau** gender of nouns

cenedlaethau *gw.* **cenhedlaeth**

cenedlaethol *a.* national. **Llyfrgell Genedlaethol Cymru** National Library of Wales

cenedlaetholdeb *e.b.* nationalism

cenedlaetholwr *e.g. ll.* **cenedlaetholwyr** a nationalist

cenedlaetholwyr *gw.* **cenedlaetholwr**

cenedligrwydd *e.g.* nationality

cenfigennus *a.* jealous

cenhadaeth *e.b. ll.* **cenadaethau** mission; embassy

cenhadol *a.* missionary

cenhadon *gw.* **cenhadwr**

cenhadu *be.* **(cenhadaf)** to conduct a mission

cenhadwr *e.g. ll.* **cenhadon** a missionary; **cenhades** a female missionary

cenhedlaeth

cenhedlaeth *e.b. ll.*
 cenedlaethau generation;
 nation
cenhedloedd *gw.* **cenedl**
cenhinen *e.b. ll.* **cennin** leek.
 cenhinen Bedr daffodil
cenllysg *e.torf.* hailstones
cennin *gw.* **cenhinen**
cer *bf.* go! *(singular). gw.*
 mynd
cerdyn *e.g. ll.* **cardiau** card.
 cerdyn Nadolig Christmas
 card; **cerdyn pen-blwydd**
 birthday card
cerdd *e.b. ll.* **-i** song, poem;
 music. **cerdd dafod** poetic
 art, poetry; music; **cerdd
 dant** instrumental music;
 penillion singing
cerdded *be.* **(cerddaf)** to walk
cerddi *gw.* **cerdd**
cerddor *e.g. ll.* **-ion** musician
cerddorfa *e.b. ll.*
 cerddorfeydd orchestra.
 Cerddorfa Ieuenctid Youth
 Orchestra
cerddorfeydd *gw.* **cerddorfa**
cerddoriaeth *e.b.* music
cerddorol *a.* musical
cerddwr *e.g. ll.* **cerddwyr**
 walker. **Cymdeithas
 Cerddwyr Llanelli** Llanelli
 Ramblers' Association
cerddwyr *gw.* **cerddwr**
Ceredigion (Sir) *e.b.*
 Ceredigion County
cerfio *be.* **(cerfiaf)** to carve
cerflun *e.g. ll.* **-iau** statue
cerrig *gw.* **carreg**
cerwch *bf.* go! *(plural). gw.*
 mynd

ces *bf.* I had. *gw.* **cael**
cesair *e. torf.* hailstones
 (S.W.)
cestyll *gw.* **castell**
ceubren *e.g. ll.* **-nau** hollow
 tree
cewri *gw.* **cawr**
cewyn *e.g. ll.* **-nau, -ion**
 napkin *(S.W.)*
ceyrydd *gw.* **caer**
ci *e.g. ll.* **cŵn** dog. **ci bach**
 pup, **ci defaid** sheepdog; **ci
 tywys** guide dog; **ci hela**
 hound; **corgi** corgi; **milgi**
 greyhound
cic *e.b. ll.* **-iau** kick. **cic a
 chwrs** up and under kick;
 cic adlam drop-kick; **cic am
 (yr) ystlys** kick for touch; **cic
 gornel** corner kick; **cic gosb**
 penalty kick; **cic letraws**
 diagonal kick; **cic osod** place
 kick; **cic rydd** free kick; **cic
 wib** fly kick; **cic ymlaen** kick
 ahead
cig *e.g. ll.* **-oedd** meat; gum.
 cig eidion beef; **cig oen**
 lamb; **cig moch** bacon
cigydd *e.g. ll.* **-ion** butcher
cigyddion *gw.* **cigydd**
cilio (i, rhag.) *be.* **(ciliaf)** to
 flee; to retreat (to, from).
 cilio i to flee towards; **cilio
 rhag** to flee from, to retreat
 from
ciniawau *gw.* **cinio**
cinio *e.g.b. ll.* **ciniawau**
 dinner
cipolwg *e.g. ll.* **cipolygon**
 glance
cist *e.b. ll.* **-iau** chest, coffer

clwtyn

claf 1 *e.g. ll.* **cleifion** sick person. **ystafell y cleifion** sick-room. 2 *a.* ill

clai *e.g. ll.* **cleiau, cleion** clay. **traed o glai** mortal

clasur *e.g. ll.* **-on** a classic

clasurol *a.* classical

clawdd *e.g. ll.* **cloddiau** wall made of earth, ditch. **Clawdd Offa** Offa's Dyke

clawr *e.g. ll.* **cloriau** cover, lid. **ar glawr** on record

clebran *be.* **(clebraf)** to chatter

cledr *e.b. ll.* **-au** pole, rafter; rail; palm *(of hand).* **cledrau** rails *(of railway)*

clefyd *e.g. ll.* **-au, -on** sickness. **clefyd melyn** jaundice; **clefyd melys/siwgr** diabetes

cleifion *gw.* **claf**

clêr *gw.* **cleren**

clerc *e.g. ll.* **-od** clerk

cleren *e.b. ll.* **clêr** fly *(S.W.).* **cleren lwyd** horse-fly

clir *a.* clear

clirio *be.* **(cliriaf)** to clear

clo *e.g. ll.* **-eau, -eon** lock. **ar glo** locked; **dan glo** locked, locked up, under lock and key; **yng nghlo** locked; **twll y clo** keyhole

cloc *e.g. ll.* **-iau** clock. **cloc larwm** alarm-clock

clocwedd *a.* clockwise

cloch *be. ll.* **clychau** bell. **cloch y llan** chuch-bell; **clychau'r gog** bluebells; **dau o'r gloch** two o'clock

clod *e.g.b. ll.* **-ydd** praise

clodfori *be.* **(clodforaf)** to praise

cloddiau *gw.* **clawdd**

cloeau *gw.* **clo**

cloeon *gw.* **clo**

cloff *a.* lame

cloffi 1 *be.* **(cloffaf)** to become lame. **cloffi rhwng dau feddwl** to hesitate. 2 *e.g.* lameness

clogwyn *e.g. ll.* **-au, -i** cliff, crag

clogwyni: clogwynau *gw.* **clogwyn**

clogyn *e.g. ll.* **-au** cloak

cloi *be.* **(cloaf, clof)** to lock; to conclude. **cloi allan** to lock out, to exclude; **cload allan** lock-out; **Nawr i gloi** Now to conclude

clorian *e.b. ll.* **-nau** scales

cloriau *gw.* **clawr**

clown *e.g. ll.* **-iaid** clown

clun *e.b. ll.* **-iau** hip; thigh; leg

clust *e.b. ll.* **-iau** ear. **bonclust** box on the ear

clustdlws *e.g. ll.* **clustdlysau** earring

clustog *e.b. ll.* **-au** pillow, cushion

clwb *e.g. ll.* **clybiau** club. **clwb cinio** dining club; **clwb ieuenctid** youth club

clwm *e.g. ll.* **clymau** knot; tie. *gw.* **cwlwm**

clwtyn *e.g. ll.* **clytiau** rag *(S.W.).* **clwtyn llawr** floor cloth; **clwtyn llestri** dish cloth; **clwtyn ymolch** face cloth. **ar y clwt** stranded, abandoned; without work

Clwyd

Clwyd *e.b.* Former county in N.E. Wales

clwyd *e.b. ll.* **-i, -au** gate

clwydi: clwydau *gw.* **clwyd**

clwyf *e.g. ll.* **-au** wound, injury. **clwyf y traed a'r genau** foot and mouth disease

clychau *gw.* **cloch**

clymau *gw.* **clwm, cwlwm**

clymu *be.* **(clymaf)** to tie

clytiau *gw.* **clwtyn**

clyw 1 *e.g.* hearing, earshot. **trwm ei glyw** hard of hearing; **yn fy nghlyw** within my hearing. **2** *bf.* hear! *(singular)*, listen! *(singular)*, *gw.* **clywed**

clywed (am, oddi wrth) *be.* **(clywaf)** to hear (of, from); to feel; to taste; to smell. **Clywch, clywch!** Hear, hear!

cnau *gw.* **cneuen**

cneuen *e.b. ll.* **cnau** nut

cnoc *e.g.b. ll.* **-au** a knock; a fool *(S.W.).* **tipyn o gnoc:** quite a fool; **cnocell y coed** woodpecker

cnocio; cnoco *be.* **(cnociaf: cnocaf)** to knock, to strike

cnoi *be.* **(cnoaf)** to bite, to chew. **cnoi cil** to chew the cud; to mull over

coban *e.b. ll.* **cobannau** night-shirt

cobannau *gw.* **coban**

coch *a. ll.* **-ion** red. **yn goch** obscene; of poor quality; **coch y berllan** bullfinch. *gw. At. Ansoddeiriau*

cochach *gw.* **coch**

cochaf *gw.* **coch**

coched *gw.* **coch**

cochen *e.b.* red-haired female

cochyn *e.b.* red-haired male

codi *be.* **(codaf)** to rise, to erect, to pick up; to withdraw *(money)*, to charge (fee)

coed *gw.* **coeden**

Coed-duon *e.b.* Blackwood

coeden *e.b. ll.* **coed** tree

coedwig *e.b. ll.* **-oedd** forest, wood

coes *e.b. ll.* **-au** leg. **tynnu coes** to leg pull

cof *e.g. ll.* **-ion** memory; remembrance. **er cof am** in memory of; **o fewn cof** within living memory; **o'i gof** angry; mad; **ar gof a chadw** recorded and preserved, on record; **cofion cynnes** warmest regards

cofbin *e.g. ll.* **-nau** memory stick

cofio (am) *be.* **(cofiaf)** to remember

cofion *gw.* **cof**

cofleidio *be.* **(cofleidiaf)** to embrace

cofrestr *e.b. ll.* **-au, -i** register

cofrestru *be.* **(cofrestraf)** to register

coffi *e.g.* coffee; **noson goffi** coffee evening

cog 1 *e.b. ll.* **-au** cuckoo. *gw.* **cwcw. 2** *e.g. ll.* **-au** cook

coginio *be.* **(coginiaf)** to cook

cogydd *e.g. ll.* **-ion** cook

coleg *e.g. ll.* **-au** college.

Coleg Prifysgol y Drindod
Trinity University College
coler *e.g.b. ll.* **-au, -i** collar
colofn *e.b. ll.* **-au** column,
pillar
coluro *be.* **(coluraf)** to colour,
to make up
colled *e.g.b. ll.* **-ion** loss.
Roedd colled arni She was
angry
collen *e.b. ll.* **cyll** hazel. **cnau
cyll** hazelnuts
colli *be.* **(collaf)** to lose, to
spill, to fail, to miss. **ar goll**
lost, missing, mislaid
copi *e.g. ll.* **copïau** a copy
copïo *be.* **(copïaf)** to copy
copyn *e.g. ll.* **-nau, -nod**
spider. **pryf copyn** spider
côr *e.g. ll.* **corau** choir; pew
(in church or chapel); stall,
crib. **côr cymysg** mixed
choir; **côr merched** ladies'
choir; **côr meibion** male
voice choir; **Côr y Cewri**
Stonehenge
corau *gw.* **côr**
cordyn *e.g. ll.* **-ion** cord,
string
corff *e.g. ll.* **cyrff** body;
corpse; capital. **Yr Hen Gorff**
Calvinistic Methodists
corfforol *a.* bodily, physical.
Addysg Gorfforol physical
education
corgi *e.g. ll.* **corgwn** corgi
corn *e.g. ll.* **cyrn** horn; corn;
cairn; chimney. **corn simdde**
chimney stack; **Siôn Corn**
Father Christmas
cornel *e.b.g. ll.* **-au, -i** corner

coron *e.b. ll.* **-au** crown
coroni *be.* **(coronaf)** to
crown. **i goroni'r cwbl** to cap
it all
corryn *e.g. ll.* **corynnod**
spider *(S.W.)*
corynnod *gw.* **corryn**
cosb *e.b. ll.* **-au** punishment,
penalty. **y gosb eithaf** capital
punishment; **cic gosb**
penalty kick
cosbi *be.* **(cosbaf)** to punish
cosi 1 *be.* **(cosaf)** to itch.
2 *e.g.* itch
costus *a.* expensive
cosyn *e.g. ll.* **-nau** a small
cheese. *gw.* **caws**
cot: côt *e.b. ll.* **cotau: cotiau**
coat. **cot fawr** overcoat; **cot
law** raincoat
cotau: cotiau *gw.* **cot**
cotwm *e.g. ll.* **cotymau**
cotton
crac 1 *e.g. ll.* **-au, -iau** crack.
2 *a.* angry *(S.W.)*
crachach *e.ll.* snobs *(S.W.)*
crafu 1 *be.* **(crafaf)** to scratch;
to scrape. 2 *e.g.* itch
crafiad *e.g. ll.* **-au** scratch
cragen *e.b. ll.* **cregyn** shell
craig *e.b. ll.* **creigiau** rock,
cliff. **Mae e'n graig o arian.**
He's very wealthy
cras *a. ll.* **creision** baked;
scorched; harsh. **llai cras** not
so highly baked; **tafod cras** a
harsh tongue; **llais cras** a
raucous voice. *gw.*
creisionyn
crasu *be.* **(crasaf)** to bake; to
scorch

credu

credu (yn) *be.* **(credaf)** to
believe, to trust (in)
crefydd *e.b. ll.* **-au** religion
crefft *e.b. ll.* **-au** skill, craft
crefftwr *e.g. ll.* **crefftwyr**
craftsman
crefftwyr *gw.* **crefftwr**
cregyn *gw.* **cragen**
creigiau *gw.* **craig**
creigiog *a.* rocky
creision *gw.* **cras, creisionyn**
creisionyn *e.g. ll.* **creision**
crisp, flake. **creision ŷd** corn
flakes
crempog *e.b. ll.* **-au** pancake
(N.W.). gw. **ffroesen**
creulon *a.* cruel
creulondeb *e.g. ll.* **-au** cruelty
cri *e.g.b. ll.* **-au** cry, lament.
cri'r wylan gull's cry
crib *e.b. ll.* **-au** comb; bird's
comb; crest, summit, ridge.
crib y ceiliog the cock's
comb; **crib y mynydd** the
mountain's ridge; **mynd â
chrib fân** to examine
minutely
cribo *be.* **(cribaf)** to comb; to
card
criced *e.g.* cricket (game)
cricedwr *e.g. ll.* **cricedwyr**
cricketer
cricsyn *e.g. ll.* **criciaid, crics**
a cricket *(insect)*
crio (am, ar) *be.* **(criaf)** to
shout, to weep *(N.W.)*
Cristion *e.g. ll.* **Cristnogion**
Christian
criw *e.g. ll.* **-iau** crew, crowd.
criw o bobl ifainc a gang of
young people

croen *e.g. ll.* **crwyn** skin,
hide; peel. **croendenau** thin-
skinned; sensitive; **croendew**
thick-skinned; insensitive;
croenddu black-skinned;
negroid; **croen ei din ar ei
dalcen** in a bad mood
croes *e.b. ll.* **-au** cross. **croes
Crist** Christ's cross
croesair *e.g. ll.* **croeseiriau**
crossword; **pos croeseiriau**
crossword puzzle
croesau *gw.* **croes**
croesawu *be.* **(croesawaf)** to
welcome
croesawus *a.* hospitable
croeseiriau *gw.* **croesair**
croesfan *e.g. ll.* **-nau** crossing
croesfford *e.b. ll.* **croesffyrdd**
crossroad
croeshoelio *be.* **(croeshoeliaf)**
to crucify
croesholi *be.* **(croesholaf)** to
cross-examine. **croesholiad** a
cross-examination
croesi *be.* **(croesaf)** to cross,
to oppose
croeso *e.g.* welcome. **y
Bwrdd Croeso** the Welsh
Tourist Board
Croesoswallt *e.b.* Oswestry
cron *a.b.* round. *gw.* **crwn**
cronfa *e.b. ll.* **cronfeydd**
reservoir; fund
cronfeydd *gw.* **cronfa**
crud *e.g. ll.* **-au, -iau** cradle
crwn *a.g.* round. *gw.* **cron**
crwst *e.g. ll.* **crystiau** crust.
gw. **crystyn**
crwyn *gw.* **croen**

cryd *e.g.* *ll.* **-iau** shivering, fever. **Mae'r cryd arna i** I've got the shivers; **cryd y cymalau** rheumatism

cryf *a.* *ll.* **-ion** strong, powerful. *gw. At. Ansoddeiriau*

cryfach *gw.* **cryf**

cryfaf *gw.* **cryf**

cryfed *gw.* **cryf**

crynhoi *be.* **(crynhoaf)** to collect, to gather, to summarize. **i grynhoi** to sum up

cryno *a.* tidy; suitable; compact. **ffurfiau cryno'r ferf** compact forms of the verb; **cryno ddisg** compact disc

crynodeb *e.g.b.* *ll.* **-au** precis, summary; tidiness

crynu *be.* **(crynaf)** to shiver, to quake. **daeargryn** earthquake

crys *e.g.* *ll.* **-au** shirt. **crys T** T-shirt; **Y Crysau Cochion** The Welsh Rugby team

crystiau *gw.* **crwst, crystyn**

crystyn *e.g.* *ll.* **crystiau,** crust. *gw.* **crwst**

cu *a.* dear, fond, beloved. **mam-gu** grandmother *(S.W.).* **tad-cu** grandfather *(S.W.)*

cuddio (rhag) *be.* **(cuddiaf)** to hide (from), to cover, to bury

cul *a.* *ll.* **-ion** narrow, narrow-minded. **culfor** *e.g.* strait, channel

curo (wrth) *be.* **(curaf)** to strike, to knock, to defeat. **curo dwylo** to clap hands

cusan *e.g.b.* *ll.* **-au** kiss

cusanu *be.* **(cusanaf)** to kiss

cw *gw.* **acw**

cwb *e.g.* *ll.* **cybiau** kennel, coop

cwbl 1 *a.* all, complete, entire. **cwbl iach** completely healthy; **cwbl gyfan** quite complete; **cwbl sicr** completely certain. **2** *e.g.* *ll.* *(used with the definite article)* all, everything. **y cwbl** everything, all: **y cwbl oll** everything, the whole lot; **dim o gwbl** nothing at all; **dyna'r cwbl** that's all; **Prynodd e'r cwbl** He bought everything

cwblhau *be.* **(cwblhaf)** to finish, to complete

cwcw *e.b.* *ll.* **cwcŵod** cuckoo *(S.W.). gw.* **cog**

cwch *e.g.* *ll.* **cychod** boat; hive. **cwch hwylio** sailing boat; **cwch modur** motor boat; **cwch pysgota** fishing boat; **cwch rhwyfo** rowing boat; **cwch gwenyn** beehive

cwd *e.g.* *ll.* **cydau** bag; purse; sack

cwdyn *e.g.* *ll.* **cydau** bag; purse; sack

cweryl *e.g.* *ll.* **-au, -on** quarrel

cweryla (â) *be.* **(cwerylaf)** to quarrel (with)

cwerylau

cwerylau: cwerylon *gw.*
cweryl

cwestiwn *e.g.* *ll.* **cwestiynau**
question

cwestiynu *be.* **(cwestiynaf)** to
question

cwestiynau *gw.* **cwestiwn**

cwlwm *e.g.* *ll.* **clymau** knot;
bunch. *gw.* **clwm**

cwm *e.g.* *ll.* **cymoedd** valley.
Cwm Tawe Swansea Valley

cwmni *e.g.* *ll.* **cwmnïau,**
cwmnïoedd company.
cwmni yswiriant insurance
company

cwmnïau *gw.* **cwmni**

cwmnïoedd *gw.* **cwmni**

cwmwl *e.g.* *ll.* **cymylau** cloud

cŵn *gw.* **ci**

cwningen *e.b.* *ll.* **cwningod**
rabbit

cwningod *gw.* **cwningen**

cwpan *e.g.b.* *ll.* **-au** cup

cwpla *be.* **(cwplâf)** to finish
(S.W.)

cwpwrdd *e.g.* *ll.* **cypyrddau**
cupboard. **cwpwrdd cornel**
corner cupboard

cwr *e.g.* *ll.* **cyrrau, cyrion**
corner, end; edge, border;
outskirts. **ar gwr y dref** on
the outskirts of the town

cwrdd 1 *e.g.* *ll.* **cyrddau**
meeting *(S.W.)*, religious
service, congregation. **cwrdd**
gweddi prayer-meeting;
cyrddau mawr special
preaching meetings; **tŷ cwrdd**
chapel *(nonconformist)*.
2 *be.* **(cwrddaf)** to meet, to

come together; to touch.
cwrdd â to meet, meeting

cwrensen *e.b.* *ll.* currants.
cwrens duon blackcurrants;
cwrens cochion redcurrants

cwrs *e.g.* *ll.* **cyrsau, cyrsiau**
course

cwrtais *a.* courteous

cwrw *e.g.* *ll.* **-au** beer

cwsg 1 *e.g.* sleep; numbness.
2 *a.* asleep; numb. **ynghwsg**
asleep; lifeless, numb

cwsmer *e.g.* *ll.* **-iaid** customer

cwstwm *e.g.* *ll.* **cystymau**
custom, patronage

cwt *e.b.g.* *ll.* **cytiau** hut, sty;
wound; tail; queue. **cwt ieir**
chicken coop

cwta *a.* short, abrupt

cwymp *e.g.* *ll.* **-au, -iau** fall,
slope; collapse

cwympo *be.* **(cwympaf)** to
fall; to fell

cwyn *e.b.g.* *ll.* **-au, -ion**
complaint

cwyno (am, ar) *be.* **(cwynaf)**
to complain (about, to)

cwyr *e.g.* *ll.* **-au** beeswax;
wax

cychod *gw.* **cwch**

cychwyn 1 *e.g.* beginning,
start. 2 *be.* **(cychwynnaf)**
to begin, to start. **ar y**
cychwyn at first, at the
start

cydadrodd *be.* **(cydadroddaf)**
to recite together. **parti**
cydadrodd choral speaking
party

cydau *gw.* **cwd, cwdyn**

cydio (yn) *be.* **(cydiaf)** to join, to connect, to couple, to take hold (of)

cydnabod 1 *be.* **(cydnabyddaf)** to acknowledge; to honour, to remunerate. **2** *e.g.* acquaintance

cydwybodol *a.* conscientious

cydymdeimlad *e.g.* *ll.* **cydymdeimladau** sympathy

cyfagos *a.* neighbouring

cyfaill *e.g.* *ll.* **cyfeillion** friend, companion. **Annwyl Gyfeillion** Dear Friends *(form of address)*. *gw.* **cyfeilles**

cyfan *e.g.* *ll.* **-ion** all, total, entirety. **y cyfan** all, the lot, everything: **ar y cyfan** on the whole; **wedi'r cyfan** after all

cyfangwbl *a.* altogether, complete, whole. **yn gyfangwbl** completely, wholly; **Roedd e'n gyfangwbl ddu** He was completely black

cyfansoddi *be.* **(cyfansoddaf)** to compose; to establish

cyfansoddwr *e.g.* *ll.* **cyfansoddwyr** composer

cyfanswm *e.g.* *ll.* **cyfansymiau** total, amount

cyfarch *be.* **(cyfarchaf)** to greet

cyfarchion *e.ll.* greetings

cyfarfod 1 *e.g.* *ll.* **-ydd** meeting. **2** *be.* **(cyfarfyddaf)** to meet, to encounter. **cyfarfod â** to meet

cyfarfodydd *gw.* **cyfarfod**

cyfarth *be.* **(cyfarthaf)** to bark

cyfarwyddiadur *e.g.* *ll.* **-on** directory

cyfarwyddo (â) *be.* **(cyfarwyddaf)** to familiarize, to instruct

cyfarwyddwr *e.g.* *ll.* **cyfarwyddwyr** director

cyfeilles *e.b.* *ll.* **-au** female friend. *gw.* **cyfaill**

cyfeillgar *a.* friendly, sociable. *gw. At. Ansoddeiriau*

cyfeillgarwch *e.g.* friendship

cyfeillion *gw.* **cyfaill**

cyfeiriad *e.g.* *ll.* **-au** direction, reference, address

cyfeirio (at, i) *be.* **(cyfeiriaf)** to direct, to refer

cyfenw *e.g.* *ll.* **-au** surname. **cyfenwau** Evans, Huws, Jones

cyferbyn (â) *a.* opposite, contrary. **cyferbyn â** opposite

cyfiawn *a.* righteous, just

cyfiawnder *e.g.* *ll.* **-au** righteousness, justice

cyfieithiad *e.g.* *ll.* **-au** translation

cyfieithu *be.* **(cyfieithaf)** to translate

cyfieithydd *e.g.* *ll.* **-ion** translator, interpreter

cyfle *e.g.* *ll.* **-oedd** opportunity, chance

cyfleu *be.* **(cyfleaf)** to convey, to imply

cyfleus *a.* convenient, expedient

cyflog *e.b.* *ll.* **-au** salary, wages, hire

cyflogi

cyflogi *be.* (**cyflogaf**) to employ, to hire

cyflogwr *e.g. ll.* **cyflogwyr** employer

cyflwr *e.g. ll.* **cyflyrau** state, condition, case

cyflwyno (i) *be.* (**cyflwynaf**) present (to), to dedicate (to)

cyflym *a.* quick, swift, speedy. *gw. At. Ansoddeiriau*

cyflymach *gw.* **cyflym**

cyflymaf *gw.* **cyflym**

cyflymder *e.g. ll.* **-au** speed, velocity, swiftness

cyflymed *gw.* **cyflym**

cyflymu *be.* (**cyflymaf**) to accelerate, to hasten

cyflymydd *e.g. ll.* **-ion** accelerator

cyflyrau *gw.* **cyflwr**

cyfnither *e.b. ll.* **-oedd** female cousin. *gw.* **cefnder**

cyfnod *e.g. ll.* **cyfnodau** period

cyfoeth *e.g.* wealth, riches

cyfoethog *a.* rich, wealthy

cyfradd *e.b. ll.* **-au** rate. **cyfraddau llog** interest rates

cyfraith *e.b. ll.* **cyfreithiau** law

cyfrannu (i, at) *be.* (**cyfrannaf**) to contribute; to impart

cyfreithiwr *e.g. ll.* **cyfreithwyr** solicitor, lawyer

cyfreithwyr *gw.* **cyfreithiwr**

cyfres *e.b. ll.* **-au, -i** series, suite *(musical)*. **drama gyfres** a serial

cyfresau: cyfresi *gw.* **cyfres**

cyfrif 1 *be.* (**cyfrifaf**) to count, to reckon. **2** *e.g.* account, reckoning. **cyfrif trafod** current account; **cyfrif cadw** deposit account

cyfrifiadur *e.g. ll.* **-on** computer

cyfrifiannell *e.g. ll.* **cyfrifianellau** calculator

cyfrifol *a.* responsible; calculable. **cyfrifol am** responsible for

cyfrifoldeb *e.g. ll.* **-au** responsibility

cyfrifydd *e.g. ll.* **-ion** accountant

cyfrinach *e.b. ll.* **-au** secret, mystery

cyfrinachol *a.* secret, confidential, private

cyfrol *e.b. ll.* **-au** volume, book

cyfrwng *e.g. ll.* **cyfryngau** agent; agency; medium; means. **trwy gyfrwng** through the medium of; **y cyfryngau** the media

cyfrwys *a.* cunning, crafty

cyfryngau *gw.* **cyfrwng**

cyfun *a.* agreeing, comprehensive, united. **Ysgol Gyfun Treforys** Morriston Comprehensive School

cyfuwch *gw.* **uchel**

cyfweld (â) *be.* (**cyfwelaf**) to interview

cyfweliad *e.g. ll.* **-au** interview

cyfyng *a.* narrow, confined, restricted. **Mae hi'n gyfyng arni** She is in dire straits

cyfyngiad *e.g. ll.* **-au** restriction. **cyfyngiadau cyflymder** speed restrictions

cyfyngu (ar) *be.* **(cyfyngaf)** to narrow, to confine, to restrict

cyfystyr 1 *e.g. ll.* **-on** synonym. 2 *a* synonymous. **cyfystyr â** synonymous with

cyfforddus: cyffyrddus *a.* comfortable *(S.W.)*

cyffredin *a.* common, ordinary, vulgar. **enw cyffredin** common noun; **pobl gyffredin** ordinary people

cyffrous *a.* exciting, moving

cyffur *e.g. ll.* **-iau** drug, medicine

cyffwrdd (â) *be.* **(cyffyrddaf)** to touch, to contact, to meet

cyngerdd *e.g.b. ll.* **cyngherddau** concert

cyngherddau *gw.* **cyngerdd**

cynghori (i) *be.* **(cynghoraf)** to advise, to counsel, to exhort

cynghorion *gw.* **cyngor**

cynghorwr *e.g. ll.* **cynghorwyr** adviser, councillor

cynghrair *e.g. ll.* **cynghreiriau** alliance, league

cynghreiriad *e.g. ll.* **cynghreiriaid** ally

cynghreiriau *gw.* **cynghrair**

cyngor 1 *e.g. ll.* **cynghorion** advice, counsel. 2 *e.g. ll.* **cynghorau** council. **cyngor cymuned** community council; **cyngor dosbarth** district council; **cyngor sir** county council; **Cyngor y**

Celfyddydau the Arts Council

cyhoedd 1 *a.* public. 2 *e.g.* public. **ar gyhoedd, ar goedd** publicly; **y cyhoedd** the public

cyhoeddi *be.* **(cyhoeddaf)** to announce, to proclaim; to publish

cyhoeddiad *e.g. ll.* **-au** publication; announcement; engagement

cyhoeddus *a.* public. **neuadd gyhoeddus** public hall; **cyfarfod cyhoeddus** public meeting

cyhoeddusrwydd *e.g.* publicity

cyhoeddwr *e.g. ll.* **cyhoeddwyr** publisher; announcer

cyhuddiad *e.g. ll.* **-au** accusation

cyhuddo *be.* **(cyhuddaf)** to accuse

cyhyd *gw.* **hir**

cyhyrog *a.* muscular, strong

cylch *e.g. ll.* **-au, -oedd** circle, hoop; class; region. **o gylch** around

cylchfan *e.g. ll.* **-nau** roundabout

cylchgrawn *e.g. ll.* **cylchgronau** magazine, periodical

cylchgronau *gw.* **cylchgrawn**

cylchlythyr *e.g. ll.* **-au, -on** a circular

cyll *bf.* he/she/it loses. *gw.* **collen, colli**

cyllell

cyllell *e.b. ll.* **cyllyll** knife.
cyllell boced penknife; **cyllell
fara** bread knife
cyllyll *gw.* **cyllell**
cymaint *gw.* **mawr**
cymal *e.g. ll.* **-au** joint; clause,
phrase
cymanfa *e.b. ll.* **-oedd**
assembly, singing festival
cymanfaoedd *gw.* **cymanfa**
cymar *e.g. ll.* **cymheiriaid**
partner
cymdeithas *e.b. ll.* **-au**
society, association
cymdeithaseg *e.b.* sociology
cymdogion *gw.* **cymydog**
cymeriad *e.g. ll.* **-au** character
cymryd *be.* **(cymeraf)** to
accept, to take. **cymryd ar** to
pretend *(N.W.)*
cymharu (â) *be.* **(cymharaf)** to
compare
cymhleth *a.* complex,
involved
cymhlethdod *e.g. ll.* **-au**
complication, complexity
cymhlethu *be.* **(cymhlethaf)** to
complicate
cymhorthion *gw.* **cymorth**
cymoedd *gw.* **cwm**
cymorth *e.g. ll.* **cymhorthion**
aid, assistance. **cymorth
cyntaf** first aid
Cymraeg 1 *e.b.g.* Welsh
(language). 2 *a.* Welsh *(in
language).* **Y Gymraeg** the
Welsh language; **yn Gymraeg**
in Welsh; **Cymraeg da**
good *(spoken or written)*
Welsh

Cymraes; Cymreiges *e.b. ll.*
-au Welshwoman
Cymreictod *e.g.* Welsh
quality, Welshness
Cymreig *a.* Welsh, pertaining
to Wales or to the Welsh.
arferion Cymreig Welsh
traditions; **brethyn Cymreig**
Welsh woollen cloth
Cymreiges *gw.* **Cymraes**
Cymro *e.g. ll.* **Cymry**
Welshman. **Cymro i'r carn**
thorough Welshman; **Cymro
uniaith** monoglot Welshman;
Cymry alltud exiled Welsh;
Cymry Llundain London
Welsh
Cymru *e.b.* Wales. **Cymru a'r
Cymry** Wales and the Welsh,
Wales and her people
Cymry *gw.* **Cymro**
cymryd *gw.* **cymeryd**
cymundeb *e.g. ll.* **-au**
communion, fellowship
cymuned *e.b. ll.* **-au**
community. **yr Undeb
Ewropeaidd** the European
Community
cymwynas *e.b. ll.* **-au** favour,
kindness. **talu'r gymwynas
olaf** to pay the last respects
(attendance at funeral)
cymydog *e.g. ll.* **cymdogion**
neighbour
cymylau *gw.* **cwmwl**
cymylog *a.* cloudy
cymysg *a.* mixed
cymysgu (â) *be.* **(cymysgaf)** to
mix, to confuse

cymysgwch 1 *e.g.* jumble,
medley, mixture. **2** *bf.* mix!
(plural). gw. **cymysgu**
cyn 1 *ardd.* before, previous
to. **Dewch cyn cinio** Come
before dinner. **2** *rhagdd.*
(followed by soft mutation)
first, former, ex-;
cyn-brifathro former
headteacher; **cyn-löwr**
former miner; **cyn-ŵr**
former husband; **cyn-
weinidog** former minister.
3 *c. & ad. (followed by soft
mutation)* as. **cyn dewed â
mochyn** as fat as a pig; **cyn
ddued â'r frân** as black as
the crow; **cyn goched â thân**
as red as fire; *gw. At.
Treigladau*
cynaeafau *gw.* **cynhaeaf**
cynddrwg *gw.* **drwg**
cynffon *e.b.* *ll.* -**nau** tail
(N.W.). **cynffonnau ŵyn bach**
hazel catkins. *gw.* **cwt**
cynhadledd *e.b.* *ll.*
cynadleddau conference
cynhaeaf *e.g.* *ll.* **cynaeafau**
harvest
cynhesu *be.* (**cynhesaf**) to
warm, to get warm
cynhwysion *gw.* **cynnwys**
cynhyrfus *a.* exciting, agitated
cynigion *gw.* **cynnig**
cynilion *e.ll.* savings
cynilo *be.* (**cynilaf**) to save, to
economize
cynllun *e.g.* *ll.* -**iau** plan,
design, scheme, project
cynllunio *be.* (**cynlluniaf**) to
plan, to design

cynlluniwr: cynllunydd *e.g.* *ll.*
cynllunwyr planner, designer,
architect
cynnal *be.* (**cynhaliaf**) to
support, to hold, to
maintain. **gwaith cynnal a
chadw** maintenance work
cynnar *a.* early, soon. *gw. At.
Ansoddeiriau*
cynnes *a.* warm
cynnig 1 *be.* (**cynigiaf**) to
attempt, to try, to propose.
rhoi cynnig ar to attempt to.
2 *e.g.* *ll.* **cynigion** attempt;
offer, proposal; motion, bid
cynnwys 1 *e.g.* *ll.*
cynhwysion. content,
contents. **2** *be.* (**cynhwysaf**)
to contain, to include. **gan
gynnwys** including
cynnyrch *e.g.* *ll.* **cynhyrchion**
produce
cynorthwy-ydd *e.g.* *ll.*
cynorthwywyr helper,
assistant
cynorthwywr *e.g.* *ll.*
cynorthwywyr helper,
assistant
cynradd *a.* primary. **ysgol
gynradd** primary school
cynrychioli *be.* to represent
cynt: gynt *ad.* formerly,
previously. *née.* **Siân Owen,
gynt Lewis** Siân Owen, *née*
Lewis; **y flwyddyn gynt** the
previous year. *gw.* **buan,
cynnar**
cyntaf *a.* first, chief, earliest.
gw. **cynnar**
cynted *gw.* **cynnar**

cyntedd

cyntedd *e.g. ll.* **cynteddau, cynteddoedd** porch, court, lobby, hall

cynteddau: cynteddoedd *gw.* **cyntedd**

cynulleidfa *e.b. ll.* **-oedd** congregation

cynulliad *e.g. ll.* **-au** assembly

Cynulliad Cenedlaethol Cymru National Assembly for Wales

cynwysedig *a.* included

cypyrddau *gw.* **cwpwrdd**

cyrddau *gw.* **cwrdd**

cyrff *gw.* **corff**

cyrion *gw.* **cwr**

cyrliog *a.* curly

cyrn *gw.* **corn**

cyrraedd *be.* **(cyrhaeddaf)** to reach, to arrive, to attain. **Cyrhaeddodd y tŷ** He arrived at the house

cyrrau *gw.* **cwr**

cyrsau *gw.* **cwrs**

cyrsiau *gw.* **cwrs**

cysglyd *a.* sleepy

cysgod *e.g. ll.* **-ion, -au** shadow; shelter

cysgodau *gw.* **cysgod**

cysgodi (rhag) *be.* **(cysgodaf)** to shade; to shelter

cysgodion *gw.* **cysgod**

cysgu *be.* **(cysgaf)** to sleep

cystadlaethau *gw.* **cystadleuaeth**

cystadleuaeth *e.b. ll.* **cystadlaethau** competition

cystadleuwr: cystadleuydd *e.g. ll.* **cystadleuwyr** competitor

cystadleuwyr *gw.* **cystadleuwr**

cystadlu (â) *be.* **(cystadlaf)** to compete

cystal *a.* as well. **yn ogystal** in addition. *gw.* **da**

cystymau *gw.* **cwstwm**

cysur *e.g. ll.* **-on** comfort, consolation

cysuro *be.* **(cysuraf)** to comfort, to console

cysurus *a.* comfortable

cyswllt *e.g. ll.* **cysylltau** joint, junction, connection

cytgan *e.b. ll.* **-au** chorus

cytsain 1 *e.b. ll.* **cytseiniaid** consonant.

2 *e.b. ll.* **cytseiniau** harmony

cytseiniaid *gw.* **cytsain**

cytseiniau *gw.* **cytsain**

cytundeb *e.g. ll.* **-au** agreement, pact, contract

cytuno (â) *be.* **(cytunaf)** to agree (with), consent (to)

cyw *e.g. ll.* **-ion** chick. **cyw iâr** chicken *(N.W.)*; *gw.* **ffowlyn**

cywaith *e.g. ll.* **cyweithiau** project; collective work

cyweithiau *gw.* **cywaith**

cywilydd *e.g.* shame

cywilyddus *a.* shameful

cywion *gw.* **cyw**

cywir *a.* correct, sincere, true, honest

cywiriad *e.g. ll.* **-au** correction

cywiro *be.* **(cywiraf)** to correct, to amend, to verify

CH

'ch *rhag.* you, your. *gw.* **At. Rhagenwau Personol**

chaban *gw.* **caban**

chacen *gw*. cacen
chacwn *gw*. cacwn
chacynen *gw*. cacynen
chadach *gw*. cadach
chadair *gw*. cadair
chadeirio *gw*. cadeirio
chadeiriol *gw*. cadeiriol
chadeirydd *gw*. cadeirydd
chadnawes *gw*. cadno
chadno *gw*. cadno
chadnoaid *gw*. cadno
chadw *gw*. cadw
chadwyn *gw*. cadwyn
chadwyno *gw*. cadwyno
chae *gw*. cae
chael *gw*. cael
chaer *gw*. caer
Chaerdydd *gw*. Caerdydd
Chaerfyrddin *gw*. Caerfyrddin
Chaergybi *gw*. Caergybi
chaets *gw*. caets
chaf *gw*. caf
chafodd *gw*. cafodd
chaffe *gw*. caffe
changen *gw*. cangen
changhennau *gw*. cangen
chaiff *gw*. caiff
chais *gw*. cais
chalan *gw*. calan
chaled *gw*. caled
chaledi *gw*. caledi
chaledu *gw*. caledu
chaledwch *gw*. caledwch
chalendr *gw*. calendr
chalenigion *gw*. calennig
chalennig *gw*. calennig
chaletach *gw*. caled
chaletaf *gw*. caled
chaleted *gw*. caled
chalon *gw*. calon

chall *gw*. call
challach *gw*. call
challaf *gw*. call
challed *gw*. call
cham *gw*. cam
chamarwain *gw*. camarwain
chamddeall *gw*. camddeall
chamera *gw*. camera
champ *gw*. camp
champfa *gw*. campfa
champfeydd *gw*. campfa
champus *gw*. campus
champwaith *gw*. campwaith
chamsyniad *gw*. camsyniad
chamu *gw*. camu
chân *gw*. cân
chan *gw*. can, gan
chaneuon *gw*. cân
chanfed *gw*. canfed
chanhwyllau *gw*. cannwyll
chanhwyllbren *gw*.
  canhwyllbren
chaniad *gw*. caniad
chaniadaeth *gw*. caniadaeth
chaniadau *gw*. cân, caniad
chaniatâd *gw*. caniatâd
chaniatáu *gw*. caniatáu
chaniedydd *gw*. caniedydd
chanmlwydd *gw*. canmlwydd
chanmlwyddiannau *gw*.
  canmlwydd
chanmol *gw*. canmol
chanmoliaeth *gw*. canmoliaeth
channoedd *gw*. cant
channwyll *gw*. cannwyll
chanol *gw*. canol
chanolbarth *gw*. canolbarth
chanolbwyntio *gw*.
  canolbwyntio
chanoldir *gw*. canoldir

chanolfan

chanolfan *gw.* canolfan
chanolog *gw.* canolog
chanolwr *gw.* canolwr
chanradd *gws.* canradd
chanran *gw.* canran
chanrif *gw.* canrif
chanrifau: chanrifoedd *gw.*
 canrif
chant *gw.* cant
chantor *gw.* cantor
chantores *gw.* cantores
chanu *gw.* canu
chanŵ *gw.* canŵ
chanŵio *gw.* canŵio
chanwr *gw.* canwr
chap *gw.* cap
chapel *gw.* capel
chapteiniaid *gw.* capten
chapten *gw.* capten
chapteniaid *gw.* capten
char *gw.* car
charafán *gw.* carafán
charafana *gw.* carafana
charco *gw.* carco
charcus *gw.* carcus
charchar *gw.* carchar
charcharor *gw.* carcharor
charcharu *gw.* carcharu
chardiau *gw.* cerdyn
charedig *gw.* caredig
charedigrwydd *gw.*
 caredigrwydd
chariad *gw.* cariad
chariadon *gw.* cariad
chariadus *gw.* cariadus
chario *gw.* cario
charlamu *gw.* carlamu
charol *gw.* carol
charped *gw.* carped
charreg *gw.* carreg

chartref *gw.* cartref
chartrefi *gw.* cartref
chartrefu *gw.* cartrefu
charu *gw.* caru
charwriaeth *gw.* carwriaeth
chas *gw.* cas
chasáu *gw.* casáu
chasgen *gw.* casgen
chasgenni *gw.* casgen
chasgliad *gw.* casgliad
chasglu *gw.* casglu
Chas-gwent *gw.* Cas-gwent
Chasllwchwr *gw.* Casllwchwr
Chasnewydd *gw.* Casnewydd
chastell *gw.* castell
Chastell-nedd *gw.* Castell-
 nedd
chath *gw.* cath
chau *gw.* cau
chawl *gw.* cawl
chawod *gw.* cawod
chawr *gw.* cawr
chaws *gw.* caws
chefn *gw.* cefn
chefnder *gw.* cefnder
chefndir *gw.* cefndir
chefndiroedd *gw.* cefndir
chefndyr *gw.* cefnder
chefnogi *gw.* cefnogi
chefnu *gw.* cefnu
chefnwr *gw.* cefnwr
chefnwyr *gw.* cefnwr
cheffyl *gw.* ceffyl
cheg *gw.* ceg
chegin *gw.* cegin
chei *gw.* cael, cei
cheidwad *gw.* ceidwad
cheiliog *gw.* ceiliog
Cheinewydd *gw.* Ceinewydd
cheiniog *gw.* ceiniog

cheiriosen *gw.* ceiriosen
cheisio *gw.* ceisio
chelf *gw.* celf
chelfi *gw.* celficyn
chelficyn *gw.* celficyn
Cheltaidd *gw.* Celtaidd
chelwydd *gw.* celwydd
chelwyddog *gw.* celwyddog
chelyn *gw.* celynnen
chelynnen *gw.* celynnen
chell *gw.* cell
chellau: chelloedd *gw.* cell
chemeg *gw.* cemeg
chenadaethau *gw.* cenhadaeth
chenedl *gw.* cenedl
chenedlaethau *gw.* cenhedlaeth
chenedlaethol *gw.* cenedlaethol
chenedlaetholdeb *gw.* cenedlaetholdeb
chenedlaetholwr *gw.* cenedlaetholwr

chennin *gw.* cenhinen
cher *gw.* mynd
cherdyn *gw.* cerdyn
cherdd *gw.* cerdd
cherdded *gw.* cerdded
cherddor *gw.* cerddor
cherddorfa *gw.* cerddorfa
cherddorfeydd *gw.* cerddorfa
cherddoriaeth *gw.* cerddoriaeth
cherddorol *gw.* cerddorol
cherddwr *gw.* cerddwr
cherddwyr *gw.* cerddwr
cherflun *gw.* cerflun
cherrig *gw.* carreg
cherwch *gw.* mynd
ches *gw.* ces
chesair *gw.* cesair
chestyll *gw.* castell
chewri *gw.* cawr
chewyn *gw.* cewyn
cheyrydd *gw.* caer

Insight

chi *rhag.* (pronounced as 'ch-ee') you (singular); dog. Only the context will make clear which is which!

chenedlaetholwyr *gw.* cenedlaetholwr
chenfigennus *gw.* cenfigennus
chenhadaeth *gw.* cenhadaeth
chenhadol *gw.* cenhadol
chenhadon *gw.* cenhadwr
chenhadu *gw.* cenhadu
chenhadwr *gw.* cenhadwr
chenhedlaeth *gw.* cenhedlaeth
chenhedloedd *gw.* cenedl
chenhinen *gw.* cenhinen

chi: chwi *rhag.* you. *gw.* ci
chig *gw.* cig
chigydd *gw.* cigydd
chigyddion *gw.* cigydd
chilio *gw.* cilio
chiniawau *gw.* cinio
chinio *gw.* cinio
chipolwg *gw.* cipolwg
chist *gw.* cist
chithau: chwithau *rhag.* you also

chlaf

chlaf *gw.* claf
chlai *gw.* clai
chlasur *gw.* clasur
chlasurol *gw.* clasurol
chlawdd *gw.* clawdd
chlawr *gw.* clawr
chlebran *gw.* clebran
chledr *gw.* cledr
chlefyd *gw.* clefyd
chleifion *gw.* claf
chlêr *gw.* cleren
chlerc *gw.* clerc
chleren *gw.* cleren
chlir *gw.* clir
chlirio *gw.* clirio
chlo *gw.* clo, cloi
chloc *gw.* cloc
chloch *gw.* cloch
chlod *gw.* clod
chlodfori *gw.* clodfori
chloff *gw.* cloff
chloffi *gw.* cloffi
chlogwyn *gw.* clogwyn
chlogyn *gw.* clogyn
chloi *gw.* cloi
chlorian *gw.* clorian
chloriau *gw.* clawr
chlown *gw.* clown
chlun *gw.* clun
chlust *gw.* clust
chlustog *gw.* clustog
chlwb *gw.* clwb
chlwm *gw.* clwm
chlwtyn *gw.* clwtyn
Chlwyd *gw.* Clwyd
chlwyd *gw.* clwyd
chlwydau: chlwydi *gw.* clwyd
chlwyf *gw.* clwyf
chlychau *gw.* cloch
chlymau *gw.* clwm

chlymu *gw.* clymu
chlytiau *gw.* clwtyn
chlyw *gw.* clyw
chlywed *gw.* clywed
chnau *gw.* cneuen
chneuen *gw.* cneuen
chnoc *gw.* cnoc
chnocio *gw.* cnocio
chnoi *gw.* cnoi
choban *gw.* coban
chobannau *gw.* coban
choch *gw.* coch
chochach *gw.* coch
chochaf *gw.* coch
choched *gw.* coch
chodi *gw.* codi
Choed-duon *gw.* Coed-duon
choeden *gw.* coeden
choedwig *gw.* coedwig
choes *gw.* coes
chof *gw.* cof
chofio *gw.* cofio
chofion *gw.* cof
chofleidio *gw.* cofleidio
chofrestr *gw.* cofrestr
chofrestru *gw.* cofrestru
choffi *gw.* coffi
chog *gw.* cog
choginio *gw.* coginio
chogydd *gw.* cogydd
choleg *gw.* coleg
choler *gw.* coler
cholofn *gw.* colofn
choluro *gw.* coluro
cholled *gw.* colled
chollen *gw.* collen
cholli *gw.* colli
chopïo *gw.* copïo
chopyn *gw.* copyn
chôr *gw.* côr

chusan

chorau *gw*. côr
chordyn *gw*. cordyn
chorff *gw*. corff
chorfforol *gw*. corfforol
chorgi *gw*. corgi
chorn *gw*. corn
chornel *gw*. cornel
choron *gw*. coron
choroni *gw*. coroni
chorryn *gw*. corryn
chorynnod *gw*. corryn
chosb *gw*. cosb
chosbi *gw*. cosbi
chostus *gw*. costus
chot *gw*. cot
chotau: chotiau *gw*. cot
chotwm *gw*. cotwm
chrac *gw*. crac
chrachach *gw*. crachach
chrafu *gw*. crafu
chragen *gw*. cragen
chraig *gw*. craig
chras *gw*. cras
chrasu *gw*. crasu
chredu *gw*. credu
chrefydd *gw*. crefydd
chrefft *gw*. crefft
chrefftwr *gw*. crefftwr
chrefftwyr *gw*. crefftwr
chregyn *gw*. cragen
chreigiau *gw*. craig
chreigiog *gw*. creigiog
chreision *gw*. creisionyn
chrempog *gw*. crempog
chreulon *gw*. creulon
chreulondeb *gw*. creulondeb
chri *gw*. cri
chrib *gw*. crib
chribo *gw*. cribo
chriced *gw*. criced

chricedwr *gw*. cricedwr
chrio *gw*. crio
Christion *gw*. Cristion
Christnogion *gw*. Cristion
chriw *gw*. criw
chroen *gw*. croen
chroes *gw*. croes
chroesair *gw*. croesair
chroesau *gw*. croes
chroesawu *gw*. croesawu
chroesawus *gw*. croesawus
chroeseiriau *gw*. croesair
chroesfan *gw*. croesfan
chroesffordd *gw*. croesffordd
chroesholi *gw*. croesholi
chroesi *gw*. croesi
chroeso *gw*. croeso
chron *gw*. cron
chronfa *gw*. cronfa
chronfeydd *gw*. cronfa
chrud *gw*. crud
chrwn *gw*. crwn
chrwst *gw*. crwst
chryd *gw*. cryd
chryf *gw*. cryf
chryfach *gw*. cryf
chryfaf *gw*. cryf
chryfed *gw*. cryf
chrynhoi *gw*. crynhoi
chryno *gw*. cryno
chrynodeb *gw*. crynodeb
chrynu *gw*. crynu
chrys *gw*. crys
chrystiau *gw*. crwst, crystyn
chrystyn *gw*. crystyn
chu *gw*. cu
chuddio *gw*. cuddio
chul *gw*. cul
churo *gw*. curo
chusan *gw*. cusan

chusanu

chusanu *gw*. cusanu
chwaer *e.b.* *ll*. **chwiorydd**
sister, maiden

chwarel 1 *e.b.g.* *ll* **-i, -au**
quarry. 2 *e.g.b.* *ll*. **-au, -i**
pane of glass

Insight

chwaer *e.b.* sister; nun. Augustinian, Carmelite and
Franciscan Nuns live under vows of poverty, chastity and
obedience.

chwain *gw*. chwannen
chwaith: ychwaith *ad*. neither,
nor . . . either, not . . . either
chwalu *be*. (chwalaf) to
crumble; to scatter, to
disperse. **chwalu cartref** to
break up a home; **chwalwr**
disperser, scatterer
chwaneg: ychwaneg *a. & e.g.*
more, additional
chwanegu *gw*. ychwanegu
chwannen *e.b.* *ll*. chwain flea
chwant *e.g.* *ll*. **-au** desire,
appetite; lust. **Mae chwant
bwyd arnaf i** I desire food;
Does dim chwant mynd arni
She doesn't feel like going
chwap *a. & ad*. at once,
instantly
chwarae: 1 *be*. (chwaraeaf) to
play, to perform. 2 *e.g.* *ll*.
-on game, sport; play. **amser
chwarae** playtime; **chwarae
teg** fair play; **meysydd
chwarae** playing fields
chwaraewr *e.g.* *ll*. chwaraewyr
player, actor
chwaraewyr *gw*. chwaraewr
chwarddaf *gw*. chwerthin

chwarelau: chwareli *gw*.
chwarel
chwarelwr *e.g.* quarryman
chwareus *a*. playful
chwarter *e.g.* *ll*. **-au, -i** quarter
chwb *gw*. cwb
chwbl *gw*. cwbl
chwcw *gw*. cwcw
chwch *gw*. cwch
chwd *gw*. cwd
chwdyn *gw*. cwdyn
chwe: chwech *a*. six. **chwe**
*before singular nouns
(followed by spirant
mutation)*; **chwe bachgen,
chwe llyfr; chwech** *on its
own or with* **o** + *plural noun*
**chwech o dai, chwech o
blant; chwe deg** sixty
chweched *a*. sixth
chwedl *e.b.* *ll*. **-au, -euon**
story, legend, fable; report,
rumour; saying
chwedlau: chwedleuon *gw*.
chwedl
Chwefror *e.g.* February
chwerthin 1 *be*. (chwarddaf)
to laugh, to smile. **chwerthin
am ei ben** to laugh at him. 2
e.g. laughter

chwerthinllyd *a.* laughable
chwerw *a.* bitter; severe, sharp, spiteful
chweryl *gw.* cweryl
chwerylau: chwerylon *gw.* cweryl
chwerylu *gw.* cwerylu
chwestiwn *gw.* cwestiwn
chwestiyna *gw.* cwestiyna
chwestiynau *gw.* cwestiwn
chwi *gw.* chi
chwiban *e.g. ll.* -au a whistling, whistle
chwiban: chwibanu (ar) *be.* (chwibanaf) to whistle
chwifio (at) *be.* (chwifiaf) to wave
chwilen *e.b. ll.* chwilod beetle. **Mae chwilen yn ei ben** He has a bee in his bonnet
chwilio (am) *be.* (chwiliaf) to search (for), to examine
chwiliwr *e.g. ll.* chwilwyr investigator, searcher
chwilod *gw.* chwilen
chwilota *be.* (chwilotaf) to rummage, to pry
chwilwyr *gw.* chwiliwr
chwilotwr *e.g. ll.* chwilotwyr rummager, one engaged in research
chwiorydd *gw.* chwaer
chwip 1 *e.b.g. ll.* -au, -iau whip. 2 *a.* swift, quick. 3 *ad.* instantly
chwipio *be.* (chwipiaf) to whip
chwistrelliad *e.g. ll.* -au injection

chwith *a.* left; strange; sad. **o chwith** the wrong way about, awkwardly; **tu chwith** inside out; **llaw chwith** left-handed
chwithau *gw.* chithau
chwithig *a.* strange; awkward
chwlwm *gw.* cwlwm
chwm *gw.* cwm
chwmni *gw.* cwmni
chwmnïau *gw.* cwmni
chwmnïoedd *gw.* cwmni
chwmwl *gw.* cwmwl
chŵn *gw.* ci
chwningen *gw.* cwningen
chwningod *gw.* cwningen
chwpan *gw.* cwpan
chwpla *gw.* cwpla
chwpwrdd *gw.* cwpwrdd
chwr *gw.* cwr
chwrdd *gw.* cwrdd
chwrs *gw.* cwrs
chwrtais *gw.* cwrtais
chwrw *gw.* cwrw
chwsg *gw.* cwsg
chwsmer *gw.* cwsmer
chwstwm *gw.* cwstwm
chwt *gw.* cwt
chwta *gw.* cwta
chwydu *be.* (chwydaf) to vomit
chwyddiant *e.g. ll.* chwyddiannau inflation; inflammation
chwyddo *be.* (chwyddaf) to swell, to increase
chwyddwydr *e.g. ll.* -au magnifying glass

chwyldro: chwyldroad

chwyldro: chwyldroad *e.g. ll.*
 chwyldroadau revolution.
 y Chwyldro Diwydiannol the
 Industrial Revolution; y
 Chwyldro Ffrengig the
 French Revolution
chwymp *gw.* cwymp
chwympo *gw.* cwympo
chwyn *e. torf.* weeds. *gw.*
 cwyn; *gw.* chwynnyn
chwynladdwr *e.g.* weedkiller
chwynnyn *e.g. ll. & e.torf.*
 chwyn weed
chwynnu *be.* (chwynnaf) to
 weed
chwyno *gw.* cwyno
chwyro *gw.* cwyro
chwyrnu *be.* (chwyrnaf) to
 snore, to snarl; to whirl
chwys *e.g.* perspiration,
 sweat. yn chwys domen
 dripping with perspiration
chwysu *be.* (chwysaf) to
 perspire, to sweat
chwythu *be.* (chwythaf) to
 blow
chychod *gw.* cwch
chychwyn *gw.* cychwyn
chydadrodd *gw.* cydadrodd
chydau *gw.* cwd; cwdyn
chydio *gw.* cydio
chydnabod *gw.* cydnabod
chydwybodol *gw.* cydwybodol
chydymdeimlad *gw.*
 cydymdeimlad
chyfagos *gw.* cyfagos
chyfaill *gw.* cyfaill
chyfan *gw.* cyfan
chyfangwbl *gw.* cyfangwbl
chyfansoddi *gw.* cyfansoddi

chyfansoddwr *gw.*
 cyfansoddwr
chyfanswm *gw.* cyfanswm
chyfarch *gw.* cyfarch
chyfarfod *gw.* cyfarfod
chyfarfodydd *gw.* cyfarfod
chyfarwyddiadur *gw.*
 cyfarwyddiadur
chyfarwyddo *gw.* cyfarwyddo
chyfarwyddwr *gw.*
 cyfarwyddwr
chyfeilles *gw.* cyfeilles
chyfeillgar *gw.* cyfeillgar
chyfeillgarwch *gw.*
 cyfeillgarwch
chyfeiriad *gw.* cyfeiriad
chyfeirio *gw.* cyfeirio
chyfenw *gw.* cyfenw
chyferbyn *gw.* cyferbyn
chyfiawn *gw.* cyfiawn
chyfiawnder *gw.* cyfiawnder
chyfieithiad *gw.* cyfieithiad
chyfieithu *gw.* cyfieithu
chyfieithydd *gw.* cyfieithydd
chyfle *gw.* cyfle
chyfleu *gw.* cyfleu
chyfleus *gw.* cyfleus
chyflog *gw.* cyflog
chyflogi *gw.* cyflogi
chyflogwr *gw.* cyflogwr
chyflwr *gw.* cyflwr
chyflwyno *gw.* cyflwyno
chyflym *gw.* cyflym
chyflymach *gw.* cyflym
chyflymaf *gw.* cyflym
chyflymder *gw.* cyflymder
chyflymed *gw.* cyflym
chyflymu *gw.* cyflymu
chyflymydd *gw.* cyflymydd
chyflyrau *gw.* cyflwr

chyfnither *gw.* cyfnither
chyfnod *gw.* cyfnod
chyfoeth *gw.* cyfoeth
chyfoethog *gw.* cyfoethog
chyfraith *gw.* cyfraith
chyfrannu *gw.* cyfrannu
chyfreithiwr *gw.* cyfreithiwr
chyfreithwyr *gw.* cyfreithiwr
chyfres *gw.* cyfres
chyfresau: chyfresi *gw.* cyfres
chyfrif *gw.* cyfrif
chyfrifiadur *gw.* cyfrifiadur
chyfrifiannell *gw.* cyfrifiannell
chyfrifol *gw.* cyfrifol
chyfrifoldeb *gw.* cyfrifoldeb
chyfrifydd *gw.* cyfrifydd
chyfrinach *gw.* cyfrinach
chyfrinachol *gw.* cyfrinachol
chyfrol *gw.* cyfrol
chyfrwng *gw.* cyfrwng
chyfrwys *gw.* cyfrwys
chyfryngau *gw.* cyfrwng
chyfun *gw.* cyfun
chyfuwch *gw.* uchel
chyfweld *gw.* cyfweld
chyfweliad *gw.* cyfweliad
chyfyng *gw.* cyfyng
chyfyngiad *gw.* cyfyngiad
chyfyngu *gw.* cyfyngu
chyfystyr *gw.* cyfystyr
chyfforddus *gw.* cyfforddus
chyffredin *gw.* cyffredin
chyffrous *gw.* cyffrous
chyffur *gw.* cyffur
chyffwrdd *gw.* cyffwrdd
chyffyrddus *gw.* cyffyrddus
chyngerdd *gw.* cyngerdd
chyngherddau *gw.* cyngerdd
chynghori *gw.* cynghori
chynghorion *gw.* cyngor

chynghorwr *gw.* cynghorwr
chynghrair *gw.* cynghrair
chynghreiriad *gw.*
  cynghreiriad
chyngor *gw.* cyngor
chyhoedd *gw.* cyhoedd
chyhoeddi *gw.* cyhoeddi
chyhoeddiad *gw.* cyhoeddiad
chyhoeddus *gw.* cyhoeddus
chyhoeddusrwydd *gw.*
  cyhoeddusrwydd
chyhoeddwr *gw.* cyhoeddwr
chyhuddiad *gw.* cyhuddiad
chyhuddo *gw.* cyhuddo
chyhyd *gw.* cyhyd
chyhyrog *gw.* cyhyrog
chylch *gw.* cylch
chylchfan *gw.* cylchfan
chylchgrawn *gw.* cylchgrawn
chylchgronau *gw.* cylchgrawn
chylchlythyr *gw.* cylchlythyr
chyll *gw.* collen; colli
chyllell *gw.* cyllell
chyllyll *gw.* cyllell
chymaint *gw.* cymaint
chymal *gw.* cymal
chymanfa *gw.* cymanfa
chymanfaoedd *gw.* cymanfa
chymar *gw.* cymar
chymdeithas *gw.* cymdeithas
chymdeithaseg *gw.*
  cymdeithaseg
chymdogion *gw.* cymydog
chymeriad *gw.* cymeriad
chymeryd *gw.* cymryd
chymharu *gw.* cymharu
chymhleth *gw.* cymhleth
chymhlethdod *gw.*
  cymhlethdod
chymhlethu *gw.* cymhlethu

chymhorthion

chymhorthion *gw.* cymorth
chymoedd *gw.* cwm
chymorth *gw.* cymorth
Chymraeg *gw.* Cymraeg
Chymraes *gw.* Cymraes
Chymreictod *gw.* Cymreictod
Chymreig *gw.* Cymreig
Chymreiges *gw.* Cymreiges
Chymro *gw.* Cymro
Chymru *gw.* Cymru
Chymry *gw.* Cymro
chymryd *gw.* cymryd
chymundeb *gw.* cymundeb
chymuned *gw.* cymuned
chymwynas *gw.* cymwynas
chymydog *gw.* cymydog
chymylau *gw.* cwmwl
chymylog *gw.* cymylog
chymysg *gw.* cymysg
chymysgu *gw.* cymysgu
chymysgwch *gw.* cymysgwch
chyn *gw.* cyn
chynaeafau *gw.* cynhaeaf
chynddrwg *gw.* cynddrwg
chynffon *gw.* cynffon
chynhadledd *gw.* cynhadledd
chynhaeaf *gw.* cynhaeaf
chynhesu *gw.* cynhesu
chynhyrfus *gw.* cynhyrfus
chynigion *gw.* cynnig
chynilion *gw.* cynilion
chynilo *gw.* cynilo
chynllun *gw.* cynllun
chynllunio *gw.* cynllunio
chynlluniwr *gw.* cynlluniwr
chynllunydd *gw.* cynlluniwr
chynnal *gw.* cynnal
chynnar *gw.* cynnar
chynnes *gw.* cynnes
chynnig *gw.* cynnig

chynnwys *gw.* cynnwys
chynnyrch *gw.* cynnyrch
chynorthwywr *gw.*
 cynorthwywr
chynorthwy-ydd *gw.*
 cynorthwy-ydd
chynradd *gw.* cynradd
chynt *gw.* cynnar
chyntaf *gw.* cyntaf, cynnar
chynted *gw.* cynnar
chyntedd *gw.* cyntedd
chynteddau *gw.* cyntedd
chynteddoedd *gw.* cyntedd
chynulleidfa *gw.* cynulleidfa
chynwysiedig *gw.*
 cynwysiedig
chypyrddau *gw.* cwpwrdd
chyrddau *gw.* cwrdd
chyrff *gw.* corff
chyrion *gw.* cwr
chyrliog *gw.* cyrliog
chyrn *gw.* corn
chyrraedd *gw.* cyrraedd
chyrrau *gw.* cwr
chyrsau *gw.* cwrs
chyrsiau *gw.* cwrs
chysglyd *gw.* cysglyd
chysgod *gw.* cysgod
chysgodau *gw.* cysgod
chysgodi *gw.* cysgodi
chysgodion *gw.* cysgod
chysgu *gw.* cysgu
chystadlaethau *gw.*
 cystadleuaeth
chystadleuaeth *gw.*
 cystadleuaeth
chystadleuwr *gw.* cystadleuwr
chystadleuwyr *gw.*
 cystadleuwr
chystadleuydd *gw.*
 cystadleuwr

chystadlu *gw*. cystadlu
chystal *gw*. cystal
chystymau *gw*. cwstwm
chysur *gw*. cysur
chysuro *gw*. cysuro
chysurus *gw*. cysurus
chyswllt *gw*. cyswllt
chytgan *gw*. cytgan
chytsain *gw*. cytsain
chytseiniaid *gw*. cytsain
chytseiniau *gw*. cytsain
chytundeb *gw*. cytundeb
chytuno *gw*. cytuno
chyw *gw*. cyw
chywaith *gw*. cywaith
chyweithiau *gw*. cywaith
chywilydd *gw*. cywilydd
chywion *gw*. cyw
chywir *gw*. cywir
chywiriad *gw*. cywiriad
chywiro *gw*. cywiro

D

da 1 *a*. good, well. **bore da**
good morning; **da iawn** very
good, very well (*in health*);
Mae'n dda gen i weld I'm
glad to see. *gw. At.
Ansoddeiriau*. 2 *e.g.* good,
goodness. 3 *e. torf.* goods,
stock; cattle (*S.W.*)

dabl *gw*. tabl
dablet *gw*. tablet
dacl *gw*. tacl
daclo *gw*. taclo
daclu *gw*. taclu
daclus *gw*. taclus
dacluso *gw*. tacluso
daclwr *gw*. taclwr
dacsi *gw*. tacsi
dacw *ad*. There is/are, behold
(*far away*) (*followed by soft
mutation*)
Dachwedd *gw*. Tachwedd
dad *gw*. tad
dadansoddi *be*. (dadansoddaf)
to analyse
dad-cu *gw*. tad-cu
dadl *e.b. ll.* -euon debate,
argument, dispute
dadlau *be*. (dadleuaf) to
argue, to debate, to dispute
dadrewi *be*. (dadrewaf) to
defrost
daear *e.b. ll.* -oedd earth,
ground, soil, land. **Beth ar y
ddaear ydy e?** What on
earth is it? **Ble ar y ddaear
mae e?** Where on earth is
he/it?
daeareg *e.b.* geology
daeargryn *e.g.b. ll.* -fâu,
-feydd earthquake

Insight

da *a.; e.ll.g.* good; goods; cattle, namely the farmer's goods. Even
a tenant farmer owns his cows – his 'goods'.
Da in this context is a plural noun *m*.

daearyddiaeth

daearyddiaeth *e.b.* geography
daeth *bf.* he/she/it came. *gw.*
 dod
dafad *e.b.* *ll.* **defaid** sheep,
 ewe; wart
dafarn *gw.* **tafarn**
dafarnwr *gw.* **tafarnwr**
dafell *gw.* **tafell**
daflegryn *gw.* **taflegryn**
daflen *gw.* **taflen**
daflu *gw.* **taflu**
dafod *gw.* **tafod**
dafodiaith *gw.* **tafodiaith**
dafol *gw.* **tafol**
dagfa *gw.* **tagfa**
dagrau *gw.* **deigryn**
dagu *gw.* **tagu**
dangnefedd *gw.* **tangnefedd**
daid *gw.* **taid**
dail *gw.* **dalen, deilen**
daioni *e.g.* goodness. **er**
 daioni for the good of. *gw.*
 da
dair *gw.* **tair**
daith *gw.* **taith**
dal *gw.* **tal**
dal: dala *(S.W.)* *be.* **(daliaf,**
 dalaf) to hold, to capture, to
 seize, to catch; to maintain;
 to keep, to wager, to bet; to
 continue; to rely, to trust.
 dal annwyd to catch a cold;
 dal ati to persevere, to stick
 at it; **dal dŵr** to hold water;
 dal dig to bear or retain a
 grudge; **dal ei dir** to hold his
 ground; **dal i fyny** to bear
 up, to uphold; **dal i lawr** to
 subjugate; **dal perthynas â** to
 be related to; **dal sylw** to
 take notice; **dal wrth/at** to
adhere to, to persevere in;
 dal y slac yn dynn to
 pretend to work; **does dim**
 dal arno. He cannot be relied
 upon; **Ydy e'n dal i ganu?**
 Does he still sing?
dâl *gw.* **tâl**
dalai *gw.* **talai**
dalaith *gw.* **talaith**
dalcen *gw.* **talcen**
daleb *gw.* **taleb**
daleion *gw.* **talai**
dalen *e.b.* *ll.* **dail, -nau** leaf
 (*of a book*); sheet (*of paper*);
 leaf (*of tree, plant, etc.*). **troi**
 dalen newydd to turn over a
 new leaf; **ymyl y ddalen**
 margin of a page. *gw.* **deilen,**
 tudalen
dalent *gw.* **talent**
dalentog *gw.* **talentog**
dalgylch *e.g.* *ll.* **-oedd**
 catchment area
dalu *gw.* **talu**
dalwr *gw.* **talwr**
dalwrn *gw.* **talwrn**
dall 1 *a.* blind. 2 *e.g.* *ll.*
 deillion, deilliaid blind
 person(s)
dallu *be.* **(dallaf)** to blind, to
 dazzle
damaid *gw.* **tamaid**
dameg *e.b.* *ll.* **damhegion**
 parable
dameidiau *gw.* **tamaid**
damhegion *gw.* **dameg**
damwain *e.b.* *ll.* **damweiniau**
 accident; chance. **ar**
 ddamwain, trwy ddamwain,
 wrth ddamwain by chance
dan: tan *ardd.* **(dana, danat,**

dano/dani, danon, danoch, danyn) under, until, as far; (*followed by soft mutation*). *gw. At. Arddodiaid.* **dan + verb-noun: aeth adref dan ganu** he went home singing; **cododd hi dan chwerthin** she got up laughing; **aethon nhw i'r capel dan wylo** they went to the chapel weeping

dân *gw.* **tân**

danau *gw.* **tân**

dancer *gw.* **tancer**

danddaear *gw.* **tanddaear**

danfon *be.* (**danfonaf**) to send, to dispatch; to conduct, to accompany. *gw.* **anfon**

danfor *gw.* **tanfor**

dangos (i) *be.* (**dangosaf**) to show, to reveal

danio *gw.* **tanio**

danlinellu *gw.* **tanlinellu**

danlwybr *gw.* **tanlwybr**

danllyd *gw.* **tanllyd**

dannau *gw.* **tant**

dannedd *gw.* **dant**

dannoedd *e.b.* toothache

danseilio *gw.* **tanseilio**

dant *e.g. ll.* **dannedd** tooth; cog; tine. **dant blaen** front tooth; incisor; **dannedd gosod/dodi** false teeth; **at ei ddant** to his taste; **dant y llew** dandelion. *gw.* **tant**

danwydd *gw.* **tanwydd**

dap *gw.* **tap**

dâp *gw.* **tâp**

daran *gw.* **taran**

daranu *gw.* **taranu**

darddiad *gw.* **tarddiad**

darddu *gw.* **tarddu**

darfod (i) *be.* (**darfodaf**) to end; to finish; to die; to waste away; to happen (*N.W.*)

darganfod *be.* (**darganfyddaf**) to discover

darged *gw.* **targed**

darian *gw.* **tarian**

darlith *e.b. ll.* **-iau, -oedd** lecture

darlithio *be.* (**darlithiaf**) to lecture

darlithiwr: darlithydd *e.g. ll.* **darlithwyr** lecturer

darlun *e.g. ll.* **-iau** picture

darlunio *be.* (**darluniaf**) to describe, to draw, to illustrate

darlledu *be.* (**darlledaf**) to broadcast

darllen *be.* (**darllenaf**) to read

darllenwr: darllenydd *e.g. ll.* **darllenwyr** reader

darn *e.g. ll.* **-au** part, piece

daro *gw.* **taro**

darw *gw.* **tarw**

dasg *gw.* **tasg**

dasgu *gw.* **tasgu**

datblygiad *e.g. ll* **-au** development, evolution

datblygu *be.* (**datblygaf**) to develop, to evolve

daten *gw.* **taten**

datgan *be.* (**datganaf**) to declare, to recite

datganiad *e.g. ll.* **-au** declaration, rendering

datganoli *be.* (**datganolaf**) to devolve, to decentralize

datgelu *be.* (**datgelaf**) to reveal

datguddio

datguddio *be.* **(datguddiaf)** to reveal, to disclose
dato: datws *gw.* **taten**
datod *be.* **(datodaf)** to undo, to solve, to loose; to dissolve (*N.W.*)
datrys *be.* **(datrysaf)** to solve, to unravel
datws *gw.* **taten**
dathliad *e.g. ll.* **dathliadau** celebration
dathlu *be.* **(dathlaf)** to celebrate
dau 1 *a.g.* (*followed by soft mutation*) two. 2 *e.g. ll.* **deuoedd** two. **y ddau** both. *gw.* **dwy**
dawel *gw.* **tawel**
dawelu *gw.* **tawelu**
dawelwch *gw.* **tawelwch**
dawelydd *gw.* **tawelydd**
dawelyn *gw.* **tawelyn**
dawns *e.b. ll.* **-iau** dance. **dawns werin** folk dance
dawnsio *be.* **(dawnsiaf)** to dance. **dawnsio gwerin** folk dancing
de 1 *a.* southern; right. **y llaw dde** the right hand. 2 *e.g.* south. **pegwn y de** south pole. 3 *e.b.* right side. **ar y dde** on the right (hand) side. *gw.* **te**
deall 1 *be.* **(deallaf)** to understand. 2 *e.g.* understanding, intelligence, intellect

deallus *a.* intelligent
debot *gw.* **tebot**
debyg *gw.* **tebyg**
debygrwydd *gw.* **tebygrwydd**
decell *gw.* **tegell**
dechneg *gw.* **techneg**
dechnegol *gw.* **technegol**
dechnegwr *gw.* **technegwr**
dechnoleg *gw.* **technoleg**
dechrau 1 *be.* **(dechreuaf)** to begin, originate. **Mae e'n dechrau tyfu** He/it is beginning to grow. 2 *e.g.* beginning, origin
dechreuad *e.g.* beginning. **'Yn y dechreuad . . .'** 'In the beginning . . .'
dedwydd *a.* happy, blessed
deddf *e.b. ll.* **-au** law, statute, act. **Deddf Gwlad** law of the land; **Deddf Uno 1536** Act of Union 1536; **Deddf yr Iaith** (Welsh) Language Act
deddfu *be.* **(deddfaf)** to legislate
defnydd *e.g. ll.* **-iau** material, cloth, fabric; use, purpose
defnyddio *be.* **(defnyddiaf)** to use
defnyddiol *a.* useful
deffro *be.* **(deffroaf)** to awake, to awaken
deg: deng 1 *a.* ten. **deng mlynedd** ten years, decade; **deng mlwydd** ten years (*of age*); **deng niwrnod** ten days; **a'm deg ewin** (*doing*) my

Insight

deg *a.* ten; pretty; fair. The context should tell you which word is meant.

level best. *gw. At. Tr. Trwynol.* 2 *e.g. ll.* **degau** ten. *gw.* **teg**

degan *gw.* **tegan**

degawd *e.g. ll.* **-au** decade

degell *gw.* **tegell**

degwch *gw.* **tegwch**

deng *a.* ten; (*used before* **blwydd, blynedd** *and* **diwrnod**) (followed by nasal mutation). *gw.* **deg**

deheuol *a.* southern

dei *gw.* **tei**

deialog *e.g.b. ll.* **-au** dialogue

deiar *gw.* **teiar**

deidiau *gw.* **taid**

deigr *gw.* **teigr**

deigryn *e.g. ll.* **dagrau** tear

deilen *e.b. ll.* **dail** leaf (*of tree*); *gw.* **dalen**

deiliwr *gw.* **teiliwr**

deilsen *gw.* **teilsen**

deilwng *gw.* **teilwng**

deilwres *gw.* **teilwres**

deilyngdod *gw.* **teilyngdod**

deilliaid: deillion *gw.* **dall**

deimlad *gw.* **teimlad**

deimlo *gw.* **teimlo**

deintydd *e.g. ll.* **-ion** dentist

deipiadur *gw.* **teipiadur**

deirgwaith *gw.* **teirgwaith**

deiseb *e.b. ll.* **-au** petition

deisen *gw.* **teisen**

deitl *gw.* **teitl**

deithio *gw.* **teithio**

deithiwr *gw.* **teithiwr**

del *a.* pretty, neat (*N.W.*)

deledu *gw.* **teledu**

deleffon *gw.* **teleffon**

delw *e.b. ll.* **-au** image, idol, form, manner. **ar ddelw** in the image of

delwi *be.* (**delwaf**) to become motionless, to be paralyzed with fright

delyn *gw.* **telyn**

delyneg *gw.* **telyneg**

delynor *gw.* **telynor**

delynores *gw.* **telynores**

deml *gw.* **teml**

denau *gw.* **tenau**

deniadol *a.* attractive, enticing

denu *be.* (**denaf**) to attract, to entice

derbyn *be.* (**derbyniaf, derbynnaf**) to receive

derbynebau: derbynebion *gw.* **derbynneb**

derbyniol *a.* acceptable, approved, receptive

derbynneb *e.g. ll.* **derbynebau, derbynebion** receipt, voucher

derbynnydd *e.g. ll.* **derbynyddion** receiver; receptionist. **derbynnydd swyddogol** official receiver

derfyn *gw.* **terfyn**

deri *e. ll.* oak trees, oak. *gw.* **derwen**

derm *gw.* **term**

derw *a.* of oak, oaken. *gw.* **derwen**

derwen *e.b. ll.* **derw** oak tree, oak. *gw.* **deri, derw**

des *gw.* **tes**

desg *e.b. ll.* **-iau** desk

desog *gw.* **tesog**

destun

destun *gw.* testun

detholiad *e.g.* *ll.* **-au**
selection, anthology

deuawd *e.g.b.* *ll.* **-au** duet

deuddeg 1 *a.* twelve. 2 *e.g.*
twelve

deuddegfed *a.* twelfth

deugain 1 *a.* forty. **deugain
mlynedd** forty years. 2 *e.g.*
forty

deulu *gw.* teulu

deunaw 1 *a.* eighteen.
deunaw mlynedd eighteen
years. 2 *e.g.* eighteen

deuoedd *gw.* dau

dew *gw.* tew

dewch *bf.* come! (*plural*). *gw.*
dod

dewin *e.g.* *ll.* **-iaid** magician,
wizard, diviner

dewis 1 *be.* **(dewisaf)** to
choose, to select. 2 *e.g.* *ll.*
-au choice, desire

dewr 1 *a.* *ll* **-ion** brave,
valiant. 2 *e.g.* *ll.* **-ion** brave
man, hero

deyrnas *gw.* teyrnas

di *gw.* ti. *gw.* At. *Rhagenwau*

diacon *e.g.* *ll.* **-iaid** deacon

diafol *e.g.* *ll.* **diawliaid** devil

dial (ar) 1 *be.* **(dialaf)** to
avenge; to revenge. 2 *e.g.* *ll.*
-au, -on vengeance; **dialedd**
vengeance, retribution

dianc (rhag) *be.* **(dihangaf)** to
escape, to avoid

diarfogi *be.* **(diarfogaf)** to
disarm

diarhebion *gw.* dihareb

diawl *e.g.* *ll.* **-iaid** devil. **Cer
i'r diawl!** To hell with you!
diawl o beth a devil of a
thing

diawledig *a.* devilish

diawliaid *gw.* diafol, diawl

di-baid *a.* unceasing, constant

diben *e.g.* *ll.* **-ion** end, object,
aim. **di-ben-draw** endless,
interminable

dibennu *be.* **(dibennaf)** to
end, to finish, to terminate

di-blwm *a.* unleaded. **petrol
di-blwm** unleaded petrol

dibynnu (ar) *be.* **(dibynnaf)** to
depend (on), to rely (on)

diced *gw.* ticed

diderfyn *a.* unlimited

diddordeb *e.g.* *ll.* **-au** interest,
hobby

diddorol *a.* interesting, of
interest

dieithr *a.* strange, unfamiliar

dieithryn *e.g.* *ll.* **dieithriaid**
stranger

diferyn *e.g.* *ll.* **-nau, diferion**
drop

difetha *be.* **(difethaf)** to
destroy, to spoil

diflannu *be.* **(diflannaf)** to
vanish, to disappear

diflas *a.* distasteful, dull

difrifol *a.* serious, earnest,
solemn

difyr: difyrrus *a.* pleasant,
amusing, entertaining

difyrru *be.* **(difyrraf)** to amuse,
to entertain

diffiniad *e.g.* *ll.* **-au** definition

diffinio *be.* **(diffiniaf)** to define

dioddef

diffodd *be.* **(diffoddaf)** to
extinguish, to quench.
**diffodda'r golau/stôf/tân/
teledu** switch off the
light/stove/fire/television
diffuant *a.* genuine, sincere.
Yr eiddoch yn ddiffuant
Yours sincerely
diffyg *e.g. ll.* **-ion** defect,
want, lack, failure, flaw
digartref *a.* homeless. **y
digartref** the homeless
digidol *a.* digital
digon 1 *e.g.* enough,
sufficiency; plenty.
2 *a.* enough; plentiful,
ample. 3 *ad.* enough,
sufficiently, adequately. **Dyna
ddigon!** That's enough! **yn
ddigon da** good enough (*no
mutation*)
digonedd *e.g.* abundance,
plenty
digrif *a.* merry, amusing
digwydd *be.* **(digwyddaf)** to
happen, to occur.
Digwyddodd hi weld y dyn.
She happened to see the man
digwyddiad *e.g. ll.* **-au**
happening, event
digyfeiliant *a.* unaccompanied
dihareb *e.b. ll.* **diarhebion**
proverb
diheintydd *e.g. ll.* **-ion**
disinfectant
dihuno *be.* **(dihunaf)** to
waken, to awaken (*S.W.*)
dileu *be.* **(dileaf)** to delete, to
abolish, to exterminate, to
erase

dilyn *be.* **(dilynaf)** to follow,
to pursue
dillad *gw.* **dilledyn**
dilledyn *e.g. ll.* **dillad**
garment, dress, item of
clothing. **dillad bob dydd**
everyday clothes; **dillad
diwedydd** clothes changed
into after work; **dillad gwaith**
working clothes; **dillad gwely**
bedclothes; **dillad isa(f)**
underclothing; **dillad nos**
pyjamas; **dillad parch**
Sunday best, best clothes
dim 1 *e.g.* any, anything,
nothing. 2 *a.* any, no. **am
ddim** for nothing, gratis; **dim
byd** nothing at all; **dim ond**
nothing but, only, merely;
dim un not a single one; **i'r
dim** exactly
dinas *e.b. ll.* **-oedd** city
dinasyddion *gw.* **dinesydd**
Dinbych *e.b.* **Tref a Sir**
Denbighshire (N. Wales)
Dinbych-y-pysgod *e.b.* Tenby
dinesig *a.* civic, urban
dinesydd *e.g. ll.* **dinasyddion**
citizen
dinistrio *be.* **(dinistriaf)** to
destroy
diniwed *a.* innocent,
harmless, simple
diod *e.b. ll.* **-ydd** drink,
beverage. **diod gadarn**
strong drink; **diod o ddŵr** a
drink of water
dioddef (o) 1 *be.* **(dioddefaf)**
to suffer, to endure, to
allow. 2 *e.g. ll.* **-au, -iadau**
suffering, passion

diofal

diofal *a.* careless
diog: dioglyd *a.* lazy, sluggish, indolent
diogel *a.* safe, secure, certain
diogi 1 *be.* **(diogaf)** to be lazy or idle, to laze. 2 *e.g.* laziness
dioglyd *gw.* **diog**
diogyn *e.g. ll.* **-nod** idler, sluggard
diolch (i, am) 1 *be.* **(diolchaf)** to thank, to give thanks. 2 *e.g. ll.* **-iadau** thanks; thanksgiving. **diolch byth!** thank heaven! **diolch yn fawr** many thanks (*to you*). **diolch i'r nef (drefn)** thank goodness
diolchgar *a.* thankful, grateful
diolchgarwch *e.g.* thankfulness, thanksgiving. **Cwrdd Diolchgarwch** Harvest thanksgiving service
diolchiadau *gw.* **diolch**
diota *be.* **(diotaf)** to drink (*alcohol*)
dip *gw.* **tip**
dipyn *gw.* **tipyn**
dir *gw.* **tir**
dirgelwch *e.g. ll.* **dirgelion** mystery, secret, secrecy
dirion *gw.* **tirion**
dirlun *gw.* **tirlun**
diroedd *gw.* **tiroedd**
dirprwy *e.g. ll.* **-on** deputy, delegate, proxy, substitute. **dirprwy brifathro** deputy headmaster
dirprwyaeth *e.b. ll.* **-au** deputation, delegation

dirwasgiad *e.g. ll.* **-au; pant** *e.g. ll.* **-iau** depression
dirwy *e.b. ll.* **-on** fine, penalty
disg *e.g.b. ll.* **-iau** disc, record
disglair *a.* bright, brilliant
disgleirio *be.* **(disgleiriaf)** to shine, to glitter
disgrifiad *e.g. ll.* **-au** description
disgrifio *be.* **(disgrifiaf)** to describe
disgwyl (am) *be.* **(disgwyliaf)** to expect, to look, to wait for. **Mae hi'n disgwyl baban** She is expecting a baby. **Mae e'n disgwyl bws.** He is waiting for a bus
disgybl *g. ll.* **-ion** disciple, pupil, novice, follower, adherent
disgyblaeth *e.b. ll.* **-au** discipline
disgyn *be.* **(disgynnaf)** to descend, to fall
disian *gw.* **tisian**
distaw *a.* silent, calm, quiet
distawrwydd *e.g.* silence, quiet
distewi *be.* **(distewaf)** to silence, to be silent, to calm
diswyddo *be.* **(diswyddaf)** to dismiss, to depose, to sack, to make redundant
dithau *gw.* **tithau**
di-waith *a.* unemployed, idle
diwallu *be.* **(diwallaf)** to satisfy, to supply
diwedd 1 *e.g. ll* **-ion, -au** end, close, conclusion; death; purpose. 2 *a.* last, final. **o'r**

dodrefnyn

dechrau i'r diwedd from start to finish

diweddar *a.* recent; modern, late (*S.W.*); late (*of person*); lately, deceased. **y diweddar Tom Jones** the late Tom Jones. **Ydych chi wedi nofio'n ddiweddar?** Have you been swimming lately? **Cymraeg Diweddar** Modern Welsh

diweddglo *e.g. ll.* **diweddgloeon** conclusion, close, epilogue

diweddarach *a.* later. *gw.* **diweddar**

diwerth *a.* worthless

diwethaf *a.* last; previous; latest. **Rydw i'n dal y trên nesa achos collais yr un diwethaf** I'm catching the next train because I missed the previous one

diwrnod *e.g. ll.* **-au** day. **diwrnod braf/teg** fine day; **diwrnod gwaith** working day; **diwrnod gŵyl** holy day, holiday; **diwrnod mawr** red letter day, 'big day'; **diwrnod i'r brenin** a thoroughly enjoyable day; **y diwrnod o'r blaen** the day before, the other day; **ers diwrnodau** for many days (*past*)

diwtor *gw.* **tiwtor**

diwydiant *e.g. ll.* **diwydiannau** industry. **diwydiant dur** steel industry; **diwydiant glo** coal industry; **diwydiant ymwelwyr** tourist industry; **diwydiant ysgafn** light industry

diwygiad *e.g. ll.* **-au** reform, reformation; revival. **Diwygiad Protestannaidd** Protestant Reformation

diwygio *be.* **(diwygiaf)** to amend, to reform, to revise

diwylliant *e.g. ll.* **diwylliannau** culture

dlawd *gw.* **tlawd**

dlodi *gw.* **tlodi**

dlodion *gw.* **tlawd**

dlos *gw.* **tlos**

dlws *gw.* **tlws**

dlysau *gw.* **tlws**

do *ad.* yes (*affirmative answer to questions using verbs in the past tense*). **Fuest ti'n siopa heddiw? Do** Were you shopping today? Yes. **Welaist ti'r dyn? Do** Did you see the man? Yes. *gw.* **to**

doc *e.g. ll.* **-iau** dock. **docfa** berth

doctor *e.g. ll.* **-iaid** doctor (always used in title); **Y Dr Tom Huws** Dr Tom Huws

docyn *gw.* **tocyn**

docynnwr *gw.* **tocynnwr**

dod: dyfod (at, dros, yn, i) *be.* **(deuaf)** to come, to arrive; to occur; to become. *gw.* **At. Berfau**

dodi *be.* **(dodaf)** to put, to place (*S.W.*); to give. **dodi ar ddeall** to explain to; **dodi bai ar** to blame; **dodi (un) ar waith** to set (one) to work

dodrefnyn *e.g. ll.* **dodrefn** piece of furniture (*N.W.*). *gw.* **celficyn**

dodwy

dodwy *be.* **(dodwaf)** to lay
eggs
doddi *gw.* **toddi**
doe *ad. & e.g.b.* yesterday.
bore ddoe yesterday
morning; **echdoe** the day
before yesterday
does *gw.* **toes**
doeth *a.* wise. **Y Tri Gŵr
Doeth** The Three Wise Men
doethineb *e.g. ll.* **-au**
wisdom, discretion
dof *a. ll.* **-ion** tame,
domesticated
dogfen *e.b. ll.* **-ni, -nau**
document
doiled *gw.* **toiled**
dol *e.b. ll.* **-iau** doll
dôl *e.b. ll* **dolydd, dolau**
meadow
dôl *e.g.* dole. **ar y dôl** on the
dole
dolc *gw.* **tolc**
dolcio *gw.* **tolcio**
dolen *e.b. ll.* **-nau, -ni** handle,
link, ring. **dolen gydiol**
connecting link
dolur *e.g. ll.* **-iau** hurt,
ailment, pain, ache. **dolur
rhydd** diarrhoea; **dolur y
galon** heart disease
dolydd *gw.* **dôl**
doll *gw.* **toll**
dom *gw.* **tom**
don *gw.* **ton**
dôn *gw.* **tôn**
donau *gw.* **tôn**
donfedd *gw.* **tonfedd**
doniol *a.* witty, humorous
donnau *gw.* **ton**

dorch *gw.* **torch**
doreithiog *gw.* **toreithiog**
doreth *gw.* **toreth**
dorf *gw.* **torf**
dorfeydd *gw.* **torf**
dorheulo *gw.* **torheulo**
Dori *gw.* **Tori**
doriad *gw.* **toriad**
Dorïaid *gw.* **Torïaid**
Dorïaidd *gw.* **Torïaidd**
dorri *gw.* **torri**
dors *gw.* **tors**
dorth *gw.* **torth**
dosau *gw.* **tosyn**
dosbarth *e.g. ll.* **-au, -iadau**
class, standard; district.
dosbarth canol middle class;
dosbarth gweithiol working
class; **dosbarth isaf** lower
class; **dosbarth uchaf** upper
class; **dosbarthiadau meithrin**
nursery classes; **cyngor
dosbarth** district council;
dosbarth nos evening class
dost *gw.* **tost**
dostrwydd *gw.* **tostrwydd**
dosyn *gw.* **tosyn**
drachfen: trachefn *ad.* again
draddodiad *gw.* **traddodiad**
draddodiadol *gw.*
traddodiadol
draed *gw.* **traed**
draen *e.b. ll.* **-iau** drain.
draeniau dŵr water drains
draen: draenen *e.b. ll.* drain
thorn. **draenen ddu**
blackthorn; **draenen wen**
hawthorn; **ar bigau'r drain**
on tenterhooks
draenog *e.g. ll.* **-od, -iaid, -ion**
hedgehog

draeth *gw*. **traeth**
draethau *gw*. **traeth**
draethawd *gw*. **traethawd**
draethodau *gw*. **traethawd**
drafnidiaeth *gw*. **trafnidiaeth**
drafod *gw*. **trafod**
drafferth *gw*. **trafferth**
drafferthu *gw*. **trafferthu**
draffordd *gw*. **traffordd**
draffyrdd *gw*. **traffordd**
dragwyddol *gw*. **tragwyddol**
drai *gw*. **trai**
draig *e.b.* *ll*. **dreigiau** dragon.
  Y Ddraig Goch the Red
  Dragon.
drain *e.* *ll*. thorns; *gw*. **draen:**
  draenen
drais *gw*. **trais**
drallod *gw*. **trallod**
drallwysiad *gw*. **trallwysiad**
drama *e.b.* *ll*. **dramâu** drama.
  drama radio radio play;
  drama deledu television
  play; **drama gyfres** serial;
  drama un act one-act play
dramodwr: dramodydd *e.g.* *ll*.
  dramodwyr dramatist
dramor *gw*. **tramor**
drannoeth *gw*. **trannoeth**
drap *gw*. **trap**
draul *gw*. **traul**
draw *ad*. yonder, there,
  beyond. **Mae'r tŷ draw fanna**
  The house is over there
drawsblannu *gw*. **trawsblannu**
drawst *gw*. **trawst**
drechu *gw*. **trechu**
dref: dre *gw*. **tref**
drefi *gw*. **tref**
drefn *gw*. **trefn**

drefnu *gw*. **trefnu**
drefnus *gw*. **trefnus**
dreigiau *gw*. **draig**
dreiglad *gw*. **treiglad**
dreiglo *gw*. **treiglo**
dreisio *gw*. **treisio**
dreisgar *gw*. **treisgar**
drem *gw*. **trem**
drên *gw*. **trên**
drenau *gw*. **trên**
drennydd *gw*. **trennydd**
dreser: dresel *e.g.* *ll*. **-i, -ydd**
  dresser
dreth *gw*. **treth**
drethdalwr *gw*. **trethdalwr**
drethu *gw*. **trethu**
dreuliau *gw*. **traul**
dreulio *gw*. **treulio**
drewdod *e.g.* stink, stench
drewi (o) 1 *be*. **(drewaf)** to
  stink. 2 *e.g.* stench
dri *gw*. **tri**
driawd *gw*. **triawd**
dric *gw*. **tric**
dridiau *gw*. **tridiau**
drigain *gw*. **trigain**
drigfan *w*. **trigfan**
drigo *gw*. **trigo**
drigolion *gw*. **trigolion**
dringo *be*. **(dringaf)** to climb
dringwr *e.g.* *ll*. **dringwyr**
  climber
drin *gw*. **trin**
drindod *gw*. **trindod**
drioedd *gw*. **trioedd**
driongl *gw*. **triongl**
drist *gw*. **trist**
dristwch *gw*. **tristwch**
dro *gw*. **tro**
drochi *gw*. **trochi**

droeau

droeau *gw*. tro
droed *gw*. troed
droedfedd *gw*. troedfedd
droedffordd *gw*. troedffordd
dröedig *gw*. tröedig
dröedigaeth *gw*. tröedigaeth
droedio *gw*. troedio
droednoeth *gw*. troednoeth
droeon *gw*. tro
drogylch *gw*. trogylch
droi *gw*. troi
drom *gw*. trom
dros: tros *ardd. (followed by soft mutation)* **(drosto/droso drostot/drosot, drosto/drosti, droston, drostoch, drostyn).** over, for, instead of, on behalf of. **dros Gymru** for/over Wales. **drosodd** finished; **drosodd a throsodd** over and over again; **dros ben** exceedingly; **mynd dros ben llestri** to go over the top; **dros dro** temporary; **dros nos** overnight; **dros y Sul** over the weekend. *gw. At. Arddodiaid*
drosedd *gw*. trosedd
droseddu *gw*. troseddu
droseddwr *gw*. troseddwr
drosgais *gw*. trosgais
drosglwyddo *gw*. trosglwyddo
drosi *gw*. trosi
drosiad *gw*. trosiad
droswr *gw*. troswr
drothwy *gw*. trothwy
drowsus *gw*. trowsus
druan *gw*. truan
drud *a*. expensive, dear, precious, valuable

drudwy *e.g. ll*. -od starling
drueni *gw*. trueni
druenus *gw*. truenus
drugaredd *gw*. trugaredd
drugarhau *gw*. trugarhau
drwbl *gw*. trwbl
drwchus *gw*. trwchus
drwg 1 *e.g.* evil, iniquity, wickedness. **o ddrwg i waeth** from bad to worse; **y drwg yn y caws** the source of the evil. 2 *a*. evil; bad; wicked; rotten. **afal drwg** rotten apple; **wy drwg** rotten egg; **dyn drwg** evil man. *gw. At. Ansoddeiriau*
drwm *e.g. ll*. **drymiau** drum. *gw*. **trwm**
drws *e.g. ll*. **drysau** door, entrance, gap. **drws cefn** a back door; **drws nesaf** next door; **wrth y drws** at hand, close, near; **carreg y drws** doorstep
drwser *gw*. trwser
drwsio *gw*. trwsio
drwsiwr *gw*. trwsiwr
drwy: trwy *ardd. (followed by soft mutation)* **(drwyddoi, drwyddot, drwyddo/drwyddi, drwyddon, drwyddoch, drwyddyn)** through, by, by means of. *gw. At. Arddodiaid*
drwydded *gw*. trwydded
drwyn *gw*. trwyn
drwynol *gw*. trwynol
drych *e.g. ll*. -au mirror; image, form; spectacle; vision

dwrw

drychineb *gw*. **trychineb**
drychiolaeth *e.b.* *ll.* **-au**
  apparition, illusion
drydan *gw*. **trydan**
drydanol *gw*. **trydanol**
drydanwr *gw*. **trydanwr**
drydedd *gw*. **trydedd**
drydydd *gw*. **trydydd**
drydyddol *gw*. **trydyddol**
drygioni *e.g.* evil, wickedness.
  gw. **drwg**
drygionus *a*. bad, wicked.
  gw. **drwg**
dryloyw *gw*. **tryloyw**
dryll *e.g.b.* *ll.* **-iau** gun
  (*S.W.*), rifle (*S.W.*), cannon
drysau *gw*. **drws**
drysor *gw*. **trysor**
drysorfa *gw*. **trysorfa**
drysori *gw*. **trysori**
drysorydd *gw*. **trysorydd**
drysu *be.* **(drysaf)** to confuse,
  to entangle, to disarrange
dryw *e.g.b.* *ll.* **-od** wren
drywydd *gw*. **trywydd**
du *a*. *ll* **-on** black; dark
dudalen *gw*. **tudalen**
dueddiad *gw*. **tueddiad**
dull *e.g.* *ll* **-iau** form, mode,
  manner
dun *gw*. **tun**
dunnell *gw*. **tunnell**
duo *be.* **(duaf)** to blacken, to
  darken
duon *a.ll.* black. *gw*. **du**
dur 1 *e.g.* *ll.* **-oedd** steel. **2** *a*.
  steel
duw *e.g.* *ll.* **-iau** god. **Duw
  Dad** God the Father; **Duw
  Hollalluog** Almighty God;

Duw Tragwyddol Eternal
  God; **bendith Duw** the
  blessing of God; **Duw Duw!**
  Good God!
duwies *e.b.* *ll.* **-au** goddess
duwiol *a*. devout, godly
dwbl *a*. double, twice
dweud (am, wrth) *be.* **(dwedaf,
  dywedaf)** to say, to speak; to
  mention. **dweud a dweud** to
  keep on saying; **dweud
  anwiredd** to tell a lie; **dweud
  ei feddwl** to say what one
  thinks; **dweud yn dda (am)**
  to speak well (of); **dweud yn
  ddrwg (am)** to speak ill (of);
  **dywedais wrtho am gau ei
  geg** I told him to shut up
dwfn *a*. deep; profound
dwfr *gw*. **dŵr**
dwl *a*. dull, foolish
dwlc *gw*. **twlc**
dwll *gw*. **twll**
dwmpath *gw*. **twmpath**
dwndis *gw*. **twndis**
dwnel *gw*. **twnel**
dwp *gw*. **twp**
dwpsyn *gw*. **twpsyn**
dŵr: dwfr *e.g.* *ll.* **dyfroedd**
  water. **dŵr berw(edig)**
  boiling water, **dŵr glaw**
  rainwater; **dŵr golchi llestri**
  dishwater; **dŵr (y) môr** sea
  water; **gwneud dŵr** to
  urinate. *gw*. **tŵr**
dwr *gw*. **twr**
dwrci *gw*. **twrci**
dwristiaeth *gw*. **twristiaeth**
dwrn *e.g.* *ll.* **dyrnau** fist
dwrw *gw*. **twrw**

dwsin

dwsin *e.g. ll.* **-au** dozen
dwt *gw.* **twt**
dwy *a.b.* two. **y ddwy** the
two, both (feminine). *gw.*
dau
dwyieithog *a.* bilingual
dwyieithrwydd *e.g.*
bilingualism
dwylo *e.ll.* hands. *gw.* **llaw**
dwyll *gw.* **twyll**
dwyllo *gw.* **twyllo**
dwym *gw.* **twym**
dwymo *gw.* **twymo**
dwymyn *gw.* **twymyn**
dwyn *be.* **(dygaf)** to take
away, to bear, to convey; to
bring; to steal. **dwyn ar gof**
to bring to mind; **dwyn i ben**
to accomplish, to complete;
dwyn ffrwyth to bear fruit;
dwgyd to steal (*S.W.*)
dwyrain *e.g.* east. **y Dwyrain**
Canol the Middle East; **y**
Dwyrain Pell the Far East
dwys *a.* grave; intense;
profound; thick, dense,
concentrated. **cwrs dwys**
crash course
dwywaith *ad.* twice
dy *rhag.* (*followed by soft*
mutation) your (*singular*). **dy**
chwaer your sister; **dy lyfr**
your book; **dy hunan**
yourself
dŷ *gw.* **tŷ**
dybied: dybio *gw.* **tybied**
dychmygion *gw.* **dychymyg**
dychmygu *be.* **(dychmygaf)** to
imagine, to think, to contrive
dychrynllyd *a.* frightful,
dreadful, horrendous

dychwelyd (at, i) *be.*
(dychwelaf) to return
dychymyg *e.g. ll.*
dychmygion imagination,
fancy; idea; riddle
dydy e/hi ddim *bf.* he/she/it
does not. *gw.* **bod**
dydd *e.g. ll.* **-iau** day. **Dydd**
da! Good day; **o ddydd i**
ddydd from day to day;
dyddiau'r wythnos days of
the week; **ers dyddiau** many
days ago; **Dydd Nadolig**
Christmas Day; **Dydd Gŵyl**
Dewi St David's Day; **Dydd**
Gwener y Groglith Good
Friday; **Dydd Llun (y) Pasg**
Easter Monday
dyddiad *e.g. ll.* **-au** date,
dating
dyddiau *gw.* **dydd**
dyddio *be.* **(dyddiaf)** to date
(*something*); to become
day
dyddyn *gw.* **tyddyn**
dyddynnwr *gw.* **tyddynnwr**
dyfalu *be.* **(dyfalaf)** to
conjecture, to guess; to
devise
dyfarniad *e.g. ll.* **-au** verdict,
decision
dyfarnu *be.* **(dyfarnaf)** to
adjudicate; to decide
dyfarnwr *e.g. ll.* **dyfarnwyr**
judge, umpire
dyfiant *gw.* **tyfiant**
dyfnder *e.g. ll.* **-au, -oedd**
deep, depth
dyfod *gw.* **dod**
dyfodol 1 *a.* future, coming.
2 *e.g.* future. **amser dyfodol**

future tense; **yn y dyfodol** in
the future; **dyfodol disglair** a
brilliant future

dyfroedd *gw*. **dŵr**

dyfu *gw*. **tyfu**

dyfyniad *e.g. ll.* **-au**
quotation

dyffryn *e.g. ll.* **-noedd** valley

dynged *gw*. **tynged**

dyngedfennol *gw*.
tyngedfennol

dyngu *gw*. **tyngu**

dylanwad *e.g. ll.* **-au**
influence

dyle *gw*. **tyle**

dyled *e.b. ll.* **-ion** debt, due,
claim, obligation

dyledus *a*. due, indebted,
obligatory

dyletswydd *e.b. ll.* **-au** duty,
obligation

dylino *gw*. **tylino**

dylwyth *gw*. **tylwyth**

dyllau *gw*. **twll**

dyllu *gw*. **tyllu**

dylluan *gw*. **tylluan**

dyma *ad*. here is/are; this is;
these are (*followed by soft
mutation*)

dymer *gw*. **tymer**

dymestl *gw*. **tymestl**

dymherau *gw*. **tymheredd**

dymheredd *gw*. **tymheredd**

dymhestlog *gw*. **tymhestlog**

dymhorau *gw*. **tymor**

dymor *gw*. **tymor**

dymuniad *e.g. ll.* **-au** wish,
desire; request. **gyda phob
dymuniad da** with all best
wishes; **dymuniadau gorau**
best wishes

dymuno *be*. **(dymunaf)** to
wish, to desire

dymunol *a*. desirable,
pleasant; desired

dyn *e.g. ll.* **-ion** man, person.
dyn cyffredin common man;
dyn dieithr stranger; **dyn eira**
snowman. *gw*. **tyn(n)**

dyna *ad*. there is/are
(*followed by soft mutation*).
dyna chi there you are; **dyna
dro** what bad luck! **dyna
drueni** what a pity! **dyna fe**
there it is

dyner *gw*. **tyner**

dynerwch *gw*. **tynerwch**

dynes *e.b. ll.* **-au** woman
(*N.W.*)

dynion *gw*. **dyn**

dyn(n) *gw*. **tyn(n)**

dynnu *gw*. **tynnu**

dyrau *gw*. **tŵr**

dyrfa *gw*. **tyrfa**

dyrfau *gw*. **twrw**

dyrnaid *e.g. ll.* **dyrneidiau**
handful, little, few

dyrnau *gw*. **dwrn**

dyrneidiau *gw*. **dyrnaid**

dyrrau *gw*. **twr**

dysgedig *a*. learned

dysgl *e.b. ll.* **-au** dish, plate;
cup; disk. **dysgl de** tea cup;
dysgl gawl soup-plate, soup-
bowl

dysgu (i) *be*. **(dysgaf)** to
learn, to teach, to educate;
dysgu ar gof to learn by
heart; **dysgu rhywbeth i
rywun** to teach someone
something

dysgwr

dysgwr *e.g. ll.* dysgwyr
 learner
dysgwyr *gw.* dysgwr
dyst *gw.* tyst
dystio *gw.* tystio
dystiolaeth *gw.* tystiolaeth
dystion *gw.* tyst
dystysgrif *gw.* tystysgrif
dywediad *e.g. ll.* -au saying
dyweddïad *e.g. ll.* -au
 engagement, betrothal
dyweddïo *be.* (dyweddïaf) to
 get engaged
dywel *gw.* tywel
dywod *gw.* tywod
dywydd *gw.* tywydd
dywyll *gw.* tywyll
dywyllu *gw.* tywyllu
dywyllwch *gw.* tywyllwch
dywys *gw.* tywys
dywysog *gw.* tywysog
dywysoges *gw.* tywysoges

DD

dda *gw.* da
ddadansoddi *gw.* dadansoddi
ddadl *gw.* dadl
ddadlau *gw.* dadlau
ddadrewi *gw.* dadrewi
ddaear *gw.* daear
ddaeareg *gw.* daeareg
ddaeargryn *gw.* daeargryn
ddaearyddiaeth *gw.*
 daearyddiaeth
ddaeth *gw.* daeth
ddafad *gw.* dafad
ddagrau *gw.* deigryn
ddail *gw.* deilen

ddaioni *gw.* daioni
ddal: ddala *gw.* dal
ddalen *gw.* dalen
ddalgylch *gw.* dalgylch
ddall *gw.* dall
ddallu *gw.* dallu
ddameg *gw.* dameg
ddamhegion *gw.* dameg
ddamwain *gw.* damwain
ddanfon *gw.* danfon
ddangos *gw.* dangos
ddannedd *gw.* dant
ddannoedd *gw.* dannoedd
ddant *gw.* dant
ddarfod *gw.* darfod
ddarganfod *gw.* darganfod
ddarlith *gw.* darlith
ddarlithio *gw.* darlithio
ddarlithiwr: darlithydd *gw.*
 darlithiwr
ddarlun *gw.* darlun
ddarlunio *gw.* darlunio
ddarlledu *gw.* darlledu
ddarllen *gw.* darllen
ddarllenwr: ddarllenydd *gw.*
 darllenwr
ddarn *gw.* darn
ddatblygiad *gw.* datblygiad
ddatblygu *gw.* datblygu
ddatgan *gw.* datgan
ddatganiad *gw.* datganiad
ddatganoli *gw.* datganoli
ddatgelu *gw.* datgelu
ddatguddio *gw.* datguddio
ddatod *gw.* datod
ddatrys *gw.* datrys
ddathliad *gw.* dathliad
ddathlu *gw.* dathlu
ddau *gw.* dau
ddawns *gw.* dawns

ddawnsio *gw*. dawnsio

dde *gw*. de

ddeall *gw*. deall

ddeallus *gw*. deallus

ddechrau *gw*. dechrau

ddechreuad *gw*. dechreuad

ddedwydd *gw*. dedwydd

ddeddf *gw*. deddf

ddeddfu *gw*. deddfu

ddefnydd *gw*. defnydd

ddefnyddio *gw*. defnyddio

ddefnyddiol *gw*. defnyddiol

ddeffro *gw*. deffro

ddeg: ddeng *gw*. deg

ddegawd *gw*. degawd

ddeheuol *gw*. deheuol

ddeialog *gw*. deialog

ddeigryn *gw*. deigryn

ddeilen *gw*. deilen

ddeilliaid: ddeillion *gw*. dall

ddeintydd *gw*. deintydd

ddeiseb *gw*. deiseb

ddel *gw*. del

ddelw *gw*. delw

ddelwi *gw*. delwi

ddeniadol *gw*. deniadol

ddenu *gw*. denu

dderbyn *gw*. derbyn

dderbyniol *gw*. derbyniol

dderbynneb *gw*. derbynneb

dderbynnydd *gw*. derbynnydd

dderi *gw*. deri

dderw *gw*. derwen

dderwen *gw*. derwen

ddesg *gw*. desg

ddetholiad *gw*. detholiad

ddeuawd *gw*. deuawd

ddeuddeg *gw*. deuddeg

ddeuddegfed *gw*. deuddegfed

ddeugain *gw*. deugain

ddeunaw *gw*. deunaw

ddeuoedd *gw*. deuoedd

ddewin *gw*. dewin

ddewis *gw*. dewis

ddewr *gw*. dewr

ddiacon *gw*. diacon

ddiafol *gw*. diafol

ddial *gw*. dial

ddianc *gw*. dianc

ddiarfogi *gw*. diarfogi

ddiawl *gw*. diawl

ddiawledig *gw*. diawledig

ddiawliaid *gw*. diafol, diawl

ddi-baid *gw*. di-baid

ddiben *gw*. diben

ddibennu *gw*. dibennu

ddi-blwm *gw*. di-blwm

ddibynnu *gw*. dibynnu

ddiderfyn *gw*. diderfyn

ddiddordeb *gw*. diddordeb

ddiddorol *gw*. diddorol

ddieithr *gw*. dieithr

ddieithryn *gw*. dieithryn

ddiferyn *gw*. diferyn

ddifetha *gw*. difetha

ddiflannu *gw*. diflannu

ddiflas *gw*. diflas

ddifrifol *gw*. difrifol

ddifyr: ddifyrrus *gw*. difyr

ddifyrru *gw*. difyrru

ddiffiniad *gw*. diffiniad

ddiffinio *gw*. diffinio

ddiffodd *gw*. diffodd

ddiffuant *gw*. diffuant

ddiffyg *gw*. diffyg

ddigon *gw*. digon

ddigonedd *gw*. digonedd

ddigrif *gw*. digrif

ddigwydd *gw*. digwydd

ddigwyddiad *gw*. digwyddiad

ddigyfeiliant

ddigyfeiliant *gw.* digyfeiliant
ddihareb *gw.* dihareb
ddiheintydd *gw.* diheintydd
ddihuno *gw.* dihuno
ddileu *gw.* dileu
ddilyn *gw.* dilyn
ddillad *gw.* dilledyn
ddilledyn *gw.* dilledyn
ddim *gw.* dim
ddinas *gw.* dinas
ddinasyddion *gw.* dinesydd
ddinesig *gw.* dinesig
ddinesydd *gw.* dinesydd
ddinistrio *gw.* dinistrio
ddiniwed *gw.* diniwed
ddiod *gw.* diod
ddioddef *gw.* dioddef
ddiofal *gw.* diofal
ddiog: ddioglyd *gw.* diog
ddiogel *gw.* diogel
ddiogi *gw.* diogi
ddioglyd *gw.* diog
ddiogyn *gw.* diogyn
ddiolch *gw.* diolch
ddiolchgar *gw.* diolchgar
ddiolchgarwch *gw.*
  diolchgarwch
ddiota *gw.* diota
ddirgelwch *gw.* dirgelwch
ddirprwy *gw.* dirprwy
ddirprwyaeth *gw.* dirprwyaeth
ddirwasgiad *gw.* dirwasgiad
ddirwy *gw.* dirwy
ddisg *gw.* disg
ddisglair *gw.* disglair
ddisgleirio *gw.* disgleirio
ddisgrifiad *gw.*disgrifiad
ddisgrifio *gw.* disgrifio
ddisgwyl *gw.* disgwyl
ddisgybl *gw.* disgybl

ddisgyblaeth *gw.* disgyblaeth
ddisgyn *gw.* disgyn
ddistaw *gw.* distaw
ddistawrwydd *gw.*
  distawrwydd
ddistewi *gw.* distewi
ddiswyddo *gw.* diswyddo
ddi-waith *gw.* di-waith
ddiwallu *gw.* diwallu
ddiwedd *gw.* diwedd
ddiweddar *gw.* diweddar
ddiweddarach *gw.* diweddar
ddiweddglo *gw.* diweddglo
ddiwerth *gw.* diwerth
ddiwethaf *gw.* diwethaf
ddiwrnod *gw.* diwrnod
ddiwydiant *gw.* diwydiant
ddiwygiad *gw.* diwygiad
ddiwygio *gw.* diwygio
ddiwylliant *gw.* diwylliant
ddoc *gw.* doc
ddoctor *gw.* doctor
ddod: ddyfod *gw.* dod
ddodi *gw.* dodi
ddodrefnyn *gw.* dodrefnyn
ddodwy *gw.* dodwy
ddoe *gw.* doe
ddoeth *gw.* doeth
ddoethineb *gw.* doethineb
ddof *gw.* dof
ddogfen *gw.* dogfen
ddol *gw.* dol
ddôl *gw.* dôl
ddolen *gw.* dolen
ddolur *gw.* dolur
ddoniol *gw.* doniol
ddosbarth *gw.* dosbarth
ddraen: ddraenen *gw.* draen
ddraenog *gw.* draenog
ddraig *gw.* draig

ddrain *gw*. draen
ddrama *gw*. drama
ddramodwr *gw*. dramodwr
ddramodydd *gw*. dramodwr
ddreser: ddresel *gw*. dreser
ddrewdod *gw*. drewdod
ddrewi *gw*. drewi
ddringo *gw*. dringo
ddringwr *gw*. dringwr
ddrud *gw*. drud
ddrudwy *gw*. drudwy
ddrwg *gw*. drwg
ddrwm *gw*. drwm
ddrws *gw*. drws
ddrych *gw*. drych
ddrychiolaeth *gw*.
  drychiolaeth
ddrygioni *gw*. drygioni
ddrygionus *gw*. drygionus
ddryll *gw*. dryll
ddrylliau *gw*. dryll
ddrysau *gw*. drws
ddrysu *gw*. drysu
ddryw *gw*. dryw
ddu *gw*. du
ddull *gw*. dull
dduo *gw*. duo
ddur *gw*. dur
dduw *gw*. duw
dduwies *gw*. duwies
ddwbl *gw*. dwbl
ddweud *gw*. dweud
ddwfn *gw*. dwfn
ddwfr *gw*. dŵr
ddwl *gw*. dwl
ddŵr *gw*. dŵr
ddwrn *gw*. dwrn
ddwsin *gw*. dwsin
ddwy *gw*. dwy
ddwyieithog *gw*. dwyieithog

ddwyieithrwydd *gw*.
  dwyieithrwydd
ddwylo *gw*. dwylo
ddwyn *gw*. dwyn
ddwyrain *gw*. dwyrain
ddwys *gw*. dwys
ddwywaith *gw*. dwywaith
ddychmygion *gw*. dychymyg
ddychmygu *gw*. dychmygu
ddychrynllyd *gw*. dychrynllyd
ddychwelyd *gw*. dychwelyd
ddychymyg *gw*. dychymyg
ddydd *gw*. dydd
ddyddiad *gw*. dyddiad
ddyddiau *gw*. dydd
ddyfalu *gw*. dyfalu
ddyfarniad *gw*. dyfarniad
ddyfarnu *gw*. dyfarnu
ddyfarnwr *gw*. dyfarnwr
ddyfnder *gw*. dyfnder
ddyfod *gw*. dod
ddyfodol *gw*. dyfodol
ddyfroedd *gw*. dŵr
ddyfyniad *gw*. dyfyniad
ddyffryn *gw*. dyffryn
ddylanwad *gw*. dylanwad
ddyled *gw*. dyled
ddyledus *gw*. dyledus
ddyletswydd *gw*. dyletswydd
ddymuniad *gw*. dymuniad
ddymuno *gw*. dymuno
ddymunol *gw*. dymunol
ddyn *gw*. dyn
ddynes *gw*. dynes
ddyrnaid *gw*. dyrnaid
ddyrnau *gw*. dwrn
ddyrneidiau *gw*. dyrnaid
ddysgedig *gw*. dysgedig
ddysgl *gw*. dysgl
ddysgu *gw*. dysgu

ddysgwr

ddysgwr *gw.* **dysgwr**
ddysgwyr *gw.* **dysgwyr**
ddywediad *gw.* **dywediad**
ddyweddïad *gw.* **dyweddïad**
ddyweddïo *gw.* **dyweddïo**

E

e: **o** *gw.* **ef**
eang *a.* broad, wide,
extensive
eb: **ebe**: **ebr** *bf.* says, said (I,
he/she, they, etc.)
ebol *e.g. ll.* **-ion** colt; buck
e-bost *e.g.ll.* **e-bostiau** e-mail
Ebrill *e.g.* April
economeg *e.b.* economics.
echdoe *e.g. & ad.* the day
before yesterday
echnos *e.b. & ad.* the night
before last
edau *e.b. ll.* **edafedd** thread
edifar: **edifeiriol** *a.* sorry,
penitent, contrite. **Mae'n
edifar gen i** I regret
edmygu *be.* **(edmygaf)** to
admire
edrych *be.* **(edrychaf)** to look,
to observe, to search, to
examine; to expect. **edrych
am** to look for, to expect;
edrych ar to look on, to
look upon; **edrych ar ôl** to
look after, to mind; **edrych
at** to look towards; **edrych
dros** to overlook, to survey;
edrych allan to look out, to
seek; **edrych ymlaen** to look
forward
ef: **efe**: **efo** *rhag.* he, him, it, **y
fo** (*N.W.*), **y fe** (*S.W.*)

efallai *ad.* perhaps
efengyl *e.b. ll.* **-au** gospel.
Efengyl Iesu Grist the
Gospel of Jesus Christ
efeilliad *gw.* **gefell**
efo *ardd.* with, by means of
(*N.W.*)
efo *gw.* **ef**
Efrog *e.b.* York
Efrog Newydd *e.b.* New York
effaith *e.b. ll.* **effeithiau** effect
effeithiau *gw.* **effaith**
effeithiol *a.* effective
effro *a.* awake (*N.W.*)
egin *gw.* **eginyn**
eginyn *e.g. ll.* **egin** shoot,
sprout, (young) blade
eglur *a.* clear, evident, plain
egluro *be.* **(egluraf)** to reveal;
to explain; to manifest
eglwys *e.b. ll.* **-i** church, the
church
egni *e.g. ll.* **egnïon, egnïoedd**
energy, might; effort,
endeavour
egnïoedd *gw.* **egni**
egnïol *a.* vigorous, energetic
egnïon *gw.* **egni**
egwyddor *e.b. ll.* **-ion**
principle; rudiment; alphabet
egwyddorol *a.* having
principles. *gw.* **gwyddor**
egwyl *e.b. ll.* **-iau, -ion** break,
interval; spell
enghraifft *e.b. ll.* **enghreifftiau**
example, instance. **er
enghraifft** for example
enghreifftiau *gw.* **enghraifft**
englyn *e.g. ll.* **-ion** an
epigrammatic four-line
stanza in Welsh poetry

engyl *gw.* angel
ehedydd *e.g. ll.* **-ion** lark
ei *rhag.* his, her, its. **ei hunan**
himself/herself. *gw. At.*
Treigladau
eich *rhag.* your. **eich hunan**
yourself; **eich hunain**
yourselves
Eidal, Yr *e.b.* Italy
Eidaleg *e.b.* Italian language
Eidales *e.b. ll.* **-au** Italian
woman
Eidalwr *e.g. ll.* **Eidalwyr**
Italian man
eiddo 1 *e.g.* possession(s),
property, estate. **ei eiddo** his
possession. 2 *ad.* his, hers, etc
eifr *gw.* gafr
Eingl-Gymro *e.g. ll.* **Eingl-**
Gymry Anglo-Welshman
eiliad *e.g.b. ll.* **-au** second,
moment. **dwy eiliad** two
seconds
eilwaith *ad.* again, a second
time
ein *rhag.* our. **ein hunain**
ourselves

eirin *gw.* eirinen
eirinen *e.b. ll.* **eirin** plum,
damson; berry. **eirin gwlanog**
peaches
eirio *gw.* geirio
eirlys *e.g. ll.* **-iau** snowdrop.
gw. **tlws yr eira**
eirth *gw.* arth
eisiau *e.g.* need, want, lack,
poverty. **Rydw i eisiau –** I
need –, I want –. **Mae eisiau**
– arnaf i I need –, I want –
eisoes *ad.* already
eistedd (wrth) *be.* (eisteddaf)
to sit, to seat
eisteddfod *e.b. ll.* **-au**
eisteddfod
eisteddfodwr *e.g. ll.*
eisteddfodwyr a frequenter
of *eisteddfodau*
eitem *e.b. ll.* **-au** item
eithaf 1 *e.g. ll.* **-ion, -oedd,**
-edd end, extremity,
uttermost part. 2 *a.* farthest,
superlative. **y gosb eithaf**
capital punishment. 3 *ad.*
very, quite

Insight

eira *e.g.* snow and a girl's name
eirlys *e.g.* snowdrop, and a pretty name for a girl
enw *e.g.* name (an essential possession).

---

eira *e.g. ll.* **-oedd** snow
eirch *gw.* arch
eirchion *gw.* arch
eirfa *gw.* geirfa
eiriadur *gw.* geiriadur
eiriau *gw.* gair

eithafol *a.* extreme
eithr 1 *rhag.* except, besides.
2 *c.* but
eithrio *be.* (eithriaf) to except,
to exclude. **ac eithrio** except,
excepting

eleni

eleni *ad.* this year

elfen *e.b. ll.* **-nau** element, particle, factor, tendency. **yn fy elfen** in my element

elfennau *gw.* **elfen**

elfennol *a.* elementary, constituent, simple

eliffant *e.g. ll.* **-od** elephant

elw *e.g. ll.* **-on** profit, gain

elwa *be.* **(elwaf)** to profit, to gain

elyn *gw.* **gelyn**

elltydd *gw.* **allt**

em *gw.* **gem**

emyn *e.g. ll.* **-au** hymn. **emyn-dôn** hymn-tune

emynydd *e.g. ll.* **emynwyr** hymn-writer

ên *gw.* **gên**

enaid *e.g. ll.* **eneidiau** soul, spirit; life

enau *gw.* **genau**

enedigaeth *gw.* **genedigaeth**

eneidiau *gw.* **enaid**

eneth *gw.* **geneth**

eneuau *gw.* **genau**

enfawr *a.* enormous, vast, immense, huge

enfys *e.b. ll.* **-au** rainbow

eni *gw.* **geni**

enillwr: enillydd *e.g. ll.* **enillwyr** earner; victor, winner

ennill 1 *be.* **(enillaf)** to gain, to profit, to get; to win. 2 *e.g. ll.* **enillion** winnings; salary; profit

ennyd *e.g.b.* a while, moment

enw *e.g. ll.* **-au** name; noun. **enw anwes** pet name; **enw benywaidd** feminine noun;

enw gwrywaidd masculine noun; **enw torfol** collective noun; **ffugenw** *nom de plume*, pseudonym

enwad *e.g. ll.* **-au** religious denomination

enwedig *a.* especial

enwi *be.* **(enwaf)** to name

enwog 1 *a.* famous renowned, eminent. 2 *e.ll.* **-ion** persons of renown or fame; celebrities

enwogrwydd *e.g.* fame

enyn *gw.* **genyn**

eos *e.b. ll.* **-iaid** nightingale

epa *e.g. ll.* **-od** ape

er *ardd.* because of, for, in order to; since (*a fixed point in time*); despite. **er anrhydedd** in honour; **er bod** although; **er cof** in memory, *in memoriam*; **er gwaethaf** in spite of, despite; **er hynny** yet, since then; **er lles/budd** for the benefit of; **er mwyn** for the sake of, in order to; **er dydd Llun** since Monday

eraill *gw.* **arall**

erbyn *ardd.* against, facing, opposite; by, for, in preparation for. **erbyn hyn** by this time, by now; **mynd yn erbyn** to oppose, to go against; **erbyn meddwl** coming to think of it

erchyll *a.* atrocious, terrible

erddi *gw.* **gardd**

erfin *gw.* **erfinen**

erfinen *e.b. ll.* **erfin** turnip, swede

erfyn 1 *be.* **(erfyniaf)** to beg, to entreat, to expect, to implore. 2 *e.g. ll.* **arfau** weapon, tool. *gw.* **arf**

ergyd *e.g.b. ll.* **-ion** blow, knock, shot, hit, bang, detonation

erioed *ad.* ever

erlid *be.* **(erlidiaf)** to pursue, to persecute

erlyn *be.* **(erlynaf)** to prosecute

erlyniad *e.g. ll.* **-au** prosecution

erlynydd *e.g. ll.* **-ion** prosecutor

ernes *e.b. ll.* **-au** security, pledge; deposit

ers *ardd.* for, since (*a continuing period*). **ers pythefnos** for the last fortnight. **ers tro** for some time

erthygl *e.b. ll.* **-au** article, literary composition; clause

erthyliad *e.g. ll.* **-au** abortion, miscarriage

erthylu *be.* **(erthylaf)** to abort, to miscarry

erw *e.b. ll.* **-au** acre

eryr *e.g. ll.* **-od** eagle

Eryri *e.b.* Snowdonia.

es i *bf.* I went. *gw.* **mynd**

esboniad *e.g. ll.* **-au** commentary; explanation, exposition

esbonio (i) *be.* **(esboniaf)** to explain (to)

esgeulus *a.* negligent

esgeuluso *be.* **(esgeulusaf)** to neglect

esgeulustod: esgeulustra *e.g.* negligence

esgid *e.b. ll.* **-iau** boot; shoe: **esgidiau mawr/uchel** high boots; **esgidiau ysgafn** light boots or shoes; **yr esgid yn gwasgu** a difficult financial situation

esgob *e.g. ll.* **-ion** bishop. **Esgob Tyddewi** Bishop of St David's; **esgobaeth** diocese; **Esgob!** Oh Lord!

esgus *e.g. ll.* **-ion, -odion** excuse; pretence (*S.W.*). **mae e'n esgus cysgu** he's pretending to sleep

esgusion *gw.* **esgus**

esgusodi *be.* **(esgusodaf)** to make an excuse, to excuse; **Esgusodwch fi** Excuse me

esgusodion *gw.* **esgus**

esgyrn *gw.* **asgwrn. Esgyrn Dafydd!** Good heavens!

esiampl *e.b. ll.* **-au** example

esmwyth *a.* soft, easy, comfortable

estron *e.g. ll.* **-iaid** foreigner, alien, stranger

estyn *be.* **(estynnaf)** to extend, to reach; to stretch, to lengthen; to give

estyniad *e.g. ll.* **-au** extension

etifeddu *be.* **(etifeddaf)** to inherit

eto *c. & ad.* again a second time, yet, still, nevertheless

ethol *be.* **(etholaf)** to elect, to choose, to select

etholaeth *e.b. ll.* **-au** constituency; electorate

etholiad

etholiad *e.g. ll.* **-au** election;
etholiad cyffredinol general
election; **is-etholiad** by-
election

eu *rhag.* (*words beginning
with a vowel are aspirated
when preceded by* **eu**) their.
eu hafalau their apples; **eu
hemynau** their hymns; **eu
hysgolion** their schools. **eu
hunain** themselves. *gw. At.
Rhagenwau*

euog *a.* guilty; **euog neu
ddieuog** guilty or not guilty

euogrwydd *e.g.* guilt

euraid: euraidd *a.* gold,
golden

ewch *bf.* go! (*plural*). *gw.
mynd*

ewin *e.g.b. ll.* **-edd** nail, claw,
talon; hoof. **â'i ddeg ewin**
with all his might

Ewrop *e.b.* Europe

ewyllys *e.b. ll.* **-iau, -ion** will;
desire; testament. **yn erbyn ei
ewyllys** against his will

ewyn *e.g.* foam, froth. *gw.
gewyn*

ewythr *e.g. ll.* **-edd, -od** uncle

F

fab *gw.* **mab**
faban *gw.* **baban**
fabanaidd *gw.* **babanaidd**
fabi *gw.* **babi**
fabolgamp *gw.* **mabolgamp**
facio *gw.* **bacio**
fach *gw.* **bach**
fachau *gw.* **bach, bachyn**

fachgen *gw.* **bachgen**
fachgennaidd *gw.*
bachgennaidd
fachlud *gw.* **machlud**
fachu *gw.* **bachu**
fachyn *gw.* **bach**
fad *gw.* **bad**
fadarch *gw.* **madarch**
fae *gw.* **bae**
faer *gw.* **maer**
faeres *gw.* **maeres**
faes *gw.* **maes**
faestref *gw.* **maestref**
fafon *gw.* **mafonen**
fag *gw.* **bag**
fagddu, y *e.b.* utter darkness
fagiau *gw.* **bag**
fagu *gw.* **magu**
Fai *gw.* **Mai**
fai *gw.* **bai**
faich *gw.* **baich**
fain *gw.* **main**
faint *rhag. gof.* how much?
how many? *gw.* **maint**
falch *gw.* **balch**
falchder *gw.* **balchder**
faldod *gw.* **maldod**
faldodi *gw.* **maldodi**
faled *gw.* **baled**
faledwr *gw.* **baledwr**
falot *gw.* **balot**
falu *gw.* **malu**
falŵn *gw.* **balŵn**
falwoden *gw.* **malwoden**
fam *gw.* **mam**
fam-gu *gw.* **mam-gu**
famiaith *gw.* **mamiaith**
fân *gw.* **mân**
fan *e.b. ll.* **-iau** van. *gw.* **ban,
man**

fedrus

fanana *gw.* banana
fanc *gw.* banc
fancio *gw.* bancio
fand *gw.* band
fandal *e.g. ll.* -iaid vandal
fandaleiddio *be.* (fandaleiddiaf)
  to vandalize
fandaliaeth *e.b.* vandalism
faneg *gw.* maneg
faner *gw.* baner
fannau *gw.* ban, man
fannod *gw.* bannod
fans *gw.* mans
fantais *gw.* mantais
fanteisio *gw.* manteisio
fanteision *gw.* mantais
fantell *gw.* mantell
fanwl *gw.* manwl
fanylion *gw.* manylyn
fanylu *gw.* manylu
fanylyn *gw.* manylyn
fap *gw.* map
far *gw.* bar
fara *gw.* bara
farbeciw *gw.* barbeciw
farc *gw.* marc
farcio *gw.* marcio
farchnad *gw.* marchnad
farchog *gw.* marchog
fardd *gw.* bardd
farddoniaeth *gw.* barddoniaeth
farf *gw.* barf
farn *gw.* barn
farnwr *gw.* barnwr
farrau *gw.* bar
fart *gw.* mart
farw *gw.* marw
farwaidd *gw.* marwaidd
farwol *gw.* marwol
farwolaeth *gw.* marwolaeth

fas *gw.* bas
fasged *gw.* basged
fasn *gw.* basn
fasnach *gw.* masnach
fasnachwr *gw.* masnachwr
fasnau: fasnys *gw.* basn
faswr *gw.* baswr, maswr
fat *gw.* bat, mat
fater *gw.* mater
fatsen: fatsien *gw.* matsen
fath *gw.* bath, math
fathdy *gw.* bathdy
fathemateg *gw.* mathemateg
fathemategol *gw.*
  mathemategol
fathemategwr *gw.*
  mathemategwr
fathodyn *gw.* bathodyn
fathu *gw.* bathu
faw *gw.* baw
fawd *gw.* bawd
fawl *gw.* mawl
fawn *gw.* mawn
fawr *gw.* mawr
fawredd *gw.* mawredd
Fawrth *be.* Mawrth
fe 1 *rhag.* he, him, it. 2 *geir.*
  particle (*may be used before
  verbs* (S.W.)). **fe welais; fe
  glywais; fe gwympodd.** *gw.
  At. Berfau* – Fe/Mi
feallai *ad.* perhaps
fecso *gw.* becso
fechan *gw.* bechan
fechgyn *gw.* bachgen
fechnïaeth *gw.* mechnïaeth
Fedi *gw.* Medi
fedi *gw.* medi
fedru *gw.* medru
fedrus *gw.* medrus

fedwen

fedwen *gw*. bedwen
fedyddio *gw*. bedyddio.
Fedyddiwr *gw*. Bedyddiwr
fedd *gw*. bedd, meddu
feddal *gw*. meddal
feddalu *gw*. meddalu
feddalwedd *gw*. meddalwedd
feddu *gw*. meddu
feddw *gw*. meddw
feddwi *gw*. meddwi
feddwl *gw*. meddwl
feddyg *gw*. meddyg
feddygfa *gw*. meddygfa
feddyginiaeth *gw*.
  meddyginiaeth
feddylgar *gw*. meddylgar
feddyliau *gw*. meddwl
fefus *gw*. mefusen
Fehefin *gw*. Mehefin
feiau *gw*. bai
feibion *gw*. mab
Feibl *gw*. Beibl
feic *gw*. beic
feicrodon *gw*. meicrodon
feichiau *gw*. baich
feichiog *gw*. beichiog
feiddio *gw*. meiddio
feim *gw*. meim
feinir *gw*. meinir
feio *gw*. beio
feirdd *gw*. bardd
feirioli *gw*. meirioli
feirniad *gw*. beirniad
feirniadu *gw*. beirniadu
feirniaid *gw*. beirniad
feistr *gw*. meistr
feistres *gw*. meistres
feistri: feistriaid *gw*. meistr
feistroli *gw*. meistroli
feithrin *gw*. meithrin

fel *c*. as, so, like. **fel arfer** as
  usual, usually; **fel pe**
  bai/petai/petasai as if
fêl *gw*. mêl
felen *gw*. melen
felin *gw*. melin
felyn *gw*. melyn
felys *gw*. melys
felysfwyd *gw*. melysfwyd
fellten *gw*. mellten
felltith *gw*. melltith
felly *ad*. so, thus
fendigedig *gw*. bendigedig
fendith *gw*. bendith
fenig *gw*. maneg
fenter *gw*. menter
fentrau *gw*. menter
fentro *gw*. mentro
fentrus *gw*. mentrus
fenthyca *gw*. benthyca
fenyn *gw*. menyn
fenyw *gw*. benyw, menyw
fenywaidd *gw*. benywaidd,
  menywaidd
fer *gw*. ber
fêr *gw*. mêr
ferch *gw*. merch
Fercher *gw*. Mercher
ferchetaidd *gw*. merchetaidd
ferf *gw*. berf
ferfa *gw*. berfa
ferfenw *gw*. berfenw
ferlod *gw*. merlyn
ferlota *gw*. merlota
ferlotwr *gw*. merlotwr
ferlyn *gw*. merlyn
fersiwn *e.g*. *ll*. fersiynau
  version
ferthyr *gw*. merthyr
ferw *gw*. berw

flinedig

ferwi *gw*. berwi

fes *gw*. mesen

fesen *gw*. mesen

festri *e.b*. *ll*. **festrïoedd** vestry

fesul *gw*. mesul

fesur *gw*. mesur

fesurydd *gw*. mesurydd

fetel *gw*. metel

fetr *gw*. metr

fetrig *gw*. metrig

fethiant *gw*. methiant

fewn *gw*. mewn

fewnwr *gw*. mewnwr

feysydd *gw*. maes

finlliw *gw*. minlliw

finnau *gw*. minnau

fiola *e.b*. *ll*. **-s** viola

fioled *e.b*. *ll*. **-au** violet

fioleg *gw*. bioleg

firi *gw*. miri

firws *e.g*. *ll*. **-au** virus

fis *gw*. mis

fisged *gw*. bisged

fisgïen *gw*. bisgïen

fisglwyf *gw*. misglwyf

fisoedd *gw*. mis

fisol *gw*. misol

fisolyn *gw*. misolyn

Insight

fi *rhag*. I, me (of utmost importance)

fy *rhag*. my, of me. *Fy Mam* My Mother.

---

fi: mi *rhag*. I, me. *gw*. mi

ficer *e.g*. *ll*. **-iaid** vicar

ficerdai *gw*. ficerdy

ficerdy *e.g*. *ll*. **ficerdai** vicarage

ficro-don *gw*. micro-don

fideo *e.g*. *ll*. **-s** video. **fideocasét** video cassette

figwrn *gw*. migwrn

fil *gw*. mil

filfeddyg *gw*. milfeddyg

filgi *gw*. milgi

filiwn *gw*. miliwn

filoedd *gw*. mil

filwr *gw*. milwr

filltir *gw*. milltir

fin *gw*. bin

fin *gw*. min

finegr *e.g*. *ll*. **-au** vinegar

finiog *gw*. miniog

fitw *gw*. bitw

fiwsig *gw*. miwsig

flaen *gw*. blaen

flaendal *gw*. blaendal

flaenor *gw*. blaenor

flaenwr *gw*. blaenwr

flaguro *gw*. blaguro

flaguryn *gw*. blaguryn

flaidd *gw*. blaidd

flanced *gw*. blanced

flas *gw*. blas

flasu *gw*. blasu

flasus *gw*. blasus

flawd *gw*. blawd

fleiddiaid *gw*. blaidd

flew *gw*. blewyn

flewyn *gw*. blewyn

flin *gw*. blin

flinder *gw*. blinder

flinedig *gw*. blinedig

flino

flino *gw.* blino
flodau *gw.* blodyn
flodeugerdd *gw.* blodeugerdd
flodfresychen *gw.* blodfresychen
flodyn *gw.* blodyn
floedd *gw.* bloedd
floeddio *gw.* bloeddio
flows *gw.* blows
flwch *gw.* blwch
flwydd *gw.* blwydd
flwyddyn *gw.* blwyddyn
flychau *gw.* blwch
flynedd *gw.* blwyddyn
flynyddoedd *gw.* blwyddyn
fo *rhag.* he, him, it (*N.W.*)
focs *gw.* bocs
foch *gw.* boch, mochyn
fochyn *gw.* mochyn
fod *gw.* bod
fodau *gw.* bod
fodfedd *gw.* modfedd
fodiau *gw.* bodiau
fodio *gw.* bodio
fodlon: foddlon *gw.* bodlon
fodloni *gw.* bodloni
fodrwy *gw.* modrwy
fodryb *gw.* modryb
fodur *gw.* modur
fodurwr *gw.* modurwr
fodd *gw.* bodd, modd
foddhad *gw.* boddhad
foddi *gw.* boddi
foddion *gw.* moddion
foel *gw.* moel
foelni *gw.* moelni
foes *gw.* moes
foesol *gw.* moesol
foethus *gw.* moethus
fogi *gw.* mogi

fol *gw.* bol
fola *gw.* bola
foli *gw.* moli
foliau *gw.* bol
follt *gw.* bollt
folltau *gw.* bollt
fom *gw.* bom
Fôn *gw.* Môn
fôn *gw.* bôn
foneddiges *gw.* boneddiges
foneddigion *gw.* bonheddwr
fonheddig *gw.* bonheddig
fonheddwr *gw.* bonheddwr
fonion *gw.* bôn
fôr *gw.* môr
ford *gw.* bord
fordaith *gw.* mordaith
fordau: fordydd *gw.* bord
forddwyd *gw.* morddwyd
fore *gw.* bore
forfa *gw.* morfa
forfil *gw.* morfil
forgais *gw.* morgais
Forgannwg *gw.* Morgannwg
forgeisiau *gw.* morgais
forgrugyn *gw.* morgrugyn
fôr-leidr *gw.* môr-leidr
fôr-ladron *gw.* môr-leidr
forio *gw.* morio
foroedd *gw.* môr
foron *gw.* moronen
foronen *gw.* moronen
forthwyl *gw.* morthwyl
forwr *gw.* morwr
forwyn *gw.* morwyn
forwyr *gw.* morwr
fory: yfory *ad. & e.g.* tomorrow
fos *gw.* bos
fotwm *gw.* botwm

fotymu *gw.* botymu
fowlen *gw.* bowlen
fragdy *gw.* bragdy
fraich *gw.* braich
fraint *gw.* braint
frân *gw.* brân
fras *gw.* bras
fraslun *gw.* braslun
fraster *gw.* braster
fraw *gw.* braw
frawd *gw.* brawd
frawddeg *gw.* brawddeg
frecwast *gw.* brecwast
frech *gw.* brech
frechdan *gw.* brechdan
frechiad *gw.* brechiad
freichiau *gw.* braich
freichled *gw.* breichled
freiniau: freintiau *gw.* braint
frenhines *gw.* brenhines
frenhinoedd *gw.* brenin
frenhinol *gw.* brenhinol
frenin *gw.* brenin
fres *gw.* bres
frest *gw.* brest
fresychen *gw.* bresychen
frethyn *gw.* brethyn
freuddwyd *gw.* breuddwyd
freuddwydio *gw.* breuddwydio
freuddwydion *gw.* breuddwyd
frifo *gw.* brifo
frig *gw.* brig
frigau *gw.* brig, brigyn
frigyn *gw.* brigyn
fritho: frithio *gw.* britho
friwsion *gw.* briwsionyn
friwsionyn *gw.* briwsionyn
fro *gw.* bro
frodor *gw.* brodor
frodyr *gw.* brawd

froga *gw.* broga
fron *gw.* bron
fronfraith *gw.* bronfraith
fronnau: fronnydd *gw.* bron
frown *gw.* brown
fröydd *gw.* bro
frwdfrydig *gw.* brwdfrydig
frwnt *gw.* brwnt
frws: frwsh *gw.* brws
frwsio: frwshio *gw.* brwsio
frwsys: frwshys *gw.* brws
frwydr *gw.* brwydr
frwydrau *gw.* brwydr
fryd *gw.* bryd
fryn *gw.* bryn
fryniau *gw.* bryn
frys *gw.* brys
frysio *gw.* brysio
fuan *gw.* buan
fuarth *gw.* buarth
fuchod *gw.* buwch
fud *gw.* mud
fudiad *gw.* mudiad
fudr *gw.* budr
fudd-dâl *gw.* budd-dâl
fuddsoddi *gw.* buddsoddi
fuddugol *gw.* buddugol
fuddugoliaeth *gw.*
  buddugoliaeth
fues i *bf.* I was, I have been.
  gw. bod
fugail *gw.* bugail
fugeiliad *gw.* bugail
fugeilio *gw.* bugeilio
ful *gw.* mul
fûm: fues *bf.* I was, I have
  been. *gw.* bod
funud *gw.* munud
fur *gw.* mur
fusnes *gw.* busnes

fuwch

fuwch *gw.* buwch

fwced *gw.* bwced

fwg *gw.* mwg

fwgwd *gw.* mwgwd

fwlch *gw.* bwlch

fwnci *gw.* mwnci

fwrdeistref *gw.* bwrdeistref

fwrdd *gw.* bwrdd

fwriad *gw.* bwriad

fwriadu *gw.* bwriadu

fwrw *gw.* bwrw

fws *gw.* bws

fwstash *gw.* mwstash

fwstwr *gw.* mwstwr

fwthyn *gw.* bwthyn

fwy *gw.* mawr

fwyaf *gw.* mawr

fwyar *gw.* mwyaren

fwyaren *gw.* mwyaren

fwyd *gw.* bwyd

fwydo: fwyda *gw.* bwydo

fwydlen *gw.* bwydlen

fwydydd *gw.* bwyd

fwydyn *gw.* mwydyn

fwyn *gw.* mwyn

fwynhad *gw.* mwynhad

fwynhau *gw.* mwynhau

fwyta: fyta *gw.* bwyta

fwyty *gw.* bwyty

fy *rhag.* (*followed by nasal mutation*) my, of me. *gw. At. Rhagenwau*

fychan *gw.* bychan

fyd *gw.* byd

fydoedd *gw.* byd

fydd e/o/hi *bf.* he/she/it will be. *gw.* bod

fyddar *gw.* byddar

fyddin *gw.* byddin

fyddinoedd *gw.* byddin

fyfyrdod *gw.* myfyrdod

fyfyrio *gw.* myfyrio

fyfyriwr *gw.* myfyriwr

fyglyd *gw.* myglyd

fygu *gw.* mygu

fygydau *gw.* mwgwd

fylchau *gw.* bwlch

fynach *gw.* mynach

fynachlog *gw.* mynachlog

fynachod *gw.* mynach

fynaich *gw.* mynach

fynd: fyned *gw.* mynd

fynedfa *gw.* mynedfa

fynedfeydd *gw.* mynedfa

fynediad *gw.* mynediad

fynegai *gw.* mynegai

fynegeion *gw.* mynegai

fynegi *gw.* mynegi

fynnu *gw.* mynnu

fynwent *gw.* mynwent

fyny, i *ad.* up, upwards. **oddi fyny** from above; **ar i fyny** upwards; in good spirits, in a cheerful mood

fynychu *gw.* mynychu

fynydd *gw.* mynydd

fynyddig: fynyddog *gw.* mynyddig

fyr *gw.* byr

fyrbryd *gw.* byrbryd

fyrddau *gw.* bwrdd

fyrfodd *gw.* byrfodd

fyrr *gw.* myrr

fys *gw.* bys

fysedd *gw.* bys

fystyrau *gw.* mwstwr

fysys *gw.* bws

fyth, *gw.* byth, *gw.* myth

fythynnod *gw.* bwthyn

fyw *gw.* byw

fywiog *gw.* bywiog
fywyd *gw.* bywyd
fywydeg *gw.* bywydeg

FF

ffa *gw.* ffäen
ffäen: ffeuen *e.b. ll.* ffa bean.
ffa pob baked beans
ffactor *e.g.b. ll.* -au factor
ffaelu (â) *be.* (ffaelaf) to fail,
to miss, to mistake (*S.W.*)
ffafr *e.b. ll.* -au favour,
respect
ffair *e.b. ll.* ffeiriau fair. ffair
haf summer fair; ffair lyfrau
book fair; ffair sborion
jumble sale; fel ffair an utter
mess, very busy
ffaith *e.b. ll.* ffeithiau fact
ffarm: fferm *e.b. ll.* ffermydd
farm. tŷ fferm farmhouse
ffarmio: ffermio *be.* (ffarmiaf:
ffermiaf) to farm
ffarmwr: ffermwr *e.g. ll.*
ffermwyr farmer,
agriculturist
ffárwel: ffarwél *e.b.* farewell.
Ffárwel haf Michaelmas
daisy
ffarwelio (â) *be.* (ffarweliaf) to
bid farewell; to say goodbye
ffatri *e.b. ll.* ffatrïoedd
factory
ffau *e.b. ll.* ffeuau den, lair,
burrow, set
ffawydden *e.b. ll.* ffawydd
beech tree
ffefryn *e.g. ll.* -nau favourite
ffeil *e.b. ll.* -iau file

ffeilio *be.* to file
ffeiriau *gw.* ffair
ffeithiau *gw.* ffaith
ffel *a.* dear; knowing –
especially of a dog
ffenestr *e.b. ll.* -i window
fferm *gw.* ffarm
ffermdai *gw.* ffermdy
ffermdy *e.g. ll.* ffermdai
farmhouse
ffermio *gw.* ffarmio
ffermwr *gw.* ffarmwr
ffermwyr *gw.* ffarmwr
fferyllydd *e.g. ll.* -ion
pharmacist, chemist
ffeuau *gw.* ffau
ffeuen *gw.* ffäen
ffiaidd *a.* foul, loathsome,
odious
ffigur *e.g. ll.* -au figure, type,
form; diagram
ffin *e.b. ll.* -iau boundary,
border, frontier, limit
ffiniau *gw.* ffin
ffiniol *a.* bordering
ffiseg *e.b.* physics
fflachio *be.* (fflachiaf) to flash
fflam *e.b. ll.* -au, -iau flame,
blaze
fflamau: fflamiau *gw.* fflam
Fflint *e.b.* Tref a Sir Flintshire
(N. Wales)
ffoadur *e.g. ll.* -iaid fugitive,
refugee; deserter
ffoaduriaid *gw.* ffoadur
ffodus *a.* fortunate, lucky,
prosperous
ffoi (rhag) *be.* (ffoaf) to flee,
to escape; to desert
ffôl *a.* foolish, unwise, silly,
foolhardy

ffolineb

ffolineb *e.g. ll.* **-au**
foolishness, folly
ffon *e.b. ll.* **ffyn** stick,
walking-stick, staff; rod; club
ffôn *e.g. ll.* **ffonau** telephone,
phone. **ffôn symudol** mobile
phone. *gw.* **teleffon**
ffonio *be.* (**ffoniaf**) to phone
fforc *e.b. ll.* **ffyrc** fork
fforchio *be.* (**fforchiaf**) to
fork; to straddle
ffordd *e.b. ll.* **ffyrdd** road,
way, street, route. **ffordd
allan** exit; **ffordd fawr**
highway; **ffordd osgoi**
bypass; **priffordd** highway;
ffordd dda good way;
traffordd motorway; **ffordd
ddeuol** dual carriageway;
pontffordd viaduct;
trosffordd fly-over

Ffrances *e.b. ll.* **-au**
Frenchwoman
Ffrancod *gw.* **Ffrancwr**
Ffrancwr *e.g. ll.* **Ffrancwyr,
Ffrancod** Frenchman
Ffrancwyr *gw.* **Ffrancwr**
Ffrengig *a.* French
ffres *a.* fresh
ffrind *e.g. ll.* **-iau** friend
ffrindiau *gw.* **ffrind**
ffrio *be.* (**ffriaf**) to fry
ffroen *e.b. ll.* **-au** nostril
ffroesen *e.b. ll.* **ffroes**
pancake *(S.W.). gw.*
crempog
ffrog: ffroc *e.b. ll.* **-iau** frock.
ffrog felen a yellow frock;
ffrog wen a white frock
ffroga *e.g. ll.* **ffrogaod** frog.
gw. **broga**

ffortiwn *e.b. ll.* **ffortiynau**
fortune
ffortiynau *gw.* **ffortiwn**
ffos *e.b. ll.* **-ydd** ditch, trench
ffosydd *gw.* **ffos**
ffowls *gw.* **ffowlyn**
ffowlyn *e.g. ll.* **ffowls**
chicken, fowl *(S.W.)*
ffraeo (â) *be.* (**ffraeaf**) to
quarrel, to bicker
Ffrangeg *e.b.* French
(language)
Ffrainc *e.b.* France

ffrwd *e.b. ll.* **ffrydiau** swift
stream; torrent, flood;
current
ffrwydro *be.* (**ffrwydraf**) to
explode
ffrwyth *e.g. ll.* **ffrwythau**
fruit; produce; result, effect
ffrwythlon *a.* fruitful, fertile
ffrwythloni *be.* (**ffrwythlonaf**)
to become or be fruitful; to
fertilize
ffrydiau *gw.* **ffrwd**

ffrynt *e.g.b.* *ll.* **-iau** front.
ffrynt gynnes warm front;
ffrynt oer cold front; **drws
(y) ffrynt** front door; **o'r
ffrynt** from the front

ffug *a.* deceptive, sham,
counterfeit, false. **dogfen ffug**
forged document

ffug-bas *e.b.* *ll.* **-ys** dummy-
pass (*rugby*)

ffugenw *e.g.* *ll.* **-au**
pseudonym, *nom de plume*

ffugio *be.* (**ffugiaf**) to pretend,
to disguise, to forge, to feign

ffuglen *e.b.* fiction. **ffuglen
wyddonol** *e.b.* science fiction

ffurf *e.b.* *ll.* **-iau** form, shape;
appearance, likeness;
substance

ffurfafen *e.b.* *ll.* **-nau** sky;
heavens

ffurfiau *gw.* **ffurf**

ffurfio *be.* (**ffurfiaf**) to form, to
fashion, to create

ffurflen *e.b.* *ll.* **-ni** form,
chart. **ffurflen gais**
application form

ffurflenni *gw.* **ffurflen**

ffwdan *e.g.* fuss, flurry

ffŵl *e.g.* *ll.* **ffyliaid** fool

ffwr *e.g.* *ll.* **ffyrrau** fur

ffwrdd, i *ad.* away. **ffwrdd-â-
hi** *a. & ad.* slapdash,
precipitate

ffwrn *e.b.* *ll.* **ffyrnau,
ffwerneisi,** oven, furnace.
ffwrn microdon microwave
oven

ffws *e.g.* fuss

ffydd *e.b.* *ll.* **-iau** faith, belief,
confidence

ffyddlon *a.* faithful, loyal

ffyliaid *gw.* **ffŵl**

ffyn *gw.* **ffon**

ffynhonnau *gw.* **ffynnon**

ffynhonnell *e.b.* *ll.* **ffynonellau**
source, spring, fount; origin

ffynidwydden *e.b.* *ll.*
ffynidwydd fir tree, pine tree

ffynnon *e.b.* *ll.* **ffynhonnau**
spring, fountain,well; source,
origin

ffynonellau *gw.* **ffynhonnell**

ffyrc *gw.* **fforc**

ffyrdd *gw.* **ffordd**

ffyrnau *gw.* **ffwrn**

ffyrnig *a.* fierce, savage,
furious, wild.

ffyrnigrwydd *e.g.* ferocity

ffyrrau *gw.* **ffwr**

G

ga i *bf.* may I . . .? *gw.* **cael**

gaban *gw.* **caban**

gacen *gw.* **cacen**

gacwn *gw.* **cacynen**

gacynen *gw.* **cacynen**

gadach *gw.* **cadach**

gadael *be.* (**gadawaf**) to leave,
to desert; to allow. **gadewais**
I left; **gadewaist** you left

gadair *gw.* **cadair**

gadeiriau *gw.* **cadair**

gadeirio *gw.* **cadeirio**

gadeiriol *gw.* **cadeiriol**

gadeirydd *gw.* **cadeirydd**

gadno *gw.* **cadno**

gadw *gw.* **cadw**

gadwyn *gw.* **cadwyn**

gadwyno *gw.* **cadwyno**

gae

gae *gw.* **cae**

gaeaf *e.g. ll.* **-au** winter

gaeau *gw.* **cae**

gael *gw.* **cael**

gaer *gw.* **caer**

Gaer *gw.* **Caer**

Gaerdydd *gw.* **Caerdydd**

Gaeredin *gw.* **Caeredin**

Gaerfyrddin *gw.* **Caerfyrddin**

Gaergybi *gw.* **Caergybi**

gaets *gw.* **caets**

gaf *gw.* **cael**

gafael (yn) *be.* **(gafaelaf)** to hold tight, to clutch; to grip. **Gafael yn fy llaw** Take my hand

gafaelgar *a.* gripping

gafodd *gw.* **cael**

gafr *e.b. ll.* **geifr** goat

gaffe *gw.* **caffe**

gangen *gw.* **cangen**

ganghennau *gw.* **cangen**

gaiff *gw.* **caiff**

gair *e.g. ll.* **geiriau** word. **gair bach** short address, brief note; **geirda** good report, commendation, reference; **gair drwg** bad reputation; **ar y gair** instantly: **cadw at ei air** to keep his word; **dweud gair** to speak or address (a meeting, etc.); **Gair Duw** God's word; **gair yn ei bryd** timely advice

gais *gw.* **cais**

galan *gw.* **calan**

galar *e.g.* mourning, grief

galaru *be.* **(galaraf)** to mourn

galed *gw.* **caled**

galedi *gw.* **caledi**

galedwch *gw.* **caledwch**

galendr *gw.* **calendr**

galennig *gw.* **calennig**

galetach *gw.* **caled**

galetaf *gw.* **caled**

galeted *gw.* **caled**

galon *gw.* **calon**

galw (ar, am) *be.* **(galwaf)** to call, to summon; to visit; to name

galwad *e.b.g. ll.* **-au** a call; vocation, calling, profession. **Cafodd y gweinidog alwad i Lanelli** The minister received a call to Llanelli

galwedigaeth *e.b. ll.* **-au** occupation, vocation

galwyn *e.g. ll.* **-i, -au** gallon

gall *gw.* **call**

gallach *gw.* **call**

gallaf *gw.* **call.** *gw.* **gallu**

galled *gw.* **call**

gallu 1 *be.* **(gallaf)** to be able. **2** *e.g. ll.* **-oedd** ability, power, wealth

galluog *a.* able, powerful

gam *gw.* **cam**

gamarwain *gw.* **camarwain**

gamddeall *gw.* **camddeall**

gamera *gw.* **camera**

gamp *gw.* **camp**

gampfa *gw.* **campfa**

gampfeydd *gw.* **campfa**

gampus *gw.* **campus**

gampwaith *gw.* **campwaith**

gampweithiau *gw.* **campwaith**

gamsyniad *gw.* **camsyniad**

gamu *gw.* **camu**

gan *ardd.* *(followed by soft mutation)* *(personal forms:*

gen i, gen ti, ganddo/ganddi,
gennyn, gennych, ganddyn).
with, by, from, since. **gan
amlaf** usually, mostly: **gan
hynny** therefore; **gan mwyaf**
mostly, almost. *gw. At.
Arddodiaid; gw.* **can; cant**
gân *gw.* **cân**
ganddi: ganddo *gw.* **gan**
ganddyn *gw.* **gan**
ganed *bf.* he/she was born
ganeuon *gw.* **cân**
ganfed *gw.* **canfed**
ganhwyllbren *gw.*
  canhwyllbren
ganiad *gw.* **caniad**
ganiadaeth *gw.* **caniadaeth**
ganiadau *gw.* **cân, caniad**
ganiatâd *gw.* **caniatâd**
ganiatáu *gw.* **caniatáu**
ganiedydd *gw.* **caniedydd**
ganmlwydd *gw.* **canmlwydd**
ganmlwyddiannau *gw.*
  canmlwyddiant
ganmlwyddiant *gw.*
  canmlwyddiant
ganmol *gw.* **canmol**
ganmoliaeth *gw.* **canmoliaeth**
gannoedd *gw.* **cant**
gannwyll *gw.* **cannwyll**
ganhwyllau *gw.* **cannwyll**
ganol *gw.* **canol**
ganolbarth *gw.* **canolbarth**
ganolbwyntio *gw.*
  canolbwyntio
ganoldir *gw.* **canoldir**
ganolfan *gw.* **canolfan**
ganolog *gw.* **canolog**
ganolwr *gw.* **canolwr**
ganradd *gw.* **canradd**

ganran *gw.* **canran**
ganrif *gw.* **canrif**
ganrifau: ganrifoedd *gw.*
  canrif
gant *gw.* **cant**
gânt *gw.* **cael**
gantor *gw.* **cantor**
gantores *gw.* **cantores**
ganu *gw.* **canu**
ganŵ *gw.* **canŵ**
ganŵio *gw.* **canŵio**
ganwr *gw.* **canwr**
ganwriad *gw.* **canwriad**
ganwyd *bf.* he/she was born.
  Ganwyd ef yng Nghymru He
  was born in Wales. *gw.* **geni**
gap *gw.* **cap**
gapel *gw.* **capel**
gapten *gw.* **capten**
gar *gw.* **car**
garafán *gw.* **carafán**
garafana *gw.* **carafana**
garco *gw.* **carco**
garcus *gw.* **carcus**
garchar *gw.* **carchar**
garcharor *gw.* **carcharor**
garcharu *gw.* **carcharu**
gardiau *gw.* **cerdyn**
gardd *e.b. ll.* **gerddi** garden;
  Gardd Fotaneg Genedlaethol
  National Botanic Garden of
  Wales
garddio *be.* **(garddiaf)** to
  garden, to cultivate a garden
garddwr *e.g. ll.* **garddwyr**
  gardener
garedig *gw.* **caredig**
garedigrwydd *gw.*
  caredigrwydd
garej *e.g. ll.* **-ys** garage

gariad

gariad *gw.* cariad
gariadon *gw.* cariad
gariadus *gw.* cariadus
gario *gw.* cario
garlleg *e.g.* garlic. ewin(-edd)
 garlleg clove of garlic
garol *gw.* carol
garped *gw.* carped
garreg *gw.* carreg
gartref *ad.* at home. Mae e'n
 byw gartref He's living at
 home. *gw.* cartref

the old gate; dwy gât two
gates; y gât wen the white
gate. *gw.* clwyd. *gw.* iet
gath *gw.* cath
gau *a.* (*precedes noun*) false.
 gau broffwyd a false
 prophet. *gw.* cau
gawl *gw.* cawl
gawod *gw.* cawod
gawr *gw.* cawr
gaws *gw.* caws
gefell *e.g.b.* *ll.* gefeilliaid

Insight

gartref *ad.* at home; ('home' is cartref); 'homeward' is mynd
adref or mynd tua thref
gwefan *e.b.* website. ar y we on the web
gyda *ardd.* together, with. gyda'i gilydd all together.

---

gartrefi *gw.* cartref
gartrefu *gw.* cartrefu
garu *gw.* caru
garw *a.* *ll.* geirwon coarse,
 rough, harsh
garwriaeth *gw.* carwriaeth
gas *gw.* cas
gasáu *gw.* casáu
gasgen *gw.* casgen
gasgenni *gw.* casgen
gasgliad *gw.* casgliad
gasglu *gw.* casglu
Gas-gwent *gw.* Cas-gwent
Gasllwchwr *gw.* Casllwchwr
Gasnewydd *gw.* Casnewydd
gastell *gw.* castell
Gastell-nedd *gw.* Castell-nedd
gât *e.b.* *ll.* gatiau, gâts,
 gatsys (*never undergoes soft
 mutation*) gate. yr hen gât

twin. gefell twin brother;
 gefeilles twin sister; yr
 efeilliaid the twins
gefn *gw.* cefn
gefnder *gw.* cefnder
gefndir *gw.* cefndir
gefndiroedd *gw.* cefndir
gefndyr *gw.* cefnder
gefnogi *gw.* cefnogi
gefnu *gw.* cefnu
gefnwr *gw.* cefnwr
geffyl *gw.* ceffyl
geg *gw.* ceg
gegin *gw.* cegin
gei *gw.* cei
geidwad *gw.* ceidwad
geifr *gw.* gafr
geiliog *gw.* ceiliog
Geinewydd *gw.* Ceinewydd
geiniog *gw.* ceiniog

geir *gw.* **car**

geirfa *e.b.* *ll.* **-oedd**
vocabulary

geiriadur *e.g.* *ll.* **-on**
dictionary

geiriau *gw.* **gair**

geirio *be.* **(geiriaf)** to word, to
phrase

geiriosen *gw.* **ceiriosen**

geirwon *gw.* **garw**

geisiadau: geisiau *gw.* **cais**

geisio *gw.* **ceisio**

gelf *gw.* **celf**

gelfi *gw.* **celficyn**

gelficyn *gw.* **celficyn**

Geltaidd *gw.* **Celtaidd**

gelwydd *gw.* **celwydd**

gelwyddog *gw.* **celwyddog**

gelyn *e.g.* *ll.* **-ion** enemy.
gelyn pennaf chief enemy.
gw. **celynnen**

gelynnen *gw.* **celynnen**

gell *gw.* **cell**

gellau: gelloedd *gw.* **cell**

gem *e.b.g.* *ll.* **-au** gem

gêm *e.b.* *ll.* **gêmau** (*doesn't
mutate*) game. **Dyma gêm
dda** Here's a good game;
dwy gêm rygbi two rugby
games; **dewch i gêmau'r
ysgol** Come to the school's
games

gemeg *gw.* **cemeg**

gen *gw.* **gan**

gên *e.b.* *ll.* **genau** chin, jaw

genau *e.g.* *ll.* **geneuau**
mouth; *gw.* **gên**

genedigaeth *e.b.* *ll.* **-au** birth

genedl *gw.* **cenedl**

genedlaethol *gw.*
cenedlaethol

genedlaetholdeb *gw.*
cenedlaetholdeb

genedlaetholwr *gw.*
cenedlaetholwr

genetig: genetaidd: genynnol
a. genetic

geneth *e.b.* *ll.* **-od** girl (*N.W.*)

geneuau *gw.* **genau**

genfigennus *gw.* **cenfigennus**

genhadaeth *gw.* **cenhadaeth**

genhadol *gw.* **cenhadol**

genhadu *gw.* **cenhadu**

genhadwr *gw.* **cenhadwr**

genhedlaeth *gw.* **cenhedlaeth**

genhedloedd *gw.* **cenedl**

genhinen *gw.* **cenhinen**

geni *be.* to be born, to give
birth to. **dyddiad geni** date
of birth

gennin *gw.* **cenhinen**

gennych *gw.* **gan**

gennym *gw.* **gan**

genyn *e.g.* *ll.* **-au** gene

ger *ardd.* at, by, near, before,
in front of. **gerllaw** close to

gêr *e.ll.* gear, tackle; rubbish

gerbron *gw.* **ger**

gerdyn *gw.* **cerdyn**

gerdd *gw.* **cerdd**

gerdded *gw.* **cerdded**

gerddi *gw.* **cerdd, gardd**

gerddor *gw.* **cerddor**

gerddorfa *gw.* **cerddorfa**

gerddoriaeth *gw.* **cerddoriaeth**

gerddorol *gw.* **cerddorol**

gerddwr *gw.* **cerddwr**

gerddwyr *gw.* **cerddwr**

gerfio *gw.* **cerfio**

gerflun *gw.* **cerflun**

gerllaw *gw.* **ger**

germ

germ *e.g. ll.* **-au** germ
gerrig *gw.* **carreg**
ges *gw.* **cael**
gesair *gw.* **cesair**
gestyll *gw.* **castell**
gewri *gw.* **cawr**
gewyn *gw. ll.* **-nau, -ion**
sinew, tendon, ligament;
nerve. *gw.* **cewyn**
geyrydd *gw.* **caer**
gi *gw.* **ci**
gig *gw.* **cig**
gigydd *gw.* **cigydd**
gilio *gw.* **cilio**
gilydd *rhag.* other, another,
another of the same class or
kind. **ei gilydd** each other;
gyda'i gilydd together (they);
gyda'ch gilydd together
(you); **gyda'n gilydd** together
(we)
ginio *gw.* **cinio**
gipolwg *gw.* **cipolwg**
gist *gw.* **cist**
glaf *gw.* **claf**
glai *gw.* **clai**
glan *e.b. ll.* **-nau, glennydd**
bank, shore. **glan y môr**
seashore; **glan yr afon** river's
bank; **glan y bedd** the grave-
side; **gwyliwr y glannau**
coastguard
glân *a.* clean, pure, holy;
beautiful, fair
glanhau *be.* **(glanhaf)** to
clean, to purify; to heal
glanio *be.* **(glaniaf)** to land, to
come or go ashore,
disembark; bring to land
glannau *gw.* **glan**

glas 1 *a. ll.* **gleision** blue,
green, grey, silver; wan,
pallid; raw. **arian gleision**
silver (money), silver coins;
glas y dorlan kingfisher.
2 *e.g.* blue
glaswelltyn *e.g. ll.* **glaswellt**
green grass
glasur *gw.* **clasur**
glasurol *gw.* **clasurol**
glaw *e.g. ll.* **-ogydd** rain.
bwrw glaw to rain; **eirlaw**
sleet; **glaw mân** drizzle
glawdd *gw.* **clawdd**
glawr *gw.* **clawr**
glebran *gw.* **clebran**
glefyd *gw.* **clefyd**
gleison *gw.* **glas**
glendid *e.g.* cleanness,
cleanliness, purity; beauty;
piety, holiness
glennydd *gw.* **glan**
glêr *gw.* **cleren**
glerc *gw.* **clerc**
gleren *gw.* **cleren**
glin *e.g.b. ll.* **-iau** knee
gliniadur *e.b. ll.* **-on** laptop.
gw. **sgrîn ben-glin**
glir *gw.* **clir**
glirio *gw.* **clirio**
glo *e.g.* coal. **glo brig** open-
cast coal; **glo carreg**
anthracite coal; **glo mân**
small coal; **glo rhwym**
bituminous coal. *gw.* **clo**
gloc *gw.* **cloc**
glocwedd *gw.* **clocwedd**
gloch *gw.* **cloch**
glod *gw.* **clod**
glodfori *gw.* **clodfori**

gloddiau *gw.* **clawdd**

glofa *e.b.* *ll.* **glofeydd** colliery

glofeydd *gw.* **glofa**

gloff *gw.* **cloff**

gloffi *gw.* **cloffi**

glogwyn *gw.* **clogwyn**

glogyn *gw.* **clogyn**

gloi *gw.* **cloi**

glorian *gw.* **clorian**

glown *gw.* **clown**

glöwr *e.g.* *ll.* **glowyr** collier, coal-miner

glöyn byw *e.g.* *ll.* **glöynnod byw** butterfly (*N.W.*)

gloyw *a.* *ll.* **-on** clear, bright, shiny. **Cymro glân gloyw** a thoroughbred Welshman

glud *e.g.* *ll.* **-ion** glue

gludio: gludo *be.* **(gludiaf: gludaf)** to glue; to adhere

glun *gw.* **clun**

glust *gw.* **clust**

glustog *gw.* **clustog**

glwb *gw.* **clwb**

glwm *gw.* **clwm**

glwtyn *gw.* **clwtyn**

Glwyd *gw.* **Clwyd**

glwyd *gw.* **clwyd**

glwyf *gw.* **clwyf**

glychau *gw.* **cloch**

glymau *gw.* **clwm, cwlwm**

glymu *gw.* **clymu**

glyn *e.g.* *ll.* **-noedd** valley, glen

Glynebwy *e.b.* Ebbw Vale

glynu (wrth) *be.* **(glynaf)** to adhere, to cling

glyw *ge.* **clyw**

glywed *gw.* **clywed**

gnau *gw.* **cneuen**

gneuen *gw.* **cneuen**

gnoc *gw.* **cnoc**

gnocio *gw.* **cnocio**

gnoi *gw.* **cnoi**

go *ad.* (*precedes noun and causes soft mutation*) rather, somewhat; small, little, exceeding (*N.W.*). **go ddrud** somewhat expensive

gobaith *e.g.* *ll.* **gobeithion** hope

goban *gw.* **coban**

gobeithio (am) *be.* **(gobeithiaf)** to hope

gobeithion *gw.* **gobaith**

gobennydd *e.g.* *ll.* **gobenyddion** pillow, bolster

goch *gw.* **coch**

gochach *gw.* **coch**

gochaf *gw.* **coch**

goched *gw.* **coch**

godi *gw.* **codi**

godidog *gw.* excellent, splendid

godre *e.g.* *ll.* **-on** edge, hem, fringe; foot or bottom (*of mountain, hill, etc.*); foot (*of page*)

godro *be.* **(godraf)** to milk

goddef *be.* **(goddefaf)** to suffer, to bear, to endure, to tolerate

goddefgar *a.* tolerant

goddrych *e.g.* *ll.* **-au** subject

Goed-duon *gw.* **Coed-duon**

goeden *gw.* **coeden**

goedwig *gw.* **coedwig**

goes *gw.* **coes**

gof *e.g.* *ll.* **-aint** smith, blacksmith. *gw.* **cof**

gofal

gofal *e.g. ll.* **-on** care; charge

gofalu (am) *be.* **(gofalaf)** to take care; to worry, to vex

gofalus *a.* careful, anxious, worried

gofalwr *e.g. ll.* **gofalwyr** caretaker, custodian

gofbin *gw.* **cofbin**

gofid *e.g. ll.* **-iau** trouble, sorrow, grief, affliction

gofidio (am) *be.* **(gofidiaf)** to grieve, to vex

gofio *gw.* **cofio**

gofleidio *gw.* **cofleidio**

gofod *e.g. ll.* **-au** space, gap. *gw.* **gwagle**

gofodwr *e.g. ll.* **gofodwyr** astronaut

gofrestr *gw.* **cofrestr**

gofrestru *gw.* **cofrestru**

gofyn (am, i) 1 *be.* **(gofynnaf)** to ask (for). 2 *e.g. ll.* **-ion** request, requirement, demand. **yn ôl y gofyn** according to demand; **Gofyn bendith** to say grace

goffi *gw.* **coffi**

gog *gw.* **cog**

goginio *gw.* **coginio**

gogledd 1 *e.g.* north. 2 *a.* north, northern. **Pegwn y Gogledd** North Pole

gogleddol *a.* northern

gogleddwr *e.g. ll.* **gogleddwyr** northerner

gogleisio *be.* **(gogleisiaf)** to tickle

gogoniant *e.g. ll.* **gogoniannau** glory

gogydd *gw.* **cogydd**

gogystal *a.* comparable

gohirio *be.* **(gohiriaf)** to postpone

gôl *e.b. ll.* **goliau** goal (*soccer*)

golau 1 *e.g.* light. 2 *a.* light, fair (*colour*). *gw.* **goleuni**. **golau diogelwch** safety light; **golau dydd** daylight; **golau (l)leuad** moonlight; **golau llachar** bright light

golchi *be.* **(golchaf)** to wash; to flow over or past

goleg *gw.* **coleg**

goler *gw.* **coler**

goleudy *e.g. ll.* **goleudai** lighthouse

goleuni *e.g.* light; *gw.* **golau**

goleuo *be.* **(goleuaf)** to light, to enlighten; to set fire to

goliau *gw.* **gôl**

golofn *gw.* **colofn**

golud *e.g. ll.* **-oedd** wealth, riches

goluro *gw.* **coluro**

golwg *e.g.b. ll.* **golygon** sight; appearance, view. **golygon** eyes; **i bob golwg** to all appearances; **o'r golwg** out of sight; **y fath olwg!** what a sight; **rhagolygon y tywydd** weather prospects; **roedd golwg wael arni** she looked ill; **allan o olwg** out of sight

golygfa *e.b. ll.* **golygfeydd** view, scenery, scene

golygon *gw.* **golwg**

golygu *be.* **(golygaf)** to view; to mean, to imply, to intend; to edit. **Beth rwyt ti'n ei olygu?** What do you mean?

golygus *a.* handsome
golygydd *e.g.* *ll.* **-ion** editor
golled *gw.* **colled**
gollen *gw.* **collen**
golli *gw.* **colli**
gollwng *be.* **(gollyngaf)** to
release; to leak
gonest *a.* honest, sincere
gopïo *gw.* **copïo**
gopyn *gw.* **copyn**
gôr *gw.* **côr**
gorau *a.* best. **o'r gorau**
okay. *gw.* **da.** *gw.* **côr**
gorchfygu *be.* **(gorchfygaf)** to
defeat, to conquer, to
subdue, to beat
gorchymyn (i) 1 *be.*
(gorchmynnaf) to command,
to order, to decree, to
charge. *gw.* **archebu** 2 *e.g.*
ll. **gorch(y)mynion**
commandment, command,
decree, order. **Y Deg
Gorchymyn** The Ten
Commandments; *gw.* **archeb**
gordyn *gw.* **cordyn**
gorfod 1 *e.g.b.* *ll.* **-au**
compulsion, obligation.
2 *be.* **(gorfodaf)** to be
obliged, forced or
compelled to, to
have (to). **Rwyt ti'n
gorfod mynd** You have to
go. **Rydw i'n gorfod
gwerthu'r tŷ.** I'm forced to
sell the house.
gorfodaeth *e.b.g.* *ll.* **-au**
compulsion, obligation.
gorfodaeth filwrol military
conscription
gorfodi (i) *be.* **(gorfodaf)** to

compel, to oblige, to
constrain, to force
gorfodol *a.* compulsory,
obligatory
gorfoleddus *a.* joyful
gorff *gw.* **corff**
gorffen *be.* **(gorffennaf)** to
finish, to conclude
Gorffennaf *e.g.* July
gorffennol 1 *e.g.* the past.
2 *a.* past
gorfforol *gw.* **corfforol**
gorffwys *e.g.* rest
gorffwyso *be.* **(gorffwysaf)** to
rest
gorgi *gw.* **corgi**
gorlawn *a.* overflowing,
overcrowded
gorllewin *e.g.* west. **Gorllewin
Cymru** West Wales
gormod 1 *e.g.* excess; too
many. 2 *a. & ad.* too much,
excessive. **gormod o gwynion**
too many complaints;
gormod o straeon too many
stories; **gormod o stŵr** too
much noise; **gormod o
drafferth** too much trouble;
bwyta gormod to eat too
much
gorn *gw.* **corn**
gornel *gw.* **cornel**
gornest *e.b.* *ll.* **-au** contest,
battle; match
goron *gw.* **coron**
goroni *gw.* **coroni**
gorryn *gw.* **corryn**
gorsaf *e.b.* *ll.* **-oedd** station.
gorsaf betrol petrol station;
gorsaf bŵer power station;
gorsaf dân fire station

gorsedd

gorsedd *e.b. ll.* **-au** throne.
Gorsedd y Beirdd the
Gorsedd of Bards (*bardic institution*)

goruchaf *a.* most high, supreme

goruwchnaturiol *a.* supernatural

gorwedd *be.* **(gorweddaf)** to lie, to lie down

gorwel *e.g. ll.* **-ion** horizon

gorymdaith *e.b. ll.* **gorymdeithiau** procession

gosb *gw.* **cosb**

gosbi *gw.* **cosbi**

gosi *gw.* **cosi**

gosod 1 *be.* **(gosodaf)** to put; to plant; to let; to bestow; to fix. **gosod gerbron** to set before; **gosod mewn trefn** to set in order; **gosod pris** to fix a price; **gosod yr ardd** to plant the garden. 2 *a.* false, artificial, applied. **dannedd gosod** false teeth, denture. **gwallt gosod** false hair, wig

gostus *gw.* **costus**

gostwng *be.* **(gostyngaf)** to lower, to reduce; to diminish; to ease

gostyngedig *a.* humble

gostyngiad *e.g. ll.* **-au** reduction

gosyn *gw.* **cosyn**

got: gôt *gw.* **cot**

gotwm *gw.* **cotwm**

grac *gw.* **crac**

grachach *gw.* **crachach**

gradd *e.b. ll.* **-au** step, grade, degree, university degree.
gradd anrhydedd an honours degree; **i'r fath raddau** to such an extent; **mewn graddau** by degrees, gradually; **o radd i radd** step by step, by degrees

graddfa *e.b. ll.* **graddfeydd** scale. **ar raddfa eang** on a large scale; **graddfa Celsius** Celsius Scale

graddio *be.* **(graddiaf)** to graduate, to grade, to scale

graddol *a.* gradual. **yn raddol** by degrees

graenus *a.* of good quality, glossy, sleek

grafu *gw.* **crafu**

gragen *gw.* **cragen**

graig *gw.* **craig**

gramadeg *e.g. ll.* **-au** grammar. **llyfr gramadeg** grammar book

gramadegol *a.* grammatical

grant *e.g. ll.* **-iau** grant

gras *e.g. ll.* **-au, -usau** grace. *gw.* **cras**

grasu *bw.* **crasu**

grawnffrwyth *e.g. ll.* **-au** grapefruit

gredu *gw.* **credu**

grefydd *gw.* **crefydd**

grefft *gw.* **crefft**

grefftwr *gw.* **crefftwr**

gregyn *gw.* **cragen**

greigiau *gw.* **craig**

greigiog *gw.* **creigiog**

greision *gw.* **cras, creisionyn**

grempog *gw.* **crempog**

gresyn *e.g. ll.* **-au** pity (*N.W.*). **Gresyn iddo farw**

Pity that he died; **Gresyn o beth** It's a shame

gresynu *be.* **(gresynaf)** to deplore, to be sorry, to pity

greulon *gw.* **creulon**

greulondeb *gw.* **creulondeb**

gri *gw.* **cri**

grib *gw.* **crib**

gribo *gw.* **cribo**

griced *gw.* **criced**

gricedwr *gw.* **cricedwr**

grio *gw.* **crio**

gris *e.g. ll.* **-iau** step, stair

Gristion *gw.* **Cristion**

griw *gw.* **criw**

Groeg 1 *e.b.* Greece. **2** *e.b. & a.* the Greek language, Greek; pertaining to the Greek language, to Greece or to the Greeks

Groegaidd *a.* Grecian, Greek

Groeges *e.b. ll.* **-au** Greek female

Groegwr *e.g. ll.* **Groegwyr** Greek, Grecian

groen *gw.* **croen**

groes *gw.* **croes**

groesair *gw.* **croesair**

groesawu *gw.* **croesawu**

groesawus *gw.* **croesawus**

groesfan *gw.* **croesfan**

groesffordd *gw.* **croesffordd**

groesholi *gw.* **croesholi**

groesi *gw.* **croesi**

groeso *gw.* **croeso**

gron *gw.* **cron**

gronfa *gw.* **cronfa**

grud *gw.* **crud**

grudd *e.b.g. ll.* **-iau** cheek

grug *e.g.* heather

grwn *gw.* **crwn**

grŵp *e.g. ll.* **grwpiau** group. **grŵp pop** pop group

grwst *gw.* **crwst**

gryd *gw.* **cryd**

gryf *gw.* **cryf**

gryfach *gw.* **cryf**

gryfaf *gw.* **cryf**

gryfed *gw.* **cryf**

grym *e.g. ll.* **-oedd** force; energy; power

grymus *a.* powerful, strong, mighty

grynhoi *gw.* **crynhoi**

gryno *gw.* **cryno**

grynodeb *gw.* **crynodeb**

grynu *gw.* **crynu**

grys *gw.* **crys**

grystyn *gw.* **crystyn**

gu *gw.* **cu**

guddio *gw.* **cuddio**

gul *gw.* **cul**

guro *gw.* **curo**

gusan *gw.* **cusan**

gusanu *gw.* **cusanu**

gwadu *be.* **(gwadaf)** to deny, to disown

gwaed *e.g.* blood. **yn y gwaed** in the blood as a family trait; **Cymro o waed coch cyfan** a thoroughbred Welshman

gwaedu *be.* **(gwaedaf)** to bleed. **gwaedu fel mochyn** to bleed like a (slaughtered) pig

gwaedd *e.b. ll.* **-au** shout

gwael *a.* poor; miserable; sick; vile. **tro gwael â** an unworthy act (with)

gwaelod

gwaelod *e.g. ll.* **-ion** bottom,
base, foundation. **ar waelod**
at the bottom; **yng ngwaelod**
in the bottom; **gwaelodion**
sediment, dregs

gwaeth *gw.* **drwg**

gwaethaf *gw.* **drwg. er**
gwaethaf in spite of;
gwaetha'r modd the more
the pity; worse luck

gwaethed *gw.* **drwg**

gwaethygu *be.* **(gwaethygaf)**
to worsen

gwag *a. ll.* **gweigion** empty;
desolate; vacant

gwagedd *e.g. ll.* **-au** vanity;
void

gwagio: gwagu *be.* **(gwagiaf:**
gwagaf) to empty

gwagle *e.g. ll.* **-oedd** space,
void. *gw.* **gofod**

gwagu *gw.* **gwagio**

gwahân *e.g.* separation;
difference. **ar wahân** apart;
separately; independently;
byw ar wahân to live apart

gwahaniaeth *e.g.* difference,
separation

gwahaniaethu *be.*
(gwahaniaethaf) to differ

gwahanol *a.* different, various

gwahanu *be.* **(gwahanaf)** to
separate

gwahardd *be.* **(gwaharddaf)** to
prohibit

gwahodd 1 *be.* **(gwahoddaf)**
to invite, to ask. 2 *e.g. ll.*
-ion invitation, bidding

gwahoddedig *e.g. ll.* **-ion**
invited, bidden, called.
gwahoddedigion guests

gwahoddiad *e.g. ll.* **-au**
invitation

gwahoddion *gw.* **gwahodd**

gwair *e.g. ll.* **gweiriau** grass
(*grown for harvesting*); hay
(*S.W.*)

gwaith 1 *e.g. ll.* **gweithiau**
work; composition; works.
gwaith annwyd cold sores;
gwaith cartref homework;
gwaith glo coal-mine,
colliery; **gwaith tŷ** house
work. 2 *e.b. ll.* **gweithiau**
time, occasion, turn. **unwaith**
once; **dwywaith** twice;
teirgwaith three times;
canwaith a hundred times;
y waith honno that occasion.
3 *c.* for, because

gwal *e.b. ll.* **gwaliau, gwelydd**
wall

gwâl *e.b. ll.* **gwalau** lair; bed

gwall *e.g. ll.* **-au** mistake,
defect, want

gwallgof *a.* insane, mad

gwallt *e.g. ll.* **-au, -iau** hair.
blewyn (*one*) hair

gwallus *a.* faulty, inaccurate,
erroneous

gwan *a. ll.* **gweiniaid,**
gweinion weak, feeble.
esgus wan a feeble excuse

gwanwyn *e.g. ll.* **-au** spring

gwar *e.b.g. ll.* **-rau** nape of
the neck

gwâr *a.* cultured

gwarchod *be.* **(gwarchodaf)** to
watch, to guard, to baby-sit

gwaredu (rhag) *be.* **(gwaredaf)**
to save, to redeem, to
deliver, to rid

gwaredwr *e.g.* *ll.* **gwaredwyr**
saviour, deliverer
gwario *be.* **(gwariaf)** to spend
(*money*)
gwarrau *gw.* **gwar**
gwartheg *e.ll.* cattle. *gw.*
buwch, da
gwarthus *a.* shameful
gwas *e.g.* *ll.* **gweision** male
servant; boy, lad. **gwas**
ffarm farm labourer. *gw.*
morwyn
gwasanaeth *e.g.* *ll.* **-au**
service; use
gwasanaethu *be.*
(gwasanaethaf) serve, to
minister
gwasg 1 *e.b.* *ll.* **-au, -oedd,**
gweisg press, pressure;
waist. **gwasg argraffu**
printing-press; **gwasg gaws**
cheese-press; **gwŷr y wasg**
the press (*reporters*). 2 *e.g.*
ll. **-au, -oedd** stress; waist
gwasgedd *e.g.* *ll.* **-au**
pressure. **gwasgedd isel** low
pressure; **gwasgedd uchel**
high pressure
gwasgfa *e.b.* *ll.* **gwasgfeydd**
squeeze. **gwasgfa gredyd**
credit crunch
gwasgod *e.b.* *ll.* **-au**
waistcoat
gwasgu *be.* **(gwasgaf)** to
press, to squeeze, to wring,
to crush
gwastad 1 *e.g.ll.* **-au** plain. 2
a. flat, level, even; constant.
yn wastad always (*S.W.*)

gwastraff *e.g.* *ll.* **-au, -oedd**
waste. **gwastraff niwclear**
nuclear waste
gwastraffu *be.* **(gwastraffaf)**
to waste
gwau *be.* **(gweaf, gweuaf)** to
weave; to knit. **dillad gwau**
knitted garments. *gw.* **gweu**
gwaun *e.b.* *ll.* **gweunydd**
meadow; moor
gwawd *e.g.* *ll.* **-iau, -ion**
scorn, satire
gwawdio *be.* **(gwawdiaf)** to
scorn, to mock, to jeer
gwawr *e.b.g.* *ll.* **-iau, -oedd**
dawn; hue; shade. **ar doriad**
gwawr at daybreak; **roedd**
gwawr las yn y brethyn there
was a shade of blue in the
material
gwawrio *be.* **(gwawriaf)** to
dawn
gwawroedd *gw.* **gwawr**
gwb *gw.* **cwb**
gwbl *gw.* **cwbl**
gwcw *gw.* **cwcw**
gwch *gw.* **cwch**
gwd *gw.* **cwd**
gwdihŵ *e.b.* *ll.* **-aid, -s** owl
(*S.W.*). *gw.* **tylluan**
gwdyn *gw.* **cwdyn**
gwddf *e.g.* *ll.* **gyddfau** neck,
throat; neckline. **gwddf crwn**
round neck; **gwddf ffrog**
neckline; **gwddf sgwâr**
square neck; **gwddf V**
V-neck
gwddwg *e.g.* *ll.* **gwddygau**
neck, throat; neckline (*S.W.*)

gwe

gwe *e.b.* *ll.* **-oedd** web, cobweb. **gwe corryn: gwe pry' cop** cobweb; **safle ar y we: gwefan** a website. *gw.* **gwefan**

gweddi *e.b.* *ll.* **gweddïau** prayer. **Gweddi'r Arglwydd** The Lord's Prayer; **cwrdd gweddi** prayer meeting

gweddill *e.g.* *ll.* **-ion** remnant

gweddïo (dros, ar) *be.* **(gweddïaf)** to pray

gweddol 1 *a.* fair. **pris gweddol** a fairly good price; **cyflog gweddol** a fairly good wage. 2 *ad. (precedes the adjective and is followed by soft mutation).* **yn weddol dawel** fairly quiet; **yn weddol gyflym** fairly quick

gweddw 1 *e.b.* *ll.* **-on** widow. 2 *a.* widowed. **gŵr gweddw** widower *gw.* **widw: gwidw**

gwefan *e.b.* *ll.* **-nau** website

gwefus *e.b.* *ll.* **-au** lip

gweiddi *be.* **(gwaeddaf)** to shout

gweigion *gw.* **gwag**

gweiniaid *gw.* **gwan**

gweinidog *e.g.* *ll.* **-ion** minister, servant. **Gweinidog yr Efengyl** Minister of the Gospel; **Prif Weinidog** Prime Minister; **Gweinidog Gwladol** Minister of State

gweinion *gw.* **gwan**

gweinydd *e.g.* *ll.* **-ion** waiter

gweinyddes *e.b.* *ll.* **-au** waitress, female attendant; nurse. **gweinyddes feithrin** nursery nurse

gweiriau *gw.* **gwair**

gweisg *gw.* **gwasg**

gweision *gw.* **gwas**

gweithdy *e.g.* *ll.* **gweithdai** workshop

gweithgar *a.* hardworking, industrious

gweithiau *gw.* **gwaith**

gweithio *be.* **(gweithiaf)** to work; to ferment; to operate

gweithiwr *e.g.* *ll.* **gweithwyr** worker

gweithred *e.b.* *ll.* **-oedd** act, deed

gweithredu *be.* **(gweithredaf)** to act, to operate, to execute

gweithwyr *gw.* **gweithiwr**

gwelâu *gw.* **gwely**

gweld: gweled *be.* **(gwelaf)** to see, to perceive. **gweler** see (*when referring to something*)

gwelw *a.* pale

gwely *e.g.* *ll.* **-au, gwelâu** bed

gwelydd *gw.* **gwal**

gwell *a.* better (*note: nouns following* **gwell** *do not mutate*)

gwella *be.* **(gwellaf)** to improve, to better; to cure; to mend

gwellt *e. torf.* grass, sward; straw. *gw.* **gwelltyn**

gwelltyn *e.g.* *ll.* **gwellt** blade of grass; a straw. *gw.* **gwellt**

gwen *a.b.* white. **ffrog wen** a white frock; **torth wen** a white loaf. *gw.* **gwyn**

gwên *e.b.* *ll.* **gwenau** smile

gwenau *gw.* **gwên**

gwendid *e.g. ll.* **-au**
weakness; wane (*of the
moon*). **y lleuad yn ei
gwendid** the wane of the
moon

Gwener *e.b.* Venus. **dydd
Gwener** Friday

gwenith *e.ll.* wheat.
gwenithen a grain of wheat

gwennol *e.b. ll.* **gwenoliaid**
swallow

Gwent *e.b.* a former county
in S.E. Wales, now
Monmouthshire

gwenu (ar) *be.* **(gwenaf)** to
smile

gwenwyn *e.g. ll.* **-au** poison;
venom; malice; spite

gwenwynig: gwenwynol *a.*
poisonous

gwenynen *e.b. ll.* **gwenyn**
bee

gwêr *e.g. ll.* **gwerau** tallow

gwerdd *a.b.* green. **ffrog
werdd** a green frock; **deilen
werdd** a green leaf; **y Blaid
Werdd** The Green Party. *gw.*
gwyrdd

gwerin *e.b. & e.torf. ll.*
-oedd, -edd ordinary people,
peasantry, folk; proletariat.
amgueddfa werin folk
museum; **cân werin** folk
song

gweriniaeth *e.b. ll.* **-au**
democracy, republic

Gweriniaeth Iwerddon *e.b.*
Eire

gwers *e.b. ll.* **-i** lesson; stanza
of poetry. **gwers Gymraeg**
Welsh lesson; **gwers hanes**
history lesson

gwerslyfr *e.g. ll.* **-au** textbook

gwersyll *e.g. ll.* **-oedd** camp

gwerth *e.g. ll.* **-oedd** worth,
value. **mae'n werth y
drafferth** it's worth the
trouble; **ar werth** for sale;
mae'n werth punt It's worth
a pound; **Ga i werth pum
punt o betrol?** May I have
five pounds' worth of petrol?

gwerthfawr *a.* valuable,
precious

gwerthfawrogi *be.*
(gwerthfawrogaf) to
appreciate

gwerthfawrogiad *e.g. ll.* **-au**
appreciation

gwerthiant *e.g. ll.*
gwerthiannau sale

gwerthoedd *gw.* **gwerth**

gwerthu *be.* **(gwerthaf)** to sell

gwerthwr *e.g. ll.* **gwerthwyr**
seller, salesman

gweryl *gw.* **cweryl**

gweryla *gw,* **cweryla**

gwestai *e.g. ll.* **gwesteion**
guest. *gw.* **gwesty**

gwesteion *gw.* **gwestai**

gwesteiwr *e.g. ll.* **gwesteiwyr**
host. **gwesteiwraig** hostess

gwestiwn *gw.* **cwestiwn**

gwestiynau *gw.* **cwestiwn**

gwestiynu *gw.* **cwestiynu**

gwesty *e.g. ll.* **gwestai,
gwestyau** hotel, inn

gweu *be.* **(gweuaf)** to weave;
to knit. *gw.* **gwau**

gweunydd *gw.* **gwaun**

gwg

gwg *e.g. ll.* **-on, gygau** frown, scowl

gwgu (ar) *be.* **(gwgaf)** to frown, to scowl, to glower

gwiail *gw.* **gwialen**

gwialen *e.b. ll.* **gwiail, gwialennod** rod, cane, stick. **gwialen fedw** birch-rod

gwialennod *gw.* **gwialen**

gwidman *e.g. ll.* **-od** widower. *gw.* **gŵr gweddw**

gwin *e.g. ll.* **-oedd** wine. **gwin coch** red wine; **gwin gwyn** white wine

gwir 1 *e.g.* truth. **yn wir** in truth, indeed. 2 *a.* true; real; net. **stori wir** a true story; (*the adjective may also precede a noun and convey additional emphasis; it then causes a soft mutation*). **gwir bwysau** net weight; **gwir Gymro** a real Welshman; **y gwir ystyr** the real meaning

gwirionedd *e.g. ll.* **-au** truth, reality

gwisg *e.b. ll.* **-oedd** dress. **gwisg briodas** wedding-dress; **gwisg nos** night-dress

gwisgo (am) *be.* **(gwisgaf)** to dress; to wear

gwiwer *e.b. ll.* **-od** squirrel. **y wiwer goch** the red squirrel; **y wiwer lwyd** the grey squirrel

gwlad *e.b. ll.* **gwledydd** country, land. **gwlad fy nhadau** land of my fathers

Gwlad Belg *e.b.* Belgium

gwladfa *e.b. ll.* **gwladfaoedd,**

gwladfeydd colony; settlement. **Y Wladfa** Patagonia

gwladgarwr *e.g. ll.* **gwladgarwyr** patriot

gwladol *a.* civil; country; state; national. **Ysgrifennydd Gwladol** Secretary of State

Gwlad Pwyl *e.b.* Poland

Gwlad y Basg *e.b.* Basque Country

Gwlad yr Haf *e.b.* Somerset

Gwlad yr Iâ *e.b.* Iceland

gwlân *e.g. ll.* **gwlanoedd** wool

gwlanen *e.b. ll.* **-ni** home-spun, home-made cloth or flannel. **gwlanen goch** red flannel; **gwlanen wen** white flannel; **gwlanen ymolchi** face-cloth; **crys gwlanen** flannel shirt

gwledig *a.* rural; rustic; boorish. **Cymru Wledig** Rural Wales

gwledydd *gw.* **gwlad**

gwledd *e.b. ll.* **-oedd** feast; **gwledd briodas** marriage-feast

gwledda (ar) *be.* **(gwleddaf)** to feast

gwleidydd *e.g. ll.* **-ion** politician, statesman

gwleidyddiaeth *e.b.* politics

gwleidyddol *a.* political

gwlff *e.g. ll.* **gylffau** gulf

gwlith *e.g. ll.* **-oedd** dew

gwlwm *gw.* **cwlwm**

gwlyb *a. ll.* **-ion** wet

gwlybaniaeth *e.g.* moisture, wet, humidity

gwlychu *be.* **(gwlychaf)** to wet, to moisten; to get wet

gwm *e.g.* *ll.* **gymiau** gum. *gw.* **cwm**

gwmni *gw.* **cwmni**

gwmnïau *gw.* **cwmni**

gwmnïoedd *gw.* **cwmni**

gwmwl *gw.* **cwmwl**

gwn *e.g.* *ll.* **gynnau** gun. *gw.* **gwybod**

gŵn *e.g.* *ll.* **gynau** gown. **gŵn gwisgo** dressing gown; **gŵn nos** night-gown; *gw.* **ci**

gwneud: gwneuthur *be.* **(gwnaf)** to make; to do. *gw. At. Berfau*

gwningen *gw.* **cwningen**

gwniadyddes: gwniyddes *e.b.* *ll.* **-au** dressmaker, seamstress

gwnïo *be.* **(gwnïaf)** to sew, to stitch. **peiriant gwnïo** sewing machine

gwniyddes *gw.* **gwniadyddes**

gwobr *e.b.* *ll.* **-au** prize, reward. **y wobr gyntaf** the first prize; **gwobr gysur** consolation prize

gwobrwyo *be.* **(gwobrwyaf)** to reward, to award prize to

gwpan *gw.* **cwpan**

gwpla *gw.* **cwpla**

gwpwrdd *gw.* **cwpwrdd**

gwr *gw.* **cwr**

gŵr *e.g.* *ll.* **gwŷr** man; husband. **gŵr dieithr** stranger; **gŵr gwadd** guest, guest speaker; **gwŷr a gwraig** man and wife; **gŵr gweddw** *e.g.* *ll.* **gwŷr gweddw** widower. *gw.* **gwidman**

gwrach *e.b.* *ll.* **-od, -ïod** hag, witch

gwragedd *gw.* **gwraig**

gwraidd *gw.* **gwreiddyn**

gwraig *e.b.* *ll.* **gwragedd** wife; woman

gwrandawiad *e.g.* *ll.* **-au** listening, hearing

gwrandawr *e.g.* *ll.* **gwrandawyr** listener, hearer

gwrando (ar) *be.* **(gwrandawaf)** to listen. **Gwrandewais ar** I listened to; **Gwrandewaist ar** You listened to

gwrdd *gw.* **cwrdd**

gwreichionen *e.b.* *ll.* **gwreichion** spark

gwreiddiau *gw.* **gwreiddyn**

gwreiddio *be.* **(gwreiddiaf)** to root, to ground

gwreiddiol *a.* original

gwreiddyn *e.g.* *ll.* **gwraidd, gwreiddiau** root; stock

gwres *e.g.* *ll.* **-au** heat, warmth; zeal. **gwres canolog** central heating

gwresog *a.* hot, warm; fervent

gwresogi *be.* **(gwresogaf)** to heat

gwresogydd *e.g.* *ll.* **-ion** heater

gwrido *be.* **(gwridaf)** to blush

gwridog *a.* rosy-cheeked, ruddy

gwrol *a.* brave, courageous

gwrs *gw.* **cwrs**

gwrtais *gw.* **cwrtais**

gwrtaith *e.g.* *ll.* **gwrteithiau** manure, fertilizer

gwrth

gwrth *rhagdd.* (*Prefix with the sense 'against, contra-, counter-, anti-' in nouns, adjectives and verbs, and followed by soft mutation*).
gwrth-ddweud to contradict
gwrthblaid *e.b. ll.*
gwrthbleidiau opposition (*party*)
gwrthchwyswr *e.b. ll.*
gwrthchwyswyr antiperspirant
gwrthdaro *be.* (**gwrthdrawaf**) to clash, to collide
gwrthdystio *be.* (**gwrthdystiaf**) to protest. *gw.* **protest**
gwrthglocwedd *a.* anticlockwise
gwrthod *be.* (**gwrthodaf**) to refuse; to reject. **Fe wrthododd e fynd adref** He refused to go home
gwrthrych *e.g. ll.* **-au** object
gwrthrychol *a.* objective
gwrthryfel *e.g. ll.* **-oedd** rebellion, mutiny, insurrection
gwrthryfela *be.* (**gwrthryfelaf**) to rebel
gwrthwyneb 1 *e.g. ll.* **-au** in opposition to. 2 *a.* contrary, opposite. **i'r gwrthwyneb** to the contrary, in the opposite direction.
gwrthwynebu *be.* (**gwrthwynebaf**) to oppose; to object
gwrthwynebwr: gwrthwynebydd *e.g. ll.* **gwrthwynebwyr** opponent;

objector; antagonist.
gwrthwynebydd cydwybodol conscientious objector
gwrw *gw.* **cwrw**
gwrych *e.g. ll.* **-oedd** hedge; *e.ll.* bristles
gwryw 1 *e.g. ll.* **-od** male. **gwryw a benyw** male and female. 2 *a.* male
gwrywaidd: gwrywol *a.* male
gwrywgydiaeth *e.b.* homosexuality. **gwrywgydiwr** homosexual
gwsg *gw.* **cwsg**
gwsmer *gw.* **cwsmer**
gwstwm *gw.* **cwstwm**
gwt *gw.* **cwt**
gwta *gw.* **cwta**
gwthiad *e.g. ll.* **-au** heave, thrust, push
gwthio *be.* (**gwthiaf**) to push, to thrust
gwthiwr *e.g. ll.* **gwthwyr** pusher
gwybedyn *e.g. ll.* **gwybed** gnat
gwybod (am) 1 *be.* (**gwn**) to know. *gw.* At. Berfau. 2 *e.g. ll.* **-au** knowledge. **heb yn wybod (i)** without knowing, unwittingly
gwybodaeth *e.b. ll.* **-au** knowledge
gwych *a.* fine, splendid; brilliant
gwydr *e.g. ll.* **-au** glass. **gwydr gwin** wineglass; **gwydr lliw** coloured glass, stained glass; **gwydr nadd** cut-glass; **tŷ gwydr** glasshouse

gwydrau *gw.* **gwydr, gwydryn**

gwydryn *e.g. ll.* **gwydrau**
drinking-glass. **gwydraid**
glassful

gŵydd 1 *e.b. ll.* **gwyddau**
goose. **croen gŵydd** goose-
flesh. **2** *e.g.* presence. **yng
ngŵydd fy ngelynion** in the
presence of my enemies

gwyddbwyll *e.b.* chess

Gwyddel *e.g. ll.* **-od, Gwyddyl**
Irishman

Gwyddeleg *e.g.* Irish
language

Gwyddeles *e.b. ll.* **-au**
Irishwoman

Gwyddelig *a.* Irish

gwyddoniaeth *e.b.* science

gwyddonol *a.* scientific

gwyddonydd *e.g. ll.*
gwyddonwyr scientist

gwyddor *e.b. ll.* **-ion**
rudiment, science: **yr wyddor**
the alphabet

gwyfyn *e.g. ll.* **-od** moth

gŵyl *e.b. ll.* **gwyliau** feast,
festival; holiday. **Gŵyl Dewi**
Saint David's Day. **gŵyl y
banc** bank holiday

gwylan *e.b. ll.* **-od** gull

gwyliadwrus *a.* watchful,
cautious

gwyliau *gw.* **gŵyl**

gwylio (dros, rhag) *be.*
(gwyliaf) to mind; watch
(over); to guard

gwyliwr *e.g. ll.* **gwylwyr**
sentry, guard, watchman

gwylnos *e.b. ll.* **-au** vigil,
watchnight

gwylwyr *gw.* **gwyliwr**

gwyll *e.g.* darkness

gwyllt *a.* wild, mad. **yn wyllt
gacwn** furiously cross, in a
mad rage

gwylltio: gwylltu *be.* **(gwylltiaf:
gwylltaf)** to lose one's
temper, to excite violently

gwymon *e.g.* seaweed

gwymp *gw.* **cwymp**

gwympo *gw.* **cwympo**

gwyn *a. ll.* **-ion** white; holy.
Gwlad y menig gwynion
Land of the white gloves
(*alluding to the frequent
presentation of white gloves
to assize judges in Wales,
when there were no cases for
trial*). *gw.* **cwyn.** *gw.* **gwen**

Gwynedd *e.b.* county and
local authority in N. W.
Wales

gwynegon *e.g.* rheumatism
(*S.W.*)

gwynegu *be.* **(gwynegaf)** to
ache (*S.W.*)

gwynfa *e.b.* paradise

gwynfyd *e.g. ll.* **-au**
blessedness, bliss. **Y
Gwynfydau** The Beatitudes

gwyngalch *e.g.* white-lime,
whitewash

gwynion *gw.* **cwyn.** *gw.* **gwyn**

gwynnu *be.* **(gwynnaf)** to
whiten, to bleach

gwynt *e.g. ll.* **-oedd** wind;
smell. **a'i wynt yn ei ddwrn**
breathless, panting, having
one's heart in one's mouth;
prin ei wynt short of breath

gwyntog

gwyntog *a.* windy;
bombastic; **hirwyntog**
longwinded

gwyr *gw.* cwyr

Gŵyr *e.b.* Gower

gŵyr 1 *a.* crooked, inclined,
aslant. 2 *bf.* he/she/it knows.
gw. gwybod

gwŷr *gw.* gŵr

gwyrdd 1 *a. ll.* -ion green.
2 *e.g.* green. *gw.* gwerdd

gwyriad *e.g. ll.* -au deviation

gwyro: gwyrio *be.* (gwyraf:
gwyriaf) to bend, to deviate,
to incline, to swerve

gwyrth *e.b. ll.* -iau miracle

gwyrthiol *a.* miraculous.
Roedd hi'n wyrthiol ei weld
It was miraculous to see him

gwyryf *e.b. ll.* -on virgin

gwysion *gw.* gwŷs

gwŷs *e.b. ll.* gwysion
summons

gwystl *e.g. ll.* -on hostage;
pledge.

gwywo *be.* (gwywaf) to
wither, to fade

gychod *gw.* cwch

gychwyn *gw.* cychwyn

gyd, i *ad.* (*always immediately
follows the noun to which it
refers*) all. **Roedd y plant i
gyd yn dost** All the children
were ill; **Mae'r cŵn i gyd yma**
All the dogs are here

gyda: gydag *ardd.* together
with; in company of; **gyda'i
gilydd** all together, not
gyda'u gilydd

gydadrodd *gw.* cydadrodd

gydio *gw.* cydio

gydnabod *gw.* cydnabod

gyddfau *gw.* gwddf

gyfaill *gw.* cyfaill

gyfan *gw.* cyfan

gyfangwbl *gw.* cyfangwbl

gyfansoddi *gw.* cyfansoddi

gyfansoddwr *gw.*
cyfansoddwr

gyfanswm *gw.* cyfanswm

gyfarch *gw.* cyfarch

gyfarfod *gw.* cyfarfod

gyfarwyddiadur *gw.*
cyfarwyddiadur

gyfarwyddo *gw.* cyfarwyddo

gyfarwyddwr *gw.*
cyfarwyddwr

gyfeilles *gw.* cyfeilles

gyfeillgar *gw.* cyfeillgar

gyfeillgarwch *gw.*
cyfeillgarwch

gyfeillion *gw.* cyfaill

gyfeiriad *gw.* cyfeiriad

gyfeirio *gw.* cyfeirio

gyfenw *gw.* cyfenw

gyferbyn (â) *ardd.* opposite.
yn y tŷ gyferbyn in the
opposite house; **gyferbyn â'n
tŷ ni** opposite our house

gyfiawn *gw.* cyfiawn

gyfiawnder *gw.* cyfiawnder

gyfieithiad *gw.* cyfieithiad

gyfieithu *gw.* cyfieithu

gyfieithydd *gw.* cyfieithydd

gyfle *gw.* cyfle

gyfleu *gw.* cyfleu

gyfleus *gw.* cyfleus

gyflog *gw.* cyflog

gyflogi *gw.* cyflogi

gyflogwr *gw.* cyflogwr

gyflwr *gw*. cyflwr

gyflwyno *gw*. cyflwyno

gyflym *gw*. cyflym

gyflymach *gw*. cyflym

gyflymaf *gw*. cyflym

gyflymder *gw*. cyflymder

gyflymed *gw*. cyflym

gyflymu *gw*. cyflymu

gyflymydd *gw*. cyflymydd

gyfnither *gw*. cyfnither

gyfnod *gw*. cyfnod

gyfoeth *gw*. cyfoeth

gyfoethog *gw*. cyfoethog

gyfraith *gw*. cyfraith

gyfrannu *gw*. cyfrannu

gyfreithiwr *gw*. cyfreithiwr

gyfres *gw*. cyfres

gyfrif *gw*. cyfrif

gyfrifiadur *gw*. cyfrifiadur

gyfrifol *gw*. cyfrifol

gyfrifoldeb *gw*. cyfrifoldeb

gyfrifydd *gw*. cyfrifydd

gyfrinach *gw*. cyfrinach

gyfrinachol *gw*. cyfrinachol

gyfrol *gw*. cyfrol

gyfrwng *gw*. cyfrwng

gyfrwys *gw*. cyfrwys

gyfun *gw*. cyfun

gyfuwch *gw*. uchel

gyfweld *gw*. cyfweld

gyfweliad *gw*. cyfweliad

gyfyng *gw*. cyfyng

gyfyngiad *gw*. cyfyngiad

gyfyngu *gw*. cyfyngu

gyfystyr *gw*. cyfystyr

gyfforddus *gw*. cyfforddus

gyffredin *gw*. cyffredin

gyffrous *gw*. cyffrous

gyffur *gw*. cyffur

gyffwrdd *gw*. cyffwrdd

gygau *gw*. gwg

gyngerdd *gw*. cyngerdd

gynghori *gw*. cynghori

gynghorwr *gw*. cynghorwr

gyngor *gw*. cyngor

gyhoedd *gw*. cyhoedd

gyhoeddi *gw*. cyhoeddi

gyhoeddiad *gw*. cyhoeddiad

gyhoeddus *gw*. cyhoeddus

gyhoeddusrwydd *gw*.
 cyhoeddusrwydd

gyhoeddwr *gw*. cyhoeddwr

gyhyd *gw*. cyhyd

gyhyrog *gw*. cyhyrog

gylch *gw*. cylch

gylchgrawn *gw*. cylchgrawn

gylchlythyr *gw*. cylchlythyr

gyll *gw*. cyll

gyllell *gw*. cyllell

gyllyll *gw*. cyllell

gymaint *gw*. mawr

gymal *gw*. cymal

gymanfa *gw*. cymanfa

gymdeithas *gw*. cymdeithas

gymdeithaseg *gw*.
 cymdeithaseg

gymdogion *gw*. cymydog

gymeriad *gw*. cymeriad

gymharu *gw*. cymharu

gymhleth *gw*. cymhleth

gymhlethdod *gw*.
 cymhlethdod

gymhlethu *gw*. cymhlethu

gymoedd *gw*. cwm

gymorth *gw*. cymorth

Gymraeg *gw*. Cymraeg

Gymraes *gw*. Cymraes

Gymreictod *gw*. Cymreictod

Gymreig *gw*. Cymreig

Gymreiges *gw*. Cymraes

Gymro

Gymro *gw.* **Cymro**
Gymru *gw.* **Cymru**
Gymry *gw.* **Cymro**
gymryd *gw.* **cymryd**
gymundeb *gw.* **cymundeb**
gymuned *gw.* **cymuned**
gymwynas *gw.* **cymwynas**
gymydog *gw.* **cymydog**
gymylau *gw.* **cwmwl**
gymylog *gw.* **cymylog**
gymysg *gw.* **cymysg**
gymysgu *gw.* **cymysgu**
gymysgwch *gw.* **cymysgwch**
gyn *gw.* **cyn**
gynaeafau *gw.* **cynhaeaf**
gynau *gw.* **gŵn**
gynddrwg *gw.* **cynddrwg**
gynffon *gw.* **cynffon**
gynhadledd *gw.* **cynhadledd**
gynhaeaf *gw.* **cynhaeaf**
gynhesu *gw.* **cynhesu**
gynhyrfus *gw.* **cynhyrfus**
gynigion *gw.* **cynnig**
gynilion *gw.* **cynilion**
gynilo *gw.* **cynilo**
gynllun *gw.* **cynllun**
gynllunio *gw.* **cynllunio**
gynlluniwr *gw.* **cynlluniwr**
gynllunydd *gw.* **cynlluniwr**
gynnal *gw.* **cynnal**
gynnar *gw.* **cynnar**
gynnau *ad.* a short while ago, just now. *gw.* **gwn**
gynnes *gw.* **cynnes**
gynnig *gw.* **cynnig**
gynradd *gw.* **cynradd**
gynt *ad.* formerly; *née*; long since; ages ago. **Rhian Smith (gynt Jones)** Rhian Smith (*née* Jones); **yr hen ddyddiau**

gynt the old days, ages ago. *gw.* **cynnar**
gyntaf *gw.* **cynnar**
gynted *gw.* **cynnar**
gyntedd *gw.* **cyntedd**
gynulleidfa *gw.* **cynulleidfa**
gynulliad *gw.* **cynulliad**
gyrddau *gw.* **cwrdd**
gyrfa *e.b.* *ll.* -oedd, gyrfeydd race; career; course
gyrfeydd *gw.* **gyrfa**
gyrff *gw.* **corff**
gyrion *gw.* **cwr**
gyrliog *gw.* **cyrliog**
gyrn *gw.* **corn**
gyrraedd *gw.* **cyrraedd**
gyrrau *gw.* **cwr**
gyrru *be.* **(gyrraf)** to drive; to send; to push
gyrrwr *e.g.* *ll.* **gyrwyr** driver; sender
gyrwyr *gw.* **gyrrwr**
gysglyd *gw.* **cysglyd**
gysgod *gw.* **cysgod**
gysgodi *gw.* **cysgodi**
gysgu *gw.* **cysgu**
gystadleuaeth *gw.* **cystadleuaeth**
gystadleuwr *gw.* **cystadleuwr**
gystadleuydd *gw.* **cystadleuwr**
gystadlu *gw.* **cystadlu**
gystal *gw.* **da**
gystymau *gw.* **cwstwm**
gysur *gw.* **cysur**
gysuro *gw.* **cysuro**
gysurus *gw.* **cysurus**
gyswllt *gw.* **cyswllt**
gytgan *gw.* **cytgan**
gytsain *gw.* **cytsain**
gytundeb *gw.* **cytundeb**

gytuno *gw*. cytuno
gyw *gw*. cyw
gywaith *gw*. cywaith
gywir *gw*. cywir
gywiriad *gw*. cywiriad
gywiro *gw*. cywiro

NG

ngadael *gw*. gadael
ngaeaf *gw*. gaeaf
ngafael *gw*. gafael
ngafr *gw*. gafr
ngair *gw*. gair
ngalar *gw*. galar
ngalw *gw*. galw
ngalwad *gw*. galwad
ngalwedigaeth *gw*.
 galwedigaeth
ngalwyn *gw*. galwyn
ngallu *gw*. gallu
ngardd *gw*. gardd
ngarddio *gw*. garddio
ngarddwr *gw*. garddwr
ngarej *gw*. garej
ngarlleg *gw*. garlleg
ngât *gw*. gât
ngefeilliaid *gw*. gefell
ngeirfa *gw*. geirfa
ngeiriadur *gw*. geiriadur
ngeiriau *gw*. gair
ngelyn *gw*. gelyn
ngên *gw*. gên
ngenau *gw*. gên, genau
ngenetaidd *gw*. genetig
ngenetig *gw*. genetig
ngeneth *gw*. geneth
ngeneuau *gw*. genau
ngeni *gw*. geni
ngenyn *gw*. genyn

ngenynnol *gw*. genetig
ngêr *gw*. gêr
ngewyn *gw*. gewyn
nghaban *gw*. caban
nghacen *gw*. cacen
nghacwn *gw*. cacynen
nghacynen *gw*. cacynen
nghadach *gw*. cadach
nghadair *gw*. cadair
nghadeirio *gw*. cadeirio
nghadeirydd *gw*. cadeirydd
nghadnawes *gw*. cadno
nghadno *gw*. cadno
nghadw *gw*. cadw
nghadwyn *gw*. cadwyn
nghadwyno *gw*. cadwyno
nghae *gw*. cae
nghael *gw*. cael
Nghaer *gw*. Caer
nghaer *gw*. caer
Nghaerdydd *gw*. Caerdydd
Nghaerfyrddin *gw*.
 Caerfyrddin
Nghaergybi *gw*. Caergybi
Nghaerloyw *gw*. Caerloyw
Nghaersalem *gw*. Caersalem
nghaets *gw*. caets
nghaffe *gw*. caffe
nghangen *gw*. cangen
nghais *gw*. cais
nghalan *gw*. calan
nghaledi *gw*. caledi
nghaledu *gw*. caledu
nghaledwch *gw*. caledwch
nghalendr *gw*. calendr
nghalennig *gw*. calennig
nghalon *gw*. calon
ngham *gw*. cam
nghamarwain *gw*. camarwain
nghamddeall *gw*. camddeall

nghamera

nghamera *gw.* camera
nghamp *gw.* camp
nghampfa *gw.* campfa
nghampwaith *gw.* campwaith
nghamsyniad *gw.* camsyniad
nghan *gw.* can
nghân *gw.* cân
nghaneuon *gw.* cân
nghanfed *gw.* canfed
nghanhwyllau *gw.* cannwyll
nghanhwyllbren *gw.*
 canhwyllbren
nghaniad *gw.* caniad
nghaniadaeth *gw.* caniadaeth
nghaniadau *gw.* cân. *gw.*
 caniad
nghaniatâd *gw.* caniatâd
nghaniatáu *gw.* caniatáu
nghaniedydd *gw.* caniedydd
nghanmlwydd *gw.* canmlwydd
nghanmol *gw.* canmol
nghanmoliaeth *gw.*
 canmoliaeth
nghannoedd *gw.* cant
nghannwyll *gw.* cannwyll
nghanol *gw.* canol
nghanolbarth *gw.* canolbarth
nghanoldir *gw.* canoldir
nghanolfan *gw.* canolfan
nghanolwr *gw.* canolwr
nghanradd *gw.* canradd
nghanran *gw.* canran
nghanrif *gw.* canrif
nghanrifau: nghanrifoedd *gw.*
 canrif
nghant *gw.* cant
nghantor *gw.* cantor
nghantores *gw.* cantores
nghanu *gw.* canu
nghanŵ *gw.* canŵ

nghanŵio *gw.* canŵio
nghanwr *gw.* canwr
nghap *gw.* cap
nghapel *gw.* capel
nghapten *gw.* capten
nghar *gw.* car
ngharafán *gw.* carafán
ngharafana *gw.* carafana
ngharco *gw.* carco
ngharchar *gw.* carchar
ngharcharor *gw.* carcharor
ngharcharu *gw.* carcharu
nghardiau *gw.* cerdyn
ngharedigrwydd *gw.*
 caredigrwydd
nghariad *gw.* cariad
nghariadon *gw.* cariad
nghariadus *gw.* cariadus
nghario *gw.* cario
ngharol *gw.* carol
ngharped *gw.* carped
ngharreg *gw.* carreg
nghartref *gw.* cartref
nghartrefi *gw.* cartref
nghartrefu *gw.* cartrefu
ngharu *gw.* caru
ngharwriaeth *gw.* carwriaeth
nghas *gw.* cas
nghasáu *gw.* casáu
nghasgen *gw.* casgen
nghasgliad *gw.* casgliad
nghasglu *gw.* casglu
Nghas-gwent *gw.* Cas-gwent
Nghasllwchwr *gw.* Casllwchwr
Nghasnewydd *gw.*
 Casnewydd
nghastell *gw.* castell
Nghastell-nedd *gw.* Castell-
 nedd
nghath *gw.* cath

nghau *gw*. cau
nghawl *gw*. cawl
nghawod *gw*. cawod
nghawr *gw*. cawr
nghaws *gw*. caws
nghefn *gw*. cefn
nghefnder *gw*. cefnder
nghefndir *gw*. cefndir
nghefndiroedd *gw*. cefndir
nghefndyr *gw*. cefnder
nghefnogi *gw*. cefnogi
nghefnu *gw*. cefnu
nghefnwr *gw*. cefnwr
nghefnwyr *gw*. cefnwr
ngheffyl *gw*. ceffyl
ngheg *gw*. ceg
nghegin *gw*. cegin
nghei *gw*. cei
ngheidwad *gw*. ceidwad
ngheiliog *gw*. ceiliog
Ngheinewydd *gw*. Ceinewydd
ngheiniog *gw*. ceiniog
ngheiriosen *gw*. ceiriosen
ngheisio *gw*. ceisio
nghelf *gw*. celf
nghelfi *gw*. celficyn
nghelficyn *gw*. celficyn
nghelwydd *gw*. celwydd
nghelyn *gw*. celynnen
nghelynnen *gw*. celynnen
nghell *gw*. cell
nghellau: nghelloedd *gw*. cell
nghemeg *gw*. cemeg
nghenedl *gw*. cenedl
nghenedlaetholdeb *gw*.
 cenedlaetholdeb
nghenedlaetholwr *gw*.
 cenedlaetholwr
nghenhadaeth *gw*.
 cenhadaeth

nghenhadon *gw*. cenhadwr
nghenhadu *gw*. cenhadu
nghenhadwr *gw*. cenhadwr
nghenhedlaeth *gw*.
 cenhedlaeth
nghenhinen *gw*. cenhinen
nghennin *gw*. cennin
ngherdyn *gw*. cerdyn
ngherdd *gw*. cerdd
ngherddor *gw*. cerddor
ngherddorfa *gw*. cerddorfa
ngherddoriaeth *gw*.
 cerddoriaeth
ngherddwr *gw*. cerddwr
ngherfio *gw*. cerfio
ngherflun *gw*. cerflun
ngherrig *gw*. carreg
nghesair *gw*. cesair
nghestyll *gw*. castell
nghewri *gw*. cawr
nghewyn *gw*. cewyn
ngheyrydd *gw*. caer
nghi *gw*. ci
nghig *gw*. cig
nghigydd *gw*. cigydd
nghinio *gw*. cinio
nghipolwg *gw*. cipolwg
nghist *gw*. cist
nghlaf *gw*. claf
nghlai *gw*. clai
nghlasur *gw*. clasur
nghlawdd *gw*. clawdd
nghlawr *gw*. clawr
nghlebran *gw*. clebran
nghledr *gw*. cledr
nghlefyd *gw*. clefyd
nghleifion *gw*. claf
nghlêr *gw*. cleren
nghlerc *gw*. clerc
nghleren *gw*. cleren

nghlirio

nghlirio *gw.* clirio
nghlo *gw.* clo
nghloc *gw.* cloc
nghloch *gw.* cloch
nghlod *gw.* clod
nghlodfori *gw.* clodfori
nghloddiau *gw.* clawdd
nghloffi *gw.* cloffi
nghlogwyn *gw.* clogwyn
nghlogyn *gw.* clogyn
nghloi *gw.* cloi
nghlorian *gw.* clorian
nghloriau *gw.* clawr
nghlown *gw.* clown
nghlun *gw.* clun
nghlust *gw.* clust
nghlustdlws *gw.*clustdlws
nghlustog *gw.* clustog
nghlwb *gw.* clwb
nghlwm *gw.* clwm
nghlwtyn *gw.* clwtyn
Nghlwyd *gw.* Clwyd
nghlwyd *gw.* clwyd
nghlwydau: nghlwydi *gw.*
 clwyd
nghlwyf *gw.* clwyf
nghlychau *gw.* cloch
nghlymau *gw.* clwm
nghlymu *gw.* clymu
nghlytiau *gw.* clwtyn
nghlyw *gw.* clyw
nghlywed *gw.* clywed
nghnau *gw.* cneuen
nghneuen *gw.* cneuen
nghnoc *gw.* cnoc
nghnocio *gw.* cnocio
nghnoi *gw.* cnoi
nghoban *gw.* coban
nghoch *gw.* coch
nghodi *gw.* codi

nghoed *gw.* coeden
Nghoed-duon *gw.* Coed-duon
nghoeden *gw.* coeden
nghoedwig *gw.* coedwig
nghoes *gw.* coes
nghof *gw.* cof
nghofbin *gw.* cofbin
nghofion *gw.* cof
nghofleidio *gw.* cofleidio
nghofrestr *gw.* cofrestr
nghofrestru *gw.* cofrestru
nghoffi *gw.* coffi
nghog *gw.* cog
nghoginio *gw.* coginio
nghogydd *gw.* cogydd
ngholeg *gw.* coleg
ngholer *gw.* coler
nghololofn *gw.* colofn
nghololuro *gw.* coluro
nghololled *gw.* colled
nghololen *gw.* collen
nghololli *gw.* colli
nghopïo *gw.* copïo
nghopyn *gw.* copyn
nghôr *gw.* côr
nghorau *gw.* côr
nghordyn *gw.* cordyn
nghorff *gw.* corff
nghorgi *gw.* corgi
nghorn *gw.* corn
nghornel *gw.* cornel
nghoron *gw.* coron
nghoroni *gw.* coroni
nghorryn *gw.* corryn
nghosb *gw.* cosb
nghosbi *gw.* cosbi
nghot *gw.* cot
nghôt *gw.* cot
nghotwm *gw.* cotwm
nghrac *gw.* crac

nghrachach *gw*. crachach
nghrafu *gw*. crafu
nghragen *gw*. cragen
nghraig *gw*. craig
nghrasu *gw*. crasu
nghredu *gw*. credu
nghrefydd *gw*. crefydd
nghrefft *gw*. crefft
nghrefftwr *gw*. crefftwr
nghregyn *gw*. cragen
nghreigiau *gw*. craig
nghreision *gw*. creision
nghrempog *gw*. crempog
nghreulondeb *gw*.
  creulondeb
nghri *gw*. cri
nghrib *gw*. crib
nghribo *gw*. cribo
nghriced *gw*. criced
nghricedwr *gw*. cricedwr
nghricsyn *gw*. cricsyn
nghrio *gw*. crio
Nghristion *gw*. Cristion
Nghristnogion *gw*. Cristion
nghriw *gw*. criw
nghroen *gw*. croen
nghroes *gw*. croes
nghroesair *gw*. croesair
nghroesau *gw*. croes
nghroesawu *gw*. croesawu
nghroesfan *gw*. croesfan
nghroesffordd *gw*.
  croesffordd
nghroesholi *gw*. croesholi
nghroesi *gw*. croesi
nghroeso *gw*. croeso
nghronfa *gw*. cronfa
nghronfeydd *gw*. cronfa
nghrud *gw*. crud
nghrwst *gw*. crwst

nghrwyn *gw*. croen
nghryd *gw*. cryd
nghrynodeb *gw*. crynodeb
nghrynu *gw*. crynu
nghrys *gw*. crys
nghrystiau *gw*. crwst, crystyn
nghrystyn *gw*. crystyn
nghuddio *gw*. cuddio
nghuro *gw*. curo
nghusan *gw*. cusan
nghusanu *gw*. cusanu
nghwb *gw*. cwb
nghwbl *gw*. cwbl
nghwcw *gw*. cwcw
nghwch *gw*. cwch
nghwd *gw*. cwd
nghwdyn *gw*. cwdyn
nghweryl *gw*. cweryl
nghwestiwn *gw*. cwestiwn
nghwestiyna *gw*. cwestiyna
nghwestiynau *gw*. cwestiwn
nghwlwm *gw*. cwlwm
nghwm *gw*. cwm
nghwmni *gw*. cwmni
nghwmnïau: nghwmnïoedd
  gw. cwmni
nghwmwl *gw*. cwmwl
nghŵn *gw*. ci
nghwningen *gw*. cwningen
nghwningod *gw*. cwningen
nghwpan *gw*. cwpan
nghwpla *gw*. cwpla
nghwpwrdd *gw*. cwpwrdd
nghwr *gw*. cwr
nghwrdd *gw*. cwrdd
nghwrs *gw*. cwrs
nghwrw *gw*. cwrw
nghwsg *gw*. cwsg
nghwsmer *gw*. cwsmer
nghwstwm *gw*. cwstwm

nghwt

nghwt *gw.* cwt
nghwymp *gw.* cwymp
nghwyn *gw.* cwyn
nghwyno *gw.* cwyno
nghwyr *gw.* cwyr
nghychod *gw.* cwch
nghychwyn *gw.* cychwyn
nghydadrodd *gw.* cydadrodd
nghydau *gw.* cwd, cwdyn
nghydnabod *gw.* cydnabod
nghyfaill *gw.* cyfaill
nghyfan *gw.* cyfan
nghyfansoddi *gw.* cyfansoddi
nghyfansoddwr *gw.*
 cyfansoddwr
nghyfanswm *gw.* cyfanswm
nghyfarch *gw.* cyfarch
nghyfarfod *gw.* cyfarfod
nghyfarfodydd *gw.* cyfarfod
nghyfarwyddiadur *gw.*
 cyfarwyddiadur
nghyfarwyddo *gw.*
 cyfarwyddo
nghyfarwyddwr *gw.*
 cyfarwyddwr
nghyfeilles *gw.* cyfeilles
nghyfeillgarwch *gw.*
 cyfeillgarwch
nghyfeillion *gw.* cyfaill
nghyfeiriad *gw.* cyfeiriad
nghyfeirio *gw.* cyfeirio
nghyfenw *gw.* cyfenw
nghyfiawnder *gw.* cyfiawnder
nghyfieithiad *gw.* cyfieithiad
nghyfieithu *gw.* cyfieithu
nghyfieithydd *gw.* cyfieithydd
nghyfle *gw.* cyfle
nghyflog *gw.* cyflog
nghyflogi *gw.* cyflogi
nghyflogwr *gw.* cyflogwr

nghyflwr *gw.* cyflwr
nghyflwyno *gw.* cyflwyno
nghyflymder *gw.* cyflymder
nghyflymu *gw.* cyflymu
nghyflymydd *gw.* cyflymydd
nghyfnither *gw.* cyfnither
nghyfoeth *gw.* cyfoeth
nghyfraith *gw.* cyfraith
nghyfreithiwr *gw.* cyfreithiwr
nghyfres *gw.* cyfres
nghyfrif *gw.* cyfrif
nghyfrifiadur *gw.* cyfrifiadur
nghyfrifiannell *gw.*
 cyfrifiannell
nghyfrifoldeb *gw.* cyfrifoldeb
nghyfrifydd *gw.* cyfrifydd
nghyfrinach *gw.* cyfrinach
nghyfrol *gw.* cyfrol
nghyfrwng *gw.* cyfrwng
nghyfyngiad *gw.* cyfyngiad
nghyfweliad *gw.* cyfweliad
nghyfyngu *gw.* cyfyngu
nghyffur *gw.* cyffur
nghyffwrdd *gw.* cyffwrdd
nghyngerdd *gw.* cyngerdd
nghynghori *gw.* cynghori
nghynghorwr *gw.* cynghorwr
nghynghrair *gw.* cynghrair
nghyngor *gw.* cyngor
nghyhoeddi *gw.* cyhoeddi
nghyhoeddiad *gw.*
 cyhoeddiad
nghyhoeddusrwydd *gw.*
 cyhoeddusrwydd
nghyhoeddwr *gw.* cyhoeddwr
nghylch *gw.* cylch
nghylchfan *gw.* cylchfan
nghylchgrawn *gw.*
 cylchgrawn
nghylchgronau *gw.*
 cylchgrawn

nghylchlythyr *gw.* cylchlythyr
nghyll *gw.* collen
nghyllell *gw.* cyllell
nghyllyll *gw.* cyllell
nghymal *gw.* cymal
nghymanfa *gw.* cymanfa
nghymdeithas *gw.*
 cymdeithas
nghymdeithaseg *gw.*
 cymdeithaseg
nghymdogion *gw.* cymydog
nghymeriad *gw.* cymeriad
nghymharu *gw.* cymharu
nghymhlethdod *gw.*
 cymhlethdod
nghymoedd *gw.* cwm
nghymorth *gw.* cymorth
Nghymraeg *gw.* Cymraeg
Nghymraes *gw.* Cymraes
Nghymreictod *gw.* Cymreictod
Nghymreiges *gw.* Cymreiges
Nghymro *gw.* Cymro
Nghymru *gw.* Cymru
Nghymry *gw.* Cymro
nghymryd *gw.* cymryd
nghymundeb *gw.* cymundeb
nghymwynas *gw.* cymwynas
nghymydog *gw.* cymydog
nghymylau *gw.* cwmwl
nghymysgu *gw.* cymysgu
nghymysgwch *gw.*
 cymysgwch
nghyn- *gw.* cyn-
nghynaeafau *gw.* cynhaeaf
nghynffon *gw.* cynffon
nghynhadledd *gw.*
 cynhadledd
nghynhaeaf *gw.* cynhaeaf
nghynhesu *gw.* cynhesu
nghynilion *gw.* cynilion

nghynllun *gw.* cynllun
nghynllunio *gw.* cynllunio
nghynlluniwr *gw.* cynlluniwr
nghynnal *gw.* cynnal
nghynnig *gw.* cynnig
nghynnwys *gw.* cynnwys
nghynorthwywr *gw.*
 cynorthwywr
nghynorthwy-ydd *gw.*
 cynorthwy-ydd
nghyntaf *gw.* cyntaf
nghyntedd *gw.* cyntedd
nghynulleidfa *gw.* cynulleidfa
nghypyrddau *gw.* cwpwrdd
nghyrddau *gw.* cwrdd
nghyrff *gw.* corff
nghyrn *gw.* corn
nghyrraedd *gw.* cyrraedd
nghyrsau: nghyrsiau *gw.* cwrs
nghysgod *gw.* cysgod
nghysgodi *gw.* cysgodi
nghysgodion *gw.* cysgod
nghysgu *gw.* cysgu
nghystadlaethau *gw.*
 cystadleuaeth
nghystadleuaeth *gw.*
 cystadleuaeth
nghystadleuwr *gw.*
 cystadleuwr
nghystadlu *gw.* cystadlu
nghystymau *gw.* cwstwm
nghysur *gw.* cysur
nghysuro *gw.* cysuro
nghyswllt *gw.* cyswllt
nghytgan *gw.* cytgan
nghytsain *gw.* cytsain
nghytundeb *gw.* cytundeb
nghytuno *gw.* cytuno
nghyw *gw.* cyw
nghywaith *gw.* cywaith

nghywiriad

nghywiriad *gw*. cywiriad
nghywiro *gw*. cywiro
nglan *gw*. glan
nglân *gw*. glân
nglanhau *gw*. glanhau
nglanio *gw*. glanio
nglannau *gw*. glan
nglas *gw*. glas
nglaswelltyn *gw*. glaswelltyn
nglaw *gw*. glaw
nglendid *gw*. glendid
nglin *gw*. glin
nglo *gw*. glo
nglofa *gw*. glofa
nglöwr *gw*. glöwr
nglöyn byw *gw*. glöyn byw
nglud *gw*. glud
ngludio *gw*. gludio
ngludo *gw*. gludio
nglyn *gw*. glyn
nglynu *gw*. glynu
ngobaith *gw*. gobaith
ngobeithion *gw*. gobaith
ngobennydd *gw*. gobennydd
ngodre *gw*. godre
ngodro *gw*. godro
ngoddef *gw*. goddef
ngoddrych *gw*. goddrych
ngof *gw*. gof
ngofaint *gw*. gof
ngofal *gw*. gofal
ngofalwr *gw*. gofalwr
ngofid *gw*. gofid
ngofidio *gw*. gofidio
ngofod *gw*. gofod
ngofodwr *gw*. gofodwr
ngofynion *gw*. gofyn
ngogledd *gw*. gogledd
ngogleisio *gw*. gogleisio
ngogogiant *gw*. gogoniant

ngôl *gw*. gôl
ngolau *gw*. golau
ngolchi *gw*. golchi
ngoleudy *gw*. goleudy
ngoleuni *gw*. goleuni
ngoleuo *gw*. goleuo
ngolud *gw*. golud
ngolwg *gw*. golwg
ngolygfa *gw*. golygfa
ngolygfeydd *gw*. golygfa
ngolygon *gw*. golwg
ngolygydd *gw*. golygydd
ngollwng *gw*. gollwng
ngorau *gw*. gorau
ngorchfygu *gw*. gorchfygu
ngorchymyn *gw*. gorchymyn
ngorfodaeth *gw*. gorfodaeth
ngorfodi *gw*. gorfodi
Ngorffennaf *gw*. Gorffennaf
ngorffennol *gw*. gorffennol
ngorffwys *gw*. gorffwys
ngorffwyso *gw*. gorffwyso
ngorllewin *gw*. gorllewin
ngornest *gw*. gornest
ngorsaf *gw*. gorsaf
ngorsedd *gw*. gorsedd
ngorwel *gw*. gorwel
ngosod *gw*. gosod
ngostwng *gw*. gostwng
ngostyngiad *gw*. gostyngiad
ngradd *gw*. gradd
ngraddfa *gw*. graddfa
ngramadeg *gw*. gramadeg
ngrant *gw*. grant
ngras *gw*. gras
ngrawnffrwyth *gw*.
  grawnffrwyth
ngris *gw*. gris
Ngroeg *gw*. Groeg
ngrudd *gw*. grudd

ngwên

ngrug *gw.* grug
ngrŵp *gw.* grŵp
ngrym *gw.* grym
ngwadu *gw.* gwadu
ngwaed *gw.* gwaed
ngwaedu *gw.* gwaedu
ngwaedd *gw.* gwaedd
ngwaelod *gw.* gwaelod
ngwaelodion *gw.* gwaelod
ngwaethaf *gw.* gwaethaf
ngwagedd *gw.* gwagedd
ngwagle *gw.* gwagle
ngwahanol *gw.* gwahanol
ngwahodd *gw.* gwahodd
ngwahoddedigion *gw.*
 gwahoddedig
ngwahoddiad *gw.*
 gwahoddiad
ngwair *gw.* gwair
ngwaith *gw.* gwaith
ngwal *gw.* gwal
ngwâl *gw.* gwâl
ngwalau *gw.* gwâl
ngwaliau *gw.* gwal
ngwall *gw.* gwall
ngwallt *gw.* gwallt
ngwanwyn *gw.* gwanwyn
ngwar *gw.* gwar
ngwarchod *gw.* gwarchod
ngwaredu *gw.* gwaredu
ngwaredwr *gw.* gwaredwr
ngwario *gw.* gwario
ngwartheg *gw.* gwartheg
ngwas *gw.* gwas
ngwasanaeth *gw.* gwasanaeth
ngwasanaethu *gw.*
 gwasanaethu
ngwasg *gw.* gwasg
ngwasgedd *gw.* gwasgedd
ngwasgfa *gw.* gwasgfa

ngwasgod *gw.* gwasgod
ngwasgu *gw.* gwasgu
ngwastraff *gw.* gwastraff
ngwastraffu *gw.* gwastraffu
ngwau *gw.* gwau
ngwaun *gw.* gwaun
ngwawdio *gw.* gwawdio
ngwawr *gw.* gwawr
ngwdihŵ *gw.* gwdihŵ
ngwddf *gw.* gwddf
ngwddwg *gw.* gwddwg
ngweddi *gw.* gweddi
ngweddill *gw.* gweddill
ngweddïo *gw.* gweddïo
ngwefus *gw.* gwefus
ngweiddi *gw.* gweiddi
ngweigion *gw.* gwag
ngweiniaid *gw.* gwan
ngweinidog *gw.* gweinidog
ngweinion *gw.* gwan
ngweinydd *gw.* gweinydd
ngweinyddes *gw.* gweinyddes
ngweiriau *gw.* gwair
ngweisg *gw.* gwasg
ngweision *gw.* gwas
ngweithdy *gw.* gweithdy
ngweithiau *gw.* gwaith
ngweithio *gw.* gweithio
ngweithiwr *gw.* gweithiwr
ngweithred *gw.* gweithred
ngweithwyr *gw.* gweithiwr
ngwelâu *gw.* gwely
ngweld *gw.* gweld
ngwely *gw.* gwely
ngwelyau *gw.* gwely
ngwell *gw.* da
ngwella *gw.* gwella
ngwellt *gw.* gwellt, gwelltyn
ngwelltyn *gw.* gwelltyn
ngwên *gw.* gwên

ngwenau

ngwenau *gw*. gwên
ngwendid *gw*. gwendid
Ngwener *gw*. Gwener
ngwenith *gw*. gwenith
ngwennol *gw*. gwennol
Ngwent *gw*. Gwent
ngwenu *gw*. gwenu
ngwenwyn *gw*. gwenwyn
ngwenynen *gw*. gwenynen
ngwêr *gw*. gwêr
ngwerin *gw*. gwerin
ngweriniaeth *gw*. gweriniaeth
ngwers *gw*. gwers
ngwerslyfr *gw*. gwerslyfr
ngwersyll *gw*. gwersyll
ngwerth *gw*. gwerth
ngwerthfawrogi *gw*.
 gwerthfawrogi
ngwerthfawrogiad *gw*.
 gwerthfawrogiad
ngwerthiant *gw*. gwerthiant
ngwerthu *gw*. gwerthu
ngwerthwr *gw*. gwerthwr
ngwestai *gw*. gwestai, gwesty
ngwesteion *gw*. gwestai
ngwesteiwr *gw*. gwesteiwr
ngwesteiwraig *gw*. gwesteiwr
ngwesty *gw*. gwesty
ngweu *gw*. gweu
ngweunydd *gw*. gwaun
ngwg *gw*. gwg
ngwgu *gw*. gwgu
ngwiail *gw*. gwialen
ngwialen *gw*. gwialen
ngwialennod *gw*. gwialen
ngwin *gw*. gwin
ngwir *gw*. gwir
ngwirionedd *gw*. gwirionedd
ngwisg *gw*. gwisg

ngwisgo *gw*. gwisgo
ngwiwer *gw*. gwiwer
ngwlad *gw*. gwlad
ngwladfa *gw*. gwladfa
ngwladgarwyr *gw*.
 gwladgarwr
ngwlân *gw*. gwlân
ngwlanen *gw*. gwlanen
ngwledydd *gw*. gwlad
ngwledd *gw*. gwledd
ngwledda *gw*. gwledda
ngwleidydd *gw*. gwleidydd
ngwleidyddiaeth *gw*.
 gwleidyddiaeth
ngwlff *gw*. gwlff
ngwlith *gw*. gwlith
ngwlybaniaeth *gw*.
 gwlybaniaeth
ngwlychu *gw*. gwlychu
ngwn *gw*. gwn
ngŵn *gw*. gŵn
ngwneud *gw*. gwneud
ngwniadyddes *gw*.
 gwniadyddes
ngwnïo *gw*. gwnïo
ngwniadyddes *gw*.
 gwniyddes
ngwobr *gw*. gwobr
ngwobrwyo *gw*. gwobrwyo
ngŵr *gw*. gŵr
ngwrach *gw*. gwrach
ngwragedd *gw*. gwraig
ngwraidd *gw*. gwreiddyn
ngwraig *gw*. gwraig
ngwrandawiad *gw*.
 gwrandawiad
ngwrandawr *gw*. gwrandawr
ngwrando *gw*. gwrando
ngwreichion *gw*.

ngyrwyr

gwreichionen
ngwreiddiau *gw.* gwreiddyn
ngwreiddio *gw.* gwreiddio
ngwreiddyn *gw.* gwreiddyn
ngwres *gw.* gwres
ngwresogi *gw.* gwresogi
ngwresogydd *gw.*
  gwresogydd
ngwrtaith *gw.* gwrtaith
ngwrthblaid *gw.* gwrthblaid
ngwrthdystio *gw.* gwrthdystio
ngwrthod *gw.* gwrthod
ngwrthrych *gw.* gwrthrych
ngwrthryfel *gw.* gwrthryfel
ngwrthwyneb *gw.*
  gwrthwyneb
ngwrthwynebu *gw.*
  gwrthwynebu
ngwrthwynebwr *gw.*
  gwrthwynebwr
ngwrthwynebydd *gw.*
  gwrthwynebwr
ngwrywgydiaeth *gw.*
  gwrywgydiaeth
ngwthiad *gw.* gwthiad
ngwthio *gw.* gwthio
ngwthiwr *gw.* gwthiwr
ngwybod *gw.* gwybod
ngwybodaeth *gw.*
  gwybodaeth
ngwydr *gw.* gwydr
ngwydrau *gw.* gwydr,
  gwydryn
ngwydryn *gw.* gwydryn
ngŵydd *gw.* gŵydd
ngwyddbwyll *gw.* gwyddbwyll
Ngwyddel *gw.* Gwyddel
Ngwyddeleg *gw.* Gwyddeleg
ngwyddoniaeth *gw.*
  gwyddoniaeth

ngwyddonydd *gw.*
  gwyddonydd
ngwyddor *gw.* gwyddor
ngwyfyn *gw.* gwyfyn
ngŵyl *gw.* gŵyl
ngwylan *gw.* gwylan
ngwyliau *gw.* gŵyl
ngwylio *gw.* gwylio
ngwyliwr *gw.* gwyliwr
ngwylnos *gw.* gwylnos
ngwylwyr *gw.* gwyliwr
ngwyll *gw.* gwyll
ngwylltio *gw.* gwylltio
ngwymon *gw.* gwymon
ngwyn *gw.* gwyn
Ngwynedd *gw.* Gwynedd
ngwynegon *gw.* gwynegon
ngwynfa *gw.* gwynfa
ngwynfyd *gw.* gwynfyd
ngwyngalch *gw.* gwyngalch
ngwynt *gw.* gwynt
ngwŷr *gw.* gŵr
ngwyrdd *gw.* gwyrdd
ngwyriad *gw.* gwyriad
ngwyro *gw.* gwyro
ngwyrth *gw.* gwyrth
ngwŷs *gw.* gwŷs
ngwystlon *gw.* gwystl
ngynau *gw.* gŵn
ngynnau *gw.* gwn
ngyrfa *gw.* gyrfa
ngyrfeydd *gw.* gyrfa
ngyrru *gw.* gyrru
ngyrrwr *gw.* gyrrwr
ngyrwyr *gw.* gyrrwr

had

H

In certain circumstances **h** is prefixed to words beginning with a vowel. If the word you require does not appear in this section ignore the initial **h** and look it up in the appropriate section, for example, **hawr**, see **awr**. See **Personal Pronouns** in the Supplement.

had *e. torf.* seed. *gw.* **hadyn, hedyn**

hadu *be.* **(hadaf)** to sow, to propagate; to run to seed

hadyn; hedyn *e.g. ll.* **had** a seed. *gw.* **had**

haearn 1 *e.g. ll.* **heyrn** iron. 2 *a.* of iron, iron

haeddu *be.* **(haeddaf)** to deserve, to merit. **haeddu ennill** to deserve to win; **haeddu clod** to deserve praise

hael *a.* generous, liberal

haelioni *e.g.* generosity, liberality

haelionus *a.* generous, liberal

haenen *e.b. ll.* **haenau** layer, stratum, seam (*of rock*)

haerllug *a.* impudent

haerllugrwydd *e.g.* cheek, impudence

haeru *be.* **(haeraf)** to assert, to affirm

haf *e.g. ll.* **-au** summer, summertime

hafaidd *a.* summer-like, summery

hafal 1 *a.* like, similar, equal. 2 **cydradd** *e.g. b. ll.* **-au: cyfartal** *e.g. b. ll.* **-au, -ion** equal. 3 *bf.* **bod yn hafal** (i) being equal (to)

hafaliad *e.g. ll.* **-au** equation. **hafaliad cydamserol** simultaneous equation; **hafaliad dwyradd** quadratic equation; **hafaliad syml** simple equation; **hafaliad unradd** linear equation

hafan *e.b. ll.* **-au** haven, port, harbour

hafdy *e.g. ll.* **hafdai** summerhouse. **tŷ haf** holiday cottage

hafddydd *e.g. ll.* **-iau** summer's day

hafod *e.g. ll.* **-ydd** (*often seen in place names*) summer residence formerly occupied by the family and its stock during the summer months only. *gw.* **hendref**

hafoty *e.g. ll.* **hafotai** chalet, holiday cottage

Hafren *e.b.* Severn. **Afon Hafren** River Severn, the Severn; **Pont Hafren** Severn Bridge

hagr *a.* ugly, unsightly (*N.W.*)

hagrwch *e.g.* ugliness

haid *e.b. ll.* **heidiau** swarm, flock, drove. **haid o wenyn** swarm of bees

haidd *e. torf.* barley. *gw.* **heidden**

haig *e.b. ll.* **heigiau** shoal. **haig o bysgod** shoal of fish

haint *e.b.* *ll.* **heintiau** disease, infection, plague; faint, fit.
Fe ges i haint pan welais i'r ysbryd I had a fit when I saw the ghost

hala *be.* **(halaf)** to spend; to send; to drive; to spread (*S.W.*)

halen *e.g.* *ll.* **-au** salt, brine. **halen y ddaear** salt of the earth

hallt *a.* salty, briny; harsh, severe. **talu'n hallt** to pay dearly

halltu *be.* **(halltaf)** to salt, to cure

hamdden *e.g.b.* leisure, respite. **canolfan hamdden** leisure centre; **oriau hamdden** leisure hours, spare time

hamddena *be.* **(hamddenaf)** to concern oneself with leisure pursuits

hamddenol *a.* leisurely

hances *e.b.* *ll.* **-i** handkerchief

hanerau *gw.* **hanner**

haneri *gw.* **hanner**

hanerwr *e.g.* *ll.* **hanerwyr** half-back (games)

hanes *e.g.* *ll.* **-ion** history; story of the past, tale, record, report. **Glywaist ti'r hanes am Wil?** Did you hear the tale about Wil?

haneswyr *gw.* **hanesydd**

hanesydd: haneswr *e.g.* *ll.* **hanesyddion: haneswyr** historian

hanesyn *e.g.* *ll.* **-nau** story, anecdote, tale

hanfodol *a.* essential; integral

haniaethol *a.* abstract

hanner *e.g.* *ll.* **hanerau, haneri** half. **hanner awr** half an hour; **hanner call** foolish, half-witted; **hanner cylch** semicircle; **hanner dydd** midday, noon; **hanner munud!** half-a-minute! half-a-moment! **hanner nos** midnight; **hanner-pan** half-soaked; half-wit; **hanner pris** half-price

hap *e.b.* *ll.* **-au, -iau** chance, luck, fortune. **chwarae hap** to gamble. **ar hap a damwain** by chance, by luck

hapus *a.* happy, cheerful

hapusrwydd *e.g.* happiness, bliss, blessedness

harbwr *e.g.* *ll.* **-s** harbour, port

hardd *a.* *ll.* **heirdd** beautiful, comely, handsome, fine, splendid (*of person or object*)

harddwch *e.g.* beauty, fairness, comeliness

hau: heu *be.* **(heuaf)** to sow, to scatter; to disseminate

haul *e.g.* *ll.* **heuliau** sun

hawdd *a.* easy. **Mae'n hawdd gweld** It is easy to see; **Mae'n hawdd nofio** It is easy to swim; **Mae'n hawdd siopa** It is easy to shop. *gw. At. Ansoddeiriau*

hawl

hawl *e.b.g.* *ll.* **-iau** legal claim, right, demand; question. **hawliau dyn/dynol** the rights of man, human rights; **hawliau sifil** civil rights

hawlfraint *e.b.* *ll.* **hawlfreintiau** privilege; copyright

hawlio *be.* **(hawliaf)** to claim, to demand

haws *gw.* **hawdd**

hawsaf *gw.* **hawdd**

hawsed *gw.* **hawdd**

heb *ardd.* (*followed by soft mutation*) **(hebddo, hebddot, hebddo/hebddi, hebddon, hebddoch, hebddyn)** without, minus, free from, besides. *gw. At. Arddodiaid*

heblaw *ardd.* besides, without

hebog *e.g.* *ll.* **-au, -iaid** hawk, falcon. **gwylio fel hebog** to watch like a hawk, to watch intensely

Hebrëwr *e.g.* *ll.* **Hebrëwyr** Hebrew; **Hebrëes** female Hebrew

hebrwng *be.* **(hebryngaf)** to lead, to accompany, to escort. **cynhebrwng** funeral, funeral procession; **tŷ hebrwng** funeral home, chapel of rest

hecsagon *e.g.* *ll.* **-au** hexagon

hedeg *be.* **(hedaf)** to fly

hedfan *be.* **(hedfanaf)** to fly

hedydd *e.g.* *ll.* **-ion** lark. *gw.* **ehedydd**

hedyn *gw.* **hadyn**

hedd *e.g.b.* *ll.* **-au** peace, tranquillity, serenity, calm

heddiw *ad. & e.g.* today

heddlu *e.g.* *ll.* **-oedd** police force

heddwas *e.g.* *ll.* **heddweision** policeman

heddwch *e.g.* peace, tranquillity, stillness

Insight

heddwch *e.g.* peace. The Archdruid's cry in the annual National Eisteddfod is, 'A oes heddwch?' 'Are you all in agreement with the adjudication, is there peace?' The anticipated reply from the 3,500 listeners in the pavilion is: 'HEDDWCH!'

Hebraeg *e.g.* Hebrew language

Hebreig *a.* Hebrew

heddweision *gw.* **heddwas**

hefo *gw.* **efo** (*N.W.*)

hefyd *c. & ad.* also, too, in addition; likewise

heibio *ad.* past; aside, beside, by. **heibio i'r tŷ** past the house

heidiau *gw.* **haid**

heidden *e.b.* *ll.* **haidd** grain of barley

heigiau *gw.* **haig**

heini *a.* active, lively, agile, nimble. **dosbarth cadw'n heini** keep fit class

heintiau *gw.* **haint**

heintus *a.* diseased, infectious, contagious

heirdd *gw.* **hardd**

hel: hela *be.* **(heliaf: helaf)** to drive; to chase, to pursue; to send; to hunt; to gather, to collect; to fetch. **hel achau** to genealogize (*N.W.*). **hel straeon** to gossip (*N.W.*)

helaeth *a.* ample, large, broad; plentiful

helfa *e.b.* *ll.* **helfâu, helfeydd** a hunting, hunt, chase, catch. **helfa drysor** treasure hunt; **helfa dda** a good catch

helgi *e.g.* *ll.* **helgwn** hound

heliwr *e.g.* *ll.* **helwyr** huntsman, gatherer

help *e.g.b.* help, aid; assistance; support. **help llaw** helping hand

help (i) *be.* **(helpaf)** to help, to assist

helygen *e.b.* *ll.* **helyg** willow

helynt *e.g.* *ll.* **-ion** course or way (*of life, etc.*); fuss, bother; business. **Beth yw ei hynt a'i helynt?** What has become of him?

hem *e.b.* *ll.* **-iau** hem, border, seam

hen *a.* old, aged; ancient (*precedes the noun and causes soft mutation*) **hen bryd** high time; **hen ddigon** quite enough; **henffasiwn** old-fashioned; **hen gariad** former sweetheart, 'old flame'; **hen gownt** outstanding account, debit; grudge; **hen lanc** (old) bachelor; **wedi hen farw** long since dead; **yr Hen Wlad** the Old Country, term of endearment for Wales. *gw. At. Ansoddeiriau*

henach *gw.* **hen**

henaf *gw.* **hen**

henaidd *a.* oldish, old-fashioned

henaint *e.g.* old age; senility

hendaid *e.g.* *ll.* **hendeidiau** great-grandfather; forefather, ancestor

hendeidiau *gw.* **hendaid**

hendref *e.b.* *ll.* **hendrefi, hendrefydd** winter dwelling located in the valley, to which the family and its stock returned after the summer months in the **hafod** on the mountain. *gw.* **hafod**

hendrefi *gw.* **hendref**

hendrefydd *gw.* **hendref**

henebion *e.ll.* ancient monuments

hened *gw.* **hen**

heneiddio *be.* **(heneiddiaf)** to grow old, to become old

heneiniau *gw.* **hennain**

henffasiwn

henffasiwn *gw.* **hen**

hennain *e.b. ll.* **heneiniau**
great-grandmother (*N.W.*)

heno *ad. & e.b.* tonight, (on)
this night

henoed *e.g. & e.torf. & a.*
old age, great age; old
person; old people, old,
elderly. **cartref henoed** old
people's home

henwr *e.g. ll.* **henwyr** old
man

heol: hewl *e.b. ll.* **-ydd** street,
road, way. **heol ddeuol** dual
carriageway; **heol fawr**
highway; **heol gefn** back-
road, byway

heolydd *gw.* **heol**

her *e.b. ll.* **-iau** challenge,
defiance, provocation

hercyd *be.* **(hercaf)** to fetch,
to reach (*S.W.*)

herio *be.* **(heriaf)** to challenge,
to defy, to dare

herwfilwr *e.g. ll.* **herwfilwyr**
guerilla

herwgipiad *e.g. ll.* **-au** hijack

herwgipio *be.* **(herwgipiaf)** to
hijack

herwgipiwr *e.g. ll.*
herwgipwyr hijacker

herwgydiad *e.g. ll.* **-au**
kidnap

herwgydio *be.* **(herwgydiaf)** to
kidnap

herwgydiwr *e.g. ll.*
herwgydwyr kidnapper

herwydd *ardd.* according to,
by. **o'r herwydd** on account
of that

het *e.b. ll.* **-au, -iau** hat

heu *gw.* **hau**

heuad *e.g.* a sowing

heulog *a.* sunny

heuliau *gw.* **haul**

heulwen *e.b.* sunshine; a
girl's name. **Heulwen ydy
enw'r ferch** The girl's name
is Heulwen

heuwr *e.g. ll.* **heuwyr** sower

hewl *gw.* **heol**

hewlydd *gw.* **heol**

heyrn *gw.* **haearn**

hi *rhag.* she, her, it

hidio (am) *be.* **(hidiaf)** to heed,
to care, to mind (*S.W.*)

hil *e.b. ll.* **-ion, -iau** race,
lineage; offspring,
descendants

hiliol *a.* racial

hin *e.b. ll.* **-oedd** weather

hindda *e.b.* fine weather.
hindda a drycin fair weather
and foul

hinsawdd *e.b. ll.* **hinsoddau**
climate. **newid hinsawdd**
climate change

hir *a. ll.* **-ion** long, lengthy.
gw. At. Ansoddeiriau

hirach *gw.* **hir**

hiraeth *e.g. ll.* **-au** longing,
nostalgia, homesickness,
grief

hiraethu (am) *be.* **(hiraethaf)**
to long (for), to yearn (for),
to sorrow, to grieve

hiraf *gw.* **hir**

hirbell *a.* distant, remote. **o
hirbell** from afar; **dysgu o
hirbell** distance learning

hired *gw.* **hir**

hirgylch *e.g. ll.* **-au, -oedd** ellipse

hirion *gw.* **hir**

hirlwm *e.g.* lean period at the end of winter

hirnod *e.g. ll.* **-au** circumflex accent (^)

hithau *rhag.* she, she too

hiwmor *e.g.* humour

hoe *e.g. ll.* **-au** pause, break, respite. **Sioni hoe** a layabout (*S.W.*)

hoel: hoelen *e.g.b. ll.* **hoelion, hoelon** nail. **taro'r hoelen ar ei phen** to comment appropriately with a fitting remark; to hit the nail on the head

hoelio *be.* **(hoeliaf)** to nail

hofrennydd *e.g. ll.* **hofrenyddion** helicopter

hoff *a. (precedes the noun and causes soft mutation)* dear, beloved, favourite. **fy hoff le bwyta** my favourite eating place

hoffi *be.* **(hoffaf)** to like, to be pleased (with)

hoffter *e.g. ll.* **-au** liking, fondness

hogen *e.b. ll.* **-nod** girl, lass (*N.W.*)

hogi *be.* **(hogaf)** to sharpen, to whet. **carreg hogi** whetstone

hogiau *gw.* **hogyn**

hogyn *e.g. ll.* **hogiau, hogynnau** boy, lad (*N.W.*)

hongian *be.* **(hongiaf)** to hang, to suspend

hôl *be.* **(holaf)** to fetch (*S.W.*). *gw.* **holi, nôl**

holi *be.* **(holaf)** to question, to inquire, to ask (about). **holi am** to ask about, to ask after

holiadur *e.g. ll.* **-on** questionnaire

holwr *e.g. ll.* **holwyr** questioner, examiner, interrogator

holwyddoreg *e.b. ll.* **-au** catechism

holl *a. (precedes the noun and causes soft mutation)* all, whole. **yr holl bobl** all the people; **yr holl fyd** the whole world

hollalluog *a.* almighty

hollfyd *e.g.* universe

holliach *a.* whole, sound (of health)

hollol *a. & ad. (precedes the adjective and causes soft mutation)* whole, entire, complete. **yn hollol dawel** completely quiet; **yn hollol gywir** wholly correct

hollt *e.g. ll.* **-au** a split

hollti *be.* **(holltaf)** to split

hon *a.b. & rhag.* this (one), she (her), it. *gw.* **hwn**

honedig *a.* alleged, reputed

honiad *e.g. ll.* **-au** assertion, claim

honni *be.* **(honnaf)** to allege, to assert, to profess, to pretend, to claim

honno, honna

honno, honna *a.b. & rhag.* that (one), she (her), it. *gw.* **hwnnw**

hosan *e.b. ll.* **-au** stocking, sock

hoyw *a.* lively, sprightly; gay, homosexual

hud *e.g. ll.* **-ion** magic, charm, spell

hudo *be.* (**hudaf**) to charm, to allure

hudol *a.* enchanting

huddygl *e.g.* soot

hufen *e.g. ll.* **-nau** cream. **hufen iâ** ice-cream

hugain *gw.* **ugain**

hun: hunan 1 *rhag. ll.* **hunain** self. **fi fy hun(an)** I myself; **ti dy hun(an)** you yourself; **ef ei hun(an)** he himself; **nhw eu hunain** they themselves; **ei hunan bach** alone. 2 *a.* self-. **hunanwasanaeth** self-service

hunain *gw.* **hun**

hunanarlwyol *a.* self-catering

hunan-barch *e.g.* self-respect

hunangofiant *e.g.* autobiography

hunanhyderus *a.* self-confident

hunanladdiad *e.g. ll.* **-au** suicide

hunanlanhaol *a.* self-cleaning

hunanol *a.* selfish

hunllef *e.b.* nightmare

huno *be.* (**hunaf**) to sleep, to fall asleep

Hunodd, 5 Mai 1940 Died 5 May 1940 (*on gravestones*)

hurt *a.* stupid, dull, stunned. **hurtyn** stupid person, blockhead

hwch *e.b. ll.* **hychod** sow. **Mae hi'n hen hwch** She is slovenly

hwiangerdd *e.b. ll.* **-i** lullaby; nursery-rhyme

hwn *a.g. & rhag.* this (one), he (him), it. *gw.* **hon**

hwnnw, hwnna *a.g. & rhag.* that (one). *gw.* **honno**

hwnt *ad.* beyond, aside, away. **tu hwnt** beyond; **yn gyflym tu hwnt** exceedingly fast

hwp *e.g.* push, thrust, shove

hwrdd *e.g. ll.* **hyrddod**. ram (*S.W.*)

hwrê *ebych. & e.b.* hooray!

hwy: hwynt: nhw *rhag.* they, them. *gw.* **hir**

hwyaf *gw.* **hir**

hwyad: hwyaden *e.b. ll.* **hwyaid** duck

hwyaid *gw.* **hwyad**

hwyl *e.b. ll.* **-iau** sail; journey; religious fervour; mood; fun; goodbye. **mewn hwyliau da** in a good mood; **hwyl!** bye! **Pob hwyl ichi** All the best

hwyliau *gw.* **hwyl**

hwylio *be.* (**hwyliaf**) to sail, to set out on a journey

hwylus *a.* ease, comfortable, expedient, convenient

hwyluso *be.* (**hwylusaf**) to facilitate

hwylustod *e.g.* ease, convenience, facility, expediency

hwynt *gw.* **hwy**

hwyr 1 *a.* late. 2 *e.g.* (late) evening

hwyrach *ad.* perhaps (*N.W.*).
gw. At. Ansoddeiriau

hwythau *rhag.* they, they also

hyblyg *a.* flexible, pliable,
pliant

hybu *be.* **(hybaf)** to recover;
to promote

hychod *gw.* **hwch**

hyd 1 *ardd.* (*followed by soft
mutation*) to, till, for, as far
as. **hyd yn hyn** up till now;
hyd at bum punt up to £5.
gw. At. Treigladau. **2** *e.g. ll.*
-au, -oedd, -ion length; while

hyder *e.g.* confidence, trust

hyderu *be.* **(hyderaf)** to be
confident; to trust, rely or
depend (on)

hyderus *a.* confident

Hydref *e.g.* October

hydref *e.g. ll.* **-au** autumn

hydrefol *a.* autumnal

hydrogen *e.g.* hydrogen

hydd *e.g. ll.* **-od** stag

hyddysg *a.* learned, well-
versed

hyf *a.* bold

hyfdra *e.g.* boldness

hyfryd *a.* pleasant, delightful,
fine, agreeable

hyfrydwch *e.g.* delight,
pleasure

hyfforddi *be.* **(hyfforddaf)** to
train, to direct, to instruct

hyfforddiant *e.g. ll.*
hyfforddiannau training,
instruction

hyfforddwr *e.g. ll.*
hyfforddwyr instructor,
guide, trainer, coach

hyhi *rhag.* she, her (*emphatic*)

hylif *a. & e.g. ll.* **-au** liquid,
flowing; fluid; a liquid, a
fluid; a flow

hyll *a.* ugly, hideous

hyn *a. & rhag.* this, these

hŷn *gw.* **hen**

hynaf *gw.* **hen**

hynafiad *e.g. ll.* **hynafiaid**
ancestor

hynafol *a.* ancient

hyned *gw.* **hen**

hynny *a. & rhag.* that, those

hynod *a.* remarkable,
notable; exceptional. **yn
hynod o dda** exceptionally
well; **yn hynod o gyfoethog**
exceptionally rich

hynt *e.b. ll.* **-au, -oedd** way,
course, journey; career;
(one's) fate or lot, condition,
state. **Beth yw ei hynt erbyn
hyn?** What's his fate by
now?

hyrddod *gw.* **hwrdd**

hysbyseb *e.b.g. ll.* **-ion**
advertisement,
announcement

hysbysebiad *e.g. ll.* **-au**
advertisement

hysbysebu *be.* **(hysbysebaf)**
to advertise

hysbysebwr *e.g. ll.*
hysbysebwyr advertiser

hysbysfwrdd *e.g. ll.*
hysbysfyrddau noticeboard

hysbysiad *e.g. ll.* **-au**
announcement, notice,
advertisement

hysbysu *be.* **(hysbysaf)** to
announce, to inform; to
advertise

hytrach *ad.* rather; more so

i

I

i 1 *ardd. (followed by soft
mutation)*
**(i fi/mi, i ti, iddo/iddi, i ni, i
chi, iddyn nhw)** to, into, for.
i'r dim exactly, precisely; **i
fyny** up, upwards; **i ffwrdd**
away; **i gyd** all; **i lawr** down;
i mewn into; **i fod i**
supposed to; **i'w gilydd** to
each other. *gw. At.
Arddodiaid.* 2 *rhag.* I, me.
gw. At. Rhagenwau Personol
iâ *e.g.* ice. **cloch iâ** icicle
iach *a.* healthy, well
iacháu *be.* **(iachâf)** to heal, to
cure
iachawdwr *e.g. ll.* **iachawdwyr**
saviour
iachawdwriaeth:
iechydwriaeth *e.b.* salvation,
healing
iachus *a.* healthy, wholesome
iaith *e.b. ll.* **ieithoedd**
language. **iaith lafar** spoken
language; **mamiaith** first
language, mother tongue; **ail
iaith** second language;
dwyieithog bilingual
iâr *e.b. ll.* **ieir** hen. **iâr fach yr
haf** butterfly

iard *e.b. ll.* **ierdydd** yard (of
school, etc.)
iarll *e.g. ll.* **ieirll** earl
iarlles *e.b. ll.* **-au** countess
ias *e.b. ll.* **-au** thrill, shiver;
temper
iasol *a.* thrilling; intensely
cold
Iau *e.g.* Thursday
iau 1 *e.g. ll.* **ieuau** liver. 2
e.b. ll. **ieuau** yoke. *gw.*
ieuanc
iawn 1 *ad.* very. **yn dda iawn**
very good. 2 *e.g.* rightness,
truth; compensation;
atonement; **talu'r iawn am** to
compensate. 3 *a.* right, true,
correct
iawndal *e.g. ll.* **-oedd**
compensation, damages,
indemnity
iawnder *e.g. ll.* **-au** justice,
right, rightness. **iawnderau
dynol: iawnderau sifil** civil
rights, civil liberties
idiom *e.b. ll.* **-au** idiom
Iddew *e.g. ll.* **-on** Jew
Iddewes *e.b. ll.* **-au** Jewess
Iddewig *a.* Jewish
Iddewaeth *e.b.* Judaism
ie *ad.* yes (*positive response
to a question that does not
begin with a verb*)

Insight

ie *ad.* (a two syllable word pronounced 'i-e') yes. There are
many other ways of saying 'yes', but this is the correct
response to a question that does *not* begin with a verb. **Ai
melyn yw ei liw?** *Ie.* (Is its colour yellow? Yes.) **Onid yn y
bws y daeth hi?** *Ie.* (Was it not in the bus she came? Yes.)

iechyd *e.g.* health, soundness, well-being

iechyd da! good health! (*in drinking a toast*)

ieir *gw.* iâr

ieirll *gw.* iarll

ieithoedd *gw.* iaith

ierdydd *gw.* iard

Iesu *e.g.* Jesus. **Iesu Grist** Jesus Christ; **Iesu Mab Duw** Jesus Son of God

iet *e.b.* *ll.* **-au, -iau** gate. *gw.* **clwyd**

ieuangach *gw.* ieuanc

ieuangaf *gw.* ieuanc

ieuanged *gw.* ieuanc

ieuainc *gw.* ieuanc

ieuanc: ifanc *a.* *ll.* **ieuainc: ifainc.** young. *gw.* At. Ansoddeiriau

ieuau *gw.* iau

ieuenctid *e.g. & e.ll.* youth. **côr ieuenctid** youth choir

ifainc *gw.* ieuanc

ifanc *gw.* ieuanc

ifancach *gw.* ieuanc

ifancaf *gw.* ieuanc

ig *e.b.* *ll.* **-ion** hiccup

igam-ogam *a.* zigzag

igian *be.* (**igiaf**) to hiccup

ing *e.g.* *ll.* **-oedd** anguish, agony, distress

ildio *be.* (**ildiaf**) to yield

ill *rhag.* both, they, them. **ill dau (dwy)** both of them

imwnedd *e.g.* immunity

imwneiddiad *e.g.* *ll.* **-au** immunisation

imwneiddio *be.* (**imwneiddiaf**) to immunise

incwm *e.g.* income. **Treth Incwm** Income Tax

India, Yr *e.b.* India

Indiad *e.g.* *ll.* **Indiaid** an Indian. **Un o'r India yw e/hi** He/she is Indian

injan: injin *e.b.* *ll.* **-s** engine

Ionawr *e.g.* January

iorwg *e.g.* ivy (*S.W.*)

iro *be.* (**iraf**) to grease; to anoint; to oil; to lubricate

is 1 *ardd.* below, under. *gw.* **isel.** 2 *rhagdd.* (*followed by soft mutation*) sub-, under-, vice-

isaf *gw.* isel

ised *gw.* isel

isel *a.* low; humble; base; depressed. *gw.* At. Ansoddeiriau

Iseldiroedd, Yr *e.b.* The Netherlands

is-etholiad *e.g.* *ll.* **-au** by-election

is-gadeirydd *e.g.* *ll.* **-ion** vice-chairman

islaw *ardd.* below, beneath

is-lywydd *e.g.* *ll.* **-ion** vice-president

israddol *a.* inferior; subordinate

isymwybod *e.g.* subconscious

Iwerddon *e.b.* Ireland. **byw yn Iwerddon** to live in Ireland; **dod o Iwerddon** to come from Ireland; **mynd i Iwerddon** to go to Ireland

J

jac: Jac *e.g. ll.* -s jack
jac-codi-baw *e.g.* 'J.C.B.',
  mechanical excavator
jac-do: jac-y-do *e.g. ll.* -s
  jackdaw
jac-y-do *gw.* jac-do
jam *e.g. ll.* -iau jam
Japan *e.b.* Japan
Japanead *e.g. ll.* Japaneaid a
  Japanese
Japaneaidd *a.* Japanese
Japanaeg *e.b.* Japanese
  (language)
jar: jâr *e.b. ll.* jariau, jarrau
  jar
jas *e.g.* jazz
jeli *e.g. ll.* -s, jeliau jelly
jersi: jyrsi: siersi *e.b. ll.* -s
  jersey
jet *e.g. ll.* -iau jet (of water,
  gas, etc.); jet (nozzle); jet
  plane. awyren jet jet aircraft,
  jet plane; peiriant jet jet
  engine
ji-binc *e.b. ll.* -od chaffinch
jig-so *e.g.* jigsaw: pos jig-so
  jigsaw puzzle
jîns *e.g.* jeans
jîp *e.g.* jeep
jiráff *e.g. ll.* jiraffod giraffe
jiwbilî: jubilî *e.b. ll.* jiwbilïau
  jubilee, occasion or season of
  rejoicing
job *e.g.b. ll.* -iau, -s job,
  piece of work; occupation
jobyn *e.g. ll.* jobiau a small
  job. Jobyn da! Good job!
jôc *e.b. ll.* -s a joke,

witticism; object of ridicule
jocan *bf.* (jocaf) to joke
  (*S.W.*)
joio *bf.* (joiaf) to enjoy
jubilî *gw.* jiwbilî
jwg: siwg *e.b. ll.* jygiau:
  siygiau jug. jwg laeth milk
  jug
jygiau *gw.* jwg
jyngl *e.b. ll.* -oedd jungle
jyrsi *gw.* jersi

L

labed *gw.* llabed
label *e.g. ll.* -i label
labelu *be.* (labelaf) to label
labordy *e.g. ll.* labordai
  laboratory
labrwr *e.g. ll.* labrwyr
  labourer
lac *gw.* llac
lacio *gw.* llacio
lacs *gw.* llacs
lacsog *gw.* llacsog
lachar *gw.* llachar
Ladin *gw.* Lladin
ladrad *gw.* lladrad
ladrata *gw.* lladrata
ladron *gw.* lleidr
ladd *gw.* lladd
ladd-dy *gw.* lladd-dy
laes *gw.* llaes
laesu *gw.* llaesu
laeth *gw.* llaeth
lafant *e.g.* lavender
lafar *gw.* llafar
lafariad *gw.* llafariad
lafn *gw.* llafn
lafur *gw.* llafur

lafurio *gw.* llafurio
lafurus *gw.* llafurus
lafurwr *gw.* llafurwr
lai *gw.* llai
lain *gw.* llain
lais *gw.* llais
laith *gw.* llaith
lam *gw.* llam
lamp *e.b.* *ll.* -au lamp. lamp
  ôl rear-lamp, tail-light of
  vehicle; lamp olew oil lamp
lamplen *e.b.* lampshade
lamu *gw.* llamu
lan *ad.* up; *gw.* glan, llan
lân *gw.* glân
lanastr *gw.* llanastr
lanc *gw.* llanc
lances *gw.* llances
lanciau *gw.* llanc
lanhau *gw.* glanhau
lanio *gw.* glanio
lannau *gw.* glan, llan
lanw *gw.* llanw
lapio (am) *be.* (lapiaf) to lap,
  to wrap. papur lapio
  wrapping paper
larwm *e.g.* alarm: cloc larwm
  alarm-clock
las *gw.* glas
laswelltyn *gw.* glaswelltyn
lathen *gw.* llathen
lau *gw.* lleuen
law *gw.* glaw, llaw
lawdriniaeth *gw.* llawdriniaeth
lawen *gw.* llawen
lawenhau *gw.* llawenhau
lawenydd *gw.* llawenydd
lawer *gw.* llawer
lawes *gw.* llawes
lawfeddyg *gw.* llawfeddyg

lawfeddygaeth *gw.*
  llawfeddygaeth
lawfeddygol *gw.* llawfeddygol
lawlif *gw.* llawlif
lawlyfr *gw.* llawlyfr
lawn *gw.* llawn
lawrlwytho *gw.* llawrlwytho
lawnder *gw.* llawnder
lawnt *e.g.b.* *ll.* -iau, -ydd
  lawn
lawrlwytho *gw.* llawrlwytho
lawr, i *ad.* down. *gw.* llawr
lawysgrif *gw.* llawysgrif
lawysgrifen *gw.* llawysgrifen
le *gw.* lle
lecyn *gw.* llecyn
lechen *gw.* llechen
lechi *gw.* llechen
led *gw.* lled
ledled *gw.* lledled
ledr *gw.* lledr
ledrith *gw.* lledrith
ledu *gw.* lledu
lef *gw.* llef
lefain *e.g.b.* leaven. *gw.*
  llefain
lefaru *gw.* llefaru
lefarwr *gw.* llefarwr
lefarwyr *gw.* llefarwr
lefarydd *gw.* llefarydd
lefau *gw.* llef
lefel *e.b.g.* *ll.* -au, -ydd, leflau
  level. lefel y môr sea-level
lefelyn *gw.* llefelyn
leflau *gw.* lefel
lefrith *gw.* llefrith
lefydd *gw.* lle
leiaf *gw.* bach
leiafrif *gw.* lleiafrif
leian *gw.* lleian.
leidr *gw.* lleidr

leihau

leihau *gw.* lleihau

lein *e.b.* *ll.* -iau, leins line, cord; telephone line; line-out. **lein ddillad** clothes line; **lein fach** narrow-gauge railway

leiniau *gw.* lein, llain

leinio *be.* (leiniaf) to line up; to form a line-out; to thrash, to give (one) a hiding (*N.W.*)

leisiau *gw.* llais

leisio *gw.* lleisio

leithder *gw.* lleithder

len *gw.* llen

lên *gw.* llên

lencyndod *gw.* llencyndod

lendid *gw.* glendid

lenni *gw.* llen

lennydd *gw.* glan

lenor *gw.* llenor

lenwi *gw.* llenwi

lenyddiaeth *gw.* llenyddiaeth

lenyddol *gw.* llenyddol

leoedd *gw.* lle

leol *gw.* lleol

leoli *gw.* lleoli

leoliad *gw.* lleoliad

Lerpwl *e.b.* Liverpool

les 1 *e.b.* *ll.* -oedd lease. 2 *e.b.* *ll.* -au lace. *gw.* lles

lesol *gw.* llesol

lestr *gw.* llestr

letchwith *gw.* lletchwith

lety *gw.* llety

letya *gw.* lletya

letys *gw.* letysen

letysen *e.b.* *ll.* letys lettuce

leuad *gw.* lleuad

leuen *gw.* lleuen

lew *gw.* llew

lewygu *gw.* llewygu

lewyrch *gw.* llewyrch

lewyrchu *gw.* llewyrchu

lewyrchus *gw.* llewyrchus

lewys *gw.* llawes

liain *gw.* lliain

lid *gw.* llid

lieiniau *gw.* lliain

lif *gw.* llif

lifio *gw.* llifio

lifo *gw.* llifo

lifogydd *gw.* llif

lifft *e.g.* *ll.* -iau lift

lili *e.b.* *ll.* -s, liliau lily; **lili wen fach** snowdrop

lin *gw.* glin

lindysyn *e.g.* (*b.* lindysen) *ll.* lindys caterpillar

linell *gw.* llinell

linyn *gw.* llinyn

lio *gw.* llio

litr *e.g.* *ll.* -au litre

lithren *gw.* llithren

lithriad *gw.* llithriad

lithrig *gw.* llithrig

lithro *gw.* llithro

liw *gw.* lliw

liwgar *gw.* lliwgar

liwiau *gw.* lliw

liwio *gw.* lliwio

liwiog *gw.* lliwiog

liwo *gw.* lliwo

lo *gw.* glo, llo

loches *gw.* lloches

lochesu *gw.* llochesu

Loegr *gw.* Lloegr

loer *gw.* lloer

loeren *gw.* lloeren

lofa *gw.* glofa

lofnod *gw.* llofnod

lofnodi *gw.* llofnodi

lofrudd *gw.* llofrudd
lofruddiaeth *gw.* llofruddiaeth
lofruddio *gw.* llofruddio
lofft *gw.* llofft
log *gw.* llog
logi *gw.* llogi
long *gw.* llong
longddrylliad *gw.*
  llongddrylliad
longwr *gw.* llongwr
loi *gw.* llo
lol *e.b.* frivolity; nonsense.
  Paid â siarad lol! Don't talk
  nonsense!.
lolfa *e.b.* *ll.* lolfeydd lounge,
  sitting-room
lolan: lolian *be.* (lolaf: loliaf)
  to lounge; to joke, to talk
  nonsense (*S.W.*)
lon *gw.* llon
lôn *e.b.* *ll.* lonydd lane, road.
  y Lôn Goed the Tree-Lined
  Way (*place name in N.W.
  Wales*); **y lôn gefn** the back-
  lane; **lôn ddianc** escape lane
loncian *be.* (lonciaf) to jog
lonciwr *e.g.* *ll.* loncwyr
  jogger
lond *gw.* llond
longyfarch *gw.* llongyfarch
longyfarchiad *gw.*
  llongyfarchiad
lonydd *gw.* lôn. *gw.* llonydd
lonyddwch *gw.* llonyddwch
loriau *gw.* llawr
lorïau *gw.* lorri
lorri *e.b.* *ll.* lorïau, lorris
  lorry. **lorri laeth** milk-lorry;
  lorri lo coal-lorry; **lorri
  wartheg** cattle-lorry

losg *gw.* llosg
losgi *gw.* llosgi
losin *gw.* losinen
losinen: losen *e.b.* *ll.* losin
  sweet, lozenge
löwr *gw.* glöwr
löyn byw *gw.* glöyn byw
loyw *gw.* gloyw
lu *gw.* llu
lud *gw.* glud
ludio: ludo *gw.* gludio
ludw *gw.* lludw
Lun *gw.* Llun
lun *gw.* llun
Lundain *gw.* Llundain
luniaidd *gw.* lluniaidd
lunio *gw.* llunio
luoedd *gw.* llu
luosi *gw.* lluosi
luosog *gw.* lluosog
lusern *gw.* llusern
lusgo *gw.* llusgo
luwch *gw.* lluwch
luwchfa *gw.* lluwchfa
lw *gw.* llw
lŵans: lwfans *e.g.b.*
  allowance, concession
lwc *e.b.g.* luck, fate, chance.
  Pob lwc i ti! Good luck to
  you! **Lwc dda!** Good luck!
  Prosperity! Success!
lwcus *a.* lucky, fortunate
lwch *gw.* llwch
lwfans *gw.* lŵans
lwfr *gw.* llwfr
lwgu *gw.* llwgu
lwnc *gw.* llwnc
lwncdestun *gw.* llwncdestun
lwon *gw.* llw
lwy *gw.* llwy

lwyaid

lwyaid *gw.* llwyaid
lwybr *gw.* llwybr
lwyd *gw.* llwyd
lwydo *gw.* llwydo
lwydrew *gw.* llwydrew
lwydrewi *gw.* llwydrewi
lwydd *gw.* llwydd
lwyddiannus *gw.*
 llwyddiannus
lwyddiant *gw.* llwydd
lwyddo *gw.* llwyddo
lwyfan *gw.* llwyfan
lwyfannu *gw.* llwyfannu
lwyn *gw.* llwyn
lwynog *gw.* llwynog
lwyr *gw.* llwyr
lwyrymwrthodwr *gw.*
 llwyrymwrthodwr
lwyth *gw.* llwyth
lwytho *gw.* llwytho
lwythog *gw.* llwythog
lydan *gw.* llydan
lydanu *gw.* llydanu
Lydaw *gw.* Llydaw
lyfelyn *gw.* llyfelyn
lyfn *gw.* llyfn
lyfr *gw.* llyfr
lyfrgell *gw.* llyfrgell
lyfrgellydd *gw.* llyfrgellydd
lyfryn *gw.* llyfryn
lyfu *gw.* llyfu
lyffant *gw.* llyffant
lygad *gw.* llygad
lygadu *gw.* llygadu
lygaid *gw.* llygad
lygod *gw.* llygoden
lygoden *gw.* llygoden
lygredig *gw.* llygredig
lygredd *gw.* llygredd
lygru *gw.* llygru

lynges *gw.* llynges
lyn *gw.* glyn, llyn
lynciau *gw.* llwnc
lyncu *gw.* llyncu
lynnau *gw.* llyn
lynnoedd *gw.* glyn, llyn
lynu *gw.* glynu
lys *gw.* llys
lysenw *gw.* llysenw
lysenwi *gw.* llysenwi
lysfam *gw.* llysfam
lysfwytäwr *gw.* llysfwytäwr
lysgenhadaeth *gw.*
 llysgenhadaeth
lysgennad *gw.* llysgennad
lysiau *gw.* llysieuyn
lysieuol *gw.* llysieuol
lysieuyn *gw.* llysieuyn
lythrennau *gw.* llythyren
lythrennog *gw.* llythrennog
lythyr *gw.* llythyr
lythyren *gw.* llythyren
lyw *gw.* llyw
lywio *gw.* llywio
lywodraeth *gw.* llywodraeth
lywodraethu *gw.* llywodraethu
lywodraethwr *gw.*
 llywodraethwr
lywydd *gw.* llywydd
lywyddu *gw.* llywyddu

LL

llabed *e.b.* *ll.* -au lapel, flap
llac *a.* slack, loose; lax
llacio *be.* (llaciaf) to slacken;
 to loosen; to relax
llacs *e.g.* mud, dirt (*S.W.*)
llacsog *a.* muddy, dirty
 (*S.W.*)

llain

llachar a. bright, brilliant, dazzling

Lladin e.b. & a. Latin. **America Ladin** Latin America

lladrad e.g. ll. -au theft, robbery

lladrata be. (**lladrataf**) to rob, to steal, to thieve

lladron gw. **lleidr**

lladd be. (**lladdaf**) to kill, to slay, to slaughter; to cut, to mow, to fell. **lladd ar** to run down, to criticize adversely; **lladd gwair** to mow (hay); **lladd mawn** to cut peat; **fel lladd nadroedd** at full speed, with might and main (lit. like killing snakes)

lladd-dy e.g. ll. **lladd-dai** slaughterhouse

llaes a. loose, long, flowing

llaesu be. (**llaesaf**) to slacken, to loosen, to relax. **llaesu dwylo** to become idle, weak or indifferent, to stay one's hand(s)

llaeth e.g. ll. -au milk (S.W.) **llaeth y fuwch** cow's milk. gw. **llefrith**

llafar the spoken language. **2** a. loud, clear, vociferous; pertaining to the voice; oral **arholiad llafar** oral (as opposed to written) examination

llafariad e.b. ll. **llafariaid** vowel

llafn e.g. ll. -au blade

llafur e.g. ll. -iau labour, toil; tillage; corn. **llafur cariad** labour of love; **Y Blaid Lafur** The Labour Party

llafurio: llafuro be. (**llafuriaf: llafuraf**) to labour, to toil, to work

llafurus a. laborious, painstaking, industrious

llafurwr e.g. ll. **llafurwyr** labourer, worker, husbandman

llai gw. **bach**

llain e.b. ll. **lleiniau** (long narrow) strip of land, cloth & c., piece, patch, pitch, wicket (cricket), plot (of land). **llain galed** hard shoulder (of motorway); **llain lanio** landing-strip, airstrip; **llain o dir** strip of land,

---

Insight

llaeth: llefrith e.g. milk. llaeth y fuwch cow's milk; llaeth glas: llaeth sgim skimmed milk; llaeth enwyn butter-milk; llaeth gafr goat's milk; llaeth oer cold milk; llaeth y fam mother's milk.

---

llafar 1 e.g. (verbal) expression, spoken or colloquial language. **iaith**

isthmus; **Llain Gasa** Gaza Strip

llais

llais *e.g. ll.* **lleisiau** voice, sound

llaith *a.* damp, moist, dank

llall *rhag. ll.* **lleill** the other (*one*), another. **y llall** the other (*person, thing*); **y lleill** the others, the other persons/things

llam *e.g. ll.* **-au** leap, jump, bound, stride

llamu *be.* (**llamaf**) to leap, to jump, to bound, to stride

llan *e.b. ll.* **-nau** (parish) church, churchyard; enclosure, yard

llanast(r) *e.g.* mess

llanc *e.g. ll.* **-iau** youth, lad

llances *e.b. ll.* **-i, -au** young woman, lass

llanciau *gw.* **llanc**

llannau *gw.* **llan**

llanw 1 *e.g. ll.* **-au** flow (of tide). **trai a llanw** ebb and flow. 2 *be.* (**llanwaf**) to fill, to fill up

llathen *e.b. ll.* **-ni** yard, yardstick. **Doedd e ddim yn llawn llathen** He wasn't all there

llau *gw.* **lleuen**

llaw *e.b. ll.* **dwylo** hand. **i law** to hand: **llawchwith** left-handed; **llawdde** skilful, dextrous; **llawfer** shorthand; **llaw galed** trouble, rough time, hard time (*especially with sick person*); **llaw yn llaw** hand in hand; **ail-law** second hand; **hen law ar** one who possesses the 'know

how', (*lit. an old hand*); **rhoi help llaw** to give a helping hand

llawdriniaeth *e.b. ll.* **-au** surgery. *gw.* **llawfeddygaeth**

llawen *a.* cheerful, merry, glad. **Nadolig Llawen!** Merry Christmas!

llawenhau (â, yn) *be.* (**llawenhaf**) to rejoice, to be joyful. *gw.* **ymhyfrydaf**

llawenydd *e.g.* joy, jubilation, rejoicing

llawer 1 *e.g. ll.* **-oedd** many, much; abundant. 2 *ad.* by far, much (*with comparative adjective*). **o lawer** by far, by a great deal, by much; **llawer gwaith** many times; **yn llawer gwell** much better; **llawer tro** many a time

llawes *e.b. ll.* **llewys** sleeve

llawfeddyg *e.g. ll.* **-on** surgeon. *gw.* **llawdriniaeth**

llawfeddygaeth *e.b.* surgery

llawfeddygol *a.* surgical

llawlif *e.b. ll.* **-iau** hand-saw

llawlyfr *e.g. ll.* **-au** handbook, manual

llawn *a. ll.* **-ion** full; **yn llawn bryd** high time

llawnder *e.g.* abundance, fullness

llawnion *gw.* **llawn**

llawr *e.g. ll.* **lloriau** floor, ground; storey; earth. **ar lawr** down, exhausted, on (to) the ground, on the ground floor, downstairs, up (*from bed*), not yet gone to bed; **ar lawr**

gwlad on the lowlands; **y llawr cyntaf** the first floor

llawrlwytho *be.* (**llawrlwythaf**) to download

llawysgrif *e.g. ll.* **-au** manuscript

llawysgrifen *e.b. ll.* **llawysgrifennau** handwriting

lle *e.g. ll.* **-oedd, llefydd** place, room, accommodation

lle bwyd café, restaurant. **lle chwech** toilet; **lle tân** fireplace; **o'i le** out of (its) place or order, wrong, inappropriate

llecyn *e.g. ll.* **-nau** spot, place

llechen *e.b. ll.* **llechi** slate

llechi *gw.* **llechen**

lled 1 *e.g. ll.* **-au** breadth, width. **Mae stori ar led yn a pentref** There is a story going around the village. 2 *ad.* rather, partly, almost

lledled *ardd.* throughout. **lledled y byd** throughout the world

lledr *e.g. ll.* **-au** leather

lledrith *e.g. ll.* **-oedd** magic, enchantment; spectre; fantasy: **hud a lledrith** magic and fantasy

lledu *be.* (**lledaf**) to spread, to widen, to open, to expand

llef *e.g. ll.* **-au** voice, cry

llefain *be.* (**llefaf**) to cry (*S.W.*)

llefaru (wrth) *be.* (**llefaraf**) to speak, to utter

llefarwr *e.g. ll.* **llefarwyr** speaker

llefarwyr *gw.* **llefarwr**

llefarydd *e.g. ll.* **-ion** speaker, spokesman. **Y Llefarydd** (the) Speaker of the House of Commons

llefau *gw.* **llef**

llefelyn *e.g. ll* **-od** stye (*in eye*). *gw.* **llyfelyn, llefrithen**

llefrith *e.g.* milk (*N.W.*). *gw.* **llaeth**

llefrithen *e.b.* stye (in eye) (*N.W.*); *gw.* **llefelyn, llyfelyn**

llefydd *gw.* **lle**

lleiaf *a.* smallest, least. **o leiaf** at least; **gorau po leiaf** the fewer the better

lleiafrif *e.g. ll.* **-au, -oedd** minority

lleian *e.b. ll.* **-od** nun

lleidr *e.g. ll.* **lladron** thief, robber, bandit. **lleidr pen ffordd** highwayman

lleihau *be.* (**lleihaf**) to become smaller, to diminish, to shrink

lleill *gw.* **llall**

lleiniau *gw.* **llain**

lleisiau *gw.* **llais**

lleisio *be.* (**lleisiaf**) to use the voice (*in speaking, shouting, etc.*), to sound, to cry out

lleithder *e.g. ll.* **-au** damp, moisture

llen *e.b. ll.* **-ni** curtain, veil, sheet. **Y Llen Haearn** The Iron Curtain

llên *e.b.* literature. **llên gwerin** folklore; **ffuglen** fiction

llencyndod *e.g.* adolescence

llenni

llenni *gw.* **llen**
llenor *e.g.* *ll.* **-ion** author, writer, literary person
llenwi *be.* **(llenwaf)** to fill
llenyddiaeth *e.b.* *ll.* **-au** literature
llenyddol *a.* literary
lleoedd *gw.* **lle**
lleol *a.* local. **llywodraeth leol** local government
lleoli *be.* **(lleolaf)** to locate, to localise, to place
lleoliad *e.g.* *ll.* **-au** location, setting.
lles *e.g.* *ll.* **-au** benefit, profit, advantage, welfare. **er lles** for the benefit of, to the advantage of: **o les** of benefit; **Y Wladwriaeth Les** The Welfare State
llesol *a.* beneficial, profitable, advantageous
llestr *e.g.* *ll.* **-i** vessel; cup, dish, pot
lletchwith *a.* awkward, clumsy
llety *e.g.* *ll.* **-au** lodging(s)
lletya *be.* **(lletyaf)** to lodge
lleuad *e.b.* *ll.* **-au** moon. **lleuad lawn** full moon; **lleuad newydd** new moon. *gw.* **lloer**
lleuen *e.b.* *ll.* **llau** louse
llew *e.g.* *ll.* **-od** lion. **llewes** lioness
llewygu *be.* **(llewygaf)** to faint, to swoon
llewyrch *e.g.* brightness, light, gleam, lustre
llewyrchu *be.* **(llewyrchaf)** to shine, to gleam

llewyrchus *a.* bright, prosperous
llewys *gw.* **llawes**
lliain *e.g.* *ll.* **llieiniau** line, cloth, towel, napkin
llid *e.g.* *ll.* **-iau, -ion** wrath; irritation, inflammation; passion. **llid yr ymennydd** meningitis
llieiniau *gw.* **lliain**
llif 1 *e.g.* *ll.* **-ogydd** stream, flow, flood, deluge, current. 2 *e.b.* *ll.* **-iau** saw. **llif gadwyn** chainsaw
llifio *be.* **(llifiaf)** to saw; to rasp, to file
llifo *be.* **(llifaf)** to flow, to stream, to flood
llifogydd *gw.* **llif**
llinell *e.b.* *ll.* **-au** line, axis; line-out. **llinell gam** crooked line; **llinell syth** straight line
llinyn *e.g.* *ll* **-nau** line, string, cord, tape, twine. **llinyn mesur** measuring tape
llio *be.* **(lliaf)** to lick
llithren *e.b.* *ll.* **-nau** chute, slide
llithriad *e.g.* *ll.* **-au** a slip, glide, slur; error, mistake
llithrig *a.* slippery; fluent
llithro *be.* **(llithraf)** to slip, to slide; to slur
lliw *e.g.* *ll.* **-iau** colour, countenance, hue. **liw dydd** by day; **liw nos** by night; **lliwiau'r hydref** autumn colours; **lliw llachar** bright colour
lliwgar *a.* colourful

lliwiau *gw.* **lliw**

lliwio: lliwo *be.* **(lliwiaf: lliwaf)**
to colour, to dye

lliwiog *a.* coloured, tinted

lliwo *gw.* **lliwio**

llo *e.g. ll.* **lloi, lloeau** calf; **fel
llo** gormless

lloches *e.g. ll.* **-au** refuge,
shelter, lair

llochesu *be.* **(llochesaf)** to
harbour, to shelter

lloeau *gw.* **llo**

Lloegr *e.b.* England

lloer *e.b. ll.* **-au** moon
(*literary usage*); *gw.* **lleuad**

lloeren *e.b. ll.* **-ni, -nau**
satellite, sputnik

llofnod *e.b. ll.* **-au, -ion**
signature

llofnodi *be.* **(llofnodaf)** to sign

llofrudd *e.g. ll.* **-ion** murderer

llofruddiaeth *e.g. ll.* **-au**
murder

llofruddio *be.* **(llofruddiaf)** to
murder

llofft *e.b. ll.* **-ydd** loft,
upstairs; gallery; bedroom:
ar y llofft upstairs; **lan llofft**
upstairs (*S.W.*)

llog *e.g. ll.* **-au** interest, hire;
ar log for hire

llogi *be.* **(llogaf)** to hire

llong *e.b. ll.* **-au** ship. **llong
hwyliau** sailing ship; **llong
danfor** submarine; **llong ryfel**
warship

llongddrylliad *e.g. ll.* **-au**
shipwreck

llongwr *e.g. ll.* **llongwyr**
sailor

lloi *gw.* **llo**

llon *a.* merry, cheerful

llond *e.g.* as much as
something will hold; fullness,
sufficiency. **llond llwy de o
siwgr** a teaspoonful of
sugar; **llond tŷ o blant** a
houseful of children

llongyfarch (ar) *be.*
(llongyfarchaf) to
congratulate

llongyfarchiad *e.g. ll.* **-au**
congratulation.
Llongyfarchiadau!
Congratulations!

llonydd *a.* quiet, still, calm;
Gad lonydd i fi! Let me have
some peace!

llonyddwch *e.g.* stillness,
tranquillity, quietness; peace

lloriau *gw.* **llawr**

llosg 1 *e.g. ll.* **-iadau**
burning, arson. 2 *a.* burning,
burnt. **llosgfynydd** volcano;
pwnc llosg burning
issue

llosgi *be.* **(llosgaf)** to burn, to
scorch, to smart

llosgydd *e.g. ll.* **-ion**
incinerator, burner

llu *e.g. ll.* **-oedd** host,
multitude; (*follows plural
noun and undergoes soft
mutation*) crowd. **Daeth
milwyr lu o rywle** A host of
soldiers came from
somewhere

lluched *e. torf.* flash of
lightning; lightning flashes

lludw

lludw *e.g.* ash, ashes. **lludw i ludw** ashes to ashes; **dydd Mercher y Lludw** Ash Wednesday; **lorri ludw** ashcart

Llun *e.g.* Monday. **Llun y Pasg** Easter Monday

llun *e.g. ll.* **-iau** picture, drawing, image

Llundain *e.b.* London

lluniaidd *a.* shapely, graceful

lluniau *gw.* **llun**

llunio *be.* **(lluniaf)** to form, to fashion, to shape

lluoedd *gw.* **llu**

lluosi *be.* **(lluosaf)** to multiply

lluosog *a.* numerous, plural

llusern *e.b. ll.* **-au** lamp, lantern

llusgo *be.* **(llusgaf)** to drag, to trail, to draw, to crawl: **llusgo traed** to drag (one's) feet

lluwch *e.g. ll.* **-au** snowdrift; dust, specks

lluwchfa *e.b. ll.* **lluwchfeydd** snowdrift

llw *e.g. ll.* **-on** oath; curse. **ar fy llw** on oath, on my word; **cymryd llw** to take an oath

llwch *e.g. ll.* **llychau** dust, powder; ashes; lake, loch

llwfr *a.* cowardly, timid

llwgu *be.* **(llwgaf)** to starve, to be ravenously hungry

llwm *a.* poor, bare

llwnc *e.g. ll.* **llynciau** gullet, throat; draught, gulp

llwncdestun *e.g. ll.* **-au** toast (health)

llwon *gw.* **llw**

llwy *e.b. ll.* **-au** spoon. **llwy bren** wooden spoon; **llwy de** teaspoon; **llwy gawl** soup-spoon; **llwy garu** love-spoon; **llwy arian** silver spoon

llwyaid *e.b. ll.* **llwyeidiau** spoonful

llwybr *e.g. ll.* **-au** path, track, route. **llwybr tarw** straight path, short cut; **ar y llwybr iawn** on the right track

llwyd *a.* grey, pale, hoary. **Brawd Llwyd** Grey Friar, Cistercian Friar

llwydo *be.* **(llwydaf)** to turn grey; to become mouldy

llwydrew *e.g. ll.* **-ogydd** hoarfrost (*S.W.*)

llwydrewi *be.* **(llwydrewaf)** to cast a hoarfrost, to be frosty (*S.W.*)

llwydd: llwyddiant *e.g. ll.* **llwyddiannau** success, prosperity

llwyddiannus *a.* successful, prosperous

llwyddo (i) *be.* **(llwyddaf)** to succeed, to prosper

llwyfan *e.g.b. ll.* **-nau** platform, stage. **llwyfan olew** oil rig

llwyfannu *be.* **(llwyfannaf)** to stage

llwyn 1 *e.g. ll.* **-i** grove, bush. **o lech i lwyn** furtively, stealthily, slyly (*literally from rock to bush*).
2 *e.b. ll.* **-au** loin

llwynog *e.g. ll.* **-od** fox (*N.W.*). **llwynoges** vixen

llynnoedd

llwyr 1 *a.* complete, entire, utter, total. **2** *ad.* entirely, altogether, utterly. **3** *rhagdd.* total

llwyrymwrthodwr *e.g. ll.* **llwyrymwrthodwyr** teetotaller

llwyth *e.g. ll.* **-au** tribe, clan; *e.g. ll.* **-i** load, burden, freight

llwytho *be.* **(llwythaf)** to load, to burden

llwythog *a.* laden, burdened

llydan *a.* wide, broad

llydanu *be.* **(llydanaf)** to widen

Llydaw *e.b.* Britanny

Llydäwr *e.g.* Breton

Llydawes *e.b.* Breton woman

Llydaweg *e.b.* Breton language

llyfelyn *e.g. ll.* **llyfelod** stye (in eye). *gw.* **llefelyn, llefrithen**

llyfn *a.* smooth, sleek

llyfr *e.g. ll.* **-au** book. **llyfr emynau** hymn-book; **llyfr gosod** set book (*in syllabus*); **llyfr lloffion** scrapbook; **llyfr lluniau** picture book; **llyfr sieciau** cheque book; **llawlyfr** handbook, manual

llyfrgell *e.b. ll.* **-oedd** library. **llyfrgell y sir** county library

llyfrgellydd *e.g. ll.* **-ion, llyfrgellwyr** librarian

llyfryn *e.g. ll.* **-nau** booklet, pamphlet

llyfu *be.* **(llyfaf)** to lick

llyffant *e.g. ll.* **-od, llyffaint** frog. *gw.* **broga: ffroga**

llygad *e.g.b. ll.* **llygaid** eye. **llygad tro** squint; **llygad y ffynnon** fountain head, original source of information; **yn llygad ei le** perfectly right, quite correct. **yn llygaid i gyd** all eyes, all attention; **(dim ond) dau lygad a thrwyn** '(only) two eyes and a nose', said of a thin person

llygadu *be.* **(llygadaf)** to eye, to watch, to have (one's) eye upon

llygaid *gw.* **llygad**

llygod *gw.* **llygoden**

llygoden *e.b. ll.* **llygod** mouse. **llygoden fach** mouse; **llygoden fawr/Ffrengig** rat

llygredig *a.* corrupt, degraded, defiled

llygredd *e.g. ll.* **-au** corruption; pollution, contamination

llygru *be.* **(llygraf)** to corrupt, to pollute, to contaminate

llynges *e.b. ll.* **-au** fleet, navy. **Y Llynges** The Navy

llym *a.* sharp, keen, severe

llyn *e.g.b. ll.* **-noedd, -nau** lake, pool

llynciau *gw.* **llwnc**

llyncu *be.* **(llyncaf)** to swallow, to devour, to gulp

llynedd *ad.* (*the definite article is used with the adverb*) last year. **Gwelais ef y llynedd** I saw him last year

llynnau *gw.* **llyn**

llynnoedd *gw.* **llyn**

llyo

llyo *be.* **(llyaf)** to lick (*S.W.*)
llys *e.g.* *ll.* **-oedd** court, hall, place. **Llys y Goron** The Crown Court; **Llys yr Ynadon** The Magistrates' Court; **Yr Uchel Lys** The High Court
llysenw *e.g.* *ll.* **-au** nickname
llysenwi *be.* **(llysenwaf)** to nickname
llysfam *e.b.* *ll.* **-au** stepmother
llysfwytäwr *e.g.* *ll.* **llysfwytawyr** vegetarian (male). **llysfwytäwraig** vegetarian (female)
llysgenhadaeth *e.b.* *ll.* **llysgenadaethau** embassy
llysgennad *e.g.* *ll.* **llysgenhadon** ambassador
llysiau *gw.* **llysieuyn**
llysieuol *a.* herbal, vegetable, botanical; spiced. **te llysieuol** herbal tea
llysieuyn *e.g.* *ll.* **llysiau** vegetable, herb
llythrennau *gw.* **llythyren**
llythrennog *a.* literate
llythyr *e.g.* *ll.* **-au, -on** letter, epistle. **llythyr caru** love-letter; **llythyr cyfreithiwr** solicitor's letter
llythyren *e.b.* *ll.* **llythrennau** letter of the alphabet. **llythrennau'r abiec** letters of the alphabet; **priflythrennau** capital letters; **llythyren y ddeddf** letter of the law
llyw *e.g.* *ll.* **-iau** leader, ruler; rudder, helm. **(bod) wrth y**

llyw (to be) at the helm, (to be) in charge
llywio *be.* **(llywiaf)** to govern, to rule; to steer, to pilot
llywodraeth *e.b.* *ll.* **-au** government. **llywodraeth ganolog** central government; **llywodraeth leol** local government
llywodraethu *be.* **(llywodraethaf)** to govern, to rule, to control
llywodraethwr *e.g.* *ll.* **llywodraethwyr** governor
llywydd *e.g.* *ll.* **-ion** president (*of society*). *gw.* **arlywydd**
llywyddu *be.* **(llywyddaf)** to preside

M

mab *e.g.* *ll.* **meibion** boy, son, man, male
maban *gw.* **baban**
mabi *gw.* **babi**
mabolgamp *e.b.* *ll.* **-au** game, sport, feat. **mabolgampau'r ysgol** school sports
mach *gw.* **bach**
machau *gw.* **bach; bachyn**
machgen *gw.* **bachgen**
machlud *e.g.* *ll.* **-oedd** setting (*of the sun*), going down. **machlud haul** sunset
machu *gw.* **bachu**
machyn *gw.* **bachyn**
mad *gw.* **bad**
madarch *e.* *torf.* *g.* mushroom(s); toadstool(s); **madarchen** *e.b.* mushroom; toadstool

manana

maddau (i) *be.* **(maddeuaf)** to forgive

mae *gw.* **bae, bod**

maer *e.g.* *ll.* **meiri** mayor. **maer y dre** the town mayor

maeres *e.b.* *ll.* **-au** mayoress

maes *e.g.* *ll.* **meysydd** field, square; syllabus. **maes chwarae** playing field; **maes o law** shortly

maestref *e.b.* *ll.* **-i, -ydd** suburb

mafonen *e.b.* *ll.* **mafon** raspberry

mag *gw.* **bag**

magiau *gw.* **bag**

magu *be.* **(magaf)** to breed, to nurse, to gain. **magu bola** to acquire a pot belly; **magu hyder** to gain confidence

Mai *e.g.* May

mai *c.* that (*emphatic*). **rwy'n sicr mai Tom yw e** I'm sure that it is Tom (and nobody else). *gw.* **bai**

maich *gw.* **baich**

main *a.* thin, lean, slim, shrill, fine

maint *e.g.b.* *ll.* **meintiau** size, dimension; magnitude; amount, quantity; extent

malchder *gw.* **balchder**

maldod *e.g.* indulgence, pampering, spoiling; caresses; affectation

maldodi *be.* **(maldodaf)** to pamper, to fondle, to pet

maled *gw.* **baled**

maledwr *gw.* **baledwr**

malot *gw.* **balot**

malu *be.* **(malaf)** to grind, to crush, to smash. **malu awyr** to talk nonsense, to talk idly

malwn *gw.* **balwn**

malwen: (*N.W.*) **malwoden** (*S.W.*) *e.b.* *ll.* **malwod** snail, slug

malwoden (*S.W.*) *gw.* **malwen**

mam *e.b.* *ll.* **-au** mother. **mam faeth** foster-mother; **mam-yng-nghyfraith** mother-in-law

mam-gu *e.b.* *ll.* **mam-guod** grandmother (*S.W.*); *gw.* **nain**

mamiaith *e.b.* *ll.* **mamieithoedd** mother tongue

mân *a.* tiny, small, minute; fine; petty. **arian mân** small change, small coin; **glaw mân** fine rain, drizzle; **glo mân** small coal, slack; **yn fân ac yn fuan** quickly and in short gasps (*of breath*); with small quick steps or movements

man *e.g.b.* *ll.* **-nau** place, spot; mark; blemish. **man a man (i fi, i ti . . .)** (it is) all the same (to me, to you . . .), (it makes) no difference; **man cychwyn** starting-point; **man cyfarfod** meeting place; **man gwan** weak spot; **yn y fan a'r lle** in the (very) place, on the (very) spot; **yn y man** soon, before (very) long, presently; on the spot, immediately, at once, now. *gw.* **ban**

manana *gw.* **banana**

manc

manc *gw.* **banc**

mancio *gw.* **bancio**

mand *gw.* **band**

mandiau *gw.* **band**

maneg *e.b. ll.* **menig** glove, gauntlet. **Gwlad y menig gwynion** Land of the white gloves (alluding to the frequent presentation of white gloves to assize judges in Wales, when there were no cases for trial)

maner *gw.* **baner**

mannau *gw.* **ban, man**

mans *e.g.* manse

mantais *e.b. ll.* **manteision** advantage. **o fantais** of advantage; **cymryd mantais (ar)** to take advantage (of)

manteisio (ar) *be.* **(manteisiaf)** to take advantage, to profit (from)

manteision *gw.* **mantais**

mantell *e.b. ll.* **-oedd, mentyll** mantle, cloak, robe

manwl *a.* exact, careful, strict; fine; particular; **yn fanwl** in detail

manylion *e.ll.* details, particulars

manylu (ar) *be.* **(manylaf)** to particularize, to go into detail (about), to be exact

manylyn *e.g. ll.* **manylion** detail

map *e.g. ll.* **-iau** map

mar *gw.* **bar**

mara *gw.* **bara**

marbeciw *gw.* **barbeciw**

marc *e.g. ll.* **-iau, -au** mark. **gwneud marc** to make one's mark

marcio *be.* **(marciaf)** to mark, to mark out

marcut coch *gw.* **barcut coch**

marchnad *e.b. ll.* **-oedd** market. **y Farchnad Gyffredin** the Common market; **y farchnad rydd** the free market

marchog *e.g. ll.* **-ion** horseman, rider; knight

mardd *gw.* **bardd**

marddoniaeth *gw.* **barddoniaeth**

marf *gw.* **barf**

marn *gw.* **barn**

marnwr *gw.* **barnwr**

mart *e.g. ll.* **-iau** mart (*S.W.*)

marw 1 *be.* **(marwaf)** to die; **wedi marw: yn farw** dead. 2 *a. ll.* **meirw, meirwon** dead, deceased. 3 *e.g. ll.* **meirw, meirwon** the dead

marwaidd *a.* lifeless, listless, sluggish

marwol *a.* deadly, fatal, mortal. **ergyd farwol** mortal blow

marwolaeth *e.b. ll.* **-au** death

mas *gw.* **bas**

masged *gw.* **basged**

masn *gw.* **basn**

masnach *e.b. ll.* **-au** trade, commerce

masnachwr *e.g. ll.* **masnachwyr** merchant, tradesman, dealer

masnau: masnys *gw.* **basn**

maswr *e.g. ll.* **maswyr** outside-half (*rugby*)

mat *e.g. ll.* **-iau** mat. *gw.* **bat**

mater *e.g. ll.* **-ion** matter, subject

meddyginiaeth

matsen: matsien *e.b.* *ll.*
matsys match. **fel matsien**
wild tempered, fiery (*lit. like
a match*)

math *e.g.* *ll.* **-au** sort, kind,
species. *gw.* **bath**

mathemateg *e.g.* mathematics

mathemategol
a. mathematical

mathemategwr *e.g.*
ll. **mathemategwyr**
mathematician

mathodyn *gw.* **bathodyn**

maw *gw.* **baw**

mawd *gw.* **bawd**

mawl *e.g.* praise

mawn *e.g.* peat. **lladd mawn**
to cut peat

mawnog *e.b.* *ll.* **-ydd** a peat
bog

mawr *a.* *ll.* **-ion** great, big,
large. *gw.* *At. Ansoddeiriau*

mawredd *e.g.* greatness,
majesty, grandeur. **Mawredd
mawr!** Good gracious!

Mawrth *e.g.* March; Tuesday;
Mars. **Mawrth y Cyntaf** St
David's Day

mecso *gw.* **becso**

mechan *gw.* **bechan**

mechgyn *gw.* **bachgen**

mechnïaeth *e.b.* bail,
suretyship

Medi *e.g.* September

medi *be.* **(medaf)** to reap, to
harvest, to cut

medru *be.* **(medraf)** to be able
to do or accomplish (*a
thing*); to be able to speak,
know (*a language*), to be
conversant with. **medru'r**

Gymraeg to know Welsh, to
be able to speak Welsh

medrus *a.* skilful, able, clever
(*with one's hand*); correct

medw *gw.* **bedwen**

medwen *gw.* **bedwen**

medyddio *gw.* **bedyddio**

medd *e.g.* mead. *gw.* **bedd,
meddaf**

meddaf (wrth) *bf.* I say, I
said. **meddwn i** I would say;
medd he/she/it says/said. *gw.*
meddu

meddai *bf.* he/she/it was
saying, he/she/it was used to
saying

meddal *a.* soft, tender, pliable

meddalu *be.* **(meddalaf)** to
soften, to become soft; to
thaw

meddalwedd *e.b.* software

meddu *be.* **(meddaf)** to
possess, to own

meddw *a.* *ll.* **-on** drunk. **yn
feddw gaib** blind drunk

meddwi (ar) *be.* **(meddwaf)** to
be drunk, to become drunk

meddwl (am) 1 *be.* **(meddyliaf,
meddylaf)** to think, to mean,
to intend. **meddwl y byd o** to
think the world of. 2 *e.g.* *ll.*
meddyliau thought, mind,
meaning, opinion

meddyg *e.g.* *ll.* **-on** doctor of
medicine

meddygfa *e.b.*
ll. **meddygfeydd** surgery *gw.*
llawdriniaeth

meddyginiaeth *e.b.* *ll.* **-au**
remedy, medicine

meddylgar

meddylgar *a.* thoughtful, pensive

meddyliau *gw.* **meddwl**

mefusen *e.b.* *ll.* **mefus** strawberry

Mehefin *e.g.* June

meiau *gw.* **bai**

meibion *gw.* **mab**

Meibl *gw.* **Beibl**

meic *e.g.* *ll.* **-iau** microphone. *gw.* **beic**

meicrodon *gw.* **microdon**

meichiau *gw.* **baich**

meiddio *be.* **(meiddiaf)** to dare, to venture. *gw.* **beiddio**

meim *e.g.b.* *ll.* **-iau** mime

meinir *e.b.* maiden

meintiau *gw.* **maint**

meio *gw.* **beio**

meirdd *gw.* **bardd**

meiri *gw.* **maer**

meirioli *be.* **(meiriolaf)** to thaw, to melt

meirniad *gw.* **beirniad**

meirniadu *gw.* **beirniadu**

meirniaid *gw.* **beirniad**

meistr *e.g.* *ll.* **-i, -iaid** master, owner

meistres *e.b.* *ll.* **-i** mistress

meistri: meistriaid *gw.* **meistr**

meistroli *be.* **(meistrolaf)** to master

meithrin *be.* **(meithrinaf)** to nurture, to rear, to foster. **meithrinfa** nursery; **ysgol feithrin** nursery school

mêl *e.g.* honey. **mis mêl** honeymoon; **yn fêl ar ei fysedd** music to his ears, to his extreme gratification

melen *a.b.* yellow: **ffrog felen** yellow frock. *gw.* **melyn**

melin *e.b.* *ll.* **-au** mill: **melin ddŵr** water mill; **melin wlân** woollen mill; **melin wynt** windmill; **gwneud melin ac eglwys** to make a great to-do of, to make a fuss about nothing

melyn *a.g.* yellow. **crys melyn** yellow shirt, **cyw melyn olaf** youngest child of family, last of the brood; **melynwy** yolk of an egg. *gw.* **melen**

melys *a.* sweet; **melysion** sweets

melysfwyd *e.g.* *ll.* **-ydd** dessert

mellt *gw.* **mellten**

mellten *e.b.* *ll.* **mellt** lightning. **fel mellten** like a flash (*of lightning*), fast

melltith *e.b.* *ll.* **-ion** curse. **Melltith arno!** Curse him!

menig *gw.* **maneg**

menter *e.b.* *ll.* **mentrau** venture, hazard

mentrau *gw.* **menter**

mentro (ar) *be.* **(mentraf)** to venture.

mentrus *a.* venturesome

mentyll *gw.* **mantell**

menthyca *gw.* **benthyca**

menyn: ymenyn *e.g.* butter. **blodau menyn** buttercups

menyw 1 *e.b.* *ll.* **-od** woman. 2 *a.* female (*S.W.*)

mêr *e.g.* *ll.* **merion** marrow (*bone*)

merch *e.b.* *ll.* **-ed** girl, daughter

metel *e.g.* *ll.* **-oedd, -au** metal; mettle

Insight

meistr *e.g.* master. meistres mistress; meistroli to master
merch *e.b.* girl, daughter. Meinir, Rhian – *proper nouns* meaning 'girl' and used as girls' names.

Mercher *e.g.* Wednesday; Mercury. **Dydd Mercher Lludw** Ash Wednesday
merchetaidd *a.* effeminate
merf *gw.* **berf**
merfa *gw.* **berfa**
merfenw *gw.* **berfenw**
merlod *gw.* **merlyn**
merlota *bf.* to go pony-trekking
merlotwr *e.g.* *ll.* **merlotwyr** pony-trekker
merlyn *e.g.* *ll.* **-nod, merlod** pony
merthyr *e.g.* *ll.* **-on** martyr. **Merthyr Tudful** town *&* county borough (S. W.)
merw *gw.* **berw**
merwi *gw.* **berwi**
mesen *e.b.* *ll.* **mes** acorn
mesul *ad.* in the measure of. **Daeth y plant i mewn fesul un** The children came in one by one; **fesul tri** three at a time
mesur 1 *e.g.* *ll.* **-au** measure, metre. **ffon fesur** rule, ruler. 2 *be.* to measure
mesurydd *e.g.* *ll.* **-ion** measurer, meter, gauge. **mesurydd glaw** rain gauge

metr *e.g.* *ll.* **-au** metre. **metr sgwâr** square metre
metrig *a.* metric
methiant *e.g.* *ll.* **methiannau** failure
methu (â) *be.* **(methaf)** to fail
meudwy *e.g.* *ll.* **-aid, -od** hermit, recluse
mewian *be.* **(mewiaf)** to mew
mewn *ardd.* in, within. **i mewn: i fewn** in, inward(s): **mewn a maes** in and out; **mewn bod** in being, extant; **mewn cariad** in love; **mewn eiliad** in a moment, at once, instantly; **mewn gwaith** in work, employed; **mewn llaw** in hand, receiving attention, under consideration; **mewn trefn** in order; **o fewn y mis** within the month; **y tu mewn: y tu fewn** inside
mewnwr *e.g.* *ll.* **mewnwyr** scrum-half (*rugby*), inside-forward (*soccer*)
meysydd *gw.* **maes**
mha *gw.* **pa**
Mhab *gw.* **Pab**
mhabell *gw.* **pabell**
mhabi *gw.* **pabi**

mhabydd

mhabydd *gw*. pabydd
mhac *gw*. pac
mhaced *gw*. paced
mhacio *gw*. pacio
mhadell *gw*. padell
mhader *gw*. pader
mhaent *gw*. paent
mhafiliwn *gw*. pafiliwn
mhafin *gw*. pafin
mhagan *gw*. pagan
mhais *gw*. pais
mhâl *gw*. pâl
mhalas *gw*. palas
mhalau: mhalod *gw*. pâl
mhalu *gw*. palu
mhamffled *gw*. pamffled
mhamffledyn *gw*. pamffledyn
mhanasen *gw*. panasen
mhanel *gw*. panel
mhannas *gw*. panasen
mhant *gw*. pant
mhapur *gw*. papur
mhapuro *gw*. papuro
mhâr *gw*. pâr
mharadwys *gw*. paradwys
mharagraff *gw*. paragraff
mharatoi *gw*. paratoi
mharc *gw*. parc
mharch *gw*. parch
mharchu *gw*. parchu
mharchus *gw*. parchus
mhardwn *gw*. pardwn
mharhad *gw*. parhad
mharsel *gw*. parsel
mharti *gw*. parti
Mhasg *gw*. Pasg
mhasiant *gw*. pasiant
mhatrwm *gw*. patrwm
mhatrwn *gw*. patrwn
mhatrymau *gw*. patrwm

mhatrynau *gw*. patrwn
mhawb *gw*. pawb
mhawen *gw*. pawen
mhebyll *gw*. pabell
mhecyn *gw*. pecyn
mhechadur *gw*. pechadur
mhechod *gw*. pechod
mhedair *gw*. pedair
mhedol *gw*. pedol
mhedwar *gw*. pedwar
mhedwaredd *gw*. pedwaredd
mhedwerydd *gw*. pedwerydd
mheg *gw*. peg
mhegwn *gw*. pegwn
mhegynau *gw*. pegwn
mheilot *gw*. peilot
mheint *gw*. peint
mheintio *gw*. peintio
mheintiwr *gw*. peintiwr
mheiriannau *gw*. peiriant
mheiriannydd *gw*. peiriannydd
mheiriant *gw*. peiriant
mheisiau *gw*. pais
mhêl *gw*. pêl
mhelydr *gw*. pelydr
mhellter *gw*. pellter
mhen *gw*. pen
mhenaethiaid *gw*. pennaeth
mhenawdau *gw*. pennawd
mhen-blwydd *gw*. pen-blwydd
mhencadlys *gw*. pencadlys
mhencampwr *gw*. pencampwr
mhenderfyniad *gw*.
  penderfyniad
mhenelin *gw*. penelin
mhenillion *gw*. pennill
mhennaeth *gw*. pennaeth
mhennau *gw*. pen
mhennawd *gw*. pennawd
mhennill *gw*. pennill

mhennod *gw*. pennod
mhenodau *gw*. pennod
mhenodi *gw*. penodi
mhenodiad *gw*. penodiad
mhenrhyn *gw*. penrhyn
mhensaer *gw*. pensaer
mhensil *gw*. pensil
mhensiwn *gw*. pensiwn
mhensiynwr *gw*. pensiynwr
mhenteulu *gw*. penteulu
mhentref *gw*. pentref
mhentwr *gw*. pentwr
mhenwythnos *gw*.
 penwythnos
mhêr *gw*. pêr
mherchen: mherchennog *gw*.
 perchen
mheren *gw*. peren
mhererin *gw*. pererin
mherfedd *gw*. perfedd
mherffaith *gw*. perffaith
mherffeithio *gw*. perffeithio
mheri *gw*. peri
mherl *gw*. perl
mherlysiau *gw*. perlysiau
mherllan *gw*. perllan
mhersli *gw*. persli
mherson *gw*. person
mhersonoliaeth *gw*.
 personoliaeth
mherth *gw*. perth
mherthynas *gw*. perthynas
mherygl *gw*. perygl
mheswch *gw*. peswch
mhesychiad *gw*. pesychiad
mheth *gw*. peth
mhiano *gw*. piano
mhianydd *gw*. pianydd
mhib *gw*. pib
mhiben *gw*. piben

mhicil *gw*. picil
mhictiwr *gw*. pictiwr
mhicwn *gw*. picwnen
mhicwnen *gw*. picwnen
mhigiad *gw*. pigiad
mhigo *gw*. pigo
mhil *gw*. pil
mhiler *gw*. piler
mhilion *gw*. pil
mhili-pala *gw*. pili-pala
mhilsen *gw*. pilsen
mhilyn *gw*. pilyn
mhin *gw*. pin
mhîn *gw*. pîn
mhînafal *gw*. pînafal
mhinnau *gw*. pin
mhinsio *gw*. pinsio
mhinwydden *gw*. pinwydden
mhioden *gw*. pioden
mhisyn *gw*. pisyn
mhlaid *gw*. plaid
mhlan *gw*. plan
mhlanced *gw*. blanced,
 planced
mhlanhigyn *gw*. planhigyn
mhlannu *gw*. plannu
mhlant *gw*. plant
mhlas *gw*. plas
mhlasty *gw*. plasty
mhlât *gw*. plât
mhlatiau *gw*. plât
mhleidiau *gw*. plaid
mhleidlais *gw*. pleidlais
mhleidleisiau *gw*. pleidlais
mhleidleisio *gw*. pleidleisio
mhleidleisiwr *gw*. pleidleisiwr
mhlentyn *gw*. plentyn
mhleser *gw*. pleser
mhleserus *gw*. pleserus
mhlesio *gw*. plesio

mhlisgyn

mhlisgyn *gw*. plisgyn

mhlisman: mhlismon *gw*.
 plisman

mhlu *gw*. pluen

mhluen *gw*. pluen

mhluf *gw*. plufyn

mhlufyn *gw*. plufyn

mhlwc *gw*. plwc

mhlwg *gw*. plwg

mhlwm *gw*. plwm

mhlwyf *gw*. plwyf

mhlygu *gw*. plygu

mhob *gw*. pob

mhobi *gw*. pobi.

mhobl *gw*. pobl

mhoblogaeth *gw*. poblogaeth

mhobman *gw*. pobman

mhobydd *gw*. pobydd

mhoced *gw*. poced

mhoen *gw*. poen

mhoeni *gw*. poeni

mhoenus *gw*. poenus

mhoenydio *gw*. poenydio

mhoer: mhoeri *gw*. poer, poeri

mhoethi *gw*. poethi

mholyn *gw*. polyn

mhont *gw*. pont

mhopeth *gw*. popeth

mhopty *gw*. popty

mhorfa *gw*. porfa

mhorfeydd *gw*. porfa

mhorffor *gw*. porffor

mhortread *gw*. portread

mhorth *gw*. porth

mhorthladd *gw*. porthladd

mhos *gw*. pos

mhosibilrwydd *gw*.
 posibilrwydd

mhost *gw*. post

mhostman: mhostmon *gw*.

postman

mhostyn *gw*. postyn

mhotel *gw*. potel

mhowdr: mhowdwr *gw*. powdr

mhowdrau *gw*. powdr

mhowlen *gw*. bowlen

mhraidd *gw*. praidd

mhram *gw*. pram

mhrawf *gw*. prawf

mhregeth *gw*. pregeth

mhregethu *gw*. pregethu

mhregethwr *gw*. pregethwr

mhreiddiau *gw*. praidd

mhren *gw*. pren

mhrennau *gw*. pren

mhrentis *gw*. prentis

mhrentisiaeth *gw*. prentisiaeth

mhrentisiaid *gw*. prentis

mhres *gw*. pres

mhreseb *gw*. preseb

mhresennol *gw*. presennol

mhresenoldeb *gw*.
 presenoldeb

mhresgripsiwn *gw*.
 presgripsiwn

mhreswyl: mhreswylfod *gw*.
 preswyl

mhridwerth *gw*. pridwerth

mhridd *gw*. pridd

mhrifardd *gw*. prifardd

mhrifathrawes *gw*.
 prifathrawes

mhrifathro *gw*. prifathro

mhrifddinas *gw*. prifddinas

mhrifeirdd *gw*. prifardd

mhrifysgol *gw*. prifysgol

mhriffordd *gw*. priffordd

mhrinder *gw*. prinder

mhrintio *gw*. printio

mhriod *gw*. priod

milfeddyg

mhriodas *gw.* priodas
mhriodi *gw.* priodi
mhriodol *gw.* priodol
mhris *gw.* pris
mhroblem *gw.* problem
mhrofi *gw.* profi
mhrofiad *gw.* profiad
mhrofion *gw.* prawf
mhrofocio : mhryfocio *gw.* profocio
mhroffid *gw.* proffid
mhroffwyd *gw.* proffwyd
mhrotest *gw.* protest
mhryd *gw.* pryd
Mhrydain *gw.* Prydain
mhrydau *gw.* pryd
mhryder *gw.* pryder
mhrydferthwch *gw.* prydferthwch
mhrydiau *gw.* pryd
mhryf: mhryfedyn: mhryfyn *gw.* pryf
mhryfocio *gw.* profocio
mhrynhawn *gw.* prynhawn
mhrynu *gw.* prynu
mhrynwr *gw.* prynwr
mhrysurdeb *gw.* prysurdeb
mhulpud *gw.* pulpud
mhum: mhump *gw.* pum
mhunnau *gw.* punt
mhunnoedd *gw.* punt
mhunt *gw.* punt
mhupur *gw.* pupur
mhurfa *gw.* purfa
mhuro *gw.* puro
mhwdin *gw.* pwdin
mhwdryn *gw.* pwdryn
mhŵer *gw.* pŵer
mhwll *gw.* pwll
mhwllyn *gw.* pwllyn

mhwmp *gw.* pwmp
mhwnc *gw.* pwnc
mhwrpas *gw.* pwrpas
mhwrs *gw.* pwrs
mhwyll *gw.* pwyll
mhwyllgor *gw.* pwyllgor
mhwynt *gw.* pwynt
mhwys *gw.* pwys
mhwysedd *gw.* pwysedd
mhwysigrwydd *gw.* pwysigrwydd
mhwyslais *gw.* pwyslais
mhwyso *gw.* pwyso
mhwyth *gw.* pwyth
mhyllau *gw.* pwll *gw.* pyllyn
mhyllyn *gw.* pyllyn
mhymtheg *gw.* pymtheg
mhymthegfed *gw.* pymthegfed
mhynciau *gw.* pwnc
mhyped *gw.* pyped
mhyrsau *gw.* pwrs
mhyrth *gw.* porth
mhys *gw.* pysen
mhysen *gw.* pysen
mhysgodyn *gw.* pysgodyn
mhysgota *gw.* pysgota
mhysgotwr *gw.* pysgotwr
mhyst *gw.* postyn
mhythefnos *gw.* pythefnos
mi *gw.* fi; *geiryn (particle used before a verb)* (N.W.). *gw.* fe
micro-don *e.b.g.* microwave; microwave oven
migwrn *e.g. ll.* migyrnau. ankle, knuckle
mil *e.b. ll.* -oedd thousand
mil *gw.* bil
milfeddyg *e.g. ll.* -on veterinary surgeon

milgi

milgi *e.g.* *ll.* milgwn
greyhound. **fel milgi** swift,
like a greyhound
miliwn *e.b.* *ll.* miliynau
million. **miliynydd**
millionaire
miloedd *gw.* mil
milwr *e.g.* *ll.* milwyr soldier
milltir *e.b.* *ll.* -oedd mile.
 milltir sgwâr square mile;
 immediate locality
min *e.g.* *ll.* -ion lip; side,
 bank; (cutting) edge (of
 blade). **min y gyllell** the edge
 of the knife; **min y ffordd** the
 wayside; **min y môr** the sea-
 shore, seaside; **byw wrth fin y**
 gyllell to live from hand to
 mouth. *gw.* **bin**
miniog *a.* sharp, keen, edged
minlliw *e.g.* lipstick
minnau *rhag.* I also, me
mioleg *gw.* bioleg
miri *e.g.* merriment, fun
mis *e.g.* *ll.* -oedd month.
 Mis Bach February
misged *gw.* bisged
misgedi *gw.* bisged
misgïen *gw.* bisgïen
misglwyf *e.g.* menstruation,
 period
misoedd *gw.* mis
misol *a.* monthly
misolyn *e.g.* *ll.* misolion
 monthly (magazine)
miwsig *e.g.* music
mlaen *gw.* blaen
mlaendal *gw.* blaendal
mlaenor *gw.* blaenor
mlaenwr *gw.* blaenwr

mlagur *gw.* blaguryn
mlaguryn *gw.* blaguryn
mlaidd *gw.* blaidd
mlanced *gw.* blanced
mlas *gw.* blas
mlasu *gw.* blasu
mlawd *gw.* blawd
mleiddiaid *gw.* blaidd
mlew *gw.* blewyn
mlewyn *gw.* blewyn
mlinder *gw.* blinder
mlino *gw.* blino
mlodau *gw.* blodyn
mlodeugerdd *gw.*
 blodeugerdd
mlodfresychen *gw.*
 blodfresychen
mlodyn *gw.* blodyn
mloedd *gw.* bloedd
mloeddio *gw.* bloeddio
mlows *gw.* blows
mlwch *gw.* blwch
mlwydd *gw.* blwydd
mlwyddyn *gw.* blwyddyn
mlychau *gw.* blwch
mlynedd *gw.* blwyddyn
mlynyddoedd *gw.* blwyddyn
mocs *gw.* bocs
moch *gw.* boch, mochyn
mochyn *e.g.* *ll.* moch pig. **fel**
 mochyn dirty, filthy, fat, like
 a pig
mod *gw.* bod
modfedd *e.b.* *ll.* -i inch
modiau *gw.* bawd
modloni *gw.* bodloni
modrwy *e.b.* *ll.* -on ring.
 modrwy aur gold ring;
 modrwy briodas wedding-
 ring; **modrwy glust**
 earring

modryb *e.b.* *ll.* **-edd** aunt

modur *e.g.* *ll.* **-on** motor

modurwr *e.g.* *ll.* **modurwyr** motorist

modd *e.g.* *ll.* **-ion** manner; means, wealth. **gwaetha'r modd** worse luck; **modd bynnag** however; **pa fodd?** how? *gw.* **bodd**

moddhad *gw.* **boddhad**

moddi *gw.* **boddi**

moddion *e.ll.* means; medicine: **moddion gras** means of grace. *gw.* **modd**

moel *a.* bare; bald

moelni *e.g.* bareness; baldness

moes *e.b.* *ll.* **-au** usual behaviour, habit, wont; *in plural:* manners; morals. **moesau da** good manners; good morals

moesol *a.* ethical; moral

moethus *a.* luxurious, comfortable

mogi *be.* **(mogaf)** to suffocate, to smother; **Brawd mogi yw tagu** Suffocating is akin to choking, one is as bad as the other

mol *gw.* **bol**

mola *gw.* **bola**

moli *be.* **(molaf)** to praise

moliau *gw.* **bol**

mollt *gw.* **bollt**

mom *gw.* **bom**

Môn, Ynys *e.b.* Anglesey. **Môn Mam Cymru** Anglesey Mother of Wales

môn *gw.* **bôn**

moneddiges *gw.* **boneddiges**

moneddigion *gw.* **bonheddwr**

monheddwr *gw.* **bonheddwr**

môr *e.g.* *ll.* **moroedd** sea, ocean. **Y Môr Canoldir** Mediterranean Sea; **Môr Iwerydd** Atlantic Ocean; **Môr Tawel** Pacific Ocean

mor *ad.* (*followed by soft mutation, except for adjectives beginning with* **ll** *and* **rh**) as, so, how. **mor dew â mochyn** as fat as a pig; **mor ddu â'r nos** as black as the night; **mor goch â thân** as red as fire; **mor wyn ag eira** as white as snow

mord *gw.* **bord**

mordaith *e.b.* *ll.* **mordeithiau** (sea) voyage

mordau: mordydd *gw.* **bord**

morddwyd *e.b.* *ll.* **-ydd** thigh

more *gw.* **bore**

morfa *e.b.g.* *ll.* **morfeydd** sea-marsh, bog, fen

morfeydd *gw.* **morfa**

morfil *e.g.* *ll.* **-od** whale

morgais *e.g.* *ll.* **morgeisiau** mortgage

Morgannwg *e.b.* Glamorgan. **De Morgannwg** South Glamorgan; **Gorllewin Morgannwg** West Glamorgan; **Morgannwg Ganol** Mid Glamorgan (*1974–96*); **Prifysgol Morgannwg** Glamorgan University

morgeisiau *gw.* **morgais**

morgrugyn *e.g.* *ll.* **morgrug** ant

morio

morio *be*. **(moriaf)** to sail

môr-leidr *e.g. ll*. **môr-ladron**
pirate

morlo *e.g. ll*. **morloi** seal

moroedd *gw*. **môr**

moron *gw*. **moronen**

moronen *e.b. ll*. **moron**
carrot

morthwyl *e.g. ll*. **-ion** hammer

morwr *e.g. ll*. **morwyr** sailor,
seaman

morwyn *e.b. ll*. **morynion**
maid, girl, virgin. **y Forwyn
Fair** the Virgin Mary

morwyr *gw*. **morwr**

mos *gw*. **bos**

mosys *gw*. **bos**

motwm *gw*. **botwm**

motymau *gw*. **botwm**

mowlen *gw*. **bowlen**

mragdy *gw*. **bragdy**

mraich *gw*. **braich**

mrain *gw*. **brân**

mraint *gw*. **braint**

mrân *gw*. **brân**

mraslun *gw*. **braslun**

mraster *gw*. **braster**

mraw *gw*. **braw**

mrawd *gw*. **brawd**

mrawddeg *gw*. **brawddeg**

mrecwast *gw*. **brecwast**

mrech *gw*. **brech**

mrechdan *gw*. **brechdan**

mrechiad *gw*. **brechiad**

mreichiau *gw*. **braich**

mreichled *gw*. **breichled**

mrenhines *gw*. **brenhines**

mrenin *gw*. **brenin**

mres *gw*. **bres**

mrest *gw*. **brest**

mresychen *gw*. **bresychen**

mrethyn *gw*. **brethyn**

mreuddwyd *gw*. **breuddwyd**

mreuddwydio *gw*.
breuddwydio

mreuddwydion *gw*.
breuddwyd

mrifo *gw*. **brifo**

mrig *gw*. **brig**

mrigau *gw*. **brig, brigyn**

mrigyn *gw*. **brigyn**

mriwsionyn *gw*. **briwsionyn**

mro *gw*. **bro**

mrodorion *gw*. **brodor**

mrodyr *gw*. **brawd**

mroga *gw*. **broga**

mron *gw*. **bron**

mronfraith *gw*. **bronfraith**

mronnau: mronnydd *gw*. **bron**

mrown *gw*. **brown**

mröydd *gw*. **bro**

mrws: mrwsh *gw*. **brws**

mrwsio: mrwsho *gw*. **brwsio**

mrwsys: mrwshys *gw*. **brws**

mrwydr *gw*. **brwydr**

mrwydrau *gw*. **brwydr**

mryd *gw*. **bryd**

mryn *gw*. **bryn**

mryniau *gw*. **bryn**

mrys *gw*. **brys**

mrysio *gw*. **brysio**

muarth *gw*. **buarth**

muchod *gw*. **buwch**

mud *a*. dumb, mute

mudiad *e.g. ll*. **-au**
movement. **Mudiad Ysgolion
Meithrin** (Welsh) Nursery
Schools' Movement

mudd-dâl *gw*. **budd-dâl**

muddugoliaeth *gw*.
buddugoliaeth

mugail *gw.* **bugail**
mugeiliaid *gw.* **bugail**
mugeilio *gw.* **bugeilio**
mul *e.g.* *ll.* **-od** donkey; mule
munud *e.g.b.* *ll.* **-au** minute.
  Arhoswch funud! Wait a
  minute! **ugain munud** twenty
  minutes
mur *e.g.* *ll.* **-iau** wall
musnes *gw.* **busnes**
muwch *gw.* **buwch**
mwced *gw.* **bwced**
mwg *e.g.* smoke
mwgwd *e.g.* *ll.* **mygydau**
  mask
mwlch *gw.* **bwlch**
mwnci *e.g.* *ll.* **mwncïod**
  monkey
mwrdeistref *gw.* **bwrdeistref**
mwrdd *gw.* **bwrdd**
mwriad *gw.* **bwriad**
mws *gw.* **bws**
mwstash *e.g.* *ll.* **mwstashis**
  moustache
mwstwr *e.g.* *ll.* **mystyrau**
  noise, commotion, bustle
  (*S.W.*)
mwthyn *gw.* **bwthyn**
mwy 1 *a.* bigger, larger,
  greater, more, louder, longer,
  further. **2** *ad.* more (*often
  followed by* **na**). **mwy na**
  more than. **mwy na digon**
  too much, excessive; **mwy na
  mwy** a lot, a great deal, very
  many, too much,
  exceedingly; **mwy na thebyg**
  more than likely; **mwy neu
  lai** more or less. *gw.* **mawr**
mwyach *ad.* any more, any
  longer, again, henceforth

mwyaf *gw.* **mawr**
mwyar *gw.* **mwyaren**
mwyaren *e.b.* *ll.* **mwyar**
  blackberry
mwyd *gw.* **bwyd**
mwydlen *gw.* **bwydlen**
mwydo: mwyda *gw.* **bwydo**
mwydod *gw.* **mwydyn**
mwydyn *e.g.* *ll.* **mwydod**
  worm
mwyn 1 *e.g.* *ll.* **-au** mineral;
  ore. **2** *e.g.* sake. **er mwyn**
  for the sake of; **er mwyn Duw**
  for God's sake. **3** *a.* gentle,
  mild, dear
mwynhad *e.g.* enjoyment,
  pleasure
mwynhau *be.* (**mwynhaf**) to
  enjoy; to become mild
mwyta: myta *gw.* **bwyta**
mwyty *gw.* **bwyty**
mychan *gw.* **bychan.** *gw.*
  bechan
myd *gw.* **byd**
myddin *gw.* **byddin**
myfi *rhag.* I, me, myself
myfyrdod *e.g.* *ll.* **-au**
  meditation
myfyrio (ar) *be.* (**myfyriaf**) to
  study, to meditate
myfyriwr *e.g.* *ll.* **myfyrwyr**
  student. **myfyriwr hŷn**
  mature student
myglyd *a.* smoky, close,
  stifling
mygu *be.* (**mygaf**) to smoke;
  to smother; to suffocate
mygydau *gw.* **mwgwd**
mylchau *gw.* **bwlch**
mynach *e.g.* *ll.* **-od, mynaich**
  monk

mynachlog

mynachlog *e.b. ll.* -ydd
monastery
mynachod *gw.* mynach
mynaich *gw.* mynach
mynd: myned (â, at, i, yn) *be.*
(af) to go, to proceed. *gw.*
At. Berfau
mynedfa *e.b. ll.* mynedfeydd
entrance, passage
mynedfeydd *gw.* mynedfa
mynediad *e.g. ll.* -au
admission, access, entry;
going. **mynediad am ddim**
admission free
mynegai *e.g. ll.* mynegeion
index, concordance
mynegeion *gw.* mynegai
mynegi (i) *be.* (mynegaf) to
tell, to indicate
mynnu *be.* (mynnaf) to will,
to insist, to wish, to obtain
mynwent *e.b. ll.* -ydd
graveyard, churchyard,
cemetery
Mynwy (Sir) *e.b.*
Monmouthshire
mynychu *be.* (mynychaf) to
attend
mynydd *e.g. ll.* -oedd
mountain; **llosgfynydd**
volcano
mynyddig: mynyddog *a.*
mountainous

myrbryd *gw.* byrbryd
myrddau *gw.* bwrdd
myrfodd *gw.* byrfodd
myrfoddau *gw.* byrfodd
myrr *e.g.* myrrh
mys *gw.* bys
mysedd *gw.* bys
mysiau *gw.* bws
mystyrau *gw.* mwstwr
mysys *gw.* bws
myta *gw.* bwyta
myth *e.g. ll.* -au myth
mythynnod *gw.* bwthyn
myw *gw.* byw
mywyd *gw.* bywyd
mywydeg *gw.* bywydeg

N

na 1 *c.* (*followed by spirant
mutation*) nor, neither, than.
2 *ad.* no, not. *gw.* da.
gw. At. Treigladau
nabod *gw.* adnabod
nac 1 *c.* neither, nor. 2 *ad.*
no, not
nad *ad.* not
nadansoddi *gw.* dadansoddi
nadl *gw.* dadl
nadlau *gw.* dadlau
Nadolig *e.g. ll.* -au Christmas.
Nadolig Llawen Merry
Christmas

Insight

Nadolig *e.g.* Christmas. **Gŵyl y Nadolig** Christmas Holiday;
Bendithion y Nadolig the Blessings of Christmas; **Carolau'r
Nadolig** Christmas Carols; **Teisen Nadolig** Christmas Cake.

nadredd: nadroedd *gw.* **neidr**
naddo *ad.* no (*negative answer to questions using verbs in the past tense*) **Fuest ti yn y dre ddoe? Naddo** Were you in the town yesterday? No. **Ganodd e gyda'r côr? Naddo** Did he sing with the choir? No. **Fuoch chi yn Rhos erioed? Naddo** Were you ever in Rhos? No
naddu *be.* (**naddaf**) to chip, to hew, to whittle
naear *gw.* **daear**
naeareg *gw.* **daeareg**
naeargryn *gw.* **daeargryn**
naearyddiaeth *gw.* **daearyddiaeth**
nafad *gw.* **dafad**
nag *c.* than
nage *ad.* not so, no
nagrau *gw.* **deigryn**
nai *e.g.* *ll.* **neiaint** nephew
naid *e.g.* *ll.* **neidiau** jump, leap, bound
nail *gw.* **dalen, deilen**
naill *rhag.* the one, either: **y naill neu'r llall** the one or the other; **naill ai Ebrill neu Fai** either April or May
nain *e.b.* *ll.* **neiniau** grandmother (*N.W.*). *gw.* **mam-gu**
naioni *gw.* **daioni**
nal: nala *gw.* **dal**
nalen *gw.* **dalen**
nalgylch *gw.* **dalgylch**
nallu *gw.* **dallu**
nam *e.g.* *ll.* **-au** flaw, blemish, mark

nameg *gw.* **dameg**
namhegion *gw.* **dameg**
namwain *gw.* **damwain**
nanfon *gw.* **danfon**
nangos *gw.* **dangos**
nannedd *gw.* **dannedd**
nannoedd *gw.* **dannoedd**
nant *e.b.* *ll.* **nentydd** brook, stream. *gw.* **dant**
narganfod *gw.* **darganfod**
narlith *gw.* **darlith**
narlithio *gw.* **darlithio**
narlithiwr: narlithydd *gw.* **darlithiwr**
narlun *gw.* **darlun**
narlunio *gw.* **darlunio**
narlledu *gw.* **darlledu**
narllen *gw.* **darllen**
narllenwr: narllenydd *gw.* **darllenwr**
narn *gw.* **darn**
natblygiad *gw.* **datblygiad**
natblygu *gw.* **datblygu**
natgan *gw.* **datgan**
natganiad *gw.* **datganiad**
natganoli *gw.* **datganoli**
natguddio *gw.* **datguddio**
natod *gw.* **datod**
natrys *gw.* **datrys**
natur *e.b.* nature; temper
naturiol *a.* natural
nathliad *gw.* **dathliad**
nathlu *gw.* **dathlu**
nau *gw.* **dau**
naw 1 *a.* nine. **2** *e.g.* nine. **naw deg** ninety; **naw deg un** ninety one; **deunaw** eighteen; **naw wfft ichi!** blow you!
nawdd *e.g.* refuge; patronage, support

nawns

nawns *gw*. **dawns**
nawnsio *gw*. **dawnsio**
nawr *ad*. now. *gw*. **rŵan**

neidiwr *e.g. ll*. **neidwyr**
jumper, leaper

Insight

nawr : rŵan *ad*. now. If we ignore the accent, we have a palindrome. **Nawr amdani!** Now for it!

---

naws *e.b. ll*. **-au** feeling, nature, tingle, disposition, nuance. **naws y gaeaf** feeling of winter; **naws oer** cold feeling
ne *gw*. **de**
neall *gw*. **deall**
neb *e.g.* anyone, no one. **Does neb yma** There's no one here
nechrau *gw*. **dechrau**
nechreuad *gw*. **dechreuad**
neddf *gw*. **deddf**
neddfu *gw*. **deddfu**
nef: nefoedd *e.b.* heaven. **Nefoedd Wen!** Good heavens!
nefol: nefolaidd *a.* heavenly
nefnydd *gw*. **defnydd**
nefnyddio *gw*. **defnyddio**
neffro *gw*. **deffro**
neg: neng *gw*. **deg**
negawd *gw*. **degawd**
neges *e.b. ll*. **-au, -euon** message, errand. **negesydd** messenger
negyddol *a.* negative
neiaint *gw*. **nai**
neialog *gw*. **deialog**
neidiau *gw*. **naid**
neidio *be.* **(neidiaf)** to jump, to leap

neidr *e.b. ll*. **nadroedd, nadredd** snake
neidwyr *gw*. **neidiwr**
neigryn *gw*. **deigryn**
neilen *gw*. **deilen**
neilliaid: neillion *gw*. **dall**
neilltu *e.g.* one side. **o'r neilltu** apart, aside
neilltuo *be.* **(neilltuaf)** to reserve, to set aside, to earmark
neilltuol *a.* special, particular, peculiar. **yn neilltuol o oer** particularly cold
neiniau *gw*. **nain**
neintydd *gw*. **deintydd**
neis *a.* nice
neiseb *gw*. **deiseb**
neithiwr *ad.* last night
nelw *gw*. **delw**
nen *e.b. ll*. **-nau, -noedd** ceiling; heaven, sky
nenfwd *e.g. ll*. **nenfydau** ceiling
nentydd *gw*. **nant**
nenu *gw*. **denu**
nerbyn *gw*. **derbyn**
nerbynneb *gw*. **derbynneb**
nerbynnydd *w.* **derbynnydd**
nerf *e.b. ll*. **-au** nerve

nerfus *a.* nervous
neri *gw.* **deri**
nerth *e.g.* *ll.* **-oedd** strength,
  might, power
nerthoedd *gw.* **nerth**
nerw *gw.* **derw**
nerwen *gw.* **derwen**
nes *c. & ardd.* until. *gw.*
  agos
nesaf *a.* next. *gw.* **agos**
nesáu (at) *be.* **(nesâf)** to
  approach, to draw near
nesed *gw.* **agos**
nesg *gw.* **desg**
netholiad *gw.* **detholiad**
neu *c.* *(followed by soft*
  mutation) or. **bachgen neu**
  ferch boy or girl; **eira neu**
  law rain or snow. (*Note:*
  conjugated forms of verbs do
  not *mutate after* **neu**)
  Rhedodd neu cerddodd He
  walked or ran; **Holais neu**
  gofynnais I questioned or
  asked
neuadd *e.b.* *ll.* **-au** hall:
  Neuadd Gyhoeddus Public
  Hall; **Neuadd Les** Welfare
  Hall
neuawd *gw.* **deuawd**
neuddeg *gw.* **deuddeg**
neuddegfed *gw.* **deuddegfed**
neugain *gw.* **deugain**
neunaw *gw.* **deunaw**
neuoedd *gw.* **dau**
newid 1 *be.* **(newidiaf)** to
  change, to alter. **2** *e.g.* *ll.*
  -iadau change
newin *gw.* **dewin**
newis *gw.* **dewis**

newydd 1 *a.* new. **newydd**
  sbon brand new. **2** *e.g.* *ll.*
  -ion news. **papur newydd**
  newspaper. **Mae e newydd**
  ganu. He has just sung
newydd-ddyfodiad *e.g.* *ll.*
  newydd-ddyfodiaid
  newcomer
newyddiadurwr *e.g.* *ll.*
  newyddiadurwyr journalist
newyddion *gw.* **newydd**
newyn *e.g.* famine, hunger
nhabl *gw.* **tabl**
nhabled *gw.* **tabled**
nhacl *gw.* **tacl**
nhaclo *gw.* **taclo**
nhaclu *gw.* **taclu**
nhaclwr *gw.* **taclwr**
nhacsi *gw.* **tacsi**
Nhachwedd *gw.* **Tachwedd**
nhad *gw.* **tad**
nhad-cu *gw.* **tad-cu**
nhafarn *gw.* **tafarn**
nhafarnwr *gw.* **tafarnwr**
nhafell *gw.* **tafell**
nhaflegryn *gw.* **taflegryn**
nhaflen *gw.* **taflen**
nhaflu *gw.* **taflu**
nhafod *gw.* **tafod**
nhafodiaith *gw.* **tafodiaith**
nhafol *gw.* **tafol**
nhagfa *gw.* **tagfa**
nhagu *gw.* **tagu**
nhangnefedd *gw.* **tangnefedd**
nhai *gw.* **tŷ**
nhaid *gw.* **taid**
nhair *gw.* **tair**
nhaith *gw.* **taith**
nhâl *gw.* **tâl**
nhalai *gw.* **talai**

nhalaith

nhalaith *gw.* talaith	nhechneg *gw.* techneg
nhalcen *gw.* talcen	nhechnegwr *gw.* technegwr
nhaleb *gw.* taleb	nhechnoleg *gw.* technoleg
nhalent *gw.* talent	nhegan *gw.* tegan
nhaloedd *gw.* tâl	nhegell *gw.* tecell
nhalu *gw.* talu	nhegwch *gw.* tegwch
nhalwr *gw.* talwr	nhei *gw.* tei
nhalwrn *gw.* talwrn	nheiar *gw.* teiar
nhamaid *gw.* tamaid	nheidiau *gw.* taid
nhameidiau *gw.* tamaid	nheigr *gw.* teigr
nhân *gw.* tân	nheiliwr *gw.* teiliwr
nhanau *gw.* tân	nheilsen *gw.* teilsen
nhancer *gw.* tancer	nheilwres *gw.* teilwres
nhanio *gw.* tanio	nheilyngdod *gw.* teilyngdod
nhannau *gw.* tant	nheimlad *gw.* teimlad
nhanseilio *gw.* tanseilio	nheimlo *gw.* teimlo
nhant *gw.* tant	nheipiadur *gw.* teipiadur
nhanwydd *gw.* tanwydd	nheisen *gw.* teisen
nhap *gw.* tap	nheitl *gw.* teitl
nhâp *gw.* tâp	nheithiau *gw.* taith
nhapiau *gw.* tap, tâp	nheithio *gw.* teithio
nharan *gw.* taran	nheithiwr *gw.* teithiwr
nharddiad *gw.* tarddiad	nhelediad *gw.* telediad
nharged *gw.* targed	nheledu *gw.* teledu
nharian *gw.* tarian	nheleffon *gw.* teleffon
nhariannau *gw.* tarian	nhelyn *gw.* telyn
nharo *gw.* taro	nhelyneg *gw.* telyneg
nharw *gw.* tarw	nhelynor *gw.* telynor
nhasg *gw.* tasg	nhelynores *gw.* telynores
nhasgu *gw.* tasgu	nhelynorion *gw.* telynor
nhaten *gw.* taten	nheml *gw.* teml
nhato: nhatws *gw.* taten	nherfyn *gw.* terfyn
nhawelu *gw.* tawelu	nherfysg *gw.* terfysg
nhawelwch *gw.* tawelwch	nherfysgaeth *gw.* terfysgaeth
nhawelydd *gw.* tawelydd	nherfysgwr *gw.* terfysgwr
nhawelyn *gw.* tawelyn	nherm *gw.* term
nhe *gw.* te	nhes *gw.* tes
nhebot *gw.* tebot	nhestun *gw.* testun
nhebygrwydd *gw.* tebygrwydd	nheulu *gw.* teulu
nhecell *gw.* tecell	nheyrnas *gw.* teyrnas

nhiced *gw*. ticed
nhîm *gw*. tîm
nhip *gw*. tip
nhipyn *gw*. tipyn
nhir *gw*. tir
nhirlun *gw*. tirlun
nhiroedd *gw*. tir
nhiwtor *gw*. tiwtor
nhlodi *gw*. tlodi
nhlws *gw*. tlws
nhlysau *gw*. tlws
nho *gw*. to
nhocyn *gw*. tocyn
nhocynnwr *gw*. tocynnwr
nhoddi *gw*. toddi
nhoes *gw*. toes
nhoiled *gw*. toiled
nholc *gw*. tolc
nholl *gw*. toll
nhon *gw*. ton
nhôn *gw*. tôn
nhonau *gw*. tôn
nhonfedd *gw*. tonfedd
nhonnau *gw*. ton
nhorch *gw*. torch
nhorf *gw*. torf
nhorfeydd *gw*. torf
nhoriad *gw*. toriad
nhorri *gw*. torri
nhors *gw*. tors
nhorth *gw*. torth
nhosau *gw*. tosyn
nhost *gw*. tost
nhostrwydd *gw*. tostrwydd
nhosyn *gw*. tosyn
nhrachwant *gw*. trachwant
nhraddodiad *gw*. traddodiad
nhraed *gw*. troed
nhraeth *gw*. traeth
nhraethau *gw*. traeth

nhraethawd *gw*. traethawd
nhrafnidiaeth *gw*. trafnidiaeth
nhrafod *gw*. trafod
nhrafferth *gw*. trafferth
nhrafferthu *gw*. trafferthu
nhraffordd *gw*. traffordd
nhraffyrdd *gw*. traffordd
nhrai *gw*. trai
nhrais *gw*. trais
nhrallod *gw*. trallod
nhrallwysiad *gw*. trallwysiad
nhrap *gw*. trap
nhraul *gw*. traul
nhrawsblannu *gw*.
  trawsblannu
nhrawst *gw*. trawst
nhrechu *gw*. trechu
nhref: nhre *gw*. tref
nhrefn *gw*. trefn
nhrefnu *gw*. trefnu
nhrefnydd *gw*. trefnydd
nhrefydd *gw*. tref
nhreial *gw*. treial
nhreiglad *gw*. treiglad
nhreiglo *gw*. treiglo
nhreisio *gw*. treisio
nhrên *gw*. trên
nhrenau *gw*. trên
nhreth *gw*. treth
nhrethdalwr *gw*. trethdalwr
nhrethu *gw*. trethu
nhreuliau *gw*. traul
nhreulio *gw*. treulio
nhri *gw*. tri
nhriawd *gw*. triawd
nhric *gw*. tric
nhrigain *gw*. trigain
nhrigfan *gw*. trigfan
nhrigolion *gw*. trigolion
nhrin *gw*. trin

nhrindod

nhrindod *gw.* trindod
nhrioedd *gw.* trioedd
nhriongl *gw.* triongl
nhristwch *gw.* tristwch
nhro *gw.* tro
nhrochi *gw.* trochi
nhroeau *gw.* tro
nhroed *gw.* troed
nhroedfedd *gw.* troedfedd
nhroedffordd *gw.* troedffordd
nhröedigaeth *gw.* tröedigaeth
nhroedio *gw.* troedio
nhroeon *gw.* tro
nhrogylch *gw.* trogylch
nhroi *gw.* troi
nhrosedd *gw.* trosedd
nhroseddwr *gw.* troseddwr
nhrosgais *gw.* trosgais
nhrosglwyddo *gw.*
  trosglwyddo
nhrosiad *gw.* trosiad
nhroswr *gw.* troswr
nhrothwy *gw.* trothwy
nhrowsus *gw.* trowsus
nhruan *gw.* truan
nhrueni *gw.* trueni
nhrugaredd *gw.* trugaredd
nhrwbl *gw.* trwbl
nhrwser *gw.* trwser
nhrwsiwr *gw.* trwsiwr
nhrwydded *gw.* trwydded
nhrwyn *gw.* trwyn
nhrychineb *gw.* trychineb
nhrydan *gw.* trydan
nhrydanwr *gw.* trydanwr
nhrydedd *gw.* trydedd
nhrydydd *gw.* trydydd
nhrysor *gw.* trysor
nhrysorfa *gw.* trysorfa
nhrysori *gw.* trysori

nhrysorydd *gw.* trysorydd
nhrywydd *gw.* trywydd
nhudalen *gw.* tudalen
nhueddiad *gw.* tueddiad
nhun *gw.* tun
nhunnell *gw.* tunnell
nhw: hwy *rhag.* they, them.
  Ble maen nhw? Where are
  they? **Gwelodd nhw** He/she
  saw them
nhwlc *gw.* twlc
nhwll *gw.* twll
nhwmpath *gw.* twmpath
nhwndis *gw.* twndis
nhwnel *gw.* twnel
nhwpsyn *gw.* twpsyn
nhŵr *gw.* tŵr
nhwr *gw.* twr
nhwrci *gw.* twrci
nhwristiaeth *gw.* twristiaeth
nhwrw *gw.* twrw
nhwyll *gw.* twyll
nhwyllo *gw.* twyllo
nhwymo *gw.* twymo
nhwymyn *gw.* twymyn
nhŷ *gw.* tŷ
nhybied: nhybio *gw.* tybied
nhyddyn *gw.* tyddyn
nhyddynnwr *gw.* tyddynnwr
nhyfiant *gw.* tyfiant
nhyfu *gw.* tyfu
nhynged *gw.* tynged
nhyle *gw.* tyle
nhylwyth *gw.* tylwyth
nhyllau *gw.* twll
nhyllu *gw.* tyllu
nhylluan *gw.* tylluan
nhymer *gw.* tymer
nhymestl *gw.* tymestl
nhymheredd *gw.* tymheredd

niswyddo

nhymhorau *gw.* **tymor**
nhymor *gw.* **tymor**
nhyner *gw.* **tyner**
nhynerwch *gw.* **tynerwch**
nhynnu *gw.* **tynnu**
nhyrfa *gw.* **tyrfa**
nhyst *gw.* **tyst**
nhystiolaeth *gw.* **tystiolaeth**
nhystysgrif *gw.* **tystysgrif**
nhywel *gw.* **tywel**
nhywod *gw.* **tywod**
nhywydd *gw.* **tywydd**
nhywyllu *gw.* **tywyllu**
nhywyllwch *gw.* **tywyllwch**
nhywys *gw.* **tywys**
nhywysog *gw.* **tywysog**
nhywysoges *gw.* **tywysoges**
ni *rhag.* we, us
ni: nid *ad.* not
niacon *gw.* **diacon**
niafol *gw.* **diafol**
nial *gw.* **dial**
nianc *gw.* **dianc**
niawl *gw.* **diawl**
niawliaid *gw.* **diafol, diawl**
niben *gw.* **diben**
nid *gw.* **ni**
niddordeb *gw.* **diddordeb**
nieithryn *gw.* **dieithryn**
nifer (o) *e.g.b.* *ll.* -oedd, -i
  number, quantity. **nifer o**
  fechgyn a number of boys
niferyn *gw.* **diferyn**
nifetha *gw.* **difetha**
nifyrru *gw.* **difyrru**
niffiniad *gw.* **diffiniad**
niffinio *gw.* **diffinio**
niffodd *gw.* **diffodd**
niffyg *gw.* **diffyg**
nigon *gw.* **digon**

nigonedd *gw.* **digonedd**
nigwyddiad *gw.* **digwyddiad**
nihareb *gw.* **dihareb**
niheintydd *gw.* **diheintydd**
nihuno *gw.* **dihuno**
nileu *gw.* **dileu**
nilyn *gw.* **dilyn**
nillad *gw.* **dilledyn**
nilledyn *gw.* **dilledyn**
nim *gw.* **dim**
ninas *gw.* **dinas**
ninasyddion *gw.* **dinesydd**
ninesydd *gw.* **dinesydd**
ninistrio *gw.* **dinistrio**
ninnau *rhag.* we also
niod *gw.* **diod**
nioddef *gw.* **dioddef**
niogi *gw.* **diogi**
niogyn *gw.* **diogyn**
niolch *gw.* **diolch**
niolchgarwch *gw.*
  diolchgarwch
nirgelwch *gw.* **dirgelwch**
nirprwy *gw.* **dirprwy**
nirprwyaeth *gw.* **dirprwyaeth**
nirwasgiad *gw.* **dirwasgiad**
nirwy *gw.* **dirwy**
nis *ad.* not . . . him/her/it/
  them. **nis gwelais** I did not
  see him/etc
nisg *gw.* **disg**
nisgrifiad *gw.* **disgrifiad**
nisgrifio *gw.* **disgrifio**
nisgwyl *gw.* **disgwyl**
nisgybl *gw.* **disgybl**
nisgyblaeth *gw.* **disgyblaeth**
nisgyn *gw.* **disgyn**
nistawrwydd *gw.* **distawrwydd**
nistewi *gw.* **distewi**
niswyddo *gw.* **diswyddo**

nith

nith *e.b.* *ll.* **-oedd** niece
niwallu *gw.* **diwallu**
niwed *e.g.* *ll.* **niweidiau** harm,
   damage, injury. **gwneud**
   niwed i to harm
niwedd *gw.* **diwedd**
niweddglo *gw.* **diweddglo**
niweidiau *gw.* **niwed**
niwl *e.g.* *ll.* **-oedd** mist, haze.
   niwl trwchus fog
niwlog *a.* misty, foggy, hazy
niwrnod *gw.* **diwrnod**
niwydiant *gw.* **diwydiant**
niwygiad *gw.* **diwygiad**
niwygio *gw.* **diwygio**
niwylliant *gw.* **diwylliant**
noc *gw.* **doc**
noctor *gw.* **doctor**
nod *e.g.b.* *ll.* **-au, -ion** note;
   mark, token, aim
nodau *gw.* **nod, nodyn**
nodedig *a.* remarkable, noted,
   appointed, specified
nodi *be.* **(nodaf)** to note, to
   mark, to appoint, to state.
   gw. **dodi**
nodrefn *gw.* **dodrefnyn**
nodrefnyn *gw.* **dodrefnyn**
nodwedd *e.b.* *ll.* **-ion**
   character, feature,
   characteristic. **rhaglen**
   nodwedd feature programme
nodweddiadol *a.*
   characteristic, typical
nodwydd *e.b.* *ll.* **-au** needle
nodyn *e.g.* *ll.* **nodau** note
noddwr *e.g.* *ll.* **noddwyr**
   protector, patron
noe *gw.* **doe**
noeth *a.* naked, bare,
   exposed, raw, sheer

noethineb *gw.* **doethineb**
nofel *e.b.* *ll.* **-au** novel
nofelwr: nofelydd *e.g.*
   ll. **nofelwyr** novelist
nofiad *e.g.* a swim
nofio *be.* **(nofiaf)** to swim
nogfen *gw.* **dogfen**
nol *gw.* **dol**
nôl: hôl *be.* **(nolaf: holaf)** to
   fetch; *gw.* **dôl**
nolen *gw.* **dolen**
nolur *gw.* **dolur**
Norman *e.g.* *ll.* **-iaid** Norman.
   castell Normanaidd Norman
   castle
nos *e.b.* *ll.* **-au** night. **nos da**
   good night; **nos Sul** Sunday
   night; **nos yfory** tomorrow
   night; **nos dywyll** dark
   night *gw.* **noson**
nosbarth *gw.* **dosbarth**
noson: noswaith *e.b.* *ll.*
   nosweithiau evening:
   noswaith dda good evening;
   noson lawen merry evening;
   am ddwy noson for two
   evenings
nosweithiau *gw.* **noson**
nraen: nraenen *gw.* **draen**
nraenog *gw.* **draenog**
nraig *gw.* **draig**
nrain *gw.* **draen**
nrama *gw.* **drama**
nramodwr *gw.* **dramodwr**
nramodydd *gw.* **dramodwr**
nreigiau *gw.* **draig**
nreser: nresel *gw.* **dreser**
nrewdod *gw.* **drewdod**
nringwr *gw.* **dringwr**
nrudwy *gw.* **drudwy**
nrwg *gw.* **drwg**

o

nrwm *gw.* **drwm**
nrws *gw.* **drws**
nrych *gw.* **drych**
nrychiolaeth *gw.* **drychiolaeth**
nrygioni *gw.* **drygioni**
nryll *gw.* **dryll**
nryllau *gw.* **dryll**
nrysau *gw.* **drws**
nrysu *gw.* **drysu**
nryw *gw.* **dryw**
null *gw.* **dull**
nuo *gw.* **duo**
nur *gw.* **dur**
nuw *gw.* **duw**
nuwies *gw.* **duwies**
nwfr *gw.* **dŵr**
nŵr *gw.* **dŵr**
nwrn *gw.* **dwrn**
nwsin *gw.* **dwsin**
nwy *e.g. ll.* **-on, -au** gas. **Nwy Môr y Gogledd** North Sea gas. *gw.* **dwy**
nwyau *gw.* **nwy**
nwydd *e.g. ll.* **-au** material, article. **nwyddau** goods (*note: only the plural form is used*)
nwyon *gw.* **nwy**
nwyieithrwydd *gw.* **dwyieithrwydd**
nwylo *gw.* **dwylo**
nwyn *gw.* **dwyn**
nwyrain *gw.* **dwyrain**
nychmygion *gw.* **dychymyg**
nychmygu *gw.* **dychmygu**
nychymyg *gw.* **dychymyg**
nydd *gw.* **dydd**
nyddiad *gw.* **dyddiad**
nyfarniad *gw.* **dyfarniad**
nyfarnu *gw.* **dyfarnu**
nyfarnwr *gw.* **dyfarnwr**
nyfnder *gw.* **dyfnder**

nyfodol *gw.* **dyfodol**
nyfroedd *gw.* **dŵr**
nyfyniad *gw.* **dyfyniad**
nyffryn *gw.* **dyffryn**
nylanwad *gw.* **dylanwad**
nyled *gw.* **dyled**
nyletswydd *gw.* **dyletswydd**
nymuniad *gw.* **dymuniad**
nyn *gw.* **dyn**
nynes *gw.* **dynes**
nyni *rhag.* we, us
nyrnaid *gw.* **dyrnaid**
nyrnau *gw.* **dwrn**
nyrs *e.b.g. ll.* **-ys** nurse
nyrsio *be.* (**nyrsiaf**) to nurse
nysgl *gw.* **dysgl**
nysgu *gw.* **dysgu**
nysgwr *gw.* **dysgwr**
nyth *e.b. ll.* **-od** nest. **nyth y dryw** the wren's nest
nywediad *gw.* **dywediad**
nyweddïad *gw.* **dyweddïad**
nyweddïo *gw.* **dyweddïo**

O

o *ardd.* (*followed by soft mutation*) (*personal forms:* **ohono, ohonot, ohono/ohoni, ohonon, ohonoch, ohonyn**) from, of, out of. **o amgylch** around; **o chwith** wrongly, the wrong way about; **o flaen** before, ahead of; **o gwbl** at all; **o gwmpas** around, round about; **o hyd** still; **o'r blaen** beforehand, earlier, previously; **o'r diwedd** at last; **o'r gloch** o'clock; **o'r gorau** very well. *gw. At. Arddodiaid. gw.* **ef**

obaith

obaith *gw.* gobaith
obeithio *gw.* gobeithio
obeithion *gw.* gobaith
obennydd *gw.* gobennydd
oblegid *c. & ardd.* because,
for
ochenaid *e.b. ll.* ocheneidiau
sigh
ochneidio *be.* (ochneidiaf) to
sigh, to groan
ochr *e.b. ll.* -au side. ochr yn
ochr side by side; wrth ochr
beside; yr ochr draw i (on)
the other side to
od *a.* odd, bizarre;
remarkable
odidog *gw.* godidog
odl *e.b. ll.* -au rhyme; ode,
song

oddrych *gw.* goddrych
oed *e.g. ll.* -au age; time.
blwydd oed year old; saith
oed seven years of age;
gwneud oed â to arrange a
tryst, to make a date
oedfa *e.b. ll.* -on, oedfeuon
service, meeting
oedi *be.* (oedaf) to delay, to
postpone; to linger
oedolion *gw.* oedolyn
oedolyn *e.g. ll.* oedolion adult
oedran *e.g. ll.* -nau age
oedrannus *a.* aged, elderly
oedd *bf.* was, were. *gw.* bod
oen *e.g. ll.* ŵyn lamb
oer *a.* cold, chill, chilly; frigid
oerfel *e.g.* cold
oergell *e.b. ll.* -oedd

odli *be.* (odlaf) to rhyme
odre *gw.* godre
odro *gw.* godro
oddef *gw.* goddef
oddefgar *gw.* goddefgar
oddeutu *ardd. & ad.* about,
around
oddi *ardd.* out of, from. oddi
allan outside; oddi ar from
off; since; oddieithr except,
unless; oddi mewn within;
oddi wrth from; oddi yma
from here

refrigerator
oeri *be.* (oeraf) to cool, to
become cold
oes 1 *e.b. ll.* -au, -oedd age,
lifetime. ers oes from an
age; o oes i oes from age to
age; yn oes oesoedd for ever
and ever. 2 *bf.* is, are. *gw.*
bod. *gw. At. Berfau –
Affirmative & Negative
answers*
of *gw.* gof
ofal *gw.* gofal

ôl-nodiad

ofalu *gw.* **gofalu**
ofalus *gw.* **gofalus**
ofalwr *gw.* **gofalwr**
ofer *a.* vain; prodigal; waste.
 ymgais ofer a vain attempt
oferedd *e.g.* vanity,
 dissipation, frivolity
ofergoel *e.b.* *ll.* **-ion**
 superstition
ofergoeledd: ofergoeliaeth *e.g.*
 superstition
ofergoelus *a.* superstitious
ofid *gw.* **gofid**
ofidio *gw.* **gofidio**
ofn *e.g.* *ll.* **-au** fear, terror,
 dread. **Mae ofn arno fe** He is
 afraid; **Mae ofn llygod arna i**
 I am afraid of mice
ofnadwy *a.* awful, dreadful,
 horrendous
ofnau *gw.* **ofn**
ofni *be.* **(ofnaf)** to fear, to
 dread
ofnus *a.* timid, nervous
ofod *gw.* **gofod**
ofodwr *gw.* **gofodwr**
ofyn *gw.* **gofyn**
offeiriad *e.g.* *ll.* **offeiriaid**
 priest, parson
offer *gw.* **offeryn**
offeren *e.b.* mass (*Roman
 Catholic*)
offeryn *e.g.* *ll.* **-nau, offer**
 instrument, tool, apparatus,
 equipment. **offeryn cerdd**
 musical instrument; **offeryn
 chwyth** wind instrument;
 offeryn llinynnol stringed
 instrument; **offerynnau taro**
 percussion instruments

offerynnol *a.* instrumental.
 darn offerynnol instrumental
 piece (*of music*)
ogledd *gw.* **gogledd**
ogleddol *gw.* **gogleddol**
ogleddwr *gw.* **gogleddwr**
ogleisio *gw.* **gogleisio**
ogof *e.b.* *ll.* **-âu, -eydd** cave,
 cavern; den
ogoniant *gw.* **gogoniant**
ogylch *ardd.* about
ogystal *gw.* **gogystal**
ongl *e.b.* *ll.* **-au** angle. **ongl
 sgwâr** right angle; **triongl**
 triangle
onglog *a.* angular
oherwydd *c. & ardd.*
 because, for
ohirio *gw.* **gohirio**
ôl 1 *e.g.* *ll.* **olion** mark, print;
 track; trace. **ôl bysedd**
 finger-marks; **ôl traed**
 footprints. 2 *a.* back, hind:
 ar ôl after; **pen ôl** behind,
 bottom (buttocks); **yn ôl**
 according to; ago; **y tu ôl**
 behind
olaf *a.* last (*the very last*). *gw.*
 hwyr
olau *gw.* **golau**
olchi *gw.* **golchi**
oleudy *gw.* **goleudy**
oleuni *gw.* **goleuni**
oleuo *gw.* **goleuo**
olew *e.g.* *ll.* **-au** oil. **maes
 olew** oilfield
olion *gw.* **ôl**
ôl-nodiad *e.g.* *ll.* **ôl-nodiadau**
 postscript

ôl-ofal

ôl-ofal *e.g. ll.* ôl-ofalon aftercare
olrhain *be.* (olrheiniaf) to
trace, to track
olud *gw.* golud
olwg *gw.* golwg
olwr *e.g. ll.* olwyr back
(*rugby, etc.*)
olwyn *e.b. ll.* -ion wheel.
cadair olwyn/olwynion
wheelchair; olwyn fesur
trundle wheel
olwyr *gw.* olwr
olygfa *gw.* golygfa
olygon *gw.* golwg
olygu *gw.* golygu
oll *ad.* all, wholly; ever, at all
ollwng *gw.* gollwng
ond 1 *c.* but, only. 2 *ardd.*
except; save; but
onest *gw.* gonest
oni: onid 1 *ad.* not? is it not?
2 *c.* if not, unless. 3 *ardd.*
except; save; but: onid e?
otherwise; else; is it not?
onibai (am) *c.* were it not
(for)
onid *gw.* oni
onnen *e.b. ll.* ynn ash tree
opera *e.b. ll.* operâu opera.
opera ddigri comic opera;
opera fawreddog grand
opera; opera ysgafn light
opera; opera sebon soap
opera
optegwr: optegydd *e.g. ll.*
optegwyr optician
orau *gw.* da
orchfygu *gw.* gorchfygu
orchymyn *gw.* gorchymyn

oren *e.g. ll.* -au orange
orfod *gw.* gorfod
orfodaeth *gw.* gorfodaeth
orfodi *gw.* gorfodi
orfodol *gw.* gorfodol
orfoleddus *gw.* gorfoleddus
orffen *gw.* gorffen
Orffennaf *gw.* Gorffennaf
orffennol *gw.* gorffennol
orffwys *gw.* gorffwys
orffwyso *gw.* gorffwyso
organ *e.g.b. ll.* -au organ.
organ geg mouth-organ
organig *a.* organic
organydd *e.g. ll.* -ion
organist
oriau *gw.* awr
oriel *e.b. ll.* -au gallery
orlawn *gw.* gorlawn
orllewin *gw.* gorllewin
ormod *gw.* gormod
ornest *e.b. ll.* -au contest,
combat, duel, match. *gw.*
gornest
orsaf *gw.* gorsaf
orsedd *gw.* gorsedd
oruchaf *gw.* goruchaf
oruwchnaturiol *gw.*
goruwchnaturiol
orwedd *gw.* gorwedd
orwel *gw.* gorwel
orymdaith *gw.* gorymdaith
os *c.* if (*definite not
conjecture*). Os daw Tom, dof
i hefyd If Tom comes, I will
come too
osgoi *be.* (osgoaf) to avoid,
to swerve, to evade; to shirk.
ffordd-osgoi bypass
osod *gw.* gosod

ostwng *gw.* **gostwng**
ostyngedig *gw.* **gostyngedig**
ostyngiad *gw.* **gostyngiad**
owns *e.b.* *ll.* **-ys** ounce; **dwy owns** two ounces

P

pa *a.* Which? What? **(Pa) beth?** What (thing)? **Pa bryd? Pryd?** When? **Pa fodd?** How? **P'un?** Which one? *gw.* **pam**
Pab *e.g.* *ll.* **-au** Pope
pabell *e.b.* *ll.* **pebyll** tent, pavilion
pabi *e.b.* *ll.* **pabïau** poppy
pabydd *e.g.* *ll.* **-ion** papist
pac *e.g.* *ll.* **-au, -iau** pack, bundle
paced *e.g.* *ll.* **-i** packet, package
paciau *gw.* **pac**
pacio *be.* **(paciaf)** to pack
padell *e.b.* *ll.* **-i** bowl, pan
pader *e.g.* *ll.* **-au** the Lord's prayer, prayers. **dweud pader/dysgu pader i berson** 'to teach your grandmother to suck eggs'
paent *e.g.* *ll.* **-iau** paint
pafiliwn *e.g.* pavilion
pafin *e.g.* *ll.* **-au** pavement *(S.W)*
pagan *e.g.* **-iaid** pagan
paham *gw.* **pam**
pais *e.b.* *ll.* **peisiau** petticoat
pâl 1 *e.b.* *ll.* **palau** spade *(S.W.).* 2 *e.g.* *ll.* **palod** puffin

palas *e.g.* *ll.* **-au, -oedd** palace
palau *gw.* **pâl**
palmant *e.g.* *ll.* **-au** pavement *(N.W.)*
palod *gw.* **pâl**
palu *be.* **(palaf)** to dig over *(not down)*
pallu *be.* **(pallaf)** to refuse, to fail, to cease, to lack
pam: paham: pa *ad.* why?
pamffled *e.g.* *ll.* **-i, -au** pamphlet
pamffledyn *e.g.* pamphlet
pan *c.* when
panasen *e.b.* *ll.* **pannas** parsnip
panel *e.g.* *ll.* **-i** panel
pannas *gw.* **panasen.**
pant *e.g.* *ll.* **-au, -iau** valley, hollow; depression, dent. *undergoing soft mutation after* **i** > **i bant, bant** *ad.* away, off. **Mae e bant** He's away; **o bant** from away; **o bant i bentan** everywhere, from pillar to post
papur *e.g.* *ll.* **-au** paper. **papur newydd** newspaper; **papur deg punt** ten-pound note; **papur wal** wallpaper
papuro *be.* **(papuraf)** to paper
pâr *e.g.* *ll.* **parau** pair
para (i): parhau (i) *be.* **(paraf)** to continue (to)
paradwys *e.b.* *ll.* **-au** paradise
paragraff *e.g.* *ll.* **-au** paragraph

paratoi

paratoi *be.* **(paratoaf)** to prepare to. **paratoi i fynd** to prepare to go

parau *gw.* **pâr**

parc *e.g.* *ll.* **-au, -iau** park; field *(S.W.W.)*

parch *e.g.* respect. **dillad parch** Sunday best, best clothes *(lit. the clothes of respect)*

parchedig *a.* *ll.* **-ion** *(often abbreviated to* **y parchg**) reverend, reverent. **Y Parchedig Ifan Rhys** Reverend Ifan Rhys

parchu *be.* **(parchaf)** to respect

parchus *be.* respectable, respectful

pardwn *e.g.* *ll.* **pardynau** pardon

parhad *e.g.* continuation

parhau *gw.* **para**

parod *a.* ready, willing, prepared. **yn barod** already; **arian parod** ready cash

parsel *e.g.* *ll.* **-au, -i** parcel

parti *e.g.* *ll.* **-ion** party

Pasg *e.g.* Easter. **Dydd Llun y Pasg** Easter Monday; **wy Pasg** Easter egg; **Gwyliau'r Pasg** Easter holidays; **y Pasg** Easter

pasiannau *gw.* **pasiant**

pasiant *e.g.* *ll.* **pasiannau** pageant

patrwm *e.g.* *ll.* **patrymau** pattern

patrwn *e.g.* *ll.* **patrynau** pattern

patrymau *gw.* **patrwm**

patrynau *gw.* **patrwn**

pawb *e.g.* everybody, all

pawen *e.b.* *ll.* **-nau** paw

pe *c.* if. **Pe bawn i yno** If I were there

pebyll *gw.* **pabell**

pecyn *e.g.* *ll.* **-nau** package, packet

pechadur *e.g.* *ll.* **-iaid** sinner

pechod *e.g.* *ll.* **-au** sin: **Dyna bechod!** What a pity!

pechu *be.* **(pechaf)** to sin; **pechu yn erbyn** to sin against

pedair *eb. & a.b.* *(adjective placed before feminine noun)* four. **pedair merch** four girls; **pedair cadair** four chairs. *gw.* **pedwar**

pedol *e.b.* *ll.* **-au** horseshoe

pedwar *e.g.* *ll. & a.g.* four. *gw.* **pedair**

pedwaredd *a.b.* fourth. **y bedwaredd ferch** the fourth girl

pedwerydd *a.g.* fourth. **y pedwerydd bachgen** the fourth boy

peg *e.g.* *ll.* **-iau** peg

pegwn *e.g.* *ll.* **pegynau** pole. **Pegwn y De** South Pole; **Pegwn y Gogledd** North Pole

pegynau *gw.* **pegwn**

peidio (â) *be.* **(peidiaf)** to cease, to stop. **Paid (â) siarad** Don't talk

peilot *e.g.* *ll.* **-iaid** pilot

peint *e.g.* *ll.* **-iau** pint. **peint a hanner** a pint and a half

peintio *be.* **(peintiaf)** to paint
peintiwr *e.g.* *ll.* **peintwyr**
painter
peiriannau *gw.* **peiriant**
peiriannydd: peiriannwr *e.g.*
ll. **peirianwyr** engineer
peiriant *e.g.* *ll.* **peiriannau**
engine, machine. **peiriant**
golchi washing machine;
peiriant car car engine;
peiriant gwnïo sewing
machine
peisiau *gw.* **pais**
pêl *e.b.* *ll.* **peli, pelau** ball.
pêl-droed football; **pêl rygbi**
rugby ball
pelydr *e.g.* *ll.* **-au** ray, beam.
pelydr X X ray
pell *a.* far. *gw.* *At.*
Ansoddeiriau. **nid nepell o**
not far from
pellach *gw.* **pell**
pellaf *gw.* **pell**
pelled *gw.* **pell**
pellter *e.g.* *ll.* **-au, -oedd**
distance. **yn y pellter** in the
distance. **o bellter** from a
distance
pen 1 *e.g.* *ll.* **-nau** head, top,
end, mouth. **ar ben** on top
of, ended; **ar ei phen ei hun**
by herself; **pen y bryn** top of
the hill; **pen ôl** behind,
bottom (buttocks). **2** *a.*
chief, supreme
penaethiaid *gw.* **pennaeth**
penawdau *gw.* **pennawd**
pen-blwydd *e.g.* *ll.* **-i**
birthday
pencadlys *e.g.* *ll.* **-oedd**
headquarters

pencampwr *e.g.* *ll.*
pencampwyr champion
pendant *a.* positive, definite,
emphatic
penderfyniad *e.g.* *ll.* **-au**
resolution, determination
penderfynol *a.* resolute,
determined. **yn benderfynol o**
determined to
penderfynu *be.* **(penderfynaf)**
to decide, to resolve: **Fe**
benderfynodd fynd He
decided to go
penelin *e.g.b.* *ll.* **-oedd** elbow
penfoel *a.* bald-headed
Penfro *e.b.* **Tref a Sir**
Pembrokeshire (S. Wales)
pen-glin: pen-lin *e.b.* *ll.*
pengliniau: penliniau knee
penigamp *a.* splendid,
excellent
penillion *gw.* **pennill**
pen-lin *gw.* **pen-glin**
penlinio *be.* **(penliniaf)** to
kneel
pennaeth *e.g.* *ll.* **penaethiaid**
chief
pennaf *a.* principal, chief
pennau *gw.* **pen**
pennawd *e.g.* *ll.* **penawdau**
heading; headline;
penawdau'r newyddion the
news headlines
pennill *e.g.* *ll.* **penillion**
stanza, verse
pennod *e.b.* *ll.* **penodau**
chapter
penodau *gw.* **pennod**
penodi *be.* **(penodaf)** to
appoint

penodiad

penodiad *e.g. ll.* **-au**
appointment
penrhyn *e.g. ll.* **-au**
promontory, headland
pensaer *e.g. ll.* **penseiri**
architect
penseiri *gw.* **pensaer**
pensil *e.g. ll.* **-iau** pencil
pensiwn *e.g. ll.* **pensiynau**
pension
pensiynau *gw.* **pensiwn**
pensiynwr *e.g. ll.* **pensiynwyr**
pensioner
penteulu *e.g. ll.* **-oedd** head
of family
pentref *e.g. ll.* **-i** village
pentwr *e.g. ll.* **pentyrrau**
heap, mass, pile

perchenogaeth *e.b.*
ownership
perchenogi *be.* to own
peren *e.b. ll.* **pêr** pear
pererin *e.g. ll.* **-ion** pilgrim
pererindod *e.b. ll.* **-au**
pilgrimage
pererindota *be.* to go on a
pilgrimage
perfedd *e.g. ll.* **-ion** entrails,
guts, middle. **perfedd gwlad**
heart of countryside; **perfedd
nos** dead of night
perffaith *a.* perfect
perffeithio *be.* **(perffeithiaf)** to
perfect
peri (i) *be.* **(peraf)** to cause
perl *e.g. ll.* **-au** pearl

Insight

penrhyn *e.g.* promontary, headland, peninsula. **Penrhyn
Gŵyr** Gower peninsula; **Penrhyn Llŷn** Lleyn Peninsula.
pererin e.g. pilgrim. **Taith y Pererin** – *Pilgrim's Progress*,
John Bunyan (1678)
person e.g. person, parson. **Person y plwyf** the parish Vicar
or Rector; **person enwog** famous person.

---

pentyrrau *gw.* **pentwr**
penwythnos *e.g. ll.* **-au**
weekend
pêr *a.* sweet *(of sound). gw.*
peren
perlysiau *e.ll.* herbs
perchen: perchennog *e.g. ll.*
perchenogion owner,
proprietor. **Roedd e'n
berchen ar dŷ** He was a
house owner

perllan *e.b. ll.* **-nau** orchard
persawr *e.g. ll.* **-au** perfume,
fragrance
persli *e.g.* parsley
person 1 *e.g. ll.* **-au** person.
2 *e.g. ll.* **-iaid** parson
personol *a.* personal
personoliaeth *e.b. ll.* **-au**
personality
pert *a.* pretty

perth *e.b. ll.* **-i** bush; hedge
(*S.W.*)

perthnasau *gw.* **perthynas**

perthnasol *a.* relevant

perthyn (i) *be.* **(perthynaf)** to
belong, to be related

perthynas *e.b.g. ll.*
perthnasau relation;
relationship

perygl *e.g. ll.* **peryglon**
danger

peryglus *a.* dangerous

peswch 1 *be.* **(pesychaf)** to
cough. 2 *e.g.* a cough

pesychiad *e.g. ll.* **-au** cough

petai *bf.* if it were
(*conjecture*). **pe bai** if; **pe
basai** if

petrol *e.g. ll.* **-au** petrol.
petrol di-blwm unleaded
petrol

peth *e.g. ll.* **-au** thing, some,
part. **pa beth?** what (thing)?
oes peth ar ôl is there some
left?

piano *e.g.b. ll.* **-s** piano

pianydd *e.g. ll.* **-ion** pianist

pib *e.b. ll.* **-au: pibell** *e.b. ll.*
-au, -i pipe (*smoking,
musical variety*). **canu'r
pibau** to play the pipes;
tanio pib to light a pipe

piben *e.b. ll.* **-ni** pipe
(*drainpipe, etc.*)

picil *e.g.* pickle, trouble.
mewn picil in trouble

pictiwr *e.g. ll.* **pictiyrau**
picture

picwn *gw.* **picwnen**

picwnen *e.b. ll.* **picwn** wasp
(*S.W.*). **nyth picwn** wasps'
nest. *gw.* **cacynen**

pigfain *a.* tapering

pigiad *e.g. ll.* **-au** prick, sting;
injection

pigo *be.* **(pigaf)** to pick, to
sting, to prick, to peck

pigog *a.* prickly, irritable

pil *e.g. ll.* **-ion** peel

piler *e.g. ll.* **-au** pillar,
column. **o biler i bost** from
pillar to post

pilio *be.* **(piliaf)** to peel

pilion *gw.* **pil**

pili-pala *e.g. ll.* **pili-palod**
butterfly (*S.W.*)

pilsen *e.b. ll.* **pils** pill

pilyn *e.g. ll.* **-nau** garment
(*S.W.*) rag. **pilyn gorau** best
garment; **pilyn parch** Sunday
garment, best garment

pin *e.g. ll.* **-nau** pin; pen. **pin
ysgrifennu** writing pen;
pinnau bawd drawing pins

pîn *gw.* **pinwydden**

pînafal *e.g. ll.* **-au** pineapple

pinc *a.* pink: **yn y pinc** in
very good health

pinnau *gw.* **pin**

pinsio *be.* **(pinsiaf)** to pinch

pinwydden *e.b. ll.* **pîn,
pinwydd** pine

piod *gw.* **pioden**

pioden *e.b. ll.* **piod** magpie

pisyn *e.g. ll.* **-nau** piece
(*S.W.*). **Mae hi'n bisyn!** She's
good looking!

piti *e.g.* pity

plaid

plaid *e.b. ll.* **pleidiau** party, side. **o blaid** in favour; **Y Blaid Geidwadol** The Conservative Party; **Y Blaid Lafur** The Labour Party; **Y Blaid (Plaid Cymru)** The Welsh Nationalist Party; **Y Blaid Werdd** The Green Party

plan *e.g. ll.* **-iau** plan

planced *e.b. ll.* **-i** blanket. *gw.* **blanced**

planhigyn *e.g. ll.* **planhigion** plant

planiau *gw.* **plan**

plannu *be.* **(plannaf)** to plant

plant *gw.* **plentyn**

plas *e.g. ll.* **-au** palace, mansion

plastai *gw.* **plasty**

plasty *e.g. ll.* **plastai** palace, mansion

plât *e.g. ll.* **platiau** plate

platiau *gw.* **plât**

pleidiau *gw.* **plaid**

pleidlais *e.b. ll.* **pleidlesiau** vote

pleidleisiau *gw.* **pleidlais**

pleidleisio *be.* **(pleidleisiaf)** to vote. **bwrw pleidlais** to cast a vote

pleidleisiwr *e.g. ll.* **pleidleiswyr** voter

plentyn *e.g. ll.* **plant** child

plentynnaidd *a.* childish

pleser *e.g. ll.* **-au** pleasure. **rhoi pleser i** to give pleasure to

pleserus *a.* pleasant, pleasurable

plesio *be.* **(plesiaf)** to please

plisgyn *e.g. ll.* **plisg** shell, pod, casing

plisman: plismon *e.g. ll.* **plismyn** policeman

plismyn *gw.* **plisman**

plith *e.g.* midst. **i blith** into the midst of; **o blith** from among; **ymhlith** among; **blith draphlith** in confusion, intermingled

plu *gw.* **pluen**

pluen *e.b. ll.* **plu** feather; fly *(fishing-bait)*. **clymu plu** to fashion fishing-flies; **yn ysgafn fel pluen** light as a feather

pluf *gw.* **plufyn**

plufyn *e.g. ll.* **pluf** feather *(S.W.)*

plwc *e.g. ll.* **plyciau** pull, jerk

plwg *e.g. ll.* **plygiau** plug

plwm 1 *e.g.* lead; 2 *a.* leaden; vertical

plwyf *e.g. ll.* **-i** parish. **ar y plwyf** on the parish, destitute

plyciau *gw.* **plwc**

plygiau *gw.* **plwg**

plygu *be.* **(plygaf)** to fold, to bend, to stoop, to bow, to submit

pob *a.* each, every, all; roast. **pob cynnig** every attempt, every offer; **pob dydd** every day; **pob tro** every occasion; **pob un** everyone; **tatws pob** roast potatoes

pobi *be.* **(pobaf)** to bake, to roast

pobl *e.b.* *ll.* **-oedd** people. **y bobl hyn** these people

poblogaeth *e.b.* *ll.* **-au** population

poblogaidd *a.* popular

pobman *ad.* everywhere

pobydd *e.g.* *ll.* **-ion** baker

poced *e.b.* *ll.* **-i** pocket

poen *e.g.b.* *ll.* **-au** pain, ache, agony

poeni (am) *be.* **(poenaf)** to pain, to worry, to tease. **Paid poeni!** Don't worry!

poenus *a.* painful

poenydio *be.* **(poenydiaf)** to torture, to torment

poer: poeri *e.g.* spittle, saliva

poeri (at, i'r) *be.* **(poeraf)** to spit. *gw.* **poer**

poeth *a.* hot

poethi *be.* **(poethaf)** to heat, to be heated

polion *gw.* **polyn**

politicaidd *a.* political

polyn *e.g.* *ll.* **polion** pole, stake

pont *e.b.* *ll.* **-ydd** bridge

pontydd *gw.* **pont**

Pont-y-pŵl *e.b.* Pontypool

popeth *e.g.* everything

poptai *gw.* **popty**

popty *e.g.* *ll.* **poptai** bakehouse; oven; **popty ping** microwave oven

porfa *e.b.* *ll.* **porfeydd** pasture; grass *(S.W.)*

porfeydd *gw.* **porfa**

porffor *e.g. & a.* purple

pori *be.* **(poraf)** to graze

portread *e.g.* *ll.* **-au** portrait, portrayal

porth *e.g.* *ll.* **pyrth** door; porch

porthladd *e.g.* *ll.* **-oedd** harbour

pos *e.g.* *ll.* **posau** puzzle, riddle. **pos croeseiriau** crossword puzzle

posibilrwydd *e.g.* possibility

posibl *a.* possible

post 1 *e.g.* *ll.* **pyst** post, pillar. 2 *e.g.* *ll.* **-iau** post, mail; **blwch postio/llythyrau** post box; **e-bost** e-mail

postio *be.* **(postiaf)** to post

postman: postmon *e.g.* *ll.* **postmyn** postman

postmyn *gw.* **postman**

postyn *e.g.* *ll.* **pyst** post. **fel postyn** deaf *(as a post)*

potel *e.b.* *ll.* **-i** bottle. **potel ddŵr poeth** hotwater bottle

powdr: powdwr *e.g.* *ll.* **powdrau** powder

powdrau *gw.* **powdr**

powlen *gw.* **bowlen**

Powys (Sir) *e.b.* Powys County, the largest Welsh County

praidd *e.g.* *ll.* **preiddiau** flock

pram *e.g.* *ll.* **-iau** pram

prawf *e.g.* *ll.* **profion** trial, test, proof. **prawf darllen** reading test; **prawf gyrru** driving test; **ar brawf** on trial, on probation; **blwyddyn brawf** probationary year; **Gwasanaeth Prawf** Probation Service; **swyddog prawf** probation officer

pregeth

pregeth *e.b.* *ll.* **-au** sermon
pregethu (ar) *be.* **(pregethaf)**
to preach
pregethwr *e.g.* *ll.* **pregethwyr**
preacher
preiddiau *gw.* **praidd**
preifat *a.* private
pren *e.g.* *ll.* **-nau** tree, wood,
timber. **pren afalau** apple
tree; **pren caled** hardwood;
pren meddal softwood; **llwy**
bren a wooden spoon
prennau *gw.* pren
prentis *e.g.* *ll.* **-iaid**
apprentice
prentisiaeth *e.b.* *ll.* **-au**
apprenticeship
prentisiaid *gw.* **prentis**
pres 1 *e.g.* brass, bronze;
money. 2 *a.* brass. **band**
pres brass band; **jwg bres**
brass jug
preseb *e.g.* *ll.* **-au** crib, stall,
manger
presennol *a.* present. **yr**
amser presennol the present
tense
presenoldeb *e.g.* *ll.* **-au**
presence, attendance
presgripsiwn *e.g.* *ll.*
presgripsiynau prescription
preswyl: preswylfod *e.g.* *ll.*
preswylfeydd dwelling place.
preswylfan dwelling place;
ysgol breswyl boarding
school; **neuadd breswyl** hall
of residence
pridwerth *e.g.* ransom
pridd *e.g.* *ll.* **-oedd** soil, earth
prif *a.* *(precedes the noun it*

qualifies and is followed by
soft mutation) prime, chief,
major, principal. **prif**
ddiddordeb chief interest;
prif westeion principal
guests; **Prif Weinidog** Prime
Minister
prifardd *e.g.* *ll.* **prifeirdd** chief
bard *(one who has won*
chair or crown at National
Eisteddfod)
prifathrawes *e.b.* *ll.* **-au**
headmistress, principal
prifathro *e.g.* *ll.* **prifathrawon**
headmaster, principal
prifddinas *e.b.* *ll.* **-oedd**
capital city
prifeirdd *gw.* **prifardd**
prifio *be.* **(prifiaf)** to grow
(S.W.)
prifysgol *e.b.* *ll.* **-ion**
university: **Prifysgol Cymru**
University of Wales
priffordd *e.b.* *ll.* **priffyrdd**
highway
priffyrdd *gw.* **priffordd**
prin *a.* rare, scarce, hardly
prinder *e.g.* *ll.* **-au** scarcity
printio *be.* **(printiaf)** to print
priod 1 *a.* own, proper;
married. 2 *e.g.b.* husband or
wife. **ei phriod** her husband;
fy mhriod my partner
(husband/wife). **ei briod le**
his proper place; **priodfab**
bridegroom; **priodferch**
bride; **gŵr priod** married
man; **gwraig briod** married
woman; **Ydych chi'n briod?**
Are you married?

priodas *e.b.* *ll.* **-au** marriage, wedding

priodi (â) *be.* **(priodaf)** to marry

priodol *a.* appropriate, proper

pris *e.g.* *ll.* **-iau, -oedd** price

problem *e.b.* *ll.* **-au** problem

profi *be.* **(profaf)** to prove, to test, to taste

profiad *e.g.* *ll.* **-au** experience

profiadol *a.* experienced

profion *gw.* **prawf**

profocio: pryfocio *be.* **(profociaf: pryfociaf)** to provoke

proffid *e.b.* *ll.* **-iau** profit

proffidiol *a.* profitable

proffwyd *e.g.* *ll.* **-i** prophet; **proffwydes** prophetess

proffwydo *be.* **(proffwydaf)** to prophesy

protest 1 *e.b.* *ll.* **-iadau** protest. 2 **protestio** be. **(protestiaf)** to protest *gw.* **gwrthdystio**

Protestant *e.g.* *ll.* **Protestaniaid** Protestant

prudd *a.* sad, grave, serious

pryd 1 *e.g.* *ll.* **-au** meal. **byrbryd** snack; **tamaid i aros pryd** temporary provision while awaiting arrival of something more substantial. 2 *e.g.* *ll.* **-iau** time, season: **Pryd? Pa bryd?** What time? **mewn pryd** in time; **ar y pryd** at the time; impromptu; **hen bryd** about time

Prydain *e.b.* Britain

prydau *gw.* **pryd**

Prydeinig *a.* British

pryder *e.g.* *ll.* **-on** anxiety, care, worry

pryderu (am) *be.* **(pryderaf)** to be anxious

pryderus *a.* anxious

prydferth *a.* beautiful, handsome

prydferthwch *e.g.* beauty

prydiau *gw.* **pryd**

prydlon *a.* **punctual**

pryf: pryfedyn: pryfyn *e.g.* *ll.* **pryfed** insect; vermin; animal; worm. **pryf copyn** spider *(N.W.)*

pryfed *gw.* **pryf**

pryfocio *gw.* **profocio**

pryfyn *gw.* **pryf**

prynhawn *e.g.* *ll.* **-au** afternoon. **prynhawn da!** good afternoon!

prynu *be.* **(prynaf)** to buy

prynwr *e.g.* *ll.* **prynwyr** buyer, redeemer

prysur *a.* busy, hasty; diligent, serious

prysurdeb *e.g.* haste, hurry; busyness

prysuro (i) *be.* **(prysuraf)** to hasten (to), to hurry. **Rwy'n prysuro i esbonio** I hasten to explain

pulpud *e.g.* *ll.* **-au** pulpit

pum: pump *e.g.* *ll. & a.* five. **pumed** fifth

p'un *gw.* **pa**

punnau *gw.* **punt**

punnoedd *gw.* **punt**

punt

punt *e.b.* *ll.* **punnau,
punnoedd** pound *(£)*

pupur *e.g.* *ll.* **-au** pepper. **fel
melin bupur** very talkative

pur 1 *a.* pure, sincere. **Yr
eiddoch yn bur** Yours
sincerely. 2 *ad.* very, fairly.
yn bur wael very poorly; **yn
bur dda** fairly good

purfa *e.b.* *ll.* **purfeydd**
refinery. **purfa olew** oil
refinery

puro *be.* **(puraf)** to purify

pwdin *e.g.* *ll.* **-au** pudding,
sweet *(after dinner)*. **Bydd
pwdin yn dilyn** There's a
sweet to follow

pwdr *a.* rotten, corrupt, lazy
(S.W.)

pwdryn *e.g* idler, sluggard
(S.W.)

pwdu *be.* **(pwdaf)** to sulk, to
pout

pŵer *e.g.* *ll.* **-au** power

pwll *e.g.* *ll.* **pyllau** pit, pool,
pond. **pwll glo** coal-pit, coal-
mine

pwmp *e.g.* *ll.* **pympiau** pump

pwnc *e.g.* *ll.* **pynciau** subject,
topic. **pynciau craidd** core
subjects; **pynciau sylfaen**
foundation subjects;
Cymanfa Bwnc assembly for
cathechizing and discussing
prepared portions of
Scripture

pwrpas *e.g.* *ll.* **-au** purpose

pwrs *e.g.* *ll.* **pyrsau** purse

pwy *rhag. gof.* who? **pwy
bynnag** whosoever

pwyll *e.g.* sense, discretion.
colli ei bwyll to lose his
senses, to become enraged;
cymryd pwyll to take time;
mynd gan bwyll to go
steadily

pwllgor *e.g.* *ll.* **-au**
committee. **pwllgor addysg**
education committee;
pwyllgor brys emergency
committee; **pwyllgor gwaith**
executive committee

pwyllo *be.* **(pwyllaf)** to pause,
to consider, to reflect

pwynt *e.g.* *ll.* **-iau** point. **dau
bwynt pump** 2.5 (two point
five); **rhewbwynt** freezing-
point

pwys 1 *e.g.* *ll.* **-au** weight,
importance. **ar bwys** near;
ennill pwysau to put on
weight; **o bwys** important;
codi pwys ar to make one
feel sick. 2 *e.g.* *ll.* **-i** pound
(lb)

pwysedd *e.g.* pressure.
pwysedd gwaed blood
pressure

pwysig *a.* important

pwysigrwydd *e.g.* importance

pwyslais *e.g.* *ll.* **pwysleisiau**
emphasis

pwyso (ar) *be.* **(pwysaf)** to
weigh, to lean (on), to rest

pwyth *e.g.* *ll.* **-au** stitch. **talu'r
pwyth** to avenge; retaliate

pydru *be.* **(pydraf)** to rot, to
decay

pyllau *gw.* **pwll,** *gw.* **pyllyn**

pyllyn *e.g.* *ll.* **pyllau** pool,
pond

pympiau *gw.* pwmp
pymtheg 1 *e.g.* *ll.* -au fifteen
  2 *a.* fifteen
pymthegfed *a.* fifteenth
pynciau *gw.* pwnc
pyped *e.g.* *ll.* -au puppet
pyrsau *gw.* pwrs
pyrth *gw.* porth
pys *gw.* pysen
pysen *e.b.* *ll.* pys pea. pys
  pêr sweet peas
pysgod *gw.* pysgodyn
pysgodyn *e.g.* *ll.* pysgod a
  fish. pysgodyn aur a
  goldfish
pysgota *be.* (pysgotaf) to fish
pysgotwr *e.g.* *ll.* pysgotwyr
  fisherman
pyst *gw.* post, postyn
pythefnos *e.g.b.* *ll.* -au
  fortnight

PH

pha *gw.* pa
Phab *gw.* Pab
phabell *gw.* pabell
phabi *gw.* pabi
phabydd *gw.* pabydd
phac *gw.* pac
phaced *gw.* paced
phacio *gw.* pacio
phadell *gw.* padell
phader *gw.* pader
phaent *gw.* paent
phafiliwn *gw.* pafiliwn
phafin *gw.* pafin
phagan *gw.* pagan
phaham *gw.* paham
phais *gw.* pais

phâl *gw.* pâl
phalas *gw.* palas
phalau *gw.* pâl
phalod *gw.* pâl
phalu *gw.* palu
phallu *gw.* pallu
pham *gw.* pam
phamffled *gw.* pamffled
phamffledyn *gw.* pamffled
phan *gw.* pan
phanasen *gw.* panasen
phanel *gw.* panel
phannas *gw.* panasen
phant *gw.* pant
phapur *gw.* papur
phapuro *gw.* papuro
phâr *gw.* pâr
phara *gw.* para
pharadwys *gw.* paradwys
pharagraff *gw.* paragraff
pharatoi *gw.* paratoi
pharc *gw.* parc
pharch *gw.* parch
pharchedig *gw.* parchedig
pharchu *gw.* parchu
pharchus *gw.* parchus
pharhad *gw.* parhad
pharhau *gw.* parhau
pharod *gw.* parod
pharsel *gw.* parsel
pharti *gw.* parti
Phasg *gw.* Pasg
phasiannau *gw.* pasiant
phasiant *gw.* pasiant
phatrwm *gw.* patrwm
phatrwn *gw.* patrwn
phatrymau *gw.* patrwm
phatrynau *gw.* patrwn
phawb *gw.* pawb
phawen *gw.* pawen

phe

phe *gw*. pe
phebyll *gw*. pabell
phecyn *gw*. pecyn
phechadur *gw*. pechadur
phechod *gw*. pechod
phechu *gw*. pechu
phedair *gw*. pedair
phedol *gw*. pedol
phedwar *gw*. pedwar
phedwaredd *gw*. pedwaredd
phedwerydd *gw*. pedwerydd
pheg *gw*. peg
phegwn *gw*. pegwn
phegynau *gw*. pegwn
pheidio *gw*. peidio
pheilot *gw*. peilot
pheint *gw*. peint
pheintio *gw*. peintio
pheintiwr *gw*. peintiwr
pheiriannydd: pheiriannwr *gw*.
  peiriannydd
pheiriannau *gw*. peiriant
pheiriant *gw*. peiriant
pheisiau *gw*. pais
phêl *gw*. pêl
phelydr *gw*. pelydr
phell *gw*. pell
phellach *gw*. pell
phellaf *gw*. pell
phelled *gw*. pell
phellter *gw*. pellter
phen *gw*. pen
phenaethiaid *gw*. pennaeth
phenawdau *gw*. pennawd
phen-blwydd *gw*. pen-blwydd
phencadlys *gw*. pencadlys
phencampwr *gw*. pencampwr
phendant *gw*. pendant
phenderfyniad *gw*.
  penderfyniad

phenderfynol *gw*. penderfynol
phenderfynu *gw*. penderfynu
phenelin *gw*. penelin
phenfoel *gw*. penfoel
phen-glin *gw*. pen-glin
phenigamp *gw*. penigamp
phenillion *gw*. pennill
phen-lin *gw*. pen-glin
phenlinio *gw*. penlinio
phennaeth *gw*. pennaeth
phennaf *gw*. pennaf
phennau *gw*. pen
phennawd *gw*. pennawd
phennill *gw*. pennill
phennod *gw*. pennod
phenodau *gw*. pennod
phenodi *gw*. penodi
phenodiad *gw*. penodiad
phenrhyn *gw*. penrhyn
phensaer *gw*. pensaer
phenseiri *gw*. pensaer
phensil *gw*. pensil
phensiwn *gw*. pensiwn
phensiynau *gw*. pensiwn
phensiynwr *gw*. pensiynwr
phenteulu *gw*. penteulu
phentref *gw*. pentref
phentwr *gw*. pentwr
phenwythnos *gw*.
  penwythnos
phêr *gw*. pêr
pherchen *gw*. perchen
pherchennog *gw*. perchen
pheren *gw*. peren
phererin *gw*. pererin
pherfedd *gw*. perfedd
pherffaith *gw*. perffaith
pherffeithio *gw*. perffeithio
pheri *gw*. peri
pherl *gw*. perl

phlufyn

pherlysiau *gw.* perlysiau	phîn *gw.* pîn
pherllan *gw.* perllan	phînafal *gw.* pînafal
phersli *gw.* persli	phinc *gw.* pinc
pherson *gw.* person	phinnau *gw.* pin
phersonol *gw.* personol	phinsio *gw.* pinsio
phersonoliaeth *gw.* personoliaeth	phinwydden *gw.* pinwydden
phert *gw.* pert	phioden *gw.* pioden
pherth *gw.* perth	phisyn *gw.* pisyn
pherthnasau *gw.* perthynas	phiti *gw.* piti
pherthnasol *gw.* perthnasol	phlaid *gw.* plaid
pherthyn *gw.* perthyn	phlan *gw.* plan
pherthynas *gw.* perthynas	phlanced *gw.* blanced
pherygl *gw.* perygl	phlanhigyn *gw.* planhigyn
pheryglus *gw.* peryglus	phlaniau *gw.* plan
pheswch *gw.* peswch	phlannu *gw.* plannu
phesychiad *gw.* pesychiad	phlant *gw.* plant
phetai *gw.* petai	phlas *gw.* plas
phetrol *gw.* petrol	phlastai *gw.* plasty
pheth *gw.* peth	phlasty *gw.* plasty
phiano *gw.* piano	phlât *gw.* plât
phianydd *gw.* pianydd	phlatiau *gw.* plât
phib *gw.* pib	phleidiau *gw.* plaid
phiben *gw.* piben	phleidlais *gw.* pleidlais
phicil *gw.* picil	phleidleisiau *gw.* pleidlais
phictiwr *gw.* pictiwr	phleidleisio *gw.* pleidleisio
phicwn *gw.* picwnen	phleidleisiwr *gw.* pleidleisiwr
phicwnen *gw.* picwnen	phlentyn *gw.* plentyn
phigfain *gw.* pigfain	phlentynnaidd *gw.* plentynnaidd
phigiad *gw.* pigiad	
phigo *gw.* pigo	phleser *gw.* pleser
phigog *gw.* pigog	phleserus *gw.* pleserus
phil *gw.* pil	phlesio *gw.* plesio
philer *gw.* piler	phlisgyn *gw.* plisgyn
philio *gw.* pilio	phlisman: phlismon *gw.* plisman
philion *gw.* pil	
phili-pala *gw.* pili-pala	phlismyn *gw.* plisman
philsen *gw.* pilsen	phlu *gw.* pluen
philyn *gw.* pilyn	phluen *gw.* pluen
phin *gw.* pin	phluf *gw.* plufyn
	phlufyn *gw.* plufyn

phlwc

phlwc *gw.* plwc.
phlwg *gw.* plwg
phlwm *gw.* plwm
phlwyf *gw.* plwyf
phlyciau *gw.* plwc
phlygiau *gw.* plwg
phlygu *gw.* plygu
phob *gw.* pob
phobi *gw.* pobi
phobl *gw.* pobl
phoblogaeth *gw.* poblogaeth
phoblogaidd *gw.* poblogaidd
phobman *gw.* pobman
phobydd *gw.* pobydd
phoced *gw.* poced
phoen *gw.* poen
phoeni *gw.* poeni
phoenus *gw.* poenus
phoenydio *gw.* poenydio
phoer *gw.* poer
phoeri *gw.* poer, poeri (at, i'r)
phoeth *gw.* poeth
phoethi *gw.* poethi
pholion *gw.* polyn
pholiticaldd *gw.* politicaidd
pholyn *gw.* polyn
phont *gw.* pont
phontydd *gw.* pont
Phont-y-pŵl *gw.* Pont-y-pŵl
phopeth *gw.* popeth
phoptai *gw.* popty
phopty *gw.* popty
phorfa *gw.* porfa
phorfeydd *gw.* porfa
phorffor *gw.* porffor
phori *gw.* pori
phortread *gw.* portread
phorth *gw.* porth
phorthladd *gw.* porthladd
phos *gw.* pos

phosibilrwydd *gw.*
  posibilrwydd
phosibl *gw.* posibl
phost *gw.* post
phostio *gw.* postio
phostman: phostmon *gw.*
  postman
phostmyn *gw.* postman
phostyn *gw.* postyn
photel *gw.* potel
phowdr: phowdwr *gw.* powdr
phowdrau *gw.* powdr
phowlen *gw.* bowlen
phraidd *gw.* praidd
phram *gw.* pram
phrawf *gw.* prawf
phregeth *gw.* pregeth
phregethu *gw.* pregethu
phregethwr *gw.* pregethwr
phreiddiau *gw.* praidd
phreifat *gw.* preifat
phren *gw.* pren
phrennau *gw.* pren
phrentis *gw.* prentis
phrentisiaeth *gw.* prentisiaeth
phrentisiaid *gw.* prentis
phres *gw.* pres
phreseb *gw.* preseb
phresennol *gw.* presennol
phresenoldeb *gw.*
  presenoldeb
phresgripsiwn *gw.*
  presgripsiwn
phreswyl: phreswylfod *gw.*
  preswyl
phridwerth *gw.* pridwerth
phridd *gw.* pridd
phrif *gw.* prif
phrifardd *gw.* prifardd
phrifathrawes *gw.*
  prifathrawes

phrifathro *gw*. prifathro
phrifddinas *gw*. prifddinas
phrifeirdd *gw*. prifardd
phrifio *gw*. prifio
phrifysgol *gw*. prifysgol
phriffordd *gw*. priffordd
phriffyrdd *gw*. priffordd
phrin *gw*. prin
phrinder *gw*. prinder
phrintio *gw*. printio
phriod *gw*. priod
phriodas *gw*. priodas
phriodi *gw*. priodi
phriodol *gw*. priodol
phris *gw*. pris
phroblem *gw*. problem
phrofi *gw*. profi
phrofiad *gw*. profiad
phrofiadol *gw*. profiadol
phrofion *gw*. prawf
phrofocio *gw*. profocio
phroffid *gw*. proffid
phroffidiol *gw*. proffidiol
phroffwyd *gw*. proffwyd
phroffwydo *gw*. proffwydo
phrotest *gw*.protest
Phrotestant *gw*. Protestant
phrudd *gw*. prudd
phryd *gw*. pryd
Phrydain *gw*. Prydain
phrydau *gw*. pryd
Phrydeinig *gw*. Prydeinig
phryder *gw*. pryder
phryderu *gw*. pryderu
phryderus *gw*. pryderus
phrydferth *gw*. prydferth
phrydferthwch *gw*.
  prydferthwch
phrydiau *gw*. pryd
phrydlon *gw*. prydlon

phryf: phryfedyn: phryfyn *gw*.
  pryf
phryfed *gw*. pryf
phryfocio *gw*. profocio
phryfyn *gw*. pryf
phrynhawn *gw*. prynhawn
phrynu *gw*. prynu
phrynwr *gw*. prynwr
phrysur *gw*. prysur
phrysurdeb *gw*. prysurdeb
phrysuro *gw*. prysuro
phulpud *gw*. pulpud
phum: phump *gw*. pum
ph'un *gw*. pa
phunnau *gw*. punt
phunnoedd *gw*. punt
phunt *gw*. punt
phupur *gw*. pupur
phur *gw*. pur
phurfa *gw*. purfa
phuro *gw*. puro
phwdin *gw*. pwdin
phwdr *gw*. pwdr
phwdryn *gw*. pwdryn
phwdu *gw*. pwdu
phŵer *gw*. pŵer
phwll *gw*. pwll
phwllyn *gw*. pwllyn
phwmp *gw*. pwmp
phwnc *gw*. pwnc
phwrpas *gw*. pwrpas
phwrs *gw*. pwrs
phwy *gw*. pwy
phwyll *gw*. pwyll
phwyllgor *gw*. pwyllgor
phwyllo *gw*. pwyllo
phwynt *gw*. pwynt
phwys *gw*. pwys
phwysedd *gw*. pwysedd
phwysig *gw*. pwysig

phwysigrwydd

phwysigrwydd *gw.*
 pwysigrwydd
phwyslais *gw.* pwyslais
phwyso *gw.* pwyso
phwyth *gw.* pwyth
phwytho *gw.* pwytho
phydru *gw.* pydru
phyllau *gw.* pwll, pyllyn
phyllyn *gw.* pyllyn
phympiau *gw.* pwmp
phymtheg *gw.* pymtheg
phymthegfed *gw.* pymthegfed
phynciau *gw.* pwnc
phyped *gw.* pyped
phyrsau *gw.* pwrs
phyrth *gw.* porth
phys *gw.* pysen
physgod *gw.* pysgodyn
physgodyn *gw.* pysgodyn
physgota *gw.* pysgota
physgotwr *gw.* pysgotwr
physt *gw.* post, postyn
phythefnos *gw.* pythefnos

R

raca *gw.* rhaca
raced *e.b.g. ll.* -i racket
racs *gw.* rhecsyn
rad *gw.* rhad
radio *e.g. ll.* -s radio
radd *gw.* gradd
raddfa *gw.* graddfa
raddio *gw.* graddio
raddol *gw.* graddol
raeadr *gw.* rhaeadr
raenus *gw.* graenus
raff *gw.* rhaff
ragair *gw.* rhagair
ragbrawf *gw.* rhagbrawf

ragbrofion *gw.* rhagbrawf
ragenw *gw.* rhagenw
ragfarn *gw.* rhagfarn
ragfarnllyd *gw.* rhagfarnllyd
ragflas *gw.* rhagflas
Ragfyr *gw.* Rhagfyr
raglen *gw.* rhaglen
raglenni *gw.* rhaglen
ragor *gw.* rhagor
ragori *gw.* rhagori
ragorol *gw.* rhagorol
rai *gw.* rhai
raid *gw.* rhaid
ramadeg *gw.* gramadeg
ramadegol *gw.* gramadegol
ramantaidd *gw.* rhamantus
ramantus *gw.* rhamantus
ran *gw.* rhan
ranbarth *gw.* rhanbarth
randir *gw.* rhandir
raniad *gw.* rhaniad
rannau *gw.* rhan
rannu *gw.* rhannu
ras *e.b. ll.* -ys race
 (competitive). **ras-gyfnewid**
 relay race. *gw.* **gras**
raw *gw.* rhaw
rawnffrwyth *gw.* grawnffrwyth
record *e.b. ll.* -iau record
recsyn *gw.* rhecsyn
redeg *gw.* rhedeg
redwr *gw.* rhedwr
redyn *gw.* rhedynen
redynen *gw.* rhedynen
reg *gw.* rheg
regfeydd *gw.* rheg
regi *gw.* rhegi
reidiau *gw.* rhaid
reilffordd *gw.* rheilffordd
reilffyrdd *gw.* rheilffordd

reis *e.g.* rice. **pwdin reis** rice
 pudding
reol *gw.* **rheol**
reolaidd *gw.* **rheolaidd**
reoli *gw.* **rheoli**
reolwr *gw.* **rheolwr**
reolwyr *gw.* **rheolwr**
res *gw.* **rhes**
resi *gw.* **rhes**
restr *gw.* **rhestr**
restrau *gw.* **rhestr**
restri *gw.* **rhestr**
reswm *gw.* **rheswm**
resymau *gw.* **rheswm**
resynu *gw.* **gresynu**
rew *gw.* **rhew**
rewgell *gw.* **rhewgell**
rewi *gw.* **rhewi**
rewlif *gw.* **rhewlif**
rëydr *gw.* **rhaeadr**
riant *gw.* **rhiant**
rieni *gw.* **rhiant**
rif *gw.* **rhif**
rifau *gw.* **rhif**
rifo *gw.* **rhifo**
rifyddeg *gw.* **rhifyddeg**
rifyn *gw.* **rhifyn**
rifynnau *gw.* **rhifyn**
riffl *e.g.* *ll.* **-au** rifle
rigwm *gw.* **rhigwm**
rigymau *gw.* **rhigwm**
rihyrsal *e.b.* *ll.* **-s** rehearsal
rinwedd *gw.* **rhinwedd**
ris *gw.* **gris**
risiau *gw.* **gris**

riw *gw.* **rhiw**
robin goch *e.g.* robin
roced *e.b.* *ll.* **-i, -au** rocket
rodd *gw.* **rhodd**
roddi *gw.* **rhoddi**
roddion *gw.* **rhodd**
roedd -e/-hi *bf.* he/she/it/was.
 gw. **bod**
Roeg *gw.* **Groeg**
Roegaidd *gw.* **Groegaidd**
Roegwr *gw.* **Groegwr**
rofiau *gw.* **rhaw**
roi *gw.* **rhoddi**
Romania *e.b.* Romania
rolio *gw.* **rholio**
ros *gw.* **rhos**
rosydd *gw.* **rhos**
rosyn *gw.* **rhosyn**
rosynnau *gw.* **rhosyn**
ruban *e.g.* *ll.* **-au** ribbon
rudd *gw.* **grudd**
Rufain *gw.* **Rhufain**
Rufeinig *gw.* **Rhufeinig**
rug *gw.* **grug**
ruo *gw.* **rhuo**
ruthro *gw.* **rhuthro**
rŵan *ad.* now *(N.W.)*. *gw.*
 nawr
rwbio *gw.* **rhwbio**
rwber *e.g.* rubber
Rwsia *e.b.* Russia
Rwsiad *e.g.* *ll.* **Rwsiaid** a
 Russian
Rwsieg *e.g.* Russian
 (language)

Insight

Rwsiaid sy'n siarad Rwsieg yn Rwsia Russians speak Russian
in Russia.

rwyd

rwyd *gw.* rhwyd
rwydi *gw.* rhwyd
rwydd *gw.* rhwydd
rwyfo *gw.* rhwyfo
rwyfus *gw.* rhwyfus
rwygo *gw.* rhwygo
rwymo *gw.* rhwymo
rwystr *gw.* rhwystr
rybudd *gw.* rhybudd
rybuddio *gw.* rhybuddio
ryd *gw.* rhyd
rydw i *bf.* I am. *gw.* **bod**
Rydychen *gw.* Rhydychen
rydd *gw.* rhydd
ryddhau *gw.* rhyddhau
ryddid *gw.* rhyddid
ryddion *gw.* rhydd
ryfedd *gw.* rhyfedd
ryfeddod *gw.* rhyfeddod
ryfeddol *gw.* rhyfeddol
ryfeddu *gw.* rhyfeddu
ryfel *gw.* rhyfel
ryngwladol *gw.* rhyngwladol
rym *gw.* grym
rymus *gw.* grymus
rysáit *eb.* *ll.* **-s**. recipe,
 prescription
ryw *gw.* rhyw
rywbeth *gw.* rhywbeth
rywbryd *gw.* rhywbryd
rywdro *gw.* rhywdro
rywfaint *gw.* rhywfaint
rywiol *gw.* rhywiol
rywle *gw.* rhywle
rywrai *gw.* rhywun
rywsut *gw.* rhywsut
rywun *gw.* rhywun

RH

rhaca *e.b.* *ll.* **-nau** rake. **fel
 rhaca** very thin, like a rake
rhacs *gw.* **rhecsyn**
rhad 1 *a.* cheap; free. **yn rhad
 ac am ddim** absolutely free.
 2 *e.g.* *ll.* **-au** blessing, grace.
 rhadffôn free phone;
 rhadbost freepost
rhaeadr *e.b.* *ll.* **-au, rhëydr**
 cataract, waterfall
rhaff *e.b.* *ll.* **-au** rope
rhag 1 *ardd.* before; lest;
 against, from. 2 *rhagdd.*
 pre-, for-, ante-
rhagair *e.g.* preface
rhagbrawf *e.g.* *ll.* **rhagbrofion**
 preliminary test; foretaste
rhagbrofion *gw.* **rhagbrawf**
rhagenw *e.g.* *ll.* **-au** pronoun.
 rhagenw gofynnol
 interrogative pronoun;
 rhagenw perthynol relative
 pronoun
rhagfarn *e.b.* *ll.* **-au** prejudice
rhagfarnllyd *a.* prejudiced
rhagflas *e.g.* foretaste
Rhagfyr *e.g.* December
rhaglen *e.b.* *ll.* **-ni**
 programme. **rhaglen deledu**
 television programme;
 rhaglen fyw live programme;
 rhaglen nodwedd feature
 programme
rhaglenni *gw.* **rhaglen**
rhagor *e.g.* *ll.* **-au, -ion**
 difference, more, excess.
 rhagor o fwyd more food
rhagori (ar) *be.* (**rhagoraf**) to
 excel, to surpass

rhagorol *a.* excellent, splendid

rhai 1 *rhag.* ones. **y rhai da** the good ones. **2** *a.* some. **Mae rhai pobl yn oer** Some people are cold

rhaid *e.g. ll.* **rheidiau** necessity, need. **Mae rhaid i ti fynd** You must go

rhain, y *rhag.* these. **Ble mae'r rhain i fod?** Where are these to go? **y rheina** those

rhamantus: rhamantaidd *a.* romantic

rhan *e.b. ll.* **-nau** part, share; rôle. **y rhan fwyaf** the greatest part

rhanbarth *e.g. ll.* **-au** division, region, area, district

rhandir *e.g. ll.* **-oedd** region, division, district; allotment

rhandiroedd *gw.* **rhandir**

rhaniad *e.g. ll.* **-au** division; parting

rhannau *gw.* **rhan**

rhannu *be.* **(rhannaf)** to divide, to share, to distribute

rhaw *e.b. ll.* **-iau, rhofiau** shovel; spade

rhecsyn *e.g. ll.* **rhacs** rag

rhedeg *be.* **(rhedaf)** to run; to flow

rhedwr *e.g. ll.* **rhedwyr** runner

rhedyn *e.ll.* fern, bracken. *gw.* **rhedynen**

rhedynen *e.b. ll.* **rhedyn** fern

rheg *e.b. ll.* **-feydd** curse, swearword

rhegfeydd *gw.* **rheg**

rhegi *be.* **(rhegaf)** to curse, to swear

rheidiau *gw.* **rhaid**

rheiddiadur *e.g. ll.* **-on** radiator

rheilffordd *e.b. ll.* **rheilffyrdd** railway

rheiffyrdd *gw.* **rheilffordd**

rheina, y *gw.* **rhain**

rheini, y *rhag.* those (*not present.*)

rheol *e.b. ll.* **-au** rule, order. **Rheolau'r Ffordd Fawr** the Highway Code

rheolaidd *a.* regular, constant, orderly, proper

rheoli *be.* **(rheolaf)** to control, to manage

rheolwr *e.g. ll.* **rheolwyr** manager, ruler, controller, governor; referee

rheolwyr *gw.* **rheolwr**

rhes *e.b. ll.* **-i** row, rank; stripe, line

rhesi *gw.* **rhes**

rhestr *e.b. ll.* **-au, -i** row, rank; list. **rhestr fer** short list

rhestrau *gw.* **rhestr**

rhestri *gw.* **rhestr**

rheswm *e.g. ll.* **rhesymau** reason, cause. **y rheswm dros** the reason for

rhesymau *gw.* **rheswm**

rhesymol *a.* reasonable

rhew *e.g. ll.* **-iau, -ogydd** frost, ice. **rhewbwynt** freezing-point. **rhewfwyd** frozen food; **rhewlif** glacier; **Siôn Rhew** Jack Frost

rhewgell *eb. ll.* **-oedd** deep freeze cabinet, freezer

rhewi

rhewi *be.* **(rhewaf)** to freeze
rhewiau *gw.* **rhew**
rhewlif *e.g. ll.* **-iau** glacier
rhewogydd *gw.* **rhew**
rhëydr *gw.* **rhaeadr**
rhiant *e.g. ll.* **rhieni** parent
rhieni *gw.* **rhiant**
rhif *e.g. ll.* **-au** number,
numeral
rhifau *gw.* **rhif**
rhifo *be.* **(rhifaf)** to count, to
number, to reckon
rhifyddeg *e.b.g.* arithmetic
rhifyn *e.g. ll.* **-nau** number
(*of magazine*)
rhifynnau *gw.* **rhifyn**
rhigwm *e.g. ll.* **rhigymau**
rhyme; rigmarole
rhigymau *gw.* **rhigwm**
rhiniog *e.b. ll.* **-au** threshold
rhinwedd *e.b.g. ll.* **-au** virtue
rhisgl *e.ll.* bark (*of tree*)
rhiw *e.b. ll.* **-iau** hill, ascent,
slope (*S.W.*)
rhodd *e.b. ll.* **-ion** gift,
donation
rhoddi: rhoi *be.* **(rhoddaf:**
rhoiaf) to give, to bestow, to
put. **rhoi benthyg** to lend;
rhoi'r gorau i to relinquish.
gw. At. **Berfau**
rhoddion *gw.* **rhodd**
rhofion *gw.* **rhaw**
rhoi *gw.* **rhoddi**
rholio *be.* **(rholiaf)** to roll
rhos *e.b. ll.* **-ydd.** moor,
heath, plain. *gw.* **rhosyn**
rhosod *gw.* **rhosyn**
rhosydd *gw.* **rhos**
rhosyn *e.g. ll.* **-nau, rhos,**
rhosod rose

rhosynnau *gw.* **rhosyn**
Rhufain *e.b.* Rome
Rhufeinig *a.* Roman
rhugl *a.* fluent
rhuo *be.* **(rhuaf)** to roar, to
bellow
rhuthro *be.* **(rhuthraf)** to rush
rhwbio *be.* **(rhwbiaf)** to rub
rhwng *ardd.* (*personal forms:*
rhyngo, rhyngot,
rhyngddo/rhyngddi,
rhyngom, rhyngoch,
rhyngddyn) between,
among. *gw. At.* **Arddodiaid**
rhwyd *e.b. ll.* **-au, -i** net,
snare
rhwydd *a.* easy; fluent;
generous; fast (*S.W.*)
rhwyfo *be.* **(rhwyfaf)** to row
rhwyfus *a.* restless
rhwygo *be.* **(rhwygaf)** to tear,
to rip
rhwym *a.* bound, tied;
constipated
rhwymo *be.* **(rhwymaf)** to
bind, to tie; to constipate
rhwystr *e.g. ll.* **-au** hindrance,
obstacle
rhwystrau *gw.* **rhwystr**
rhy 1 *e.g.* excess. 2 *ad.* too.
yn rhy drwm too heavy
rhybudd *e.g. ll.* **-ion** warning,
notice, caution
rhybuddio (rhag) *be.*
(rhybuddiaf) to warn, to
caution
rhyd *e.b. ll.* **-au** ford
Rhydychen *e.b.* Oxford
rhydd *a. ll.* **-ion** free, liberal.
Y Seiri Rhyddion
Freemasons

saethwr

rhyddhau *be.* **(rhyddhaf)** to free, to release, to loose
rhyddid *e.g.* freedom, liberty
rhyddion *gw.* **rhydd**
rhyfedd: rhyfeddol *a.* wonderful, strange
rhyfeddod *e.g.* *ll.* **-au** wonder, surprise

rhywun *e.g.* *ll.* **rhywrai** someone, anyone. **rhywun neu'i gilydd** someone or other; **rhywrai** some

---

Insight

rhyfeddod *e.g.*wonder, surprise. **Saith o ryfeddodau'r byd** The seven wonders of the world.

---

rhyfeddol *gw.* **rhyfedd**
rhyfeddu (at) *be.* **(rhyfeddaf)** to wonder, to marvel
rhyfel *e.g.b.* *ll.* **-oedd** war, warfare. **Rhyfel y Gwlff** The Gulf War; **Yr Ail Ryfel Byd** The Second World War; **Y Rhyfel Mawr** The Great War
rhyngo i *gw.* **rhwng**
rhyngrwyd *e.b.* internet
rhyngwladol *a.* international
rhyw 1 *e.b.g.* *ll.* **-au** sort, kind; sex; gender. **2** *a.* some, certain. **Roedd rhyw ddyn yma ddoe** A certain man was here yesterday
rhywbeth *e.g.* something
rhywbryd *ad.* sometime
rhywdro *ad.* sometime
rhywfaint *e.g.* some amount
rhywiol *a.* sexual
rhywle *ad.* somewhere, anywhere
rhywrai *gw.* **rhywun**
rhywsut *ad.* somehow, anyhow

S

Sabath: Saboth *e.g.* *ll.* **-au** Sabbath
sach *e.b.* *ll.* **-au** sack. **sach gysgu** sleeping bag
Sadwrn *e.g.* *ll.* **Sadyrnau.** Saturn; Saturday
saer *e.g.* *ll.* **seiri** carpenter, joiner; wright; mason. **saer coed** carpenter; **saer maen** stonemason; **pensaer** architect
Saesneg 1 *e.b.* English (*language*). **2** *a.* English (*in language*)
Saesnes *e.b.* *ll.* **-au** Englishwoman.
Saeson *e.ll.* English people *gw.* **Sais**
saeth *e.b.* *ll.* **-au** arrow
saethu (at) *be.* **(saethaf)** to shoot, to fire
saethwr *e.g.* *ll.* **saethwyr** shooter; archer; goal shooter

safbwynt

safbwynt *e.g. ll.* **-iau** standpoint, viewpoint, perspective

safle *e.g. ll.* **-oedd** position, station, situation, rank

safon *e.b. ll.* **-au** standard, class; criterion. **Y Safon Aur** The Gold Standard; **Safon A** A level

safonol *a.* standard

saib *e.g. ll.* **seibiau** pause, rest

sail *e.b. ll.* **seiliau** base, foundation; ground. **ar sail** on the basis of

saim *e.g. ll.* **seimiau** grease, fat. **saim gŵydd** goose grease

sain *e.b. ll.* **seiniau** sound, tone

sant *e.g. ll.* **saint, seintiau** saint. **Dewi Sant** Saint David; **Sant Ioan** Saint John

santes *e.b. ll.* **-au** female saint; **Santes Dwynwen** Saint Dwynwen, patron saint of lovers

sarff *e.b. ll.* **seirff** serpent

sarhad *e.g. ll.* **-au** insult, disgrace

sarnu (ar) *be.* **(sarnaf)** to trample, to litter, to spill (*S.W.*)

sathru (ar) *be.* **(sathraf)** to trample, to tread. **sathru dan draed** to trample underfoot; **sathru ar gyrn** to offend

sawdl *e.g.b. ll.* **sodlau** heel

sawl *rhag. & ad. (followed by a singular noun)* he that, *(the*

Insight

Sadwrn *e.g.* Saturday. 'Sydyn daw dydd Sadwrn.' 'Saturday comes suddenly.'

sant *e.g.* saint. Dewi Sant; Dyfrig Sant; Illtud Sant ... Saint David; Saint Dyfrig; Saint Illtud ...

---

saint *gw.* **sant**

Sais *e.g. ll.* **Saeson** Englishman

saith *a. & e.g.* seven

sâl 1 *a.* poorly, sick; mean. **2** *e.g.* sale (*N.W.*)

salm *e.b. ll.* **-au** psalm. **salmdôn** chant

salw *a.* ugly, vile, mean (*S.W.*)

salwch *e.g.* illness

sanctaidd *a.* holy

one) who, that which; several, a number (of); how many? many. **Sawl car sy 'da chi?** How many cars do you have? **Sawl tŷ sy ar y bryn?** How many houses are there on the hill? **Roedd sawl llyfr yn y pentwr** There were many books in the pile; **Y sawl a gododd a gollodd ei le** The one that got up lost his seat

saws *e.g. ll.* **-iau** sauce
Sbaen *e.g.* Spain
Sbaeneg *e.b.* Spanish language
Sbaenes *e.b. ll.* **-au** Spanish woman
Sbaenwr *e.g. ll.* **-wyr** Spanish man, Spaniard
sbardun *e.g. ll.* **-au** accelerator; spur
sbectol *e.b.* spectacles
sbio (ar) *be.* **(sbiaf)** to spy
sbon *ad.* (*as used with the adjective* **newydd**) wholly. **newydd sbon** brand new
sbot: sbotyn *e.g. ll.* **sbotiau** spot
sebon *e.g. ll.* **-au** soap. **sebon dannedd** toothpaste
sedd *e.b. ll.* **-au** seat, pew. **sedd fawr** deacons' pew
sef *c.* namely, that is to say
sefydliad *e.g. ll.* **-au** establishment, institution, induction
sefydlog *a.* fixed, settled, stationary
sefydlu *be.* **(sefydlaf)** to establish, to settle
sefyll (am) *be.* **(safaf)** to stand; to stop; to stay, to wait (for) (*S.W.*). **sefyll arholiad** to sit an examination
sefyllfa *e.b. ll.* **-oedd** situation, position
segur *a.* idle
segura *be.* **(seguraf)** to idle
segurdod *e.g.* idleness
sengl *a.* single

seiat *e.b. ll.* **seiadau** fellowship, meeting, society
seibiant *e.g. ll.* **-au, seibiannau** leisure, respite, pause
seibiannau *gw.* **seibiant**
seibiau *gw.* **saib**
seiciatreg *e.b.* psychiatry
seiciatrydd *e.g. ll.* **-ion** psychiatrist
seicoleg *e.b.g.* psychology
seicolegydd *e.g. ll.* **seicolegwyr** psychologist
seiliau *gw.* **sail**
seilio *be.* **(seiliaf)** to base, to found, to ground
seimiau *gw.* **saim**
seimlyd: seimllyd *a.* greasy
seiniau *gw.* **sain**
seindorf *eb. ll.* **-eydd, seindyrf.** band (*musical*). **seindorf bres** brass band; **band un dyn** one-man band
seintiau *gw.* **sant**
seirff *gw.* **sarff**
seiri *gw.* **saer**
Seisnig *a.* English, pertaining to England
Seisnigeiddio: Seisnigo *be.* **(Seisnigeiddiaf: Seisnigaf)** to Anglicize
seithfed *a.* seventh
sêl *e.b.* zeal
Seland Newydd *e.b.* New Zealand
seld *e.b. ll.* **-au** dresser
sen *e.b. ll.* **-nau** rebuke, snub, censure. **bwrw sen ar** to cast a rebuke at
senedd *e.b. ll.* **-au** parliament, senate

sennau

sennau *gw.* **sen**

sêr *gw.* **seren**

serch 1 *e.g.* *ll.* **-iadau** love.
2 *c. & ardd.* although,
notwithstanding. **serch ei fod
e'n briod** although he was
married

serchog *a.* affectionate,
loving

serchu (yn) *be.* **serchaf** to
love

serchus *a.* affectionate,
loving; pleasant

seremoni *e.b.* *ll.* **seremonïau**
ceremony

seren *e.b.* *ll.* **sêr** star;
asterisk. **seren wib** shooting
star

serennog *a.* starry

serth *a.* steep; unclean;
obscene

set *e.b.* *ll.* **-iau** set. **set deledu**
television set

sêt *e.b.* *ll.* **seti** seat, pew: **sêt
fawr** deacons' seat

seti *gw.* **sêt**

setiau *gw.* **set**

setlo *be.* **(setlaf)** to settle

sgarff *e.b.* *ll.* **-iau** scarf

sgert *e.b.* *ll.* **-i, -iau** skirt. *gw.*
sgyrt

sgets *e.b.* *ll.* **-ys** sketch

sgi *e.b.g.* ski

sgil *e.g.* *ll.* **-iau** skill, device,
trick

sgil *ad.* in the wake of,
behind. **Daeth tlodi yn sgil y
rhyfel** There was poverty in
the wake of the war

sgïo *be.* **(sgïaf)** to ski

sgipio *be.* **(sgipiaf)** to skip

sgiw 1 *e.b.* *ll.* **-iau** settle.
2 *a.* askew

sgïwr *e.g.* *ll.* **sgïwyr** skier

sglefrio *be.* **(sglefriaf)** to
skate, to slide

sglodion *gw.* **sglodyn**

sglodyn *e.g.* *ll.* **sglodion**
chips. **pysgod a sglodion**
fish and chips

sgôr *e.b.* *ll.* **sgoriau** score

sgorio *be.* **(sgoriaf)** to score

sgrech *e.b.* *ll.* **-iadau** yell,
scream. **sgrech y coed** jay

sgrechain: sgrechian *be.*
(sgrechaf: sgrechiaf) to yell,
to scream

sgrifennu: ysgrifennu (ar, at)
be. **(sgrifennaf: ysgrifennaf)**
to write

sgrîn ben-glin *e.b.* *ll.* **sgriniau
pen-glin** laptop *gw.* **gliniadur**

sgript *e.b.* *ll.* **-iau** script

sgrym *e.b.* *ll.* **-iau** scrum
(*rugby*)

sgrymio *be.* **(sgrymiaf)** to
scrum

sgubo *be.* **(sgubaf)** to sweep,
to brush

sgwâr *e.g.b.* *ll.* **-iau** square

sgwd *e.g.* *ll.* **sgydau**
waterfall, cataract

sgwrs *e.b.* *ll.* **sgyrsiau** talk,
chat; conversation

sgwrsio (â) *be.* **(sgwrsiaf)** to
talk, to chat

sgydau *gw.* **sgwd**

sgyrsiau *gw.* **sgwrs**

sgyrt *e.b.* *ll.* **-iau, -s** skirt.
gw. **sgert**

si *e.g. ll.* **sïon** buzz, rumour, murmur

siaced *e.b. ll.* **-i** jacket, coat

sialc *e.g. ll.* **-iau** chalk. **sialciau lliw** coloured chalks

siampl *e.b. ll.* **-au** example

sianel *e.b. ll.* **-i** channel. **Sianel Pedwar Cymru** S4C (Welsh TV Channel 4)

siâp *e.g. ll.* **-iau** shape

siâr *e.b.* share. **Ga i siâr o'r bwyd?** May I have a share of the food?

siarad *be.* **(siaradaf)** to talk, to speak. **siarad â** to speak with; **siarad am** to speak about

siaradwr *e.g. ll.* **siaradwyr** talker, speaker

sibrwd *be.* **(sibrydaf)** to whisper

sicr: siŵr *a.* sure, certain; secure

sicrhau *be.* **(sicrhaf)** to assure, to confirm, to obtain, to fix, to secure.

sicrwydd *e.g.* certainty, assurance, security

sidan *e.g. ll.* **-au** silk

Siôn *e.p. g.* John, Ioan, Ieuan. **Siôn Barrug: Siôn Rhew** Jack Frost; **mae Siôn Cwsg yn dod** the sandman is coming

sipsi *e.g. ll.* **sipsiwn** gipsy

siswrn *e.g. ll.* **sisyrnau** scissors

siwd *gw.* **sut**

siwg: jwg *e.g. ll.* **-iau** jug. **siwg laeth** milk jug

siwgr *e.g.* sugar; **siwgr brown** brown sugar

siŵr *gw.* **sicr**

siwrnai 1 *e.g. ll.* **siwrneiau, siwrneion** journey. **Siwrnai dda ichi!** Have a good trip! 2 *ad.* once. **Siwrnai roedd tawelwch, fe gododd i siarad** Once there was silence he rose to speak (*S.W.)*

sliper *e.b. ll.* **-i** slipper

smotyn *e.g. ll.* **smotiau** spot

sodlau *gw.* **sawdl**

sôn (am, wrth) 1 *be.* **(soniaf)** to mention, to talk, to rumour. 2 *e.g.* mention, talk, rumour: **Does dim sôn amdani** There is no sign of her

sosban *e.b. ll.* **-au, sosbenni** saucepan

sosbenni *gw.* **sosban**

soser *e.b. ll.* **-i** saucer

sosialaeth *e.b.* socialism

sosialaidd *a.* socialist

sosialwyr *gw.* **sosialydd**

sosialydd *e.g. ll.* **sosialwyr** socialist

sothach *e.torf.* trash, rubbish

stabl *e.b. ll.* **-au** stable

stafell: ystafell *e.b. ll.* **-oedd** room. **stafell ffrynt** front room; **stafell gefn** back room; **stafell wely** bedroom; **stafell ymolchi** bathroom

stamp *e.g. ll.* **-iau** stamp

stampio *be.* **(stampiaf)** to stamp

stôl *e.b. ll.* **stolau** stool

stondin

stondin *e.b. ll.* **-au** stall.
stondin farchnad market
stall

stopio *be.* **(stopiaf)** to stop

stôr *e.g. ll.* **storau** store. **stôr
celfi** furniture store

stordy *e.g. ll.* **stordai**
storehouse, warehouse

storfa *e.b. ll.* **storfeydd** store;
storage

stori *eb. ll.* **storiáu, storïau,
straeon** story. **stori arswyd**
horror story; **stori fer** short
story

storiáu: storïau *gw.* **stori**

storïwr *e.g. ll.* **storïwyr**
storyteller

storm *e.b. ll.* **-ydd** storm

stormus *a.* stormy,
tempestuous

stormydd *gw.* **storm**

straeon *gw.* **stori**

strategaeth *e.b.* strategy

streic *e.b. ll.* **-iau** strike

strwythur *e.g. ll.* **-au**
structure

strwythuro *be.* **(strwythuraf)**
to structure

stryd *e.b. ll.* **-oedd** street

stumog *e.b. ll.* **-au** stomach

stumogi *be.* **(stumogaf)** to
stomach

stŵr *e.g.* stir, noise, bustle,
fuss

su *e.g. ll.* **suon** buzz,
murmur, rumour. *gw.* **si**

suddo *be.* **(suddaf)** to sink, to
dive; to invest

sugno *be.* **(sugnaf)** to suck,
to absorb

Sul *e.g. ll.* **-iau** Sunday. **Dydd
Sul** Sunday; **Sul y Blodau**
Palm Sunday; **Sul y Mamau**
Mothering Sunday

Sulgwyn *e.g.* Whitsunday

Suliau *gw.* **Sul**

suo *be.* **(suaf)** to hum, to
buzz; to lull

suon *gw.* **su**

sur *a. ll.* **-ion** sour, bitter,
acid

suro *be.* **(suraf)** to sour

sut: siwd *rhag.gof.* how?
Sut/Siwd mae? How are
things?

sŵ *e.g.b. ll.* **-au** zoo

swil *a.* shy, bashful

Swistir Y, *e.b.* Switzerland

swm *e.g. ll.* **symiau** sum

sŵn *e.g. ll.* **synau** sound,
noise

swnio *be.* **(swniaf)** to sound,
to pronounce

swper *e.g.b. ll.* **-au** supper: **Y
Swper Olaf** The Last Supper

sws *e.g.* kiss (*N.W.*)

swydd *e.b. ll.* **-i** post, office,
job; county (*in England*).
gw. **sir. Swydd Gaerloyw**
Gloucestershire; **swydd
Buckingham**
Buckinghamshire

swyddfa *e.b. ll.* **swyddfeydd**
office. **Y Swyddfa Gymreig**
The Welsh Office

swyddfeydd *gw.* **swyddfa**

swyddi *gw.* **swydd**

swyddog *e.g. ll.* **-ion** officer,
official. **swyddog prawf**
probation officer. **swyddog y
llys** officer of the court

swyddogol *a.* official. **llythyr swyddogol** official letter

swyn *e.g. ll.* **-ion** charm, magic, spell

swyno *be.* **(swynaf)** to charm, to enchant, to bewitch

swynol *a.* charming, fascinating

sy: sydd *bf.* is, are. *gw.* **bod**

sych *a.* dry. **tywydd sych** dry weather

syched *e.g.* thirst: **mae syched ar Tom** Tom is thirsty

sychedig *a.* thirsty, parched

sychu *be.* **(sychaf)** to dry, to dry up; to wipe

sydyn *a.* sudden, abrupt

sydd *gw.* **sy**

syfrdanol *a.* stupefying, stunning

sylfaen *e.b. ll.* **sylfeini** foundation, base

sylfaenol *a.* basic, fundamental

sylfeini *gw.* **sylfaen**

sylw *e.g. ll* **-adau** notice, remark, observation, attention. **Gadewch e dan sylw.** Don't take notice of him

sylwadau *gw.* **sylw**

sylwebaeth *e.b. ll.* **-au** commentary

sylwebu (ar) *be.* **(sylwebaf)** to give a commentary (on)

sylwebydd: sylwebwr *e.g. ll.* **sylwebwyr** commentator

sylwedd *e.g. ll.* **-au** substance, foundation

sylweddol *a.* substantial

sylweddoli *be.* **(sylweddolaf)** to realize

sylwi (ar) *be.* **(sylwaf)** to observe, to notice. **Sylwch arnyn nhw** Notice them

syllu (ar) *be.* **(syllaf)** to gaze

symiau *gw.* **swm**

syml *a.* simple

symud 1 *be.* **(symudaf)** to move, to remove; **2** *e.g.* movement, action

symudiad *e.g. ll.* **-au** movement, removal

symudol *a.* mobile, portable. **ffôn symudol** mobile phone

syn *a.* amazed, astonishing, surprising

synau *gw.* **swn**

syndod *e.g. ll.* **-au** surprise, amazement

synhwyrau *gw.* **synnwyr**

synhwyro *be.* **(synhwyraf)** to sense; to sniff, to smell

synhwyrol *a.* sensible

syniad *e.g. ll.* **-au** idea, notion, thought

synnu (at) *be.* **(synnaf)** to be surprised, to marvel, to wonder. **Rwy'n synnu atoch chi** I'm surprised at you

synnwyr *e.g. ll.* **synhwyrau** sense

syr *e.g.* sir. **Annwyl Syr** Dear Sir.

syrcas *e.b. ll.* **-au** circus

syrffed *e.g.* surfeit

syrffedu (ar) *be.* **(syrffedaf)** to surfeit, to be fed up (with)

syrthio

syrthio *be.* **(syrthiaf)** to fall.
syrthio mewn cariad to fall
in love; **syrthio ar fai** to
admit to blame

syth *a.* stiff, straight, erect.
Dewch yn syth Come at
once

sythlyd *a.* cold, chilled

sythu *a.* to become chilled, to
straighten *(S.W.)*. **Rwyf bron
â sythu** I'm perished

T

tabl *e.g. ll.* **-au** table
tabled *e.b. ll.* **-au, -i** tablet
tacl *e.b.g. ll.* **-au** tackle, gear
taclo *be.* **(taclaf)** to tackle
taclu *be.* **(taclaf)** to put in
order; to dress *(S.W.)*
taclus *a.* neat, tidy
tacluso *be.* **(taclusaf)** to trim,
to tidy
taclwr *e.g. ll.* **taclwyr** tackler
(rugby)
tacsi *e.g. ll.* **-s** taxi
Tachwedd *e.g.* November
tad *e.g. ll.* **-au** father: **tad
maeth** foster-father; **llystad**
stepfather; **tad-yng-
nghyfraith** father-in-law
tad-cu *e.g. ll.* **tad-cuod**
grandfather *(S.W.)*. *gw.* **taid**
tafarn *e.g.b. ll.* **tafarnau**
tavern, public house, inn
tafarnwr *e.g. ll.* **tafarnwyr**
publican, inn-keeper
tafell *e.b. ll.* **-au, -i, tefyll**
slice, slab

taflegryn *e.g. ll.* **taflegrau**
missile
taflen *e.b. ll.* **-ni** leaflet, list,
table. **taflen amser** timetable
taflu (at) *be.* **(taflaf)** to throw
(to), to fling, to cast; to
dislocate
tafod *e.g. ll.* **-au** tongue,
tang, spit. **tafod llym** sharp
tongue
tafodiaith *e.b. ll.*
tafodieithoedd dialect
tafodieithoedd *gw.* **tafodiaith**
tafol *e.b. ll.* **-au** scales
tagfa *e.b. ll.* **tagfeydd**
strangulation, choking;
bottleneck
tagu *be.* **(tagaf)** to strangle, to
choke
tangnefedd *e.g.b.* peace
tai *gw.* **tŷ**
taid *e.g. ll.* **teidiau**
grandfather *(N.W.)*; *gw.* **tad-
cu** *(S.W.)*
tair *a.b. & e.b.* three. **tair
merch** three girls. *gw.* **tri**
taith *e.b. ll.* **teithiau** journey,
tour, voyage
tal *a.* tall, lofty, high
tâl 1 *e.g. ll.* **taloedd, taliadau**
pay, payment, charge, rates.
Tâl Cymunedol Community
Charge. 2 *e.g. ll.* **talau**
forehead, front, end
talai *e.g. ll.* **taleion** payee
talaith *e.b. ll.* **taleithiau**
province, state. **Yr Unol
Daleithiau** The United States
talcen *e.g. ll.* **-nau, -ni**
forehead; gable, pine-end.

tarw

talcen tŷ pine-end of house
talcennau *gw.* **talcen**
talcenni *gw.* **talcen**
taleb *e.b. ll.* **-au, -ion** receipt
taleion *gw.* **talai**
taleithiau *gw.* **talaith**
talent *e.b. ll.* **-au** talent
talentog *a.* gifted, talented
talfyriad *e.g. ll.* **-au**
abbreviation
taliadau *gw.* **tâl**
taloedd *gw.* **tâl**
talu (am) *be.* **(talaf)** to pay
talwr *e.g. ll.* **talwyr** payer
talwrn *e.g. ll.* **talyrnau** spot,
place; cock-fighting pit:
Talwrn y Beirdd the Poet's
Place (*for competition*)
tamaid *e.g. ll.* **tameidiau**
piece, bit, bite. **tamaid i aros
pryd** temporary provision
while awaiting arrival of
something more substantial
tameidiau *gw.* **tamaid**
tan *ardd. (followed by soft
mutation)* until, as far;
under. *gw.* **dan**
tân *e.g. ll.* **tanau** fire, light.
tân siafins short-lived
enthusiasm and transitory
zeal (*lit.* a blaze of wood
shavings)
tanau *gw.* **tân**
tanbaid *a.* hot, fervent, fiery,
brilliant
tanc *e.g. ll.* **-iau** tank
tancer *e.g. ll.* **-i** tanker
tanddaear: tanddaearol *a.*
subterranean, underground
tanfor *a.* submarine. **llong**

danfor submarine
tanio *be.* **(taniaf)** to ignite, to
fire, to stoke, to light. **tanio'r
dychymyg** to fire the
imagination
tanlinellu *be.* **(tanlinellaf)** to
underline
tanlwybr *e.g. ll.* **-au** subway
tanllyd *a.* fiery, fervent
tannau *gw.* **tant**
tanseilio *be.* **(tanseiliaf)** to
sap, to undermine
tant *e.g. ll.* **tannau** chord,
string. **tant telyn** harp string
tanwydd *e.g.* fuel, firewood
tap *e.g. ll.* **-iau** tap. **tap dŵr
oer** cold water tap
tâp *e.g. ll.* **tapiau** tape
tapiau *gw.* **tap, tâp**
taran *e.b. ll.* **-au** (peal of)
thunder. **mellt a tharanau**
thunder and lightning
taranu *be.* **(taranaf)** to
thunder, to threaten
tarddiad *e.g. ll.* **-au** source,
derivation
tarddu *be.* **(tarddaf)** to spring,
to sprout, to derive from, to
issue
targed *e.g. ll.* **-au** target
tarian *e.b. ll.* **tariannau** shield
tariannau *gw.* **tarian**
taro 1 *be.* **(trawaf)** to strike,
to hit, to tap; to suit. **Mae
e'n dy daro'n iawn** It suits
you well. **2** *e.g.* difficulty,
crisis; **mewn taro** in an
emergency
tarw *e.g. ll.* **teirw** bull. **llwybr
tarw** a short cut

tasg

tasg *e.b.* *ll.* **-au**

tasgu *be.* **(tasgaf)** to splash, to start, to bolt; to spark; to lose one's temper. **Roedd e'n tasgu pan glywodd e** He was mad when he heard

taten *e.b.* **tatws, tato** potato. **tatws drwy'r croen/pil** jacket potatoes; **tatws rhost** roast potatoes; **tatws wedi'u berwi** boiled potatoes; **tatws wedi'u ffrio** fried potatoes; **creision tatws** potato crisps

tato: tatws *gw.* **taten**

tawel *a.* quiet, calm, still, peaceful

tawelu *be.* **(tawelaf)** to calm, to grow calm

tawelwch *e.g.* quiet, calm, stillness, tranquillity

tawelydd *e.g.* *ll.* **-ion** tranquillizer

tawelyddion gw. **tawelydd**

tawelyn *e.g.* *ll.* **-nau** tranquillizer

tawelynnau *gw.* **tawelyn**

te *e.g.* tea

te-parti *e.g.* *ll.* **te-partïon, te-partis** tea-party

tebot *e.g.* *ll.* **-au** teapot

tebyg *a.* like, similar, likely. **yn debyg i** like, similar to; **yn debyg o** likely to

tebygol *a.* likely, probable. **yn debygol o ennill** likely to win

tebygrwydd *e.g.* likeness, similarity, resemblance

tecell: tegell *e.g.* *ll.* **-au, -i** kettle

techneg *e.b.* *ll.* **-au** technique

technegol *a.* technical

technegwr *e.g.* *ll.* **technegwyr** technician

technoleg *e.b.* technology

teg *a.* fair, fine, beautiful. **chwarae teg** fair play; **teg o bryd** beautiful in appearance

tegan *e.g.* *ll.* **-au** toy, plaything

tegell *gw.* **tecell**

tegwch *e.g.* beauty, fairness

tei *e.g.b.* *ll.* **teis** tie

teiar *e.g.* *ll.* **-s** tyre

teidiau *gw.* **taid**

teigr *e.g.* *ll.* **-od** tiger

teiliwr *e.g.* *ll.* **teilwriaid** tailor

teilsen *e.b.* *ll.* **teils** tile

teilwng *a.* worthy, deserved. **yn deilwng o** worthy of

teilwres *e.b.* *ll.* **-au** tailoress

teilwriaid *gw.* **teiliwr**

teilyngdod *e.g.* *ll.* **-au** merit, worthiness

teimlad *e.g.* *ll.* **-au** feel, emotion, feeling, sensation

teimlo *be.* **(teimlaf)** to feel, to handle, to touch. **teimlo fel** to feel like

teipiadur *e.g.* *ll.* **-on** typewriter

teirgwaith *ad.* three times

teirw *gw.* **tarw**

teis *gw.* **tei**

teisen *e.b.* *ll.* **-nau** cake, tart. **teisen ddwbl** sandwich cake; **teisen ffrwythau** fruit cake; **teisennau cri** Welsh cakes

teitl *e.g.* *ll.* **-au** title

teithiau *gw.* **taith**

teithio *be.* **(teithiaf)** to travel, to journey

teithiwr *e.g.* *ll.* **teithwyr** traveller

telediad *e.g.* *ll.* **-au** telecast

teledu 1 *be.* **(teledaf)** to televise. 2 *e.g.* television. **set deledu lliw** colour television set

teleffon: ffôn *e.g.* *ll.* **-au** telephone. *gw.* **ffôn**

teleffonio: ffonio *be.* **(teleffoniaf: ffoniaf)** to telephone, to phone

telyn *e.b.* *ll.* **-au** harp

telyneg *e.b.* *ll.* **-ion** lyric

telynor *e.g.* *ll.* **-ion** harpist

telynores *e.b.* *ll.* **-au** female harpist

telynorion *gw.* **telynor**

teml *e.b.* *ll.* **-au** temple

tenau *a.* thin, slender, lean; rare

terfyn *e.g.* *ll.* **-au** end, boundary, extremity

terfynol *a.* ultimate, last. **y taliad terfynol** the last instalment

terfysg *e.g.* *ll.* **-oedd** tumult, commotion, riot

terfysgaeth *e.g.* terrorism

terfysgwr *e.g.* *ll.* **terfysgwyr** terrorist

term *e.g.* *ll.* **-au** term. **termau technegol** technical terms

tes *e.g.* heat, sunshine, haze

tesog *a.* hot, sunny

testun *e.g.* *ll.* **-au** text, subject. **testun sgwrs** subject for debate; **testun siarad** subject of gossip

teulu *e.g.* *ll.* **-oedd** family

tew *a.* fat

teyrnas *e.b.* *ll.* **-oedd** kingdom. **Teyrnas Nefoedd** Kingdom of Heaven; **Y Deyrnas Unedig** The United Kingdom

ti *rhag.* you *(singular)*

ticed *e.g.* *ll.* **-i** ticket

tîm *e.g.* *ll.* **timau** team

tip *e.g.* *ll.* **-iau** tip

tipiau *gw.* **tip, tipyn**

tipyn *e.g.* *ll.* **-nau, tipiau** little, bit. **tipyn bach** a little; **bob yn dipyn** little by little

tir *e.g.* *ll.* **-oedd** land, earth, ground, territory. **tir neb** no man's land; **colli tir** to lose ground

tirion *a.* tender, kind, gentle, gracious

tirlun *e.g.* *ll.* **-iau** landscape

tiroedd *gw.* **tir**

tisian *be.* **(tisiaf)** to sneeze

tithau *rhag.* you also *(singular)*

tiwtor *e.g.* *ll.* **-iaid** tutor

tlawd *a.* *ll.* **tlodion** poor, needy. **y tlodion** the poor

tlodi *e.g.* poverty

tlodion *gw.* **tlawd**

tlos *a.b.* pretty. **merch dlos** a pretty girl *(N.W.).* *gw.* **tlws.**

tlws 1 *e.g.* *ll.* **tlysau** gem, jewel, brooch. **tlws aur** a gold brooch; **tlws yr eira** snowdrop; **clustdlysau** earrings. 2 *a.g.* pretty. *gw.* **tlos**

tlysau

tlysau. *gw.* tlws

to 1 *e.g.* *ll.* -eau, -eon roof.
2 *e.g.b.* generation. **y to sy'n
codi** the rising generation

tocyn *e.g.* *ll.* -nau ticket,
token. **tocyn dwyffordd**
return ticket

tocynnau *gw.* tocyn

tocynnwr *e.g.* *ll.* tocynwyr
ticket collector, conductor

tocynwyr *gw.* tocynnwr

toddi *be.* (toddaf) to melt, to
thaw, to dissolve

toeau *gw.* to

toeon *gw.* to

toes *e.g.* dough. **toesenni**
doughnuts; **tylino toes** to
knead dough

toiled *e.g.* *ll.* -au toilet

tolc *e.g.* *ll.* -iau dent

tolcio *be.* (tolciaf) to dent

toll *e.b.* *ll.* -au toll, custom,
duty. **tollborth/tollglwyd** tollgate

tom *e.b.* manure

ton *e.b.* *ll.* **tonnau** wave,
breaker

tôn *e.b.* *ll.* **tonau** tune. **tôn
gron** a round (tune)

tonau *gw.* tôn

tonfedd *e.b.* *ll.* -i wavelength

tonnau *gw.* ton

torch *e.b.* *ll.* -au wreath, coil,
torque

toreithiog *a* abundant,
teeming

toreth *e.b.* abundance

torf *e.b.* *ll.* -eydd crowd,
multitude

torfeydd *gw.* torf

torfol *a.* collective, mass. **enw
torfol** collective noun

torheulo *be.* (torheulaf) to
sunbathe

Tori *e.g.* *ll.* **Torïaid** Tory

toriad *e.g.* *ll.* -au break, cut

Torïaid *gw.* Tori

Torïaidd *a.* Tory,
Conservative

torri *be.* (torraf) to break, to
cut, to sever; to go bankrupt.
torri ar draws to interrupt;
torri enw to sign; **torri gwynt**
to break wind

tors *e.g.b.* *ll.* **tyrs** torch

torth *e.b.* *ll.* -au loaf. **torth
wen** white loaf

tosau *gw.* tosyn

tost 1 *a.* severe, sharp, sore;
ill *(S.W.)*. 2 *e.g.* toast
(bread)

tostrwydd *e.g.* illness, severity

tosyn *e.g.* *ll.* **tosau** pimple
(S.W.)

tra 1 *ad.* extremely, over,
very. **Dw i'n dra diolchgar**
I'm very grateful; 2 *c.* while,
whilst. **Ewch tra bod
heddwch** Go whilst there is
peace

trachefn *gw.* drachefn

trachwant *e.g.* *ll.* -au lust,
greed, covetousness

trachwantus *a.* covetous,
lustful

traddodiad *e.g.* *ll.* -au
tradition; delivery

traddodiadol *a.* traditional

traed *gw.* troed

traeth *e.g.* *ll.* -au beach,
shore

traethau *gw.* **traeth**

traethawd *e.g.* *ll.* **traethodau** essay, treatise, tract

traethodau *gw.* **traethawd**

trafnidiaeth *e.b.* traffic, commerce

trafod *be.* **(trafodaf)** to handle, to discuss, to negotiate, to transact. **cylch trafod** discussion group

trafferth *e.b.g.* *ll.* **-ion** trouble, toil, bother

trafferthu (i) *be.* **(trafferthaf)** to trouble, to bother, to take pains

trafferthus *a.* troublesome, laborious; troubled

traffordd *e.b.* *ll.* **traffyrdd** motorway

traffyrdd *gw.* **traffordd**

tragwyddol *a.* eternal, everlasting.
  o dragwyddol bwys of everlasting importance

trai *e.g.* *ll.* **treiau** ebb, decrease. **trai a llanw** ebb and flow

trais *e.g.* *ll.* **treisiau** violence, oppression; rape

trallod *e.g.* *ll.* **-au, -ion** tribulation, trouble

trallodau *gw.* **trallod**

trallodion *gw.* **trallod**

trallwysiad *e.g.* *ll.* **-au** transfusion. **Gwasanaeth Trallwyso Gwaed** Blood Transfusion Service

tramor *a.* overseas, foreign

trannoeth *ad.* next day. **Daeth e drannoeth** He came the next day

trap *e.g.* *ll.* **-iau** trap

traul *e.b.* *ll.* **treuliau** wear; cost, expense

trawsblannu *be.* **(trawsblannaf)** to transplant

trawst *e.g.* *ll.* **-iau** beam, crossbar

tre *gw.* **tref**

trechu *be.* **(trechaf)** to overcome, to defeat

tref: tre *e.b.* *ll.* **trefi, trefydd** town, home. **tua thre** homeward; **tre farchnad** market town; **gartref** at home

trefi *gw.* **tref**

trefn *e.b.* *ll.* **-au** order, arrangment, system, method. **dweud y drefn** to scold

trefnu (i) *be.* **(trefnaf)** to order, to arrange, to organize, to sort

trefnus *a.* orderly, methodical

trefnydd *e.g.* *ll.* **-ion** organizer

trefol *a.* urban

trefydd *gw.* **tref**

treial *e.g.* *ll.* **-on** trial, contest. **treialon cŵn defaid** sheepdog trials

treiglad *e.g.* *ll.* **-au** mutation; rolling. **treiglad llaes** spirant mutation; **treiglad meddal** soft mutation; **treiglad trwynol** nasal mutation

treiglo *be.* **(treiglaf)** to mutate; to roll

treisgar *a.* violent

treisiau *gw.* **trais**

treisio *be.* **(treisiaf)** to force, to violate, to oppress; to rape.

trem *e.b.* *ll.* **-iau** sight, look

trên

trên *e.g. ll.* **trenau** train
trenau *gw.* **trên**
trennydd *ad.* two days hence
treth *e.b. ll.* **-i** rate, tax, levy; strain. **treth ar werth** value added tax; **treth incwm** income tax; **treth y pen** community charge/poll tax; **treth gyngor** council tax; **Roedd e'n dreth ar fy amynedd** He was a strain on my patience
trethdalwr *e.g. ll.* **trethdalwyr** ratepayer
trethu *be.* **(trethaf)** to tax, to rate
treuliau *gw.* **traul**
treulio *be.* **(treuliaf)** to wear; to spend; to digest
tri *a.g. & e.g.* **-oedd** *(followed by spirant mutation)* three. **tri chap** three caps; **tri pheint** three pints; **tri thŷ** three houses; **tri chynnig i Gymro** three tries for a Welshman. *gw. At. Treigladau. gw.* **tair**
triawd *e.g. ll.* **-au** trio, threesome
tric *e.g. ll.* **-iau** trick
tridiau *e.ll.* three days
trigain *a. & e.g.* sixty. **trigain mlynedd yn ôl** sixty years ago. *gw. At. Treiglad Trwynol*

trigfan *e.b. ll.* **-nau** dwelling-place
trigo *be.* **(trigaf)** to dwell, to reside; to die (of animal)
trigolion *e.ll.* inhabitants
trin *be.* **(triniaf)** to treat; to handle; to dress; to till; to revile. **siop trin gwallt** hairdresser's shop; **trin y tir** to cultivate the land
trindod *e.b. ll.* **-au** trinity. **Coleg y Drindod** Trinity College
trioedd *e.ll.* triads
triongl *e.g.b. ll.* **-au** triangle
trist *a.* sad, sorrowful, unhappy
tristwch *e.g.* sadness, sorrow. **tristwch o'r mwyaf** the greatest sorrow
tro *e.g. ll.* **troeau, troeon** turn, twist, bend; conversion. **gweld tro ar fyd** to experience a change in circumstances. **llygad tro** a squint; **tro gwael** an unworthy act; **tro yn ei gwt** a twist in his tail
trochi *be.* **(trochaf)** to dip, to plunge; to soil *(S.W.)*; to bathe *(N.W.)*
troeau *gw.* **tro**
troed *e.g.b. ll.* **traed** foot, base; handle

Insight

troed *e.b.* (pronounced 'troid') foot, base; handle. **troed y baban** the baby's foot; **troed y bryn** the foot of the hill; **troed y gwely** the foot of the bed; **troed y grisiau** the foot of the stairs; **troed caib** hoe handle.

troedfedd *e.b.* *ll.* **-i** foot *(measure)*

troedffordd *e.g.* *ll.* **troedffyrdd** footpath

tröedig *a.* turned, converted

tröedigaeth *e.b.* *ll.* **-au** conversion, turning

troedio *be.* **(troediaf)** to walk, to tread, to trudge

troednoeth *a.* barefooted

troeon *gw.* **tro**

trogylch *e.g.* *ll.* **-oedd, -au** roundabout

troi (at) *be.* **(troaf)** to turn, to revolve, to convert; to plough; to translate. *gw. At. Berfau*

trom *a.b.* *ll.* **trymion** heavy, sad. **calon drom** heavy heart *gw.* **trwm**

tros *gw.* **dros**

trosedd *e.b.* *ll.* **-au** crime, offence, transgression

troseddu *be.* **(troseddaf)** to offend, to transgress

troseddwr *e.g.* *ll.* **troseddwyr** criminal, transgressor

trosgais *e.g.* *ll.* **trosgeisiau** converted try *(rugby)*

trosglwyddo *be.* **(trosglwyddaf)** to convey, to transfer

trosi *be.* **(trosaf)** to turn, to translate, to transfer; to convert *(rugby)*

trosiad *e.b.* *ll.* **-au** translation; conversion *(rugby)*

troswr *e.g.* *ll.* **troswyr** switch *(electricity)*

trothwy *e.g.* *ll.* **-au, -on** threshold. **ar drothwy'r Nadolig** on the threshold of Christmas

trowsus *e.g.* *ll.* **-au** trousers. **trowsus byr** short trousers

truan *e.g.* *ll.* **trueiniaid** wretch. **Druan ohono!** Poor fellow! **Jac druan!** Poor Jack!

trueiniad *gw.* **truan**

trueni *e.g.* wretchedness, pity, misery. **trueni ei fod** a pity that; **trueni iddo** a pity that

truenus *a.* wretched, pitiful

trugaredd *e.g.* *ll.* **-au** mercy, compassion. **drwy drugaredd** fortunately

trugarhau (wrth) *be.* **(trugarhaf)** to be merciful (to), to take pity (on)

trwbl *e.g.* trouble

trwchus *a.* thick; dense

trwm *a.g.* *ll.* **trymion** heavy, sad, wretched. *gw.* **trom**

trwser *e.g.* *ll.* **-i** trousers. *gw.* **trowsus**

trwsio *be.* **(trwsiaf)** to mend, to trim, to dress

trwsiwr *e.g.* *ll.* **trwswyr** repairer

trwy *gw.* **drwy**

trwydded *e.b.* *ll.* **-au** licence, dispensation. **trwydded yrru** driving licence

trwyn *e.g.* *ll.* **-au** nose, snout; point, cape

trwynol *a.* nasal. **treiglad trwynol** nasal mutation

trychineb *e.g.b.* *ll.* **-au** disaster, calamity

trydan

trydan 1 *e.g.* electricity.
2 *a.* electric. **Y Bwrdd Trydan**
The Electricity Board
trydanol *a.* electrical
trydanwr *e.g.* *ll.* **trydanwyr**
electrician
trydedd *a.b. (used before
feminine nouns)* third. **y
drydedd bennod** the third
chapter
trydydd *a.g. (used before
masculine nouns)* third. **y
trydydd tro** the third time
trydyddol *a.* tertiary. **Coleg
Trydyddol** Tertiary College
tryloyw *a.* transparent
trymaidd *a.* heavy, close,
sultry, muggy; sad
trymion *gw.* **trwm**
trysor *e.b.* *ll.* **-au** treasure
trysorfa *e.b.* *ll.* **trysorfeydd**
treasury, fund
trysori *be.* **(trysoraf)** to
treasure
trysorydd *e.g.* *ll.* **-ion**
treasurer
trywydd *e.g.* *ll.* **-ion** scent,
trail.
ar drywydd on the trail of
tu *e.g.* side, region. **tu draw i:
tu hwnt** beyond; **tu fewn: tu
mewn** inside; **tu faes** *(S.W.)*:
tu allan *(N.W.)*. outside
tua: tuag *ardd. (followed by
spirant mutation)* towards;
about. **tua thre: adre**
homewards; **tuag at**
towards; **tua mis** about a
month
tudalen *e.g.b.* *ll.* **-nau** page.

tudalen flaen front page. *gw.*
dalen.
tueddiad *e.g.* *ll.* **-au** tendency,
proneness
tun 1 *e.g.* **-iau** tin, can. 2 *a.*
tin
tunnell *e.g.* *ll.* **tunelli** ton
twlc *e.g.* *ll.* **tylciau** sty. **twlc
mochyn** pigsty
twll *e.g.* *ll.* **tyllau** hole
twmffat *e.g.* funnel
twmpath *e.g.* *ll.* **-au** tump,
hillock. **Twmpath Dawns**
folk dancing event
twndis *e.g.* *ll.* **-au** funnel
twnel *e.g.* *ll.* **-au, -i** tunnel
twp *a.* dull, stupid *(S.W.)*
twpsyn *e.g.* stupid person
twr *e.g.* *ll.* **tyrrau** heap;
group; crowd
twr *e.g.* *ll.* **tyrau** tower
twrci *e.g.* *ll.* **twrcïod, tyrcwn**
turkey
twristiaeth *e.b.* tourism. **Y
Bwrdd Croeso** The Tourist
Board
twrw *e.g.* *ll.* **tyrfau** noise,
tumult, roar, crash. **tyrfau:
taranau** thunder
twt *a.* neat, tidy. **tŷ bach twt**
a Wendy house *(lit. a neat
little house)*; **twt a lol**
nonsense, rubbish
twyll *e.g.* deceit, fraud,
treachery
twyllo *be.* **(twyllaf)** to deceive,
to cheat, to defraud
twyllodrus *a.* deceitful, false,
fraudulent
twym *a.* warm *(S.W.)*. **twym
iawn** hot *(S.W.)*

tyst

twymo *be.* **(twymaf)** to warm

twymyn *e.b.* *ll.* **-au** fever

tŷ *e.g.* *ll.* **tai** house. **tŷ newydd** new house; **tŷ bach** toilet; **tŷ tafarn** public house; **tŷ cwrdd** religious meeting house

tybed *ad.* I wonder: is that so? **Tybed a ddaw hi?** I wonder whether she will come?

tybied: tybio *be.* **(tybiaf)** to suppose, to think, to imagine

tydi *rhag.* you yourself

tyddyn *e.g.* *ll.* **-nod, -nau** small holding, small farm, croft. **ty'n cwm: tyddyn y cwm** the valley smallholding; **ty'n y waun** the moor croft

tyddynnwr *e.g.* *ll.* **tyddynwyr** smallholder, crofter

tyddynwyr *gw.* **tyddynnwr**

tyfiannau *gw.* **tyfiant**

tyfiant *e.g.* *ll.* **tyfiannau** growth, increase

tyfu *be.* **(tyfaf)** to grow, to increase

tynged *e.b.* *ll.* **tynghedau** destiny, fate

tyngedfennol *a.* fateful, fatal

tynghedau *gw.* **tynged**

tyngu (i, wrth) *be.* **(tyngaf)** to swear, to vow

tylciau *gw.* **twlc**

tyle *e.g.* *ll.* **-au** hill, ascent, slope *(S.W.)*

tylino *be.* **(tylinaf)** to knead *(dough)*

tylwyth *e.g.* *ll.* **-au** family, ancestry, kindred. **Tylwyth Teg** fairies

tyllau *gw.* **twll**

tyllu *be.* **(tyllaf)** to hole, to bore, to perforate

tylluan *e.b.* *ll.* **-od** owl *(N.W.)*. *gw.* **gwdihŵ**

tymer *e.b.* *ll.* **tymherau** temper, temperament

tymereddau *gw.* **tymheredd**

tymestl *e.b.* *ll.* **tymhestloedd** tempest, storm

tymherau *gw.* **tymer**

tymheredd *e.g.* *ll.* **tymereddau** temperature, temperament

tymhestloedd *gw.* **tymestl**

tymhestlog *a.* tempestuous, stormy

tymhorau *gw.* **tymor**

tymor *e.g.* *ll.* **tymhorau** season, term. **Tymor yr Haf** Summer Term; **yn ei thymor** in season *(of animal)*

tyn 1 *a.* tight, mean, perverse. 2 *bf.* pull! tighten! *gw.* **tynnu**

tyner *a.* gentle, tender

tynerwch *e.g.* gentleness, tenderness

tynnu (at) *be.* **(tynnaf)** to pull, to draw, to remove; take off. **Tynnwch eich cot** Take off your coat

tyrau *gw.* **twr**

tyrfa *e.b.* *ll.* **-oedd** crowd, multitude

tyrfau *gw.* **twrw**

tyrrau *gw.* **twr**

tyst *e.g.* *ll.* **-ion** witness

tystio

tystio *be.* **(tystiaf)** to testify,
to witness. **tystio bod** to
testify that
tystiolaeth *e.b.* *ll.* **-au**
evidence; testimony
tystion *gw.* **tyst**
tystysgrif *e.b.* *ll.* **-au**
certificate. **tystysgrif geni**
birth certificate; **tystysgrif
marwolaeth** death certificate;
tystysgrif priodias marriage
certificate **Tystysgrif
Gyffredinol Addysg Uwch**
(TGAU) General Certificate
of Secondary Education
(GCSE)
tywel *e.g.* *ll.* **-ion** towel
tywod *e.g.* sand
tywydd *e.g.* weather. **tywydd
mawr** stormy weather;
tywydd teg fair weather
tywyll *a.* dark, obscure; blind,
sad
tywyllu *be.* **(tywyllaf)** to
darken
tywyllwch *e.g.* darkness
tywys *be.* **(tywysaf)** to lead,
to guide
tywysydd *e.g.* *ll.* **-ion** guide.
tywysog *e.g.* *ll.* **-ion** prince.
Tywysog Cymru Prince of
Wales
tywysoges *e.b.* *ll.* **-au**
princess. **Tywysoges Cymru**
Princess of Wales

TH

thabl *gw.* **tabl**
thabled *gw.* **tabled**

thacl *gw.* **tacl**
thaclo *gw.* **taclo**
thaclu *gw.* **taclu**
thaclus *gw.* **taclus**
thacluso *gw.* **tacluso**
thaclwr *gw.* **taclwr**
thacsi *gw.* **tacsi**
Thachwedd *gw.* **Tachwedd**
thad *gw.* **tad**
thad-cu *gw.* **tad-cu**
thafarn *gw.* **tafarn**
thafarnwr *gw.* **tafarnwr**
thafell *gw.* **tafell**
thaflegryn *gw.* **taflegryn**
thaflen *gw.* **taflen**
thaflu *gw.* **taflu**
thafod *gw.* **tafod**
thafodiaith *gw.* **tafodiaith**
thafodieithoedd *gw.* **tafodiaith**
thafol *gw.* **tafol**
thagfa *gw.* **tagfa**
thagu *gw.* **tagu**
thangnefedd *gw.* **tangnefedd**
thai *gw.* **tŷ**
thaid *gw.* **taid**
thair *gw.* **tair**
thaith *gw.* **taith**
thai *gw.* **tai**
thâl *gw.* **tâl**
thalai *gw.* **talai**. *gw.* **talu**
thalaith *gw.* **talaith**
thalcen *gw.* **talcen**
thalcennau: thalcenni *gw.*
talcen
thaleb *gw.* **taleb**
thalent *gw.* **talent**
thalentog *gw.* **talentog**
thaliadau: thaloedd *gw.* **tâl**
thalu *gw.* **talu**
thalwr *gw.* **talwr**

thalwrn *gw*. talwrn

thamaid *gw*. tamaid

thameidiau *gw*. tamaid

than *gw*. dan

thân *gw*. tân

thanau *gw*. tân

thanbaid *gw*. tanbaid

thanc *gw*. tanc

thancer *gw*. tancer

thanddaear *gw*. tanddaear

thanddaearol *gw*. tanddaear

thanfor *gw*. tanfor

thanio *gw*. tanio

thanlinellu *gw*. tanlinellu

thanlwybr *gw*. tanlwybr

thanllyd *gw*. tanllyd

thannau *gw*. tant

thanseilio *gw*. tanseilio

thant *gw*. tant

thanwydd *gw*. tanwydd

thap *gw*. tap

thâp *gw*. tâp

thapiau *gw*. tap. *gw*. tâp

tharan *gw*. taran

tharanu *gw*. taranu

tharddiad *gw*. tarddiad

tharddu *gw*. tarddu

tharged *gw*. targed

tharian *gw*. tarian

tharianau *gw*. tarian

tharo *gw*. taro

tharw *gw*. tarw

thasg *gw*. tasg

thasgu *gw*. tasgu

thaten *gw*. taten

thato *gw*. taten

thatws *gw*. taten

thawel *gw*. tawel

thawelu *gw*. tawelu

thawelwch *gw*. tawelwch

thawelydd *gw*. tawelydd

thawelyddion *gw*. tawelydd

thawelyn *gw*. tawelyn

the *gw*. te

theatr *eb*. *ll*. -au theatre,
 playhouse

thebot *gw*. tebot

thebyg *gw*. tebyg

thebygrwydd *gw*. tebygrwydd

thecell *gw*. tecell

thechneg *gw*. techneg

thechnegol *gw*. technegol

thechnegwr *gw*. technegwr

thechnoleg *gw*. technoleg

theg *gw*. teg

thegan *gw*. tegan

thegell *gw*. tecell

thegwch *gw*. tegwch

thei *gw*. tei

theiar *gw*. teiar

theidiau *gw*. taid

theigr *gw*. teigr

theiliwr *gw*. teiliwr

theilsen *gw*. teilsen

theilwng *gw*. teilwng

theilwres *gw*. teilwres

theilwriaid *gw*. teiliwr

theilyngdod *gw*. teilyngdod

theimlad *gw*. teimlad

theimlo *gw*. teimlo

theipiadur *gw*. teipiadur

theirgwaith *gw*. teirgwaith

theirw *gw*. tarw

theis *gw*. tei

theisen *gw*. teisen

theitl *gw*. teitl

theithiau *gw*. taith

theithio *gw*. teithio

theithiwr *gw*. teithiwr

thelediad *gw*. telediad

theledu

theledu *gw*. teledu
theleffon *gw*. teleffon
theleffonio *gw*. teleffonio
thelyn *gw*. telyn
thelyneg *gw*. telyneg
thelynor *gw*. telynor
thelynores *gw*. telynores
thelynorion *gw*. telynor
thema *e.b* *ll*. themâu theme
theml *gw*. teml
thenau *gw*. tenau
therapydd *e.g.* *ll*. -ion
  therapist
therfyn *gw*. terfyn
therfysg *gw*. terfysg
therfysgaeth *gw*. terfysgaeth
therfysgwr *gw*. terfysgwr
therm *gw*. term
thermomedr *e.g.* *ll*. -au
  thermometer
thes *gw*. tes
thesog *gw*. tesog
thestun *gw*. testun
theulu *gw*. teulu
thew *gw*. tew
theyrnas *gw*. teyrnas
thi *gw*. ti
thiced *gw*. ticed
thîm *gw*. tîm
thipiau *gw*. tip. *gw*. tipyn
thipyn *gw*. tipyn
thir *gw*. tir
thirion *gw*. tirion
thirlun *gw*. tirlun
thiroedd *gw*. tir
thisian *gw*. tisian
thithau *gw*. tithau
thiwtor *gw*. tiwtor
thlawd *gw*. tlawd
thlodi *gw*. tlodi

thlodion *gw*. tlawd
thlos *gw*. tlos
thlws *gw*. tlws
thlysau *gw*. tlws
tho *gw*. to
thocyn *gw*. tocyn
thocynnau *gw*. tocyn
thocynnwr *gw*. tocynnwr
thocynwyr *gw*. tocynnwr
thoddi *gw*. toddi
thoeau *gw*. to
thoeon *gw*. to
thoes *gw*. toes
thoiled *gw*. toiled
tholc *gw*. tolc
tholcio *gw*. tolcio
tholl *gw*. toll
thom *gw*. tom
thon *gw*. ton
thôn *gw*. tôn
thonau *gw*. tôn
thonfedd *gw*. tonfedd
thonnau *gw*. ton
thorch *gw*. torch
thoreithiog *gw*. toreithiog
thoreth *gw*. toreth
thorf *gw*. torf
thorfeydd *gw*. torf
thorfol *gw*. torfol
thorheulo *gw*. torheulo
Thori *gw*. Tori
thoriad *gw*. toriad
Thorïaid *gw*. Tori
Thorïaidd *gw*. Torïaidd
thorri *gw*. torri
thors *gw*. tors
thorth *gw*. torth
thosau *gw*. tosyn
thost *gw*. tost
thostrwydd *gw*. tostrwydd

throedffordd

thosyn *gw.* tosyn
thrachefn *gw.* trachefn
thrachwant *gw.* trachwant
thrachwantus *gw.*
  trachwantus
thraddodiad *gw.* traddodiad
thraddodiadol *gw.*
  traddodiadol
thraed *gw.* troed
thraeth *gw.* traeth
thraethau *gw.* traeth
thraethawd *gw.* traethawd
thraethodau *gw.* traethawd
thrafnidiaeth *gw.* trafnidiaeth
thrafod *gw.* trafod
thrafferth *gw.* trafferth
thrafferthu *gw.* trafferthu
thrafferthus *gw.* trafferthus
thraffordd *gw.* traffordd
thraffyrdd *gw.* traffordd
thragwyddol *gw.* tragwyddol
thrai *gw.* trai
thrais *gw.* trais
thrallod *gw.* trallod
thrallodau *gw.* trallod
thrallodion *gw.* trallod
thrallwysiad *gw.* trallwysiad
thramor *gw.* tramor
thrannoeth *gw.* trannoeth
thrap *gw.* trap
thraul *gw.* traul
thrawsblannu *gw.*
  trawsblannu
thrawst *gw.* trawst
thre *gw.* tref
threchu *gw.* trechu
thref *gw.* tref
threfi *gw.* tref
threfn *gw.* trefn
threfnu *gw.* trefnu

threfnus *gw.* trefnus
threfnydd *gw.* trefnydd
threfol *gw.* trefol
threfydd *gw.* tref
threial *gw.* treial
threiau *gw.* trai
threiglad *gw.* treiglad
threiglo *gw.* treiglo
threisgar *gw.* treisgar
threisiau *gw.* trais
threisio *gw.* treisio
threm *gw.* trem
thrên *gw.* trên
threnau *gw.* trên
thrennydd *gw.* trennydd
threth *gw.* treth
threthdalwr *gw.* trethdalwr
threthu *gw.* trethu
threuliau *gw.* traul
threulio *gw.* treulio
thri *gw.* tri
thriawd *gw.* triawd
thric *gw.* tric
thridiau *gw.* tridiau
thrigain *gw.* trigain
thrigfan *gw.* trigfan
thrigo *gw.* trigo
thrigolion *gw.* trigolion
thrin *gw.* trin
thrindod *gw.* trindod
thrioedd *gw.* trioedd
thriongl *gw.* triongl
thrist *gw.* trist
thristwch *gw.* tristwch
thro *gw.* tro
throchi *gw.* trochi
throeau *gw.* tro
throed *gw.* troed
throedfedd *gw.* troedfedd
throedffordd *gw.* troedffordd

thröedig

thröedig *gw.* tröedig

thröedigaeth *gw.* tröedigaeth

throedio *gw.* troedio

throednoeth *gw.* troednoeth

throeon *gw.* tro

throgylch *gw.* trogylch

throi *gw.* troi

thros *gw.* tros

throsedd *gw.* trosedd

throseddu *gw.* troseddu

throseddwr *gw.* troseddwr

throsgais *gw.* trosgais

throsglwyddo *gw.*

 trosglwyddo

throsi *gw.* trosi

throsiad *gw.* trosiad

throswr *gw.* troswr

throthwy *gw.* trothwy

throwsus *gw.* trowsus

thruan *gw.* truan

thrueiniaid *gw.* truan

thrueni *gw.* trueni

thruenus *gw.* truenus

thrugaredd *gw.* trugaredd

thrugarhau *gw.* trugarhau

thrwbl *gw.* trwbl

thrwchus *gw.* trwchus

thrwm *gw.* trwm

thrwser *gw.* trwser

thrwsio *gw.* trwsio

thrwsiwr *gw.* trwsiwr

thrwy *gw.* drwy

thrwydded *gw.* trwydded

thrwyn *gw.* trwyn

thrwynol *gw.* trwynol

thrychineb *gw.* trychineb

thrydan *gw.* trydan

thrydanol *gw.* trydanol

thrydanwr *gw.* trydanwr

thrydedd *gw.* trydedd

thrydydd *gw.* trydydd

thrydyddol *gw.* trydyddol

thryloyw *gw.* tryloyw

thrymaidd *gw.* trymaidd

thrymion *gw.* trwm

thrysor *gw.* trysor

thrysorfa *gw.* trysorfa

thrysorydd *gw.* trysorydd

thrywydd *gw.* trywydd

thu *gw.* tu

thua *gw.* tua

thuag *gw.* tua

thudalen *gw.* tudalen

thueddiad *gw.* tueddiad

thun *gw.* tun

thunnell *gw.* tunnell

thus *e.g.* frankincense

thwlc *gw.* twlc

thwll *gw.* twll

thwmpath *gw.* twmpath

thwndis *gw.* twndis

thwnel *gw.* twnel

thwp *gw.* twp

thwpsyn *gw.* twpsyn

thwr *gw,* twr

thŵr *gw.* tŵr

thwrci *gw.* twrci

thwristiaeth *gw.* twristiaeth

thwrw *gw.* twrw

thwt *gw.* twt

thwyll *gw.* twyll

thwyllo *gw.* twyllo

thwyllodrus *gw.* twyllodrus

thwym *gw.* twym

thwymo *gw.* twymo

thwymyn *gw.* twymyn

thŷ *gw.* tŷ

thybied *gw.* tybied

thybio *gw.* tybied

thydi *gw.* tydi

thyddyn *gw.* **tyddyn**
thyddynnwr *gw.* **tyddynnwr**
thyddynwyr *gw.* **tyddynnwr**
thyfiannau *gw.* **tyfiant**
thyfiant *gw.* **tyfiant**
thyfu *gw.* **tyfu**
thynged *gw.* **tynged**
thyngedfennol *gw.*
 tyngedfennol
thynghedau *gw.* **tynged**
thyngu *gw.* **tyngu**
thylciau *gw.* **twlc**
thyle *gw.* **tyle**
thylino *gw.* **tylino**
thylwyth *gw.* **tylwyth**
thyllau *gw.* **twll**
thyllu *gw.* **tyllu**
thylluan *gw.* **tylluan**
thymer *gw.* **tymer**
thymereddau *gw.* **tymheredd**
thymestl *gw.* **tymestl**
thymherau *gw.* **tymer**
thymheredd *gw.* **tymheredd**
thymhestloedd *gw.* **tymestl**
thymhestlog *gw.* **tymhestlog**
thymhorau *gw.* **tymor**
thymor *gw.* **tymor**
thyn *gw.* **tyn**
thyner *gw.* **tyner**
thynerwch *gw.* **tynerwch**
thynnu *gw.* **tynnu**
thyrau *gw.* **tŵr**
thyrfa *gw.* **tyrfa**
thyrfaoedd *gw.* **tyrfa**
thyrfau *gw.* **twrw**
thyrrau *gw.* **twr**
thyst *gw.* **tyst**
thystio *gw.* **tystio**
thystiolaeth *gw.* **tystiolaeth**
thystion *gw.* **tyst**

thystysgrif *gw.* **tystysgrif**
thystysgrifau *gw.* **tystysgrif**
thywel *gw.* **tywel**
thywod *gw.* **tywod**
thywydd *gw.* **tywydd**
thywyll *gw.* **tywyll**
thywyllu *gw.* **tywyllu**
thywyllwch *gw.* **tywyllwch**
thywys *gw.* **tywys**
thywysog *gw.* **tywysog**
thywysoges *gw.* **tywysoges**

U

uchaf *a.* uppermost, highest;
 loudest. **am yr uchaf** for the
 loudest
uchafbwynt *e.g.* *ll.* **-iau**
 climax; zenith
uchder *e.g.* *ll.* **-au** height,
 altitude
uchel *a.* high; loud
uchelder *e.g.* *ll.* **-au** highness
ucheldir *e.g.* *ll.* **-oedd**
 highland
uchelgais *e.g.b.* *ll.*
 uchelgeisiau ambition
uchelgeisiol *a.* ambitious
uchelion *e.ll.* heights
uchelwr *e.g.* *ll.* **uchelwyr**
 gentleman, nobleman
uchod *ad.* above. **yn y rhestr**
 uchod in the above list
udo *be.* **(udaf)** to howl, to
 moan, to wail
ufudd *a.* obedient
ufuddhau (i) *be.* **(ufuddhâf)** to
 obey
uffern *e.b.* *ll.* **-au** hell. **Uffern**
 dân! Hell fire!

uffernol

uffernol *a.* infernal, hellish.
Roedd hi'n ddrud uffernol It
was extremely expensive.
ugain *a. & e.g. ll.* **ugeiniau**
twenty. **tri ar hugain** twenty-
three; **deg ar hugain** thirty
ugeinfed *a.* twentieth. **yr**
ugeinfed ganrif the 20th
century
ugeiniau *gw.* **ugain**
un *a. & e.g. ll.* **-au** one. **un**
tro one turn; once; **yr un** the
one, the same; **yr un faint** as
much, the same; **yr un pryd**
the same time

uned *e.b. ll.* **-au** unit
unedig *a.* united
unfarn *a.* unanimous
unfryd: unfrydol *a.* unanimous
unffordd *a.* one-way. **stryd**
unffordd one-way street
uniaethu (â) *be.* **(uniaethaf)** to
identify (with)
unig *a. (precedes noun and*
causes soft mutation) only,
sole; alone, lonely. **yr unig**
fab the only son; **mab unig**
lonely son
unigol *a.* singular; individual
unigolyn *e.g. ll.* **unigolion**
individual

unawd *e.g. ll.* **-au** solo
unawdwr: unawdydd *e.g. ll.*
unawdwyr soloist
unben *e.g. ll.* **-iaid** dictator,
despot
undeb *e.g. ll.* **-au** union,
unity. **Undeb yr Athrawon**
the Teachers' Union; **Undeb**
y Mamau the Mothers' Union
undebwr *e.g. ll.* **undebwyr**
unionist
undod *e.g. ll.* **-au** unit, unity
Undodwr *e.g. ll.* **Undodwyr**
Unitarian
undonog *a.* monotonous
undydd *a.* one-day. **ysgol**
undydd a one-day school

unigrwydd *e.g.* loneliness
unigryw *a.* unique
union *a.* direct, straight;
exact. **yr union fan** the exact
place
unioni *be.* **(unionaf)** to rectify,
to straighten
unman *ad.* anywhere
unnos *a.* of or for one night.
tŷ unnos habitable cabin
built between dusk and
dawn
uno *be.* **(unaf)** to unite, to
join
unrhyw *a.* same; any;
homogeneous. **mewn unrhyw**

warthus

wlad in any country; **unrhyw beth** anything

unwaith *ad.* once. **ar unwaith** at once; **unwaith ac am byth** once and for all

urdd *e.b. ll.* **-au** order, guild. **Urdd Gobaith Cymru** Welsh League of Youth

urddas *e.g. ll.* **-au** dignity, honour

urddo *be.* **(urddaf)** to ordain, to bestow honour on

us *e.ll.* chaff

ustus *e.g. ll.* **-iaid** magistrate

uwch *a.* higher, senior, superior; advanced. **uwchgapten** major (army officer); **uwchnormal** superior. *gw.* **uchel**

uwchben *ardd. & ad.* above

uwchfarchnad *e.b. ll.* **-oedd** supermarket

uwchlaw *ardd.* above

uwchradd *a.* secondary. **ysgol uwchradd** secondary school

uwd *e.g. ll.* **-iau** porridge

W

wadu *gw.* **gwadu**
waed *gw.* **gwaed**
waedu *gw.* **gwaedu**
waedd *gw.* **gwaedd**
wael *gw.* **gwael**
waelod *gw.* **gwaelod**
waeth *gw.* **drwg**
waethaf *gw.* **drwg**
waethed *gw.* **drwg**
waethygu *gw.* **gwaethygu**

wag *gw.* **gwag**
wagedd *gw.* **gwagedd**
wagio *gw.* **gwagio**
wagle *gw.* **gwagle**
wagu *gw.* **gwagio**
wahân *gw.* **gwahân**
wahanlaeth *gw.* **gwahaniaeth**
wahaniaethu *gw.* **gwahaniaethu**
wahanol *gw.* **gwahanol**
wahanu *gw.* **gwahanu**
wahardd *gw.* **gwahardd**
wahodd *gw.* **gwahodd**
wahoddedig *gw.* **gwahoddedig**
wahoddedigion *gw.* **gwahoddedig**
wahoddiad *gw.* **gwahoddiad**
wahoddion *gw.* **gwahodd**
wair *gw.* **gwair**
waith *gw.* **gwaith**
wal *e.b. ll.* **-iau** wall. *gw.* **gwal**
wâl *gw.* **gwâl**
walau *gw.* **gwâl**
waliau *gw.* **gwal, wal**
wall *gw.* **gwall**
wallgof *gw.* **gwallgof**
wallt *gw.* **gwallt**
wallus *gw.* **gwallus**
wan *gw.* **gwan**
wanwyn *gw.* **gwanwyn**
war *gw.* **gwar**
wâr *gw.* **gwâr**
warchod *gw.* **gwarchod**
waredu *gw.* **gwaredu**
waredwr *gw.* **gwaredwr**
wario *gw.* **gwario**
warrau *gw.* **gwar**
wartheg *gw.* **gwartheg**
warthus *gw.* **gwarthus**

was

was *gw*. gwas
wasanaeth *gw*. gwasanaeth
wasanaethu *gw*. gwasanaethu
wasg *gw*. gwasg
wasgedd *gw*. gwasgedd
wasgfa *gw*. gwasgfa
wasgod *gw*. gwasgod
wasgu *gw*. gwasgu
wastad *gw*. gwastad
wastraff *gw*. gwastraff
wastraffu *gw*. gwastraffu
wats *e.g*. *ll*. **-ys** watch
wau *gw*. gwau
waun *gw*. gwaun
wawd *gw*. gwawd
wawdio *gw*. gwawdio
wawr *gw*. gwawr
wawrio *gw*. gwawrio
wawroedd *gw*. gwawr
wdihŵ *gw*. gwdihŵ
wddf *gw*. gwddf
wddwg *gw*. gwddwg
we *gw*. gwe
wedi *ardd*. after. **wedi deg**
after ten; **Mae wedi chwech
arno** He has lost his chance;
*the preposition is also used
as follows:* (forms of **bod**) +
(**wedi**) + *(be.)*; **Rydw i wedi
blino** I am tired; **Dwyt ti
ddim wedi cysgu** You have
not slept; **Roedd ef wedi troi**
He turned; **Maen nhw wedi
marw** They are dead
wedyn *ad*. afterwards, then
weddi *gw*. gweddi
weddïau *gw*. gweddi
weddill *gw*. gweddill
weddïo *gw*. gweddïo
weddol *gw*. gweddol

weddw *gw*. gweddw
wefus *gw*. gwefus
weiddi *gw*. gweiddi
weigion *gw*. gwag
weiniaid *gw*. gwan
weinidog *gw*. gweinidog
weinion *gw*. gwan
weinydd *gw*. gweinydd
weinyddes *gw*. gweinyddes
weiriau *gw*. gwair
weisg *gw*. gwasg
weision *gw*. gwas
weithdy *gw*. gweithdy
weithgar *gw*. gweithgar
weithiau *ad*. sometimes. *gw*.
  gwaith
weithio *gw*. gweithio
weithiwr *gw*. gweithiwr
weithred *gw*. gweithred
weithredu *gw*. gweithredu
weithwyr *gw*. gweithiwr
wel *ebych*. well!
welâu *gw*. gwely
weld *gw*. gweld
wele *ebych*. behold!
weled *gw*. gweld
welw *gw*. gwelw
wely *gw*. gwely
welyau *gw*. gwely
welydd *gw*. gwal
well *gw*. gwell
wella *gw*. gwella
wellt *gw*. gwellt
welltyn *gw*. gwelltyn
wen *gw*. gwen
wên *gw*. gwên
wenau *gw*. gwên
wendid *gw*. gwendid
Wener *gw*. Gwener
wenith *gw*. gwenith

wobrwyo

wennol *gw*. gwennol
Went *gw*. Gwent
wenu *gw*. gwenu
wenwyn *gw*. gwenwyn
wenwynig *gw*. gwenwynig
wenwynol *gw*. gwenwynig
wenyn *gw*. gwenynen
wenynen *gw*. gwenynen
wêr *gw*. gwêr
werdd *gw*. gwerdd
werin *gw*. gwerin
weriniaeth *gw*. gweriniaeth
wers *gw*. gwers
werslyfr *gw*. gwerslyfr
wersyll *gw*. gwersyll
werth *gw*. gwerth
werthfawr *gw*. gwerthfawr
werthfawrogi *gw*.
 gwerthfawrogi
werthfawrogiad *gw*.
 gwerthfawrogiad
werthiant *gw*. gwerthiant
werthu *gw*. gwerthu
werthwr *gw*. gwerthwr
werthwyr *gw*. gwerthwr
westai *gw*. gwestai. *gw*.
 gwesty
westeion *gw*. gwestai
westeiwr *gw*. gwesteiwr
westeiwyr *gw*. gwesteiwr
westy *gw*. gwesty
weu *gw*. gweu
weunydd *gw*. gwaun
wg *gw*. gwg
wgu *gw*. gwgu
whilber *e.b*. *ll*. -au
 wheelbarrow. *gw*. **berfa**
wiail *gw*. gwialen
wialen *gw*. gwialen
wialennod *gw*. gwialen

wiced *e.b*. *ll*. -i wicket
wicedwr *e.g*. *ll*. wicedwyr
 wicket-keeper
widw: gwidw *e.b*. *ll* -od
 widow *(S.W.) gw*. gweddw
win *gw*. gwin
winwnsyn *e.g*. *ll*. winwns
 onion
wir *gw*. gwir
wirionedd *gw*. gwirionedd
wisg *gw*. gwisg
wisgo *gw*. gwisgo
wiwer *gw*. gwiwer
wlad *gw*. gwlad
wladfa *gw*. gwladfa
wladgarwr *gw*. gwladgarwr
wladol *gw*. gwladol
wlân *gw*. gwlân
wlanen *gw*. gwlanen
wledig *gw*. gwledig
wledydd *gw*. gwlad
wledd *gw*. gwledd
wledda *gw*. gwledda
wleidydd *gw*. gwleidydd
wleidyddiaeth *gw*.
 gwleidyddiaeth
wleidyddol *gw*. gwleidyddol
wlith *gw*. gwlith
wlyb *gw*. gwlyb
wlybaniaeth *gw*. gwlybaniaeth
wlychu *gw*. gwlychu
wn *gw*. gwn
ŵn *gw*. gŵn
wneud *gw*. gwneud
wneuthur *gw*. gwneud
wniadyddes *gw*. gwniadyddes
wnïo *gw*. gwnïo
wniyddes *gw*. gwniadyddes
wobr *gw*. gwobr
wobrwyo *gw*. gwobrwyo

ŵr

ŵr *gw*. gŵr
wrach *gw*. gwrach
wragedd *gw*. gwraig
wraidd *gw*. gwreiddyn
wraig *gw*. gwraig
wrandawiad *gw*. gwrandawiad
wrandawr *gw*. gwrandawr
wrando *gw*. gwrando
wreichion *gw*. gwreichionen
wreichionen *gw*.
 gwreichionen
wreiddiau *gw*. gwreiddyn
wreiddio *gw*. gwreiddio
wreiddiol *gw*. gwreiddiol
wreiddyn *gw*. gwreiddyn
wres *gw*. gwres
wresog *gw*. gwresog
wresogi *gw*. gwresogi
wresogydd *gw*. gwresogydd
wrido *gw*. gwrido
wridog *gw*. gwridog
wrol *gw*. gwrol
wrtaith *gw*. gwrtaith
wrth *ardd*. by; with; to;
 because; since. **wrth gwrs** of
 course; **wrth law** at hand, in
 reserve; **wrth lwc** luckily
wrthblaid *gw*. gwrthblaid
wrthchwyswr *gw*.
 gwrthchwyswr
wrthdaro *gw*. gwrthdaro
wrthdystio *gw*. gwrthdystio
wrthglocwedd *gw*.
 gwrthglocwedd
wrthod *gw*. gwrthod
wrthrych *gw*. gwrthrych
wrthrychol *gw*. gwrthrychol
wrthryfel *gw*. gwrthryfel
wrthryfela *gw*. gwrthryfela
wrthwyneb *gw*. gwrthwyneb

wrthwynebu *gw*.
 gwrthwynebu
wrthwynebwr *gw*.
 gwrthwynebwr
wryw *gw*. gwryw
wrywaidd *gw*. gwrywaidd
wrywgydiaeth *gw*.
 gwrywgydiaeth
wrywol *gw*. gwrywaidd
wthiad *gw*. gwthiad
wthio *gw*. gwthio
wthiwr *gw*. gwthiwr
wy *e.g*. *ll*. **-au** egg. **wy clwc**
 addled egg; **wy Pasg** Easter
 egg; **wy wedi'i falu** beaten
 egg; **wy wedi'i ferwi** boiled
 egg; **wy wedi'i ffrio** fried egg
wybedyn *gw*. gwybedyn
wybod *gw*. gwybod
wybodaeth *gw*. gwybodaeth
wybren *e.b*. *ll*. **-nau, -nydd**
 sky, firmament *(literary
 usage)*
wybrennau *gw*. wybren
wybrennydd *gw*. wybren
wych *gw*. gwych
wydr *gw*. gwydr
wydrau *gw*. gwydr. *gw*.
 gwydryn
wydryn *gw*. gwydryn
ŵydd *gw*. gŵydd
wyddau *gw*. gŵydd
wyddbwyll *gw*. gwyddbwyll
Wyddel *gw*. Gwyddel
Wyddeleg *gw*. Gwyddeleg
Wyddeles *gw*. Gwyddeles
Wyddelig *gw*. Gwyddelig
Wyddfa, Yr *e.b*. Snowdon
Wyddgrug, Yr *e.b*. Mold
wyddoniaeth *gw*.
 gwyddoniaeth

wyddonol *gw.* gwyddonol
wyddonydd *gw.* gwyddonydd
wyddor *gw.* gwyddor
wyf (i) *bf.* I am. *gw.* bod
wyfyn *gw.* gwyfyn
ŵyl *gw.* gŵyl
wylan *gw.* gwylan
wyliadwrus *gw.* gwyliadwrus
wyliau *gw.* gŵyl
wylio *gw.* gwylio
wyliwr *gw.* gwyliwr
wylnos *gw.* gwylnos
wylo (dros) *be.* (wylaf) to
  weep, to cry *(N.W.)*
wylwyr *gw.* gwyliwr
wyll *gw.* gwyll
wyllt *gw.* gwyllt
wylltio *gw.* gwylltio
wylltu *gw.* gwylltio
wymon *gw.* gwymon
wyn *gw.* gwyn
ŵyn *gw.* oen
wyneb *e.g.* *ll.* -au face;
  surface. dauwynebog
  deceitful; wyneb-ddalen title
  page; wynebgaled barefaced;
  wyneb i waered upside-
  down

wynfyd *gw.* gwynfyd
wyngalch *gw.* gwyngalch
wynion *gw.* gwyn
wynnu *gw.* gwynnu
wynt *gw.* gwynt
wyntog *gw.* gwyntog
wŷr *gw.* gwŷr
ŵyr *e.g.* *ll.* wyrion grandson
wyrion *gw.* ŵyr
wyrdd *gw.* gwyrdd
wyres *e.b.* *ll.* -au granddaughter
wyresau *gw.* wyres
wyriad *gw.* gwyriad
wyrio *gw.* gwyro
wyro *gw.* gwyro
wyrth *gw.* gwyrth
wyrthiol *gw.* gwyrthiol
wyryf *gw.* gwyryf
wŷs *gw.* gwŷs
Wysg *e.b.* Usk (river)
wystl *gw.* gwystl
wyt (ti) *bf.* you are *(singular).*
  Wyt ti gartref? Are you at
  home? *gw.* bod.
wyth *a. & e.g.* eight. wyth
  deg eighty
wythawd *e.g.* *ll.* -au octave;
  octet

Insight

wyneb *e.g.* face wyneb serchus pleasant face; wyneb trist sad
face; wyneb agored open face; wyneb cloc clock face.

wynebu *be.* (wynebaf) to face,
  to confront
Wynedd *gw.* Gwynedd
wynegon *gw.* gwynegon
wynegu *gw.* gwynegu
wynfa *gw.* gwynfa

wythfed *a.* eighth
wythnos *e.b.* *ll.* -au week. yr
  wythnos diwethaf last week;
  yr wythnos hon this week; yr
  wythnos nesaf next week

wythnosol

wythnosol *a.* weekly.
 cyfarfod wythnosol weekly
 meeting; **papur wythnosol**
 weekly paper
wythwr *e.g. ll.* **wythwyr**
 number eight *(rugby
 forward)*
wythwyr *gw.* **wythwr**
wywo *gw.* **gwywo**

Y

y: yr: 'r, 1 *y fan.* the. **y** *before
a consonant:* **y dyn** the man;
 y ferch the girl; **y tai** the
houses; **yr** *before a vowel
and h:* **yr afal** the apple; **yr
esgid** the shoe; **yr haul** the
sun; **yr heol** the road; **'r** *after
a vowel:* **a'r plant** and the
children; **o'r llyfr** from the
book; **i'r cae** to the field; **y**
and **'r** *are followed by soft
mutation of feminine
singular nouns:* **y dorth** the
loaf; **tŷ'r fam** the mother's
house; **gyda'r gath** with the
cat; *nouns beginning with ll
and rh do not mutate after* **y**
and **'r.** *gw. At. Treiglad
Meddal.* **2** *geir. used with
forms of the verb* **bod: y
mae...; yr oedd...; rwyf...**
y: yr *geir. perth.* **Dyma'r tŷ y
trigaf ynddo** Here is the
house in which I live
ychwaith *gw.* **chwaith**
ychwaneg *gw.* **chwaneg**
ychwanegu: chwanegu (at) *be.*
 (ychwanegaf: chwanegaf) to
add, to augment

ychydig *a.* little, few. **ychydig
 o lyfrau** a few books;
 ychydig fara a little bread;
 ychydig lai a little less
ŷd *e.g. ll.* **ydau** corn. **creision
ŷd** cornflakes
ydy *bf.* is, are. *gw.* **bod**
yddfau *gw.* **gwddf**
yfed *be.* **(yfaf)** to drink
yfory: fory *ad. & e.g.*
tomorrow
yfflon *e.ll.* fragments, pieces,
bits *(S.W.).* **yn yfflon racs** in
smithereens. *gw.* **yfflyn**
yfflyn *e.g. ll.* **yfflon** fragment,
piece, bit. **heb yfflyn o
wahaniaeth** without a scrap
of difference
ygau *gw.* **gwg**
yng *gw.* **yn**
ynghanol *ardd.* in the midst
of
ynghyd *ad.* together. **ynghyd
â** together with
ynghylch *ardd.* about,
concerning
ynglŷn (â) *ad.* in connection
(with), concerning
ym *gw.* **yn**
yma *ad.* here, this
ymadael (â) *be.* **(ymadawaf)**
to depart
ymadrodd *e.g. ll.* **-ion** speech,
saying, expression
ymaelodi (â) *be.* **(ymaelodaf)**
to become a member, to join
ymaith *ad.* away
ymarfer (â) 1 *be.* **(ymarferaf)**
to practise. **2** *e.b.g. ll.* **-ion**
practice, exercise. **ymarfer
corff** physical exercise

ymgais

ymarferiad *e.g. ll.* **-au** practice, exercise
ymarferol *a.* practical
ymateb (i) 1 *be.* **(ymatebaf)** to respond. 2 *e.g. ll.* **-ion** reaction; response
ymbelydredd *e.g.* radiation
ymbelydrol *a.* radioactive
ymbil (ar) *be.* **(ymbiliaf)** to implore
ymchwil *e.b.* research, search, quest
ymchwiliad *e.g. ll.* **-au** investigation; inquiry
ymchwilio (i) *be.* **(ymchwiliaf)** to research; to search
ymdaith 1 *e.b. ll.* **ymdeithiau** journey, march. 2 *be.* **(ymdeithiaf)** to travel, to march
ymdrech *e.b. ll.* **-ion** effort, endeavour, struggle:
  ymdrech deg valiant effort
ymdrechu (i) *be.* **(ymdrechaf)** to strive, to endeavour
ymdrin (â) *be.* **(ymdriniaf)** to deal (with)
ymddangos (i) *be.* **(ymddangosaf)** to appear, to seem
ymddangosiad *e.g. ll.* **-au** appearance
ymddeol *be.* **(ymddeolaf)** to retire
ymddeoliad *e.g. ll.* **-au** retirement
ymddiheuriad *e.g. ll.* **-au** apology
ymddiheuro *be.* **(ymddiheuraf)** to apologize

ymddiried (yn) *be.* **(ymddiriedaf)** to trust, to confide *(in)*
ymddiriedaeth *e.b. ll.* **-au** trust, confidence
ymddiriedolaeth *e.b. ll.* **-au** trust *(charity)*;
  Ymddiriedolaeth Genedlaethol National Trust
ymddiriedolwr *e.b. ll.* **ymddiriedolwyr** trustee
ymddiswyddiad *e.g. ll.* **-au** resignation
ymddiswyddo *be.* **(ymddiswyddaf)** to resign
ymddwyn *be.* **(ymddygaf)** to behave
ymddygiad *e.g. ll.* **-au** behaviour
ymennydd *e.g. ll.* **ymenyddion** brain
ymenyddion *gw.* **ymennydd**
ymenyn: menyn *e.g.* butter.
  bara menyn bread and butter
ymerodraeth *e.b. ll.* **-au** empire
ymestyn (at) *be.* **(ymestynnaf)** to stretch, to reach, to extend
ymfudo *be.* **(ymfudaf)** to emigrate
ymfudwr *e.g. ll.* **ymfudwyr** emigrant
ymffrost *e.g.* boast
ymffrostio (yn) *be.* **(ymffrostiaf)** to boast
ymffrostiwr *e.g. ll.* **ymffrostwyr** boaster
ymffrostwyr *gw.* **ymffrostiwr**
ymgais *e.b.* effort, attempt

ymgeiswyr

ymgeiswyr *gw.* ymgeisydd
ymgeisydd *e.g. ll.* ymgeiswyr
candidate, applicant.
  ymgeisydd seneddol
parliamentary candidate
ymgeledd *e.g. ll.* **-au** care,
succour. **ymgeledd parod**
first aid
ymgom *e.b. ll.* **-ion**
conversation, chat. **ymgom â**
a conversation with
ymgomio (â) *be.* **(ymgomiaf)**
to chat, to converse
ymgorffori *be* **(ymgorfforaf)** to
incorporate
ymgrymu *be.* **(ymgrymaf)** to
stoop, to bow down
ymgynghori (â) *be.*
  (ymgynghoraf) to consult, to
confer
ymgymryd (â) *be.*
  (ymgymeraf) to undertake
ymgyrch *e.g.b. ll.* **-oedd**
campaign, expedition
ymhel (â) *be.* **(ymhelaf)** to be
concerned; to meddle *(with)*
ymhell *ad.* far, afar
ymhellach *ad.* furthermore,
further
ymhlith *ardd.* among
ymholi *be.* **(ymholaf)** to
inquire
ymholiad *e.g. ll.* **-au** inquiry
ymhyfrydu (yn) *b.e.*
  (ymhyfrydaf) to rejoice
ymlacio *be.* **(ymlaciaf)** to relax
ymladd (â) 1 *be.* **(ymladdaf)** to
fight (with). 2 *e.g. ll.* **-au**
fight, battle
ymladdwr *e.g. ll.* **ymladdwyr**
fighter

ymlaen *ad.* on, onward. **yn ôl
ac ymlaen** backward and
forward
ymolch: ymolchi *be.*
  (ymolchaf) to wash oneself
ymosod (ar) *be.* **(ymosodaf)**
to attack
ymosodiad *e.g. ll.* **-au** attack.
  ymosodiadau awyr air
attacks
ymosodwr *e.g. ll.* **ymosodwyr**
attacker
ymosodwyr *gw.* ymosodwr
ymostwng (i) *be.* **(ymostyngaf)**
to stoop; to submit, to
capitulate
ymryson (â) 1 *be.* **(ymrysonaf)**
to contend; to strive, to
compete. 2 *e.g. ll.* **-au**
competition, rivalry; strife,
contention. **Ymryson y
Beirdd** poets' contest
ymuno (â) *be.* **(ymunaf)** to
unite; to join
ymweld (â) *be.* **(ymwelaf)** to
visit
ymweliad *e.g. ll.* **-au** visit,
visitation
ymwelwr: ymwelydd *e.g. ll.*
  ymwelwyr visitor
ymwelwyr *gw.* ymwelwr
ymwelydd *gw.* ymwelwr
ymwneud (â) *be.* **(ymwnaf)** to
deal (with), to be connected
(with)
ymyl *e.g.b. ll.* **-on** edge,
border, margin. **ymyl y
ddalen** edge of the page; **yn
ymyl** close by, near

ymyrraeth *e.b.* *ll.*
ymyrraethau interference,
intervention
ymyrru: ymyrryd (â) *be.*
(ymyrraf) to interfere, to
intervene, to meddle
ymysg *ardd.* among, amid
yn:'n:yng: ym 1 *ardd.*
(personal forms: **yno, ynot,
ynddo/ynddi, ynom, ynoch,
ynddyn)** in, at, into; for; *the
prepostion* **yn** *is followed by
nasal mutation:* **yn** + Corwen
yng Nghorwen in Corwen;
yn + Pen-bre **ym Mhen-bre** in
Pen-bre; **yn** + Treorci **yn
Nhreorci** in Treorchy; **yn** +
Gŵyr **yng Ngŵyr** in Gower;
yn + Dinbych **yn Ninbych** in
Denbigh; **yn** + Bangor **ym
Mangor** in Bangor. *gw. At.
Treiglad Trwynol.* 2 *geiryn.*
(not translated). *An adjective
or noun following the
predicative particle* **yn** *takes
soft mutation:* **Mae Twm yn
ddoniol** Tom is amusing;
Ydy Alun yn ddyn da? Is
Alun a good man? *gw. At.
Treiglad Meddal. No
mutation occurs when* **yn** *is
followed by a be.* (verb-
noun): **Mae'r ci yn cyfarth**
The dog is barking; **Mae'r
gath yn cysgu** The cat is
sleeping; **Mae Mair yn canu**
Mair is singing; **Rydw i'n
darllen** I am reading; **Maen
nhw'n gwrando** They are
listening

yna *ad.* there; then;
thereupon; that
ynad *e.g.* *ll.* **-on** judge,
justice, magistrate. **Ynad
Heddwch (Y.H.)** Justice of
the Peace (J.P.).
Llys yr Ynadon the
Magistrates' Court
ynau *gw.* **gŵn**
yn awr *ymadrodd ad.* now, at
present. *gw.* **rwan**
ynn *gw.* **onnen**
ynnau *gw.* **gwn**
ynni *e.g.* energy, vigour
yno *ad.* there. *gw.* **yn**
yntau *rhag.* he, he also
ynte: ynteu *c.* or, or else,
otherwise; then
ynys *e.b.* *ll.* **-oedd** island.
Ynys Bŷr Caldey Island;
Ynys Enlli Bardsey Island;
Ynys Wyth Isle of Wight;
Ynysoedd Heledd the
Hebrides
ynysoedd *gw.* **ynys**
yr *gw.* **y**
yrfa *gw.* **gyrfa**
yrfeydd *gw.* **gyrfa**
yrru *gw.* **gyrru**
yrrwr *gw.* **gyrrwr**
yrwyr *gw.* **gyrrwr**
ysbardun *e.g.* *ll.* **-au** spur,
accelerator *(in car)*
ysbïo *be.* **(ysbïaf)** to spy, to
look
ysbïwr *e.g.* *ll.* **ysbïwyr** spy
ysbïwyr *gw.* **ysbïwr**
ysblander *e.g.* splendour,
glory

ysbryd

ysbryd *e.g. ll* **-ion, -oedd**
spirit, ghost. **Yr Ysbryd Glân**
The Holy Spirit
ysbrydion *gw.* **ysbryd**
ysbrydoedd *gw.* **ysbryd**
ysbrydol *a.* spiritual; high-
spirited.
ysbrydoli *be.* **(ysbrydolaf)** to
inspire; to spiritualise
ysbwriel *e.g.* refuse, rubbish
ysbytai *gw.* **ysbyty**
ysbyty *e.g. ll.* **ysbytai**
hospital, hospice
ysfa *e.b. ll.* **ysfeydd** itching;
hankering; urge
ysfeydd *gw.* **ysfa**
ysgafn *a.* light *(weight)*
ysgafnhau: ysgafnu *be.*
(ysgafnhaf: ysgafnaf) to
lighten
ysgall *gw.* **ysgallen**
ysgallen *e.b. ll.* **ysgall** thistle
ysgariad *e.g. ll.* **-au** divorce
ysgol *e.b. ll.* **-ion** school;

school; **ysgol gynradd**
primary school; **ysgol iau**
junior school; **ysgol nos**
night-school; **ysgol Sul**
Sunday school; **ysgol**
uwchradd secondary school
ysgolfeistr *e.g. ll.* **-i**
schoolmaster
ysgolfeistres *e.b. ll.* **-au**
schoolmistress
ysgolhaig *e.g. ll.*
ysgolheigion scholar
ysgolheigion *gw.* **ysgolhaig**
ysgolor *e.g. ll.* **-ion** scholar
ysgoloriaeth *e.b. ll.* **-au**
scholarship
ysgolorion *gw.* **ysgolor**
ysgrech *e.b. ll.* **-feydd**
scream, shriek
ysgrechfeydd *gw.* **ysgrech**
ysgrif *e.b. ll.* **-au** article,
essay
ysgrifennu (ar, at) *be.*
(ysgrifennaf) to write

Insight

ysgrifennu *be.* to write 'Darllen a wna ddyn llawn ... ac
ysgrifennu ddyn manwl' 'Reading maketh a full man ... and
writing an exact man' Francis Bacon (1625).

ladder. **ysgol annibynnol**
independent school; **ysgol**
arbennig special school;
ysgol breifat private school;
ysgol breswyl boarding
school; **ysgol feithrin**
nursery school; **ysgol gyfun**
comprehensive school; **ysgol**
Gymraeg Welsh medium

ysgrifennydd *e.g. ll.*
ysgrifenyddion secretary
ysgrifenyddes *e.b. ll.* **-au**
female secretary
ysgrifenyddion *gw.*
ysgrifennydd
ysgrythur *e.b. ll.* **-au**
scripture

ysgubo *be.* **(ysgubaf)** to
sweep

ysgubor *e.b. ll.* **-iau** barn

ysgwyd *be.* **(ysgydwaf)** to
shake, to sway, to wag

ysgwydd *e.b. ll.* **-au** shoulder

ysgyfaint *e.ll.* lungs

ysgyfarnog *e.b. ll.* **-od** hare.
codi ysgyfarnog to raise a
red herring *(fig. – irrelevant
diversion)*

ysgytwad *e.g. ll* **-au** shock,
shaking

ysmala *a.* funny, amusing;
droll

ystadegau *e.ll.* statistics

ystafell *e.b. ll.* **-oedd** room.
ystafell ddosbarth
classroom; **ystafell wely**
bedroom; **ystafell ymolchi**
bathroom

ystlum *e.g. ll.* **-od** bat
(animal)

ystlys *e.b. ll.* **-au** side, flank;
touchline

ystlyswr *e.g. ll.* **ystlyswyr**
linesman; sidesman

ystod *e.b. ll.* **-ion, -au** course,
space of time, span, range;
swath. **yn ystod** during;
ystod oed age range

ystrydeb *e.b. ll.* **-au** cliché;
stereotype

ystwyth *a.* flexible, supple,
agile, pliant

ystyr *e.g.b. ll.* **-on** sense,
meaning

ystyriaeth *e.b. ll.* **-au**
consideration, heed

ystyried *be.* **(ystyriaf)** to
consider, to heed

ystyriol *a.* heedful, mindful

ystyrlon *a.* meaningful

ysu *be.* **(ysaf)** to consume, to
crave, to itch. **yn ysu am
wybod** itching to know

yswiriannau *gw.* **yswiriant**

yswiriant *e.g. ll.* **yswiriannau**
insurance. **yswiriant cyfun**
comprehensive insurance;
yswiriant trydydd person
third-party insurance

yswirio: yswiro *be.* **(yswiriaf:
yswiraf)** to insure

yw *bf.* is, are. *gw.* **bod.** *gw.*
ywen

ywen *e.b. ll.* **yw** yew.

English–Welsh dictionary

Abbreviations

a.	adjective	*ansoddair*
ad.	adverb	*adferf*
c.	conjunction	*cysylltair*
def. art.	definite article	*y fannod*
e.g. (exempli gratia)	for example	*er enghraifft*
i.	interjection	*ebychiad*
int. pn.	interrogative pronoun	*rhagenw gofynnol*
n.	noun	*enw*
coll.	collective	*torfol*
f.	feminine	*benywaidd*
m.	masculine	*gwrywaidd*
n.pl.	noun plural	*enw lluosog*
N.W.	North Wales	*Gogledd Cymru*
pn.	pronoun	*rhagenw*
p.n.	proper noun	*enw priod*
prp.	preposition	*arddodiad*
px.	prefix	*rhagddodiad*
rel. pn.	relative pronoun	*rhagenw perthynol*
S.W.	South Wales	*De Cymru*
v.	verb	*berf).*

abbreviation

If the gender of the Welsh noun is not specified, that noun has the same gender as the noun(s) immediately following it in the definition.

A

abbreviation *n.* byrfodd, talfyriad *m.*
abdomen *n.* bol *m.*
ability *n.* gallu *m.*
able *a.* galluog, medrus. **to be able** gallu, medru
abode *n.* cartref, preswyl, preswylfod *m.*
abolish *v.* dileu
abort *v.* erthylu
abortion *n.* erthyliad *m.*
about *prp. & ad.* am, o gwmpas, oddeutu, tua, ogylch, ynghylch
above 1 *prp.* dros, i fyny, uwchben, uwchlaw. 2 *ad.* uchod
abrupt *a.* sydyn, cwta. **abrupt reply** ateb cwta
absent *a.* absennol
abstract *a.* haniaethol
abundance *n.* toreth *f.*
abundant *a.* helaeth, aml, toreithiog
accelerate *v.* cyflymu
accelerator *n.* cyflymydd, sbardun *m.*

accent *n.* acen *f.*
accept *v.* derbyn, cymryd
acceptable *a.* derbyniol
access *n.* mynedfa *f.* mynediad *m.*
accident *n.* damwain *f.*
accommodation *n.* llety, lle *m.*
accomplish *v.* cyflawni, gorffen
account *n.* cyfrif, cownt; adroddiad *m.*
accountant *n.* cyfrifydd *m.*
accusation *n.* cyhuddiad *m.*
accuse *v.* cyhuddo
accustom *v.* cyfarwyddo, arfer
ache 1 *n.* poen *mf,* dolur *m.* 2 *v.* poeni, brifo, gwynegu
acid 1 *n.* asid *m.* 2 *a.* sur
acknowledge *v.* cydnabod
acorn *n.* mesen *f.*
acquaintance *n.* cydnabod *m.*
acre *n.* erw, acer *f.*
across *prp.* draw, ar draws
act 1 *n.* act *(drama)*; deddf *(law)*; gweithred *f.* 2 *v.* actio *(drama)*; gweithredu
active *a.* bywiog, heini
actor *n.* actor, chwaraewr *m.*

Insight

accelerator *n.* One of the terms offered is *sbardun* e.g. This word is found in literature as far back as the thirteenth century when it referred to the pointed spurs attached to the horseman's heels, used to prick the horse's flanks to urge it on to a faster gallop.

add *v.* ychwanegu, chwanegu
address 1 *n.* cyfeiriad. *m.*
  2 *n. & v.* annerch
adequately *ad.* digonol
adhere *v.* glynu wrth
adjective *n.* ansoddair *m.*
adjudge *v.* dyfarnu
adjudicate *v.* beirniadu
adjudicator *n.* beirniad *m.*
admire *v.* edmygu
admit *v.* derbyn, cyfaddef
adolescence *n.* llencyndod
  m.
adult *n.* oedolyn *m.*
advantage *n.* mantais *f.* **to
  take advantage** manteisio
advantageous *a.* llesol,
  manteisiol
adventure *n.* antur *mf.*
adventurous *a.* anturus
adverb *n.* adferf *fm.*
advertise *v.* hysbysebu
advertisement *n.* hysbyseb *f.*
advertiser *n.* hysbysebwr *m.*
advice *n.* cyngor *m.*
advise *v.* cynghori
adviser *n.* ymgynghorwr *m.*
aeroplane *n.* awyren *f.*
afar *ad.* ymhell
affair *n.* carwriaeth *f.*; mater,
  peth, busnes *m.*; helynt *f.*
affectation *n.* maldod *m.*
affection *n.* cariad, serch *m.*
affectionate *a.* serchus,
  serchog, cariadus
after 1 *ad.* wedyn, yna.
  2 *prp.* ar ôl, wedi
aftercare *n.* ôl-ofal *m.*
afternoon *n.* prynhawn *m.*
afterwards *ad.* wedyn, wedi
  hynny

again *ad.* eto, drachefn,
  eilwaith
against *prp.* erbyn, yn erbyn
age 1 *n.* oed, oedran *m;* oes
  f.
  2 *v.* heneiddio
aged *a.* hen, oedrannus. **the
  aged** yr oedrannus, yr
  henoed
agency *n.* cyfrwng
  m, asiantaeth *f.*
agent *n.* asiant, cyfrwng *m.*
agile *a.* heini
agitated *a.* cynhyrfus
ago *ad.* yn ôl
agony *n.* ing, poen mawr *m.*
agree *v.* cytuno (â)
agreement *n.* cytundeb *m.*
agriculturalist *n.* ffarmwr,
  ffermwr, amaethwr *m.*
agriculture *n.*
  amaethyddiaeth *f.*
aid 1 *n.* cymorth, help *m.* 2
  v. helpu. **First Aid** Cymorth
  Cyntaf.
ailment *n.* afiechyd, dolur *m.*
aim *n.* amcan, bwriad, diben,
  nod *m.*
air *n.* awyr; aer; alaw *f.*
  fresh air awyr iach
alarm *n.* braw, ofn; larwm *m.*
  alarm-clock cloc larwm
alien *n. & a.* estron *m.*
all 1 *n.* pawb; y cwbl, y cyfan
  m. 2 *a.* holl, i gyd, pob.
  3 *ad.* yn hollol
allege *v.* honni
alleged *a.* honedig
alliance *n.* cynghrair *m.*
allotment *n.* rhandir *m.*

allow *v.* caniatáu, goddef, gadael (i)

allowance *n.* lŵans, lwfans *m.*

allure *v.* hudo

ally *n.* cynghreiriad *m.*

almighty *a.* hollalluog.
Almighty God Hollalluog Dduw

almost *ad.* bron, braidd, lled

alone *a.* unig, ar ei ben ei hun, wrtho'i hun

along 1 *ad.* ymlaen; ar hyd.
2 *prp.* ar hyd.
all along o'r cychwyn

alphabet *n.* yr wyddor, abiéc *f.*

already *ad.* eisoes, yn barod

also *ad. & c.* hefyd

alter *v.* newid

although *prp. & c.* serch, er

altitude *n.* uchder *m.*

altogether *ad.* yn gyfan gwbl, i gyd

always *ad.* bob amser, yn wastad

am, I *v.* rydw i, dw i

amazed *a.* syn

amazement *n.* syndod *m.*

amazing *a.* rhyfedd, rhyfeddol

ambassador *n.* llysgennad *m.*

ambition *n.* uchelgais *m.*

ambitious *a.* uchelgeisiol

ambulance *n.* ambiwlans *m.*

amend *v.* gwella, diwygio, cywiro

American 1 *n.* Americanwr *m,* Americanes *f.* **2** *a.* Americanaidd

amid *prp.* ymhlith, rhwng, ynghanol, ymysg

among *prp.* rhwng, ymhlith, ymysg

amount *n.* swm, cyfanswm, cyfrif *m.*

ample *a.* helaeth, digon, digonedd

amuse *v.* difyrru

amusing *a.* difyr, difyrrus, digrif, ysmala

analyse *v.* dadansoddi

ancestor *n.* hynafiad *m.*

ancient *a.* hynafol, hen iawn.
ancient monument henebyn

and *c.* a, ac

anecdote *n.* hanesyn *m.*

angel *n.* angel *m.*

angle *n.* ongl *m.* **right angle** ongl sgwâr

Anglesey *n.* Môn *f.*

Anglicize *v.* Seisnigeiddio, Seisnigo

Anglo- *a.* Eingl-

Anglo-Welshman *n.* Eingl-Gymro *m.*

angry *a.* crac, dig

anguish *n.* ing *m.*

angular *a.* onglog

animal *n.* anifail *m.*

animate *a.* byw

ankle *n.* migwrn, pigwrn *m.*

announce *v.* cyhoeddi; datgan; hysbysu

announcement *n.* cyhoeddiad, hysbysiad *m.*

announcer *n.* cyhoeddwr *m.*

anoint *v.* iro

another *a. & pn.* arall, llall

answer *n. & v.* ateb *m.*

ant *n.* morgrugyn *m.*

antagonist *n.* gwrthwynebwr, gwrthwynebydd *m.*

anthology *n.* blodeugerdd *f*, detholiad *m*.
anti- *px.* gwrth-, yn erbyn
anticlockwise *a.* gwrthglocwedd
antiperspirant *n.* gwrthchwyswr *m*.
anxiety *n.* pryder *m*.
any *a.* unrhyw, rhyw, peth, dim. **I don't see her any longer/more** Ni fyddaf yn ei gweld mwyach
anyone *n. & pn.* rhywun, unrhyw un, neb *m*.
anywhere *ad.* unman, rhywle, unrhyw le
apart *ad.* ar wahân, o'r neilltu
ape *n.* epa *m*.
aperture *n.* agoriad, twll *m*.
apologize *v.* ymddiheuro
apology *n.* ymddiheuriad *m*.
apparatus *n.* offer *m*.
apparition *n.* drychiolaeth *f*, ysbryd *m*.
appear *v.* ymddangos
appearance *n.* ymddangosiad *m*.
appendix *n.* atodiad *m*.
apple *n.* afal *m*.
applicant *n.* ymgeisydd *m*.
appoint *v.* penodi; trefnu, nodi
appointed *a.* penodedig
appointment *n.* penodiad *m*.
appreciate *n.* gwerthfawrogi
appreciation *n.* gwerthfawrogiad *m*.
apprentice *n.* prentis *m*.
apprenticeship *n.* prentisiaeth *f*.

approach *v.* agosáu, nesáu
appropriate *a.* addas, priodol
approximate *a.* bras, agos
April *n.* Ebrill *m*.
archer *n.* saethwr *m*.
architect *n.* pensaer, cynlluniwr, cynllunydd *m*.
are *v.* mae, maen, maent, oes, sy, sydd, ydy, ydynt, ydyw, yw. *see* **bod**
argue *v.* dadlau
argument *n.* dadl *f*.
arithmetic *n.* rhifyddeg *f*.
ark *n.* arch *f*. **Noah's Ark** Arch Noa
arm *n.* braich *f*; arf *m*. **nuclear arms** arfau niwclear
armed *a.* arfog. **armed forces** lluoedd arfog
army *n.* byddin *f*.
around *ad. & prp.* am, o amgylch, o gwmpas, o gylch
arrange *v.* trefnu
arrive at *v.* cyrraedd
arrow *n.* saeth *f*.
art *n.* celf *f*. **art exhibition** arddangosfa gelf
article *n.* erthygl, ysgrif *f*; nwydd *m*. **definite article** y fannod (y, yr, 'r)
as *c. & ad.*, â, ag, fel, mor, cyn. **as if** fel pe bai, fel petai, fel petasai
ascent *n.* rhiw *f*, tyle *m*.
ash *n.* lludw *m*; onnen *f*.
ashes *n.* llwch, lludw *m*.
aside *ad.* o'r neilltu
ask *v.* gofyn, holi, gwahodd
askew *a.* ar gam, gŵyr
asleep *ad.* yn cysgu, yng nghwsg

ass *n*. asyn *m*.
assembly *n*. cymanfa *f*. cynulliad *m*. **Assembly Member** Aelod o'r Cynulliad
assert *v*. honni, haeru
assertion *n*. honiad *m*.
assess *v*. asesu
assist *v*. helpu
assistance *n*. cymorth, help *m*.
assistant *n*. cynorthwywr, cynorthwy-ydd *m*.
association *n*. cymdeithas *f*.
assurance *n*. sicrwydd *m*.
assure *v*. sicrhau
asterisk *n*. seren *f*.
astonishing *a*. rhyfedd, rhyfeddol, syn
astronaut *n*. gofodwr *m*, gofodwraig *f*.
at *prp*. am, ar, ger, wrth, yn, yng, ym
atonement *n*. iawn *m*.
atrocious *a*. erchyll
attack 1 *n*. ymosodiad *m*. 2 *v*. ymosod (ar)
attacker *n*. ymosodwr *m*.
attain *v*. ennill, cyrraedd
attempt 1 *n*. cais, cynnig *m*; ymgais *f*. 2 *v*. ceisio, cynnig.
attend *v*. mynychu
attendance *n*. presenoldeb *m*.
attention *n*. sylw *m*.
attitude *n*. agwedd *m*.
attract *v*. denu, tynnu
attractive *a*. deniadol, atyniadol
augment *v*. ychwanegu at, chwanegu at
August *n*. Awst *m*.

aunt *n*. modryb *f*.
author *n*. awdur, llenor *m*.
authoress *n*. awdures, llenores, *f*.
authority *n*. awdurdod *m*: **Education Authority** Awdurdod Addysg
autobiography *n*. hunangofiant *m*.
autumn *n*. hydref *m*.
autumnal *a*. hydrefol
avenge *v*. dial (ar)
avoid *v*. osgoi
awake 1 *v*. deffro, dihuno, 2 *a*. effro, ar ddi-hun
away *ad*. ymaith, i ffwrdd
awful *a*. ofnadwy
awkward *a*. lletchwith; chwithig

B

baby *n*. baban, babi *m*.
baby-sit *v*. gwarchod.
babysitter *n*. gwarchodwr babanod *m*.
bachelor *n*. dyn dibriod, hen lanc *m*.
back 1 *n*. cefn; cefnwr *m*. 2 *ad*. yn ôl
background *n*. cefndir *m*.
bacon *n*. cig moch, bacwn *m*.
bad *a*. drwg, drygionus; sâl, gwael
badge *n*. bathodyn *m*.
bag *n*. bag, cwd, cwdyn *m*.
bail *n*. mechnïaeth *f*.
bake *v*. crasu, pobi
baked *a*. cras, pob

bakehouse *n.* popty *m.*

baker *n.* pobydd *m.*

bald *a.* moel, penfoel. **bald-headed** penfoel

baldness *n.* moelni *m.*

ball *n.* dawns; pêl *f.* **football** pêl droed; **rugby ball** pêl rygbi

ballad *n.* balad *f.* **ballad-monger** baledwr

ballot *n.* balot *m.*

banana *n.* banana *m.*

band *n.* band *m.*; seindorf *f.* **brass band** band pres

bangle *n.* breichled *f.*

bank 1 *n.* glan *f.*; clawdd; banc *m.* 2 *v.* bancio. **bank statement** adroddiad banc

banner *n.* baner *f.*

banquet 1 *n.* gwledd *f.* 2 *v.* gwledda

Baptist *n.* Bedyddiwr *m.*

baptize *v.* bedyddio

bar 1 *n.* bar *m.* 2 *v.* atal

barbecue *n.* barbeciw *m.*

bard *n.* bardd *m.*

barn *n.* ysgubor *f.*

barrel *n.* casgen *f,* baril *mf.*

barrow *n.* berfa, whilber *f.*

base 1 *n.* bôn, gwaelod *m.*; sail, sylfaen *f.*; canolfan *mf.* 2 *a.* isel. 3 *v.* seilio

bashful *a.* swil

basic *a.* sylfaenol

basin *n.* basn *m.*

basket *n.* basged *f.*

Basque Country *n.* Gwlad y Basg *f.*

bass *n.* bas, baswr *m.*

baste *v.* iro

bat 1 *n.* ystlum; bat *m.* 2 *v.* batio

bath *n.* bath, baddon *m.*

bathe *v.* ymolch, ymolchi, golchi

bathroom *n.* ystafell ymolchi *f.*

battle 1 *n.* ymladdfa *m,* brwydr *f.* 2 *v.* ymladd *m.*

bay *n.* bae *m.* **Swansea Bay** Bae Abertawe

be *v.* bod

Insight

bard *n.* of Celtic origin (Irish *bard*; Scottish *bard*; Welsh *bardd!*)

---

bare *a.* noeth, llwm, moel, prin

barefooted *a.* troednoeth

barely *ad.* prin

bareness *n.* moelni *m.*

bark 1 *n.* cyfarthiad; rhisgl *m.* 2 *v.* cyfarth

barley *n.* haidd, barlys *m.coll.*

beach *n.* traeth *m,* glan y môr *f.*

beam *n.* pelydr: trawst *m.*

bean *n.* ffäen, ffeuen *f.*

bear 1 *n.* arth *m,* arthes *f.* 2 *v.* cario; geni; goddef. **polar bear** arth gwyn

beard *n.* barf *f.*

beat

beat *v*. taro; gorchfygu

beautiful *a*. hardd, glân, teg, prydferth

beauty *n*. harddwch, prydferthwch, tegwch *m*.

because *prp*. er, oherwydd, o achos, gan, am, oblegid

become *v*. dyfod, dod (yn)

bed *n*. gwely *m*.

bedding *n*. dillad gwely *m*.

bedroom *n*. ystafell wely, llofft *f*.

bedsitter *n*. ystafell un gwely *f*.

bee *n*. gwenynen *f*.

beech *n*. ffawydden *f*.

been, I have *v*. bues i, fues i, bûm, *see* bod

beer *n*. cwrw *m*.

beeswax *n*. cwyr *m*.

beetle *n* chwilen *f*.

before 1 *prp*. cyn, gerbron, o flaen, rhag. 2 *ad*. o'r blaen.
 before long cyn bo hir

beforehand *ad*. ymlaen llaw

beg *v*. erfyn (ar)

begin *v*. cychwyn, dechrau

beginning *n*. dechreuad *m*.

behave *v*. ymddwyn

behaviour *n*. ymddygiad *m*.

behind 1 *prp*. tu ôl (i), tu cefn (i), 2 *ad*. ar ôl

behold 1 *i*. wele! 2 *v*. gweld, edrych

being *n*. bod *m*.

Belgium *n*. Gwlad Belg *f*.

believe *v*. credu (yn)

bell *n*. cloch *f*.

bellow *v*. rhuo

belly *n*. bol, bola *m*.

belong *v*. perthyn (i)

beloved 1 *n*. anwylyd *mf*. 2 *a*. annwyl, anwylaf, cariadus, cu, hoff. **beloved ones** anwyliaid

below *prp*. islaw, dan

bend 1 *n*. tro *m*. 2 *v*. plygu

beneath *prp*. islaw, dan.

beneficial *a*. llesol

benefit 1 *n*. elw, lles *m*. 2 *v*. elwa

berry *n*. aeronen, mwyaren *f*.

berserk *a*. gwyllt.

beside *prp*. ger, gerllaw, wrth, heibio, yn ymyl

besides *prp*. heb, heblaw

best *a*. gorau

bestow *v*. rhoddi, rhoi, cyflwyno

betrothal *n*. dyweddïad *m*.

better 1 *a*. gwell. 2 *ad*. yn well

between *prp*. rhwng

beverage *n*. diod *f*.

bewitch *v*. swyno

beyond *prp*. draw, dros, tu hwnt

Bible *n*. Beibl *m*.

bicker *v*. cweryla, ffraeo

bicycle *n*. beic *m*.

bid *n & v*. cynnig *m*.

bide *v*. aros, disgwyl

big *a*. mawr. **bigger** mwy; **biggest** mwyaf

bilingual *a*. dwyieithog. **bilingual education** addysg ddwyieithog

bilingualism *n*. dwyieithrwydd *m*.

bill *n*. bil; mesur *m*; rhaglen *f*.

bin *n.* bin *m.* **rubbish bin** bin ysbwriel

bind *v.* rhwymo, clymu

biological *a.* biolegol

biology *n.* bioleg, bywydeg *f.*

birch *n.* bedwen, bedw *f.*

bird *n.* aderyn *m.*

birthday *n.* pen-blwydd *m.* **birthday card** cerdyn pen-blwydd

biscuit *n.* bisged, bisgïen *f.*

bishop *n.* esgob *m.*

bit *n.* tamaid, darn, tipyn, yfflyn *m.*

bite 1 *n.* tamaid *m.* 2 *v.* cnoi

bitter *a.* chwerw, sur

bizarre *a.* od, rhyfedd, chwithig

black 1 *n.* du; dyn du *m.* 2 *a.* du, tywyll. 3 *v.* duo

blackberry *n.* mwyaren *f.*

blackbird *n.* aderyn du *m.*

blackboard *n.* bwrdd du *m.*

blacken *v.* duo

blacksmith *n.* gof *m.*

Blackwood *n.* Y Coed-duon *f.*

blade *n.* eginyn; llafn *m.*

blame 1 *n.* bai *m.* 2 *v.* beio

blameless *a.* di-fai

blanch *v.* gwynnu

blank *a.* gwag; syn. **blank cheque** siec wag

blanket *n.* blanced, planced *f.*

blaze *n.* fflam *f.*

bleach 1 *n.* cannydd *m.* 2 *v.* cannu, gwynnu

bleed *v.* gwaedu

blemish *n.* nam; bai *m.*

blend *v.* cymysgu

blessed *a.* bendigedig

blessedness *n.* gwynfyd *m.*

blessing *n.* bendith *f.*

blind 1 *a.* dall, tywyll. 2 *n.* person dall *m.* 3 *v.* dallu

bliss *n.* gwynfyd *f.*

blizzard *n.* storm o wynt ac eira *f.*

blog 1 *n.* blog *m.* 2 *v.* blogio

blood *n.* gwaed *m.* **blood pressure** pwysedd gwaed

bloom *n.* blodyn *m.*

blossom *n.* blodyn *m.*

blouse *n.* blows, blowsen *f.*

blow 1 *n.* ergyd *mf.* 2 *v.* chwythu

blow-dry *v.* chwythu'n sych

blue *n. & a.* glas *m.*

blush *v.* gwrido, cochi

blushing *a.* gwridog

blustery *a.* stormus

board *n.* bwrdd *m,* bord *f;* bwyd *m.*

boarding house *n.* llety *m.*

boast 1 *n.* ymffrost *m.* 2 *v.* ymffrostio

boaster *n.* ymffrostiwr *m.*

boat *n.* bad, cwch *m.*

bodily *a.* corfforol

body *n.* corff *m.*

boil *v.* berwi

boiling *n. & a.* berw *m.*

bold *a.* hyf

boldness *n.* hyfdra *m.*

bolster *n.* clustog hir *f,* gobennydd mawr *m.*

bolt 1 *n.* bollt *m.* 2 *v.* bolltio

bomb 1 *n.* bom *m.* 2 *v.* bomio

bone *n.* asgwrn *m.*

book *n.* llyfr *m*; cyfrol *f*.
booklet *n.* llyfryn *m*.
boot *n.* esgid *f*.
booth *n.* caban *m*. stondin *f*.
border *n.* ffin *f*, ymyl *mf*.
border *m*.
bordering *a.* ffiniol
bore 1 *n.* twll; dyn diflas *m*.
2 *v.* tyllu; blino
boring *a.* diflas
born *a.* wedi ei eni; ganed
borough *n.* bwrdeistref *f*.
Borough Council Cyngor
Bwrdeistref
borrow *v.* benthyca, cael
benthyg
boss *n.* meistr, pennaeth, bos
m.
botanical *a.* llysieuol
both *a. & ad. &. pn.* y ddau,
y ddwy. **they both** ill dau, ill
dwy
bother 1 *n.* helynt *f*, trafferth
m. 2 *v.* trafferthu
bottle *n.* potel *f*.
bottleneck *m*. tagfa *f*.
bottom *n.* gwaelod: godre *m*.
boulder *n.* carreg fawr *f*.
bound 1 *n.* llam; terfyn *m*,
ffin *f*. 2 *v.* llamu, neidio;
ffinio
boundary *n.* ffin *f*, terfyn *m*.
bow 1 *n.* bwa; clwm *m*. 2 *v.*
plygu, ymgrymu
bowl 1 *n.* bowlen, powlen *f*.
2 *v.* bowlio
box *n.* blwch, bocs; pren bocs
m. **box office** swyddfa
docynnau
boy *n.* bachgen, hogyn, mab;
gwas *m*.

boyish *a.* bachgennaidd
brace *n.* bres; pâr *m*.
braces *n.* bresys *m*.
bracelet *n.* breichled *f*.
brain *n.* ymennydd *m*.
branch *n.* cangen *f*.
brandy *n.* brandi *m*.
brass *n.* pres *m*.
brave *a.* dewr, gwrol
bread *n.* bara *m*. **daily bread**
bara beunyddiol
breadth *n.* lled *m*.
break 1 *n.* egwyl, hoe *f*,
toriad *m*. 2 *v.* torri
breaker *n.* ton *f*.
breakfast *n.* brecwast *m*.
breast *n.* bron; brest *f*.
breath *n.* anadl *mf*, gwynt *m*.
breathe *v.* anadlu, chwythu
breed *v.* magu, bridio
breeze *n.* awel *f*.
brewery *n.* bragdy *m*.
bride *n.* priodferch *f*.
bridge 1 *n.* pont *f*. 2 *v.* pontio
brief *a.* byr, cryno
bright *a.* disglair, gloyw,
llachar, llewyrchus
brightness *n.* llewyrch,
disgleirdeb *m*.
brilliant 1 *n.* gem *f*. 2 *a.*
disglair, llachar; gwych
bring *v.* dwyn, dod (â)
brink *n.* ymyl *mf*, min *m*.
Britain *n.* Prydain *f*.
British *a.* Prydeinig
Brittany *a.* Llydaw *f*.
broad *a.* llydan, eang, bras
broadcast 1 *n.* darllediad *m*.
2 *v.* darlledu
brochure *n.* llyfryn *m*.

bronze *n.* pres, efydd *m.*
brooch *n.* tlws *m.*
brook *n.* nant *f.*
broom *n.* brws, brwsh *m,* ysgub *f.*
broth *n.* cawl *m.*
brother *n.* brawd *m.* **brother-in-law** brawd-yng-nghyfraith
brow *n.* ael *f,* talcen *m;* crib *mf.*
brown *a.* brown
brush 1 *n.* brws, brwsh *m,* ysgub *f.* **2** *v.* brwsio, brwshio, sgubo, ysgubo. **paint brush** brws paent, brwsh paent
bucket *n.* bwced *m.*
bud 1 *n.* blaguryn *m.* **2** *v.* blaguro.
bug *n.* byg *m.*
build *v.* adeiladu, codi
builder *n.* adeiladwr *m.*
building *n.* adeilad *m.*
bull *n.* tarw *m.* **bulldozer** tarw dur
bungalow *n.* tŷ unllawr, byngalo *m.*
burden 1 *n.* baich, llwyth *m.* **2** *v.* llwytho
burdened *a.* llwythog
bureau *n.* swyddfa *f.*
burglar *n.* lleidr tŷ *m.*
burn 1 *n.* llosg *m;* nant *f.* **2** *a.* llosg. **3** *v.* llosgi
burner *n.* llosgydd *m.*
burrow 1 *n.* twll cwningen *m.* **2** *v.* tyllu
bus *n.* bws *m.* **bus-stop** arhosfan *f.* bysus.
bush *n.* llwyn *m,* perth *f.*

business *n.* busnes *m.*
busy *a.* prysur
but *c.* ond, onid
butcher *n.* cigydd
butter *n.* menyn, ymenyn *m.*
butterfly *n.* glöyn byw *m,* iâr fach yr haf, pili-pala *f.*
button 1 *n.* botwm *m.* **2** *v.* botymu
buy *v.* prynu
buyer *n.* prynwr *m.*
buzz 1 *n.mf.* si, su, sŵn gwenyn **2** *v.* sio, suo
by *prp.* erbyn, ger, gerllaw, drwy, trwy, gan, heibio, wrth, â
by-election *n.* is-etholiad *m.*
bypass *n.* ffordd osgoi *f.*

C

cabbage *n.* bresychen; bresych *f.*
cabin *n.* caban *m* .
café *n.* caffe *m.*
cake *n.* cacen, teisen *f.* **birthday cake** teisen pen-blwydd
calamity *n.* trychineb *mf.*
calculate *v.* cyfrif, rhifo
calculation *n.* cyfrif *m.*
calculator *n.* cyfrifiannell *m.*
calendar *n.* calendar *m.*
calf *n.* llo (anifail) *m;* croth (coes) *f.*
call 1 *n.* galwad *mf,* galw *m.* **2** *v.* galw, ymweld (â)
calling *n.* galwad *mf;* galwedigaeth *f.*

calm 1 *n.* tawelwch; hedd *m.*
2 *a.* tawel; **3** *v.* tawelu,
distewi
camera *n.* camera *m.*
camp 1 *n.* gwersyll *m.* **2** *v.*
gwersyllu
campaign *n.* ymgyrch *mf.*
can *n.* can, tun *m.*
candidate *n.* ymgeisydd *m.*
candle *n.* cannwyll *f.*
candlestick *n.* canhwyllbren
m.
cane *n.* gwialen *f.*
canoe 1 *n.* canŵ *m.* **2** *v.*
canŵio
cap *n.* cap *m.*
capital 1 *n.* prifddinas *f;* corff
(arian), cyfalaf *m;*
priflythyren *f.* **2** *a.* prif, pen
capitulate *v.* ymostwng, ildio
captain *n.* capten *m.*
captivate *v.* swyno, hudo,
denu
capture *v.* dal, dala
car *n.* car *m.* **car park** maes
parcio
caravan *n.* carafán *f.* **caravan**
site maes carafanau *m.*
carbon *n.* carbon *m.*
card *n.* cerdyn *m,* carden *f.*
Cardiff *n.* Caerdydd *f.*
care 1 *n.* gofal, pryder *m.*
2 *v.* gofalu, carco, hidio,
pryderu
career 1 *n.* gyrfa *f.* **2** *v.*
rhuthro
careful *a.* carcus, gofalus,
manwl
careless *a.* diofal, esgeulus
caretaker *n.* gofalwr *m.*

caring *a.* gofalus
Carmarthen *n.* Caerfyrddin *f.*
carol *n.* carol *f.*
carpenter *n.* saer coed *m.*
carpet 1 *n.* carped *m.* **2** *v.*
carpedu
carrot *n.* moronen *f.*
cartoon *n.* cartŵn *m.*
carry *v.* cario
carve *v.* cerfio
case *n.* cas; achos; cyflwr *m;*
dadl *f.*
cash 1 *n.* arian parod *m.* **2** *v.*
newid
casing *n.* plisgyn; casin *m.*
cast *v.* taflu
castle *n.* castell *m.*
cat *n.* cath *f.*
catalogue *n.* catalog *m.*
cataract *n.* rhaeadr *f,* sgwd *m;*
pilen *(ar lygad) f.*
catch *v.* dal, dala
catchment *n.* dalgylch;
catchment area dalgylch
catechism *n.* holwyddoreg *f.*
caterpillar *n.* lindysen *m.*
cathedral *n.* eglwys gadeiriol
f.
catholic 1 *n.* pabydd *m.*
2 *a.* pabyddol; catholig
cattle *n.pl.* gwartheg, da
cauliflower *n.* blodfresychen *f.*
cause 1 *n.* achos; achlysur;
rheswm *m.* **2** *v.* achosi, peri
caution 1 *n.* pwyll; rhybudd
m. **2** *v.* rhybuddio
cautious *a.* gofalus,
gwyliadwrus
cave *n.* ogof *f.*
cavity *n.* gwagle *m.*

cease *v.* peidio (â)

ceaseless *a.* di-baid

ceiling *n.* nen *f.*

celebrate *v.* dathlu

celebrated *a.* enwog

celebration *n.* dathliad *m.*

cell *n.* cell *f.*

Celt *n.* Celtes *f.*

Celt *n.* Celt *m.*

Celtic *a.* Celtaidd

Celtic language *n.* Celteg *f.*

cemetery *n.* mynwent *f.*

censure 1 *n.* cerydd *m*, sen *f.*
2 *v.* ceryddu.

centenary *n.* canmlwyddiant
m.

centigrade *a.* canradd,
sentigred. **20°C** ugain gradd
Celsius

central *a.* canol, canolog.
central heating gwres
canolog

centre *n.* canol *m*; canolfan *f*;
canolwr *m*. **shopping centre**
canolfan siopa; **job centre**
canolfan gwaith.

centurion *n.* canwriad *m.*

century *n.* cant *m*; canrif *f.*

ceremony *n.* seremoni *f.*

certain *a.* sicr, siŵr; rhyw,
rhai

certainly *ad.* yn sicr, yn siŵr

certainty *n.* sicrwydd *m.*

certificate *n.* tystysgrif *f.*

chaff *n.* us *m. mân us*

chaffinch *n.* ji-binc, asgell
fraith *f.*

chain 1 *n.* cadwyn *f.* 2 *v.*
cadwyno

chair 1 *n.* cadair, stôl *f.* 2 *v.*
cadeirio, llwyddu. **Chairing
of the Bard** Cadeirio'r Bardd

chaired *a.* cadeiriol

chairman *n.* cadeirydd *m.*

chalet *n.* hafoty, bwthyn (haf)
m.

chalk 1 *n.* sialc *m.* 2 *v.*
sialcio

challenge 1 *n.* her *f.* 2 *v.*
herio

chamber *n.* ystafell, siambr *f.*
chamber orchestra cerddorfa
siambr

champion *n.* pencampwr *m.*

chance 1 *n.* hap, siawns, lwc
f, cyfle *m*, damwain *f.* 2 *v.*
digwydd gwneud rhywbeth

change *n. & v.* newid *m.*

changing-room *n.* ystafell
newid *f.*

channel *n.* sianel *f.* gwely *m.*

chapel *n.* capel *m.*

chapter *n.* pennod *f.*

character *n.* cymeriad, nod
m; llythyren *f.*

characteristic 1 *n.* nodwedd *f.*
2 *a.* nodweddiadol

charge 1 *n.* gofal;
gorchymyn; pris; tâl; ergyd
m. 2 *v.* gofalu, gorchymyn;
codi

charm 1 *n.* hud, swyn *m.* 2 *v.*
hudo, swyno

charming *a.* swynol

chase 1 *n.* helfa *f.* 2 *v.* hel,
hela, erlid

chat 1 *n.* sgwrs *f*, siarad, sôn
m, ymgom *mf.* 2 *v.* sgwrsio,
siarad, ymgomio

chatter *v.* clebran

cheap *a.* rhad

cheat 1 *n.* twyllwr *m.* 2 *v.* twyllo

cheek *n.* grudd *mf*, boch *f*, haerllugrwydd *m.*

cheerful *a.* llawen, llon, siriol

cheese *n.* caws *m.*

cheers! *i.* iechyd da!

chemist *n.* fferyllydd; cemegwr *m.*

chemistry *n.* cemeg *f.*

Chepstow *n.* Cas-Gwent *f.*

cheque *n.* siec *f.* **cheque book** llyfr sieciau; **cheque card** cerdyn sieciau

cherry *n.* ceiriosen *f.*

chest *n.* cist; brest *f*;

Chester *n.* Caer *f.*

chew *v.* cnoi

chick *n.* cyw *m.*

chicken *n.* cyw iâr *m.* ffowlyn *f.* **chickenpox** brech yr ieir

chief 1 *n.* pen, pennaeth *m.* 2 *a.* prif, pen, pennaf. **chief bard** prifardd

child *n.* plentyn *m.*

childish *a.* plentynnaidd

chill 1 *a.* oer. 2 *v.* oeri

chilled *a.* sythlyd, wedi ei oeri

chilly *a.* oer, oerllyd

chimney *n.* simdde, simnai *f.*, corn (mwg) *m.*

chin *n.* gên *f.*

China *n.* Tseina, China *f.*

china *n.* llestri te *m.*

chip *n.* sglodyn *m.* **fish and chips** pysgod a sglodion

chocolate *n.* siocled *m.*

choice *n.* dewis *m.*

choir *n.* côr *m.*

choke *v.* tagu

choose *v.* dewis, ethol

chop *v.* torri

chord *n.* tant, cord *m.*

chorus *n.* cytgan *f*; côr, corws *m.*

Christ *n.* Crist *m.*

christen *v.* bedyddio, enwi.

Christian 1 *n.* Cristion *m.* 2 *a.* Cristnogol. **Christian Aid** Cymorth Cristnogol; **Christian name** enw bedydd

Christmas *n.* y Nadolig *m.* **Christmas Day** Dydd Nadolig; **Christmas Eve** Noswyl Nadolig; **Christmas Holidays** gwyliau'r Nadolig; **Christmas presents** anrhegion Nadolig; **Christmas tree** coeden Nadolig

chum *n.* cyfaill, ffrind *m.*

church *n.* eglwys, llan *f.*

churchyard *n.* mynwent *f.*

chute *n.* llithren *f.*

cigar *n.* sigâr *f.*

cigarette *n.* sigarét *f.*

cinema *n.* sinema *f.*

circle *n.* cylch *m.*

circular 1 *n.* cylchlythyr *m.* 2 *a.* cylchog.

circumflex *n.* hirnod *mf.* (^)

circus *n.* syrcas *f.*

citizen *n.* dinesydd *m.*

city *n.* dinas *f.*

civic *a.* dinesig

civil *a.* gwladol; cwrtais

civilian *n.* dinesydd *m.*

civil war *n.* rhyfel cartref *mf.*
claim 1 *n.* hawl *m.* **2** *v.*
hawlio
clamber *v.* dringo
clash *v.* gwrthdaro
class 1 *n.* dosbarth *m;* adran
f, cylch *m,* safon *f.* **2** *v.*
dosbarthu
classic *n.* clasur, campwaith
m.
classical *a.* clasurol
classics *n.* clasuron *m.pl.*
clause *n.* cymal *m.* adnod,
adran *f.*
clay *n.* clai *m.*
clean 1 *a.* glân. **2** *v.* glanhau
cleanliness *n.* glendid *m.*
cleanly *ad.* yn lân
clear 1 *a.* amlwg, clir, eglur,
gloyw. **2** *v.* clirio
clef *n.* allwedd *f,* cleff *m.*
clerk *n.* clerc *m.*
clever *a.* medrus, clyfar
cliché *n.* ystrydeb *f.*
cliff *n.* clogwyn *m,* craig *f.*
climate *n.* hinsawdd *f.*
climax *n.* uchafbwynt *m.*
climb *v.* dringo
climber *n.* dringwr *m.*
cling *v.* glynu, cydio
clinic *n.* meddygfa *f,* clinig *m.*
cloak *n.* clogyn *m,* mantell *f.*
clock *n.* cloc *m.* **o'clock** o'r
gloch; **six o'clock** chwech o'r
gloch; **alarm clock** cloc
larwm
clockwise *a.* clocwedd
close 1 *n.* diwedd, terfyn *m.*
2 *v.* cau
close 1 *n.* clos, buarth *m,*
iard *f.* **2** *a.* agos, clòs, tyn

cloth *n.* brethyn, defnydd,
lliain, clwtyn *m.*
clothes *n.pl.* dillad *m.pl.,*
gwisgoedd *f.pl.*
clothing *n.* dillad *m.*
cloud 1 *n.* cwmwl *m.* **2** *v.*
cymylu
cloudy *a.* cymylog
clown *n.* clown *m.*
clumsy *a.* lletchwith
coach 1 *n.* hyfforddwr *m;*
coets *f.* **2** *v.* hyfforddi
coal *n.* glo *m.*
coalfield *n.* maes glo *m.*
coarse *a.* garw, bras
coast *n.* arfordir *m,* glan môr *f.*
coat *n.* cot, siaced *f.*
cobweb *n.* gwe. *f.*
cockerel *n.* ceiliog *m.*
coffee *n.* coffi *m.*
coffin *n.* arch, coffin *f.*
cog *n.* dant, còg *m.*
coil 1 *n.* torch *m.* **2** *v.* torchi
coin 1 *n.* darn arian *m.* **2** *v.*
bathu; **pound coin** darn punt
cold 1 *n.* oerfel; annwyd *m.*
2 *a.* oer, sythlyd. **to become
cold** oeri; **to catch a cold** dal
annwyd
collar *n.* coler *f.* **collar bone**
pont yr ysgwydd
collect 1 *n.* colect *m*
(gweddi). **2** *v.* casglu,
crynhoi, hel
collection *n.* casgliad *m.*
college *n.* coleg *m.*
collide *n.* gwrthdaro
collier *n.* glöwr m; llong lo *f.*
colliery *n.* glofa *f,* pwll glo,
gwaith glo *m.*

colloquial *a.* llafar

colony *n.* gwladfa *f.*

colour 1 *n.* lliw *m.* **2** *v.* lliwio, lliwio, coluro

coloured *a.* lliwiog

colourful *a.* lliwgar

colt *n .* ebol *m.*

column *n.* colofn *f,* piler *m.*

columnist *n.* newyddiadurwr *m.*

comb 1 *n.* crib *mf.* **2** *v.* cribo

combat *n.* gornest, brwydr *f.*

come *v.* dod, dyfod. **to come across** dod ar draws; **to come to an end** dod i ben

comely *a.* teg, glân, hardd

comfort 1 *n.* cysur *m.* **2** *v.* cysuro

comfortable *a.* cyfforddus, cyffyrddus, cysurus

command *n. & v.* gorchymyn *m.* **commandment** *n.* gorchymyn *m:* **The Ten Commandments** Y Deg Gorchymyn

commence *v.* dechrau

commend *v.* canmol

comment 1 *n.* sylw *m.* **2** *v.* sylwi, esbonio

commentary *n.* sylwebaeth *f;* esboniad *m.* **to commentate** sylwebu

commentator *n.* sylwebydd, sylwebwr *m.*

committee *n.* pwyllgor *m.*

common *a.* cyffredin. **common sense** synnwyr cyffredin

commons *n.* y cyffredin *m.pl.* **House of Commons** Tŷ'r Cyffredin

commotion *n.* terfysg *m.*

communion *n.* cymun, cymundeb *m.*

community *n.* cymdeithas, cymuned *f.* **Member of the European Union** Aelod o'r Gymuned Ewropeaidd

compact *a.* cryno. **compact disc** cryno ddisg

companion *n.* cyfaill *m,* cyfeilles *f.*

company *n.* cwmni *m.*

compare *v.* cymharu (â)

compassion *n.* trugaredd *m.*

compel *v.* gorfodi

compensate *v.* talu iawn

compensation *n.* iawn, iawndal *m.*

compete *v.* cystadlu

competition *n.* cystadleuaeth *f,* ymryson *m.*

competitor *n.* cystadleuwr, cystadleuydd *m.*

complain *v.* cwyno

complaint *n.* cwyn *mf.*

complete *a.* hollol, llwyr

completely *ad.* yn hollol, yn llwyr

complex *a.* cymhleth

complexity *m.* cymhlethdod *m.*

complicate *v.* cymhlethu

complicated *a.* cymhleth

complication *n.* cymhlethdod *m.*

compose *v.* cyfansoddi

composer *n.* cyfansoddwr *m.*

comprehensive *a.* cyfun, cynhwysfawr.

Comprehensive School Ysgol Gyfun

compulsion *n.* gorfod *m,*
gorfodaeth *f.*
compulsory *a.* gorfodol
computer *n.* cyfrifiadur *m.*
conceal *v.* cuddio
concentrate *v.* canolbwyntio
concerning *prp.* ynglŷn â,
ynghylch
concert *n.* cyngerdd *mf.*
concession *n.* lŵans, lwfans
m.
conclude *v.* gorffen
conclusion *n.* casgliad;
diwedd, diweddglo *m.*
concrete *n.* concrit *m.*
condition *n.* cyflwr *m;* amod
mf.
conduct 1 *n.* ymddygiad *m.*
2 *v.* arwain
conductor *n.* arweinydd;
tocynnwr *m.*
cone *n.* côn *m.*
confer *v.* ymgynghori
conference *n.* cynhadledd *f.*
confide *v.* ymddiried (yn)
confidence *n.* hyder *m,*
ymddiriedaeth *f.* **self-
confidence** hunanhyder
confident *a.* hyderus: **to be
confident** hyderu
confidential *a.* cyfrinachol
confine *v.* cyfyngu, carcharu
confined *a.* cyfyng
confluence *n.* cymer *m.*
confront *v.* wynebu
confuse *v.* drysu, cymysgu
congratulate *v.* llongyfarch
congratulation *n.*
llongyfarchiad *m.*
Congratulations!
Llongyfarchiadau!

congregation *n.* cynulleidfa *f.*
Congregationalist *n.*
Annibynnwr *m.*
conjecture *v.* dychmygu,
dyfalu
conjunction *n.* cysylltair *m.*
connection *n.* cysylltiad *m,*
perthynas *mf.* **in connection
with** ynglŷn â
conquer *v.* gorchfygu, trechu
conquest *n.* buddugoliaeth,
concwest *f.*
conscientious *a.* cydwybodol
conscription *n.* gorfodaeth
filwrol *f.*
consent 1 *n.* caniatâd *m.* **2** *v.*
caniatáu
conservative 1 *n.* ceidwadwr;
Tori *m.* **2** *a.* cadwrol,
ceidwadol.
conservatory *n.* tŷ gwydr *m.*
conserve *v.* cadw, amddiffyn
consider *v.* ystyried
considerable *a.* cryn
consideration *n.* ystyriaeth *f.*
considering *prp.* ag ystyried
consolation *n.* cysur *m.*
consolation prize gwobr
gysur
console *v.* cysuro
consonant *n.* cytsain *f.*
constituency *n.* etholaeth *f.*
construct *v.* ffurfio, llunio,
adeiladu
consult *v.* ymgynghori (â)
consume *v.* bwyta;
defnyddio; treulio
contact *v.* cyffwrdd (â)
contain *v.* cynnwys, dal
contaminate *v.* llygru

contamination *n.* llygredd *m.*
content *n.* cynnwys *m.*
content 1 *a.* bodlon. **2** *v.*
  bodloni
contention *n.* ymryson *m.*
contents *n.* cynnwys *m.pl.*
contest 1 *n.* gornest, ornest,
  cystadleuaeth, ymryson *f.*
  2 *v.* ymryson; ymladd
contestant *n.* cystadleuwr,
  cystadleuydd *m.*
context *n.* cyd-destun *m.*
continual *a.* parhaus
continually *ad.* byth a hefyd
continuation *n.* parhad *m.*
continue *v.* para, parhau, dal
  (ati)
continuous *a.* parhaol
contra- *px.* gwrth-, croes-
  (followed by soft mutation).
contradiction *n.*
  gwrthddywediad *m.*
contract *n.* cytundeb *m.*
contrary *a.* gwrthwyneb,
  croes. **on the contrary** i'r
  gwrthwyneb
contribute *v.* cyfrannu
contrite *a.* edifeiriol
control *v.* rheoli
controller *n.* rheolwr *m.*
convenient *a.* cyfleus, hwylus
conversation *n.* ymgom *mf,*
  sgwrs *f.*
converse 1 *n.* gwrthwyneb *m.*
  2 *v.* ymgomio, sgwrsio,
  ymddiddan
conversion *n.* trosiad *m;*
  tröedigaeth *f.*
convert *v.* troi, newid, trosi
converted *a.* wedi ei addasu.
  converted try trosgais

convey *v.* cyfleu; trosglwyddo
cook 1 *n.* cogydd *m;*
  cogyddes *f.* **2** *v* coginio,
  gwneud bwyd.
cool 1 *a.* oer. **2** *v.* oeri
copy 1 *n.* copi *m.* **2** *v.* copïo
copyright *n.* hawlfraint *f.*
cord *n.* cordyn *m;* lein *f,*
  llinyn *m.*
corgi *n.* corgi *m.*
corn *n.* llafur, corn, ŷd *m.*
corner *n.* cornel *mf,* cwr *m,*
  congl *f.*
cornflakes *n.* creision ŷd
  m.pl.
corpse *n.* corff *m.*
correct 1 *a.* cywir, iawn,
  priodol. **2** *v.* cywiro
correction *n.* cywiriad *m.*
corrupt 1 *a.* llygredig. **2** *v.*
  llygru
corruption *n.* llygredd,
  llygredigaeth *m.*
cost 1 *n.* pris *m,* traul, cost *f.*
  2 *v.* costio
costume *n.* gwisg *f.*
cottage *n.* bwthyn *m.*
cotton *n.* cotwm *m;* edau *f.*
  cotton wool gwlân cotwm
cough 1 *n.* peswch, pesychiad
  m. **2** *v.* peswch
council *n.* cyngor *m.* **council
  house** tŷ cyngor; **county
  council** cyngor sir
councillor *n.* cynghorwr *m.*
  County Councillor
  Cynghorwr Sir
counsel 1 *n.* cyngor *m.* **2** *v.*
  cynghori
count 1 *n.* cyfrif; iarll *m.*
  2 *v.* rhifo; cyfrif

counter- *px.* gwrth- (*followed by soft mutation*): **counteract** gwrthweithio;
counterclockwise gwrthgloc
counterfeit *n. & a.* ffug *m.*
counterfoil *n.* bôn *m* (*siec/ derbynneb . . .*)
countess *n.* iarlles *f.*
country *n.* gwlad, bro *f.*
Country Music Canu Gwlad
county *n.* sir, swydd (*English county*) *f:* **Carmarthenshire** Sir Gaerfyrddin, Sir Gâr; **Lancashire** Swydd Gaerhirfryn; **Yorkshire** Swydd Efrog; **Buckinghamshire** Swydd Buckingham
courageous *a.* dewr, gwrol
course *n.* cwrs *m*, hynt; ystod; gyrfa *f.* **in the course of** yn ystod; **of course** wrth gwrs; **crash course** cwrs carlam
court 1 *n.* llys *m.* **2** *v.* caru, canlyn. **Magistrates' Court** Llys Ynadon
courteous *a.* cwrtais
cousin *n.* cefnder *m;* cyfnither *f.*
cover 1 *n.* clawr *m.* **2** *v.* gorchuddio
covetous *a.* trachwantus
covetousness *n.* trachwant *m.*
cow *n.* buwch *f.*

cowardly *a.* llwfr
crack 1 *n.* crac *m.* **2** *v.* cracio
cradle *n.* crud *m.*
craft *n.* crefft; llong; awyren *f.*
craftsman *n.* crefftwr *m.*
crafty *a.* cyfrwys
crag *n.* craig *f*, clogwyn *m.*
cream *n.* hufen *m.*
crematorium *n.* amlosgfa *f.*
cress *n.* berw *m.*
crest *n.* brig *m*, crib *mf.*
crew *n.* criw *m.*
crib *n.* preseb *m.*
cricket *n.* criced; cricsyn *m.*
cricketer *n.* cricedwr *m.*
crime *n.* trosedd *f.*
criminal *n.* troseddwr *m.*
crisps *n.* creision (tatws) *m.pl.*
critic *n.* beirniad *m.*
criticize *v.* beirniadu
crockery *n.* llestri *pl.m.*
croft *n.* tyddyn *m.*
crook *n.* troseddwr; ffon fugail *m.*
crooked *a.* cam
cross 1 *n., *croes *f.* **2** *v.* croesi
cross-examine *v.* croesholi
crossing *n.* croesfan *f.*
crossroad *n.* croesffordd *f.*
crossword *n.* croesair, pos croeseiriau *m.*
crow *n.* brân *f.*

Insight

cow *n.* buwch. One plural form is *buchod*, the other is *da*. *Da* is also an adjective meaning 'good'; a farmer owns his cows – his 'goods'. *Da* in this context is a plural noun *m.*

crowd *n.* torf *f*, twr *m*, tyrfa *f*, llu *m*.

crown 1 *n.* coron *f*. 2 *v.* coroni: **Crown land** tir y Goron; **Triple Crown** Coron Driphlyg

cruel *a.* creulon

cruelty *n.* creulondeb *m*.

crumb *n.* briwsionyn *m*.

crumble *v.* chwalu; briwsioni

crush *v.* malu, gwasgu

crust *n.* crwst, crystyn *m*.

cry 1 *n.* cri *mf*, llef, sgrech *f*. 2 *v.* crio, llefain, wylo

cuckoo *n.* cog, cwcw *f*.

cultured *a.* gwâr

cunning *a.* cyfrwys

cup *n.* cwpan *mf*, dysgl *f*.

custom *n.* arfer, cwstwm *m*; toll *f*.

customary *a.* arferol

customer *n.* cwsmer *m*.

customs *n.* y tollau *f.pl.*

customs officer swyddog tollau

cut 1 *n.* toriad *m*. 2 *v.* torri

cycle 1 *n.* cylch; beic *m*. 2 *v.* seiclo

cylinder *n.* silindr *m*.

cylindrical *a.* silindrog

D

dad: daddy *n.* tad *m*.

daffodil *n.* cenhinen Bedr *f*, daffodil *m*.

Insight

daffodil *n.m.* is the national flower of Wales. Its leaves on a dull day may be mistaken for those of a leek, so they say! No one has eaten daffodil leaves, but *cawl* without leeks should be prohibited! Leeks are delicious cooked or raw; even Shakespeare savoured them.

---

cupboard *n.* cwpwrdd *m*.

cure *v.* gwella, iacháu

curly *a.* cyrliog

currants *n.* cwrens f. pl.

current 1 *n.* ffrwd *f*. llif *m*. 2 *a.* cyfoes: **current affairs** materion cyfoes

currently *ad.* ar hyn o bryd

curse 1 *n.* llw *m*, melltith, rheg *f*. 2 *v.* rhegi

curtain *n.* llen *f*.

cushion *n.* clustog *f*.

daisy *n.* llygad y dydd *m*.

dale *n.* cwm, dyffryn *m*, dôl, bro *f*. **hill and dale** bryn a dôl

damage *n.* niwed, difrod *m*.

damages *n.pl.* iawndal, iawn *m*.

damp *a.* llaith

damson *n.* eirinen ddu *f*.

dance 1 *n.* dawns *f*. 2 *v.* dawnsio. **public folk dance** twmpath dawns; **folk dancing** dawnsio gwerin

dandelion *n.* dant y llew *m.*
danger *n.* perygl *m.*
dangerous *a.* peryglus
dank *a.* llaith, gwlyb
dare *v.* beiddio, meiddio, mentro
dark *a.* tywyll
darkness *n.* tywyllwch, gwyll *m.*
darling 1 *n.* anwylyd *mf,* cariad *m.* 2 *a.* annwyl
date *n.* dyddiad *m.*
daughter *n.* merch *f.*
dawn 1 *n.* gwawr *f.* 2 *v.* gwawrio
day *n.* diwrnod, dydd *m.* **day before yesterday** echdoe; **yesterday** doe, ddoe; **today** heddiw; **tomorrow** yfory; **day after tomorrow** trennydd; **three days hence** tradwy; **by day** liw dydd; **next day** trannoeth; **Good day!** Dydd da!
daybreak *n.* gwawr *f,* toriad dydd *m.*
daylight *n.* golau dydd *m.*
dazzle *v.* dallu; disgleirio
dazzling *a.* llachar, disglair
deacon *n.* diacon; blaenor *m.*
deaconess diacones
dead *n. & a.* marw, meirw, meirwon *m.pl.*
deadly *a.* marwol
deaf *n. & a.* byddar *m.*
deal *v.* ymwneud (â), delio (â), ymdrin (â)
dear 1 *n.* anwylyd *mf,* cariad *m.* 2 *a.* annwyl, bach, cu, ffel, hoff; drud

dearest *n. & a.* anwylaf *mf.*
dearest ones anwyliaid
death *n.* angau *m,* marwolaeth *f.*
debate 1 *n.* dadl *f.* 2 *v.* dadlau, ymryson
debt *n.* dyled *f.*
decade *n.* degawd *m.*
decay *v.* pydru
deceased *a.* y diweddar
deceit *n.* twyll *m.*
deceitful *a.* twyllodrus
deceive *v.* twyllo
decelerate *v.* arafu
December *n.* Rhagfyr *m.*
decentralize *v.* datganoli
decide *v.* penderfynu, dyfarnu
decision *n.* penderfyniad, dyfarniad *m.*
deck *n.* bwrdd; dec *m.*
declaration *n.* datganiad *m.*
declare *v.* datgan, mynegi
decompose *v.* pydru
decree *n.* gorchymyn *m.*
dedicate *v.* cyflwyno; cysegru
deed *n.* gweithred *f.*
deep 1 *n.* dyfnder *m.* 2 *a.* dwfn. **deep freeze cabinet** rhewgell
Deeside *n.* Glannau Dyfrdwy *f.*
defeat *v.* gorchfygu, trechu
defect *n.* nam, diffyg, gwall *m.*
defence *n.* amddiffyn, amddiffyniad *m;* amddiffynfa *f.*
defend *v.* amddiffyn
defiance *n.* her *f.*
define *v.* diffinio

definite *a.* pendant
definitely *ad.* yn bendant
definition *n.* diffiniad *m.*
defraud *v.* twyllo
defrost *v.* dadrewi
deft *a.* medrus
degree *n.* gradd *f.*
de-ice *v.* toddi
deity *n.* duwdod; duw *m.*
delay *v.* oedi
delectable *a.* hyfryd
delegate 1 *n.* dirprwy *m.* **2** *v.* dirprwyo
delegation *n.* dirprwyaeth *f.*
delete *v.* dileu
delicious *a.* blasus
delightful *a.* hyfryd, braf
deliver *v.* gwaredu (rhag); danfon, trosglwyddo
deliverer *n.* gwaredwr
demand 1 *n.* gofyn, galw *m.* arch; gofynneb *f.* **2** *v.* mynnu, gofyn
demi- *px.* hanner
demise *n.* marwolaeth *f.*
den *n.* ffau *f.*
denomination *n.* enwad *m.*
dense *a.* trwchus; hurt
dent 1 *n.* pant, tolc *m.* **2** *v.* tolcio
dentist *n.* deintydd *m.*
dentures *n.* dannedd gosod, dannedd dodi *m.pl.*
deny *v.* gwadu, gwrthod
depart *v.* ymadael (â); cychwyn (am rywle)
department *n.* adran *f.* dosbarth *m.*
depend *v.* dibynnu (ar)
deplore *v.* gresynu

depose *v.* diswyddo; tystio
deposit *n.* ernes *f.* blaendal *m.*
depressed *a.* isel, digalon.
depression *n.* dirwasgiad *m.*; pant *m.*
depth *n.* dyfnder *m.*
deputation *n.* dirprwyaeth *f.*
deputy *n.* dirprwy *m.* **Deputy Director** Dirprwy Gyfarwyddwr; **Deputy Headteacher** Dirprwy Brifathro, Dirprwy Brifathrawes
derivation *n.* tarddiad *m.*
derive *v.* derbyn, cael; tarddu
descend *v.* disgyn
describe *v.* disgrifio, darlunio
description *n.* disgrifiad *m.*
desert *n.* anialwch *m.*
desert *v.* cilio, ffoi (rhag)
deserter *n.* ffoadur *m.*
deserve *v.* haeddu
deserved *a.* teilwng
design 1 *n.* cynllun *m.* **2** *v.* cynllunio
designer *n.* cynlluniwr, cynllunydd *m.*
desirable *a.* dymunol
desire 1 *n.* dymuniad, chwant, ewyllys *m.* **2** *v.* dymuno
desirous *a.* awyddus
desk *n.* desg *f.*
desolate *a.* gwag
despite *prp.* er, er gwaethaf
despot *n.* unben *m.*
dessert *n.* pwdin, melysfwyd *m.*
destiny *n.* tynged *f.*
destroy *v.* dinistrio, difetha

detached *a.* ar wahân
detail 1 *n.* manylyn *m.* **2** *v.*
manylu. **details** manylion; **in
detail** yn fanwl
detective *n.* ditectif *m.*
detective story stori dditectif
determination *n.* penderfyniad
m.
determine *v.* penderfynu
determined *a.* penderfynol
detest *v.* casáu
develop *v.* datblygu
development *n.* datblygiad *m.*
deviate *v.* gwyro, gwyrio
deviation *n.* gwyriad *m.*
devil *n.* diafol, diawl *m.*
devilish *a.* diawledig
devolution *n.* datganoli *m.*
devolve *v.* datganoli
devour *v.* llyncu, ysu
dew 1 *n.* gwlith *m.* **2** *v.*
gwlitho
diagnose *v.* adnabod
diagnosis *n.* diagnosis *m.*
dialect *n.* tafodiaith *f.*
dialogue *n.* deialog, sgwrs *f.*
diarrhoea *n.* dolur rhydd *m.*
diary *n.* dyddiadur *m.*
dictator *n.* unben *m.*
dictionary *n.* geiriadur *m.*
die *v.* marw, darfod, trigo
differ *v.* gwahaniaethu
difference *n.* gwahaniaeth *m.*
different *a.* gwahanol
difficult *a.* anodd, caled
difficulty *n.* anhawster *m.*
dig *v.* palu
digest *v.* treulio
digital *a.* digidol
dignity *n.* urddas *m.*

diligent *a.* prysur, diwyd
dimension *n.* maint *m.*
diminish *v.* lleihau
diminutive *a.* bychan
dingle *n.* cwm, glyn, pant *m.*
dinner *n.* cinio *mf.*
dip *v.* trochi, golchi
direct 1 *a.* union. **2** *v.*
cyfeirio
direction *n.* cyfeiriad;
hyfforddiant *m.*
directly *ad.* yn union
director *n.* cyfarwyddwr *m.*
directory *n.* cyfarwyddiadur *m.*
dirt *n.* baw, llacs *m.*
dirty *a.* brwnt, budr
disability *n.* anabledd *m.*
disabled *a.* anabl, methedig
disappear *v.* diflannu
disappoint *v.* siomi
disappointed *a.* siomedig
disappointing *a.* siomedig
disappointment *n.* siom *mf.*
disarm *v.* diarfogi
disaster *n.* trychineb *mf.*
disc *n.* disg *mf.*
disciple *n.* disgybl *m.*
discipline *n.* disgyblaeth *f.*
disclaim *v.* gwadu
disclose *v.* datguddio
discontented *a.* anfodlon
discover *v.* darganfod
discretion *n.* doethineb, pwyll
m.
discuss *v.* trafod
discussion *n.* trafodaeth,
sgwrs *f.*
disease *n.* afiechyd, clefyd,
dolur *m.* haint *f.*
disembark *v.* glanio

dish *n.* dysgl *f.*
disinfectant *n.* diheintydd *m.*
disk *n.* disg *mf.*
dislike *v.* casáu
dismiss *v.* diswyddo;
rhyddhau; gwrthod
disown *v.* gwadu, diarddel
dispatch 1 *n.* neges *f.* 2 *v.*
anfon, danfon
dispute 1 *n.* dadl *f.* 2 *v.*
dadlau, amau, ymryson
disseminate *v.* hau
dissimilar *a.* annhebyg,
gwahanol
dissolve *v.* toddi; datod
distance *n.* pellter *m.*
distant *a.* pell, hirbell. **from
far** o hirbell
distasteful *a.* diflas
distinct *a.* arbennig; eglur;
gwahanol
distribute *v.* rhannu,
dosbarthu
district *n.* ardal *f.* dosbarth,
cylch, rhanbarth, rhandir *m.*
ditch *n.* ffos *f.*
diverse *a.* gwahanol
divide *v.* rhannu
diviner *n.* dewin, dyn hysbys
m.
division *n.* adran, rhan *f,*
rhaniad, rhanbarth, rhandir
m.
divorce *n.* ysgariad *m.*
do *v.* gwneud, gwneuthur
dock *n.* doc *m.*
doctor *n.* meddyg, doctor *m.*
Dr John Jones y Dr John
Jones
document *n.* dogfen *f.*

dog *n.* ci *m.* **guide dog** ci
tywys
doll *n.* dol *f.*
domesticated *a.* dof
donation *n.* rhodd *f,*
cyfraniad *m.*
donkey *n.* asyn, mul *m.*
door *n.* drws, porth *m.*
double *a.* dwbl
doubt 1 *n.* amheuaeth, amau.
2 *v.* amau.
dough *n.* toes *m.*
down *ad.* i lawr
download *v.* llawrlwytho
dozen *n.* dwsin, deuddeg *m.*
drag *v.* llusgo
dragon *n.* draig *f.*
drama *n.* drama *f.* **drama
festival** gŵyl ddrama
dramatist *n.* dramodydd *m.*
draw *v.* darlunio, llunio,
tynnu; llusgo
drawing *n.* llun *m.*
dread 1 *n.* ofn *m.* 2 *v.* ofni
dreadful *a.* ofnadwy
dream 1 *n.* breuddwyd *mf.*
2 *v.* breuddwydio
dregs *n.* gwaelodion *m.pl.,*
gwaddod *m.*
dress 1 *n.* gwisg *f,* dilledyn *m,*
ffrog *f.* 2 *v.* gwisgo, taclu;
trin
dresser *n.* seld, dreser, dresel
f; gwisgwr *m.*
dressmaker *n.* gwniadyddes,
gwniyddes *f.*
drink 1 *n.* diod *f.* 2 *v.* yfed;
diota
drive 1 *n.* dreif *m.* 2 *v.* gyrru,
hala

driver *n.* gyrrwr *m.*
driving licence *n.* trwydded
yrru *f.*
droll *a.* ysmala, digrif
drop 1 *n.* cwymp; diferyn *m.*
2 *v.* cwympo. **drop goal** gôl
adlam
drown *v.* boddi
drug *n.* cyffur *m.*
drum *n.* drwm *m.*
drunk *a.* meddw. **to get drunk**
meddwi
drunkard *n.* meddwyn *m.*
dry 1 *a.* sych, cras. **2** *v.* sychu
Dublin *n.* Dulyn *f.*
duck *n.* hwyad, hwyaden *f.*
duckling cyw hwyaden *m.*
due 1 *n.* dyled, hawl *f,* tâl *m.*
2 *a.* dyledus
duel *n.* gornest *f.*
duet *n.* deuawd *mf.*
dull *a.* dwl, hurt; diflas,
cymylog. **dull man** dyn dwl;
dull day diwrnod cymylog
dumb *a.* mud
dummy-pass *n.* ffug-bas *f.*
during *prp.* yn ystod
dust *n.* llwch, dwst *m.*
dustbin bin ysbwriel *m.*
duty *n.* dyletswydd; toll *f.*
dwell *v.* cartrefu, trigo, byw
dwelling *n.* preswylfa, trigfa,
trigfan *f.*
dye *v.* lliwio, lliwo
dyke *n.* clawdd, morglawdd
m. **Offa's Dyke** Clawdd Offa

E

each *a. & pn* pob un, pob
eager *a.* awyddus

eagle *n.* eryr *m.*
ear *n.* clust *f.*
earl *n.* iarll *m.*
earliest *a.* cyntaf
early 1 *a.* cynnar, bore,
boreol. **2** *a.* yn fore
earmark 1 *n.* clustnod *mf.*
2 *v.* clustnodi, neilltuo
earn *v.* ennill
earner *n.* enillwr, enillydd *m.*
earnings *n.* enillion *pl.*
earring *n.* clustlws *m.*
earshot *n.* clyw *m.*
earth *n.* daear, Y Ddaear *f,*
pridd, tir, y byd *m.*
earthquake *n.* daeargryn *mf.*
earthwork *n.* clawdd *m.*
east 1 *n.* dwyrain *m.* **2** *a.*
dwyreiniol
Easter *n.* y Pasg *m.* **Easter**
egg wy Pasg; **Easter**
holidays gwyliau'r Pasg
easy *a.* hawdd, rhwydd
easy chair *n.* cadair esmwyth *f.*
eat *v.* bwyta.
ebb *n.* trai *m.*
echo *n.* adlais, atsain *m.*
carreg ateb *f.*
economics *n.* economeg *f.*
economize *v.* cynilo
edge *n.* cwr, blaen, min *m,*
ymyl *mf.*
Edinburgh *n.* Caeredin *f.*
edit *v.* golygu
edition *n.* argraffiad *m.*
editor *n.* golygydd *m.*
education *n.* addysg *f.*
effect 1 *n.* effaith *f.* **2** *v.*
effeithio

effective *a.* effeithiol
effeminate *a.* merchetaidd
effort *n.* ymdrech, ymgais *f.*
e.g. *(exempli gratia), ad.*
  er enghraifft *(e.e.)*
egg *n.* wy *m.*
egg cup *n.* cwpan wy *mf.*
eight *n. & a.* wyth *m.*
eighteen *n. & a.* deunaw, un
  deg wyth *m.*

ellipse *n.* hirgylch *m.*
else *ad.* arall
e-mail *n.* e-bost *m.*
embankment *n.* clawdd, cob
  m.
embassy *n.* llysgenhadaeth *f.*
embrace *v.* cofleidio
emigrant *n.* ymfudwr *m.*
emigrate *v.* ymfudo
eminent *a.* enwog, amlwg

Insight

eighteen *n. & a. deunaw* (two nines), less idiomatically un
deg wyth (one ten [and] eight). Thankfully all school
children now count *un deg un* (11), *un deg dau* (12), *un deg
tri* (13) and so on. eighteenth *un deg wythfed.*

eighth *n. & a.* wythfed *m.*
eighty *n. & a.* wyth deg,
  pedwar ugain *m.*
either 1 *a. & pn.* un o'r ddau,
  naill ai . . . neu. **2** *ad. & c.*
  na, nac, chwaith, ychwaith
elbow *n.* penelin *mf.*
elderly *a.* oedrannus
elect *v.* ethol, dewis
election *n.* etholiad *m.*
electorate *n.* etholaeth *f.*
electric *n. & a.* trydan *m.*
  electric fire tân trydan
electrical *a.* trydanol
electrician *n.* trydanwr *m.*
electricity *n.* trydan *m.*
element *n.* elfen *f.*
elementary *a.* elfennol
elephant *n.* eliffant
eleven *n. & a.* un ar ddeg *m.*
eleventh *n. & a.* unfed ar
  ddeg *m.*

emphasis *n.* pwys, pwyslais
  m.
emphatic *a.* pendant
empire *n.* ymerodraeth *f.*
employ *v.* cyflogi
employee *n.* gŵr cyflog *m.*
employer *n.* cyflogwr *m.*
employment *n.* gwaith *m.*
empty 1 *a.* gwag. **2** *v.*
  gwagio, arllwys. **empty-
  handed** gwaglaw
enchant *v.* swyno, hudo
enchanting *a.* hudol, swynol
enchantment *n.* lledrith, swyn
  m.
enclose *v.* amgáu
enclosed *a.* amgaeëdig
encore 1 *n.* encôr *m.* **2** *ad.*
  eto
end 1 *n.* diwedd, diben, pen,
  terfyn *m.* **2** *v.* dibennu,
  gorffen

endeavour 1 *n.* ymdrech *f.*
2 *v.* ymdrechu
endless *a.* diddiwedd
endure *v.* dioddef, goddef
enemy *n.* gelyn *m.*
energetic *a.* egnïol
energy *n.* egni, ynni *m.*
enforce *v.* gorfodi
enforced *a.* gorfod
enforcement *n.* gorfodaeth *f.*
engagement *n.* dyweddïad;
ymrwymiad *m.*
engine *n.* peiriant *m*, injan,
injin *f.*
England *n.* Lloegr *f.*
English 1 *n.* Saesneg *f.* 2 *a.*
Saesneg, Seisnig. **English
people** Saeson; **English
language** Saesneg
Englishman *n.* Sais *m.*
Englishwoman *n.* Saesnes *f.*
enjoy *v.* mwynhau, joio
enjoyment *n.* mwynhad *m.*
enlighten *v.* goleuo; hysbysu
enormous *a.* enfawr, anferth
enough 1 *n.* digon, digonedd
m. 2 *a. & ad.* digon
enquire *v.* gofyn, holi
entangle *v.* drysu
enter *v.* mynd i mewn
entertain *v.* difyrru
entertaining *a.* difyr, difyrrus
entertainment *n.* adloniant *m.*
enthusiastic *a.* brwdfrydig
entice *v.* denu, hudo
enticing *a.* deniadol, dengar
entire *a.* cyfan, hollol, llwyr
entirely *ad.* yn gyfan gwbl, yn
hollol, yn llwyr
entrails *n.* perfedd *pl.m.*

entrance *n.* mynedfa *f.*
mynediad, drws, porth; tâl *m.*
entrance *v.* swyno
entreat *v.* erfyn
entry *n.* mynediad *m,*
mynedfa *f.*
envelop *v.* amgáu
envelope *n.* amlen *f.*
environment *n.* amgylchedd
m.
environs *n.* amgylchoedd *pl.*
envoy *n.* negesydd, cennad *m.*
epilogue *n.* diweddglo, epilog
m.
epistle *n.* llythyr, epistol *m.*
equal *a.* cydradd, yr un faint,
hafal. *See* hafal *n. & v.*
equation *n.* hafaliad *m.*
simple equation hafaliad
syml
equipment *n.* offer *m.pl.*
erase *v.* dileu.
erect 1 *a.* syth. 2 *v.* codi
errand *n.* neges *f.*
error *n.* camsyniad; bai, gwall
m.
escape *v.* dianc, ffoi
escort *v.* hebrwng
especial *a.* arbennig,
enwedig, neilltuol
especially *ad.* yn arbennig, yn
enwedig
essay *n.* traethawd *m.* ysgrif
mf.
essential *a.* hanfodol
establish *v.* sefydlu
establishment *n.* sefydliad *m.*
estate *n.* eiddo *m*, ystad, stad
f.
estuary *n.* aber *m.*

eternal *ad*. yn dragwyddol, yn oes oesoedd

Europe *n*. Ewrop *f*.

evade *v*. osgoi

eve *n*. min nos *m*, noswyl *f*.
  Christmas Eve Noswyl Nadolig

even 1 *n*. yr hwyr *m*. **2** *a*. gwastad, llyfn; tawel. **3** *ad*. hyd yn oed

evening *n*. hwyr *m*, noson, noswaith *f*. **evening class** dosbarth nos

event *n*. digwyddiad *m*.

eventually *ad*. o'r diwedd

ever *ad*. byth, erioed

evergreen *n. & a*. bythwyrdd *m*.

everlasting *a*. tragwyddol

evermore *ad*. byth, byth bythoedd

every *a*. pob

everybody *pn*. pawb, pob un

everyday *a*. bob dydd

everyone *pn* pawb, pob un

everything *pn*. pob peth, popeth

everywhere *ad*. ym mhobman

evidence *n*. tystiolaeth *f*, prawf *m*.

evident *a*. amlwg, eglur

evil 1 *n*. drwg, drygioni *m*.
  2 *a*. drwg, drygionus

evolve *v*. datblygu; esblygu

ewe *n*. dafad, mamog *f*.

ex- *px*. cyn-

exact *a*. cywir, manwl, union.
  to be exact manylu

exactly *ad*. yn union, i'r dim

examination *n*. arholiad, archwiliad *m*.

examine *v*. arholi, chwilio, archwilio

examiner *n*. arholwr, holwr *m*.

example *n*. enghraifft, esiampl *f*. **for example, e.g.** er enghraifft, e.e.

excavator *n*. jac-codi-baw *m*.

excel *v*. rhagori

excellent *a*. ardderchog, campus, godidog, gwych, penigamp, rhagorol

excellently *ad*. yn ardderchog

except 1 *v*. eithrio. **2** *prp*. ac eithrio. **3** *pn*. eithr

excess *n*. gormod *m*.

exciting *a*. cyffrous, cynhyrfus

exclaim *v*. llefain, gweiddi, bloeddio

exclamation *n*. llef, gwaedd *f*.

exclude *v*. eithrio, cau allan

excuse 1 *n*. esgus *m*. **2** *v*. esgusodi

execute *v*. gweithredu; dienyddio

exercise 1 *n*. ymarfer *mf*. ymarferiad *m*. **2** *v*. ymarfer. **exercise book** llyfr ymarfer, llyfr ysgrifennu

exile 1 *n*. alltud *m*. **2** *v*. alltudio

exist *v*. bod

existence *n*. bod *m*, bodolaeth *f*.

exit 1 *n*. allanfa *f*, mynediad allan *m*. **2** *v*. mynd allan

expect *v*. disgwyl

expediency *n*. hwylustod *m*.

expedient *a*. hwylus, cyfleus

expense *n*. traul, cost *f*.

expenses *n.* treuliau *f.pl.*
expensive *a.* costus, drud
experience *n.* profiad *m.*
experienced *a.* profiadol
explain *v.* egluro, esbonio
explanation *n.* esboniad,
eglurhad *m.*
explode *v.* ffrwydro
expose *v.* amlygu, dinoethi
exposed *a.* agored, noeth
exposition *n.* esboniad *m.*
express 1 *a.* cyflym. 2 *v.*
mynegi. 3 *n.* trên cyflym *m.*
extend *v.* estyn, ymestyn
extension *a.* estyniad *m.*
extensive *a.* eang, helaeth
extent *n.* maint, hyd,
mesur *m.* **to some extent**
i raddau
exterior 1 *n.* y tu allan *m.*
2 *a.* allanol
external *a.* allanol. **external
exam** arholiad allanol
extinguish *v.* diffodd; dileu
extreme 1 *n.* eithaf *m.* 2 *a.*
eithafol
extremely *ad.* dros ben, gor-
extremity *n.* eithaf, terfyn,
pen *m.*
eye 1 *n.* llygad *mf.* 2 *v.*
llygadu, sylwi ar
eyesight *n.* golwg *mf.*
eyewitness *n.* llygad-dyst *m.*

F

fable *n.* chwedl *f.*
fabric *n.* defnydd *m.*
face 1 *n.* wyneb *m.* 2 *v.*

wynebu. **face-cloth** clwtyn
ymolch
facilitate *v.* hwyluso
fact *n.* ffaith *f*, gwirionedd *m.*
as a matter of fact mewn
gwirionedd
factor *n.* elfen, ffactor *f.*
factory *n.* ffatri *f.*
fade *v.* gwywo, colli lliw
fail *v.* methu, ffaelu
failure *n.* methiant *m.*
faint 1 *a.* gwan. 2 *v.* llewygu.
fair 1 *n.* ffair *f.* 2 *a.* teg, glân;
gweddol; golau
fairly *ad.* yn deg, yn lân, yn
weddol, eithaf-, go-, lled-.
fairly good eithaf da, go dda,
lled dda. **fairly rare** go brin.
fairly quiet lled dawel;
*see Appendix for mutation of
Adjectives following certain
Adverbs.*
fairness *n.* harddwch; tegwch
m.
faith *n.* ffydd *f.*
faithful *a.* ffyddlon, cywir
faithfully *ad.* yn ffyddlon, yn
gywir. **Yours faithfully** Yr
eiddoch yn gywir
fake 1 *a.* ffug. 2 *v.* ffugio
falcon 1 *n.* hebog *m.*
fall 1 *n.* cwymp *m.* 2 *v.*
cwympo, syrthio
false *a.* ffug, gau, twyllodrus.
false teeth dannedd gosod,
dannedd dodi *m. pl.*
fame *n.* enwogrwydd, clod *m.*
familiarize *v.* cyfarwyddo
family *n.* teulu *m.*
famine *n.* newyn *m.*

famish *v.* llwgu
famous *a.* enwog
fanciful *a.* ffansïol
fancy 1 *n.* dychymyg *m,*
ffansi *f,* serch *m.* **2** *v.*
dychmygu, ffansïo, serchu
fantasy *n.* ffantasi *f.*
far *a. & ad.* pell, ymhell. **as
far as** hyd at; **from afar** o
hirbell; **not far from** nid
nepell o
farewell 1 *n.* ffárwel, ffarwél *f.*
2 *v.* ffarwelio. **to bid farewell**
canu'n iach
farm 1 *n.* ffarm, fferm *f.* **2** *v.*
ffarmio, ffermio
farmer *n.* amaethwr, ffarmwr,
ffermwr *m.*
farmhouse *n.* ffermdy, tŷ
ffarm *m.*
farming *n.* ffermio, gwaith
ffarm *m,* amaethyddiaeth *f.*
farmyard *n.* buarth, clos *m.*
farthest *a.* pellaf, eithaf
fascinate *v.* hudo, swyno
fascinating *a.* hudol, swynol
fashion 1 *n.* llun, ffasiwn *m;*
arfer *mf.* **2** *v.* llunio, ffurfio,
gwneud.
fast *a.* cyflym, buan; tyn
fat 1 *n.* braster, saim *m.* **2** *v.*
bras, tew. **fat meat** cig bras,
cig gwyn
fatal *a.* marwol
fatality *n.* marwolaeth *f.*
fate *n.* tynged *f.*
fateful *a.* tyngedfennol
father *n.* tad *m.* **father-in-law**
tad-yng-nghyfraith;
stepfather llystad. **Father
Christmas** *n.* Siôn Corn *m.*

fault *n.* bai, nam, diffyg *m.*
faultless *a.* di-fai
faulty *a.* gwallus
favour *n.* cymwynas, ffafr *f.*
favourite 1 *n.* ffefryn *m.* **2** *a.*
hoff
fear 1 *n.* ofn, braw *m.* **2** *v.*
ofni
feast 1 *n.* gwledd, gŵyl *f.*
2 *v.* gwledda
feat *n.* camp *f.*
feather 1 *n.* pluen, plufyn *m.*
2 *v.* pluo, plufio
feature *n.* nodwedd
fee *n.* tâl *m,* cyflog *mf,* ffi *f.*
February *n.* Chwefror, Mis
Bach *m.*
feeble *a.* gwan, egwan,
bregus
feed *v.* bwydo, bwyda; bwyta
feel 1 *n.* teimlad *m.* **2** *v.*
teimlo, clywed
feeling *n.* teimlad *m,* naws *f.*
feign *v.* cymryd ar; ffugio
fell *v.* cwympo, syrthio, torri
female 1 *n.* benyw, menyw *f.*
2 *a.* benywaidd, menywaidd
feminine *a.* benywaidd,
menywaidd
fence 1 *n.* clawdd *m,* ffens *f.*
2 *v.* cau, amgáu
fern *n.* rhedynen *f,* rhedyn *pl.*
ferocious *a.* ffyrnig, gwyllt
fertile *a.* ffrwythlon, bras,
toreithiog
fertilize *v.* ffrwythloni;
gwrteithio
fertilizer *n.* gwrtaith *m.*
fervent *a.* gwresog, tanllyd,
tanbaid, selog

festival *n.* gŵyl *f.*, dydd gŵyl *m.* **singing festival** cymanfa ganu

fetch *v.* hôl, nôl, hercyd

fever *n.* twymyn *f,* clefyd, gwres *m.*

few *a.* ychydig

fiancé *n.* darpar-ŵr, dyweddi *m.*

fiancée *n.* darpar wraig, dyweddi *f.*

fiction *n.* ffluglen *f.*

fictitious *a.* ffug, ffugiol

field *n.* cae, maes, parc *m.*

fierce *a.* ffyrnig

fiery *a.* tanllyd, tanbaid

fifteen *n. & a.* pymtheg *m.*

fifteenth *n. & a.* pymthegfed *m.*

final 1 *n.* rownd derfynol *f.* 2 *a.* terfynol, olaf

finale *n.* diweddglo

finally *ad.* o'r diwedd, yn olaf

find *v.* darganfod, cael, dod o hyd

fine 1 *n.* dirwy *f.* 2 *v.* dirwyo. 3 *a.* mân, manwl; main; braf; gwych; hardd, hyfryd, teg

finger *n.* bys *m.* **fingerprint** ôl bys

finish 1 *n.* diwedd, terfyn *m.* 2 *v.* gorffen, dibennu, cwpla

fir *n.* ffynidwydden *f.*

fire 1 *n.* tân *m.* 2 *v.* tanio; saethu. **fire-brigade** brigâd dân *f.* **fire exit** allanfa dân *f.*

fireplace *n.* lle tân *m.*

Insight

fifteenth *n. & a. pymthegfed*, less idiomatically *un deg pumed*.

---

fifth *n. & a.* pumed *m.*

fifty *n. & a.* hanner cant, pum deg *m.*

fight 1 *n.* brwydr *f.* ymladd *m.* 2 *v.* brwydro, ymladd

fighter *n.* ymladdwr *m.*

fighting *n.* ymladd *m.*

figure 1 *n.* ffigur *mf;* ffurf *f,* llun *m.* 2 *v.* ffurfio; rhifo

file 1. *n.* ffeil *f.* 2 *v.* ffeilio

fill 1 *n.* digon, digonedd *m.* 2 *v.* llanw, llenwi

film 1 *n.* ffilm *f.* 2 *v.* ffilmio

filth *n.* baw, budreddi, mochyndra *m.*

firewood *n.* coed tân *f.pl.*

fireworks *n.* tân gwyllt *m.pl.*

firm 1 *n.* cwmni, ffyrm *m.* 2 *a.* cadarn, cryf. 3 *v.* nerthu, cryfhau.

firmament *n.* ffurfafen *f.*

first 1 *n. & a.* cyntaf *m.* 2 *ad.* yn gyntaf

fish 1 *n.* pysgodyn *m.* 2 *v.* pysgota

fisherman *n.* pysgotwr *m.*

fishing *n.* pysgota *m.*

fist *n.* dwrn *m.*

fitting *a.* addas, priodol

five *n. & a.* pump *m.*

fix *v.* gosod, sicrhau, sefydlu

fixed *a.* sefydlog

flabby *a.* llac, llipa, llaes

flag *n.* baner *f.* **Union Jack** Jac-yr-Undeb

flakes *n.* creision *m.pl.* **cornflakes** creision ŷd; **snowflakes** plu eira

flame 1 *n.* fflam *f.* 2 *v.* fflamio

flank *n.* ystlys, ochr *f.*

flannel *n.* gwlanen *f.*

flap 1 *n.* llabed *f.* fflap *m.* 2 *v.* fflapio

flash 1 *n.* fflach *f.* 2 *v.* fflachio

flat 1 *n.* fflat *f.* 2 *a.* fflat, gwastad

flavour 1 *n.* blas *m.* 2 *v.* blasu

flaw *n.* bai, diffyg, nam *m.*

flea *n.* chwannen *f.*

flee *v.* cilio, dianc, ffoi

fleet *n.* llynges *f.*

flesh *n.* cig, cnawd *m.* **flesh and blood** cig a gwaed

flexible *a.* hyblyg, ystwyth

fling *v.* taflu

flock *n.* haid *f;* praidd *m.*

flood 1 *n.* llif *m.* 2 *v.* llifo, gorlifo

floor *n.* llawr *m.*

flour *n.* blawd, can *m.*

flow 1 *n.* llif *m.* 2 *v.* llifo, rhedeg

flower *n.* blodyn *m.* **flower pot** pot blodau

flowing *a.* llithrig; llaes, llac, rhydd

fluent *a.* rhwydd, llithrig, rhugl

fluid *n. & a.* hylif *m.*

fly 1 *n.* cleren *f,* pryf, gwybedyn *m.* 2 *v.* hedfan

foam *n.* ewyn *m.* **sea-foam** ewyn môr

focus 1 *n.* canolbwynt, ffocws *m.* 2 *a.* canolbwyntio

foe *n.* gelyn *m.*

fog *n.* niwl, ffog *m.* **thick fog** niwl trwchus

foggy *a.* niwlog

fold *v.* plygu

folk *n.* gwerin *coll.f.,* pobl *f.*

folklore *n.* llên gwerin *f.*

folksong *n.* cân werin *f.*

follow *v.* dilyn

follower *n.* dilynwr *m.*

folly *n.* ffolineb *m.*

fond *a.* hoff, cu, annwyl

fondle *v.* anwesu, anwylo

fondness *n.* hoffter; anwes *m.*

food *n.* bwyd *m.*

fool 1 *n.* ffŵl *m.* 2 *v.* twyllo

foolish *a.* ffôl, dwl

foolishness *n.* ffolineb, dwli *m.*

foot *n.* troed *mf;* troedfedd *f.*

football *n.* pêl-droed *f.* **footballer** pêldroediwr *m.*

footpath *n.* troedffordd *f,* llwybr *m.* **public footpath** llwybr cyhoeddus

footprint *n.* ôl troed *m.*

for 1 *prp.* am, dros, tros, er, ers, erbyn, hyd, i, yn, lle. 2 *c.* achos, gan, oblegid, oherwydd

force *n.* grym; llu *m.* **armed forces** lluoedd arfog

ford *n.* rhyd *f.* **Ammanford** Rhydaman: **Oxford** Rhydychen

forehead *n.* talcen, tâl *m.*

foreign *a.* estron, tramor. **foreign affairs** materion tramor

foreigner *n.* estron *m.*

forest *n.* coedwig, fforest *f.*

foretaste *n.* rhagflas, rhagbrawf *m.*

forge 1 *n.* gefail *f.* **2** *v.* ffugio, twyllo

forget *v.* anghofio. **forget-me-not** glas y gors

forgive *v.* maddau

fork *n.* fforc, fforch *f.*

form 1 *n.* ffurf *f*; modd, dull *m*; ffurflen *f*; dosbarth *m.* **2** *v.* ffurfio, llunio. **application form** ffurflen gais *f.*

former *px.* cyn

formerly *ad.* gynt

fort *n.* caer *f.*

forthcoming *a.* ar ddod, gerllaw

fortnight *n.* pythefnos *mf.*

fortnightly *ad.* bob pythefnos

fortunate *a.* ffodus, lwcus

fortunately *ad.* yn ffodus, yn lwcus

fortune *n.* ffortiwn *f.*

forty *n. & a.* deugain, pedwar deg *m.*

forward 1 *n.* blaenwr *m.* **2** *a.* blaen; eofn. **3** *ad.* ymlaen. **4** *v.* anfon ymlaen. **wing forward** blaenasgellwr: **number eight** wythwr

foster *v.* meithrin, rhoi ar faeth

foster-mother *n.* mam-faeth *f.*

foul *a.* brwnt, budr, ffiaidd

found *v.* dechrau, sefydlu

foundation *n.* sail *f,* sylfaen *mf.*

fountain *n.* ffynnon, ffynhonnell *f.*

four *n. & a.* pedair *f.,* pedwar *m.*

fourteen *n. & a.* pedwar ar ddeg, pedair ar ddeg, un deg pedwar *m.*

fourth *n. & a.* pedwaredd *f.,* pedwerydd *m.*

fowl *n.* ffowlyn *m.*

fox *n.* cadno, llwynog. **vixen** cadnawes, cadnöes, llwynoges

fraction *n.* ffracsiwn *m.*

fragment *n.* darn, tamaid *m,* yfflyn *m.*

France *n.* Ffrainc *f.*

frankincense *n.* thus *m.*

fraud *n.* twyll *m.*

fraudulent *a.* twyllodrus

free 1 *a.* rhad, rhydd, di-dâl. **2** *v.* rhyddhau. **free kick** cic rydd. **free phone** rhadffôn; **freepost** rhadbost

freedom *n.* rhyddid *m.*

freely *ad.* yn rhydd

freeze *v.* rhewi

freezer *n.* rhewgell *f.*

freight *n.* llwyth *m.*

French 1 *n.* Ffrangeg *f.* **2** *a.* Ffrengig

Frenchman *n.* Ffrancwr *m.*

Frenchwoman *n.* Ffrances *f.*

frequent *a.* aml

fresh *a.* ffres, newydd

Friday *n.* dydd Gwener *m.*

friend *n.* cyfaill *m*, cyfeilles *f*, ffrind *m.*

friendly *a.* cyfeillgar

friendship *n.* cyfeillgarwch *m.*

fright *n.* braw, ofn *m.*

frighten *v.* codi ofn ar, brawychu

frightful *a.* dychrynllyd

frigid *a.* oer, rhewllyd

frivolity *n.* lol *f.*

frock *n.* ffrog *f.*

frog *n.* broga, ffroga *m.*

from *prp.* o, oddi, gan, oddi wrth, rhag

front 1 *n.* ffrynt, talcen, tu blaen *m.* **2** *a.* ffrynt, blaen. **front door** drws ffrynt: **front page** tudalen flaen; **front room** ystafell flaen: **front row** rhes flaen: **cold front** ffrynt oer: **warm front** ffrynt cynnes

frontier *n.* ffin *f.*

frost *n.* rhew *m.* **hoarfrost** barrug; **to cast hoar frost** llwydrewi

frosty *a.* rhewllyd

froth *n.* ewyn *m.*

frown 1 *n.* gwg *m.* **2** *v.* gwgu

frozen *a.* wedi rhewi

fruit *n.* ffrwyth *m*, ffrwythau *pl.* **fruit juice** sudd ffrwythau *m.*

fruitful *a.* ffrwythlon

fry *v.* ffrio

frying pan *n.* padell ffrio *f.*

fuel *n.* tanwydd *m.*

fugitive *n.* ffoadur *m.*

full *a.* llawn

full-back *n.* cefnwr *m.*

fullness *n.* llawnder, cyflawnder *m.*

fully *ad.* yn gyfan gwbl, yn hollol

fun *n.* hwyl *f*, miri *m.*

fund *n.* cronfa *f.*

fundamental *a.* sylfaenol

funeral *n.* angladd *mf.*

funnel *n.* twndis, corn, twmffat *m.*

funny *a.* digrif, ysmala, doniol

fur *n.* ffwr, blew *m.*

furious *a.* ffyrnig, yn gacwn wyllt, crac

furnace *n.* ffwrn, ffwrnais *f.*

furnishings *n.* dodrefn *pl. m.*

furniture *n.* celfi, dodrefn *pl. m.* **piece of furniture** celficyn, dodrefnyn.

furry *a.* blewog

further *ad.* bellach, ymhellach. **further education** addysg bellach

fuss *n.* helynt *f*, trafferth, ffws, stŵr *m.* ffwdan *f.*

fussy *a.* ffyslyd, ffwdanus

future *n. & a.* dyfodol *m.*

G

gain 1 *n.* elw, ennill *m*, enillion *pl.* **2** *v.* elwa, ennill

gale *n.* gwynt cryf *m.* tymestl *f.*

gallery *n.* oriel *f*, galeri *m*, llofft *f.*

gallon *n.* galwyn *m.*

gallop *v.* carlamu

gamble *v.* hapchwarae, gamblo

game *n.* gêm *f*, chwarae *m*, camp *f*.

gang *n.* mintai *f*, torf, haid, gang *f*.

gaol 1 *n.* carchar *m*. 2 *v.* carcharu

gap *n.* bwlch, adwy *m*.

garage *n.* garej *f*.

garbage *n.* ysbwriel, sothach *m*.

garden 1 *n.* gardd *f*. 2 *v.* garddio; **National Botanic Garden of Wales** Gardd Fotaneg Genedlaethol

gardener *n.* garddwr *m*.

garlic *n.* garlleg *m*.

garment *n.* pilyn *m*, gwisg *f*, dilledyn *m*.

gas *n* nwy *m*. **Gas Board** Bwrdd Nwy; **gas mask** mwgwd nwy

gate *n.* clwyd, gât, iet, llidiart *f*.

gateway *n.* mynedfa *f*.

gather *v.* casglu, crynhoi, cynnull, hel

gathering *n.* casgliad, cynulliad *m*.

gem *n.* gem *f*, tlws *m*.

gender *n.* rhyw *mf*, cenedl *f*.

gene *n.* genyn *m*.

general 1 *n.* cadfridog *m*. 2 *a.* cyffredin, cyffredinol. **general election** etholiad cyffredinol; **General Certificate of Secondary Education (GCSE)** Tystysgrif Gyffredinol Addysg Uwch (TGAU)

generally *ad.* yn gyffredinol

generation *n.* cenhedlaeth, to *m*.

generosity *n.* haelioni *m*.

generous *a.* hael, haelionus

genetic *a.* genetig

genial *a.* tyner, tirion, hynaws

genteel *a.* bonheddig

gentle *a.* tyner, mwyn

gentleman *n.* bonheddwr, gŵr bonheddig, uchelwr *m*.

gentleness *n.* tynerwch, addfwynder *m*.

gently *ad.* yn dyner, yn addfwyn; gan bwyll

gents *n.* toiledau dynion *m.pl*.

Insight

gathering *n. casgliad, cynulliad m.* The Welsh Assembly (*Y Cynulliad*) is a collection or gathering of public representatives from different parts of Wales and the political spectrum.

---

gaunt *a.* llwm, tenau

gauntlet *n.* maneg *f*.

gay *a.* llon, bywiog, hoyw

gaze *v.* edrych, syllu, rhythu

gear *n.* gêr *mf*, offer *pl*.

genuine *a.* diffuant, cywir, pur

geography *n.* daearyddiaeth *f*.

geology *n.* daeareg *f*.

geometry *n.* geometreg *mf*.

germ *n.* germ *m.*

German 1 *n.* Almaeneg *(iaith)* *f.* Almaenwr *(person)* *m.* **2** *a.* Almaenaidd

Germany *n.* yr Almaen *f.*

get *v.* cael, ennill

ghost *n.* ysbryd *m,* drychiolaeth *f.*

giant *n.* cawr *m.*

gift *n.* anrheg, rhodd *f.*

gifted *a.* talentog, dawnus

gigantic *a.* anferth

gipsy *n.* sipsi *m.*

giraffe *n.* jiráff *m.*

girder *n.* trawst *m.*

girl *n.* merch, geneth, croten, hogen, llances *f.*

give *v.* rhoddi, rhoi. **to give generously** rhoi'n hael. **to give up** rhoi'r gorau i

glad *a.* llawen, llon, balch

gladly *ad.* yn llawen, â phleser

Glamorgan *n.* Morgannwg *f.* **Mid Glamorgan** Morgannwg Ganol; **South Glamorgan** De Morgannwg; **West Glamorgan** Gorllewin Morgannwg *(1974–1996)*

glance *n.* cipolwg *m,* trem *f,* cip *m.*

glass *n.* gwydr, gwydryn *m.*

gleam 1 llewyrch *m.* **2** *v.* llewyrchu

glen *n.* glyn, cwm, dyffryn *m.*

glide 1 *n.* llithriad *m.* **2** *v.* llithro dros

glitter *v.* disgleirio, serennu

glorious *a.* gogoneddus

glory *n.* gogoniant, ysblander *m.*

Gloucester *n.* Caerloyw *f.*

glove *n.* maneg *f.*

glower *v.* gwgu, cuchio

glue 1 *n.* glud *m.* **2** *v.* gludo, gludio, glynu

gnat *n.* gwybedyn *m.*

go *v.* cer! dos! *(unigol)*; cerwch! ewch! *(lluosog); see* mynd

goal *n.* gôl *f.* **goalkeeper** golgeidwad, golwr *m.*

goat *n.* gafr *f.*

god *n.* duw *m.* **God** Duw

goddess *n.* duwies *f.*

godly *a.* duwiol

gold *n.* aur *m.*

golden *a.* euraid, euraidd

goldfish *n.* pysgod aur *m.pl.*

golf *n.* golff *m.* **golf course** maes golffio

golfer *n.* golffwr *m.*

good *n. & a.* da. **good afternoon** prynhawn da; **good day** dydd da; **good evening** noswaith dda; **good morning** bore da; **good night** nos da; **good luck** lwc dda; **good weather** tywydd da; **Good gracious!** Bobol annwyl! **Good health!** Iechyd da!

goodbye 1 *n.* ffarwél *m.* **2** *i.* da bo chi! hwyl! yn iach!

goodness *n.* daioni *m.*

goods *n.* eiddo *m,* nwyddau, da *m.pl.*

goodwill *n.* ewyllys da *m.*

goose *n.* gŵydd *f.*

gosling *n.* cyw gŵydd *m.*

gospel *n.* efengyl *f.* **the Gospel according to John** yr Efengyl yn ôl Ioan

govern *v.* llywodraethu, rheoli

government *n.* llywodraeth *f.*

governor *n.* llywodraethwr, rheolwr *m.*

Gower *n.* Gŵyr *f.*

gown *n.* gŵn *f.*

grace *n.* gras *m.*

graceful *a.* lluniaidd, urddasol

grade 1 *n.* gradd, safon *f.* 2 *v.* graddio

gradual *a.* graddol

graduate 1 *n.* gŵr gradd *m.* 2 *v.* graddio

gram *n.* gram *m.*

grammar *n.* gramadeg *m.* **Grammar School** Ysgol Ramadeg

grammatical *a.* gramadegol

grand *a.* mawreddog, ardderchog, crand; prif, uchel. **grand concert** cyngerdd mawreddog

grandchild *n.* ŵyr *m,* wyres *f.*

granddaughter *n.* wyres *f.*

grandeur *n.* mawredd *m.*

grandfather *n.* tad-cu, taid *m.*

grandmother *n.* mam-gu, nain *f.*

grandson *n.* ŵyr *m.*

grant 1 *n.* rhodd *f,* grant, cymhorthdal *m.* 2 *v.* caniatáu.

grapefruit *n.* grawnffrwyth *m.*

grapes *n.pl.* grawnwin

grass *n.* glaswellt *m,* porfa *f:* **grasshopper** ceiliog y rhedyn, sioncyn y gwair

grateful *a.* diolchgar

gratefulness *n.* diolchgarwch *m.*

gratitude *n.* diolchgarwch *m.*

grave 1 *n.* bedd *m.* 2 *a.* difrifol, dwys, prudd

gravestone *n.* carreg fedd *f.*

graveyard *n.* mynwent *f.*

graze *v.* pori

grease 1 *n.* saim *m.* 2 *v.* iro

greasy *a.* seimlyd, seimllyd

great *a.* mawr. **a great many** llawer iawn

great-grandfather *n.* hen dad-cu, hendaid *m.*

great-grandmother *n.* hen fam-gu, hennain *f.*

greatly *ad.* yn fawr

greatness *n.* mawredd *m.*

Grecian 1 *n.* Groegwr *m.* 2 *a.* Groegaidd

Greece *n.* Groeg, Gwlad Groeg *f.*

greed *n.* trachwant *m.*

greedy *a.* trachwantus

Greek 1 *n.* Groeg *f (iaith);* Groegwr *m. (person).* 2 *a.* Groeg, Groegaidd

green 1 *a.* gwyrdd, gwerdd, glas. 2 *v.* glasu

greenhouse *n.* tŷ gwydr *m.*

greet *v.* cyfarch, annerch

greeting *n.* cyfarchiad *m.*

grey *a.* llwyd, glas: **to turn grey** llwydo, britho, brithio

greyhound *n.* milgi *m.*

grief *n.* galar, gofid, hiraeth *m.*

grievance *n.* cwyn *mf.*

grieve *v.* gofidio, hiraethu

grievous *a.* gofidus, poenus, blin, difrifol

grind *v.* malu

grip 1 *n.* gafael *f.* 2 *v.* gafael (yn), gwasgu

gripping *a.* gafaelgar

groan *v.* ochneidio, griddfan

gross 1 *n.* gros *m.* 2 *a.* bras.
gross weight pwysau gros

ground 1 *n.* daear *f*, tir *m*; sail *f*; cae chwarae *m.* 2 *v.* gwreiddio, seilio

groundless *a.* di-sail

group *n.* grŵp, twr *m.*

grove *n.* llwyn *m*, celli *f.*

grow *v.* tyfu, prifio, codi

growing *a.* yn tyfu

growth *n.* tyfiant *m.*

grubby *a.* brwnt, budr

guard 1 *n.* gwyliwr, gard *m.* 2 *v.* gwarchod, gwylio

guerilla *n.* herwfilwr *m.*

guess 1 *n.* amcan, dyfaliad *m.* 2 *v.* dyfalu

guest *n.* gwestai, gŵr gwadd *m*, gwraig wadd *f.*

guests *n.* gwesteion, gwahoddedigion *m.pl.*

guide 1 *n.*, arweinydd, hyfforddwr, tywysydd *m.* 2 *v.* arwain, tywys

guild *n.* cymdeithas, urdd *f.*

guilt *n.* euogrwydd, bai *m.*

guilty *a.* euog

guitar *n.* gitâr *m.*

gulf *n.* gwlff *m.*

gull *n.* gwylan *f.*

gulp *v.* llyncu, traflyncu

gum *n* gwm, glud; cig (y dannedd) *m.*

gun *n.* dryll, gwn *m.*

guts *n.* perfedd *m.*

gymnasium *n.* campfa *f.*

H

habit *n.* arfer *mf;* gwisg *f.*

had, he/she/it *v.* cafodd. **I had** ces i, cefais: *see* cael

hag *n.* gwrach *f.*

hail 1 *n.* cesair, cenllysg *coll.& pl.* 2 *v.* bwrw cesair; cyfarch, galw. 3 *i.* henffych well!

hailstones *n.* cesair *coll. & pl.*

hair *n.* gwallt; blewyn *m.*

hairbrush *n.* brwsh gwallt *m.*

hairy *a.* blewog

half *n.* hanner *m.*

half-back *n.* hanerwr *m.*

hall *n.* neuadd *f*, llys, plas; cyntedd *m.*

Hallowe'en *n.* Nos Galan Gaeaf *f.*

hammer 1 *n.* morthwyl *m.* 2 *v.* morthwylio

hand *n.* llaw *f; (of clock)* bys *m.* **hands** dwylo. **in hand** mewn llaw, ar waith

handbag *n.* bag llaw *m.*

handbook *n.* llawlyfr *m.*

handful *n.* dyrnaid *m*, llond llaw *f.*

handkerchief *n.* cadach *m*, hances, neisied *f*, macyn *m.*

handle *n.* dolen *f.* 2 *v.* trafod, trin

handsome *a.* hardd, glân, prydferth, golygus

handwork *n.* gwaith llaw *m.*

handwriting *b.* llawysgrifen *f.*
hang *v.* hongian; crogi
hankering *n.* ysfa *f.*
happen *v.* digwydd
happening *n.* digwyddiad *m.*
happily *ad.* yn hapus
happiness *n.* hapusrwydd, llawenydd *m.*
happy *a.* dedwydd, hapus, llawen, wrth ei fodd, wrth ei bodd
harbour 1 *n.* harbwr *m*, hafan *f*, porth, porthladd *m.* **2** *v.* llochesu
hard *a.* caled, anodd
harden *v.* caledu
hardly *ad.* o'r braidd
hardness *n.* caledwch *m.*
hardship *n.* caledi *m.*
hard shoulder *n.* llain galed *f.*
hard-up *a.* prin o arian
hardwood *n.* pren caled *m.*
hardworking *a.* gweithgar
hardy *a.* caled
hare *n.* ysgyfarnog *f.*
harm *n.* cam, drwg, niwed *m.*
harmless *a.* diniwed
harp 1 *n.* telyn *f.* **2** *v.* canu'r delyn
harpist *n.* telynor *m.*, telynores *f.*
harsh *a.* llym, garw, cras
harvest *n.* cynhaeaf
haste 1 *n.* brys, prysurdeb *m.* **2** *v.* brysio, prysuro, cyflymu
hasten *v.* brysio
hastily *ad.* yn frysiog
hasty *a.* brysiog
hat *n.* het *f.*
hate 1 *n.* cas, casineb *m.* **2** *v.* casáu

hatred *n.* cas, casineb *m.*
haul *v.* tynnu, llusgo
have, I *v.* caf. **he/she/it will have** caiff; *see* cael
haven *n.* hafan *f.*
hawk *n.* hebog *m.*
hawthorn *n.* draenen wen *f.*
hay *n.* gwair *m*, porfa *f.*
hazard *n.* perygl *m*, antur *mf.*
haze *n.* niwl, tawch *m.*
hazel *n.* collen *f.*
hazy *a.* niwlog
he *pn.* ef, fe, efe, efo, fo, yntau
head 1 *n.* pen, pennaeth *m.* **2** *a.* prif
headache *n.* pen tost, cur yn y pen *m.*
heading *n.* pennawd, teitl *m.*
headland *n.* penrhyn *m.*
headline *n.* pennawd, teitl *m.* **news headlines** penawdau'r newyddion
headmaster *n.* prifathro *m.*
headmistress *n.* prifathrawes *f.*
headquarters *n.* pencadlys *m.*
heal *v.* iacháu, gwella
health *n.* iechyd. **Health Service** Gwasanaeth Iechyd
healthy *a.* iach, iachus
heap *n.* pentwr, twr *m.*
hear *v.* clyw! *(unigol)*, clywch! *(lluosog); see* clywed
hearer *n.* gwrandawr *m.*
hearing *n.* clyw; gwrandawiad *m.* **hearing aid** cymorth clywed
heart *n.* calon *f.* **heart attack** trawiad ar y galon

hearth *n.* aelwyd *f.*

heat 1 *n.* gwres *m.* **2** *v.* poethi, twymo, gwresogi

heater *n.* gwresogydd *m.*

heath *n.* rhos *f,* rhostir *m.*

heather *n.* grug *m.*

heave 1 *n.* gwthiad, hwb *m.* **2** *v.* gwthio, codi

heaven *n.* nef, nefoedd, nen *f.*

heavenly *a.* nefol, nefolaidd

heavens *n.* ffurfafen, wybren *f.*

heavy *a.* trwm *m.* trom *f.*

Hebrew 1 *n.* Hebraeg *f.* *(iaith);* Hebrëwr, *m.* Hebrëes *f.* **2** *a.* Hebraeg, Hebreig

hedge *n.* perth *f,* clawdd, gwrych *m.*

hedgehog *n.* draenog *m.*

heed 1 *n.* sylw *m.* ystyriaeth *f.* **2** *v.* sylwi, ystyried, hidio

heedful *a.* ystyriol, gofalus

heel 1 *n.* sawdl *mf.* **2** *v.* sodli

height *n.* uchder, uchelder *m.*

heir *n.* aer, etifedd *m.*

heiress *n.* aeres, etifeddes *f.*

helicopter *n.* hofrennydd *f.*

hell *n.* uffern *f.*

hellish *a.* uffernol

hello *i.* helô! hylô! clyw! gwrando!

helm *n.* llyw *m.*

help 1 *n.* cymorth, help *m.* **2** *v.* cynorthwyo, helpu

helper *n.* cynorthwywr, cynorthwy-ydd, helpwr *m.*

hem *n.* hem *f,* godre *m,* ymyl *mf.*

hen *n.* iâr *f.*

henceforth *ad.* mwyach, o hyn ymlaen

her *pn.* ei, hi, hithau

herb *n.* llysieuyn *m.*

herbal *a.* llysieuol

herbs *n.* llysiau pêr, perlysiau *m.pl.*

herd *n.* gyr *m,* cenfaint *f.*

here *ad* yma, yn y man hwn

hermit *n.* meudwy *m.*

hero *n.* arwr *m.*

heroine *n* arwres *f.*

hers *pn.* ei, ei heiddo

hew *v.* torri, naddu

hexagon *n.* hecsagon *m.*

hiccup *n.* yr ig *m.*

hide 1 *n.* croen *m.* **2** *v.* cuddio. **hide and seek** chwarae mig

high *a.* uchel; mawr; cryf; llawn. **most high** goruchaf

higher *a.* uwch

highest *a.* uchaf

highland *n.* ucheldir *m.*

highly *ad.* yn fawr, yn uchel

highness *n.* uchder, uchelder; mawrhydi *m.* **His Highness** Ei Fawrhydi

highway *n.* priffordd *f.*

highwayman *n.* lleidr penffordd *m.*

hijack 1 *n.* herwgipiad *m.* **2** *v.* herwgipio

hill *n.* allt *f,* bryn *m,* rhiw *f,* tyle *m.*

hillock *n.* bryncyn, twmpath *m.*

him *pn.* ef, fe, efe, efô, fo, yntau

hindrance *n.* rhwystr *m.*
hint 1 *n.* awgrym *m.* **2** *v.* awgrymu.
hip *n.* clun *f.*
hire 1 *n.* cyflog *mf.* **2** *v.* cyflogi, llogi
his *pn.* ei, ei eiddo
historian *n.* hanesydd, haneswr *m.*
history *n.* hanes *m.* **History of Wales** Hanes Cymru
hit 1 *n.* ergyd *mf,* trawiad *m.* **2** *v.* taro
hoarfrost *n.* llwydrew, barrug *m.*
hoary *a.* llwyd
hoax 1 *n.* tric, twyll *m.* **2** *v.* twyllo
hold 1 *n.* gafael *f.* **2** *v.* dal, dala, gafael
hole 1 *n.* twll *m;* ffau *f.* **2** *v.* tyllu
holiday *n.* gŵyl *f.*
holidays *n.* gwyliau *pl.* **Christmas holidays** gwyliau Nadolig: **summer holidays** gwyliau haf
hollow 1 *n.* pant *m.* **2** *a.* gwag, cau
holly *n.* celyn *pl,* celynnen *f.* **holly bush** llwyn celyn
holy *a.* sanctaidd, glân, gwyn: **Holy Spirit** Ysbryd Glân
Holyhead *n.* Caergybi *f.*

home 1 *n.* cartref *m,* aelwyd *f.* **2** *ad.* adref, tua thref. **at home** gartref: **going home** mynd adref, mynd tua thref
homeless *a.* digartref
homesick *a.* hiraethus
homesickness *n.* hiraeth *m.*
homestead *n.* tyddyn *m.*
homeward *ad.* adref, tua thref
homework *n.* gwaith cartref *m.* **homework book** llyfr gwaith cartref
homosexuality *n.* gwrywgydiaeth *f.*
honest *a.* cywir, gonest, onest
honesty *n.* gonestrwydd, onestrwydd *m.*
honey *n.* mêl *m.*
honeymoon *n.* mis mêl
honour 1 *n.* anrhydedd *mf.* **2** *v.* anrhydeddu; urddo; cydnabod
hook 1 *n.* bach, bachyn; cryman *m.* **2** *v.* bachu
hoop *n.* cylch *m.*
hooray *i. & n.* hwrê
hope 1 *n.* gobaith *m.* **2** *v.* gobeithio
horizon *n.* gorwel *m.*
horn *n.* corn *m. (automobile).*
horrendous *a.* dychrynllyd, ofnadwy
horrible *a.* ofnadwy
horse *n.* ceffyl, march *m.*

Insight

horse *n. ceffyl, march m.* The horse has now been displaced on most farms by the ubiquitous tractor, but is still revered as one of the most intelligent of animals.

horseman *n.* marchog *m.*
horseshoe *n.* pedol *f.*
hospice *n.* ysbyty, llety *m.*
hospitable *a.* croesawus,
lletygar
hospital *n.* ysbyty *m.*
host *n.* llu *m*, byddin *f*;
gwesteiwr, lletywr *m.*
hostage *n.* gwystl *m.*
hostel *n.* neuadd breswyl *f.*
hostess *n.* gwesteiwraig *f.*
hot *a.* twym, poeth, gwresog.
hot-water bottle potel ddŵr
twym/poeth
hotel *n.* gwesty *m.*
hotelier *n.* gwestywr *m.*
hound 1 *n.* ci hela, helgi *m.*
2 *v.* hela, erlid
hour *n.* awr *f.*
hourly *ad.* bob awr
house *n.* tŷ *m.*
housework *n.* gwaith tŷ *m.*
housewife *n.* gwraig tŷ *f.*
housing *n.* tai *pl.*
how *ad.* sut, pa fodd, pa. how
many? faint?
however *ad.* sut bynnag, er
hynny, pa fodd bynnag
howl *v.* udo
hue *n.* lliw *m.* gwawr *f.*
hug *v.* cofleidio, gwasgu
huge *a.* anferth, enfawr
hum 1 *n.* si, sibrwd *m.* 2 *v.*
mwmian
humble *a.* gostyngedig, isel
humorous *a.* doniol
humour *n.* hiwmor *m*, hwyl *f.*
hundred 1 *n.* cant *m.* 2 *a.*
can. hundred years old
canmlwydd

hundredth *n. & a.* canfed
hunger 1 *n.* newyn, chwant
bwyd *m.* 2 *v.* newynu
hunt *n.* helfa *f.* 2 *v.* hel, hela,
erlid
hunter *n.* heliwr; ceffyl hela
m.
hunting *n.* hela *m.* hunting
horn corn hela
hurricane *n.* corwynt *m.*
hurry 1 *n.* brys, prysurdeb *m.*
2 *v.* brysio, prysuro
hurt 1 *n.* niwed, dolur *m.* 2 *v.*
anafu, brifo
husband *n.* gŵr, priod, gŵr
priod *m.*
hut *n.* caban, cwt *m.*
hutch *n.* cwt, cwb *m.*
hydrogen *n.* hydrogen *m.*
hymn *n.* emyn, hymn *m.*
hymnal *n.* llyfr emynau *m.*
hymn-tune *n.* emyn-dôn *f.*
hypermarket *n.* archfarchnad
f.
hyphen *n.* cyplysnod,
cysylltnod *m.*

I

I *pn.* mi, myfi; fi, i; minnau,
innau
ice *n.* iâ, rhew *m.* Ice Age
Oes yr Iâ
iceberg *n.* mynydd iâ *m.*
ice-cream *n.* hufen iâ *m.*
Iceland *n.* Gwlad yr Iâ *f.*
icy *a.* rhewllyd.
idea *n.* syniad *m.*
identical *a.* yr un *(fath).*
identify *v.* abnabod *(fel yr un
un)*, enwi, nodi; uniaethu (â)

idiom *n.* priod-ddull, idiom *f.*
idle 1 *a.* segura, diog, dioglyd. **2** *v.* segur, diogi
idler *n.* diogyn, pwdryn *m.*
idol *n.* delw *f.*
if *c.* os, pe
ignite *v.* tanio
ill *a.* claf, gwael, sâl, tost; drwg
ill-mannered *a.* anfoesgar
illness *n.* afiechyd, clefyd, dolur, salwch, tostrwydd *m.*
illustrate *v.* darlunio; egluro, esbonio
illustration *n.* darlun *m.*
image *n.* delw *f.*, llun *m.*
imagination *n.* dychymyg *m.*
imagine *v.* dychmygu, tybied, tybio
immediately *ad.* ar unwaith, yn union, yn y man
immense *a.* anferth, eang
imminent *a.* agos, gerllaw, wrth y drws
immunization *n.* imwneiddiad *m.*
immunize *v.* imwneiddio
immunity *n.* imwnedd *m.*
impart *v.* cyfrannu, rhoi
imperative 1 *n.* gorchymyn *m.* **2** *a.* gorchmynnol, gorfodol
imperfect *a.* amherffaith
impinge *v.* taro yn erbyn, cyffwrdd â
implement 1 *n.* offeryn. arf *m.* **2** *v.* gweithredu
implore *v.* erfyn (ar)
imply *v.* cyfleu, awgrymu
importance *n.* pwys, pwysigrwydd *m.*

important *a.* pwysig
impossible *a.* amhosibl
impress 1 *n.* argraff *f.* **2** *v.* argraffu, pwyso (ar)
impression *n.* argraff
imprison *v.* carcharu
improve *v.* gwella
impudence *n.* haerllugrwydd *m.*
impudent *a.* haerllug, eofn
in 1 *prp.* yn, yng, ym, mewn. **2** *ad.* i mewn. **in the midst of** ynghanol: **in time** mewn pryd
inaccurate *a.* anghywir, gwallus
inasmuch *ad.* yn gymaint (â)
inch *n.* modfedd *f.*
incident *n.* digwyddiad *m.*
incinerator *n.* llosgydd *m*, ffwrnais *f.*
include *v.* cynnwys
included *a.* cynwysedig
including *prp.* gan gynnwys
inclusive *a.* gan gynnwys, cynwysedig
income *n.* enillion *pl*, incwm *m.* **Income Tax** Treth Incwm
incorporate *v.* ymgorffori
incorrect *a.* anghywir
indebted *a.* dyledus
indeed *ad.* yn wir, iawn
indemnity *n.* iawndal *m.*
independence *n.* annibyniaeth *f.*
independent *n.* annibynnwr *m.*
independent *a.* annibynnol
independently *ad.* yn annibynnol, ar wahân
index *n.* mynegai *m.*

India *n.* Yr India *f.*
Indian 1 *n.* Indiad *m.* **2** *a.*
Indiaidd
Indicate *v.* dangos, mynegi
indigestion *n.* diffyg traul *m.*
individual 1 *n.* un, unigolyn *m.*
2 *a.* unigol
indolent *a.* diog, dioglyd,
segur, pwdr
indoor *a.* i mewn, dan do
induct *v.* sefydlu
induction *n.* sefydliad *m.*
indulgence *n.* maldod *m.*
industrious *a.* gweithgar
industry *n.* diwydiant;
diwydrwydd *m.*
ineffectual *a.* aneffeithiol
inevitable *a.* anochel

inflation *n.* chwyddiant *m.*
influence 1 *n.* dylanwad *m.*
2 *v.* dylanwadu
influenza *n.* ffliw *m.*
inform *v.* hysbysu
information *n.* gwybodaeth *f.*
infrequent *a.* anaml
ingredients *n.* defnyddiau,
cynhwysion *m.pl.*
inhabitants *n.* trigolion,
preswylwyr *m.pl.*
inhale *v.* anadlu
inherit *v.* etifeddu
iniquity *n.* drwg, drygioni,
anwiredd *m.*
injection *n.* chwistrelliad,
pigiad *m.*
injure *v.* anafu, niweidio

Insight

inevitable *a. anochel.* The word in Welsh has an ominous
sound that heralds the onset of a disaster.

inexpensive *a.* rhad
inexperience *n.* diffyg profiad
m.
inexperienced *a.* dibrofiad
infant *n.* baban, maban *m.*
Infants' school ysgol
fabanod: **Infants' teacher**
athrawes fabanod
infection *n.* haint *f.*
inferior *a.* is, israddol
infinitive *n.* berfenw *m.*
infirm *a.* gwan
infirmity *n.* gwendid, llesgedd
m.
inflammation *n.* llid *m.*
inflate *v.* chwyddo, rhoi awyr
yn

injury *n.* niwed, cam, clwyf,
anaf *m.*
inn *n.* tafarn *mf,* gwesty *m.*
inner *a.* mewnol
inn-keeper *n.* tafarnwr,
gwestywr *m.*
innocent *a.* diniwed
inoculation *n.* brechiad *m.*
inquire *v.* gofyn, holi, ymholi
inquiry *n.* ymchwiliad,
ymholiad *m.*
inquisition *n.* ymchwiliad *m.*
insane *a.* gwallgof
insect *n.* pryf, pryfedyn,
pryfyn *m.*

in-service *a.* mewn swydd. **in-service training** hyfforddiant mewn swydd
inside 1 *n.* tu mewn *m.* **2** *a.* mewnol. **3** *ad.* i mewn, o fewn. **4** *prp.* y tu mewn
inside-out *ad.* o chwith
insist *v.* mynnu
insolence *n.* haerllugrwydd *m.*
insolent *a.* haerllug
inspire *v.* ysbrydoli
instantaneous *a.* yn y man
instead *ad.* yn lle
institution *n.* sefydliad *m.*
instruct *v* . cyfarwyddo, dysgu, hyfforddi
instruction *n.* hyfforddiant *m.*
instructor *n.* hyfforddwr *m.*
instrument *n.* offeryn, arf *m.* **musical instrument** offeryn cerdd
instrumental *a.* offerynol; yn gyfrwng
insult *n.* sarhad *m.*
insurance *n.* yswiriant *m.*
insure *v.* yswiro, yswirio
insurrection *n.* terfysg, gwrthryfel *m.*
intellect *n.* deall *m.*
intelligent *a.* deallus
intelligentsia *n.* y deallus *m*, deallusion *m.pl.*
intend *v.* bwriadu, golygu
intense *a.* dwys
intent *n.* bwriad, amcan; diben *m.*
intention *n.* bwriad *m.*
interest *n.* diddordeb; llog; budd *m.* **interest rates** cyfraddau llog

interests *n.pl.* diddordebau *m.*
interfere *v.* ymhel, ymyrru, ymyrryd
interference *n.* ymyrraeth *f.*
interior 1 *n.* tu mewn, canol *m.* **2** *a.* mewnol
intermediate *a.* canol, canolradd
internal *a.* mewnol
international *a.* rhyngwladol **international eisteddfod** eisteddfod ryngwladol
internet *n.* rhyngrwyd *f.*
interpreter *n.* cyfieithydd *m.*
interrogate *v.* holi
interrogator *n.* holwr *m.*
interrupt *v.* torri ar, torri ar draws, ymyrru, ymyrryd
interval *n.* egwyl *f,* saib *m.*
intervene *v.* ymyrru, ymyrryd
interview 1 *n.* cyfweliad *m.* **2** *v.* cyfweld
into *prp.* i, i mewn
intoxicate *v.* meddwi
invalid *n.* un afiach, un methedig *mf.*
invalid *a.* di-rym
invest *v.* buddsoddi
investigate *v.* ymchwilio, chwilio
investigation *n.* ymchwiliad *m.*
investigator *n.* ymchwiliwr, ymchwilydd *m.*
invisible *a.* anweledig
invitation *n.* gwahoddiad, gwahodd *m.*
invite *v.* gwahodd
invited *a.* gwahoddedig
involved *a.* cymhleth, astrus, cywrain

inward *a.* mewnol
Ireland *n.* Iwerddon, Yr Ynys Werdd *f.*
Irish 1 *n.* Gwyddeleg *f. (iaith).* **2** *a.* Gwyddelig
Irishman *n.* Gwyddel *m.*
Irishwoman *n.* Gwyddeles *f.*
iron 1 *n. & a.* haearn *m.* **2** *v.* smwddio
ironing board *n.* bwrdd smwddio *m.*
irritable *a.* pigog, piwis
irritation *n.* poen *mf,* llid, *m,* enynfa *f.*

J

jackdaw *n.* jac-y-do *m.*
jacket *n.* siaced *f.*
jail *n.* carchar *m.*
jam 1 *n.* jam *m.;* tagfa *f.* **2** *v.* gwasgu, tagu
January *n.* Ionawr *m.*
Japan *n.* Japan *f.*
Japanese 1 *n.* Japanaeg *f. (iaith);* Japanead *m.* **2** *a.* Japaneaidd
jar 1 *n* jar, jâr *f.* **2** *v.* ysgwyd
jaundice *n.* y clefyd melyn *m.*

Insight

The Welsh equivalent for 'jaundice' emphasises the skin colour of the sick person – *y clefyd melyn m.*

is *v.* ydy, yw, mae, oes, sy, sydd
island *n.* ynys *f.* **Caldy Island** Ynys Bŷr: **Bardsey Island** Ynys Enlli
Israel *n.* Israel *f.*
Israelite *n.* Israeliad *m.*
issue 1 *n.* llif, tarddiad; plant; cyhoeddiad *m.* **2** *v.* tarddu; cyhoeddi
it *pn.* ef, efe, fe, efo, fo; hi
Italian *n.* Eidaleg *f. (iaith);* Eidalwr *m,* Eidales *f.*
Italy *n.* Yr Eidal *f.*
itch 1 *n.* crafu *m,* ysfa *f.* **2** *v.* cosi, ysu
item *n.* eitem *f.*
its *pn.* ei
itself *pn* ei hun, ei hunan
ivy *n.* iorwg, eiddew *m.*

jaw *n.* gên, cern *f.*
jay *n.* sgrech y coed *m.*
jealous *a.* cenfigennus
jeer 1 *n.* gwawd *m.* **2** *v.* gwawdio
jelly *n.* jeli *m.*
jerk 1 *n.* plwc *m.* **2** *v.* plycio
jersey *n.* jersi, jyrsi, siersi *f.*
Jerusalem *n.* Caersalem, Jerwsalem *f.*
Jesus *n.* Iesu *m.* **Jesus Christ** Iesu Grist: **Jesus Son of God** Iesu Mab Duw
Jew *n.* Iddew *m.*
Jewess *n.* Iddewes *f.*
jewel *n.* gem *f,* tlws *m.*
Jewish *a.* Iddewig
jingle *n.* rhigwm; tinc *m.*
job *n.* job, jobyn, gwaith *m,* swydd *f.* **Job Centre** Canolfan Gwaith *mf.*

jobless *a.* diwaith
jog *v.* loncian
jogger *n.* lonciwr *m.*
join *v.* cydio; ymuno; uno; ymaelodi
joiner *n.* saer coed *m.*
joint 1 *n.* cyswllt, cymal *m.* 2 *a.* cyd. cyd-. **joint authors** cydawduron. 3 *v.* torri'n ddarnau. 4 *n.* **joint of meat** darn o gig *m.*
joke 1 *n.* jôc *f.* 2 *v.* jocan, cellwair
jolly *a.* braf, llawen, llon
journalist *n.* newyddiadurwr *m.*
journey 1 *n.* hynt, siwrnai, taith *f.* 2 *v.* teithio
joy *n.* llawenydd *m.*
joyful 1 *a.* llawen, llon. 2 *v.* llawenhau
jubilation *n* . llawenydd, gorfoledd *m.*
jubilee *n.* jiwbilî *f.*
Judaism *n.* Iddewaeth *f.*
judge 1 *n.* barnwr; beirniad; dyfarnwr *m.* 2 *v.* beirniadu; dyfarnu
judgement *n.* barn *f.* dyfarniad *m.*
jug *n.* jwg, siwg *f.*
juice *n.* sudd *m.*
juicy *a.* llawn sudd
July *n.* Gorffennaf *m.*

jumble 1 *n.* cymysgwch *m,* cymysgfa *f.* 2 *v.* cymysgu: **jumble sale** ffair sborion *f.*
jump 1 *n.* naid *f.* llam *m.* 2 *v.* neidio, llamu
jumper *n.* neidiwr *m;* jersi, jyrsi, siwmper *f.*
junction *n.* cydiad *m;* cyffordd *f.*
June *n.* Mehefin *m.*
junior *a.* iau; ieuaf. **junior school** ysgol iau
just 1 *a.* cyfiawn, cywir, iawn, teg. 2 *ad.* braidd, yn union, newydd. **just now** gynnau (fach)
justice *n.* cyfiawnder; ynad *m.* **Justice of the Peace** Ynad Heddwch
juvenile *a.* ieuanc, ifanc

K

kangaroo *n.* cangarŵ *m.*
keep 1 *n.* cadw *m;* amddiffynfa *f.* 2 *v.* cadw; cynnal
keeper *n.* ceidwad *m.*
kennel *n.* cwb, cenel *m.*
kerchief *n.* cadach *m,* hances *f,* macyn *m,* neisied *f.*
kettle *n.* tegell *m.*

Insight

kettle *n. tegell m.* An 'old verse' (*Hen Bennill*) gives the universal kettle a name: 'Mari, rhowch **Morgan** ar y tân ...' 'Mari, put **Morgan** on the fire ...' (to boil in order to brew some tea). An English equivalent might be: 'Polly put the kettle on ...'

key *n.* agoriad *m*, allwedd *f;*
cywair *m.* **keyhole** twll clo
kick 1 *n.* cic *f.* 2 *v.* cicio.
  drop kick cic adlam
kidnap 1 *n.* herwgydiad *m.*
  2 *v.* herwgydio
kidnapper *n.* herwgydiwr *m.*
kidney beans *n.pl.* ffa dringo,
  cidnabêns *pl.*
kill *v.* lladd
killer *n.* lladdwr *m.*
kilogram *n.* kilogram (kg.) *m.*
kilometre *n.* kilometr (km.)
  m.
kilowatt *n.* kilowat (kW.) *m.*
kin *n.* perthynas *mf.*
kind *n.* math, rhyw *m.*
kind *a.* caredig
kindergarten *n.* ysgol feithrin
  f.
kindliness *n.* caredigrwydd *m.*
kindly *a.* caredig, tirion
kindness *n.* caredigrwydd *m;*
  cymwynas *f.*
kindred *n.* perthynas *mf;*
  perthnasau *pl.*
king *n.* brenin *m.*
kingdom *n.* teyrnas *f.*
  Kingdom of Heaven Teyrnas
  Nefoedd: **United Kingdom**
  Teyrnas Unedig
kingfisher *n.* glas y dorlan *m.*
kingly *a.* brenhinol
kipper *n.* ciper *m.*
kiss 1 *n.* cusan *mf*, sws *m*
  2 *v.* cusanu
kitchen *n.* cegin *f.*
kitchenette *n.* cegin fach *f.*
kitchen garden *n.* gardd
  lysiau *f.*

kitten *n.* cath fach *f.*
knead *v.* tylino
knee *n.* glin *mf*, pen-glin,
  pen-lin *m.*
kneel *v.* penlinio
knife *n.* cyllell *f.* **bread knife**
  cyllell fara; **pocket knife**
  cyllell boced
knight *n.* marchog *m.*
knit *v.* gwau
knock 1 *n.* cnoc, ergyd *mf.*
  2 *v.* cnocio, curo, taro
knot 1 *n.* clwm, cwlwm *m.*
  2 *v.* clymu
know *v.* adnabod; gwybod: **I**
  know gwn, mi wn, rydw i'n
  gwybod; **to know well**
  gwybod yn iawn
knowing *a.* gwybodus; ffel
knowingly *ad.* yn fwriadol
knowledge *n.* gwybodaeth *f.*
knuckle *n.* migwrn, cymal *m.*

L

label 1 *n.* llabed, label, *f.* 2 *v.*
  labelu
laboratory *n* labordy *m.*
  language laboratory labordy
  iaith
laborious *a.* llafurus
labour 1 *n.* llafur, gwaith *m.*
  2 *v.* llafurio, gweithio. **the**
  Labour Party y Blaid Lafur
labourer *n.* labrwr, gweithiwr
  m.
lace 1 *n.* les *m.* 2 *v.* cau
  (esgidiau).
lack 1 *n.* eisiau, diffyg *m.* 2 *v.*
  bod mewn eisiau

lad *n.* llanc, hogyn, gwas, bachgen *m.*
ladder *n.* ysgol *f.*

lantern *n.* llusern *f.*
lap 1 *n.* arffed *f,* glin *mf.* **2** *v.* lapio

Insight

ladder *n.* ysgol *f.* The word *ysgol* is derived from two separate sources: (i) from Latin and Breton to give 'ladder', (ii) from a different Latin root with Cornish, Breton and Irish overtones to give 'school'.

---

laden *a.* llwythog
ladies *n.* arglwyddesau; boneddigesau; toiledau merched *pl.*
lady *n.* arglwyddes; boneddiges *f.*
lair *n.* ffau, gwâl, lloches *f.*
lake *n.* llyn *m.*
lamb *n.* oen *m.* **Paschal Lamb** Oen y Pasg.
lame 1 *a.* cloff. **2** *v.* cloffi
lameness *n.* cloffi, cloffni *m.*
lamp *n.* lamp *f:* **lampshade** lamplen *f.*
lamp post *n.* postyn lamp, polyn lamp *m.*
land 1 *n.* tir *m,* daear, gwlad, glan *f.* **2** *v.* glanio
landlady *n.* gwraig llety *f.*
landlord *n.* meistr tir, lletywr, tafarnwr *m.*
landscape *n.* tirlun *m.*
lane *n.* lôn *f.* **escape lane** lôn ddianc
language *n.* iaith *f.* **first language** iaith gyntaf, mamiaith; **second language** ail iaith; **foreign language** iaith dramor, iaith estron

lapel *n.* llabed *f.*
laptop *n.* gliniadur, sgrîn ben-glin *f.*
large *a.* mawr; eang; helaeth
largely *ad.* gan mwyaf
lark *n.* ehedydd, hedydd, uchedydd *m.*
laryngitis *n.* llwnc tost *m.*
lass *n.* geneth, hogen, llances, merch *f.*
last 1 *a.* diwethaf; olaf. **2** *ad.* yn ddiwethaf, yn olaf. **3** *v.* para, parhau, dal, dala. **last night** neithiwr; **last week** yr wythnos diwethaf; **last month** mis diwethaf; **last year** y llynedd; **at last** o'r diwedd; **the last word** y gair olaf
late *a.* hwyr; diweddar
lately *ad.* yn ddiweddar
later *ad.* wedyn, eto, yn ddiweddarach
latest *a.* diweddaraf
Latin *n.* Lladin *f.*
latter *a.* diwethaf, olaf
laugh *n. & v.* chwerthin *m.*
laughable *a.* chwerthinllyd
laughter *n.* chwerthin *m.*

launderette *n* . golchdy *m*.

lavatory *n*. tŷ-bach *m*, ystafell ymolchi *f*, toiled *m*.

lavender *n*. lafant *m*.

law *n*. cyfraith, deddf *f*.

lawn *n*. lawnt *f*.

lawyer *n*. cyfreithiwr *m*.

lax *a*. llac; esgeulus

lay *v*. gosod, dodi; dodwy

layer *n*. haenen *f*.

laze *v*. diogi, segura

laziness *n*. diogi *m*.

lazy *a*. diog, dioglyd, pwdr

lead *n*. plwm *m*.

lead *v*. arwain, tywys

leaden *a*. plwm

leader *n*. arweinydd; blaenwr *m*.

leaf *n*. deilen; dalen *f*.

leaflet *n*. taflen *f*.

league *n*. cynghrair *m*.

leak *v*. gollwng, colli, diferu

lean **1** *n*. cig coch *m*. **2** *a*. main, tenau. **3** *v*. pwyso (ar)

leap **1** *n*. llam *m*, naid *f*. **2** *v*. llamu, neidio. **leap year** blwyddyn naid

learn *v*. dysgu

learned *a*. dysgedig, hyddysg

learner *n*. dysgwr *m*.

learning **1** *n*. dysg *f*. **2** *v*. dysgu

lease *n*. les, prydles *f*.

least *a*. lleiaf; *see* bach. **at least** o leiaf

leather *n*. lledr *m*.

leave **1** *n*. caniatâd *m*. **2** *v*. gadael, ymadael

leaven *n*. lefain *m*.

lecture **1** *n*. darlith *f*. **2** *v*. darlithio

lecturer *n*. darlithiwr, darlithydd *m*.

ledge *n*. silff *f*; crib *mf*.

leek *n*. cenhinen *f*.

left *a*. chwith. **left-handed** llawchwith

leg *n*. coes *f*.

legend *n*. chwedl *f*.

legislate *v*. deddfu

leisure *n*. hamdden *f*.

leisurely *a*. hamddenol

lemon *n*. lemwn *m*. **lemonade** diod lemwn; **lemon juice** sudd lemwn

lend *v*. benthyca, rhoi benthyg

length *n*. hyd *m*. **at length** o'r diwedd

lengthen *v*. estyn, ymestyn

lengthy *a*. hir

less **1** *a. & n*. llai *m*. **2** *ad*. yn llai

lesson *n*. gwers *f*. **history lesson** gwers hanes; **Welsh lesson** gwers Gymraeg

lest *c*. rhag, rhag ofn, fel na

let *v*. caniatáu; gadael; gosod ar rent

lethal *a*. marwol

letter *n*. llythyr *m*; llythyren *f*.

lettuce *n*. letysen *f*.

level *n. & a*. gwastad *m*. lefel *f*. **spirit level** lefelydd

level crossing *n*. croesfan *f*.

liable *a*. agored, atebol

liar *n*. celwyddgi *m*.

liberal *a*. hael, haelionus

liberty *n*. rhyddid *m*.

librarian *n*. llyfrgellydd *m*.

library *n*. llyfrgell *f*.

licence *n.* trwydded *f.* **driving licence** trwydded yrru
lick *v.* llyfu, llio, llyo
lid *n.* clawr *m.* **saucepan lid** clawr sosban
lie 1 *n.* celwydd, anwiredd *n.* **2** *v.* dweud celwydd, dweud anwiredd; gorwedd
life *n.* bywyd, byw *m.*
lifeboat *n.* bad achub *m.*
life insurance *n.* yswiriant bywyd *m.*
lifeless *a.* marwaidd
lifetime *n.* oes *f.*
lift 1 *n.* lifft *m.* **2** *v.* codi
ligament *n.* gewyn
light 1 *n.* golau, goleuni, llewyrch *m.* **2** *a.* golau; ysgafn. **3** *v.* goleuo; tanio
lighten *v.* ysgafnhau, ysgafnu
lighthouse *n.* goleudy *m.*
lightning *n.* mellt, lluched *pl.*
like 1 *a.* tebyg. **2** *prp.* fel. **3** *v.* hoffi, caru
likeable *a.* dymunol
likely *a. & ad.* tebygol, tebyg
likeness *n.* tebygrwydd *m.*
likewise 1 *n.* yn yr un modd. **2** *c.* hefyd
liking *n.* hoffter *m.*
lily *n.* lili *f.* **lily of the valley** lili'r dyffrynnoedd
limb *n.* aelod *m*; cangen *f*; cymal *m.*
limit *n.* ffin *f*, terfyn *m.*
limp 1 *a.* llipa. **2** *v.* cloffi
line *n.* llinell *f*, llinyn *m*, lein *f.*
linen *n.* lliain *m.*
linesman *n.* llinellwr, ystlyswr *m.*

link 1 *n.* dolen *f.* **2** *v.* cydio
lion *n.* llew *m.*
lioness *n.* llewes *f.*
lip *n.* gwefus *f*, min *m.*
lipstick *n.* minlliw *m.*
liquid 1 *n.* hylif *m.* **2** *a.* hylif; gwlyb
list *n.* rhestr *f.*
listen *v.* gwrando
listener *n.* gwrandawr *m.*
literary *a.* llenyddol
literate *a.* llythrennog
literature *n.* llên, llenyddiaeth *f.*
litre *n.* litr *m.*
litter 1 *n.* sbwriel, ysbwriel *m.* **2** *v.* sarnu
littérateur *n.* llenor *m.*
little *a.* bach, bychan, bechan; mân, tamaid, ychydig
live *a. & v.* byw
lively *a.* bywiog, heini
liver *n.* iau *m*, afu *mf.*
Liverpool *n.* Lerpwl *f.*
living *a.* byw, yn fyw
load 1 *n.* baich, llwyth *m.* **2** *v.* llwytho
loaf *n.* torth *f.*
loathsome *a.* ffiaidd
lobby *n.* cyntedd, porth *m.*
local *a.* lleol. **Local Government** Llywodraeth Leol
locality *n.* lle *m*, ardal, cymdogaeth *f.*
localize *v.* lleoli
locate *v.* lleoli, gosod
location *n.* lleoliad *m.*
loch *n.* llyn, llwch *m.*
lock 1 *n.* clo *m.* **2** *v.* cloi**

locked *a.* ar glo, dan glo, ynghlo
lodge 1 *n.* llety *m.* **2** *v.* lletya
lodger *n.* lletywr *m.*
lodging(s) *n. (pl).* llety *m.*
loft *n.* llofft *f.*
loin *n.* llwyn *f.*
London *n.* Llundain *f.*
loneliness *n.* unigrwydd *m.*
lonely *a.* unig
long 1 *a.* hir, maith. **2** *v.* hiraethu. **long since** ers amser
longing *n.* hiraeth *m.*
look 1 *n.* golwg *mf,* trem *f.* **2** *v.* edrych, ysbïo
loose 1 *a.* llac, llaes, rhydd. **2** *v.* datod, llacio, rhyddhau
loosen *v.* llacio, rhyddhau, datod
lord *n.* arglwydd *m.* **The Lord** Yr Arglwydd; **the Lord's Prayer** Gweddi'r Arglwydd; **House of Lords** Tŷ'r Arglwyddi
lord mayor *n.* arglwydd faer *m.*
lorry *n.* lorri *f.*
lorry driver *n.* gyrrwr lorri *m.*
lose *v.* colli
loss *n.* colled *mf.*
loud *a.* uchel
loudest *a.* uchaf
Loughor *n.* Casllwchwr *f.*
lounge 1 *n.* lolfa *f.* **2** *v.* lolian
louse *n.* lleuen *f.*
love 1 *n.* cariad, serch *m.* **2** *v.* caru: **love-letter** llythyr caru
lovely *a.* hyfryd, teg, prydferth; braf

lover *n.* cariad *mf,* carwr *m.*
loving *a.* cariadus, serchus, serchog
low *a.* isel
lower 1 *a.* is. **2** *v.* gostwng, gollwng
lowest *a.* isaf; lleiaf
loyal *a.* ffyddlon, teyrngar
lozenge *n.* losinen, losen *f.*
luck *n.* lwc, ffortiwn *f.* **best of luck** lwc dda, pob hwyl
luckily *ad.* yn ffodus, yn lwcus
lucky *a.* ffodus, lwcus
lull 1 *n.* gosteg *m.* **2** *v.* suo
lullaby *n.* hwiangerdd *f.*
luminous *a.* golau, disglair, llachar
lungs *n.* ysgyfaint *pl.*
lupins *n.* bysedd y blaidd *pl.*
lust *n.* chwant, trachwant *m.*
lustful *a.* trachwantus
lustre *n.* llewyrch *m.*
luxurious *a.* moethus
lyric *n.* telyneg *f.*

M

machine *n.* peiriant *m.*
machinery peiriannau
mackintosh *n.* cot law *f.*
mad *a.* gwyllt, gwallgof
magazine *n.* cylchgrawn *m.*
magic *n.* hud, lledrith, swyn *m.*
magician *n.* dewin *m.*
magistrate *n.* ustus, ynad *m.*
magnificent *a.* gwych
magnifying glass *n.* chwyddwydr *m.*

magnitude *n.* maint, ehangder *m.*

magpie *n.* pioden *m.*

maid *n.* morwyn, merch *f.* **old maid** hen ferch

mail 1 *n.* y post *m.* **2** *v.* postio. **e-mail** e-bost

main *a.* pennaf, prif, mwyaf. **main road** ffordd fawr, priffordd; **mainland** y tir mawr

mainly *ad.* yn bennaf

majesty *n.* mawredd; mawrhydi *m.* **Her Majesty** Ei Mawrhydi

major 1 *n.* uwchgapten *m.* **2** *a.* prif, mwyaf

majority *n.* mwyafrif; oedran llawn *m.*

make *v.* gwneud, gwneuthur

make-up *n. & v.* coluro *m.*

male *n.* gwryw *m.*

man *n.* dyn, gŵr, mab *m.* **man of letters** llenor

manage *v.* rheoli, trin; llwyddo

manager *n.* rheolwr *m.*

manger *n.* preseb *m.*

manifest *v.* dangos, egluro

manipulate *v.* trin, trafod

manner *n.* modd, dull *m.*

manners *n.* moesau *pl.* **good manners** moesau da

manse *n.* tŷ gweinidog, mans *m.*

mansion *n.* plas, plasty *m.*

mantle *n.* mantell *f.*

manual 1 *n.* llawlyfr *m.* **2** *a.* perthynol i'r llaw

manure *n.* gwrtaith, tail *m.* tom *f.*

manuscript *n.* llawysgrif *f.*

many 1 *n.* llawer *m.* **2** *a.* llawer, aml, sawl. **how many** sawl; **too many** gormod

map *n.* map *n.*

March *n.* Mawrth *m.*

march 1 *n.* ymdaith *f.* **2** *v.* ymdeithio

margin *n.* ffin *f,* ymyl *mf.*

mariner *n.* llongwr, morwr *m.*

mark 1 *n.* nod, nam, ôl, marc *m.* **2** *v.* nodi, marcio

market 1 *n.* marchnad *f.* **2** *v.* marchnata

marriage *n.* priodas *f.*

married *a.* priod

marrow *n.* mêr *m.* **vegetable marrow** pwmpen *f.*

marry *v.* priodi

Mars *n.* Mawrth *m.*

mart *n.* mart *m.*

martyr *n.* merthyr *m.*

marvel 1 *n.* rhyfeddod *m.* **2** *v.* rhyfeddu, synnu

Insight

manners *n. moesau m.pl.* An old proverb, 'Manners maketh man', takes no note of fine clothes or money but relates to conduct, behaviour and customs (*ymddygiad, arferion a moesau*).

marvellous *a.* rhyfeddol, gwych

masculine *a.* gwryw, gwrywaidd, gwrywol

mask 1 *n.* mwgwd *m.* **2** *v.* cuddio

mass *n.* pentwr *m;* pwysau *pl;* offeren *f.*

massive *a.* anferth

master 1 *n.* meistr, capten *(llong) m.* **2** *v.* meistroli

masterpiece *n.* campwaith *m.*

mat *n.* mat *m.*

match *n.* matsien; gêm; gornest; priodas *f.*

material *n.* defnydd, nwydd *m.*

mathematical *a.* mathemategol

mathematician *n.* mathemategwr *m.*

mathematics *n.* mathemateg *f.*

matrimony *n.* priodas *f.*

matter *n.* mater *m.* **What's the matter?** Beth sy'n bod?

mature 1 *a.* aeddfed. **2** *v.* aeddfedu

maximum *n.* uchafswm, uchafrif, uchafbwynt *m.*

May *n.* Mai *m.* **May Day** Calan Mai

maybe *ad.* efallai, hwyrach

mayor *n.* maer *f.*

mayoress *n.* maeres *f.*

me *pn.* myfi, mi, fi, i; minnau

mead *n.* medd *m.*

meadow *n.* dôl, gwaun *f*, maes *m.*

meagre *a.* cul, llwm, tenau, prin

meal *n.* pryd o fwyd; blawd *m.*

mean 1 *n.* cyfrwng, modd; canol *m.* **2** *a.* sâl; gwael; tynn. **3** *v.* bwriadu, golygu, meddwl

meaning *n.* ystyr *mf*, meddwl *m.*

meaningful *a.* ystyrlon

means *n.* modd, moddion, cyfrwng; cyfoeth *m.* **by all means** ar bob cyfrif, wrth gwrs

measles *n.* y frech goch *f.*

measure *n.* mesur *m.*

meat *n.* cig *m.*

medal *n.* bathodyn *m*, medal *f.*

meddle *v.* ymhél, ymyrru, ymyrryd

media *n.* cyfryngau *pl.*

medicine *n.* moddion, ffisig *m;* meddyginiaeth *f.*

meditate *v.* myfyrio

meditation *n.* myfyrdod *m.*

medium 1 *n.* cyfrwng; canol *m.* **2** *a.* canol

medley *n.* cadwyn o alawon *f;* cymysgwch *m.*

meet *v.* cyfarfod, cwrdd (â); cyffwrdd

meeting *n.* cyfarfod, cwrdd *m;* oedfa *f.*

melody *n.* alaw, tôn *f.*

melt *v.* toddi

member *n.* aelod *m.* **to become a member** ymaelodi: **Member of Parliament (M.P.)** Aelod Seneddol (A.S.)

membership *n.* aelodaeth *f.*

memory *n.* cof *m.*

memory stick *n.* cofbin *m.*

mend *v.* gwella, trwsio, cyweirio

meningitis *n.* llid yr ymennydd *m.*

menstruation *n.* y misglwyf *m.*

mention *n. & v.* sôn (am) *mf.*

menu *n.* bwydlen *f.*

merchant *n.* masnachwr *m.*

merciful *a.* trugarog

mercifully *ad.* drwy drugaredd

Mercury *n.* Mercher *m.*

mercury *n.* arian byw, mercwri *m.*

mercy *n.* trugaredd *f.* **to be merciful** trugarhau

merit 1 *n.* teilyngdod *m.* 2 *v.* haeddu

mermaid *n.* môr-forwyn *f.*

merriment *n.* miri *m.*

merry *a.* llawen, llon

mess *n.* llanast(r) *m.*

message *n.* neges *f.*

messenger *n.* negesydd *m.*

metal *n.* metel *m.*

meteor *n.* seren wib *f.*

meter *n.* mesurydd *m.*

method *n.* dull, modd *m*, trefn *f.* **new methods** dulliau newydd

methodical *a.* trefnus

metre *n.* mesur; metr *m.* **kilometre** kilometr (km.)

metric *a.* metrig. **metric scale** graddfa fetrig

mew *v.* mewian

micro-chip *n.* meicro-sglodyn *m.*

microphone *n.* meic, meicroffon *m.*

microscope *n.* meicrosgop *m.*

microwave *n.* meicrodon *f.*

mid *a.* canol

midday *n.* canol dydd, hanner dydd *m.*

middle *n.* canol *m.*

middle-aged *a.* canol oed

midland *n.* canolbarth *m.* **the Midlands** Canolbarth Lloegr: **Mid Wales** Canolbarth Cymru

midnight *n.* canol nos, hanner nos *f.*

midst 1 *n.* canol, plith *m.* 2 *prp.* rhwng

might *n.* nerth, gallu *m.*

mighty *a.* grymus

mild *a.* mwyn, tyner, meddal, gwan. **become mild** mwynhau, tyneru

mile *n.* milltir *f:* **milestone** carreg filltir *f.*

milk 1 *n.* llaeth, llefrith *m.* 2 *v.* godro. **milkman** dyn llaeth

mill *n.* melin *f.*

million *n.* miliwn *f.* **millionaire** miliwnydd

mime 1 *n.* meim *m.* 2 *v.* meimio

mind 1 *n.* meddwl, bryd, bwriad *m.* 2 *v.* gwylio, gofalu, hidio

mindful *a.* gofalus, ystyriol

mine 1 *n.* pwll, mwynglawdd *m.* 2 *pn.* fy, yr eiddof i

miner *n.* glöwr, mwynwr *m.*

mineral *n.* mwyn *m.*

minimum *n.* lleiafswm, isafrif, isafbwynt *m.*

minister 1 *n.* gweinidog *m.* **2** *v.* gwasanaethu

minority *n.* lleiafrif *m.*

mint *n.* bathdy; mint, mintys *m.* **Royal Mint** Bathdy Brenhinol

minute *n.* munud *mf;* cofnod *m.* **minute book** llyfr cofnodion

minute *a.* bach, mân, manwl

miracle *n.* gwyrth *f.*

miraculous *a.* gwyrthiol

mirror *n.* drych *m.*

miscarriage *n.* erthyliad *m.*

miscarry *v.* erthylu; colli

mischief *n.* drwg, drygioni *m.*

mischievous *a.* drygionus

miserable *a.* gwael, truenus, diflas

misery *n.* trallod, trueni, diflastod *m.*

mislead *v.* camarwain, twyllo

miss *v.* colli, methu, gweld eisiau

missile *n.* taflegryn *m.*

mission *n.* cenhadaeth *f.*

missionary 1 *n.* cenhadwr *m;* cenhades *f.* **2** *a.* cenhadol

mist *n.* niwl *m.*

mistake *n.* camsyniad, gwall, camgymeriad *m.*

mistress *n.* meistres, athrawes *f:* **headmistress** prifathrawes

misty *a.* niwlog

misunderstand *v.* camddeall

mix *v.* cymysgu

mixed *a.* cymysg

mob *n.* torf, tyrfa, haid *f.*

mobile *a.* symudol. **mobile phone** ffôn symudol

mock *v.* gwawdio.

mode *n.* modd, dull *m.*

modern *a.* diweddar, modern

moist *a.* llaith, gwlyb

moisten *v.* gwlychu

moisture *n.* gwlybaniaeth *f.*

Mold *n.* Yr Wyddgrug *f.*

moment *n.* eiliad *f,* ennyd *mf,* moment *f.*

monarch *n.* brenin *m.*

monastery *n.* mynachlog *f.*

Monday *n.* dydd Llun *m.*

money *n.* arian, pres *m.*

monk *n.* mynach *m.*

monkey *n.* mwnci *m.*

monoglot 1 *n.* person uniaith *m.* **2** *a.* uniaith

monotonous *a.* undonog

monstrous *a.* anferth

month *n.* mis *m.*

monthly 1 *n.* misolyn *m.* **2** *a.* misol

mood *n.* tymer, hwyl *f.*

moon *n.* lleuad, lloer *f.* **moonlight** golau leuad

moor *n.* rhos *f,* rhostir *m,* gwaun *f.*

moral *a.* moesol

morals *n.* moesau *pl.*

more 1 *n.* rhagor, ychwaneg, chwaneg *m.* **2** *a & ad.* mwy, mwyach. **more than** mwy na

morning 1 *n.* bore *m.* **2** *a.* bore, boreol. **Monday morning** bore dydd Llun: **every morning** bob bore; **Morning Service** Gwasanaeth Boreol; **next morning** bore trannoeth

morrow *n.* trannoeth
mortal 1 *n.* dyn; un marwol
m. 2 *a.* marwol
mortgage *n.* morgais *m.*
most *a.* mwyaf, amlaf
mostly *ad.* gan mwyaf
moth *n.* gwyfyn *m.*
mother *n.* mam *f.* **mother-in-law** mam-yng-nghyfraith
mother tongue *n.* mamiaith *f.*
motor *n.* modur, car *m.* **motor bike** beic modur
motorist *n.* modurwr *m.*
motorway *n.* traffordd *f.*
mountain *n.* mynydd *m.*
mountaineer *n.* mynyddwr *m.*
mountainous *a.* mynyddig
mourn *v.* galaru
mourning *n.* galar *m.*
mouse *n.* llygoden *f.*
moustache *n.* mwstash *m.*
mouth *n.* ceg *f*, genau *m.pl.*
move *v.* symud
movement *n.* mudiad; symudiad, symud *m.*
moving *a.* yn symud, cyffrous
mow *v.* lladd gwair
much 1 *n.* llawer. 2 *a.* llawer, mawr. 3 *ad.* yn fawr, llawer *(with comparative a.):* **much better** llawer gwell: **too much** gormod
mud *n.* llacs *m.*
muddy *a.* llacsog
multiply *v.* lluosi
multitude *n.* llu *m*, torf, tyrfa *f.*
munch *v.* cnoi
murder 1 *n.* llofruddiaeth *f.* 2 *v.* llofruddio
murderer *n.* llofrudd *m.*

muscular *a.* cyhyrog
museum *n.* amgueddfa *f.*
mushroom *n.* madarchen *f.*; '**magic mushroom(s)**' madarch hudol
music *n.* cerddoriaeth, cerdd, caniadaeth, alaw, miwsig *f.*
musical *a.* cerddorol
musician *n.* cerddor *m.*
must *n. & v.* rhaid *m.*
mutate *v.* treiglo
mutation *n.* treiglad, cyfnewidiad *m.*
mute *a.* mud, distaw
mutilate *v.* anafu, llurgunio
mutiny *n.* gwrthryfel, terfysg *m.*
mutton *n.* cig dafad, cig gwedder *m.*
my *pn.* fy; 'm
myrrh *n.* myrr *m.*
myself *pn.* fy hunan, mi fy hunan, myfi fy hun
mysterious *a.* rhyfedd, dirgel
mystery *n.* dirgelwch
myth *n.* chwedl, dameg, myth *f.*

N

nail 1 *n.* ewin *mf*; hoel, hoelen *f.* 2 *a.* hoelio.
naked *a.* noeth; llwm: **stark naked** noethlymun, porcyn
name 1 *n.* enw *m.* 2 *v.* enwi, galw
namely *ad.* sef
nape *n.* gwar *m.*
napkin *n.* cewyn, clwt *m.*
narrate *v.* adrodd (hanes)
narration *n.* adroddiad *m.*

narrative *n.* chwedl *f,* hanes *m,* stori *f.*

narrow 1 *a.* cul, cyfyng. **2** *v.* cyfyngu

narrow-minded *a.* cul

nasal *a.* trwynol

nasty *a.* cas, brwnt, budr, ffiaidd

nation *n.* cenedl *f.*

national *a.* cenedlaethol; gwladol. **National Assistance** Cymorth Gwladol: **National Museum** Amgueddfa Genedlaethol

nationalism *n.* cenedlaetholdeb *m.*

nationalist *n.* cenedlaetholwr *m.*

nationality *n.* cenedligrwydd *m.*

native 1 *n.* brodor *m.* **2** *a.* brodorol

nativity *n.* genedigaeth *f.*

natural *a.* naturiol

nature *n.* natur, naws *f.*

naught *n.* dim; sero *m.*

naughtiness *n.* drygioni *m.*

naughty *a.* drwg, drygionus

navy *n.* llynges *f.* **navy blue** glasddu

near 1 *a.* agos. **2** *ad.* yn agos, braidd. **3** *v.* agosáu, nesáu. **4** *prp.* ger, yn agos at

nearby *a. & ad.* yn ymyl, gerllaw

nearly *ad.* bron

neat *a.* twt, del, taclus, trefnus

Neath *n.* Castell-nedd *f.*

necessary *a.* angenrheidiol; **necessitate** gwneud yn angenrheidiol, gorfodi

necessity *n.* anghenraid, rhaid *m.*

neck *n.* gwddf, gwddwg *m.*

necklace *n.* neclis *f.* mwclis *pl.*

née *a.* gynt, cyn priodi. **Mair Puw, née Rhys** Mair Puw, gynt Rhys

need *n.* eisiau, rhaid. *m.*

needle *n.* nodwydd; gwaell *f.*

needy *a.* tlawd

negative *a.* negyddol

neglect *v.* esgeuluso

negligence *n.* esgeulustod *m.*

negligent *a.* esgeulus

negotiate *v.* trafod, trefnu

negro *n.* dyn du, negro *m.*

neighbour *n.* cymydog *m.*

neighbouring *a.* cyfagos

neither 1 *ad. & c.* na, nac, chwaith, ychwaith. **2** *pn.* nid y naill na'r llall, nid un o'r ddau

nephew *n.* nai *m.*

nerve *n.* gewyn, nerf *m.*

nervous *a.* nerfus, ofnus

nest *n.* nyth *mf.*

nestle *v.* nythu

nestling *n.* aderyn bach, cyw *m.*

net *n.* rhwyd *f.*

netball *n.* pêl rwyd *f.*

Netherlands, The *n.* Yr Iseldiroedd *f.*

never *ad.* byth, erioed

nevertheless *ad.* er hynny, eto

new *a.* newydd. **New Year** Blwyddyn Newydd; **New York** Efrog Newydd; **New Zealand** Seland Newydd; **brand new** newydd sbon

newcomer *n.* newydd-ddyfodiad *m.*

Newport (Pembs.) *n.* Trefdraeth *f.*

Newport (Mon.) *n.* Casnewydd *f.*

Newquay *n.* Ceinewydd *f.*

news *n.pl.* newyddion *pl.* newydd, hanes *m.* **good news** newyddion da; **six o'clock news** newyddion chwech

newspaper *n.* papur newydd. *m.*

next 1 *a.* nesaf. 2 *prp.* nesaf at. **next door** y drws nesaf; **Next, please** Y nesaf, os gwelwch yn dda; **next week** wythnos nesaf; **next year** y flwyddyn nesaf

nice *a.* braf, hyfryd, neis, dymunol

nickname 1 *n.* llysenw *m.* 2 *v.* llysenwi

niece *n.* nith *f.*

nigh *a, ad & prp.* agos, gerllaw, yn agos

night *n.* nos; noson, noswaith *f.* **night and day** nos a dydd; **night before last** echnos; **last night** neithiwr; **the last night** y noson olaf; **Good night!** Nos Da!

night-dress *n.* gŵn nos, coban *f.*

night-gown *n.* gŵn nos, coban *f.*

nightingale *n.* eos *f.*

nightmare *n.* hunllef *f.*

nil *n.* dim *m.*

nimble *a.* heini, sionc, ystwyth

nine *n. & a.* naw *m.*

nineteen *n. & a.* pedwar ar bymtheg, un deg naw *m.*

ninety *n. & a.* naw deg *m.*

ninth *n. & a.* nawfed *m.*

no 1 *a.* ni, nid, neb, dim. 2 *ad.* na, nad, ni, nid, nac oes, naddo, nage, nac ydy ... *(Welsh uses the verb forms to answer yes/no) e.g.* **Nia? No.** Nia? Nage. **Was she there? No** Oedd hi yno? Nac oedd. **Is Non at home? No** Ydy Non gartre? Nac ydy. **Is there food here? No** Oes bwyd yma? Nac oes. **Will they be out? No** Fyddan nhw allan? Na fyddan

noble *a.* bonheddig, ardderchog

nobleman *n.* bonheddwr, uchelwr *m.*

nobody *n.* neb *m.*

noise *n.* sŵn, mwstwr, stŵr, sain, twrw *m.*

noisy *a.* swnllyd, stwrllyd

nom de plume *n.* ffugenw *m.*

none *pn.* neb, dim, dim un

nonsense *n.* lol *f.*

nook *n.* cornel, congl *f.*

noon *n.* hanner dydd, canol dydd *m.*

no one *pn.* neb

nor *ad. & c.* na, nac

Norman 1 *n.* Norman *m.* 2 *a.* Normanaidd: **Norman church** eglwys Normanaidd

north 1 *n.* gogledd *m.* 2 *a.* gogleddol. **North Pole** Pegwn y Gogledd: **North Wales** Gogledd Cymru

northerly *a.* gogleddol
northern *a.* gogleddol.
 Northern Ireland Gogledd
 Iwerddon
Northerner *n.* Gogleddwr *m.*
nose 1 *n.* trwyn *m.* 2 *v.*
 trwyno
nostalgia *n.* hiraeth *m.*
nostril *n.* ffroen *f.*
not *ad.* na, nac, nad, ni, nid
notable *a.* hynod, enwog,
 nodedig
note 1 *n.* nodyn, nod *m.* 2 *v.*
 nodi, sylwi. **ten pound note**
 papur decpunt
noted *a.* nodedig, enwog,
 hynod
nothing *n.* dim *m.* **nothing at
 all** dim byd, dim o gwbl,
 dim yn y byd
notice 1 *n.* rhybudd,
 hysbysebiad, sylw *m.* 2 *v.*
 sylwi.
notion *n.* syniad, amcan *m.*
notwithstanding 1 *ad.* er
 hynny. 2 *prp.* er, er
 gwaethaf, serch
noun *n.* enw *m.* **collective
 noun** enw torfol; **common
 noun** enw cyffredin; **plural
 noun** enw lluosog

novel 1 *n.* nofel *f.* 2 *a.*
 newydd
novelist *n.* nofelwr, nofelydd
 m.
November *n.* Tachwedd *m.*
now *ad.* yn awr, nawr, rŵan,
 bellach, y pryd hwn. **now
 and again** nawr ac yn y
 man. **nowadays** *ad.* yn y
 dyddiau hyn. **nowhere** *ad.*
 dim yn unlle
nuance *n.* naws *f.*
nuclear *a.* niwclear. **nuclear
 energy** ynni niwclear:
 nuclear power station
 atomfa, gorsaf ynni niwclear
numb *a.* cwsg
number 1 *n.* nifer *mf,* rhif;
 rhifyn *m.* 2 *v.* rhifo, cyfrif
numeral *n.* rhifol, rhifnod *m.*
numerous *a.* lluosog, niferus;
 aml
nun *n.* lleian *f.*
nurse 1 *n.* gweinyddes, nyrs *f.*
 2 *v.* magu, nyrsio, meithrin
nursery *n.* meithrinfa *f.*
 nursery class dosbarth
 meithrin; **nursery nurse**
 gweinyddes feithrin; **nursery
 school** ysgol feithrin

Insight

nursery-rhyme: lullaby *n. hwiangerdd f.* The noted Welsh
scholar O. M. Edwards wrote: 'The literature of a nation
depends to a great extent, on its lullabies. If you seek to
understand the characteristics of a nation ... read that nation's
lullabies.' The adult learner, clutching a Welsh nursery rhyme
book, can accelerate both 'word count' and 'sentence
structure' by softly singing some of the songs daily!

nurseryman *n.* garddwr *m.*
nursery-rhyme *n.* hwiangerdd *f.*
nurture *v.* meithrin
nut *n.* cneuen; nyten *f.*
  coconut cneuen goco;
  hazelnuts cnau cyll; **monkey**
  nuts cnau mwnci; **walnut**
  cneuen ffrengig; **hexagonal**
  nut nyten hecsagonal; **square**
  nut nyten sgwâr; **nut and**
  bolt nyten a bollt

O

oak 1 *n.* derwen *f.* 2 *a.* derw.
  oak-trees derw, deri
oath *n.* llw *m.*
obedient *a.* ufudd
obey *v.* ufuddhau
object 1 *n.* gwrthrych, nod, amcan *m.* 2 *v.* gwrthwynebu
objective 1 *n.* amcan, nod *m.* 2 *a.* gwrthrychol
objector *n.* gwrthwynebwr *m.*
obligation *n.* dyletswydd, gorfodaeth *f.*
oblige *v.* gorfodi
obscene *a.* serth, brwnt
obscure 1 *a.* aneglur, tywyll 2. *v.* tywyllu
observation *n.* sylw *m.*
observe *v.* sylwi, edrych; cadw
obstacle *n.* rhwystr, maen tramgwydd *m.*
obstruct *v.* cau, tagu; rhwystro
obtain *v.* cael, ennill

obvious *a.* eglur, amlwg
occasion 1 *n.* achlysur, achos *m*, adeg *f.* 2 *v.* achosi, peri
occasional *a.* ambell
occasionally *ad.* ambell waith
occupation *n.* gwaith *m*, galwedigaeth *f.*
occur *v.* digwydd, taro
occurrence *n.* digwyddiad, achlysur *m.*
ocean *n.* môr, cefnfor, eigion *m.*
o'clock *ad.* o'r gloch
octagon *n.* wythongl *f*, octagon *m.*
octave *n.* wythawd *m.;* wythfed
octet *n.* wythawd *m.*
October *n.* Hydref *m.*
octogenarian *n.* person pedwar ugain mlwydd oed *m.*
odd *a.* od, hynod, rhyfedd
ode *n.* cerdd, awdl *f.*
odious *a.* cas, ffiaidd
of *prp.* o, gan, am, ynghylch.
  of course wrth gwrs
off 1 *a.* tu allan, tu faes. 2 *ad.* ymaith, i ffwrdd. 3 *prp.* oddi ar, oddi am, oddi wrth
offence *n.* trosedd *f.*
offend *v.* troseddu
offender *n.* troseddwr *m.*
offer *n. & v.* cynnig *m.*
office *n.* swydd; swyddfa *f.*
officer *n.* swyddog *m.*
official 1 *n.* swyddog *m.* 2 *a.* swyddogol
offspring *n.* hil *f*, plant *pl.*
often *ad.* yn aml

oil 1 *n.* olew, oel *m.* **2** *v.* iro,
oelio. **oil field** maes olew; **oil
rig** llwyfan olew

old *a.* hen, oedrannus. **old
age** henoed, henaint; **old
fashioned** henffasiwn; **old
man** hen ŵr, henwr; **of old**
gynt

omelette *n.* omled *m.*

on 1 *ad.* ymlaen. **2** *prp.* ar

once *ad.* unwaith, un tro,
gynt. **at once** ar unwaith

one 1 *n.* rhywun *m.* **2** *a.* un,
naill, unig. **3** *pn.* naill: **one
by one** bob yn un

one-way *a.* un-ffordd,
unffordd. **one-way street**
heol unffordd

onion *n.* winwnsyn, nionyn
m.

only 1 *a.* unig. **2** *ad.* yn unig,
dim ond. **the only one** yr
unig un; **one only** un yn unig

open 1 *a.* agored, ar agor.
2 *v.* agor: **open air** awyr
agored; **wide open** lled y pen

opening *n.* agoriad *m.*

opera *n.* opera *f.*

operate *v.* gweithredu,
gweithio

operation *n.* gweithred *f.*,
gweithrediad *m.*; triniaeth
lawfeddygol *f.*

opinion *n.* barn *f.*, meddwl *m.*

opponent *n.* gwrthwynebwr,
gwrthwynebydd *m.*

opportunity *n.* achlysur, cyfle
m., siawns *f.*

oppose *v.* gwrthwynebu

opposite *a. & prp.* cyferbyn,
cyferbyniol

opposition *n.* gwrthwyneb,
gwrthwynebiad *m;*
gwrthblaid *f.*

optician *n.* optegwr, optegydd
m.

option *n.* dewis, dewisiad *m.*

or *c.* neu, ynte, ynteu, ai, naill
ai

oral *a.* llafar. **oral examination**
arholiad llafar

orally *ad.* ar lafar

orange *n. & a.* oren *mf.*

orchard *n.* perllan *f.*

orchestra *n.* cerddorfa *f.*

ordain *v.* ordeinio, urddo;
penderfynu

ordeal *n.* prawf llym *m.*

order 1 *n.* trefn; urdd; rheol *f.*,
gorchymyn *m.*; archeb *f.* **2** *v.*
trefnu; gorchymyn; archebu

orderly *a.* rheolaidd, trefnus

ordinarily *ad.* fel rheol

ordinary *a.* cyffredin, arferol

ore *n.* mwyn *m.*

organ *n.* organ *f*, offeryn *m.*

organic *a.* organig

organist *n.* organydd *m.*

organization *n.* trefn;
cyfundrefn *f.*

organize *v.* trefnu

organizer *n.* trefnydd *m.*

origin *n.* ffynnon, ffynhonnell
f, dechreuad *m.*

original *a.* gwreiddiol

originate *v.* dechrau, tarddu,
hannu

other 1 *a.* arall, eraill. **2** *pn.*
arall, y llall. **each other** ei
gilydd

our *pn.* ein, ein – ni; '*n.* **Our Father** Ein Tad. **our house** ein tŷ, ein tŷ ni

ours *pn.* eiddom ni, yr eiddom

out *ad.* allan

outcrop *n.* brig *m.*

outdoor *a.* yn yr awyr agored

outline *n.* braslun *m.*

outside 1 *n.* tu allan, tu faes. *mf.* 2 *a. & ad.* allan, oddi allan. 3 *prp.* tu allan i, tu faes i

outside-half *n.* maswr *m.*

outskirts *n.* cyrrau, cyrion *pl.*

outward *a.* allanol

oven *n.* ffwrn *f*, popty *m.* **electric oven** ffwrn drydan; **gas oven** ffwrn nwy; **microwave oven** ffwrn ficrodon, popty pling

overflowing *a.* gorlawn

overhead *a. & ad.* uwchben

overjoyed *a.* llawen iawn

overlook *v.* esgeuluso; edrych dros

overnight *ad.* dros nos

overpower *v.* trechu

overseas *ad.* dros y môr, tramor

overshadow *v.* cysgodi

overweight *a.* gor-drwm

overwork *v.* gorweithio

owe *v.* bod mewn dyled

owing *a.* dyledus

owl *n.* gwdihŵ *m*, tylluan *f.* **barn owl, white owl** tylluan wen; **little owl** tylluan fechan; **long-eared owl** tylluan glustiog

own 1 *a.* eiddo dyn ei hun, priod. 2 *v.* meddu (ar)

Insight

oven *n. ffwrn f. popty m.* With the arrival of the microwave oven, a new onomatopoeic term was coined: '*popty ping*'.

---

over 1 *n.* pelawd *m. (criced).* 2 *ad.* dros ben, drosodd. 3 *prp.* dros, uwch, uwchben

over- *px,* gor-, rhag-, rhy-, tra-

overcast *a.* cymylog

overcoat *n.* cot fawr, cot uchaf *f.*

overcome *v.* gorchfygu, trechu, cael y gorau ar

overcrowded *a.* gorlawn

overdo *v.* gor-wneud

overdraw *v.* gordynnu

overflow 1 *n.* gorlif *m.* 2 *v.* gorlifo

owner *n.* perchen, perchennog *m.*

Oxford *n.* Rhydychen *f.*

oxygen *n.* ocsigen *m.*

P

pace 1 *n.* cam *m.* 2 *v.* camu, cerdded

Pacific Ocean *n.* Môr Tawel *m.*

pack 1 *n.* pac *m.* 2 *v.* pacio

package *n.* paced, pecyn *m.*

packet *n.* paced, pecyn *m.*

pact *n.* cytundeb, cynghrair *m.*

padlock *n.* clo *m.*

pagan *n.* pagan *m.*

page *n.* tudalen *mf.*; gwas bach *m.*

pageant *n.* pasiant *m.*

pail *n.* bwced *m.*

pain 1 *n.* poen *mf*, dolur *m.* **2** *v.* poeni

painful *a.* poenus

painstaking *a.* gofalus

paint 1 *n.* paent, lliw *m.* **2** *v.* peintio, lliwo

painter *n.* peintiwr, arlunydd *m.*

painting *n.* llun, darlun *m.*

pair *n.* pâr, dau, cwpl *m.*

palace *n.* llys, plas, palas, plasty *m.*

pale *a.* llwyd, glas, gwelw

Palestine *n.* Palestina *f.*

palm *n.* palmwydden *f.* **Palm Sunday** Sul y Blodau, Sul y Palmwydd

pamper *v.* maldodi, anwesu

pampering *n.* maldod, anwes *m.*

pamphlet *n.* pamffled, llyfryn *m.*

pan *n.* padell *f.*

pancake *n.* crempog, ffroesen *f.*

pane *n.* cwarel, chwarel *mf.*

panel *n.* panel *m.*

paper 1 *n.* papur *m.* **2** *v.* papuro. **newspaper** papur newydd; **toilet paper** papur toiled, papur tŷ bach;

wallpaper papur wal; **writing paper** papur ysgrifennu

paperbacks *n.* llyfrau clawr meddal *m.pl.*

papist *n.* pabydd *m.*

parable *n.* dameg *f.*

paradise *n.* gwynfa, gwynfyd *m*, paradwys *f.*

paragraph *n.* paragraff *m.*

paramount *a.* pen, pennaf, prif

parcel *n.* parsel *m.*

parch *v.* crasu, sychu

parched *a.* cras, crasboeth; sychedig

pardon 1 *n.* pardwn, maddeuant *m.* **2** *v.* maddau.

parent *n.* tad neu fam, rhiant *mf.*

parish *n.* plwyf *m.*

park 1 *n.* parc *m.* **2** *v.* parcio. **car park** maes parcio; **caravan park** maes carafanau

parliament *n.* senedd *f.* **Member of Parliament** Aelod Seneddol (A.S.)

parsley *n.* persli *m.*

parsnip *n.* panasen *f.*

parson *n.* offeiriad, person *m.*

part 1 *n.* darn *m*, rhan *f*; peth *m.* **2** *v.* rhannu; gwahanu; ymadael

particular *a.* neilltuol

particularize *v.* manylu

parting *n.* ymadael *m.*

partner *n.* cymar *m.*

party *n.* parti *m*; plaid *f.* **birthday party** parti pen-blwydd; **Christmas party**

parti Nadolig; **Conservative Party** Plaid Geidwadol; **Green Party** Plaid Werdd; **Labour Party** Plaid Lafur
pass 1 *n.* bwlch; caniatâd, pás *m.* **2** *v.* mynd heibio (i); llwyddo
passion *n.* dioddefaint; nwyd *m.*
past 1 *n. & a.* gorffennol *m.* **2** *ad.* heibio
pastor *n.* bugail *(eglwys),* gweinidog *m.*
pasture *n.* porfa *f.*
path *n.* llwybr *m.* **public footpath** llwybr cyhoeddus
patience *n.* amynedd *m.* **the patience of Job** amynedd Job
patient 1 *n.* claf *m.* **2** *a.* amyneddgar
patriot *n.* gwladgarwr *m.*
patron *n.* noddwr *m.*
patronage *n.* nawdd *m.*
pattern *n.* patrwm, patrwn *m.*
pause 1 *n.* hoe *f,* saib, seibiant *m.* **2** *v.* pwyllo, aros, gorffwys
pavement *n.* pafin *m.*
pavilion *n.* pabell *f,* pafiliwn *m.*
paw *n.* pawen *f.*
pay 1 *n.* cyflog *mf,* tâl *m.* **2** *v.* talu
payee *n.* talai *m.*
payer *n.* talwr *m.*
payment *n.* tâl, taliad *m.*
pea *n.* pysen *f.*

peace *n.* hedd, heddwch, llonyddwch *m;* tangnefedd *mf.*
peaceful *a.* tawel, llonydd, tangnefeddus
peak *n.* brig, copa *m.*
pear *n.* peren *f.*
pearl *n.* perl *m.*
peasant *n.* gwerinwr *m.*
peasantry *n.* y werin *f.*
peat *n.* mawn *m.*
peck 1 *n.* pigiad *m.* **2** *v.* pigo
peculiar *a.* od, hynod, arbennig
pedestrian 1 *n.* cerddwr *m.* **2** *a.* ar draed. **pedestrian crossing** croesfan *f.*
peel 1 *n.* croen, pil *m.* **2** *v.* pilio
peep 1 *n.* cipolwg, cip. **2** *v.* cipedrych, sbïo
peg *n.* peg *m.*
pen *n.* pin ysgrifennu *m.*
penalize *v.* cosbi
penalty *n.* cosb *f.*
pence *n.* ceiniogau *pl.*
pencil *n.* pensil *m.*
pendulum *n.* pendil *m.*
penitent *a.* edifar, edifeiriol
penknife *n.* cyllell boced *f.*
penniless *a.* heb geiniog
penny *n.* ceiniog *f.*
pension *n.* pensiwn *m.*
pensioner *n.* pensiynwr *m.*
pensive *a.* meddylgar
people *n.* pobl, gwerin *f.*
pepper *n.* pupur *m.*
per *prp.* trwy, wrth, yn ôl
perceive *n.* deall, gweld, gweled

percentage *n.* hyn a hyn y cant, canran *m.*

petition *n.* deiseb *f.*
petrol *n.* petrol *m.* **petrol**

Insight

percentage *n. hyn a hyn y cant, canran m.* 5% *pump y cant;* 7.5% *saith a hanner y cant;* 10% *deg y cant;* 15% *pymtheg y cant; un deg pump y cant;* 33% *tri deg tri y cant;* 58% *pum deg wyth y cant;* 100% *cant y cant.* <

---

perfect 1 *a.* perffaith. **2** *v.* perffeithio
perfection *n.* perffeithrwydd *m.*
perfectly *ad.* yn berffaith
perforate *v.* tyllu
perforated *a.* tyllog
perforation *n.* twll *m.*
perfume *n.* arogl; persawr *m.*
perhaps *ad.* efallai, hwyrach
period *n.* adeg *f,* amser; misglwyf, cyfnod *m.*
permanent *a.* sefydlog, parhaol
permission *n.* caniatâd *m,* hawl *f.*
permit *v.* caniatáu
perpetuate *v.* parhau
persecute *v.* erlid
person *n.* person *m.*
personal *a.* personol
personality *n.* personoliaeth *f.*
perspective *n.* safbwynt, persbectif *m.*
perspiration *n.* chwys *m.*
perspire *v.* chwysu
pester *v.* blino, poeni
pet *n.* anifail anwes *m.*
petite *a.* bychan, bechan

pump pwmp petrol; **petrol station** gorsaf betrol; **unleaded petrol** petrol di-blwm
petticoat *n.* pais *f.*
petty *a.* bach, bychan, mân, gwael
pew *n.* sedd, sêt *f,* côr *m.*
pharmacist *n.* fferyllydd *m.*
pharmacy *n.* fferyllfa *f.*
phone 1 *n.* ffôn. teleffon *m.* **2** *v.* ffonio. **phone call** galwad ffôn
photocopier *n.* llun-gopïwr, ffotogopïywr *m.*
photocopy *n.* llun-gopi, ffotogopi *m.*
photograph *n.* llun, ffotograff *m.*
photographer *n.* ffotograffydd *m.*
phrase 1 *n.* cymal, ymadrodd *m.* **2** *v.* geirio, mynegi
physical *a.* corfforol, materol. **physical education** addysg gorfforol
physics *n.* ffiseg *f.*
pianist *n.* pianydd *m.*
piano *n.* piano *m.*

pick *v.* dewis, pigo, casglu (blodau/ ffrwythau)

pick up *v.* codi

picture *n.* darlun, llun, pictiwr *m.*

piece *n.* darn, pisyn *m*, rhan *f*, tamaid *m.*

pig *n.* mochyn *m.* **piglet** mochyn bach

pile *n* . pentwr *m.*

pilgrim *n.* pererin *m.*

pilgrimage *n.* pererindod; **to go on a pilgrimage** pererindota *v.*

pill *n.* pilsen *f.*

pillar *n.* colofn *f.* piler *m.*

pillow *n.* clustog *f*, gobennydd *m.*

pilot *n.* peilot *m.*

pimple *n.* tosyn, ploryn *m.*

pin 1 *n.* pin *m.* **drawing pin** pin bawd. 2 *v.* pinio, hoelio

pinch 1 *n.* pinsiad *m.* gwasgfa *f.* 2 *v.* pinsio, gwasgu

pine *n.* ffynidwydden *f*, ffynidwydd *pl*; pinwydden *f*, pinwydd *pl*; **red pine** ffynidwydd coch

pineapple *n.* afal pîn, pîn-afal *m.*

pine-end *n.* talcen tŷ *m.*

pink *n. & a.* pinc *m.*

pint *n.* peint *m.* **pint of milk** peint o laeth

pious *a.* duwiol, crefyddol

pipe *n.* pib, piben, pibell *f.*

pirate *n.* môr-leidr *m.*

pit *n.* pwll *m.* **coal-pit** pwll glo

pity *n.* trueni, gresyn, piti *m.* **to take pity** trugarhau

place 1 *n.* lle, llecyn, man *m.* 2 *v.* dodi, gosod, lleoli

plague *n.* haint *f*, pla *m.*

plain 1 *a.* amlwg; eglur. 2 *n.* gwastad *m.*

plan 1 *n.* cynllun, plan *m.* 2 *v.* cynllunio

planet *n.* planed *f.*

planner *n.* cynlluniwr, cynllunydd *m.*

planning *n.* cynllunio *m.*

plant 1 *n.* planhigyn *m*; offer *pl.* 2 *v.* plannu; gosod

plate *n.* plât *m.*

platform *n.* llwyfan, platfform *m.*

play 1 *n.* chwarae *m*, drama *f.* **play group** grŵp chwarae; **fair play** chwarae teg; **playtime** amser chwarae. 2 *v.* chwarae, canu *(offeryn)*.

player *n.* chwaraewr *m.*

plaything *n.* tegan *m.*

pleasant *a.* pleserus, dymunol, hyfryd, serchus, siriol; braf

please *v.* bodloni, plesio. **if you please** os gwelwch yn dda

pleased *a.* bodlon, hapus

pleasurable *a.* pleserus, dymunol

pleasure *n.* pleser, boddhad *m.*

pledge 1 *n.* addewid *mf*; ernes *f.* 2 *v.* addo

plentiful *a.* helaeth

plenty *n.* digonedd, digon *m.*

pliable *a.* hyblyg

pliant *a.* ystwyth

plot 1 *n.* cynllun; cynllwyn; darn o dir *m.* 2 *v.* cynllunio; cynllwynio

plough *v.* aredig, troi

plum *n.* eirinen *f.*

plumage *n.* plu *pl.*

plume 1 *n.* pluen *f*, plufyn *m.* 2 *v.* pluo, plufio

plural *n.* lluosog *m.*

pocket 1 *n.* poced *mf.* **pocket money** arian poced. 2 *v.* pocedu

pod *n.* plisgyn *m*, coden *f.*

poem *n.* cerdd, cân *f.*

poet *n.* bardd *m.*

poetry *n.* barddoniaeth *f.*

point 1 *n.* pwynt, blaen *m.* 2 *v.* dangos

pointless *a.* dibwynt

poison 1 *n.* gwenwyn *m.* 2 *v.* gwenwyno

poisonous *a.* gwenwynig, gwenwynol

Poland *n.* Gwlad Pwyl *f.*

pole *n.* polyn; pegwn *m.* **Pole Star** Seren y Gogledd

police *n.* heddlu *m.*

policeman *n.* heddwas, plisman, plismon *m.*

policewoman *n.* heddferch, pliswraig, plismones *f.*

Polish 1 *n.* Pwyleg *f.* 2 *a.* Pwylaidd

polish 1 *n.* cwyr *m.* 2 *v.* cwyro

political *a.* gwleidyddol, politicaidd

politician *n.* gwleidydd *m.*

politics *n.* gwleidyddiaeth *f.*

pollute *v.* llygru

polluted *a.* llygredig

pollution *n.* llygredd *m.*

pond *n.* pwll, pwllyn, pownd *m.*

Pontypool *n.* Pont-y-pŵl *f.*

pony *n.* merlyn *m*, merlen *f.*

pony-trekking merlota; **pony-trekker** merlotwr

pool *n.* pwll, pwllyn *m.* **swimming pool** pwll nofio

poor *a.* gwael, llwm, tlawd

poorly *a.* gwael, sâl, tost

Pope *n.* Pab *m.*

poppy *n.* pabi *f.*

popular *a.* poblogaidd

population *n.* poblogaeth *f.*

porch *n.* cyntedd, porth *m.*

porridge *n.* uwd *m.*

port *n.* porth, porthladd *m.*

portable *a.* symudol

portrait *n.* llun, darlun, portread *m.*

portrayal *n.* portread *m.*

pose *v.* sefyll, ymddangos, cymryd ar

position *n.* safle *m*, sefyllfa, swydd *f.*

positive *a.* pendant, cadarnhaol

possess *v.* meddu

possession *n.* eiddo, meddiant *m.*

possessor *n.* perchen, perchennog *m.*

possibility *n.* posibilrwydd *m.*

possible *a.* posibl

possibly *ad.* efallai

post 1 *n.* post; postyn *m*; swydd *f.* **postcode** côd post. 2 *v.* postio

postal *a.* post. **postal order**
archeb bost
posthumous *a.* ar ôl marw
postman *n.* postman,
postmon *m.*
postmaster *n.* postfeistr *m.*
post office *n.* swyddfa'r post
f, llythyrdy *m.*
postpone *v.* oedi
postscript *n.* ôl-nodiad *m.*
potato *n.* taten *f.*
pound *n.* punt *f.* (£); pwys *m.*
(lb.); ffald *m.*
pour *v.* arllwys; bwrw
pout *v.* pwdu
poverty *n.* tlodi, eisiau *m.*
poverty-stricken *a.* tlawd,
llwm
powder *n.* llwch, powdr,
powdwr *m.*
power *n.* gallu, nerth, pŵer,
grym, ynni *m.*
powerful *a.* cryf, galluog,
grymus, nerthol
powerless *a.* dirym
power station *n.* pwerdy,
gorsaf ynni
pox *n.* brech *f.* **chicken pox**
brech yr ieir
practical *a.* ymarferol
practice *n.* ymarfer *f,*
ymarferiad, practis *m,* arfer
mf.
practise *v.* arfer, ymarfer
practising *a.* ymarferol
praise 1 *n.* canmoliaeth *f,*
clod, mawl *m.* 2 *v.* canmol,
clodfori, moli
pram *n.* pram *m.*
pray *v.* gweddïo

prayer *n.* gweddi *f.*
preach *v.* pregethu
preacher *n.* pregethwr
precarious *a.* ansicr, peryglus
precious *a.* gwerthfawr, drud,
prid; annwyl
precis *n.* crynodeb *mf.*
precise *a.* manwl
preface *n.* rhagair,
rhagymadrodd *m.*
preference *n.* dewis *m,*
ffafriaeth *f.*
preferential *a.* ffafriol
prefix *n.* rhagddodiad *m.*
pregnant *a.* beichiog
prejudice 1 *n.* rhagfarn *f;*
niwed *m.* 2 *v.* rhagfarnu;
niweidio
prejudiced *a.* rhagfarnllyd
premier 1 *n.* prif weinidog *m.*
2 *a.* prif, pennaf, blaenaf
premium *n.* gwobr *f,* tâl,
taliad *m.*
preparation *n.* paratoad *m.*
prepare *v.* paratoi *m.*
prepared *a.* parod
preposition *n.* arddodiad *m.*
prescription *n.* presgripsiwn,
rysáit *m.*
presence *n.* presenoldeb,
gŵydd *m.*
present 1 *n.* anrheg, rhodd *f;*
presennol *m.* 2 *v.* anrhegu,
cyflwyno, dangos. **at present**
ar hyn o bryd, yn awr, nawr,
rŵan
presently *ad.* yn y man, yn
union
preserve 1 *n.* jam *m.* 2 *v.*
cadw

preside *v.* llywyddu

president *n.* llywydd,
arlywydd *m.*

press 1 *n.* gwasg *f.* **2** *v.*
gwasgu. **The Press** Y Wasg
(gohebwyr)

pressure *n.* gwasgiad,
pwysedd *m.*

presumably *ad.* yn ôl pob
tebyg

presume *v.* tybio; beiddio

pretence *n.* esgus *m.*

pretend *v.* ffugio, cymryd ar;
honni

pretext *n.* esgus *m.*

prevent *v.* atal, rhwystro
(rhag)

preview *n.* rhagolwg *m.*

previous *a.* cynt; diwethaf

price 1 *n.* pris *m.* **price list**
rhestr prisoedd. **2** *v.* prisio

prick 1 *n.* pigiad *m.* **2** *v.* pigo

prickly *a.* pigog

pride *n.* balchder *m.*

priest *n.* offeiriad *m.*

primary *a.* cynradd; prif.
primary education addysg
gynradd; **primary school**
ysgol gynradd

prime *a.* prif, cyntaf; gorau

prince *n.* tywysog *m.*

princess *n.* tywysoges *f.*

principal 1 *n.* pen, prifathro
m, prifathrawes *f.* **2** *a.* prif

principle *n.* egwyddor *f.*

print 1 *n.* argraff *f*, print, ôl *m.*
2 *v.* argraffu, printio

printing-press *n.* gwasg
argraffu

prison *n.* carchar *m.*

prisoner *n.* carcharor *m.*

private *a.* cyfrinachol, preifat

privilege *n.* braint *f.*

prize *n.* gwobr *f.*

probable *a.* tebyg, tebygol

probation *n.* prawf *m.*
probation officer swyddog
prawf; **probation service**
gwasanaeth prawf

problem *n.* problem *f.*

procedure *n.* trefn *f*, arfer *mf*,
dull *m.*

proceed *v.* mynd ymlaen

proceeds *n.* enillion *pl*, elw
m.

procession *n.* gorymdaith *f.*

proclaim *v.* cyhoeddi, datgan
m.

proclamation *n.* cyhoeddiad
m.

prodigious *a.* anferth

produce *n.* cynnyrch *m.*

professor *n.* athro *m.*

profit 1 *n.* elw, ennill,
enillion, proffid *m.* **2** *v.*
elwa, ennill, manteisio

profitable *a.* proffidiol

profound *a.* dwfn, dwys

programme *n.* rhaglen *f.*

prohibit *v.* gwahardd

project 1 *n.* bwriad, cynllun;
cywaith; prosiect, project *m.*
2 *v.* bwriadu; ymestyn

proletariat *n.* y werin *f.*

prologue *n.* rhagair, prolog
m.

prominent *a.* amlwg

promise 1 *n.* addewid *mf.*
2 *v.* addo

promontory *n.* penrhyn,
pentir *m.*

proneness *n.* tueddiad *m.*

pronoun *n.* rhagenw *m.*
pronounce *v.* cyhoeddi,
datgan
pronouncement *n.*
cyhoeddiad, datganiad *m.*
proof *n.* prawf *m.*
proper *a.* addas, priod,
priodol, rheolaidd; **proper
noun** enw priod
property *n.* eiddo *m.*
prophesy *v.* proffwydo
prophet *n.* proffwyd *m.*
proportional *a.* cyfrannol.
Proportional Representation
Cynrychiolaeth Gyfrannol
proposal *n.* cynnig *m.*
propose *v.* cynnig, bwriadu
proposition *n.* cynigiad;
gosodiad *m.*
proprietor *n.* perchennog *m.*
prose *n.* rhyddiaith *f.*
prosecute *v.* erlyn
prosecution *n.* erlyniad *m.*
prosecutor *n.* erlynydd *m.*
prospect *n.* golwg *mf,* golyfga
f, rhagolwg *m.*
prosper *v.* llwyddo
prosperity *n.* llwyddiant *m.*
prosperous *a.* llwyddiannus,
llewyrchus
protect *v.* amddiffyn
protest *v.* gwrthdystio
Protestant 1 *n.* Protestant *m.*
2 *a.* Protestannaidd
proud *a.* balch
prove *v.* profi
proverb *n.* dihareb *f.*
province *n.* talaith *f;* cylch,
maes *m.*
proviso *n.* amod *mf.*

provoke *v.* profocio, pryfocio,
procio
proxy *n.* dirprwy *m.*
prudent *a.* call, doeth,
synhwyrol
pry *v.* chwilota, busnesa
psalm *n.* salm *f.*
psalter *n.* llyfr salmau *m,*
sallwyr *f.*
pseudonym *n.* ffugenw *m.*
psychiatrist *n.* seiciatrydd *m.*
psychiatry *n.* seiciatreg *f.*
psychologist *n.* seicolegwr *m.*
psychology *n.* seicoleg *f.*
public 1 *n.* y cyhoedd *m.*
2 *a.* cyhoeddus. **public hall**
neuadd gyhoeddus; **public
house** tŷ tafarn; **public place**
man cyhoeddus
publican *n* tafarnwr *m.*
publication *n.* cyhoeddiad *m.*
publicity *n.* cyhoeddusrwydd
m.
publicly *ad.* yn gyhoeddus
publish *v.* cyhoeddi
publisher *n.* cyhoeddwr *m.*
pudding *n.* pwdin *m.*
Christmas pudding pwdin
Nadolig
puddle *n.* pwllyn *m.*
pull 1 *n.* plwc; tynfa *f.* 2 *v.*
tynnu
pulpit *n.* pulpud *m.*
pulse *n.* curiad *m.*
pump 1 *n.* pwmp *m.* 2 *v.*
pwmpio
punctual *a.* prydlon
punctuality *n.* prydlondeb *m.*
puncture 1 *n.* twll *m.* 2 *v.*
tyllu

punish *v.* cosbi; poeni
punishment *n.* cosb, cosbedigaeth *f.*
pup *n.* ci bach; cenau *m.*
pupil *n.* disgybl *m;* cannwyll llygad *f.*
puppet *n.* pyped *m.*
purchase 1 *n.* pryniant *m.* **2** *v.* prynu
pure *a.* pur, glân, gwir
purge *v.* puro, glanhau
purify *v.* puro
purple *n. & a.* porffor, piws *m.*
purpose *n.* bwriad, pwrpas, amcan, diben *m.*
purr *v.* canu grwndi, canu crwth; grwnan
purse *n.* cwd, cwdyn, pwrs *m.*
pursue *v.* dilyn, erlid, erlyn, hel, hela
pursuer *n.* erlidiwr *m.*
puffin *n.* pâl *m.*
push 1 *n.* gwthiad, hwp *m.* **2** *v.* gwthio, hwpio

Q

quagmire *n.* siglen, cors *f.*
quaint *a.* od, henffasiwn
quake *v.* crynu, ysgwyd
Quaker *n.* Crynwr *m.*
Quakers Yard Mynwent y Crynwyr
qualification *n.* cymhwyster *m.*
qualified *a.* cymwys
quality *n.* rhinwedd *mf,* ansawdd *m.*
quantity *n.* swm *m,* nifer *mf,* maint, mesur *m.*
quarrel 1 *n.* cweryl, ffrae *f.* **2** *v.* cweryla, ffraeo
quarry *n.* chwarel *f,* cwar *m.*
quarryman chwarelwr
quart *n.* chwart, cwart *m.*
quarter *n.* chwarter, cwarter; cwr, man *m.* **quarter of an hour** chwarter awr
quay *n.* cei *m.* **New Quay (Ceredigion)** Ceinewydd
queen *n.* brenhines *f.*

Insight

queen *n. brenhines f.* **Queen Elizabeth II** Y *Frenhines Elisabeth yr Ail.*

pusher *n.* gwthiwr
put *v.* dodi, gosod, rhoddi, rhoi; mynegi
puzzle *n.* pos *m.* **crossword puzzle** pos croeseiriau
pyjamas *n.pl.* pyjamas *m. pl,* gwisg nos *f.*

queer *a.* od, hynod, ysmala
quench *v.* diffodd; torri (syched)
query 1 *n.* cwestiwn, ymholiad *m.* **2** *v.* holi, ymholi, amau
quest *n.* ymchwil *f,* cwest *m.*

question 1 *n.* cwestiwn *m.*
 question mark gofynnod 2 *v.*
 cwestiynu, holi
questioner *n.* holwr *m.*

radiator *n.* rheiddiadur *m.*
radio *n.* radio *m.* **radio**
 programme rhaglen radio;
 radio station gorsaf radio

Insight

radio *n.* *radio m. Radio Cymru;* **analogue radio** *radio analog;*
digital radio *radio digidol;* **local radio** *radio lleol;* **car radio**
radio'r car.

---

questionnaire *n.* holiadur *m.*
queue 1 *n.* ciw *m;* cwt *mf.*
 2 *v.* ciwio
quick *a.* cyflym, buan, byw.
 to the quick i'r byw
quickly *ad.* yn fuan
quiet 1 *n.* tawelwch,
 llonyddwch *m.* 2 *a.* tawel,
 distaw, llonydd. 3 *v.* tawelu
quietness *n.* tawelwch *m.*
quilt 1 *n.* cwilt, cwrlid *m.*
 2 *v.* cwiltio
quintet *n.* pumawd *m.*
quit *v.* gadael, symud,
 ymadael
quite *ad.* hollol, llwyr, eithaf
quiver *ad.* crynu
quiz 1 *n.* pos, cwis *m.* 2 *v.*
 holi, profocio
quotation *n.* dyfyniad *m.*
 quotation marks dyfynodau

R

rabbit *n.* cwningen *f.*
race *n.* gyrfa, ras; hil *f.*
racial *a.* hiliol
racket *n.* raced *mf.*

rag *n.* clwtyn, rhecsyn *m.* **rag**
 doll doli glwt *f.*

rail *n.* cledr, cledren, rheilen;
 canllaw *f.* **rails (of railway)**
 cledrau
railway *n.* rheilffordd *f.*
 railway station gorsaf
 reilffordd
raiment *n.* dillad *m.* gwisg *f.*
rain 1 *n.* glaw *m.* 2 *v.* glawio,
 bwrw glaw
rainbow *n.* enfys *f.*
raincoat *n.* cot law *f.*
rainy *a.* glawog, glawiog
rake 1 *n.* rhaca *mf.* 2 *v.*
 crafu, rhacanu
ram *n.* hwrdd, maharen *m.*
range *n.* amrediad; cwmpas;
 ystod *f.* **range of temperature**
 amrediad tymheredd: **age**
 range ystod oed
rank *n.* rhes, rhestr, rheng,
 gradd *f.*
ransom *n.* pridwerth *m.*
rape 1 *n.* trais *m.* 2 *v.* treisio
rapid *a.* cyflym, buan, gwyllt
rare *a.* prin; anaml

raspberry *n.* afanen, afansen, mafonen *f.*

rat *n.* llygoden fawr, llygoden Ffrengig *f.*

rate 1 *n.* treth *f*, tâl; cyflymder; cyfradd *m.* 2 *v.* trethu

ratepayer *n.* trethdalwr *m.*

rather *ad.* braidd, go, lled, yn hytrach

raw *a.* noeth, garw; amrwd

ray *n.* pelydr, pelydryn *m.*

re *prp.* ynglŷn â, mewn perthynas â

re- *px.* ail-; eto

reach 1 *n.* cyrraedd *m.* 2 *v.* cyrraedd, estyn, hercyd

reaction *n.* ymateb, adwaith *m.*

read *v.* darllen

re-address *v.* ailgyfeirio

reader *n.* darllenwr, darllenydd; llyfr darllen *m.*

readily *ad.* yn barod, yn union, yn rhwydd

reading *n.* darllen *m.*

reading-room *n.* ystafell ddarllen *f.*

ready *a.* parod, rhwydd

real *a.* gwir, real, go-iawn

reality *n.* gwirionedd, realiti *m.*

realize *v.* sylweddoli; gwerthu

really *ad.* yn wir, mewn gwirionedd

realm *n.* teyrnas, gwlad, bro *f.*

reap *v.* medi, cywain

rear 1 *n.* cefn, pen ôl, y tu ôl *m.* 2 *v.* codi, magu, meithrin

reason 1 *n.* rheswm, achos *m.* 2 *v.* rhesymu

reasonably *a.* rhesymol

rebel 1 *n.* gwrthryfelwr *m.* 2 *v.* gwrth ryfela

rebellion *n.* gwrthryfel *m.*

rebuke 1 *n.* cerydd *m*, sen *f.* 2 *v.* ceryddu

recall *v.* galw yn ôl, galw i gof, cofio

receipt *n.* derbynneb, taleb *f.*

receive *v.* derbyn

receiver *n.* derbynnydd *m.*

recent *a.* diweddar

receptionist *n.* derbynnydd *m.*

receptive *a.* derbyniol

recipe *n.* rysáit *f.*

recitation *n.* adroddiad *m.*

recite *v.* adrodd, datgan

reckon *v.* cyfrif, rhifo; barnu

recline *v.* gorwedd, gorffwys

recluse *n.* meudwy *m.*

recognize *v.* adnabod

recollect *v.* galw i gof, cofio

record 1 *n.* record *f.* 2 *v.* cofnodi, recordio

recording *n.* recordiad *m.*

re-count *v.* ailgyfrif

recreation *n.* adloniant *m.*

rectify *v.* unioni, cywiro

recurrence *n.* ailddigwyddiad, ailymddangosiad *m.*

recycle *v.* ailgylchu

red *n. & a.* coch *m.* **red kite** barcut coch

redeem *v.* gwaredu, achub, prynu (yn ôl)

redeemer *n.* prynwr, gwaredwr *m.*

reduce *v.* gostwng

reduction *n.* gostyngiad *m.*

redundant *a.* di-swydd

refer *v.* cyfeirio, cyfarwyddo
referee 1 *n.* canolwr, rheolwr *m.* **2** *v.* dyfarnu
reference *n.* cyfeiriad; geirda *m.*
refine *v.* puro
refinery *n.* purfa *f.*
reflect *v.* meddwl, myfyrio, ystyried
reform 1 *n.* diwygiad *m.* **2** *v.* diwygio, gwella
reformation *n.* diwygiad *m*; **Protestant Reformation** Diwygiad Protestannaidd
refresh *v.* adfywio
refrigerator *n.* oergell *f.*
refuge *n.* lloches, noddfa *f.*
refugee *n.* ffoadur *m.*
refuse *n.* ysbwriel, sothach *m.* **refuse bin** bin ysbwriel
refuse *v.* gwrthod, pallu
region *n.* ardal, cylch; rhanbarth *f*; rhandir *m.*
register 1 *n.* cofrestr *f.* **2** *v.* cofrestru
registrar *n.* cofrestrydd *m.*
regular *a.* rheolaidd, cyson
rehearsal *n.* rihyrsal, practis *m.*
reimburse *v.* talu yn ôl, ad-dalu
rejoice *v.* llawenhau
rejoicing *n.* llawenydd *m.*
relate *v.* adrodd, mynegi; perthyn
related *a.* yn perthyn; wedi ei ddweud
relating to *prp.* yn ymwneud â
relation *n.* perthynas *mf.*
relationship *n.* perthynas *mf.*

relative 1 *n.* perthynas *mf.* **2** *a.* perthynol; cymharol: **relative pronoun** rhagenw perthynol
relax *v.* llacio, llaesu, ymlacio
release *v.* gollwng, rhyddhau
relevant *a.* perthnasol
religion *n.* crefydd *f.*
religious *a.* crefyddol
relish 1 *n.* blas *m.* **2** *v.* blasu, hoffi, mwynhau
rely *v.* dibynnu (ar)
remain *v.* aros, bod ar ôl
remainder *n.* gweddill *m.*
remains *n.* olion, gweddillion *pl.*
remark 1 *n.* sylw *m.* **2** *v.* sylwi, dweud
remarkable *a.* hynod, nodedig; rhyfedd, od
remedy 1 *n.* meddyginiaeth *f.* **2** *v.* gwella
remember *v.* cofio
remembrance *n.* cof, coffa *m.*
remind *v.* atgoffa, atgofio, cofio
remiss *a.* esgeulus, diofal
remnant *n.* gweddill *m.*
remote *a.* pell, diarffordd, anghysbell
remotely *ad.* o bell
removal *n.* symudiad *m.*
remove *v.* symud
remunerate *v.* talu, gwobrwyo; cydnabod
rendering *n.* datganiad; trosiad *m.*
rendezvous *n.* man cyfarfod *m.*
renowned *a.* enwog, adnabyddus

repairer *n.* trwsiwr, cyweiriwr
m.

repeat *v.* ailadrodd

reply 1 *n.* ateb, atebiad *m.*
2 *v.* ateb

report 1 *n.* adroddiad; sŵn
ergyd *m.* 2 *v.* adrodd

reporter *n.* gohebydd *m.*

representation *n.*
cynrychiolaeth *f.* **Proportional
Representation**
Cynrychiolaeth Gyfrannol

republic *n.* gweriniaeth *f.*

reputed *a.* honedig

request 1 *n.* cais, dymuniad
m, arch *f.* 2 *v.* ceisio,
dymuno

require *v.* ceisio, gofyn

requirements *n.* gofynion *pl.*

rescue *v.* achub

research 1 *n.* ymchwil *f.*
research work gwaith
ymchwil. 2 *v.* ymchwilio

researcher *n.* chwilotwr *m.*

resemblance *n.* tebygrwydd
m.

reserve *v.* neilltuo, cadw wrth
gefn

reserved *a.* swil; wedi ei
gadw. **reserved seats** seddau
cadw

reservoir *n.* cronfa *f.*

reside *v.* trigo, byw,
preswylio

resident *n.* preswylydd *m.*

residential *a.* preswyl.
residential school ysgol
breswyl

residue *n.* gweddill *m.*

resign *v.* ymddiswyddo

resignation *n.*
ymddiswyddiad *m.*

resist *v.* gwrthwynebu,
gwrthsefyll

resolute *a.* penderfynol

resolution *n.* penderfyniad *m.*

resolve 1 *n.* penderfyniad *m.*
2 *v.* penderfynu

resources *n.* adnoddau *pl.*

respect 1 *n.* parch *m.* 2 *v.*
parchu

respectable *a.* parchus

respectful *a.* boneddigaidd

respectfully *ad.* yn barchus

respiration *n.* anadliad *m.*

respire *v.* anadlu

respite *n.* egwyl *f,* seibiant *m,*
hoe *f.*

respond *v.* ateb, ymateb

response *n.* ateb, atebiad *m.*

responsibility *n.* cyfrifoldeb *m*

responsible *a.* cyfrifol

rest 1 *n.* gorffwys, saib *m,*
hoe *f;* gweddill *m.* 2 *v.*
gorffwyso, pwyso

restaurant *n.* tŷ bwyta; bwyty
m.

restless *a.* rhwyfus, aflonydd

restore *v.* adfer

restrict *v.* cyfyngu

restriction *n.* cyfyngiad *m.*

result *n.* canlyniad, ateb *m.*

retain *v.* cadw, dal; llogi

retard *v.* arafu

retire *v.* ymddeol

retired *a.* wedi ymddeol

retirement *n.* ymddeoliad *m.*

retiring *a.* swil

return *v.* dychwelyd

returns *n.* enillion *pl.*

reveal *v.* datguddio, dangos, egluro, datgelu

revenge *n. & v.* dial *m.*

reverend *a.* parchedig: **Revd Ifan Puw** Parchg Ifan Puw

revise *v.* diwygio, cywiro

revival *n.* diwygiad *m.*

revive *v.* adfer

revolution *n.* chwyldro, chwyldroad *m.*

revolve *v.* troi

reward 1 *n.* gwobr *f,* tâl *m.* 2 *v.* gwobrwyo

rheumatism *n.* gwynegon, cryd cymalau *m.*

rhyme 1 *n.* odl *f;* rhigwm *m.* 2 *v.* odli; rhigymu

ribbon *n.* ruban *m.*

rice *n.* reis *m.*

rich *a.* cyfoethog, bras, ffrwythlon

riches *n.* cyfoeth, golud *pl.*

rickety *a.* simsan, sigledig

rid *v.* gwaredu, cael gwared o

riddle *n.* pos *m.*

ridge *n.* crib *mf,* cefn *m.*

rifle *n.* dryll, reiffl *m.*

right 1 *n.* hawl, iawn *m.* braint *f.* 2 *a.* iawn, cywir; de. 3 *ad.* yn gywir, yn iawn. **right angle** ongl sgwâr; **right hand** llaw dde

righteous *a.* cyfiawn

righteousness *n.* cyfiawnder *m.*

rim *n.* ymyl *mf.*

ring 1 *n.* cylch *m;* modrwy *f;* caniad *(ffôn) m.* **wedding ring** modrwy briodas. 2 *v.* canu cloch

rinse *v.* golchi

riot *n.* terfysg *m.*

rip *v.* rhwygo

ripe *a.* aeddfed

rise 1 *n.* codiad *m.* 2 *v.* codi

river *n.* afon *f.* **River Severn** Afon Hafren; **River Tawe** Afon Tawe; **River Wye** Afon Gwy

road *n.* ffordd, heol, hewl *f.* **main road** ffordd fawr, heol fawr; **narrow road** ffordd gul, heol gul; **straight road** heol syth; **winding road** heol droellog; **bypass** ffordd osgoi

roar *v.* rhuo

roast 1 *n.* rhost *m.* **roast potatoes** tatws rhost. 2 *v.* rhostio

rob *v.* lladrata, dwyn, dwgyd

robber *n.* lleidr *m.*

robbery *n.* lladrad *m.*

robe *n.* gwisg, gŵn *f.*

robin *n.* robin goch *m.*

rock 1 *n.* craig *f;* roc *m.* 2 *v.* siglo

rocky *a.* creigiog

rôle *n.* rhan, rôl *f.*

roll 1 *n.* rhôl, rhestr *f.* 2 *v.* rholio, treiglo

Roman 1 *n.* Rhufeiniwr *m.* 2 *a.* Rhufeinig. **Roman Catholic** Pabydd *n.*

romance *n.* carwriaeth *f.*

romantic *a.* rhamantus, rhamantaidd

Rome *n.* Rhufain *f.*

roof *n.* to *m,* nen *f.*

room *n.* lle *m,* ystafell, stafell *f.*

rooster *n.* ceiliog *m.*
root *n.* gwreiddyn *m.*
rope 1 *n.* rhaff *f.* **2** *v.* rhaffu, rhwymo
rose *n.* rhosyn *m.*
rosy-cheeked *a.* gwridog
rot *v.* pydru
rotten *a.* pwdr, drwg, sâl
rough *a.* garw, bras
round *a.* cron *f.*, crwn *m.*
roundabout 1 *n.* cylchfan *f.*, trogylch *m.* **2** *a.* o amgylch
route *n.* llwybr *m*, taith, ffordd *f.*
row 1 *n.* rhes, rhestr *f.* **2** *v.* rhwyfo. **rowing boat** cwch rhwyfo
row *n.* ffrae *f*, terfysg *m.*
royal *a.* brenhinol
rub *v.* rhwbio
rubber *n.* rwber *m.*
rubbish *n.* ysbwriel, sothach *coll*, lol *f*; **rubbish bin** bin ysbwriel
rudder *n.* llyw *m.*
ruddy *a.* coch, gwridog
rude *a.* anfoesgar, haerllug
rudiment *n.* egwyddor, gwyddor, elfen *f.*
rudimentary *a.* elfennol
rugby *n.* rygbi *m.* **rugby ball** pêl rygbi; **rugby match** gêm rygbi
rugged *a.* garw
ruin 1 *n.* dinistr *m*; adfail *mf.* **2** *v.* dinistrio, difetha
rule 1 *n.* llywodraeth; rheol *f*; arfer *mf*; riwl, riwler *m.* **2** *v.* llywodraethu, rheoli

ruler *n.* llywodrodaethwr, llyw, rheolwr; riwl, riwler, pren mesur *m.*
ruling *n.* dyfarniad *m.*
rummage *v.* chwilota
rummager *n.* chwilotwr *m.*
rumour *n. & v.* si, su, *m,* sôn *mf*, chwedl *f.*
run 1 *n.* rhediad *m.* **2** *v.* rhedeg, rheoli. **Run!** Rhed! (*singular*); Rhedwch! (*plural*)
runaway *n.* ffoadur *m.*
runner *n.* rhedwr *m.*
running *n.* rhediad *m.*
rural *a.* gwledig. **Rural Wales** Cymru Wledig
rush 1 *n.* rhuthr *m.* **2** *v.* rhuthro
Russia *n.* Rwsia *f.*
Russian 1 *n.* Rwsiad *m* (*person*); Rwsieg *f* (*iaith*). **2** *a.* Rwsiaidd

S

Sabbath *n.* Sabath, Saboth *m.*
sack *n.* cwd, cwdyn *m*, sach *f.*
sacred *a.* sanctaidd, glân
sacrifice 1 *n.* aberth *mf.* **2** *v.* aberthu
sad *a.* trist, blin, truenus, trwm, prudd
sadly *ad.* yn drist, yn flin, yn brudd
sadness *n.* tristwch, trymder *m.*
safe 1 *n.* cist, cell *f.* **2** *a.* diogel, saff
sail 1 *n.* hwyl *f.* **2** *v.* hwylio, morio

sailing *n.* hwylio *m.* **sailing boat** llong hwylio

sailor *n.* llongwr, morwr *m.*

saint *n.* sant *m;* santes *f.* **Saint David** Dewi Sant; **Saint John** Sant Ioan; **Saint Mary** y Santes Fair; **Saint David's** Tyddewi

sake *n.* mwyn *m.* **for the sake of** er mwyn

salary *n.* cyflog *mf.*

sale *n.* gwerthiant *m;* sâl, sêl *f,* arwerthiant *m.* **For Sale** Ar Werth

salesman *n.* gwerthwr *m.*

saliva *n.* poer, poeri *m.*

salt 1 *n.* halen *m.* **saltcellar** llestr halen. 2 *a.* hallt. **saltwater** dŵr hallt; dŵr y môr. 3 *v.* halltu

salvation *n.* iachawdwriaeth *f.* **Salvation Army** Byddin yr Iachawdwriaeth

same *a.* yr un, yr unrhyw, yr un fath

sand *n.* tywod *m.* **sand castles** cestyll tywod

sandwich 1 *n.* brechdan *f.* 2 *v.* gwthio rhwng

Santa Claus *n.* Siôn Corn *m.*

sap 1 *n.* sudd *m.* 2 *v.* sugno; tanseilio

satellite *n.* lloeren *f.*

satisfaction *n.* boddhad *m.*

satisfy *v.* bodloni

Saturday *n.* dydd Sadwrn *m.*

Saturn *n.* Sadwrn *m.*

sauce *n.* saws *m.*

saucepan *n.* sosban *f.* **small saucepan** sosban fach; **big**

saucepan sosban fawr

saucer *n.* soser *f.*

savage 1 *n.* dyn gwyllt *m.* 2 *a.* ffyrnig, gwyllt

save 1 *v.* achub, arbed, gwaredu; cynilo. 2 *prp. & c.* ond

savings *n.* cynilion *pl.*

saviour *n.* gwaredwr, iachawdwr *m.*

savoury *a.* blasus

saw 1 *n.* llif *f.* **sawdust** blawd llif; **hand-saw** llawlif. 2 *v.* llifio

say *v.* dweud (wrth). **to tell someone** dweud wrth rywun

saying *n.* dywediad, ymadrodd *m.*

scale *n.* graddfa; clorian, tafol *f.* **Celsius scale** graddfa Celsius

scales *n.* clorian, tafol *f.*

scarce *a.* prin, anaml

scarcely *ad.* braidd, prin, o'r braidd

scarcity *n.* prinder *m.*

scare 1 *n.* braw, ofn *m.* 2 *v.* ofni, dychryn

scarf *n.* sgarff *f.*

scatter *v.* chwalu

scene *n.* lle, man *m.* golygfa *f.*

scenery *n.* golygfa *f.*

scent 1 *n.* arogl, aroglau; gwynt; trywydd *m.* 2 *v.* arogli; gwynto; sawru

scheme 1 *n.* cynllun *m.* 2 *v.* cynllunio

scholar *n.* ysgolhaig, ysgolor *m.*

scholarship *n.* ysgoloriaeth *f.*
school *n.* ysgol *f.* **bilingual school** ysgol ddwyieithog; **local school** ysgol leol; **night-school** ysgol nos; **summer school** ysgol haf; **Welsh school** ysgol Gymraeg; **primary school** ysgol gynradd; **comprehensive school** ysgol gyfun
schoolboy *n.* bachgen ysgol *m.*
schooldays *n.* dyddiau ysgol *pl.*
schoolgirl *n.* merch ysgol *f.*
schoolhouse *n.* tŷ ysgol *m.*
schoolmaster *n.* athro ysgol, ysgolfeistr *m.*
schoolmistress *n.* athrawes, ysgolfeistres *f.*
science *n.* gwyddoniaeth, gwyddor *f.* **science fiction** ffuglen wyddonol

Scotland *n.* Yr Alban *f.*
scowl 1 *n.* gwg *m.* 2 *v.* gwgu
scratch 1 *n.* crafiad *m.* 2 *v.* crafu
scream 1 *n.* sgrech, ysgrech *f.* 2 *v.* sgrechian, sgrechain
screw 1 *n.* sgriw *f.* 2 *v.* sgriwio
script *n.* sgript *f.*
scripture *n.* ysgrythur *f*, y Beibl *m.*
scrum 1 *n.* sgrym *f.* 2 *v.* sgrymio
scrum-half *n.* mewnwr *m.*
sea *n.* môr *m.* **sea-level** lefel y môr; **sea trip** mordaith; **sea water** dŵr y môr
seagull *See* **gull**
seal *n.* morlo *m;* sêl *f.*
seaman *n.* morwr, llongwr *m.*
sea-marsh *n.* morfa *m.*
seamstress *n.* gwniadyddes, gwniyddes *f.*

Insight

science *n. gwyddor, gwyddoniaeth f.* **domestic science** *gwyddor cartref;* **rural science** *gwyddor gwlad;* **social science** *gwyddor cymdeithas;* **pure science** *gwyddoniaeth bur.*

scientific *a.* gwyddonol
scientist *n.* gwyddonydd *m.*
scissors *n.* siswrn *m.*
scorch *v.* crasu; rhuddo
scorched *a.* cras
score 1 *n.* sgôr; ugain *m.* 2 *v.* sgorio
scorn 1 *n.* gwawd *m.* 2 *v.* gwawdio

search 1 *n.* ymchwil *f.* 2 *v.* chwilio, edrych, ymchwilio
searcher *n.* chwiliwr *m.*
sea-shore *n.* glan y môr *f.*
seasickness *n.* salwch (y) môr. *m.*
season *n.* adeg *f*, amser, pryd, tymor *m.* **season ticket** tocyn tymor

seat 1 *n.* sedd, sêt *f.* **2** *v.* eistedd

seaweed *n.* gwymon *m.*

second 1 *n.* ail *m*; eiliad *f.* **2** *a.* ail. **second class** ail ddosbarth; isradd; **second-hand** ail-law

secret 1 *n.* cyfrinach *f.* **2** *a.* cyfrinachol

secretary *n.* ysgrifennydd *m*, ysgrifenyddes *f*. **Secretary of State** Ysgrifennydd Gwladol

section *n.* adran, rhan *f.*

secure 1 *a.* diogel, sicr, siŵr. **2** *v.* sicrhau

security *n.* sicrwydd, diogelwch *m*.; ernes *f*. **Social Security** Nawdd Cymdeithasol

sediment *n.* gwaelodion, gwaddod *m.*

see 1 *n.* esgobaeth *f.* **2** *v.* gweld, gweled.

seed 1 *n.* had *coll*, hadyn, hedyn *m.* **2** *v.* hadu

seek *v.* ceisio, chwilio

seem *v.* ymddangos

seemly *a.* addas

seething *a.* berw *m.*

seize *v.* gafael, dal. **to seize the opportunity** achub y cyfle

seldom *ad.* anaml.

select *a. & v.* dewis, dethol

selection *n.* detholiad *m.*

self *pn. & n.* hun, hunan *m.*

self-catering *a.* hunan arlwyol

self-cleaning *a.* hunan lanhaol.

self-confident *a.* hunan hyderus

selfish *a.* hunanol

self-respect *n.* hunan-barch *m.*

sell *v.* gwerthu

seller *n.* gwerthwr *m.*

semi- *px.* hanner-, go-, lled-

semicircle *n.* hanner cylch *m.*

semi-final *a.* cynderfynol

senate *n.* senedd *f.*

send *v.* anfon, danfon, gyrru, hala

sender *n.* gyrrwr *m.*

senile *a.* oedrannus, hen

senility *n.* henaint *m.*

senior *a.* hŷn, uwch, uchaf

sense 1 *n.* synnwyr, pwyll *m.* ystyr *mf.* **2** *v.* synhwyro

sensible *a.* synhwyrol, call

sentence 1 *n.* brawddeg; barn *f.* **2** *v.* dedfrydu

sentry *n.* gwyliwr *m.*

separate 1 *a.* ar wahân. **2** *v.* gwahanu

separately *ad.* ar wahân

separation *n.* gwahaniad *m.*

September *n.* Medi *m.*

serenity *n.* tawelwch, hedd, heddwch *m.*

serial 1 *n.* cyfres *f.* **2** *a.* cyfresol

series *n.* cyfres, rhes *f.*

serious *a.* difrifol, prudd, prysur

seriously *ad.* yn ddifrifol

sermon *n.* pregeth *f.*

serpent *n.* sarff *f.*

servant *n.* gwas *m*, morwyn *f.* **civil servant** gwas sifil

serve *v.* gwasanaethu

service *n.* gwasanaeth *m*; oedfa *f.*

set 1 *n.* set; *f.* **2** *v.* trefnu, gosod, dodi

setting *n.* machlud; lleoliad *m.*

settle 1 *n.* sgiw, setl *f.* **2** *v.* sefydlu; penderfynu; talu, cytuno, setlo

settled *a.* sefydlog

settlement *n.* gwladfa *f.*

seven *n. & a.* saith *m.*

seventeen *n. & a.* dau ar bymtheg, un deg saith *m.*

seventh *n. & a.* seithfed *m.*

seventy *n. & a.* deg a thrigain, saith deg *m.*

sever *v.* torri

several *a.* amryw

severe *a.* caled, llym, hallt, tost

severity *n.* caledi *m.*

Severn *n.* Afon Hafren *f.*

sew *v.* gwnïo, pwytho

sewing machine *n.* periant gwnïo *m.*

sex *n.* rhyw *m.*

sexual *a.* rhywiol

shade 1 *n.* cysgod *m.* **2** *v.* cysgodi

shadow *n.* cysgod *m.*

shady *a.* cysgodol

shake *v.* ysgwyd, siglo, crynu

shaking *n.* ysgytwad *m.*

shaky *a.* sigledig

shallow *a.* bas

sham *a.* ffug, gau

shame *n.* cywilydd

shameful *a.* gwarthus, cywilyddus

shape 1 *n.* ffurf *f*, llun *m*, siâp *f.* **2** *v.* ffurfio, llunio

shapely *a.* lluniaidd

share 1 *n.* rhan, siâr *f.* **2** *v.* rhannu

sharp *a.* llym, miniog, siarp

shawl *n.* siôl *f.*

she *pn.* hi, hithau, hyhi

shed *n.* sied, cwts *m.*

sheep 1 *n.* dafad *f.* **2** *n.* defaid *pl.*

sheer *a.* pur; glân; noeth

sheet *n.* llen *f*, lliain *m.* dalen *f*, taflen *f.*

shelf *n.* silff *f.*

shell *n.* cragen *f*; plisgyn *m.*

shelter 1 *n.* cysgod *m*, lloches *f.* **2** *v.* cysgodi, llochesu

shepherd 1 *n.* bugail *m.* **2** *v.* bugeilio

shield 1 *n.* tarian *f.* **2** *v.* cysgodi; amddiffyn

shift 1 *n.* newid, symudiad; tro *m*; shifft *f.* **2** *v.* newid, symud

shine *v.* disgleirio, llewyrchu

shiny *a.* gloyw, disglair

ship *n.* llong *f.*

shipshape *a.* taclus, trefnus, twt

shire *n.* sir (Wales), swydd (England) *f.* **Pembrokeshire** Sir Benfro (Cymru); **Gloucestershire** Swydd Gaerloyw (Lloegr)

shirk *v.* osgoi

shirt *n.* crys *m.*

shiver *v.* crynu

shivering *n.* cryd *m.*

shoal *n.* haig *f.*

shock *n.* ysgytwad, sioc *m.*

shoe *n.* esgid *f.* **pair of shoes** pâr o esgidiau

shoot 1 *n.* eginyn *m.* 2 *v.* saethu

shooter *n.* saethwr *m.*

shooting *n.* saethu

shop 1 *n.* siop *f.* 2 *v.* siopa

shopkeeper *n.* siopwr *m.*

shopper *n.* prynwr *m.*

shopping *n.* siopa *m.*

shore *n.* glan *f*, traeth *f.*

short *a.* byr, cwta, prin

shot *n.* ergyd *mf.*

shoulder *n.* ysgwydd *f.*

shout 1 *n.* bloedd *m.* gwaedd *f.* 2 *v.* bloeddio, crio, gweiddi

shove 1 *n.* hwp *m.* 2 *v.* gwthio

shovel *n.* rhaw *f.*

show 1 *n.* sioe *f.* 2 *v.* dangos, arddangos

shower *n.* cawod *f.*

shriek 1 *n.* sgrech, ysgrech *f.* 2 *v.* sgrechian, sgrechain

shrill *a.* main, llym

shut *v.* cau

shy *a.* swil

sick 1 *n.pl.* cleifion *m.* 2 *a.* claf, gwael, sâl, tost

sickness *n.* afiechyd, clefyd, dolur, anhwyldeb, anhwylder, tostrwydd *m.*

side 1 *n.* ochr *f*, ymyl, ystlys; tu *mf*, plaid *f.* 2 *v.* ochri

sidesman *n.* ystlyswr *m.*

sideways *ad.* tua'r ochr

sigh 1 *n.* ochenaid *f.* 2 *v.* ochneidio

sight 1 *n.* golwg *mf*, golygfa *f.* 2 *v.* gweld, gweled

sign 1 *n.* arwydd *m.* 2 *v.* arwyddo, llofnodi

signal *n.* arwydd *m.*

signature *n.* llofnod *m.*

silage *n.* silwair *m.*

silence 1 *n.* distawrwydd, tawelwch *m.* 2 *v.* distewi

silencer *n.* distewydd *m.*

silent *a.* distaw, tawel

silk *n.* sidan *m.*

silly *a.* ffôl, dwl, twp

silver *n.* arian *m.* **silversmith** gof arian; **silver wedding** priodas arian

similar *a.* tebyg

similarity *n.* tebygrwydd *m.*

simple *a.* syml; diniwed

sin 1 *n.* pechod *m.* 2 *v.* pechu

since 1 *c.* am, gan, oherwydd. 2 *prp.* er, ers, er pan

sincere *a.* diffuant, cywir, pur

sinew *n.* gewyn *m.*

sing *v.* canu

singer *n.* canwr, cantwr, cantor *m;* cantores *f.*

singing *n.* caniad, caniadaeth *f*, canu *m.*

single *a.* sengl, un; dibriod

singular *a.* unigol; hynod

sink 1 *n.* sinc *m.* 2 *v.* suddo

sinner *n.* pechadur *m.*

sir *n.* syr *m.*

sister *n.* chwaer *f.*

sister-in-law *n.* chwaer-yng-nghyfraith *f.*

sit *v.* eistedd

situation *n.* lle, safle *m;* sefyllfa *f.*

six *n. & a.* chwe, chwech *m.*

sixteen *n. & a.* un ar bymtheg, un deg chwech *m.*

sixth *n. & a* chweched *m.*

sixty *n. & a.* trigain, chwe deg *m.*

size *n.* maint *m.*

skate 1 *n.* sgêt *f.* 2 *v.* sglefrio. **skateboard** bwrdd sglefrio

sketch 1 *n.* llun, braslun *m;* sgets *f.* 2 *v.* braslunio

ski 1 *n.* sgi *f.* 2 *v.* sgïo

skier *n.* sgîwr *m.*

skilful *a.* medrus

skill *n.* sgil *m*, crefft *f.*

skim *v.* tynnu, codi (hufen)

skimmed milk *n.* llaeth glas *m.*

skin 1 *n.* croen *m.* 2 *v.* blingo

skip *v.* sgipio

skirt *n.* sgert, sgyrt *f.*

sky *n.* wybren, awyr, ffurfafen, nen *f.*

skylark *n.* ehedydd, uchedydd, hedydd *m.*

slack 1 *n.* glo mân *m.* 2 *a.* llac, diofal, esgeulus

slacken *v.* llacio, llaesu

slate *n.* llechen *f.*

slaughter *v.* lladd

slaughterhouse *n.* lladd-dy *m.*

slave *n.* caethwas *m.*

slay *v.* lladd

sleek *a.* llyfn

sleep 1 *n.* cwsg *m.* 2 *v.* cysgu, huno. **sleeping bag** sach gysgu

sleepy *a.* cysglyd

sleet *n.* eirlaw *m.*

sleeve *n.* llawes *f.*

slender *a.* main, tenau

slice *n.* tafell, sleisen *f.* **slice** of bread and butter tafell o fara menyn; **slice of bacon** sleisen o gig moch

slide 1 *n.* llithren *f.* 2 *v.* llithro, sglefrio

slim *a.* main

slip 1 *n.* llithriad *m.* 2 *v.* llithro dros

slipper *n.* sliper *f.*

slippery *a.* llithrig, slic

slipshod *a.* anniben

slovenly *a.* anniben

slope *n.* rhiw *f*, tyle, llethr *m.*

slow 1 *a.* araf. 2 *v.* arafu

slug *n.* malwoden *f.* slyg *m.*

sluggard *n.* diogyn, pwdryn *m.*

sluggish *a.* diog, dioglyd

slumber 1 *n.* cwsg *m.* 2 *v.* cysgu

slur 1 *n.* llithriad *m.* 2 *v.* llithro dros

sly *a.* cyfrwys

small *a.* bach, mân, bychan *m.* bechan *f.*

smallest *a.* lleiaf; *see* **bach**

smallholder *n.* tyddynnwr *m.*

smallholding *n.* tyddyn *m.*

smash *v.* malu

smell 1 *n.* arogl *m*, aroglau *pl*, gwynt *m.* 2 *v.* arogli, clywed arogl, gwynto

smile 1 *n.* gwên *f.* 2 *v.* gwenu

smith *n.* gof *m.* **smithy** gefail

smoke 1 *n.* mwg *m.* 2 *v.* mygu, ysmygu

smoky *a.* myglyd

smooth *a.* llyfn; esmwyth

smother *v.* mogi, mygu

snack *n.* byrbryd *m.*

snag *n.* rhwystr *m.*

snail *n.* malwoden *f.*

snake *n.* neidr *f.*

snarl *v.* chwyrnu

sneeze *v.* tisian

snobs *n.pl.* crachach *m.*

snore *v.* chwyrnu

snout *n.* trwyn *m.*

snow *n.* eira *m.* **snowball** pelen eira; **snowdrift** lluwch, lluwchfa, lluchfa; **snowflake** pluen eira

Snowdon *n.* Yr Wyddfa *f.*

Snowdonia *n.* Eryri *f.*

snowdrop *n.* eirlys, tlws yr eira, lili wen fach *m.*

snub *n.* sen *f.*

so *ad. & c.* fel, felly, mor

soap *n.* sebon *m.* **soap powder** powdr golchi

soccer *n.* pêl-droed *f.*

socialism *n.* sosialaeth *f.*

socialist 1 *n.* sosialydd *m.* 2 *a.* sosialaidd

society *n.* cymdeithas *f.*

sociologist *n.* cymdeithasegwr *m.*

sociology *n.* cymdeithaseg *f.*

sock *n.* hosan *f.*

soft *a.* meddal. **soft drinks** diodydd ysgafn

soften *v.* meddalu

software *n.* meddalwedd *f.*

soil 1 *n.* pridd *m*; daear *f.* 2 *v.* trochi, sarnu

soldier *n.* milwr *m.*

sole 1 *n.* gwadn *m.* 2 *a.* unig, unigol, un

solemn *a.* difrifol, dwys

solicitor *n.* cyfreithiwr *m.*

solo 1 *n.* unawd *m.* 2 *a.* unigol

soloist *n.* unawdwr, unawdydd *m.*

solve *v.* datrys, datod

some 1 *a.* rhyw, rhai, peth, ychydig. 2 *pn.* rhai, rhywrai, rhywfaint. 3 *ad.* rhyw, tua, ynghylch

somebody *n. & pn.* rhywun *m.*

someone *n. & pn.* rhywun *m.*

Somerset *n.* Gwlad yr Haf *f.*

something *n.* rhywbeth *m.*

sometime *ad.* rhywbryd, rhywdro, gynt

sometimes *ad.* weithiau, ambell waith, ar brydiau

somewhat *ad.* go, lled, braidd

somewhere *ad.* rhywle

son *n.* mab *m.*

son-in-law *n.* mab-yng-nghyfraith *m.*

soon *ad.* yn fuan, ar fyr o dro

sooner *ad.* yn gynt

soot *n.* huddygl *m.*

sore *a.* blin, tost

sorrow 1 *n.* gofid, tristwch, galar *m.* 2 *v.* gofidio, hiraethu

sorrowful *a.* trist.

sorry *a.* blin, drwg gan, edifar, trist

sort 1 *n.* math, modd, dosbarth *m.* 2 *v.* dosbarthu, trefnu

soul *n.* enaid *m.*

sound 1 *n.* sain *f*, sŵn *m.* 2 *a.* iach; cyfan. 3 *v.* swnio, seinio soup *n.* cawl *m.*

sour 1 *a.* sur. 2 *v.* suro

source *n.* ffynhonnell *f,* tarddiad *m.*

south 1 *n. & a.* de *mf,* deau *m;* **South Wales** De Cymru. 2 *ad.* tua'r de

southern *a.* deheuol

sow *n.* hwch *f.*

sow *v.* hau

sower *n.* heuwr *m.*

space *n.* gofod, gwagle, bwlch *m.*

spaceman *n.* gofodwr *m.*

spaceship *n.* llong ofod *f.*

spade *n.* pâl, rhaw *f.*

Spain *n.* Sbaen *f.*

Spaniard *n.* Sbaenwr *m.*

Spanish 1 *n.* Sbaeneg *f.* *(iaith).* 2 *a.* Sbaenaidd

spare 1 *a.* sbâr. 2 *v.* arbed

spark *n.* gwreichionen *f.*

speak *v.* llefaru, siarad

speaker *n.* llefarwr, llefarydd, siaradwr *m.*

special *a.* arbennig, neilltuol

species *n.* math *m.*

specified *a.* nodedig

specify *v.* enwi

spectacle *n.* golygfa *f.*

spectacles *n.* sbectol *f. pl.*

speech *n.* araith *f;* llafar *m,* ymadrodd *m.*

speechless *a.* mud

speed *n.* cyflymder *m.*

speedy *a.* buan, cyflym

spell 1 *n.* egwyl, hoe, sbel *f;* hud, swyn *m.* 2 *v.* cael hoe; sillafu. **to cast a spell** swyno

spend *v.* gwario, hala *(arian);* treulio *(amser).*

spiced *a.* llysieuol

spider *n.* corryn, pryf copyn *m.*

spill *v.* colli

spine *n.* asgwrn cefn *m.*

spirit *n.* ysbryd *m.*

spirited *a.* ysbrydol, nwyfus

spiritual *a.* ysbrydol

spiritualize *v.* ysbrydoli

spit *n. & v.* poeri *m.*

spittle *n.* poer, poeri *m.*

splash *v.* tasgu

splendid *a.* rhagorol, ardderchog, penigamp, campus, gwych

splendour *n.* ysblander *m.*

split 1 *n.* hollt; rhaniad; rhwyg *m.* 2 *a.* hollt; rhanedig. 3 *v.* hollti

spokesman *n.* llefarwr, llefarydd *m.*

spoon 1 *n.* llwy *f.* 2 *v.* llwyo

spoonful *n.* llwyaid *f.*

sport *n.* sbort *f.* chwarae *m,* hwyl *f.*

sports *n.* mabolgampau *pl,* chwaraeon

spot 1 *n.* man *mf,* lle, llecyn, sbot, sbotyn, smotyn *m.* 2 *v.* adnabod; smotio

spread *v.* lledu

spring 1 *n.* ffynnon, ffynhonnell; sbring; gwanwyn; neidio *f.* 2 *v.* tarddu; neidio

sprout *n.* eginyn *m,* egin *pl.* **Brussels sprouts** ysgewyll Brwsel

spur *n.* ysbardun; clogwyn *m.*

sputnik *n.* lloeren *f.*

spy 1 *n.* ysbïwr *m.* 2 *v.* ysbïo

square *n.* sgwâr *f.*

squash 1 *n.* sboncen *f.*
2 *v.* gwasgu

squirrel *n.* gwiwer *f.*

stable 1 *n.* stabl *f.*
2 *a.* sefydlog, diogel

staff *n.* ffon; staff *f.*

stag *n.* hydd *m.*

stage 1 *n.* llwyfan *m;* lefel *f.*
2 *v.* llwyfannu

stair *n.* gris *m,* staer *f.*

stall *n.* stondin *f;* côr *m.*

stamp 1 *n.* stamp *m.* 2 *v.*
stampio

stand 1 *n.* stondin *f.* 2 *v.*
sefyll

standard 1 *n.* safon; baner *f.*
2 *a.* safonol

standpoint *n.* safbwynt *m.*

stanza *n.* pennill *m.*

star 1 *n.* seren *f.* 2 *v.* serennu

starlight *n.* golau'r sêr

starling *n.* drudwy *m.*

starry *a.* serennog

start *n. & v.* cychwyn,
dechrau *m.*

starve *v.* llwgu

state 1 *n.* cyflwr *m,* ffurf;
talaith *f.* 2 *v.* mynegi, dweud

statesman *n.* gwleidydd *m.*

station *n.* gorsaf *f.* safle *m,*
sefyllfa *f.* **railway station**
gorsaf reilffordd

stationary *a.* sefydlog

stationer *n.* gwerthwr
papurau *m.*

stationery *n.* papur ysgrifennu
m.

statistics *n.pl.* ystadegau

statue *n.* cerflun *m,* delw *f.*

statute *n.* deddf, cyfraith, act
f.

stay 1 *n.* arhosiad *m.* 2 *v.*
aros, oedi, sefyll

steal *v.* lladrata, dwyn

steel *n.* dur *m.*

steep *a.* serth

steer *v.* llywio; cyfeirio

stench *n.* drewdod, drewi *m.*

step 1 *n.* cam, gris 2 *v.* camu

step- *px.* llys-

stepdaughter *n.* llysferch *f.*

stepfather *n.* llystad *m.*

stepmother *n.* llysfam *f.*

stepsister *n.* llyschwaer *f.*

stepson *n.* llysfab *m.*

steward 1 *n.* stiward *m.* 2 *v.*
stiwardio

stick 1 *n.* ffon, gwialen *f,*
pren *m.* 2 *v.* glynu

stiff *a.* syth

stiffen *v.* sythu

still 1 *a.* llonydd, tawel. 2 *ad.*
eto, er hynny; byth

stillness *n.* tawelwch,
heddwch, llonyddwch *m.*

sting 1 *n.* pigiad *m.* 2 *v.* pigo

stink 1 *n.* drewdod, drewi *m.*
2 *v.* drewi

stitch 1 *n.* pwyth *m;*
2 *v.* pwytho, gwnïo

stocking *n.* hosan *f.*

stoke *v.* tanio, gofalu am dân

stomach 1 *n.* stumog *f,* bol *m.*
2 *v.* stumogi

stone *n.* carreg *f.*

Stonehenge *p.n.* Côr y Cewri
m.

stool *n.* stôl *f.*

stoop *v.* plygu, ymostwng
stop 1 *n.* atalfa *f*, stop *m*. **full stop** atalnod llawn. 2 *v.* atal; stopio; cau; aros, sefyll; peidio (â)
storage *n.* stôr *m*, storfa *f*.
store 1 *n.* stôr *m*, storfa *f*. 2 *v.* storio
storehouse *n.* stordy *m*.
storm *n.* storm, tymestl *f*.
stormy *a.* stormus, tymhestlog
story *n.* stori *f*, hanes, hanesyn *m*, chwedl *f*.
stove *n.* ffwrn, stof *f*.
straight *a.* syth, union
straighten *v.* sythu, unioni
straightway *ad.* yn y man, yn syth
strange *a.* dieithr, rhyfedd, rhyfeddol, od, estron
stranger *n.* dieithryn, estron *m*.
strangle *v.* tagu
straw *n.* gwelltyn *m*. *(a single straw)*; gwellt *m. coll.*
strawberry *n.* mefusen *f*.
stream 1 *n.* ffrwd *f*, llif *m*, nant *f*. 2 *v.* llifo
streamer *n.* ruban *m*, baner *f*.
street *n.* stryd, heol, hewl, ffordd *f*.
strength *n.* nerth, grym *m*.
stretch *v.* estyn, ymestyn
strict *a.* cyfyng, llym, manwl
stride 1 *n.* cam *m*. 2 *v.* camu
strife *n.* ymryson *m*.
strike 1 *n.* streic *f*. 2 *v.* streicio; taro
striker *n.* streiciwr *m*.

strip *n.* llain *f*. **landing strip, airstrip** llain lanio
string *n.* cordyn, llinyn; tant *m*.
strive *v.* ymdrechu
strong *a.* cryf, grymus
structure 1 *n.* adeilad; strwythur *m*. 2 *v.* strwythuro
struggle 1 *n.* ymdrech *f*. 2 *v.* ymdrechu
student *n.* myfyriwr *m*.
study *v.* myfyrio, astudio
stump *n.* bôn *m*.
stunning *a.* syfrdanol
stupefying *a.* syfrdanol
stupid *a.* twp, dwl, hurt. **stupid person** twpsyn, hurtyn
sty *n.* twlc *m*. **pigsty** twlc mochyn
stye *n.* llefelyn, llyfelyn *m*, llefrithen *f*.
subconscious 1 *n.* isymwybod *m*. 2 *a.* isymwybodol
subject *n.* goddrych *m*.
subjective *a.* goddrychol
submarine 1 *n.* llong danfor *f*. 2 *a.* tanfor, tanforol
submit *v.* ymostwng; anfon; cyflwyno
subordinate *a.* israddol
substance *n.* sylwedd *m*.
substantial *a.* sylweddol
substantiate *v.* profi
substitute *n.* dirprwy, un yn lle rhywun arall *m*.
subterranean *a.* tanddaear, tanddaearol
suburb *n.* maestref *f*.
subway *n.* isffordd *f*, tanlwybr *m*.

succeed *v*. llwyddo; dilyn, canlyn

success *n*. llwydd, llwyddiant *m*.

successful *a*. llwyddiannus

succour *n*. ymgeledd, swcwr *m*.

such *a*. y fath, cyfryw

suck *v*. sugno

sudden *a*. sydyn

sue *v*. erlyn

suffer *v*. dioddef, caniatáu, goddef

suffering *n*. dioddef *m*, poen *mf*.

sufficient 1 *n*. digon *m*. 2 *a*. digon, digonol

sufficiently *ad*. digon

suffocate *v*. mogi, mygu, tagu

sugar 1 *n*. siwgr *m*. 2 *v*. siwgro

suggest *v*. awgrymu

suggestion *n*. awgrym, awgrymiad *m*.

suicide *n*. hunanladdiad *m*.

suitable *a*. addas, priodol

suite *n*. cyfres *f*.

sulk *v*. pwdu

sultry *a*. clòs, trymaidd

sum 1 *n*. swm *m*. 2 *v*. crynhoi

summarize *v*. crynhoi

summary *n*. crynodeb *mf*.

summer *n*. haf *m*.
 midsummer canol haf; **a summer's day** hafddydd; **summer dwelling** hafdy, hafod; tŷ haf

summery *a*. hafaidd

summit *n*. brig, pen *m*, ban *mf*, copa *m*.

summon *v*. galw, gwysio

summons *n*. gwŷs *f*.

sumptuous *a*. moethus

sun *n*. haul *m*.

sunbathe *v*. torheulo

sunburn *n*. llosg haul *m*.

Sunday *n*. dydd Sul *m*.

sunflower *n*. blodyn yr haul *m*.

sunglasses *n*. sbectol haul *f*.

sunny *a*. heulog

sunrise *n*. codiad haul *m*.

sunset *n*. machlud haul *m*.

sunshine *n*. heulwen *f*.

superb *a*. ardderchog, rhagorol

superior *a*. uwch, gwell

supermarket *n*. archfarchnad *f*.

supernatural *a*. goruwchnaturiol

superstition *n*. ofergoel, ofergoeledd, ofergoeliaeth *f*.

superstitious *a*. ofergoelus

supper *n*. swper *m*. **the Last Supper** y Swper Olaf

supple *a*. ystwyth, hyblyg

supplement 1 *n*. atodiad *m*. 2 *v*. ychwanegu

supplementary *a*. atodol, ychwanegol

support *v*. cynnal, cefnogi

suppose *v*. tybied, tybio

supreme *a*. goruchaf, prif, pennaf

sure *a*. sicr, siŵr

suretyship *n*. mechnïaeth *f*.

surface *n*. wyneb, arwyneb, arwynebedd *m*.

surfeit 1 *n*. syrffed *m*. 2 *v*. syrffedu

surgeon *n*. llawfeddyg *m*.

surgery *n.* llawfeddygaeth, llawdriniaeth; meddygfa *f.*
surgical *a.* llawfeddygol
surname 1 *n.* cyfenw *m.*
2 *v.* cyfenwi
surpass *v.* rhagori ar, trechu
surprise 1 *n.* rhyfeddod, syndod *m.* 2 *v.* synnu
surprising *a.* rhyfedd, rhyfeddol, syn
surround *v.* amgylchynu
suspect *v.* amau
suspend *v.* crogi; atal
suspension bridge *n.* pont grog *f.*
swallow 1 *n.* llwnc *m*; gwennol *f.* 2 *v.* llyncu
swamp 1 *n.* siglen, cors *f.* 2 *v.* gorlifo
swan *n.* alarch *m.*
swarm 1 *n.* haid, torf *f.* 2 *v.* heidio, tyrru
swathe 1 *n.* ystod *f.* 2 *v.* rhwymo
sway *v.* siglo
swear *v.* tyngu, rhegi
sweat 1 *n.* chwys *m.* 2 *v.* chwysu
swede *n.* erfinen, sweden, meipen *f.*
Swede *n.* Swediad *m.*
Sweden *n.* Sweden *f.*
Swedish *a.* Swedaidd
sweep 1 *n.* ysgubwr, sgubwr *f.* 2 *v.* ysgubo, sgubo, brwsio, brwshio
sweet 1 *n.* losinen, losen *f.* 2 *a.* melys
sweetheart *n.* cariad *mf.*
sweets *n.* losin *pl.*

swell *v.* chwyddo
swerve *v.* osgoi, gwyro, troi
swift 1 *n.* gwennol ddu *f.* 2 *a.* buan, cyflym
swiftness *n.* cyflymder *m.*
swim 1 *n.* nofiad *m.* 2 *v.* nofio
swimmer *n.* nofiwr *m.*
swimming *u.* nofio
swimming pool *n.* pwll nofio *m.*
swimsuit *n.* gwisg nofio *f.*
swing 1 *n.* siglen *f.* 2 *v.* siglo
switch *n.* troswr *f. (trydan)*, swits *mf.*
Switzerland *n.* Y Swistir *f.*
swoon *v.* llewygu
syllable *n.* sillaf *f.*
syllabus *n.* maes llafur *m.*
sympathy *n.* cydymdeimlad *m.*
symptom *n.* arwydd *m.*
synonym *n.* cyfystyr *m.*
synonymous *a.* cyfystyr (â)
system *a.* cyfundrefn; trefn, system *f.*

T

tabernacle *n.* tabernacl *m*, pabell *f.*
table *n.* bord *f*, bwrdd; tabl *m*; taflen *f.* **tableful** bordaid, byrddaid
tablecloth *n.* lliain bord, lliain bwrdd *m.*
tablespoon *n.* llwy fawr, llwy fwrdd *f.*
tablet *n.* tabled *m.*
tackle 1 *n.* offer *pl*, gêr, tacl *m.* 2 *v.* taclo

tackler *n.* taclwr *m.*
tail *n.* cynffon *f.*
tailback *n.* tagfa *f.*
tailor *n.* teiliwr *m.*
tailoress *n.* teilwres *f.*
take *v.* cymryd, cael, dwyn, dal
take hold *v.* cydio
tale *n.* chwedl *f*, hanes, hanesyn *m*, stori *f.*
talent 1 *n.* talent, dawn *f.* 2 *a.* talentog, dawnus
talk 1 *n.* sgwrs *f*, siarad *m.* sôn *mf.* 2 *v.* sgwrsio, siarad, sôn
talker *n.* siaradwr *m.*
tall *a.* tal, uchel
tallow *n.* gwêr *m.*
talon *n.* ewin *mf,* crafanc *f.*

target *n.* targed, nod *m.*
tart *n.* tarten, pastai *f.* **apple tart** pastai afalau; **jam tart** pastai jam
task *n.* tasg *m.*
taste 1 *n.* blas *m.* 2 *v.* blasu, clywed, profi
tasty *a.* blasus
tavern *n.* tafarn *mf*, tŷ tafarn *m.*
tax 1 *n.* treth *f.* **Income tax** Treth Incwm; **Value Added Tax** Treth Ar Werth. 2 *v.* trethu
taxi *n.* tacsi *m.*
tea *n.* te *m.* **tea bags** cydau te; **teacup** cwpan te, dysgl de; **tea leaves** dail te
teach *v.* dysgu

Insight

teach *v.* dysgu. *Dysgu* usually means to educate: **to teach someone something** – *dysgu rhywbeth i rywun*. It also means to learn: **teach me to play golf** – *dysgu imi sut i chwarae golff*. **Aled is being taught Chemistry** – *Mae Aled yn dysgu Cemeg*.

tame 1 *n.* dof. 2 *v.* dofi
tang *n.* tafod *m.*
tank *n.* tanc *m.*
tanker *n.* tancer *m;* llong olew *f.*
tap 1 *n.* tap *m.* 2 *v.* taro, tapio
tape *n.* tâp, incil *m.*
tape measure *n.* tâp mesur *m.*
tape-recorder *n.* recordydd tâp *m.*
tapering *a.* pigfain

teacher *n.* athro *m;* athrawes *f.*
team *n.* tîm *m.*
tea party *n.* te-parti *m.*
teapot *n.* tebot *m.*
tear *n.* deigryn *m.*
tear 1 *n.* rhwyg *m.* 2 *v.* rhwygo
tease *v.* poeni
teaspoon *n.* llwy de *f.*

teaspoonful *n.* llond llwy de
m.

technical *a.* technegol

technician *n.* technegwr *m.*

technique *n.* techneg *m.*

technology *n.* technoleg *f.*

teddy bear *n.* tedi *m.*

teenager *n.* un yn yr
arddegau *mf.*

teens *n.pl.* arddegau

teetotaller *n.*
llwyrymwrthodwr *m.*

telecast *n.* telediad *m.*

telephone 1 *n.* teleffon, ffôn
m. **telephone call** galwad
ffôn. **2** *v.* teleffonio, ffonio

television *n.* teledu *m.*

tell *v.* dweud (wrth), mynegi.
to tell the truth dweud y gwir

temper *n.* tymer, natur *m.*

temperature *n.* tymheredd *m.*

tempest *n.* tymestl *f.*

tempestuous *a.* tymhestlog

temple *n.* teml; arlais *f.*

ten *n. & a.* deg, deng *m.*

tendency *n.* tueddiad *m.*

tender *a.* tyner, mwyn,
meddal, tirion

tenderness *n.* tynerwch *m.*

tendon *n.* gewyn, tendon *m.*

tennis *n.* tenis *m.* **tennis ball**
pêl denis; **tennis court** cwrt
tenis; **tennis racket** raced
denis

tense 1 *n.* amser *m.*
(gramadeg). **2** *v.* tyn, tynn

tent *n.* pabell *f.*

tenth *n. & a.* degfed *m.*

term 1 *n.* tymor; term; amod
m. **2** *v.* enwi, galw

terminus *n.* terfyn *m.*

terrace *n.* rhes dai *f*, teras *m.*

terrible *a.* dychrynllyd,
ofnadwy, erchyll

terrifying *a.* dychrynllyd

territory *n.* tir *m.*

terror *n.* braw, ofn *m.*

terrorism *n.* terfysgaeth *f.*

terrorist *n.* terfysgwr *m.*

tertiary *a.* trydyddol. **tertiary
college** coleg trydyddol

test 1 *n.* prawf *m.*; **reading
test** prawf darllen; **spelling
test** prawf sillafu **2** *v.* profi

testament *n.* testament *m.*
New Testament Testament
Newydd

testify *v.* tystio

testimony *n.* tystiolaeth *f.*

text *n.* testun *m.* **textbook**
gwerslyfr

than *c.* na, nag

thank *v.* diolch. **Thanks**
Diolch! **Thanks very much**
Diolch yn fawr

thankful *a.* diolchgar

thankfulness *n.* diolchgarwch
m.

thankless *a.* diddiolch

thanksgiving *n.* diolchgarwch
m. **Thanksgiving Service**
Gwasanaeth Diolchgarwch

that 1 *a.* hwnnw, honno,
hynny, yna, acw. **2** *pn.* hwn,
hon, yna, hwn acw, hon acw,
dyna, dacw; a, y, yr. **3** *c.*
mai, taw, fel y, fel yr

thaw *v.* toddi, meddalu,
meirioli, dadmer, dadlaith

the *def. art.* y, yr, 'r

theatre *n.* theatr *f.*

thee *pn.* ti, tydi, tithau

theft *n.* lladrad *m.*

their *pn.* eu

theirs *pn.* eiddynt, yr eiddynt

them *pn.* hwy, hwynt, hwythau, nhw

themselves *pn.* eu hunain

then 1 *ad.* wedyn, yna, y pryd hwnnw. **2** *c.* yna, ynte, ynteu.

thereafter *ad.* wedyn

thereat *ad.* ar hynny, yna

thereby *ad.* trwy hynny

therefore *c.* am hynny, gan hynny, felly

therefrom *ad.* oddi yno

therein *ad.* yno, ynddo, yn hynny

thereupon *ad.* ar hynny

therewith *ad.* gyda hynny

thermometer *n.* thermomedr *f.*

these *pn. & a.* y rhai hyn, y rhain

they *pn.* hwy, hwynt, hwythau, nhw

thick *a.* tew, trwchus

thief *n.* lleidr *m.*

thieve *v.* lladrata, dwyn, dwgyd

thigh *n.* clun, morddwyd *f.*

thin *a.* main, tenau, cul

thing *n.* peth, gwrthrych *m.*

think *v.* meddwl, tybied, tybio

third *n. & a.* trydydd *m;* trydedd *f.*

thirst 1 *n.* syched *m.* **2** *v.* sychedu

thirsty *a.* sychedig

thirteen *n. & a.* tri ar ddeg,

un deg tri *m.*

thirty *n. & a.* deg ar hugain, tri deg *m.*

this *a. & pn.* hwn, hon, hyn; yma. **this minute** y funud hon, y funud yma; **this hour, (now, at present)** yr awr hon, **this day** y dydd hwn; **this week** yr wythnos hon; **this month** y mis hwn; **this year** eleni

thistle *n.* ysgallen *f.*

thorn *n.* draen, draenen *f;* **thorns** drain

those 1 *pn.* hynny, y rhai hynny, y rheini, y rheiny. **2** *a.* hynny, yna

though 1 *ad.* er, serch hynny. **2** *prp.* er, pe, cyd

thought *n.* meddwl, syniad *m.*

thoughtful *a.* meddyglar

thousand *n. & a.* mil *f.*

thread *n.* edau *f,* llinyn *m.*

three *n. & a.* tri *m,* tair *f.* **three times** teirgwaith

threesome *n.* triawd *m.*

threshold *n.* trothwy *m.* rhiniog *f.*

thrill *n.* ias *f.*

thrilling *a.* iasol

throat *n.* gwddf, gwddwg, llwnc *m.*

throne *n.* gorsedd *f.*

through 1 *ad.* trwodd. **2** *prp* drwy, trwy

throw 1 *n.* tafliad *m.* **2** *v.* taflu

thrush *n.* bronfraith *f.*

thrust 1 *n.* gwthiad, hwp *m.* **2** *v.* gwthio

thumb 1 *n.* bawd *m.* **2** *v.*
bodio

thunder 1 *n.* taran *f*, tyrfau
pl. **2** *v.* taranu

thunderbolt *n.* bollt *m*,
mellten, llucheden *f.*

thunderclap *n.* taran *f.*

thunderstorm *n.* storm fellt a
tharanau *f.*

Thursday *n.* dydd Iau

thus *ad.* fel hyn, felly

thy *pn.* dy, 'th

ticket *n.* tocyn, ticed *m.* **ticket
collector** tocynnwr; **ticket
office** swyddfa docynnau

tide *n.* llanw *m:* **high tide**
penllanw; **ebb tide** trai

tidy 1 *a.* cryno, taclus, twt.
2 *v.* tacluso

tie 1 *n.* tei; clwm, cwlwm *m.*
2 *v.* clymu, rhwymo

tiger *n.* teigr *m.*

tight *a.* tyn, tynn; cyfyng

tile *n.* teilsen *f.*

timber *n.* coed, pren *m.*

time *n.* adeg *f*, oed; amser,
pryd *m.* **at times** ar adegau,
ar brydiau; **in time** mewn
pryd

timetable *n.* amserlen *f.*

timid *a.* llwfr, ofnus

tin *n.* tun; alcam *m.* **tin of
paint** tun o baent; **tin of peas**
tun o bys

tinge *n.* naws, gwawr *f.*

tinted *a.* lliwiog

tiny *a.* bach, bychan, bitw,
mân

tip *n.* tip *m*, tomen *f*; cyngor
m; gwobr *f*; cil-dwrn *m.*

rubbish tip tomen ysbwriel,
tip ysbwriel

tire *v.* blino

tired *a.* blinedig, blin

tissue *n.* hances bapur *f.*
papur tŷ bach *m.*

title *n.* teitl, enw *m*; hawl *f.*

title-page wyneb ddalen

to *prp.* at, hyd at, i, er mwyn,
tua, wrth, yn

toad *n.* llyffant *m.* See broga:
ffroga *m.*

toadstool(s) *n.* madarch *m.*,
caws llyffant *m.*, bwyd y
boda *m. pl. coll. See*
madarch *m.*

toast 1 *n.* tost; llwncdestun
m. **2** *v.* tostio; cynnig
llwncdestun

today *ad. & n.m.* heddiw

together *ad.* gyda'i gilydd,
ynghyd. *Not* gyda'u gilydd

toil 1 *n.* llafur *m.* **2** *v.* llafurio

toilet *n.* toiled, tŷ-bach, lle
chwech, jeriw *m.*

token *n.* arwydd; tocyn *m.*

tolerate *v.* goddef, caniatáu

toll 1 *n.* toll, treth *f.* **2** *v.* canu
cloch

tollgate *n.* tollborth *m*,
tollglwyd *f.*

tomato *n.* tomato *m.*

tomb *n.* bedd, beddrod *m.*

tomcat *n.* cwrcath, gwrcath,
cwrcyn, gwrcyn *m.*

tomorrow *ad. & e.g.* fory,
yfory

ton *n.* tunnell *f.* **tonne** tunnell
fetrig

tone *n.* tôn; naws *f.*

tongue *n.* tafod *m*; tafodiaith, iaith *f*.

tonight *ad. & f.n.* heno

too *ad.* hefyd; rhy. **too much** gormod; **too little** rhy fach; **too late** rhy hwyr

tool *n.* arf, erfyn, offeryn *m*.

tooth *n.* dant *m*.

toothache *n.* dannoedd *f*.

toothbrush *n.* brwsh dannedd *m*.

toothpaste *n.* sebon dannedd, past dannedd *m*.

top *n.* pen, brig, copa, top *m*.

topic *n.* pwnc, testun *m*.

torch *n.* tors *m*.

torch-light *n.* golau tors *m*.

torment *v.* poeni, poenydio

tormentor *n.* poenydiwr *m*.

torque *n.* torch *m*.

torrid *a.* cras, poeth, crasboeth

tortoise *n.* crwban *m*.

torture *v.* poenydio

Tory 1 *n.* Tori, Ceidwadwr *m*. 2 *a.* Torïaidd

total 1 *n.* cyfanswm, y cyfan *m*. 2 *a.* cyfan, hollol, llwyr

tottering *a.* sigledig, simsan

touch 1 *n.* teimlad *m*. 2 *v.* cyffwrdd (â), teimlo

touch judge *n.* ystlyswr *m*.

touchline *n.* llinell ystlys *f*.

tour 1 *n.* taith *f*, tro *m*. 2 *v.* teithio

tourism *n.* twristiaeth *f*.

tourist 1 *n.* teithiwr, ymwelwr, ymwelydd *m*. 2 *a.* twristaidd. **Tourist Board** Bwrdd Croeso

towards *prp.* tua, at, tuag at

towel *n.* lliain, tywel *m*.

tower *n.* twr *m*.

town *n.* tref, tre *f*. **Carmarthen Town** Tre Caerfyrddin; **town centre** canol y dre; **town council** cyngor y dre; **town hall** neuadd y dre

toy 1 *n.* tegan *m*. 2 *v.* chwarae

trace *v.* olrhain

track 1 *n.* llwybr, ôl, trac *m*. 2 *v.* olrhain

tracksuit *n.* tracwisg *f*.

trade *n.* masnach; crefft *f*.

tradesman *n.* masnachwr, siopwr; crefftwr

tradition *n.* traddodiad *m*.

traditional *a.* traddodiadol

traffic *n.* trafnidiaeth, traffig *f*. **traffic jam** tagfa

trail 1 *n.* trywydd *m*. 2 *v.* llusgo

train 1 *n.* trên *m*. 2 *v.* hyfforddi; ymarfer

trainer *n.* hyfforddwr *m*.

training *n.* hyfforddiant *m*, ymarfer *f*. **in-service training** hyfforddiant mewn swydd

tramp 1 *n.* crwydryn *m*. 2 *v.* crwydro

trample *v.* sathru, sarnu

tranquillity *n.* hedd, heddwch, tawelwch, llonyddwch *m*.

tranquillizer *n.* tawelyn *m*.

transact *v.* trafod, trin, gwneud

transfer *v.* trosglwyddo

transfusion *n.* trallwysiad *m*. **blood transfusion** trallwysiad gwaed

transgress *v.* troseddu
transgression *n.* trosedd *f.*
transgressor *n.* troseddwr *m.*
translate *v.* cyfieithu, trosi
translation *n.* cyfieithiad, trosiad *m.*
translator *n.* cyfieithydd *m.*
transparent *a.* tryloyw
transplant *v.* trawsblannu
trap 1 *n.* trap *m.* 2 *v.* dal, trapio
trash *n.* sothach, ysbwriel *m.*
travel *v.* teithio
traveller *n.* teithiwr *m.*
travelling *a.* teithiol
treachery *n.* brad, twyll *m.*
treasure 1 *n.* trysor *m.* 2 *v.* trysori
treasurer *n.* trysorydd *m.*
treasury *n.* trysorfa *f.* **the Treasury** y Trysorlys
treat 1 *n.* gwledd *m.* 2 *v.* trin
treatise *n.* traethawd *m.*
tree *n.* coeden *f*, pren *m.*
tremendous *a.* dychrynllyd, ofnadwy, anferth
trench *n.* ffos *f.*
triad *n.* tri *m.*
triads *n.* trioedd *m. pl.*
trial *n.* prawf; treial *m.*
  sheepdog trials treialon cŵn defaid
triangle *n.* triongl *mf.*
triangular *a.* trionglog
tribe *n.* llwyth, tylwyth *m.*
tribulation *n.* trallod *m.*
trick *n.* tric *m.*
trickery *n.* twyll *m.*
tricky *a.* anodd
trim *v.* tacluso, trwsio

trinity *n.* trindod *f.*
trio *n.* triawd *m.*
triplet *n.* tripled *m;* triban *f.*
trouble 1 *n.* gofid *m*, helynt *f*, picil, picl, trafferth, trallod, trwbl *m.* 2 *v.* blino, gofidio, trafferthu
troublesome *a.* trafferthus
trousers *n.* trowsus, trwser *m. pl.*
trowel *n.* trywel *m.*
trudge *v.* troedio, cerdded
true *a.* gwir, cywir, iawn
truly *ad.* yn wir, yn gywir.
  Yours truly Yr eiddoch yn gywir
trunk *n.* bôn *m;* cist *f;* trwnc *m.*
trust 1 *n.* ymddiriedaeth, ymddiriedolaeth *f.* 2 *v.* ymddiried (yn); **National Trust** Ymddiriedolaeth Genedlaethol
trustee *n.* ymddiriedolwr *m.*
trusteeship *n.* ymddiriedolaeth *f.*
trusty *a.* ffyddlon, cywir
truth *n.* gwirionedd, gwir, iawn *m.*
try 1 *n.* cais *(mewn rygbi)*, cynnig *m.* **converted try** trosgais. 2 *v.* ceisio, cynnig, profi
T-shirt *n.* crys-T *m.*
Tuesday *n.* dydd Mawrth *m.*
tug 1 *n.* plwc; tynfa *m.* 2 *v.* llusgo, tynnu
tuition *n.* addysg *f*, hyfforddiant *m.*
tumble 1 *n.* cwymp *m.* 2 *v.* cwympo

tumbler *n.* gwydryn *m.*
tummy *n.* bola *m.*
tumult *n.* twrw, mwstwr, terfysg, cythrwfl *m.*
tune *n.* alaw, tôn *f.*
tunnel *n.* twnnel *m.*
turkey *n.* twrci *m.*
Turkey *n.* Twrci *f.*
Turkish *a.* Twrcaidd
turmoil *n.* berw, trafferth *m.*
turn 1 *n.* tro *m.* 2 *v.* troi
turning *n.* tro *m.* tröedigaeth *m.*
turning-point *n.* trobwynt *m.*
turnip *n.* erfinen, meipen *f.*
tutor 1 *n.* athro, tiwtor, hyfforddwr *m.* 2 *v.* dysgu, hyfforddi
twelfth *n. & a.* deuddegfed *m.*
twelve *n. & a.* deuddeg, un deg dau *m.*

two *n. & a.* dau *m:* dwy *f;* pâr *m.* **in twos, two by two** yn ddeuoedd, yn ddau a dau
typescript *n.* teipysgrif *f.*
typewriter *n.* teipiadur *m.*
typhoon *n.* corwynt *m.*
typist *n.* teipydd *m.*
tyre *n.* teiar *m.*

U

ubiquitous *a.* ym mhob man
ugliness *n.* hagrwch *m.*
ugly *a.* hagr, hyll, salw
ultra 1 *a.* eithafol. 2 *px.* gor-, dros ben, tu hwnt i
ultra-modern *a.* tra modern, modern iawn
umbrella *n.* ambarél, ymbarél, ymbrelo *m.*

Insight

umbrella *n. ymbarél m.* to put up one's umbrella *agor eich ymbarél*; to put down one's umbrella *cau eich ymbarél*. 'What colour is your umbrella? 'Light blue' *'Pa liw yw eich ymbarél?' 'Glas golau.'*

---

twentieth *n. & a.* ugeinfed *m.*
twenty *n. & a.* ugain, dau ddeg *m.*
twice *ad.* dwywaith
twig *n.* brigyn, brig *m.*
twilight *n.* cyfnos, cyfddydd *m.*
twin 1 *n.* gefell *m.* gefeilles *f.* 2 *v.* gefeillio
twine *n.* llinyn *m.*
twist 1 *n.* tro *m.* 2 *v.* troi

umpire 1 *n.* dyfarnwr, canolwr *m.* 2 *v.* dyfarnu
unaccompanied *a.* heb gwmni; digyfeiliant
unaccustomed *a.* anghyfarwydd
unacquainted *a.* anghyfarwydd
unanimous *a.* unfryd, unfrydol, unfarn

unanimously *ad.* yn ynfryd
unceasing *a.* di-baid,
diddiwedd
uncertain *a.* ansicr
uncivil *a.* anfoesgar
unclad *a.* noeth
uncle *n.* ewyrth, ewythr *m.*
unclean *a.* aflan, brwnt, budr
uncommon *a.* anghyffredin
uncover *v.* datguddio
uncultivated *a.* heb ei drin
under 1 *prp.* dan, tan, o dan,
is, islaw. 2 *ad.* danodd, oddi
tanodd. 3 *px.* is-, tan-
underclothing *n.* dillad isaf *m.*
undercurrent *n.* islif *m.*
undergo *v.* dioddef
underground *ad. a. & n.*
tanddaear, tanddaearol
underline *v.* tanlinellu,
pwysleisio
undermine *v.* tanseilio
underneath 1 *prp.* dan, tan,
oddi tan. 2 *ad.* oddi tanodd
underpass *n.* tanffordd *f.*
underskirt *n.* sgert isaf, sgyrt
isaf, pais *f.*
understand *v.* deall
understanding *n.* deall,
dealltwriaeth
undertake *v.* ymgymryd (â)
undertaker *n.* trefnydd
angladdau *m.*
undo *v.* datod; difetha
undress *v.* dadwisgo
unearned *a.* heb ei ennill
uneasy *a.* anesmwyth,
pryderus
unemployed 1 *n.* y di-waith
m. 2 *a.* di-waith, segur

unemployment *n.* diweithdra
m; **unemployment benefit**
budd-dâl di-waith
unending *a.* diddiwedd,
diderfyn
unfair *a.* annheg
unfaithful *a,* anffyddlon
unfamiliar *a.* anghyfarwydd,
dieithr
unfasten *v.* datod
unfit *a.* anaddas, anghymwys
unfortunate *a.* anffodus
unfortunately *ad.* yn anffodus
unhappy *a.* anhapus, trist
unhealthy *a.* afiach
uniform 1 *n.* gwisg swyddogol
f. 2 *a.* unffurf
unimportant *a.* dibwys
uninteresting *a.* anniddorol
union *n.* undeb *m.*
unionist *n.* undebwr *m.*
unique *a.* unigryw
unit *n.* uned *f;* un, rhif un;
undod *m.*
Unitarian *n.* Undodwr *m.*
unite *v.* uno, cysylltu, cyfuno
united *a.* unedig, unol. **the
United Kingdom** y Deyrnas
Unedig; **United States of
America** Unol Daleithiau
America
unity *n.* undod *m.*
universe *n.* bydysawd,
cyfanfyd, yr hollfyd *m*
university *n.* prifysgol *f.*
University of Wales Prifysgol
Cymru
unjust *a.* anghyfiawn
unjustly *ad.* ar gam
unkind *a.* angharedig

unleaded *a.* di-blwm.
 unleaded petrol petrol di-
 blwm
unless *c.* oni, onid
unlike *a.* annhebyg
unlimited *a.* diderfyn
unlucky *a.* anffodus, anlwcus
unmannerly *a.* anfoesgar
unmarried *a.* dibriod
unnatural *a.* annaturiol
unoccupied *a.* gwag, segur
unopened *a.* heb ei agor
unprepared *a.* amharod
unravel *v.* datod, datrys
unready *a.* amharod
unreasonable *a.* afresymol
unsatisfied *a.* anfodlon
unseen *a.* anweledig
unsightly *a.* diolwg, hyll, salw
unsteady *a.* simsan
unsuitable *a.* anaddas,
 anghymwys
untidy *a.* anniben
untie *v.* datod
until *prp. & c.* hyd, hyd oni,
 nes, tan
untrue *a.* celwyddog
untruth *n.* celwydd, anwiredd
 m.
untruthful *a.* celwyddog
unusual *a.* anarferol
unwell *a.* anhwylus, afiach,
 claf
unwholesome *a.* afiach
unwilling *a.* anfodlon
unwise *a.* annoeth, ffôl
unworthy *a.* annheilwng
up *ad. & prp.* i fyny
uphill *ad.* i fyny
uphold *v.* cynnal

upon *prp.* ar, ar warthaf, ar
 uchaf
upper *a.* uwch, uchaf
uppermost *a. & ad.* uchaf
upright *a.* syth, union,
 unionsyth; onest, cywir
upside-down *ad.* wyneb i
 waered
upstairs 1 *n.* llofft *f.* **2** *ad.* ar
 y llofft
up-to-date *a.* cyfoes, hyd yn
 hyn
upwards *ad.* i fyny
urban *a.* trefol
urge *v.* argymell
urgency *n.* brys *m.*
us *pn.* ni, ninnau, nyni, 'n
usage *n.* arfer *mf,* defnydd *m.*
use 1 *n.* arfer *mf,* defnydd,
 gwasanaeth, iws. **2** *v.* arfer,
 defnyddio
useful *a.* defnyddiol
useless *a.* diwerth
user *n.* defnyddiwr *m.*
Usk *n.* Wysg *(river)*;
 Brynbuga *(town) f.*
usual *a.* arferol. **as usual** fel
 arfer
utilize *v.* defnyddio
utmost *a.* eithaf, pellaf
U-turn *n.* tro pedol *m.*

V

vacancy *n.* lle gwag *m,*
 swydd wag *f.*
vacant *a.* gwag
vacation *n.* gwyliau *pl.*
vaccination *n.* brechiad *m,*
 brech *f.*

vacuum *n.* gwagle *m.*

vain *a.* balch; ofer

vale *n.* bro *f,* cwm, dyffryn, glyn *m.* **Vale of Glamorgan** Bro Morgannwg

valiant *a.* dewr

valley *n.* cwm, dyffryn, glyn *m.*

vengeance *n.* dial, dialedd *m.*

venom *n.* gwenwyn *m.*

venture 1 *n.* antur *m,* menter *f.* **2** *v.* mentro, beiddio, meiddio

venturesome *a.* mentrus, anturus

Venus *n.* Gwener *m.*

Insight

valley *n. cwm, dyffryn, glyn m.* the Rhondda valley *Cwm Rhondda*; the Swansea Valley *Cwm Tawe*; the valleys of South Wales *cymoedd y De*.

value *n. gwerth m.* 'A man who knows the price of everything and the value of nothing.' '*Dyn sy'n gwybod pris pob peth heb wybod gwerth dim.*' Oscar Wilde (1892)

---

valuable *a.* drud, gwerthfawr

value *n* gwerth *m.* **Value Added Tax (VAT)** Treth Ar Werth

van *n.* fan, men; y rheng flaenaf *f.*

vandal *n.* fandal *m.*

vandalize *v.* fandaleiddio

vandalism *n.* fandaliaeth *f.*

vanish *v.* diflannu

vanity *n.* gwagedd, oferedd *m.*

various *a.* amryw, gwahanol

vary *v.* newid

vast *a.* eang, enfawr, anferth

veal *n.* cig llo *m.*

vegetable *n.* llysieuyn *m.*

vegetarian *n.* llysfwytäwr *m.* llysfwytäwraig *f.*

vehicle *n.* cerbyd; cyfrwng *m.*

veil *n.* llen *f.*

velocity *n.* cyflymder *m.*

verb *n.* berf *f.*

verbally *ad.* mewn geiriau

verb-noun *n.* berfenw *m.*

verdict *n.* dyfarniad, dedfryd *m.*

vermin *n.* pryfed, llygod ... *pl.*

verse *n.* adnod *f,* pennill *m;* barddoniaeth *f.*

version *n.* fersiwn *m.*

versus *ad.* yn erbyn

vertical *a.* syth, unionsyth, plwm

very *a. & ad.* gwir, iawn, i'r dim

vessel *n.* llestr; llong *m.*

vestry *n.* festri *f.*

veterinary surgeon *n.* milfeddyg *m.*

vex *v.* blino, gofidio, poeni, becso

vexation *n.* blinder, gofid *m.*

via *prp.* trwy, ar hyd

vicar *n.* ficer *m.*

vicarage *n.* ficerdy *m.*

vice *n.* drygioni *m*; gwasg, feis *f.*

vice- *px,* is-, rhag-

vice-chairman *n.* is-gadeirydd *m.*

vice-president *n.* is-lywydd *m.*

victor *n.* buddugwr, y buddugol, enillwr, enillydd *m.*

victory *n.* buddugoliaeth *f.*

view 1 *n.* golygfa *f,* golwg *mf;* barn *f.* 2 *v.* edrych, gweld

viewer *n.* gwyliwr *m, (teledu).*

viewpoint *n.* safbwynt *m.*

vigil *n.* gwylnos, noswyl *f.*

vigour *n.* grym, nerth, egni, ynni *m.*

vigorous *a.* egnïol

vile *a.* ffiaidd, gwael, salw

village *n.* pentref *m.*

villager *n.* pentrefwr *m.*

vinegar *n.* finegr *m.*

viola *n.* fiola *f.*

violate *v.* treisio, troseddu

violence *n.* trais *m.*

violent *a.* treisiol, gwyllt. **non-violent** di-drais

violet 1 *n.* fioled *f.* 2 *a.* dulas

violin *n.* ffidil *f.*

virgin *n.* morwyn, gwyryf *f.* **the Virgin Mary** y Forwyn Fair

virtually *ad.* i bob pwrpas

virtue *n.* rhinwedd *f.*

virus *n.* firws *m.*

vision *n.* gweledigaeth *f;* golwg *mf;* gweled *m.*

visit 1 *n.* ymweliad *m.* 2 *v.* ymweld (â), galw

visitor *n.* ymwelwr, ymwelydd *m.*

vitamin *n.* fitamin *m.*

vivacious *a.* bywiog, heini

vivid *a.* byw, clir, llachar

vixen *n.* cadnawes, cadnöes, llwynoges *f.*

vocabulary *n.* geirfa *f.*

vocal *a.* llafar; lleisiol

vocalist *n.* cantor *m,* cantores *f,* canwr *m.*

vocally *ad.* â'r llais.

vocation *n.* galwedigaeth *f.*

vogue *n.* ffasiwn *m,* arfer *mf.*

voice 1 *n.* llais *m,* llef *f.* 2 *v.* lleisio, mynegi

void 1 *n.* gwagle *m.* 2 *a.* di-rym. 3 *v.* gwacáu

volcano *n.* llosgfynydd, folcano *m.*

vole *n.* llygoden y maes *f.*

volume *n.* cyfrol *f;* cyfaint; llais, sŵn; foliwm *m.*

voluntary *a.* gwirfoddol

volunteer 1 *n.* gwirfoddolwr *m.* 2 *v.* gwirfoddoli

vomit *v.* chwydu

vote 1 *n.* pleidlais *f.* 2 *v.* pleidleisio

voter *n.* pleidleisiwr *m.*

vowel *n.* llafariad *f.*

voyage 1 *n.* mordaith *f.* 2 *v.* mordeithio, mordwyo, morio. **Bon voyage** Hwyl dda! Sirwrnai dda!

vulgar *a.* cyffredin; isel, brwnt; aflednais; gwerinol

vulgarity *n.* diffyg moes *m.*

W

wag v. ysgwyd, siglo
wage n. cyflog mf.
waist n. gwasg mf, canol m.
waistcoat n. gwasgod f.
wait v. aros, disgwyl; gweini
waiter n. gweinydd m.
waitress n. gweinyddes f.
wake v. dihuno, deffro
Wales n. Cymru f.
walk 1 n. tro m. 2 v.
cerdded, mynd am dro
walker n. cerddwr m.
walking-stick n. ffon f.
wall n. gwal, wal f, mur m.
wallflowers n. blodau mam-gu
m. pl.
wallpaper n. papur wal m.
want 1 n. eisiau, diffyg m.
2 v. bod mewn eisiau
wanting a. yn eisiau
war 1 n. rhyfel mf. 2 v.
rhyfela
warehouse n. storfa, stôr f,
ystordy m.
warfare n. rhyfel mf.
warm 1 n. cynnes, gwresog,
twym. 2 v. cynhesu,
twymo
warmth n. gwres,
cynhesrwydd m.
warn v. rhybuddio
warning n. rhybudd m.
warship n. llong ryfel f.
wart n. dafaden, dafad f.
was, I v. bues i, bûm, fues i,
fûm, roeddwn; see bod
wash 1 n. golch, golchiad m.
2 v. golchi, ymolch, ymolchi

washer n. golchydd m. see
washing machine.
washing machine n peiriant
golchi m.
washing powder n. powdr
golchi m.
wash-house n. golchdy m.
wasp n. cacynen, picwnen f.
wasps' nest nyth cacwn
waste 1 n. gwastraff m.
nuclear waste gwastraff
niwclear. 2 v. gwastraffu
wasteful a. gwastraffus
watch 1 n. wats f. 2 v.
gwarchod, gwylio
watchful a. gwyliadwrus
watchman n. gwyliwr m.
watchnight n. gwylnos f.
water n. dŵr m.
waterfall n. rhaeadr, sgwd f,
pistyll m.
wave 1 n. ton f. 2 v. chwifio,
codi llaw
wavelength n. tonfedd f.
wax 1 n. cwyr m. 2 v. cwyro;
cynyddu, tyfu
way n. ffordd, heol, hewl f,
llwybr m; hynt f; arfer fm,
modd m.
wayside n. ymyl y ffordd mf.
we pn. ni, ninnau, nyni
weak a. gwan
weaken v. gwanhau
weakness n. gwendid m.
wealth n. cyfoeth, golud, da,
modd m.
wealthy a. cyfoethog, cefnog
weapon n. arf, erfyn m.
nuclear weapons arfau
niwclear

wear 1 *n.* gwisg; traul *f.* 2 *v.* gwisgo; treulio

weariness *n.* blinder *m.*

wearisome *a.* blinedig, blin, poenus

weary 1 *a.* blinedig, blin. 2 *v.* blino, diflasu

weather *n.* tywydd *m*, hin *f.* **fine weather** tywydd teg, hindda; **tempestuous weather** tywydd mawr

weave *v.* gwau, gweu

web *n.* gwe *f.*

wed *v.* priodi

website *n.* gwefan *f.*

wedding *n.* priodas *f.*

Wednesday *n.* dydd Mercher *m.*

weed 1 *n.* chwynnyn *m* 2 *v.* chwynnu

weeds *n.* chwyn *m. pl.*

week *n.* wythnos *f.* **the first week** yr wythnos gyntaf; **the second week** yr ail wythnos; **the third week** y drydedd wythnos; **the last week** yr wythnos diwethaf; **the final week** yr wythnos olaf

weekend *n.* penwythnos *m.*

weekly *a.* wythnosol

weep *v.* crio, wylo, llefain

weigh *v.* pwyso

weight *n.* pwys, pwysau *m.*

weighty *a.* pwysig; trwm

welcome 1 *n.* croeso *m.* 2 *v.* croesawu

welfare *n.* lles, budd *m.*

welfare state *n.* gwladwriaeth les *f.*

well 1 *n.* ffynnon *f.* 2 *a.* iach, da, iawn. 3 *v.* llifo, cronni. 4 *ad.*, yn dda. 5 *i.* wel! **fairly well** yn lled dda; **very well** o'r gorau

Welsh *a.* Cymraeg; Cymreig: **Welsh affairs** materion Cymreig, **Welsh books** llyfrau Cymraeg; **Welsh cakes** picau ar y maen; **Welsh office** Swyddfa Gymreig; **Welsh schools** ysgolion Cymraeg; **Welsh water** dŵr Cymru

Welsh (language) *n.* Cymraeg *f.*

Insight

week *n. wythnos f.* A period of seven consecutive days between midnight on Saturday until the same time the following Saturday. Hence the **eight nights** – wyth nos! Days during the week: **the day before yesterday** *echdoe ad. & e.g.*; **yesterday** *ddoe ad. & e.g.*; **today** *heddiw ad. & e.g.*; **tomorrow** *yfory ad. & e.g.*; **two days later, in two days' time, on the day after tomorrow** *trennydd ad. & e.g,*; **in three days' time, on the third day after today** *tradwy ad. & e.g,*; **the next day** *trannoeth ad. & e.g,*; **yesterday evening, last night** *neithiwr ad. & e.b.g.*

Welsh (people) *n.* Cymry *m.* *pl.*

Welshman *n.* Cymro *m.*

Welshness *n.* Cymreictod *m.*

Welshwoman *n.* Cymraes *f.*

west 1 *n.* gorllewin *m.* **West Wales** Gorllewin Cymru; **west or westerly wind** gwynt y gorllewin

western *a.* gorllewinol

wet 1 *n.* gwlybaniaeth *f.* 2 *a.* gwlyb. 3 *v.* gwlychu. **wetland** tir gwlyb

whale *n.* morfil *m.*

what 1 *a.* pa. 2 *pn.* pa beth. 3 *i.* beth!

whatever *pn.* beth bynnag

wheat *n.* gwenith *m.*

wheel *n.* olwyn *f.* **front wheel** olwyn flaen; **rear wheel** olwyn gefn; **spare wheel** olwyn sbâr

wheelbarrow *n.* berfa, whilber *f.*

wheelchair *n.* cadair olwyn/ olwynion *f.*

when *ad., pn & c.* pan, pa bryd

whenever *ad.* pa bryd bynnag

where *ad.* ym mha le; yn y lle, lle

whereabouts *ad.* ymhle

whereas *c.* gan, yn gymaint â

whereby *ad.* trwy yr hyn

wherefore *ad.* paham, am hynny

wherein *ad.* yn yr hyn

wherever *ad.* ble bynnag

which 1 *rel.pn.* a; y, yr. 2 *int.pn.* pa un? p'un? 3 *a.* pa

whichever *a. & pn.* pa un bynnag

whilst *ad.* cyhyd, tra

whip 1 *n.* chwip *f.* 2 *v.* chwipio

whirlpool *n.* pwll tro, trobwll *m.*

whisper 1 *n.* sisial *m.* 2 *v.* sisial, sibrwd

whistle 1 *n.* chwiban *m.* 2 *v.* chwiban, chwibanu

white *a.* gwyn, gwen, can

white-lime *n.* gwyngalch *m.*

whiten *v.* gwynnu

whitewash 1 *n.* gwyngalch *m.* 2 *v.* gwyngalchu

Whitsunday *n.* Sulgwyn *m.*

whittle *v.* naddu

whiz 1 *n.* si, su *m.* 2 *v.* sio, suo

who *pn.* a, pwy; y, yr

whole 1 *n.* cwbl, cyfan, holl *m.* 2 *a.* cyfan, holl; iach, holliach

wholesome *a.* iach, iachus

wholly *ad.* yn hollol, yn gyfan gwbl, yn llwyr

whom *rel.pn.* a; y, yr

whose *pn.* eiddo pwy? pwy biau?

whosoever *pn.* pwy bynnag

why *ad.* paham, pam

wicked *a.* drwg, drygionus

wickedness *n.* drwg, drygioni *m.*

wicket *n.* wiced; clwyd *f.* **wicket-keeper** wicedwr

wide *a.* llydan, eang

wide-awake *a.* effro, ar ddihun

widely *ad.* yn eang

widen *v.* lledu, llydanu

widow *n.* gweddw, widw, gwidw *f.*

widower *n.* gŵr gweddw, gwidman *m.*

width *n.* lled *m.*

wife *n.* gwraig, gwraig briod, priod *f.*

wild *a.* gwyllt, ffyrnig

wilderness *n.* anialwch, diffeithwch *m.*

wildfire *n.* tân gwyllt *m.*

will 1 *n.* ewyllys *m.* 2 *v.* mynnu

will be, he/she/it *v.* bydd; *see* bod

willing *a.* bodlon, parod

willow *n.* helygen *f.*

win *v.* ennill. **to win the day** cario'r dydd

wind *n.* gwynt *m;* anadl *mf.* **cold wind** gwynt oer; **the north wind** gwynt y gogledd

wind *v.* troi, dirwyn

windmill *n.* melin wynt *f.*

window *n.* ffenestr *f.* **window pane** cwarel

windy *a.* gwyntog

wine *n.* gwin *m.* **dry red wine** gwin coch sych; **sweet white wine** gwin gwyn melys

wineglass *n.* gwydr gwin *m.*

wing *n.* adain, aden, asgell *f;* asgellwr *m.*

winner *n.* enillwr, enillydd, y buddugol *m.*

winning *a.* buddugol

winnings *n.* enillion *pl.*

winter *n.* gaeaf *m.* **winter dwelling** hendref, hendre

wintry *a.* gaeafol

wipe *v.* sychu

wire *n.* gwifren *f.*

wisdom *n.* doethineb *m.*

wise *a.* call, doeth. **the Wise Men** y Doethion

wish 1 *n.* dymuniad, ewyllys *m.* 2 *v.* dymuno

witch *n.* gwrach *f.*

with *prp.* â, ag, gyda, gydag, efo, gan

withdraw *v.* tynnu yn ôl; cilio; codi arian

wither *v.* gwywo

withhold *v.* atal, dal yn ôl

within 1 *prp.* i mewn, o fewn, yn. 2 *ad.* tu mewn

without 1 *prp.* heb 2 *a.* tu allan

witness 1 *n.* tyst *m.* 2 *v.* tystio

wits *n.* synhwyrau *pl.*

witticism *n.* jôc, ffraethineb *f.*

witty *a.* doniol, ffraeth

wizard *n.* dewin *m.*

wolf *n.* blaidd *m.*

woman *n.* merch, menyw, gwraig, llances, dynes *f.*

wonder 1 *n.* rhyfeddod *m.* 2 *v.* rhyfeddu, synnu. **I wonder** tybed

wonderful *a.* rhyfedd, rhyfeddol

wood *n.* coed *pl*, coedwig *f.* pren *m.*

wooden *a.* o goed, o bren

woodwork *n.* gwaith coed, gwaith saer *m.*

wool *n.* gwlân *m.*

woollen *a.* gwlân, gwlanog.
  woollen industry diwydiant
  gwlân
word *n.* gair *m.* **a good word**
  gair da; **the last word** y gair
  olaf; **word for word** gair am
  air
work 1 *n.* gwaith, llafur *m.*
  2 *v.* gweithio, llafurio
worker *n.* gweithiwr *m.*
working *a.* gwaith, yn
  gweithio. **working class**
  dosbarth gweithiol; **working
  clothes** dillad gwaith;
  working party gweithgor
workpeople *n.* gweithwyr *pl.*
workshop *n.* gweithdy *m,*
  siop waith *f.*
world *n.* byd *m.*
worldly *a.* bydol
worldwide *a.* byd-eang
worm *n.* mwydyn, pryfyn *m.*
worried *a.* gofidus, pryderus
worry 1 *n.* gofid *m,* helynt *f,*
  pryder *m.* **2** *v.* gofidio,
  poeni, pryderu blino
worse *a.* gwaeth
worsen *v.* gwaethygu
worship *n.* addoliad *m.*
worth *n.* gwerth *m.*
worthiness *n.* teilyngdod,
  gwerth *m.*
worthless *a.* diwerth
worthy *a.* teilwng
wound 1 *n.* clwyf, anaf *m.*
  2 *v.* clwyfo, anafu
wrap *v.* lapio, rhwymo.
  wrapping paper papur lapio
wrath *n.* llid *m.*
wreath *n.* torch *f.*
wren *n.* dryw *m.*

wretch *n.* truan *m.*
wretched *a.* truan, truenus
wretchedness *n.* trueni,
  trallod *m.*
wright *n.* crefftwr, saer *m.*
  cartwright saer certiau;
  wheelwright saer olwynion
  (pren).
wrist *n.* arddwrn *m.*
write *v.* sgrifennu, ysgrifennu.
  to write a name torri enw
writer *n.* ysgrifennwr, awdur
  m, awdures *f.*
writing *n.* ysgrifen, ysgrifennu *f.*
wrong 1 *n.* cam, bai *m.* **2** *a.*
  anghywir, rong. **3** *v.* gwneud
  cam â
wrongdoer *n.* troseddwr *m.*
wrongdoing *n.* trosedd *f.*
www. *n.* (y)we byd-eang *f.*

X

X-ray *n.* pelydr X, pelydryn X
  m.
X-rays pelydrau X
xylophone *n.* seiloffon *f.*

Y

yard *n.* buarth *m,* iard *f,* clos,
  cwrt *m;* llathen *f.*
yarn *n.* chwedl, stori; edau *f.*
year *n.* blwyddyn; blwydd
  (oed) *f;* blynedd *pl (after
  numerals).* **the first year** y
  flwyddyn gyntaf; **the second
  year** yr ail flwyddyn; **three
  years old** tair blwydd oed;
  four years old pedair blwydd
  oed; **for five years** am bum

mlynedd; **for six years** am chwe blynedd; **last year** y llynedd; **leap year** blwyddyn naid; **this year** eleni; **next year** y flwyddyn nesaf
yearly *a.* blynyddol
yearn *v.* hiraethu, dyheu
yearning *n.* hiraeth *m.*
yell 1 *n.* sgrech, gwaedd *f.* 2 *v.* sgrechian, sgrechain, gweiddi
yellow *a.* melyn *m.*, melen *f.* **the yellow apple** yr afal melyn; **the yellow dress** y wisg felen

yonder *ad.* acw, draw
York *n.* Efrog *f.*
you *pn.* ti; chi, chwi. **you also** tithau, chithau, chwithau; **you yourself** tydi
young *a.* ieuanc, ifanc
younger *a.* iau
youngest *a.* ifancaf
youngster *n.* crwt, hogyn, plentyn *m.*
your *pn.* dy, 'th; eich, 'ch
yours *pn.* eiddoch, yr eiddoch. **yours faithfully** yr eiddoch yn ffyddlon; **yours truly** yr eiddoch yn gywir

---

Insight

yours *pn.* (singular) *dy un di.* This is mine and this is yours. *Dyma fy un i a dyma dy un di.* (Emphatic!) Yours truly/ Yours faithfully *Yr eiddoch yn gywir.*

---

yes *ad.* ie, byddaf, byddan, do, oes, oedd, oeddwn, ydw, ydy, ydyn . . . *(Welsh uses the verb forms to answer* yes/no) **Tom? Yes** Tom? Ie. **Was he there? Yes** Oedd e yno? Oedd. **Is Huw late? Yes** Ydy Huw'n hwyr? Ydy. **Are there dogs here? Yes** Oes cŵn yma? Oes. **Will they be cold? Yes** Fyddan nhw'n oer? Byddan
yesterday *n. & ad.* doe, ddoe. **the day before yesterday** echdoe
yet *ad.* eto, er hynny
yew *n.* ywen *f.*
yield *v.* ildio, rhoddi
yoke *n.* iau *f.*
yolk *n.* melyn wy, melynwy m

yourself *pn.* eich hun, eich hunan
yourselves *pn.* eich hunain
youth *n.* llanc; ieuenctid *m.*
youthful *a.* ieuanc, ifanc
Yuletide *n.* adeg y Nadolig *f.*

Z

zeal *n.* sêl *f.*
zero *n.* dim, sero *m.*
zigzag *a.* igam-ogam
zinc *n.* sinc *m.*
Zion *n.* Seion *f.*
zip 1 *n.* sip *m.* 2 *v.* sipio
zone *n.* cylch, rhanbarth *m.*
zoo *n.* sŵ *m.f.*
zoologist *n.* söolegwr *m.*
zoology *n.* söoleg *mf.*

supplement

Verbs

In this short introduction to the study of Welsh verbs, the irregular verb
bod (*to be*) is conjugated in the present, imperfect, future and past
tenses only. A fuller discussion of the subject may be found in
contemporary books on Welsh grammar.

Present tense (bod *to be*)

Affirmative form

	Singular			Plural	
1	*Rydw i	*I am*	Rydyn ni	*We are*
2	Rwyt ti	*You are*	Rydych chi	*You are*
3	Mae e/o	*He/It is*	Maen nhw	*They are*
	Mae hi	*She is*		

Note: 3rd Person	**mae, oes, sy,**	*is, there is*
Singular	**yw, ydyw**	*are, there are*
	Oes . . .?	*Is there . . .?*
		Are there . . .?

*Literary Form: **Yr wyf i, 'Rwyf i**. In spoken Welsh one hears **Rw
i/Dw i** and also **Ryn ni/Dyn ni; Rych chi/Dych chi** (see overleaf).

Interrogative form

	Singular			Plural	
1	Ydw i?	*Am I?*	Ydyn ni?	*Are we?*
2	Wyt ti?	*Are you?*	Ydych chi?	*Are you?*
3	Ydy e/o?	*Is he/it?*	Ydyn nhw?	*Are they?*
	Ydy hi?	*Is she?*		

Negative form

	Singular	
1	Dydw i ddim	*I am not*
2	Dwyt ti ddim	*You are not*
3	Dydy e/o ddim	*He/It is not*
	Dydy hi ddim	*She is not*

	Plural	
1	Dydyn ni ddim	*We are not*
2	Dydych chi ddim	*You are not*
3	Dydyn nhw ddim	*They are not*

Learners (**dysgwyr**) of the spoken language are introduced to the following **affirmative**, **interrogative** and **negative forms** of the above when they first encounter the verb **bod**:

Affirmative form

Singular		Plural	
1 Dw i	*I am*	Dyn ni	*We are*
2 Rwyt ti	*You are*	Dych chi	*You are*
3 Mae e/hi	*He/She/It is*	Maen nhw	*They are*

Interrogative form

Singular		Plural	
1 Ydw i?	*Am I?*	Dyn ni?	*Are we?*
2 Wyt ti?	*Are you?*	Dych chi?	*Are you?*
3 Ydy e/hi?	*Is he/she/it?*	Dyn nhw?	*Are they?*

Negative form

Singular	
1 Dw i ddim	*I'm not*
2 Dwyt ti ddim	*You're not*
3 Dydy e/hi ddim	*He's/She's/It's not*

Plural	
1 Dyn ni ddim	*We're not*
2 Dych chi ddim	*You're not*
3 Dyn nhw ddim	*They're not*

Imperfect tense (bod *to be*)

Affirmative form

Singular	
1 *Roeddwn i	*I was/used to*
2 Roeddet ti	*You were/used to*
3 Roedd e/o	*He/It was/used to*
Roedd hi	*She was/used to*

Plural	
1 Roedden ni	*We were/used to*
2 Roeddech chi	*You were/used to*
3 Roedden nhw	*They were/used to*

Note: 3rd Person Singular **roedd** *was, there was were, there were*

*Also heard in spoken Welsh: **Rown i, Roen i; Rot ti; Roedd e/hi; Ron ni; Roch chi; Ron nhw.**

Interrogative form

Singular
1	Oeddwn i?	*Was I?*
2	Oeddet ti?	*Were you?*
3	Oedd e/o?	*Was he/it?*
	Oedd hi?	*Was she?*

Plural
1	Oedden ni?	*Were we?*
2	Oeddech chi?	*Were you?*
3	Oedden nhw?	*Were they?*

Note: 3rd person singular **Oedd . . .?** *Was there . . .?*
Were there . . .?

Negative form

Singular
1	Doeddwn i ddim	*I wasn't/I used not to*
2	Doeddet ti ddim	*You weren't/You used not to*
3	Doedd e/o ddim	*He/It wasn't/It used not to*
	Doedd hi ddim	*She wasn't/She used not to*

Plural
1	Doedden ni ddim	*We weren't/We used not to*
2	Doeddech chi ddim	*You weren't/You used not to*
3	Doedden nhw ddim	*They weren't/They used not to*

Future tense (bod *to be*)

Affirmative form

	Singular			Plural	
1	Bydda i	*I shall be*	Byddwn ni	*We shall be*
2	Byddi di	*You will be*	Byddwch chi	*You will be*
3	Bydd e/o	*He/It will be*	Byddan nhw	*They will be*
	Bydd hi	*She will be*		

Note: 3rd person singular **bydd** *will be*

Interrogative form

	Singular			Plural	
1	Fydda i?	*Shall I be?*	Fyddwn ni?	*Shall we be?*
2	Fyddi di?	*Will you be?*	Fyddwch chi?	*Will you be?*
3	Fydd e/o?	*Will he/she be?*	Fyddan nhw?	*Will they be?*
	Fydd hi?	*Will she be?*		

Negative form

Singular

1	Fydda i ddim	*I shall not be*
2	Fyddi di ddim	*You will not be*
3	Fydd e/o ddim	*He/It will not be*
	Fydd hi ddim	*She will not be*

Plural

1	*Fyddwn ni ddim*	*We shall not be*
2	*Fyddwch chi ddim*	*You will not be*
3	*Fyddan nhw ddim*	*They will not be*

Imperative tense (bod *to be*)

Bydd! Bydda! (singular); **Byddwch!** (plural) *Be!*

Past tense (bod *to be*)

Affirmative form

	Singular		Plural	
1	*Bues i	*I was*	Buon ni	*We were*
2	Buest ti	*You were*	Buoch chi	*You were*
3	Buodd e/o	*He/It was*	Buon nhw	*They were*
	Buodd hi	*She was*		

*Literary form of 1st person singular past tense: **Bûm i**

Interrogative form

	Singular		Plural	
1	Fues i?	*Was I?*	Fuon ni?	*Were we?*
2	Fuest ti?	*Were you?*	Fuoch chi?	*Were you?*
3	Fuodd e/o?	*Was he/it?*	Fuon nhw?	*Were they?*
	Fuodd hi?	*Was she?*		

Negative form

Singular

1	Fues i ddim	*I wasn't*
2	Fuest ti ddim	*You weren't*
3	Fuodd e/o ddim	*He/It wasn't*
	Fuodd hi ddim	*She wasn't*

Plural

1	Fuon ni ddim	*We weren't*
2	Fuoch chi ddim	*You weren't*
3	Fuon nhw ddim	*They weren't*

Affirmative and negative answers – *yes* and *no*

The entries shown in the English–Welsh section of the dictionary under
yes and **no** may be further supplemented:

Present tense

	Singular		*Plural*	
1	Ydw/Nag ydw	*Yes/No*	Ydyn/Nag ydyn	*Yes/No*
2	Wyt/Nag wyt	*Yes/No*	Ydych/Nag ydych	*Yes/No*
3	Ydy/Nag ydy	*Yes/No*	Ydyn/Nag ydyn	*Yes/No*
	Oes/Nag oes	*Yes/No*		

Imperfect tense

	Singular	
1	Oeddwn/Nag oeddwn	*Yes/No*
2	Oeddet/Nag oeddet	*Yes/No*
3	Oedd/Nag oedd	*Yes/No*

	Plural	
1	Oedden/Nag oedden	*Yes/No*
2	Oeddech/Nag oeddech	*Yes/No*
3	Oedden/Nag oedden	*Yes/No*

Future tense

	Singular	
1	Bydda/Na fydda	*Yes/No*
2	Byddi/Na fyddi	*Yes/No*
3	Bydd/Na fydd	*Yes/No*

	Plural	
1	Byddwn/Na fyddwn	*Yes/No*
2	Byddwch/Na fyddwch	*Yes/No*
3	Byddan/Na fyddan	Yes/No

With the past tense **do** *yes* and **naddo** *no* are the forms relating to both
singular and plural usages.

For forms such as the pluperfect **Buaswn i, Fe/Mi faswn i** *I would (be)*,
see further works on contemporary Welsh grammar.

Regular verbs

Welsh verbs have inflected tenses, that is, the tenses have their own endings. These endings are added to the stem of the verbs. Most verbs follow a regular pattern but there are some irregular verbs.

In the Welsh–English section of this dictionary an entry for a verb is shown as follows:

canu *be.* **(canaf)** to sing, to play.

The stem derived from the verb-noun **canu** is **can-**. The present tense ending for the 1st person singular is **-af**, and when the ending is added to the stem, **can + af** becomes **canaf**, which is the form shown in the brackets, frequently written and pronounced **cana**.

The verb **bod** (*to be*) is used as an auxiliary in forming tenses of regular verbs such as **canu, bwyta, cysgu** . . . The present tense of **canu** is formed by using the present tense of the verb **bod**, that is, **Rydw i, Rwyt ti, Mae e** . . . followed by **yn + canu**. It also exists in compact form as shown below.

Note: **Rydw i yn canu** becomes **Rydw i'n canu/Dw i'n canu**
Rwyt ti yn canu becomes **Rwyt ti'n canu**
Mae e yn canu becomes **Mae e'n canu** . . .

Present tense (canu *to sing*)

Singular

1 Rydw/Dw i'n canu *I sing, I am singing*
2 Rwyt ti'n canu *You sing, You are singing*
3 Mae e/o'n canu *He/It sings, He/It is singing*
  Mae hi'n canu *She sings, She is singing*

Plural

1 Rydyn/Dyn ni'n canu *We sing, We are singing*
2 Rydych/Dych chi'n canu *You sing, You are singing*
3 Maen nhw'n canu *They sing, They are singing*

The imperfect tense is formed by using the imperfect tense of **bod**, that is, **Roeddwn i, Roeddet ti, Roedd e** . . . followed by **yn canu**.

Imperfect tense (canu *to sing*)

Singular

1 Roeddwn i'n canu *I was singing*
2 Roeddet ti'n canu *You were singing*
3 Roedd e/o'n canu *He/It was singing*
  Roedd hi'n canu *She was singing*

Plural

1 Roedden ni'n canu *We were singing*
2 Roeddech chi'n canu *You were singing*
3 Roedden nhw'n canu *They were singing*

The imperfect tense also conveys the meaning of continuous action. **Roedd hi'n canu** means not only *She was singing*, but also *She was going on singing*. **Roedd hi'n arfer canu** *She used to sing*.

The future tense is formed by using the future tense of **bod**, that is, **Bydda i, Byddi di, Bydd e** . . . followed by **yn + canu.**

Future tense (canu *to sing*)

Singular

1	Bydda i'n canu	*I shall be singing*
2	Byddi di'n canu	*You will be singing*
3	Bydd e/o'n canu	*He/It will be singing*
	Bydd hi'n canu	*She will be singing*

Plural

1	Byddwn ni'n canu	*We shall be singing*
2	Byddwch chi'n canu	*You will be singing*
3	Byddan nhw'n canu	*They will be singing*

Imperative (canu *to sing*)

Cana! (singular); **Canwch!** (plural) *Sing!*

The past tense of **canu** is formed by adding **-ais, -aist, -odd, -on, -och, -on** to the stem **can-**, and is used to convey completed action in the past.

Past tense (canu *to sing*)

	Singular		Plural	
1	*Cenais i	*I sang*	Canon ni	*We sang*
2	*Cenaist ti	*You sang*	Canoch chi	*You sang*
3	Canodd e/o	*He/It sang*	Canon nhw	*They sang*
	Canodd hi	*She sang*		

*In those verbs which have 'a' in the stem it is usual in literary Welsh for a > e in the 1st and 2nd person singular past tense and in the 2nd person singular present and future tenses.

The particle Fe (S.W.)/Mi (N.W.)

The verb is placed as the first word in the normal construction of the Welsh sentence:

Cerddodd Siôn i'r siop.	*Siôn walked to the shop.*
Rydw i'n darllen llyfr.	*I'm reading a book.*
Mae ci yn y cae.	*There's a dog in the field.*
Dydyn nhw ddim yma.	*They're not here.*

Usually the particle **Fe/Mi** is placed in front of the verb merely to indicate that the verb is affirmative.

Note: The particle **Fe/Mi** is not translated, and is not placed before **mae** or **maen** but may occur before other persons of the verb in speech or informal texts. Both particles are followed by soft mutation.

Golchodd Mair y dillad.
Fe olchodd Mair y dillad.   *Mair washed the clothes.*

Byddan nhw'n canu heno.
Fe fyddan nhw'n canu heno.   *They will be singing tonight.*

Canon ni yn yr eisteddfod.
Fe ganon ni yn yr eisteddfod.   *We sang in the eisteddfod.*

Compact form of verbs

The future and imperfect tenses of the verb **canu** referred to above also exist in their compact forms. These inflected verb forms are more likely to be found in formal texts than in current conversational Welsh, though they may well appear in both.

The endings for the future tense of **canu** are -af/-a, -i, -iff/ith, -wn, -wch, -an and are added to the stem *can-*.

Present and future tenses (compact form) (**canu** *to sing*)

Singular

1 Fe/Mi ganaf/gana i   *I shall sing*
2 Fe/Mi geni di/geni   *You will sing*
3 Fe/Mi gân/ganiff/ganith e/o   *He/It will sing*
   Fe/Mi gân/ganiff/ganith hi   *She will sing*

Plural

1 Fe/Mi ganwn ni   *We shall sing*
2 Fe/Mi ganwch chi   *You will sing*
3 Fe/Mi ganan nhw   *They will sing*

The endings for the imperfect tense of **canu** are -wn, -it, -ai, -en, -ech, -en and are added to the stem **can-**.

Imperfect tense (compact form) (**canu** *to sing*)

Singular

1 Canwn i   *I was singing*
2 Canit ti   *You were singing*
3 Canai e/o . . .   *He/It was singing . . .*

Plural

1 Canen ni   *We were singing*
2 Canech chi   *You were singing*
3 Canen nhw   *They were singing*

Regular verbs follow the same pattern as **canu**. The present, imperfect, future and past tenses of **bwyta** are shown below.

Present tense (bwyta *to eat*)

Singular
1 Rydw i'n bwyta   *I am eating, I eat*
2 Rwy ti'n bwyta   *You are eating*
3 Mae e'n bwyta . . .   *He/It is eating . . .* etc.

Imperfect tense (bwyta *to eat*)

Singular
1 Roeddwn i'n bwyta   *I was eating*
2 Roeddet ti'n bwyta   *You are eating*
3 Roedd e'n bwyta . . .   *He/It was eating . . .* etc.

Future tense (bwyta *to eat*)

Singular
1 Fe/Mi fydda(f) i'n bwyta   *I shall be eating*
2 Fe/Mi fyddi di'n bwyta   *You will be eating*
3 Fe/Mi fydd e'n bwyta . . .   *He/It will be eating . . .* etc.

Past tense (compact form) (bwyta *to eat*)

	Singular		*Plural*	
1	Fe/Mi fwytais i	*I ate*	Fe/Mi fwyton ni	*We ate*
2	Fe/Mi fwytaist ti	*You ate*	Fe/Mi fwytoch chi	*You ate*
3	Fe/Mi fwytodd e/o	*He/It ate*	Fe/Mi fwyton nhw	*They ate*
	Fe/Mi fwytodd hi	*She ate*		

Future tense (compact form) (bwyta *to eat*)

Singular
1 Fe/Mi fwyta(f) i   *I shall eat*
2 Fe/Mi fwyti di   *You will eat*
3 Fe/Mi fwytiff e/o   *He/It will eat*
   Fe/Mi fwytiff hi   *She will eat*

Plural
1 Fe/Mi fwytwn ni   *We shall eat*
2 Fe/Mi fwytwch chi   *You will eat*
3 Fe/Mi fwytan nhw   *They will eat*

Imperative (bwyta *to eat*)

Bwyta! (singular); **Bwyt(e)wch!** (plural) *Eat!*

Irregular verbs

Irregular verbs do not follow the same pattern as **canu** and have to be treated separately. Included below are: **cael, dod, gwneud, gwybod, mynd, rhoddi** and **troi**.

Present tense (cael *to have*)

Singular
1 Rydw i'n cael   *I am having, I have*
2 Rwyt ti'n cael   *You are having, You have*
3 Mae e'n cael . . . *He/It is having . . . etc.*

Imperfect tense (cael *to have*)

Singular
1 Roeddwn i'n cael   *I was having*
2 Roeddet ti'n cael   *You were having*
3 Roedd e'n cael . . . *He/It was having . . . etc.*

Future tense (cael *to have*)

Singular
1 Fe/Mi ga(f) i	*I shall have*
2 Fe/Mi gei di	*You will have*
3 Fe/Mi gaiff e/o	*He/It will have*
Fe/Mi gaiff hi	*She will have*

Plural
1 Fe/Mi gawn ni	*We shall have*
2 Fe/Mi gewch chi	*You will have*
3 Fe/Mi gân nhw	*They will have*

Past tense (cael *to have*)

Singular
1 Fe/Mi ges i	*I had*
2 Fe/Mi gest ti	*You had*
3 Fe/Mi gafodd/gas e/o	*He/It had*
Fe/Mi gafodd/gas hi	*She had*

Plural
1 Fe/Mi gawson ni	*We had*
2 Fe/Mi gawsoch chi	*You had*
3 Fe/Mi gawson nhw	*They had*

Imperative (cael *to have*)

Cymera! (singular); **Cymerwch!** (plural) *Have!*

Present tense (dod *to come*)

Singular

1 Rydw i'n dod   *I am coming*
2 Rwyt ti'n dod   *You are coming*
3 Mae e'n dod . . .   *He/It is coming . . . etc.*

Imperfect tense (dod *to come*)

Singular

1 Roeddwn i'n dod   *I was coming*
2 Roeddet ti'n dod   *You were coming*
3 Roedd e'n dod . . .   *He/It was coming . . . etc.*

Future tense (dod *to come*)

Singular

1 Fe/Mi ddeuaf/ddo(f) i   *I shall come*
2 Fe/Mi ddoi di   *You will come*
3 Fe/Mi ddaw e/o   *He/It will come*
  Fe/Mi ddaw hi   *She will come*

Plural

1 Fe/Mi ddown ni   *We shall come*
2 Fe/Mi ddewch/ddowch chi   *You will come*
3 Fe/Mi ddôn nhw   *They will come*

Past tense (dod *to come*)

Singular

1 Fe/Mi ddes i   *I came*
2 Fe/Mi ddest ti   *You came*
3 Fe/Mi ddaeth e/o, hi   *He/It came, She came*

Plural

1 Fe/Mi ddaethon ni   *We came*
2 Fe/Mi ddaethoch chi   *You came*
3 Fe/Mi ddaethon nhw   *They came*

Imperative (dod *to come*)

Tyrd! *(N.W.)*/**Dere!** *(S.W.)* (singular); **Dewch!** *(S.W.)*/**Dowch!** *(N.W.)* (plural) *Come!*

Present tense (gwneud *to make, to do*)

Singular

1 Rydw i'n gwneud   *I am making, I make*
2 Rwyt ti'n gwneud   *You are making, You make*
3 Mae e'n gwneud . . .   *He/It is making . . . etc.*

Imperfect tense (gwneud *to make, to do*)

Singular

1 Roeddwn i'n gwneud   *I was making*
2 Roeddet ti'n gwneud   *You were making*
3 Roedd e'n gwneud . . .   *He/It was making . . . etc.*

Future tense (gwneud *to make, to do*)

Singular

1 Fe/lMi wna(f) i   *I shall make*
2 Fe/Mi wnei di   *You will make*
3 Fe/Mi wnaiff e/o   *He/It will make*
   Fe/Mi wnaiff hi   *She will make*

Plural

1 Fe/Mi wnawn ni   *We shall make*
2 Fe/Mi wnewch chi   *You will make*
3 Fe/Mi wnân nhw   *They will make*

Past tense (gwneud *to make, to do*)

Singular

1 Fe/Mi wnes i   *I made*
2 Fe/Mi wnest ti   *You made*
3 Fe/Mi wnaeth e/o   *He/It made*
   Fe/Mi wnaeth hi   *She made*

Plural

1 Fe/Mi wnaethon ni   *We made*
2 Fe/Mi wnaethoch chi   *You made*
3 Fe/Mi wnaethon nhw   *They made*

Imperative (cael *to have*)

Gwna! (singular); Gwnewch! (plural) *Do! Make!*

Present tense (gwybod *to know*)

Singular

1 Rydw i'n gwybod   *I know*
2 Rwyt ti'n gwybod   *You know*
3 Mae e/o'n gwybod . . .   *He/It knows . . . etc.*

Present tense (compact form) (gwybod *to know*)

Singular

1 Fe/Mi wn i   *I know*
2 Fe/Mi wyddost ti   *You know*
3 Fe/Mi ŵyr e/o   *He/It knows*
   Fe/Mi ŵyr hi   *She knows*

Plural
1 Fe/Mi wyddon ni   *We know*
2 Fe/Mi wyddoch chi   *You know*
3 Fe/Mi wyddan nhw   *They know*

Imperfect tense (gwybod *to know*)

       Singular
1 Roeddwn i'n gwybod   *I knew*
2 Roeddet ti'n gwybod   *You knew*
3 Roedd e'n gwybod . . .   *He/It knows . . .* etc.

Future tense (gwybod *to know*)

       Singular
1 Bydda i'n gwybod   *I shall know*
2 Byddi di'n gwybod   *You will know*
3 Bydd e'n gwybod . . .   *He/It will know . . .* etc.

The compact form of the future and past tenses are seldom used in conversation.

Present tense (mynd *to go*)

       Singular
1 Rydw i'n mynd   *I go, I am going*
2 Rwyt ti'n mynd   *You go, You are going*
3 Mae e'n mynd . . .   *He/It goes, He/It is going . . .* etc.

Present tense (compact form) (mynd *to go*)

   Singular
1   Af/Â i   *I go, I am going*
2   Ei di   *You go, You are going*
3   *Aiff e/o   *He/It goes, He/It is going*
    *Aiff hi   *She goes, She is going . . .* etc.

The present tense follows the same pattern as the compact form of the future tense below.

Imperfect tense (mynd *to go*)

       Singular
1   Roeddwn i'n mynd   *I was going*
2   Roeddet ti'n mynd   *You were going*
3   **Roedd e'n mynd . . .   *He/It was going . . .* etc.

Future tense (mynd *to go*)

	Singular			Plural	
1	Fe/Mi af/â i	*I shall go*	Fe/Mi awn ni	*We shall go*	
2	Fe/Mi ei di	*You will go*	Fe/Mi ewch chi	*You will go*	
3	*Fe/Mi aiff e/o	*He/It will go*	Fe/Mi ân nhw	*They will go*	
	*Fe/Mi aiff hi	*She will go*			

*Literary form: **Â ef/hi** **Literary form: **Âi ef/hi**

Past tense (mynd *to go*)

	Singular			Plural	
1	Fe/Mi es i	*I went*	Fe/Mi aethon ni	*We went*	
2	Fe/lMi est ti	*You went*	Fe/Me aethoch chi	*You went*	
3	Fe/Mi aeth e/o	*He/It went*	Fe/Mi aethon nhw	*They went*	
	Fe/Mi aeth hi	*She went*			

Imperative (mynd *to go*)

Dos! *(N.W.)*/**Cer!** *(S.W.)* (singular); **Ewch!**/**Cerwch!** *(S.W.)* (plural) *Go!*

Present tense (rhoi/rhoddi *to give*)

	Singular	
1	Rydw i'n rhoi/rhoddi	*I am giving, I give*
2	Rwyt ti'n rhoi	*You are giving, You give*
3	Mae e'n rhoi . . .	*He/It is giving, He/It gives . . . etc.*

Imperfect tense (rhoi/rhoddi *to give*)

	Singular	
1	Roeddwn i'n rhoi/rhoddi	*I was giving*
2	Roeddet ti'n rhoi	*You were giving*
3	Roedd e'n rhoi . . .	*He/It was giving . . . etc.*

Future tense (rhoi/rhoddi *to give*)

	Singular	
1	Fe/Mi roia/rodda(f) i	*I shall give*
2	Fe/Mi roddi di	*You will give*
3	Fe/Mi roddiff/rydd e/o	*He/It will give*
	Fe/Mi roddiff/rydd hi	*She will give*

	Plural	
1	Fe/Mi roddwn ni	*We shall give*
2	Fe/Mi roddech chi	*You will give*
3	Fe/Mi roddan nhw	*They will give*

Past tense (rhoi/rhoddi *to give*)

	Singular	
1	Fe/Mi roiais i/roddais i	*I gave*
2	Fe/Mi roddaist ti	*You gave*

3	Fe/Mi roddodd e/o	*He/It gave*
	Fe/Mi roddodd hi	*She gave*
	Plural	
1	Fe/Mi roddon ni	*We gave*
2	Fe/Mi roddoch chi	*You gave*
3	Fe/Mi roddon nhw	*They gave*

Imperative (rhoi/rhoddi *to give*)

Rhodda! Rho! (singular); **Rhoddwch!** (plural) *Give!*

Present tense (troi *to turn*)

Singular
1 Rydw i'n troi   *I am turning, I turn*
2 Rwyt ti'n troi   *You are turning, You turn*
3 Mae e'n troi . . . *He/It is turning, He/It turns . . .* etc.

Imperfect tense (troi *to turn*)

Singular
1 Roeddwn i'n troi *I was turning*
2 Roeddet ti'n troi *You were turning*
3 Roedd e'n troi   *He/It was turning . . .* etc.

Future tense (troi *to turn*)

Singular
1 Fe/Mi droaf/droia i   *I shall turn*
2 Fe/Mi droi-i di   *You will turn*
3 Fe/Mi dröiff e/o   *He/It will turn*
  Fe/Mi dröiff hi   *She will turn*

Plural
1 Fe/Mi droiwn ni   *We shall turn*
2 Fe/Mi droiwch chi   *You will turn*
3 Fe/Mi droian nhw   *They will turn*

Past tense (troi *to turn*)

Singular
1 Fe/Mi droais i   *I turned*
2 Fe/Mi droaist ti   *You turned*
3 Fe/Mi droiodd e/o   *He/It turned*
  Fe/Mi droiodd hi   *She turned*

Plural
1 *Fe/Mi droeson ni*   *We turned*
2 *Fe/Mi droesoch chi*   *You turned*
3 *Fe/Mi droeson nhw*   *They turned*

Imperative (troi *to turn*)

Tro!/Troia! (singular); **Trowch!/Troiwch!** (plural) *Turn!*

cloi, paratoi and **rhoi** follow a similar pattern.

Imperative mood

Commands – 2nd person singular and 2nd person plural

The 2nd person singular is formed by adding **-a** to the stem of the verb-noun, while the 2nd person plural is formed by adding **-wch** to the stem:

Cysga! (2nd person singular);
Cysgwch! (2nd person plural) *Sleep!*
Brysia! (2nd person singular);
Brysiwch! (2nd person plural) *Hurry!*

Commands – other persons

The forms **Gadewch i-** *Allow-/Let* is usually used to express commands in the other persons of the verb:

Gadewch i fi weithio!   (1st person singular)   *Let me work!*
Gadewch iddo fe weithio! (3rd person singular)   *Let him work!*
Gadewch iddi hi weithio! (3rd person singular)   *Let her work!*
Gadewch i ni weithio!   (1st person plural) *Let us work!*
Gadewch iddyn nhw weithio!   (3rd person plural)
Let them work!

Verbs and mutations

The direct object of a verb in compact form takes a soft mutation:

Fe welodd e geffyl.   *He saw a horse.*
Fe brynon nhw fwyd. *They bought food.*
Mi gana i garolau 'fory.   *I'll sing carols tomorrow.*
Rhoddaf bunt iddi.   *I'll give her a pound.*

Note: When the periphrastic form of the verb (**bod** + **yn** + verb-noun) is used *no* mutation of the object occurs, as is shown in the following sentences:

Mae e'n darllen llyfr.   *He is reading a book.*
Mae nhw'n chwarae pêl-droed.   *They are playing football.*
Roedd Siân yn golchi llestri. *Siân was washing dishes.*
Rydw i'n rhoddi punt iddo. *I am giving him a pound.*

For examples involving the mutation of verbs following the particles **Fe** and **Mi**, the relative pronoun **a**, and the personal pronouns **mi, ti, ef . . .** see the section entitled **A summary of the main rules of mutation.**

Prepositions

Prepositions are followed by nouns or pronouns, for example:

gyda *with*   gyda Mam *with Mother;* gyda ni *with us*
i fyny *up*   i fyny'r bryn *up the hill;* i fyny'r ysgol *up the ladder*
i lawr *down* i lawr y cwm *down the valley;* i lawr y pwll *down the pit*
mewn *in a*   mewn cwpan *in a cup;* mewn munud *in a minute*

Some prepositions are conjugated and have personal forms:

at *to, towards* (stem **at-**)

	Singular		*Plural*	
1	ata i	*to me*	aton ni	*to us*
2	atat ti	*to you*	atoch chi	*to you*
3	ato fe/fo	*to him/it*	atyn nhw	*to them*
	ati hi	*to her/it*		

dan *under* (stem **dan-**)

	Singular		*Plural*	
1	dana i	*under me*	danon ni	*under us*
2	danat ti	*under you*	danoch chi	*under you*
3	dano fe/fo	*under him/it*	danyn nhw	*under them*
	dani hi	*under her/it*		

am *around* (stem **amdan-**)

	Singular		*Plural*	
1	amdana i	*around me*	amdanon ni	*around us*
2	amdanat ti	*around you*	amdanoch chi	*around you*
3	amdano fe/fo	*around him/it*	amdanyn nhw	*around them*
	amdani hi	*around her/it*		

ar *on* (stem **arn-**)

	Singular		*Plural*	
1	arna i	*on me*	arnon ni	*on us*
2	arnat ti	*on you*	arnoch chi	*on you*
3	arno fe/fo	*on him/it*	arnyn nhw	*on them*
	arni hi	*on her/it*		

wrth *by* (stem **wrth-**)

	Singular		*Plural*	
1	wrtho i	*by me*	wrthon ni	*by us*
2	wrthot ti	*by you*	wrthoch chi	*by you*
3	wrtho fe/fo	*by him/it*	wrthyn nhw	*by them*
	wrthi hi	*by her/it*		

drwy *and* **heb** share a similar pattern:

drwy *through* (stem **drwydd-**)

	Singular		Plural	
1	drwyddo i	*through me*	drwyddon ni	*through us*
2	drwyddot ti	*through you*	drwyddoch chi	*through you*
3	drwyddo fe/fo	*through him/it*	drwyddyn nhw	*through them*
	drwyddi hi	*through her/it*		

heb *without* (stem **hebdd-**)

	Singular		Plural	
1	hebddo i	*without me*	hebddon ni	*without us*
2	hebddot ti	*without you*	hebddoch chi	*without you*
3	hebddo fe/fo	*without him/it*	hebddyn nhw	*without them*
	hebddi hi	*without her/it*		

yn *in* (stem **yn-**)

	Singular		Plural	
1	yno i	*in me*	ynon ni	*in us*
2	ynot ti	*in you*	ynoch chi	*in you*
3	ynddo fe/fo	*in him/it*	ynddyn nhw	*in them*
	ynddi hi	*in her/it*		

i *to, for*

	Singular		Plural	
1	i fi/mi	*to me, for me*	i ni	*to us, for us*
2	i ti	*to you . . .*	i chi	*to you . . .*
3	iddo fe/fo	*to him/it . . .*	iddyn nhw	*to them . . .*
	iddi hi	*to her . . .*		

o *from* (stem **ohon-**)

	Singular		Plural	
1	ohono i	*from me*	ohonon ni	*from us*
2	ohonot ti	*from you*	ohonoch chi	*from you*
3	ohono fe/fo	*from him/it*	ohonyn nhw	*from them*
	ohoni hi	*from her/it*		

rhwng *between* (stem **rhyng-**)

	Singular		Plural	
1	rhyngo i	*between us*	rhyngon ni	*between us*
2	rhyngot ti	*between you*	rhyngoch chi	*between you*
3	rhyngddo fe/fo	*between him/it*	rhyngddyn nhw	*between them*
	rhyngddi hi	*between her/it*		

dros *over, for*

	Singular	
1	drosto/droso i	*over me, for me*
2	drostot/drosot ti	*over you, for you*
3	drosto fe/fo	*over him/it, for him*
	drosti hi	*over her/it, for her/it*

Plural

1 droston/droson ni *over us, for us*
2 drostoch/drosoch chi *over you, for you*
3 drostyn nhw *over them, for them*

gan *with*

	Singular		Plural	
1	gen i	*with me*	gennyn/gynnon ni	*with us*
2	gen ti	*with you*	gennych/gynnoch chi	*with you*
3	ganddo fe/fo	*with him/it*	ganddyn nhw	*with them*
	ganddi hi	*with her/it*		

Sometimes the preposition **gyda** is used instead of the conjugated preposition **gan** in South Wales.

The conjugated prepositions **am, ar, at, dan, dros, drwy/trwy, gan, heb, i, o, wrth** are used in their simple form when the object governed by the preposition is a noun or verb-noun. Soft mutation follows these prepositions:

> **am dro; ar bapur; at drwyn; dan wely; dros frawd; drwy fôr; heb ddiolch; i regi; o freuddwydio; wrth lusgo.**

See section **Treiglad meddal – Soft mutation.**

The conjugated preposition **rhwng** is not followed by mutation:

> rhwng cyfeillion da *between good friends*
> rhwng dau frawd *between two brothers*
> rhwng gŵr a gwraig *between husband and wife*

The conjugated preposition **yn** in its simple form is followed by nasal mutation. It becomes **yng** before **c** and **g**, and **ym** before **p** and **b**:

> yng nghornel yr ystafell *in the corner of the room*
> yng nghwrs y flwyddyn *in the course of the year*
> yng Nghorwen *in Corwen*
> yng ngardd yr ysgol *in the school's garden*
> yng nglaw mis Ebrill *in the April rain*
> yng Nglanaman *in Glanaman*
> ym mhoced y bachgen *in the boy's pocket*
> ym mhrofiad y dyn *in the man's experience*
> ym Mhorthaethwy *in Porthaethwy (Menai Bridge)*
> ym mwyd y plant *in the children's food*
> ym masged y fenyw *in the woman's basket*
> ym Mangor *in Bangor*

yn also becomes *ym* before *m*:

ym Môn; ym Mynwy; ym Môr y Gogledd; ym mynwent y plwyf

For examples of **yn** followed by soft mutation or by non-mutation, see section entitled **A summary of the main rules of mutation.**

Adjectives

In the Welsh language the adjective usually comes after the noun:

afal **sur**	*a bitter apple*
blodyn **hyfryd**	*a beautiful flower*
cadair **uchel**	*a high chair*
siwrnai **hir**	*a long journey*

When the adjective follows a singular masculine noun no mutation occurs but when the adjective follows the singular feminine noun it takes soft mutation:

bachgen bach	*a small boy*
merch fach	*a small girl*
brawd cariadus	*a loving brother*
chwaer gariadus	*a loving sister*
dyn mawr	*a big man*
menyw fawr	*a big woman*
gŵr tenau	*a thin man/husband*
gwraig denau	*a thin woman/wife*
tarw du	*a black bull*
buwch **ddu**	*a black cow*

Note: Adjectives do not mutate when they follow *plural* nouns.

When an adjective precedes a noun the noun is mutated whether it be masculine or feminine:

hen **ŵr**	*an old man*
hen **wraig**	*an old woman*
annwyl **dad**	*a dear father*
annwyl **fam**	*a dear mother*

The noun takes a soft mutation on each occasion.

The feminine form of a few adjectives is still used in everyday speech. Some are listed below:

Masculine	*Feminine*	
gwyn	gwen	*white*
melyn	melen	*yellow*
tlws	tlos	*pretty*
bychan	bechan	*little*
byr	ber	*short*

e.g. cot **wen**; ffrog **felen**; merch **dlos**; ynys **fechan**; stori **fer**.

The comparison of adjectives

There are three degrees of comparison of adjectives in Welsh. These are: equative, comparative and superlative. Adjectives may be compared by two methods:

1 Using **mor, mwy, mwya(f)** before the adjective. Adjectives of more than two syllables are also compared in this manner. Irregular adjectives, some of which are listed below, are an exception.

Positive	Equative	Comparative	Superlative
affôl (foolish)	mor ffôl	mwy ffôl	mwyaf ffôl
cryno (tidy)	mor *gryno	mwy cryno	mwyaf cryno
rhesymol (reasonable)	mor rhesymol	mwy rhesymol	mwyaf rhesymol
amlwg	mor amlwg	mwy amlwg	mwya(f) amlwg
evident	*as evident*	*more evident*	*most evident*
amyneddgar	mor amyneddgar	mwy amyneddgar	mwya(f) amyneddgar
patient	*as patient*	*more patient*	*most patient*
blasus	mor *flasus	mwy blasus	mwya(f) blasus
tasty	*as tasty*	*more tasty*	*most tasty*
cyfeillgar	mor *gyfeillgar	mwy cyfeillgar	mwya(f) cyfeillgar
friendly	*as friendly*	*more friendly*	*most friendly*
diolchgar	mor *ddiolchgar	mwy diolchgar	mwya(f) diolchgar
thankful	*as thankful*	*more thankful*	*most thankful*
doniol	mor *ddoniol	mwy doniol	mwya(f) doniol
witty	*as witty*	*more witty*	*most witty*
dyledus	mor *ddyledus	mwy dyledus	mwya(f) dyledus
indebted	*as indebted*	*more indebted*	*most indebted*
dymunol	mor *ddymuol	mwy dymunol	mwya(f) dymunol
desirable	*as desirable*	*more desirable*	*most desirable*
gwerthfawr	mor *werthfawr	mwy gwerthfawr	mwya(f) gwerthfawr
valuable	*as valuable*	*more valuable*	*most valuable*
peryglus	mor *beryglus	mwy peryglus	mwya(f) peryglus
dangerous	*as dangerous*	*more dangerous*	*most dangerous*
llawen	mor **llawen	mwy llawen	mwya(f) llawen
cheerful	*as cheerful*	*more cheerful*	*most cheerful*

*Note: **mor** *(as, so, how)* is followed by soft mutation. An alternative translation in the above context would read:

> **mor amlwg** *so evident*; **mor amyneddgar** *so patient*; **mor flasus** *so tasty*; **mor gyfeillgar** *so friendly* . . .

** **ll** and **rh** do not mutate after **mor**.

2 With regular adjectives the endings **-ed, -ach, -af** are added respectively to the adjective in its positive form in order to form the other degrees:

Positive	Equative	Comparative	Superlative
*agos	agosed	agosach	agosa(f)
near	*as near*	*nearer*	*nearest*
caled	caleted	caletach	caleta(f)
hard	*as hard*	*harder*	*hardest*
call	called	callach	calla(f)
wise	*as wise*	*wiser*	*wisest*
coch	coched	cochach	cocha(f)
red	*as red*	*redder*	*reddest*
cryf	cryfed	cryfach	cryfa(f)
strong	*as strong*	*stronger*	*strongest*
cyflym	cyflymed	cyflymach	cyflyma(f)
quick	*as quick*	*quicker*	*quickest*
eglur	eglured	eglurach	eglura(f)
clear	*as clear*	*clearer*	*clearest*
glân	glaned	glanach	glana(f)
clean	*as clean*	*cleaner*	*cleanest*
glas	glased	glasach	glasa(f)
blue	*as blue*	*bluer*	*bluest*
hapus	hapused	hapusach	hapusa(f)
happy	*as happy*	*happier*	*happiest*
oer	oered	oerach	oera(f)
cold	*as cold*	*colder*	*coldest*
pell	pelled	pellach	pella(f)
far	*as far*	*further*	*furthest*
tawel	taweled	tawelach	tawela(f)
quiet	*as quiet*	*quieter*	*quietest*
trwm	trymed	trymach	tryma(f)
heavy	*as heavy*	*heavier*	*heaviest*
tywyll	tywylled	tywyllach	tywylla(f)
dark	*as dark*	*darker*	*darkest*

Note: The final **f** of the superlative is often omitted in spelling and pronunciation.

*See end of section on adjectives for alternative forms.

cyn is used to compare adjectives which in their positive forms do not contain more than two syllables and do not end in **-en, -gar, -og, -ol** or **-us**.

cyn and **mor** are both followed by soft mutation, except when the adjective begins with **ll** or **rh**.

cyn agosed â/ag	yn agosach na(g)	yr agosa(f)
as near as	*nearer than*	*the nearest*
cyn belled â/ag	yn bellach na(g)	y pella(f)
as far as	*further than*	*the furthest*
cyn goched â/ag	yn gochach na(g)	y cocha(f)
as red as	*redder than*	*the reddest*
cyn hapused â/ag	yn hapusach na(g)	yr hapusa(f)
as happy as	*happier than*	*the happiest*
cyn llawned â/ag	yn llawnach na(g)	y llawna(f)
as full as	*fuller than*	*the fullest*

When the adjective in its positive form ends in **-g, -b** or **-d** these letters harden to **-c-, -p-** and **-t-** when the adjective is compared, as is shown below with **caled, teg, gwlyb, rhad:**

cyn galeted â/ag	yn galetach na(g)	y caleta(f)
as hard as	*harder than*	*the hardest*
cyn deced â/ag	yn decach na(g)	y teca(f)
as fair as	*fairer than*	*the fairest*
cyn wlyped â/ag	yn wlypach na(g)	y gwlypa(f)
as wet as	*wetter than*	*the wettest*
cyn rhated â/ag	yn rhatach na(g)	y rhata(f)
as cheap/free as	*cheaper/freer than*	*the cheapest/freest*

â in the equative degree and **na** in the comparative degree are used when the following word begins with a consonant, and both cause spirant mutation.

ag and **nag** are used when the following word begins with a vowel:

cyn goched â thân	*as red as fire*
yn drymach **na** phlwm	*heavier than lead*
cyn wynned **ag** eira	*whiter than snow*
yn dywyllach **nag** uffern	*darker than hell*

Irregular adjectives

There are only a few irregular adjectives in Welsh and the most important of them are listed below:

Positive	Equative	Comparative	Superlative
bach/bychan *small*	mor fach/fychan cyn lleied	llai	lleia(f)
buan/cynnar *swift/early*	mor fuan cynt	cynted	cynta(f)
da *good*	mor dda cystal	gwell	gorau
drwg *bad*	mor ddrwg cynddrwg	gwaeth	gwaetha(f)
hawdd *easy*	mor hawdd cyn hawsed	haws	hawsa(f)
hen *old*	mor hen cyn hyned	hŷn	hyna(f)
hir *long*	mor hir cyn hired	hirach	hira(f)
ifanc/ieuanc *young*	mor ifanc cyn ieuanged	ifancach ieuangach	ifanca(f) ieuanga(f)
Positive	*Equative*	*Comparative*	*Superlative*
isel *low*	mor isel cyn ised	is	isa(f)
llawer/mawr *many/big*	mor fawr cymaint	mwy	mwya(f)
uchel *high*	mor uchel cyn uched	uwch	ucha(f)

Note: **cyn** *(as)* is also used in the equative degree of comparison with the appropriate -**ed** ending. (It is already contained in such forms as **cynt**, **cystal**, **cynddrwg** and **cymaint**.) **cyn** is followed by soft mutation.

Exception: **ll** and **rh** do not mutate after **mor** and **cyn**.

The adjective **agos** also has irregular equative, comparative and superlative forms:

agos	cyn nesed â	yn nes na	y nesaf
near	*as near as*	*nearer than*	*the nearest*

Personal pronouns

There are two classes of personal pronouns in Welsh: independent and dependent.

Independent personal pronouns

These pronouns are not dependent on any other word in a sentence and may stand entirely alone.

Simple

	Singular		Plural		
1	fi, mi	*I, me*	ni	*we, us*	
2	ti, di	*you*	chi	*you*	
3	fe/e, fo/o	*he, him*	nhw	*they, them*	
	hi	*she, her*			

Reduplicated

	Singular	
1	myfi, y fi	*I, I myself*
2	tydi, y chdi (G.C.)	*you, you yourself*
3	efe, efo, y fe, y fo	*he*
	hyhi, y hi	*she, it, she herself, it itself*

	Plural	
1	nyni, y ni	*we, we ourselves*
2	chychi, y chi	*you, you yourselves*
3	y nhw	*they, them, they themselves*

The reduplicated forms are often placed at the beginning of a sentence for emphasis:

Myfi sy'n magu'r baban.   *It is I who nurses the baby.*
Tydi, O Dduw, sy'n maddau.   *It is You, O Lord, who forgives.*
Nyni sy'n troi y meysydd.   *It is we who plough the fields.*

Conjunctive

	Singular		Plural	
1	finnau, minnau	*I, me*	ninnau	*we, us*
2	tithau	*you*	chithau	*you*
3	yntau	*he, him*	nhwthau	*they, them*
	hithau	*she, her*		

The conjunctive forms frequently possess an extra meaning beyond that of the mere pronoun, the additional meaning being expressed in English by a conjunction:

minnau may mean   *I (me) also; even I (me); I (me) on the other hand; I (me) for my part; then I; but I . . .*

ninnau may mean *we (us) too, we (us) also; even we (us); we (us) on the other hand; we (us) on the contrary; we (us) for our part* . . .

Dependent personal pronouns

These pronouns are dependent on either a noun, another pronoun or personal ending of a verb or preposition, or a verb-noun.

Prefixed

	Singular		Plural	
1	fy, f'	*my*	ein	*our*
2	dy, d'	*your*	eich	*your*
3	ei	*his/her*	eu	*their*

The prefixed forms, which are always in the genitive case, are used before nouns and verb-nouns:

Darllenodd y bachgen ei lyfr.	*The boy read his book.*
Clywais fy nhad yn galw.	*I heard my father calling.*
Cafodd y gân ei chanu ar y radio.	*The song was sung on the radio.*

Affixed

	Singular		Plural	
1	i, fi	*I, me*	ni	*we, us*
2	di, ti	*you*	chi	*you*
3	e, fe, o, fo	*he, him*	nhw	*they, them*
	hi	*she, her*		

For examples of affixed forms and a fuller discussion of the subject of Welsh pronouns the reader is referred to specific works on Welsh grammar.

Words beginning with the vowels **a, e, i, o, u w** and **y** are aspirated and acquire an initial **h** when preceded by the following pronouns (or their abbreviated forms):

1	ei, 'i, 'w	*her* (feminine singular)
2	eu, 'u, 'w	*their*
3	ein, 'n	*our*

ysgol >	ei hysgol (hi) *her school;*
	Dyma 'i hysgol *Here is her school;*
	dewch i'w hysgol *Come to her school.*

ardal >	eu hardal (nhw) *their district;*
	Dyna'u hardal *That is their district;*
	Mi af i'w hardal *I shall go to their district.*

ewyllys >	ein hewyllys *our will;* a'n hewyllys da *and our goodwill.*

annwyl >	ein hannwyl blentyn *our dear child;* eu hannwyl wlad *their dear country;* ei hannwyl fam *her dear mother.*

For the mutations after the dependent personal pronouns:
    fy, dy, ei (masculine) and ei (feminine)
see the section entitled **A summary of the main rules of mutation.**

Rules of mutation

Nine initial consonants mutate. They are:
  c, p, t, g, b, d, ll, m, rh.
They mutate in the manner shown in the box below:

Initial consonant	Soft	Nasal	Spirant
cath *cat*	dy gath di *your cat*	fy nghath i *my cat*	ei chath hi *her cat*
pen *head*	dy ben di *your head*	fy mhen i *my head*	ei phen hi *her head*
tad *father*	dy dad di *your father*	fy nhad i *my father*	ei thad hi *her father*
*gardd *garden*	dy ardd di *your garden*	fy ngardd i *my garden*	
bys *finger*	dy fys di *your finger*	fy mys i *my finger*	
dant *tooth*	dy ddant di *your tooth*	fy nant i *my tooth*	
llyfr *book*	dy lyfr di *your book*		
mam *mother*	dy fam di *your mother*		
rhaff *rope*	dy raff di *your rope*		

*The consonant g disappears when soft mutation occurs, leaving the next letter (vowel or consonant) as the initial letter of the mutated word, as in:

gair > air; glo > lo; gwair > wair; gwddf > wddf; gwyrdd > wyrdd . . .

Soft mutation

Nine consonants are affected by soft mutation:

  c > g; p > b; t > d; g > (disappears); b > f; d > dd; ll > l; m > f; rh > r.

Nouns

1 Feminine singular nouns after the definite article y, yr, 'r:
   y got, y bêl, y daith, yr ardd, y fraich, o'r ddafad, i'r fam.
   ll and rh do not mutate after the definite article:
   y llaw, y llwy, y rhaglen, y rhaff, i'r rhos.

2 Nouns when preceded by adjectives:
   hen ŵr *(an old man)*; annwyl frawd *(a dear brother)*; hoff le *(a favourite place)*; unig ferch *(an only daughter)*.

3 Nouns and verb-nouns after the prepositions am, ar, at, dan, dros, drwy, gan, heb, hyd, i, o, wrth:
   am flwyddyn *(for a year)*; ar fwrdd *(on a table)*; at ddrws *(towards a door)*; dan goeden *(under a tree)*; dros Gymru *(for/over Wales)*; drwy ddŵr *(through water)*; gan ddweud *(by saying)*; heb gysgu *(without sleeping)*; wrth ganu *(by singing)*. The verb-nouns dweud, cysgu and canu mutate as nouns in this context.

4 Nouns after dyma, dyna, dacw, wele:
   Dyma le da *(Here's a good place)*. Dyna dŷ hyfryd *(There's a beautiful house)*. Dacw gi defaid *(There's a sheepdog yonder)*. Wele faban! *(Behold a babe!)*

5 Feminine singular nouns after the numeral un except those nouns beginning in ll and rh; nouns after the numerals dau and dwy; and nouns after the numerals saith and wyth beginning in c, p, t, ll and rh:
   un ferch *(one girl)*; un wraig *(one woman)*; un gadair *(one chair)*; dau fachgen *(two boys)*; dau gae *(two fields)*; dwy gath *(two cats)*; dwy dref *(two towns)*; saith gant *(seven hundred)*; wyth dudalen *(eight pages)*. Exceptions remain: un llaw *(one hand)*; un llong *(one ship)*; un rhwyd *(one net)*; un rhaw *(one shovel)*.

6 A noun when it is the direct object of an inflected verb (compact form):

Prynais lyfr.	*I bought a book.*
Gwelaf gastell.	*I see a castle.*
Agorodd ddrysau'r car.	*He opened the car's doors.*
Fe ganon nhw gân hapus.	*They sang a happy song.*

   When the verb is in a periphrastic form the object does *not* mutate:

Mae Siôn yn canu cân.	*Siôn is singing a song.*
Rydw i'n ysgrifennu llythyr.	*I'm writing a letter.*

7 Nouns after the predicative yn:

Mae Siân yn ferch hyfryd.	*Siân is a lovely girl.*
Mae'r gwaith yn fraint.	*The work is a privilege.*
Bydd hwn yn drysor am byth.	*This will be a treasure for ever.*

   Exceptions: Nouns beginning in ll and rh.

Roedd Alun yn llawen.	*Alun was happy.*

8 Nouns after the personal pronouns **dy** and **ei** (masculine) together with **'i** (masculine) and **'w** (masculine):
dy **g**ot *(your coat)*; dy **b**oced *(your pocket)*; dy **d**afod *(your tongue)*; ei **o**lwg *(his sight)*; ei **f**raich *(his arm)*; Dyma Ifan a'i **g**ŵn. *(Here is Ifan and his dogs)*; Collodd ei **f**rawd a'i **d**ad. *(He lost his brother and his father)*; Aeth e i'w **d**ŷ. *(He went to his house)*; Chwythodd y llwch i'w **l**ygaid. *(The dust blew into his eyes)*.

9 Nouns and verb-nouns after the conjunction **neu** *(or)*:
te neu **g**offi *(tea or coffee)*; mab neu **f**erch *(a son or daughter)*; ci neu **g**ath *(a dog or cat)*; ennill neu **g**olli *(win or lose)*. Inflected verbs (compact forms) are not mutated after **neu**.

10 Feminine singular nouns after ordinal numerals:
y drydedd **f**erch *(the third girl)*; y chweched **b**ennod *(the sixth chapter)*; y nawfed **g**yfrol *(the ninth volume)*; y ddegfed **w**ers *(the tenth lesson)*.

11 The numerals **dau** and **dwy** after the definite article **y**:
y **dd**au fachgen *(the two boys)*; y **dd**wy ferch *(the two girls)*.

12 Nouns used as adjectives after feminine singular nouns:
llwy **d**e *(teaspoon)*; gwisg **b**riodas *(wedding-dress)*; gardd **l**ysiau *(a vegetable garden)*; cadair **f**reichiau *(an armchair)*.

13 Nouns in the vocative case:
Fam annwyl! *(Mother dear!)*; **F**rodyr a chwiorydd! *(Brothers and sisters!)*; **L**owyr, gwrandewch! *(Miners, listen!)*; **W**eithwyr y byd! *(Workers of the world!)*.

14 After a break in the normal order of words:
Roedd croeso yno.   Roedd yno groeso.
Mae merch newydd yn yr ysgol.   Mae yna ferch newydd yn yr ysgol.

15 Nouns after **amryw, cyfryw, pa, pa fath, pa ryw, rhyw, unrhyw**:
amryw **l**iwiau *(several colours)*; cyfryw **b**ethau *(such things)*; Pa **l**e? *(What place?)*; Pa fath **f**achgen ydy e? *(What kind of a boy is he?)*.

16 Nouns after **ambell, aml, holl, naill, ychydig, y fath**:
ambell **w**aith *(sometimes)*; aml **d**ro *(frequently)*; yr holl **b**entref *(the whole village)*; y naill **g**ynllun *(the one plan)*; ychydig **f**wyd *(a little food)*; y fath **dd**yn *(such a man)*.

17 Nouns after the prefix **cyn(-)** *(former, past, ex-, pre-)*:
cyn-**b**rifathro *(former headteacher)*; cyn-**l**ywydd *(past president)*; cyn-**w**einidog *(former minister)*; cyn-**l**öwr *(ex-miner)*.

Adjectives

1 Adjectives after feminine singular nouns:
cadair **f**ach *(a small chair)*; ffordd **g**ul *(a narrow way)*; heol **f**awr *(a big road)*; merch **d**enau *(a thin girl)*; stori **dd**a *(a good story)*.

2 Adjectives after the predicative **yn**:

Mae Nia yn garedig.	*Nia is kind.*
Roedd y saer yn **dd**a.	*The carpenter was good.*
Mae'r bwyd yn **dd**iflas.	*The food is distasteful.*

ll and **rh** do *not* mutate after **yn**.

3 Adjectives in comparison after **cyn** and **mor**:

cyn **g**yflymed â *(as fast as)*; mor **g**yfeillgar â *(as friendly as)*; cyn **w**ynned â *(as white as)*; mor **d**yner â *(as tender as)*. **ll** and **rh** do not mutate after **cyn** and **mor**:

cyn llawned â *(as full as)*; mor rhad â *(as cheap as)*; mor llawen â'r gog *(as happy as the cuckoo)*.

4 Adjectives after the conjunction **neu**:

da neu **dd**rwg *(good or bad)*; gwyn neu **dd**u *(white or black)*.

5 Adjectives after the adverbs **go, gweddol, lled, mor, rhy**:

go **dd**rwg	*quite/fairly bad*
gweddol **d**awel	*fairly quiet*
lled **dd**a	*quite good/fairly well*
mor **b**wysig	*so important*
rhy lawen	*too merry*

ll and **rh** do *not* mutate after **mor**:

mor llwyddiannus	*so successful*
mor rhwydd	*so easy*

Verbs

1 Interrogative forms of inflected verbs (compact forms):

Weloch chi'r papur?	*Did you see the paper?*
Fuest ti allan heddiw?	*Were you out today?*
Ddaeth e i'r ysgol mewn pryd?	*Did he come to school in time?*

2 Verbs after the particles **Fe**(S.W.) and **Mi**(N.W.):

Fe ganodd gân.	*He sang a song.*
Mi glywais ei llais hi.	*I heard her voice.*
Fe lanwon nhw'r car.	*They filled the car.*
Mi glywson ni'r newyddion.	*We heard the news.*

3 Verbs after the relative pronoun **a** and the negative relative pronoun **na**:

Dyma'r ferch **a dd**aeth i'r parti.	*Here's the girl who came to the party.*

The relative pronoun **a** *is frequently omitted in conversational Welsh but the mutation caused by it is retained:*

Dyna'r dyn (**a**) welais i.	*There's the man whom I saw.*

The negative relative pronoun **na** causes soft mutation with verbs beginning in **g, b, d, ll, m, rh** and spirant mutation with verbs beginning in **c, p, t**:

Dyna'r ferch **na dd**aeth i'r parti.	*There's the girl who did not come to the party.*
Dyma'r dyn **na ch**anodd.	*Here's the man who did not sing.*

4 After the conjunction **pan**:
    Pan **dd**aeth Guto i'r tŷ . . .   *When Guto came to the*
                                     house . . .
    Bydda i'n hapus pan **dd**aw'r haf.   *I'll be happy when summer*
                                     comes.

5 Negative forms of inflected verbs (compact forms):
    Ddarllenodd e ddim o'r Beibl.   *He didn't read the Bible.*
    Welais i ddim yno.   *I didn't see anything there.*
    In written Welsh, the negative particle **ni** precedes these forms, as
    in 'Ni **dd**arllenodd e ddim o'r Beibl' and 'Ni welais i ddim yno', and
    causes soft mutation with verbs beginning in **g, b, d, ll, m, rh**.
    Inflected verbs beginning in **c, p, t** undergo spirant mutation.

6 Verbs after the interrogative pronouns **Beth** and **Pwy**:
    Beth weloch chi?   *What did you see?*
    Pwy brynodd y tocyn?   *Who bought the ticket?*

Nasal mutation

Six consonants are affected by Nasal Mutation:
    c > ngh; p > mh; t > nh; g > ng; b > m; d > n.

1 After the personal pronoun **fy**:
    fy **ngh**artref *(my home)*; fy **mh**oced *(my pocket)*; fy **nh**afod *(my
    tongue)*; fy **ng**obaith *(my hope)*; fy **m**rawd *(my brother)*; fy **n**rws
    (my door).

2 After the preposition **yn**:
    (In certain instances **yn** itself changes to **yng** or **ym**
      yn + c > yng ngh-
      yn + g > yng ng-
      yn + p > ym mh-
      yn + b > ym m-
    When **yn** precedes **m** it changes to **ym** even though there is no
    mutation.)
    yng **ngh**orff y dyn *(in the man's body)*; ym **mh**lwyf Llangyfelach
    (in the parish of Llangyfelach); yn **nh**re Caerfyrddin *(in
    Carmarthen town)*; yng **ng**olau'r gannwyll *(in the candlelight)*;
    ym **m**reichiau Myfanwy *(in Myfanwy's arms)*; yn **nh**ywyllwch y
    nos *(in the darkness of the night)*; yng **N**ghaerdydd; ym
    Mhontyberem; yn **N**hreorci; yng **N**gorseinon; ym **M**iwmares; yn
    Ninbych; ym **M**ynwy; ym **M**aesteg; ym mis Mai.

3 **blwydd** *(a year old)*, **blynedd** *(a year)*, and **diwrnod** *(a day)* all
    mutate after the cardinal numbers **pum, saith, wyth, naw, deng,
    deuddeng, ugain** (and numbers incorporating **ugain**, such as
    trigain), and **can**.
    pum **ml**wydd oed *(five years old)*; saith **ml**ynedd *(seven years)*;
    wyth **n**iwrnod *(eight days)*; deng **ml**wydd oed; deuddeng
    mlynedd; ugain **n**iwrnod; can **ml**ynedd.

Note: Mae Siôn yn **ddwy** flwydd oed. *Siôn is two years old.*
      Roedd Nia yma am **ddwy** flynedd. *Nia was here for two years.*
      Mae **dau dd**iwrnod cyn y parti. *There are two days before the party.*
See **soft mutation** – *treiglad meddal.*

Spirant mutation

Three consonants are affected by spirant mutation:
        c > ch; p > ph; t > th.

1 After the personal pronouns **ei** (feminine), **'i** (feminine) and **'w** (feminine):
        ei **ch**aws *(her cheese)*; ei **ph**en-blwydd *(her birthday)*; ei **th**ad-cu *(her grandfather)*; o'i **ch**artref *(from her home)*; o'i **ph**en i'w **th**raed *(from her head to her feet).*

2 After the cardinal numbers **tri, chwe:**
        tri **ch**wpan *(three cups)*; tri **ph**erson *(three persons)*; chwe **ph**lentyn *(six children)*; chwe **th**estun *(six subjects).*

3 After the prepositions **â, gyda, tua:**

torri bara â **ch**yllell	*cutting bread with a knife*
cerdded gyda **th**ad y ferch	*walking with the girl's father*
gweithio gyda **ch**yfaill	*working with a friend*
mynd tua **Ph**entre-Bach	*going towards Pentre-Bach*
aros tua **th**ymor	*waiting about a term*

4 After the conjunctions **a** *(and)*, **na** *(nor, than)*, **oni** *(until, unless)*:
        dŵr a **th**ân *(water and fire)*; ci a **ch**ath *(a dog and a cat)*; na **ph**en na **ch**wt *(nor head nor tail)*; yn fwy na **ph**unt *(more than a pound)*; yn gochach na **th**ân *(redder than fire)*; oni **ch**lywaf *(unless I shall hear).*

5 After the adverbs **â** *(as)*, **tra** *(very/exceedingly)*:

cyn drymed â **ph**lwm	*as heavy as lead*
cyn oered â **ch**lai	*as cold as clay*
tra **ch**aredig	*very kind*
tra **th**ywyll	*exceedingly dark*

6 After the negative form of the relative pronoun **na:**

Dyma'r ferch na **th**alodd am ei llyfr.	*This is the girl who did not pay for her book.*

Only verbs beginning in **c, p, t** and following **na** in this context are affected by spirant mutation. For verbs beginning in **g, b, d, ll, m, rh** after the negative pronoun **na** see **soft mutation** – *treiglad meddal.*

7 Negative forms of inflected verbs (compact forms):

Chlywais i ddim sŵn.	*I didn't hear a sound.*
Thalodd e ddim.	*He didn't pay.*
Phrynais i ddim o'r esgidiau	*I didn't buy the shoes.*

In written Welsh, the negative particle **ni** precedes these forms, as in 'Ni chlywais i ddim sŵn' and 'Ni thalodd e ddim', and causes spirant mutation with verbs beginning in **c, p, t**. Inflected verbs beginning in **g, b, d, ll, m** and **rh** undergo soft mutation.